For decades, formal theological education has
a long Christian tradition, increasing numbers
are avoiding the academy, which is seen as largely irrelevant. In p
the church is growing vibrantly, theology that developed in completely different church eras and contexts, continues to be imported en masse. In contexts where followers of the Triune God exist as a minority, an institutional model of training tends to be inappropriate and unsustainable. This important book comes from the heart and experience of thinkers who are also practitioners. It demonstrates how God is growing a different way of equipping the followers of Christ; a way that can be theologically profound, contextually relevant, and practically transformational. If we read with humility, there is much here to help all of us engaged in theological education, whether our approach is formal, informal, or non-formal.

Paul Bendor-Samuel, PhD, MBE
Executive Director, Oxford Centre for Mission Studies, UK

TEE for the 21st Century presents new trends in theological education with lessons immediately applicable to a wide variety of contexts. The text provides background on the history of TEE as a worldwide organic movement that is relevant to theological educators and church leaders. TEE refers to "Theological Education by Extension," or more recently, "Tools to Equip and Empower." It is not to be confused with distance education classes sponsored by a seminary or Bible school. Instead, the TEE model presented in this text is based on a three-part format focused on "making disciples who make disciples." This model consists of individual study, small group discussion and practical application.

The authors note that the world is rapidly changing, requiring the church to adapt discipleship strategies to unique and often complex realities. Testimony from global church leaders demonstrates that TEE empowers participants to draw closer to Jesus and experience the transforming power of the gospel on both an individual and community level.

The book presents a scholarly analysis of TEE and the educational theory behind the structure of this approach. It offers inspiration to employ the TEE philosophy and practice to the challenge of discipleship in our current context. Voices representing various parts of the globe provide a broad perspective on the growth and potential of the TEE movement in a wide range of cultural settings – "from Jordan in the west to the Philippines in the east, and from Russia in the north to New Zealand in the south."

Readers will be inspired by up-to-date stories that highlight the impact of TEE on individual and community growth in Christ around the world. Praise God for TEE as an effective tool for equipping the whole people of God to cooperate with God in God's mission in the world!

Ann E. C. Borquist, DMin
Global Consultant, International Ministries-ABCUSA

TEE for the 21st Century is fascinating tangible evidence that TEE is a credible, relevant and necessary model for equipping the people of God to be the people of God with biblical integrity, notably in the hard places where Christians seek to faithfully live the values and purposes of God's kingdom. It's a risky read if you can't cope with a contagious vision for an educationally and missionally sound form of theological education that most likely will become increasingly strategic as the world and the church establish their post-COVID-19 norms.

Allan Harkness, PhD
Founding Dean, Asia Graduate School of Theology Alliance, South East Asia
Theological Education Consultant

The strength of TEE has always been its focus on grassroots Christianity. Its insistence on integrating collaborative learning and practical ministry with theory, made accessible for diverse learners at all levels of education, from primary school to advanced university, has been particularly remarkable. This book reemphasizes that commitment and charts the development of TEE over the last century. It is essential reading for anyone who would like to bring theological education into local churches, and everyday life and ministry.

Evelyn Hibbert, EdD
Mentor, Angelina Noble Centre
Visiting Lecturer, Sydney Missionary and Bible College

What will enable the church moving forward to engage in the mission of God? *TEE for the 21st Century* provides one focused answer to this question through its examination of the foundations, frameworks and practical stories of application of the work of Theological Education by Extension. This is a multifaceted exploration of TEE.

I was struck by that fact that this is neither a history nor the story of TEE. It took me on a journey by weaving together a broad picture of the contribution and potential of this grassroots tool for the "equipping of God's people for ministry." The contribution of multiple voices enriched my understanding and gave fresh views from around the world, while calling me to look beyond traditional boundaries about knowing and creating knowledge.

For those of us involved in ministry and mission, wanting to join God in what he is doing, *TEE for the 21st Century* gives a thoughtful and provocative call to recognize and engage with the equipping of God's people through applied study of the word of God where people are.

Cathy Hine, PhD
Co-Founder, When Women Speak
Mentor, Angelina Nobel Centre

"As theological education goes – so goes the church!" Theological educators from around the globe have put together the findings of the value and variety of Theological Education by Extension – TEE. The focus of the collection of the twenty-one contributions is to match the needs of the church with an "at home" training without the traditional years of campus-based seminary or Bible school. Our times need new additional ways of training Christian leaders for the variety of ministries, especially for the fast-growing persecuted, poor (disadvantaged), and moving (diaspora) church.

The ancient question formulated by the North African church father Tertullian "What does Athens have to do with Jerusalem?" or "What emphasis should be placed on academic learning as opposed to the specific needs of the church?" has been thoroughly addressed by many of the contributors to the book.

This book is a must-read for every theologian (teachers, pastors, missionaries, and lay leaders), not only for reading and study but to put into practice the numerous excellent recommendations.

Manfred W. Kohl, ThD
Founder and President, Re-Forma

This is a comprehensive, collaborative, and compelling book on TEE! *TEE for the 21st Century* examines TEE from multi-disciplinary perspectives – theological, historical, educational, sociological, and missiological – and clearly demonstrates that TEE is an effective approach to theological education. Supported by research and accompanied by inspiring stories, this book narrates the amazing impact of TEE in building disciples and strengthening and multiplying churches, especially in restricted and needy places. The contribution from a global team of writers shows the strong support for the efficacy of TEE in equipping God's people for kingdom service. While this book is about TEE, it is likewise relevant to other modes of training, offering helpful insights to ensure that theological education does exist to serve the mission of the church in the world.

Theresa R. Lua, EdD
General Secretary, Asia Theological Association
Director, Global Theology, World Evangelical Alliance

A complete work that will be referenced for years! This is *the* orientation to TEE that I needed thirty years ago when beginning cross-cultural theological ministry. *TEE for the 21st Century* provides timely and stimulating insights for those new to TEE, experimenting with it, well versed in it, or even sceptical of it. This comprehensive volume refreshingly nurtures and re-shapes concepts of what is possible in our Covid-impacted world for equipping and empowering all God's people for all of God's mission in the context of a local church community.

New generations of learners, increasingly savvy with the online world of e-learning and m-learning, are hungry for holistic, situated learning experiences integrated into everyday life. This flows into their expectations of what ministry is, and training for that ministry. TEE, whether face to face, online or blended, firmly addresses this hunger by placing theological education on a contextual, relational and experiential foundation with an active, intentional commitment to partnership with churches.

Experienced practitioners from across Asia explore the rich history of TEE-specific accreditation, tailored for Asia, that has found fresh common ground on the global stage. We read how TEE is being effectively practiced in diverse situations in ways consistent with TEE's key pillars of group interaction, personal study and practical application. In today's world, well connected and integrated learning pathways that serve grassroots learners and churches can offer credible routes to recognized academic excellence. TEE offers this today, firmly rectifying the dated misconceptions held by many. There is much to learn in *TEE for the 21st Century* from TEE on university campuses, among people on the move, in churches wrestling with poverty and persecution, and in specific religious marketplaces. Mission workers especially will be encouraged. For theological educators and church and mission leaders who enjoy digging deeper, the bibliographies in each chapter are a rich resource for good theory and practice. I heartily recommend *TEE in the 21st Century.*

Diane Marshall, PhD

Global Director for Regional Development, SIM International

TEE for the 21st Century expertly articulates how TEE (Theological Education by Extension or Tools to Equip and Empower) emerged as a resource for newer churches experiencing rapid growth, and how it evolved to suit the contexts in which the tools were applied. It explains how TEE offers access to rapidly deployed, readily accessible, reader empowered, and relationship enhancing theological education resources.

This book confirms that TEE, guided by the Increase Association, is committed to providing quality theological education and adapting its material and methodology to suit the context, concerns and capabilities of TEE students – most of whom serve in the swelling centres of the global church, which are typically collectivist, integrated, and indigenous (including their diaspora). The authors position TEE as a trustworthy provider of biblically authentic education for the global church that engages with contemporary theologies yet remains rooted in the core tenets of historic Christianity.

The TEE method is also locally centred and applied, encouraging students to ponder theological meaning for themselves and their people, while sharing their thoughts and intentions with fellow students in their context. This mix of the macro (global) and micro (local) is powerful, providing a regulatory function that protects local churches from straying from traditional beliefs about the character of God, God's mission and the church's participation in it all as we live together in Christ by the power of the Holy Spirit. As this process matures, we can expect what is learned about God in local contexts to find its way back into the global conversation, thus completing an ecosystem of theological development for the global church. All to the glory of God.

Jay Matenga, DIS
Director, Global Witness Department, World Evangelical Alliance
Executive Director, WEA Mission Commission

TEE for the 21st Century is for anyone who wants to understand the current state of Theological Education by Extension and how it can be used to equip church leaders and lay people so that they can better serve the church and the world. Important aspects of the history, development, and acceptance of the movement are outlined and supported by worldwide reflections on its use. Importantly, the relationship between TEE and other forms of theological education – particularly formal, classroom-based methods – are clearly presented. Refusing to get mired in the past, the authors demonstrate how TEE as currently practiced engages modern learning theory and practice – concepts that benefit even those involved in traditional, formal theological education. All in all, the book offers solutions that can be globally applied for the benefit of the church. I highly recommend it.

Walter McConnell, PhD
Head of Mission Research, OMF International

TEE for the 21st Century is like a fresh, strong breeze for the sails of a beautiful ship called Theological Education by Extension (TEE). With this breeze, TEE will sail to new horizons with a motivated crew of theological educators and church leaders. The cargo, God's word, will find new ways to serve all of God's people around the world.

This book needs to be read and passed on with a word of encouragement that will be a blessing. Reading it is like feasting on a delicious spiritual meal. Everyone who starts eating will invite a friend to share this food with. Theological educators and church leaders alike will profit enormously from reading it.

This book is based on the wisdom of TEE pioneers from the past, and written by theologians and educators of today, with the goal to equip and empower the church for today and the future. This book is for all of God's people and will close the gap of the formal- and non-formal theological education divide. This is indeed a book for the twenty-first century.

Markus Völker, DMin
Director, SEAN International

TEE for the 21st Century is a multi-faceted gem – both scholarly and practical. The timing of its publication is spot-on. Church growth has long outstretched the provision of context-based biblical and theological education; persecution is a present reality for many Jesus-followers; Christian institutions face multiple pressures; and the global COVID-19 pandemic has forced us to redesign and nurture learning in new, flexible ways. "Can we do better?" ask the authors.

This book helps envision the kind of dynamic collaborations needed between the church and the training of its leaders and members, between teacher and learner, and between in-person and online learning. It speaks in highly relevant and practical ways to theological educators, church leaders, and church-based trainers. Biblical principles and contemporary learning theories are presented through a holistic perspective that sees biblical literacy and personal transformation as the hallmark of learning for all disciples of Jesus. The ideas centred on TEE are tested and grounded in years of real-life practice and the case studies and personal testimonies inform and inspire teachers and learners alike. If, like me, you have a passion to see God's people transformed and living as agents of transformation in their communities, and if you are convinced that an urgent need of the church worldwide is biblical training that addresses whole-of-life concerns in context, then you will want this resource to hand.

Ruth Wall, PhD
Chair of Executive Committee, WEA-Mission Commission
Adult Education Consultant and Chair,
International Missionary Training Network

TEE for the 21st Century should be read by anyone involved in the broad scope of theological education, not just TEE practitioners. If you have not engaged with TEE, then this is the book to take up and read. TEE is old enough to merit serious study and reflection. Though many chapters deal with TEE and its application to the Asian context, other continents are included and theological educators from around the globe will benefit from the themes presented. The context today of COVID-19 makes this book that much more relevant. The book speaks with humility and grace rather than a false triumphalism. TEE (and indeed this book) clearly challenges us to recall that theological education is for both ordained leaders and all the people of God as the universal priesthood of the Lord. This is truly a work that endeavours to engage across the board and has much to offer the global Christian community.

Jack C. Whytock, PhD
Convenor, Theological Education Commission, World Reformed Fellowship
Lecturer, African Reformation Theological Seminary, Kampala, Uganda

ICETE Series

TEE for the 21st Century

TEE for the 21st Century

Tools to Equip and Empower God's People for His Mission

General Editor

David Burke

Associate Editors

Richard Brown

Qaiser Julius

Series Editors

Riad Kassis and Michael A. Ortiz

Published 2021 by Langham Global Library
An imprint of Langham Publishing
www.langhampublishing.org

Langham Publishing and its imprints are a ministry of Langham Partnership

Langham Partnership
PO Box 296, Carlisle, Cumbria, CA3 9WZ, UK
www.langham.org

ISBNs:
978-1-83973-269-0 Print
978-1-83973-558-5 ePub
978-1-83973-559-2 Mobi
978-1-83973-560-8 PDF

British Library Cataloguing-in-Publication Data
A catalogue record for this book is available from the British Library

ISBN: 978-1-83973-269-0

Cover & Book Design: projectluz.com

In Memory of Zafar Ismail

(1948–2020)

by Tim Green[1]

Zafar Ismail was a founding member of the Increase Association, serving on its committee for eleven years and as chair from 2015 to 2017. A TEE pioneer in Pakistan, he also had a wider vision for God's people to be equipped for mission among the Muslim peoples of Asia and their worldwide diaspora. He passed away during the preparation of this book and it is fitting to mark its completion with a tribute to him.

Born in 1948 in Pakistan, Zafar grew up as a Muslim, studied engineering in university, and became Christ's follower in his twenties. He gained his Bachelor of Theology as one of the very first TEE students in Pakistan, working in the national TEE organization and becoming its first Pakistani director in

1. I had the privilege to write this tribute to Zafar as a personal friend and in my capacity as General Secretary of the Increase Association until March 2021.

1982. This growing ministry later took the name Open Theological Seminary (OTS). I joined in 1988, and Zafar became my close friend, wise mentor, and godfather to my son. Many times I ate at his table, along with his spouse, Sosan, and their children with whom I am still in touch. Zafar introduced me to a group of Christ's followers from Muslim backgrounds, with whom he shared both his teaching and his heart. He knew the challenges they faced.

Zafar loved to read widely in theology, Islam, education, history, and current affairs. He was a deep, independent thinker and a visionary, seeing beyond the next horizon, never content with the status quo but self-critically seeking improvement. His influence spread wider as he took part in international conferences from the 1980s onward and moved with his family to the UK in 1991.

Zafar had a heart for mission and a strategic mind. He stressed the key role of indigenous Christian minorities in the Muslim world, mobilized and equipped for mission; these could be "witnessing communities within cultures that would, under the mighty hand of God, change cultures from within," wrote Michael Huggins. "Zafar stressed the importance of grass-root level TEE as a key tool within such mission strategy."[2]

From 1996, Zafar helped Michael in the vision for indigenous TEE in Russia and Central Asia. A pioneering workshop they co-led in 2004 saw the launch of Russia's national TEE programme, ORTA. In 2005, with the encouragement of John Stott, they founded a charity, Matheteuo,[3] to support TEE ministries. In 2006, with others,[4] they co-launched Increase, where Zafar's continuous contribution till 2017 was appreciated by his colleagues, including myself. Zafar worked collaboratively and his influence was extended through friendship with leaders who benefitted from his insights. He also left a legacy through the organizations he helped to found and the Urdu-medium theological courses he wrote.

Zafar's heart remained in Pakistan where he continued to work for extended periods, increasingly so in his final years. His compassion for the poor

2. Michael Huggins, in a 1998 report for Oxen Ministries, email correspondence, 5 January 2021.

3. From the New Testament Greek, μαθητεύω, to be or to make a disciple.

4. Several key figures were involved; see chapter 14: Brown, Green and Aylett, "The Increase Association: A Theological Education Movement and Collaborative Network Strengthening TEE across Asia and Beyond."

was expressed through the Al Khair Trust he established to educate Christian children in Pakistan's brick-kilns, and his passion for mission through the Deir Mar Thoma organization to equip Pakistani Christian adults for mission-shaped discipleship in their Muslim environment. He was still working hard in these projects when diagnosed with cancer early in 2020. He passed away on 11 April that year.

Zafar's friends and family thank God for his generous heart, gracious hospitality, gentle patience, calm courtesy, and concern for others. We admire the breadth and depth of his searching intellect. We appreciate his humble, hard work and his commitment to equip the people of God for the mission of God. "For many he was an example and a role model of a godly Christian leader committed to prayer and God's work," writes Anneta Vysotskaya, the current Increase chairperson. "We thank God for the precious gift of brother Zafar's life, for his talents, his warm personality and kindness."[5] We do indeed.

5. Tribute found on the obituary website, https://www.gatheringus.com/memorial/zafar-ismael/3085.

Contents

Abbreviations

ARA	Action Reflection Action – methodology for theological education used in Africa
ATA	Asia Theological Association
BMB	Believer from a Muslim Background
CAED	Commission for Accreditation and Educational Development
CAMEO	Committee to Assist Ministry Education Overseas
CAVG	Central Asia Vision Group
CBT	Church-Based Training
CCTB	College of Christian Theology Bangladesh
C&MA	Christian and Missionary Alliance
CLTC	Christian Leaders' Training College
CIPEP	Corporación Instituto para la Educación Pastoral
EAAA	Euro-Asian Accrediting Agency
F2F	Face-to-face discussion in TEE learning groups
GAAMT	Global Accreditation Association for Ministries and Training
ICETE	International Council for Evangelical Theological Education
ICT	Information Communication Technology
ITEEN	Institute for TEE in Nepal
LMS	Learning Management System
MENA	Middle East and North Africa
ORTA	Open Russian Theological Academy
OTS	Open Theological Seminary (in Pakistan)
PAFTEE	Philippine Association for TEE
PTEE	Program for TEE (in the Arab World)
RPL	Recognition of Prior Learning
SEAN	Study by Extension for All Nations

SG-GETE	Standards and Guidelines for Global Evangelical Theological Education
SME	Subject matter expert
SRD	Situation Response Development (used in context-based course design)
TAFTEE	The Association for TEE (in India)
TE	theological education
TEE	Theological Education by Extension, or Tools to Equip and Empower
TEEM	TEE Malawi
TEEZ	TEE Zambia
TEF	Theological Educators' Forum (in Pakistan)
TEL	Technology Enhanced Learning
TEXT-Africa	TEE materials published by Evangel Publishing House in Kenya
WEA	World Evangelical Alliance

Foreword

On occasions, the global landscape for theological education encounters the need for adjustments. Over recent years, a significant portion of the changes have stemmed from the call for theological education that is not from the top down, but rather driven from the bottom up, namely from needs grounded in the church. Many would concur that in-residence, campus-based, formal theological education is too often inadequate to meet the scope of leaders required by current church demands, particularly due to the growth in Majority World contexts.

TEE for the 21st Century highlights a tried theological education model to be considered that distinctly addresses church demands. The editors have brought together the most experienced practitioners in TEE, along with select global theological education leaders, to offer a robust and timely collection. This book is divided into three major sections beginning with an introduction which properly sets the scene for the work. In the next section, a multidisciplinary approach outlines the theological, historical, and educational foundations for TEE so as to further extend its credible basis, no matter what the educational setting. Within this second section, various authors also tell of their creative approaches through which TEE has been utilized for unusual contexts, such as the persecuted church and diaspora communities, with proven and notable results. The final section offers TEE reflections from leaders in Asia, Africa, Latin America, and key global communities involved in theological education. These writers additionally encourage the reader to meaningfully reflect upon the vast possibilities for theological education while remaining centred on the mission of the church.

TEE for the 21st Century celebrates what TEE has accomplished for theological education, especially through its church-in-context orientation. Yet the editors and contributors alike have invested into this project not simply to celebrate, but also to inspire and challenge us all for what lies ahead. There may be portions of this book that precisely speak to a theological education need or concern a reader presently faces. Other portions of the text might cause the reader to deliberate on comprehensive considerations and perhaps shift their theological education towards a reimagined direction. For some, this text might simply lead them to make minor, though consequential, adaptations.

Throughout its history, TEE has provided accessible, relevant, practical, and contextual training for the church. *TEE for the 21st Century* reassures its reader of TEE's established model. Even so, still more remains to be done, and perhaps this work might enthuse others to innovatively draw future theological education nearer to, and for the sake of, the church.

Dr. Michael A. Ortiz

International ICETE Director

Part A

Setting the Scene

Introduction and Acknowledgments

David Burke, Richard Brown, and Qaiser Julius

Welcome to TEE for the Twenty-First Century

"TEE" stands for Theological Education by Extension (also sometimes styled as Tools to Equip and Empower) and is the subject matter of this book. Perhaps you are standing at a bookstall wondering what this book is about and whether it is worth your time to read. This chapter is designed to introduce the book and to answer some questions that you may be asking.

Who Developed the Book?

As editors and writers of this book, our backgrounds are global. Many of us have participated in traditional campus-based theological education as students and teachers and thank God for this. We are all part of the local church and value all that it brings to our lives and the opportunities of service that we find there. We have glimpsed the opportunities and challenges of developing the whole people of God in discipleship and service, and we are challenged and excited by this.

In short, we are probably in many ways rather like you, our anticipated reader. We come as friends.

We also come as part of the Increase Association, also known as Increase, which serves to connect and strengthen TEE and other church-based training across Asia. As of February 2021, the Association has thirty Core Member organizations stretching from Jordan in the west to the Philippines in the east, and from Russia in the north to New Zealand in the south. You will see we have a very generous understanding of Asia, including the Middle East, Russia and the Asia-Pacific region, as well as their far-flung diaspora peoples! We have seen the impact and potential of such training to glorify the Lord by equipping his people in his task of making disciples from all nations. We want to share that impact and potential with a wider audience, and this book is an initiative of Increase.

Why This Book?

Our earlier book, *TEE in Asia* (Increase Association, 2018; new edition, Langham, 2021) aroused widespread interest as it introduced contemporary TEE to a global audience and told some of the stories of lives changed through TEE in an array of contexts across Asia and beyond.

However, that book left a gap in explaining and exploring the academic foundations and shape of TEE. At a time when the winds of change are leading many to ask anew what forms of training best serve the church, it seemed timely to take an in-depth and scholarly look at TEE.

We want to introduce TEE to theological educators and ministry leaders as a viable approach to theological education that is contemporary in its applications, established in its track record, and well-founded in its scholarship. After a generation with almost no academic discourse on TEE, this multi-author academic book brings it back into scrutiny at a time when fundamental questions are again being asked about the future of theological education. We also want to open informed discussion about TEE and invite scrutiny from a wider educational and church audience in order to improve what we do and to serve the church better.

For Whom Do We Write?

This book is designed for several different audiences.

Theological educators

We are committed to quality-assured, multi-level, and flexible training for the whole people of God, including its leaders. We see ourselves as partners with other theological educators who daily grapple with the challenges outlined in chapter 1 and who face the following questions and more:

- Do our times call for incremental or paradigmatic change? What does that change look like?

- How can TEE help extend the mission, ministry, and reach of campus-based training and church-based training approaches?
- How can TEE adapt to partner more usefully with campus-based bodies in the task of training?

Church leaders

We are committed to the church, in all its parts and expressions, as the primary earthly means by which its Lord accomplishes his mission. We are part of the church and ask the following questions to help TEE be more effective:

- How can TEE help grow disciples and servants to serve God's mission and the mission of his church?
- How can TEE contribute to the challenge of training large numbers of leaders and workers for fast-growing churches where traditional approaches are not viable or appropriate?
- What can the church say or ask of the TEE movement to help the church fulfil its mission better?

The TEE community

We are committed to making TEE as effective as possible. As co-labourers with the global TEE network of national teams, course writers, administrators, group leaders, and students we ask anew the following questions:

- What are the roots and foundations of TEE and how are they best expressed and adapted to serve God's mission and his church in the twenty-first century?
- How can existing and new TEE programmes better serve the Lord and his church?
- How can TEE in the twenty-first century keep adapting to new developments in education and technology?

The wider community of church-based trainers

TEE is not the only form of church-based ministry training. We appreciate the approaches of other church-based trainers and want to open dialogue towards mutual advantage.

- What can different church-based training approaches learn from one another?
- How can different church-based trainers work with one another as well as with campus-based training?

How Does the Book Work?

The book is designed to introduce and discuss TEE from multiple perspectives. The book is divided into three main parts.

Part A: Setting the Scene

The words "Theological Education by Extension" themselves do not clearly define the mode of "extension." The term TEE has been used for a variety of delivery methodologies, some very different from the three-in-one methodology first described as TEE in the 1960s. The term TEE has been adapted and adopted in a myriad of ways. A short *TEE at a Glance* section in this book explains the classic definition of TEE to those who are unfamiliar with its methodology and terminology or who are confused by varying uses of the term. Some later chapters include more detail of the nature and story of TEE.

TEE fits within the wider enterprise of theological education. A group of global leaders in theological education were asked to comment on challenges that the theological education movement faces today. Chapter 1 builds on this to survey contemporary challenges, outline the fundamentals and relevance of TEE, and show how TEE can help educators address these challenges.

Part B: Multi-Disciplinary Perspectives on TEE

Theological and biblical foundations undergird and shape TEE, as befits all truly Christian education. Accordingly, chapters 2 and 3 take a broad view of the character and mission of God and how they shape the character and mission of the church. This is developed into a discussion of implications for the shape of ministry training and the contribution of TEE. Key themes that continue through the whole book are identified: God's character and mission lie at the heart of the identity of the church, all of God's people are called to serve in his mission, and the whole people of God need equipping for this task.

TEE has been on the scene since the early 1960s and has spread globally and adapted locally in response to varying contexts and changing insights. The underlying character of TEE as a church-based approach to training fits within the broader patterns of ministry training since biblical times. Chapter 4 tells the story of TEE and how it nests within historic approaches to theological education.

These theological and historical chapters lead to consideration of educational perspectives. One feature of TEE in more recent years has been its readiness to engage with contemporary insights in educational theory and practice. Chapter 5 takes a broad look at modern educational theory and how TEE relates to it. Chapter 6 complements this with a closer look at the learners, the tasks for which learners are being equipped, and how learners learn. Both these chapters engage in a two-way conversation, asking how TEE can both learn from, and contribute to, educational thinking.

The educational discussion continues in the following chapters. In its early stages, TEE arose in a particular cultural context (Latin America) and the self-study texts supporting a learner's personal study used a particular educational approach, namely programmed instruction. As earlier chapters relate, TEE has adapted to differing cultural contexts and shows readiness to be informed by current educational thinking. Chapter 7 demonstrates this adaptation through an overview of Increase's new TEE course-writing programme, illustrated by a case study from Central Asia.

The digital revolution is a fact of the present educational landscape. It presents challenges such as inequity of access, the distractions of social media, and the difficulty of discernment of truth and importance in the face of the sheer volume of information available. However, it also presents opportunities that give transformational possibilities in education. Chapter 8 has a detailed discussion of digital learning that many educators will value as an introduction to the field. It also shows how TEE is well-placed to move from its original paper-based materials to digital media, and comments on how to preserve important relational and practical aspects of the TEE approach.

Quality assurance is an important concern in TEE as for any mode of theological education. How can quality control and accountability be assured in ways that are appropriate to the particular shape of TEE? Chapter 9 engages with key questions in quality assurance and proposes a framework for TEE that is both academically defensible and suited to the unique form of TEE.

How does TEE relate to campus-based approaches in theological education? Chapter 10 argues that campus-based approaches and TEE need not be competitors but can collaborate in fruitful, mutually beneficial partnerships that contribute to the shared task of educating and equipping the whole people of God.

Two features of the present missiological landscape are discussed in chapters 11 and 12. The large-scale global movements of people challenge forms of theological training that presume a settled community of homogenous language and culture. Chapter 11 demonstrates how TEE can meet the training needs of diaspora (migrant and refugee) communities living in nations and cultures far from their homelands. From another vantage point, the present era may be described as one of the great periods of Christian persecution. The persecuted church needs ministry training so that God's people are able to stand against the forces of darkness and give a reason for their hope in Christ. How is this possible when theological training institutions may be prohibited? Chapter 12 shows how the church-based and small group-based approach of TEE enables training to be delivered to learners in hostile settings.

The theological, historical, educational, and contextual perspectives of chapters 2 to 12 are complemented by a sociological perspective in chapter 13. A religious market theory approach is combined with a case study from Central Asia to help understand the development of the TEE movement in Central Asia and to plot future trajectories.

TEE has developed historically as an organic movement with many independent branches rather than as a centrally and hierarchically controlled, multinational organization. However, growing movements need some level of framework and coordination. The Increase Association has been a key agent in providing these for the wider TEE movement across Asia. Chapter 14 tells the story of Increase and provides an analysis through a sociological lens, showing how the association developed as a movement and a network to serve TEE practitioners across Asia and beyond. This novel approach in examining Increase may be helpful to other organizations and networks wishing to evaluate and frame their development.

Part C: Church Leadership and Theological Education Perspectives on TEE

The TEE movement welcomes critical dialogue about its approach and is keen to listen to theological educators and church leaders outside Asia and the TEE community. To this end, significant contributors from among those groups were invited to read the drafts of chapters 1 to 14. In chapters 15 to 21 their comments and reflections address two questions in the present global theological education scene: "What can the wider world learn from TEE?" and "What can TEE learn from the wider world?"

Following parts A, B, and C, three appendices provide sample TEE lessons to help illustrate the methodology and to offer readers an opportunity to taste TEE.

Join the Chat

You can join the critical dialogue about TEE through the "Contact us" option on the Increase Association website (https://www.increaseassociation.org).

Acknowledgements

If it takes a village to raise a child, it takes a global community to produce a book like this. Over ninety people were involved in this project in one way or another! The whole book has a collaborative and global nature. Most chapters involved two co-writers, two external reviewers and one internal coordinator. Editorial team meetings stretched over eleven different time zones. An edited collection such as this is enriched by the diverse voices of its many writers and their passionate interest in the topics about which they have written. Within the overall flow and purposes of the book, every effort has been made to preserve those individual voices within the chapters.

The editorial team extends thanks to those who volunteered as writers and peer reviewers – and the family and friends behind them who prayed, read drafts, and allowed space for the work. Our thanks to Chen Yoke Mee, Aaron Tham and Job Chang from Kuala Lumpur Increase who gave administrative and formatting support, and much appreciation to Ross James from Perth, Western Australia, for copyediting assistance. A special thanks to the global theological educators who responded to our request for inputs to chapter 1 and to the theological educators and church leaders who read the whole draft and wrote the reflective contributions in chapters 15 to 21 and the Preface. Thanks also to Vivian Doub, along with Isobel Stevenson, Mark Arnold, and Luke Lewis from Langham Publishing, who were prompt and helpful in responding to queries and in overseeing the post-manuscript preparation and publishing of the book. Lastly, we editors record our appreciation to Graham Aylett and Tim Green from the leadership of Increase Association, for their impetus, encouragement and extensive involvement in bringing the book to publication.

Finally

Working together as editors to complete the book on target was richly rewarding and stretching. Each of our roles amicably overlapped when required. David, as general editor, provided overall leadership to the project and coordinated communications with writers and reviewers throughout the process. Richard, as associate editor, chaired editorial team meetings, managed the project schedule, and coordinated copyediting. Qaiser, as associate editor, provided helpful advice and assistance at various stages of the project.

In closing, the development of this book has been surrounded by prayer. It is published with the prayer that the Lord of the church uses it to his glory and for the strengthening of his church in his kingdom mission of discipling all nations and reconciling and renewing all things in Christ.

TEE at a Glance

Tim Green and Graham Aylett

What do we mean by "TEE?" Traditionally TEE stands for Theological Education by Extension. The term has been variously used for correspondence courses, evening classes, online lectures, or off-campus seminars delivered by campus-based faculty; all of these have value, but none conforms to the classic definition of TEE that arose in Guatemala in the 1960s. TEE, on this understanding, is a distinct mode of theological education in its own right and needs to be taken on its own terms. It is the subject of an extensive literature since its inception, and this book argues for its continuing relevance for the twenty-first century.

On this focused understanding, TEE is an integrated combination of three elements in sequence: personal study, group meetings, and practical application. These three elements are connected in a learning cycle.

The first step is *personal study*. Participants work through a carefully prepared lesson that involves active learning, not passive reading. The lesson helps them engage with Scripture, gain new knowledge, and start to connect it with their own life experience. All this becomes a springboard to the next learning step.

The second step is the *group meeting*. The group is small enough to allow every member to contribute. Helped by a trained group leader, members share what they discovered in the first step, reflect on their own experience, and learn from one another. They study Scripture together and may use role-play, learning tasks, and other group activities as well as discussion. The group leader facilitates the group interactions and does not give an extended lecture. The group time leads to the third step.

The third step is *practical application*. Whatever was learned in steps one and two must now be applied in members' daily life at home, work, church, and in the wider community. Practical application, the integration of learning and living under the Lordship of Jesus, is the goal of TEE courses. So, this step involves a specific assignment – whether for personal life, ministry, or mission. Assignments may be for individual group members, or for the group as a whole. In some cases, it may include discovery learning in preparation for the next topic in the course.

None of these three elements is exceptional on its own, but the TEE method weaves them together into a stronger cord. When integrated, they combine into a learning cycle as this diagram illustrates.

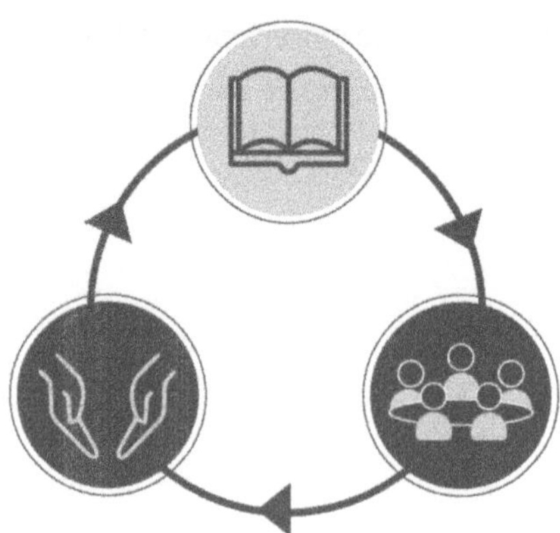

The learning cycle leads to the next cycle, typically once a week for ten to twelve weeks to complete the course, before learners proceed to the next course. Assessment reinforces learning and forms an important part of it, usually with a combined aggregate of attendance, participation in discussion, tests and exams, completion of practical assignments, and some evidence of personal development.

With repetition, this learning cycle becomes a habit, and personal study, group meetings and practical application are integrated into learners' routines.

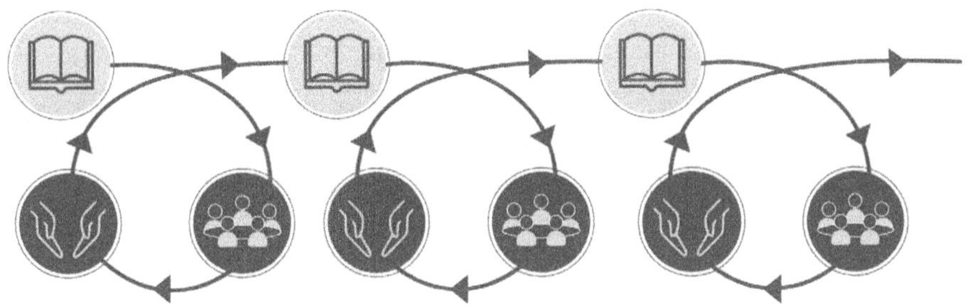

It is evident that TEE is not a form of distance learning. Rather, it is small group learning that utilizes a flipped classroom approach as described in later chapters. TEE practitioners are currently experimenting with how personal study and group meetings can take place digitally without losing the three-in-one method and the rootedness in local churches.

TEE is not an organization. Around the world various organizations publish TEE materials and many organizations serve the churches in their countries by providing TEE materials and training. But TEE itself is not an organization.

TEE is a movement. The classic term "Theological Education by Extension" may also be complemented by the phrase "Tools to Equip and Empower." This catches the dynamism of TEE's vision, to be a tool for churches to equip and empower all their members for mission and ministry, a vision that includes but is not restricted to training church leaders.

Hence TEE is *materials* using a *method* and is also a *movement* with a *vision*.

"What Excites Us about TEE"

In 2010 in Nepal, Increase ran a conference for TEE practitioners entitled "Twenty-First Century TEE in Asia: Challenges and Opportunities." The seventy participants were asked "What excites you about TEE?" Their collated responses led to the following conference statement.[1]

> We are excited about TEE!
>
> We have seen repeatedly, consistently and in many regions, the life-changing, transforming work of God in people's lives as they study through TEE. We know the joy of seeing them grow.
>
> We believe that TEE has a solid educational foundation combining home study, regular group meetings and practical application. The TEE method promotes immediate and ongoing application, and should lead to holistic, all-round growth, not just growth in knowledge. It is people-oriented and learner-centred. This method develops a whole range of skills: personal study skills, listening and communication skills, and skills of critical thinking and evaluation according to biblical values and a biblical worldview.
>
> The TEE courses we use are faithful to the Scriptures, and encourage students to engage in close, deep, regular and ongoing study of God's word. They bring sound teaching and help people to understand and apply the Bible in their context.
>
> TEE materials can be widely used across denominations, promoting the unity of faith, and have been tried and tested in many contexts and countries. There are materials at all levels, including those that are easy to use and understand, practical and not too academic. TEE is therefore a tool for training from the ground level to the highest levels of learning. TEE learning materials can also be delivered in a great variety of ways, by printed media and multi-media electronic tools.

---

1. https://www.increaseassociation.org/news-archive/31-kathmandu-2010-conference-statement.

The TEE method allows great flexibility: groups can study anywhere at any time. It can be used in all kinds of situations, city and countryside, including in a blended form alongside residential training. It is especially appropriate where there is persecution. It is a great tool for serving diaspora communities. Because the costs to the student are low, the programme is affordable. Because group meetings usually take place weekly, students can learn alongside the continuing responsibilities of their daily lives in their homes, workplaces, and communities. Through a TEE programme, training and learning are made accessible for everyone who wants to learn, regardless of location, salary, age or gender.

The TEE method provides training in the context of everyday life and ministry – training people where they live and work and serve – in this way integrating learning and living. TEE in Asia is indigenous, rooted in national movements, giving many opportunities for creating contextual training in partnership with the local churches.

Therefore, we affirm that TEE can provide a sound framework for discipleship: spiritual formation, mentoring and character development. It can help Christians grow in the knowledge of God. It is a means to go forward in obedience to the Great Commission by combining materials for discipleship, training of church leaders, and church planting. As group facilitators give rise to new facilitators there is inbuilt multiplication. It is local church related, and often local church based. Through TEE groups, relationships are deepened, and real community grows.

Above all, we believe TEE has the potential to equip all church members as agents of transformation, moving them from being passive receivers to active servants, salt and light where they are.

That's why we are excited about TEE!

1

Challenges Facing Contemporary Theological Education and the Case for TEE

David Burke, Richard Brown, and Qaiser Julius

Our greatest challenge as theologians and theological educators, is to keep God at the center of what we do.[1]

I took a deep breath and responded as best I could. "Let me put it this way," I said. "I think I know what you should not do. Don't do what we have done in the West. We know the results of that."[2]

[COVID-19] has pointed out the "chinks in the armour" of many programs.[3]

A quiet reformation has been burgeoning in western theological education for some time . . . Before long I expect the reformation won't be quiet anymore.[4]

1. Volf, "Dancing for God," 3.
2. Pratt, "Opportunities and Challenges," 2.
3. Respondent Clark.
4. Greg Forster, "Biggest Challenge," 3.

Introduction

The Old Testament refers to "sons" of the prophets gathered in what is often regarded as a school (e.g. 2 Kgs 2:5; 4:38; 6:1). Jesus took the seventy-two aside for instruction, followed by field experience with reflection (e.g. Luke 10:1–20). Priscilla and Aquila ran a home-based intensive for Apollos (Acts 18:24–26). Paul trained Timothy and Titus for leadership roles and provided continuing professional education in his letters to them. Things have changed since then. Theological education, when broadly defined as equipping the whole people of God for growth in Christ and diverse kinds and levels of service,[5] has taken many different forms historically.[6] Many present challenges give impetus to re-think established patterns.

The challenges discussed below are not new. It is sobering that the challenges identified by the International Council for Evangelical Theological Education (ICETE) since 1984 align with those identified in this chapter.[7]

The various iterations of the *ICETE Manifesto* since 1984[8] have called for renewal of theological education in words such as the following:

> Insofar as theological education concerns the formation of leadership for the church of Christ in its mission, to that extent theological education assumes a critically strategic biblical importance . . . We also recognise that there are examples in our midst, usually all too close at hand, where things are not being done right. We confess this with shame. Traditional forms are being maintained only because they are traditional, and radical

5. This book certainly defines theological education as *including* higher level training for specialized church leadership roles but argues that this is within a whole-people-of God view of ministry and training.

6. A worthwhile review of the present size and shape of global theological education is provided in Werner et al., *Handbook of Theological Education.*

7. The *ICETE Manifesto* provides a list of challenges: contextualization, church-ward orientation, strategic flexibility, theological grounding, community life, integrated programmes, servant moulding, instructional variety, a Christian mind, equipping for growth. See ICETE, *The ICETE Manifesto*.

8. We also note a range of similar concerns in *The Cape Town Commitment*. See Lausanne, *The Cape Town Commitment*, Part IIF 4, 59–60. Both ICETE and the Lausanne Movement are representative of the global evangelical church.

> forms pursued only because they are radical, and the formation of effective leadership for the church of Christ is seriously hindered.[9]

Having identified a range of contemporary challenges in theological education, the next section of the chapter introduces a presently less-known approach known as Theological Education by Extension (TEE) which previews the remainder of the book.

Challenges Faced

In preparation for this chapter some global theological educators were asked to identify contemporary challenges.[10] Their replies, with some representative literature to complement, are presented below, using questions grouped around the themes including: purpose (*why?*), learners (*with whom?*), context (*where?*), content (*what?*), methods (*how?*), and providers (*by whom?*).[11] In other words, we ask what are contemporary challenges associated with the purpose, the learners, the context, the content, the methods, and the providers of theological education?

Challenges arising from the "why?" of theological education

This section is concerned with challenges of purpose in theological education.

The high-level purpose of theological education is to serve the church as it engages in the mission of God. His mission shapes the mission of the church which is served by theological education. More is said on this in a later chapter. This high-level sense of purpose frames any discussion about purpose in theological education.

Purpose statements in theological education may reflect unexamined assumptions about Christian life and service. Such statements often talk about preparing church workers who are in a distinct category of employed church

9. All three quotes are from the *ICETE Manifesto* (2002 edition).

10. A list of the survey respondents and their role in theological education is included in the bibliography. They include diverse theological traditions and some global agencies. Both this survey and the literature reviewed are representative, rather than being exhaustive.

11. Similar questions are used to advantage by Bernard Ott in his seminal work. See Ott, *Understanding and Developing Theological Education*, 269–82. The questions will be explained in the following text.

leaders. These church workers are often seen through a professional lens, and the model for their education may be drawn from professions such as education or social work.

Does this sense of purpose reflect a theologically defensible view of Christian life and service? Does it unwittingly create a caste of religious practitioners who are in a quite separate category of Christian and whose training fosters development in just some parts of their Christian identity?

Mark 1:15–20 presents an integrated example of faith, discipleship, and service. The gospel was preached, and people were called to repentance and faith. This merges into a call to discipleship ("follow me") and a call to service ("and I will make you fishers of men"). Elsewhere, the Scriptures teach that gifts for Christian service are given through the Spirit, creating various forms of service in which every Christian is expected to have a part (1 Cor 12:4–11). The church will have its specialized leaders, but the specialist roles they perform do not exhaust the range of the Spirit's gifts or the various services to which people are called (1 Cor 12:27–30).

How can theological education keep the preparation of specialist leaders integrally tied to purposes of discipleship and service by the whole people of God? Educational models that extract students from the natural setting of discipleship in the body of believers, which equip them with knowledge and skills that distance them from disciples at large, are problematic against such concerns. Is it enough for students only to acquire some theological knowledge and professional ministry skills?[12] These models may reward academic performance more than spiritual formation and ministry skills[13] and reinforce a narrow model of ministry, with one highly trained professional minister per congregation. Such professionalization of the ministry is tragically unbiblical, crushes fulltime pastors, and fails to release the ministry of all believers.[14]

Stephen Spencer speaks of the need to move beyond Enlightenment views of people and theological knowledge and embrace personal transformation as a goal of theological education.[15] Spencer advocates a discipleship purpose of

12. Respondent Himawan.

13. Respondent Green.

14. Respondent Green.

15. Spencer, "Seminaries and Discipleship," 3, 12.

following Jesus in the domains of knowing, being, doing, and relating and notes that this will require a pedagogical shift.[16] Likewise, Richard Pratt observes the challenge to correct imbalances between attention to biblical and theological content, ministry skills and personal formation.[17] Tim Green suggests moving from both monastic and university models of theological education.[18]

Some colleges[19] recognize this and include elements of discipleship and transformation in their statements of desired learning outcomes.[20] However, is it better to tweak, or to reshape, the college model such that it better serves the discipleship and ministry of the whole people of God? Hence, Forster asks:

> Loving God and neighbour, not intellectual rectitude, is the ultimate goal. Theological knowledge used to be judged not by what kind of Bible trivia quizzes you could ace but by what kind of life you lived. How we got into this mess is a long and complicated story. One of the biggest problems is the [nineteenth century] German research university model of education, with its emphasis on abstraction, fact/value distinction, and scholarly specialization. That model is now the only model of what counts as "knowledge" in the Western world, and theological schools are not immune from its dominance. Theological educators are professionally evaluated and promoted based on whether they produce scholarly books and articles (judged by the nineteenth-century German research university model of "scholarship") much more than on whether they produce disciples.[21]

---

16. Spencer.

17. Pratt, "Opportunities and Challenges," 7.

18. Respondent Green notes how the traditional model of theological education "relies on the historical precedent of monastery for its community, and university for access to professors and books. But the former of these is not attractive to families in the twenty-first century (family upheaval, spouse career, children's education), while the latter is barely needed any longer (because teaching and learning resources are mostly on the internet)."

19. "College" is used throughout this chapter as a term inclusive of various types of campus-based institutions of theological education, including seminaries, Bible schools, etc.

20. See https://christcollege.edu.au/study/graduate-attributes/ for an example of an attempt to do this. Within this college, the desired attributes are further specified into 72 items and the whole college programme has been designed to introduce, develop and assure each attribute.

21. Forster, "Biggest Challenge," 1.

Addressing the challenges of clarity and theological soundness of purpose in theological education provides the basis for reverse engineering[22] those purposes through the whole college experience.[23] It also holds the promise of tethering theological education to the conversion-discipleship-service sequence noted above.

Challenges arising from the "with whom?" of theological education

Education involves people. They are created by God in his image, subject to the fall, saved by grace, indwelt by the Spirit, and are given gifts and calling into his service.

These people are the "with whom?" of theological education. They should be active partners in their own learning, rather than passive recipients. Their personal complexities and the complexity of theological education in the contemporary environment give rise to several challenges.

Student recruitment is a challenge to the viability of colleges. One principal from a Western context speaks of a complacency that prevents students in well-led churches from seeing how important it is that they are well-trained in basic theological disciplines, preferring instead to put their focus on a pragmatic "what works" learning.[24] Another speaks of a slowing number of people who see the need of theological formation for lifelong ministry.[25]

Others speak of generational issues. Established ministry workers may not see the need for training.[26] Older people may think that it is "too late," "too hard" and "too lengthy" to qualify for what they are already doing.[27] High academic entry standards and the academic nature of courses may be a barrier to those who are rich in life experience but low in academic orientation and experience. The tragedy is that such people have immediate potential for mature church leadership as opposed to younger students. Younger students

---

22. For more on this, see Wiggins and McTighe, *Understanding by Design*.

23. For a good example of how clarity of purpose can be reverse engineered through a college see Shaw, *Transforming Theological Education*.

24. Respondent Smith.

25. Respondent Millar.

26. Respondent Krishnan.

27. Respondent Krishnan.

hold promise of decades of service but may come to college unaware of the importance of slow formation and with less personal resilience than older people.[28] They may also be frustrated if the pedagogy of older teachers does not match their own preferred learning style which have been shaped through prior learning experiences.[29]

How can colleges serve the many students who seek education for personal growth or nonordained service?[30] How can they educate the whole people of God in a way more accessible than thirteen-week semesters of daytime classes on a centralized campus?[31] Widening access to quality education for the whole people of God can both help make colleges more educationally and financially viable and also serve the church as it implements the ministry of all.

The financial cost of traditional theological education is increasingly a barrier for students and sending churches, and a challenge for colleges.[32] Financial pressures may result in high drop-out rates as students seek or need employment.[33] Part of the solution may lie in colleges diversifying their offerings in short courses, intensives, and continuing education, and part may lie in changing the way training is packaged.[34] Is there scope for more partnership between local churches and colleges in initial ministry training, both to reduce the on-campus time and costs of the training and to cement links with church ministry?

---

28. Respondent Smith. As one respondent says, many young seminary entrants were converted in early adulthood from non-Christian backgrounds of broken homes and un-Christian behaviours. These may require more attention and extra resources in spiritual formation, counselling and other student services (Respondent Perry) which in turn increases the pastoral load on senior college leaders (Respondent Smith).

29. Sherlock et al., "Uncovering Theology," 9.

30. Sherlock et al., 9.

31. Respondent Shaw.

32. One principal reports that the costs of running a college have consistently increased by more than the consumer price index over his 30 years of involvement (Respondent Smith). Someone else comments that colleges cannot assume that unsympathetic governments will be happy to keep funding theology students via government loans endlessly or without unacceptable conditions being imposed (Respondent Perry).

33. Respondent Mishra.

34. Respondent Perry.

With increasing numbers of bi-vocational pastors,[35] challenges arise from students who are so enculturated into college and ministry that they have no capacity to be self-supporting.[36] Can theological training be delivered such that students remain fit for regular employment as they study and as they graduate to ministries lacking full financial support?[37]

A lack of access to quality theological education by most of the world's pastors[38] is a further problem. In situations of high biblical illiteracy this is a recipe for heresy and for cults to form around preachers who only do miracles and promise prosperity.[39]

Challenges arising from the "where?" of theological education

One writer of this chapter helps coordinate ministry training in Timor Leste. Scale issues make a traditional college model impossible. Pastoral students are sent abroad for training in foreign languages, which is expensive, disorienting, and leaves some reluctant to serve in remote villages on their return. Their college experiences help prepare them as church leaders, but the location of the colleges (Indonesia and Brazil) presents challenges.

Several respondents commented on challenges relating to the contexts of training and ministry. The twin dangers emerge of being so attuned to the "where?" of study and ministry that there is nothing to say beyond reinforcing messages from that context, or the opposite danger of being faithful to the Scriptures in ways that connect to ancient and distant worlds but say nothing to *these* people in *this* place. Both dangers threaten serious disconnections.

Global theological educators speak forcefully on the challenges of context.

35. Respondent Perry. Bivocational refers to the pastor who engages in everyday paid work alongside a church role that may or may not be paid.

36. Respondent Tagore.

37. One of the editors has taught in an Indonesian college that teaches self-supporting employment skills, alongside theological subjects, to students from West Papua who are preparing to be church planters.

38. David Esterline et al., "Global Survey on Theological Education 2011–2013: Summary of Main Findings," paper presented at WCC 10th Assembly, Busan, 30 October–8 November 2013, 2; Pratt, "Opportunities and Challenges," 9. Pratt reports an observation from Ralph Winter that there were two million pastors globally with no formal theological education in 1998. Many of these pastors are new converts themselves which adds to the dangers of a lack of training.

39. Respondent Tagore.

The Middle East and North Africa (MENA)

The traditional curriculum is inadequate to prepare leaders for the church in the rapidly changing context of the MENA region.[40]

India

70 percent of the Indian population lives in rural India and there is a lack of venues to provide sound and extended theological education due to challenging lifestyles and greater danger of persecution.[41]

Often theological educators from overseas and other cultural settings within India are not able to deal with relevant local issues . . . Hindi theological material is translated without considering the common usages of the word; such words may be literal in their expression but are often dreadful in communication . . . Theological materials in Hindi have to be developed, simplified, and beautified to be appealing to lay persons and trainees.[42]

Indonesia

Evangelical theological institutions find it very difficult to engage with the plurality of society (religious, cultural, etc.), and with the social and political conditions. We have no ability to integrate them into curriculum and into the praxis of the *civitas academica* [ed. academic society]. We are more concerned with pastoral-individual needs and spirituality.[43]

40. Respondent Shaw.
41. Respondent Tagore.
42. Respondent Mishra.
43. Respondent Himawan.

China

"Different Asian cultures find themselves in rapid change, yielding to the onslaught of market capitalism and what comes with it as liberal humanism in the guise of democracy, and struggling desperately at the same time to maintain their cultural identities. Sociocultural fragmentation is a common experience for many Asian people."[44]

Global Agencies

As our world continues to urbanize and become more economically interdependent, understanding and nurturing intercultural relationships will continue to grow in importance. Moreover, the Great Commission and the unity of our "one [global] body" (John 17; Acts 15; 1 Cor 12–14; Eph 2–4; Rom 12–15, etc.) gives us strong theological motivations to adjust our curriculum, faculties, and libraries in ways that recognize voices from different parts of the global church.[45]

Another challenge lies in understanding global migration, the changing ecclesial landscape and the consequences for inter-contextuality in theological education.[46]

Questions of location go beyond issues of financial cost and reluctant returnees. In many ways, it strikes at the heart of the problem. When theological education is removed from the context where ministry is conducted, its usefulness may be undermined.

Challenges arising from the "what?" of theological education

For the purposes of this chapter, the "what?" of theological education is referring to the content of the curriculum. The challenge of integration within and across the curriculum is frequently mentioned and applies at several levels.

44. Yu, "Major Issues in Asian Theological Education," 2.

45. Respondent Perry.

46. Werner, "Challenges and Major Tasks," 8.

Some comment on the danger of siloing, such that different theological disciplines are carved up like disconnected university disciplines.[47] Connection between disciplines is widely valued but remains elusive.[48]

A related fragmentation occurs between theory and practice.[49] On the university model, practical theology can become just another subject to be included on the list.[50] That can result in ecclesiastical technicians who are rich in knowledge and skills, but with a relative neglect of character and attitudes.[51]

This disconnect within the curriculum can widen to a disconnect between the curriculum and Christian ministry. If theological studies are divorced from church contexts, theology can be dissolved into religious studies that are detached from divine revelation.[52]

Yet again the traditional theological curriculum can result in the opposite disconnect. As one African commentator puts it:

> It is true that God spoke to people of ancient times in their ancient contexts, but it is also true that God is speaking to the Africans in their contemporary times. No theologian has disputed this but attempts at understanding the African to whom God is speaking to in real time and place is still a "no-go zone" for theologians. The positivist and objectivist view of knowledge continues to raise relevance-related issues for theological education in Africa.[53]

Other curriculum-related challenges identified by respondents include the problem of developing affordable non-English language materials of theological and academic quality,[54] and of including cross-cultural and communication skills and experiential learning.[55]

---

47. Respondent Himawan.
48. Respondent Smith.
49. Lausanne, *The Cape Town Commitment*, Foreword, 2–4.
50. Respondent Jusu; Lausanne, *The Cape Town Commitment*, Part IID 3, 47–48. The latter comments on the challenge of developing church leaders characterized first by character and not just "packaged knowledge, techniques and skills."
51. Respondent Himawan.
52. Buitendag, "Between the Scylla and the Charybdis," 5.
53. Respondent Jusu.
54. Respondent Ferris.
55. Esterline et al., "Global Survey," 3, 5.

Put together, these comments suggest that traditional theological curricula rely too much on the Enlightenment objectification and atomization of knowledge and are too unresponsive to context, to the needs of churches, and to changing times. As someone comments: "These uncertain times have all the more emphasized the need to re-frame the theological curriculum."[56]

Challenges arising from the "how?" of theological education

How? questions raise issues related to infrastructure, teaching and learning design, and delivery.

Infrastructure – governance

Governance (and its linked tasks of management and administration) presents several challenges.

How can theological education develop board or council members whose enthusiasm is matched by involvement in the school,[57] strategic thinking, and innovative leadership,[58] and focus on college governance?[59] What of the gap between good leadership at the levels of vision but ineffective management, as senior educational leaders are caught up in human and financial resource issues for which they are usually untrained?[60]

Infrastructure – finance

An earlier section noted financial issues affecting student access to theological education. Several respondents comment on the challenge that colleges have to achieve self-sufficiency through their own income-generation sources[61] and to avoid the temptation to replace declining access to government funds with investment in ministry activities that deliver more immediate financial results. High fees may restrict enrolments both for students and sending churches[62]

56. Respondent Feliciano-Soberano.
57. Respondent Feliciano-Soberano.
58. Respondent Feliciano-Soberano.
59. Respondent Smith.
60. Respondent Smith.
61. Respondent Harkness.
62. Pratt, "Opportunities and Challenges," 4, 10; Spencer, "Seminaries and Discipleship," 1.

and challenge the financial model of many colleges when coupled with ageing infrastructure, compliance costs,[63] and the costs of new technology.

Approaches to teaching and learning

Is education about teachers and teaching or learners and learning? Does learning only happen when "the sage is on the stage" or when "the guru is in the room"? Epistemologies of revelation as something that is "given" from God may foster top-down pedagogies that are centred on a teacher delivering content that is to be absorbed by students and repeated back in assessments.[64] While this may happen, it is neither desirable, inevitable, nor necessary.

Contemporary educational theories challenge teacher-centred approaches and point towards the effectiveness of flipped classrooms where colleges and teachers support and facilitate learning, which is primarily a student task and responsibility.[65] Many college teachers are content experts but are not necessarily well-equipped to teach in ways that connect with either educational theory or student expectations.[66]

Later chapters in this book address the challenge of reshaping theological education in the light of contemporary educational thinking. They will also show how TEE has moved away from its earlier reliance on programmed instruction and is better aligned with contemporary education theory that is consistent with its core values.

Delivery models and the role of technology

Traditional educational delivery models rely on face-to-face delivery in centralized locations. Another option is distance education where all learning is decentralized and often involves people learning only by themselves. Are there delivery systems that combine the best of both? Such systems will be accessible, affordable, flexible, promote holistic formation, and maintain appropriate academic rigour to satisfy quality assurance and accreditation issues.[67] Recent

63. Respondent Smith.

64. Raja and Rajkumar, "Relevant and Effective Theological Education," 2–3.

65. Spencer, "Seminaries and Discipleship," 12; Pratt, "Opportunities and Challenges," 6.

66. Sherlock et al., "Uncovering Theology," 9.

67. Pratt, "Opportunities and Challenges," 5–6. Pratt argues for multiple delivery systems and outlines key requirements for them.

years have seen interest in blended modes of delivery that attempt to harvest the advantages, and avoid the disadvantages, of both centralized and decentralized systems and which create whole new pedagogical possibilities.[68]

Digital technology is profoundly reshaping education at all levels globally.[69] How can theological education ride this wave to advantage? Online technology is now available globally with even the most basic communication devices having the capacity for a range of educational tasks.[70] Online technology holds rich promise in educational delivery and is further discussed in a later chapter.

Naturally, the opportunities of digital technology come with paired challenges including:

- Unequal levels of access (including to more advanced technical features).
- Faculty resistance to, and lack of training in, digital education.[71]
- Deep familiarity with biblical languages being replaced by online aids.[72]
- Creating a campus that is digitally smart and which also promotes personal connection and godly relationships.[73]
- Lack of equipment, training, and bandwidth for teachers and students.[74]
- Lack of college infrastructure for technology-assisted learning.[75]

The integration of field experience

Field experience is widespread in theological education. However, it is often amateurish if students are sent to churches with little attention given to learning objectives, assessment, or accountability, and with little integration between

68. Respondent Shaw.

69. Werner, "Challenges and Major Tasks," 9.

70. The writers of this chapter have experience in impoverished global settings where basic analogue and digital mobile phone access is widely available and is being used in creative educational practices.

71. Respondent Perry; Respondent Feliciano-Soberano; Esterline et al., "Global Survey," 4.

72. Respondent Smith.

73. Respondent Himawan.

74. Respondent Feliciano-Soberano.

75. Respondent Feliciano-Soberano.

the campus and field experience.[76] There is a growing body of literature and networking around theological field education,[77] but experience suggests that it is often a peripheral and undeveloped activity. Research in other educational fields suggests that rich learning is available from reflective practitioner approaches.[78] How can theological education foster quality, church-based field learning in ways that integrates with, draws on, and contributes to classroom experience?

This discussion of the "how?" leads us to ask what form of theological education will enable good contextual connections, fidelity to the faith once delivered to the saints, and rigour of preparation for ministry?

Challenges arising from the "by whom?" of theological education

The "by whom?" of theological education concerns parties to its provision.

Teachers

Several respondents comment on the challenge of recruiting and developing a sufficient number of suitable teachers.[79] Others address issues of teacher quality by the development of combinations of theological, pedagogical, curriculum, and pastoral competencies.[80] Others again raise qualitative issues such as developing teachers who have theological depth and discernment.[81] Beyond the classroom teacher, there is also concern for senior leaders characterized by integrity, vision, collaborative style, and contemporary relevance.[82]

76. Respondent Perry.

77. For example, see Floding, *Welcome to Theological Education!*

78. Respondent Perry. For an introduction to education using reflective practice in diverse professional applications see Schon, *The Reflective Practitioner*.

79. Yu, "Major Issues in Asian Theological Education," 1. This is in an Asian context where there is an explosion in the number of theological graduates needed.

80. Respondent Harkness.

81. Respondent Tagore; Yu, "Major Issues in Asian Theological Education," 1.

82. Esterline et al., "Global Survey," 6.

College-church relationships

Many respondents comment on the challenges this area presents and the importance of getting it right. The comments reflect an underlying view that church and college should be partners but that the partnership often suffers from significant disconnect.

Given that many students (at least in Western colleges) are not ordination candidates,[83] and given the high costs of running colleges, there is a tension as colleges diversify their activities away from training church leaders in order to raise funds, while trying to maintain connections with sending churches so that they keep sending students.[84] Many colleges are faced with increasing demands for conformity to government compliance standards, which can further widen the distance between colleges and churches.[85]

On the church side of the college-church relationship, a variety of disconnects surface. Churches (and even trained pastors)[86] may not value a classic theological education compared to a local training programme that promises immediate practical pay-offs.[87] They may dismiss the relevance of training focused on knowledge acquisition, which does not transform learners.[88] Churches may prefer to develop highly localized training that results in students without a depth of education, but that is transferable to other contexts.[89] They ask how theological education can be more affordable, accessible, practical, and creative?[90] As churches embrace the ministry of all believers, a gap may open between the training available to theological college students and the training available to the rest of a church's members and leaders.[91]

83. For example, 80 percent of students at theological colleges in Australia are not ordination candidates. See Sherlock et al., "Uncovering Theology," 9.

84. Spencer, "Seminaries and Discipleship," 2–3.

85. Respondent Millar.

86. Forster, "Biggest Challenge," 4.

87. Respondent Millar; Forster, "Biggest Challenge," 2.

88. Forster, 1.

89. Respondent Millar; Spencer, "Seminaries and Discipleship," 9.

90. Respondent Feliciano-Soberano.

91. Respondent Clark; Respondent Jusu; Raja and Rajkumar, "Relevant and Effective Theological Education," 6.

These issues suggest a disconnect between colleges with a campus-centric mindset[92] and the reality of the churches they were established to serve. Several respondents mention the need for colleges to shift to a church-centric mindset,[93] and do more listening in order to build collaborative college and church partnerships[94] as collaborators in the changing shape of church and ministry.[95]

Accreditation and government requirements

Colleges that receive government money by way of student scholarships or loans and which issue state-recognized degrees face extra burdens. Compliance costs rise[96] and external bodies may impose requirements (e.g. in staff hiring) that reflect little sympathy or understanding of the nature of Christian higher education.[97] Efforts to accommodate government requirements may further promote a college-centric mindset and widen the college-church gap. As one college principal comments: "Theological colleges struggle to see how they fit within the church's ministry . . . [they] are neither universities nor churches nor corporate businesses."[98]

Tweak or Replace?

The preceding material has shown that contemporary theological education faces significant challenges (and opportunities) in its presently dominant form of the campus-based college.

---

92. Spencer, "Seminaries and Discipleship," 14.

93. Spencer, 14.

94. Raja and Rajkumar, "Relevant and Effective Theological Education," 5–6; Sherlock et al., "Uncovering Theology," 4.

95. Sherlock et al., "Uncovering Theology," 9.

96. Respondent Smith.

97. Respondent Perry. As another respondent, Jusu, comments: "Theological education is not being theological at all. We are more occupied by systems, procedures, and formality rather than by (theological) substance. One of the reasons is because theological institutions and seminaries are under the same regulations that govern secular universities, so we are focusing on being accredited by our government, who are more interested in quantitative performances and achievements."

98. Respondent Smith.

Can other approaches also be used? Is the need of the hour simply to tweak the existing paradigms, or to explore alternative paradigms in theological education? Is it time for a Kuhnian revolution in theological education in which college-centric models are replaced by more collaborative church-college centred approaches?

The next section of this chapter introduces TEE.

The Case for TEE

Theological Education by Extension is neither traditional college education, nor distance learning. TEE is TEE! To understand the case for TEE as a valid approach to contemporary theological education it is helpful to understand its origins and conceptualization.

Ralph Winter, James Emery and Ross Kinsler pioneered TEE in the early 1960s in Guatemala in association with the Presbyterian church.[99] They saw that denominational residential seminaries were not serving the leadership training needs of rapidly growing churches.

To fill this gap, they developed seminary training that was church-based, and which became known as Theological Education by Extension. Put simply, they brought the seminary to the church. In time, TEE developed a shape of its own beyond being an extension of the seminary. TEE proceeded to expand across Latin America, Africa, and Asia and accommodates various learning levels, from the discipleship of new believers through to graduate level studies. The history of TEE is related in a later chapter.

The TEE delivery method has three main components: personal study, group meeting and practical application (Figure 1.1).[100] Various analogies are used in explanation, including a railroad track, a split rail fence, a three-legged cooking pot, a bamboo ladder, and a rope bridge.[101]

---

99. Harrison, "Forty Years On," 315-316; Kinsler, "Birth of a Movement: TEE," 24.

100. These are the terms for the three components of TEE by the Increase Association; See Van Wingerden, Green, and Aylett, eds., *TEE in Asia*, 16–18. A variation of these terms is self-study, group meetings/discussions, and practical work. See Mabuluki, "Relevance of TEE," 80.

101. Aylett and Green, "Theological Education by Extension (TEE)," 64–66; Mulholland, "TEE Come of Age."

Figure 1.1. Components of the TEE method[102]

The railroad track analogy is particularly helpful (Figure 1.2). The rails represent the personal study and the practical application, and the supporting sleepers represent group meetings.

Figure 1.2. The railroad track analogy for TEE[103]

102. Source: van Wingerden, Green and Aylett, *TEE in Asia*, 17.
103. Source: van Wingerden, Green, and Aylett, *TEE in Asia*, 18.

The personal study component involves the learner engaging in active learning and reflection through well-prepared self-study texts. Group meetings (commonly five to ten learners) take place regularly, usually weekly, with a group leader or facilitator. Group leaders direct the discussion and help learners to reflect on their personal study and to make applications. The group leader's role is not to be the subject expert but rather to facilitate the active learning process within the group.

Practical application helps students activate their learnings from the personal study and group discussion. This application component takes place in everyday life and ministry situations. The learning cycle of personal study, group meeting, and practical application promotes transformative growth in Christian maturity through reflection and integration of faith into the daily life and ministry of the learners.[104]

According to Kinsler, a chief benefit of the TEE model is its ability to overcome a wide range of access barriers including geographical, economic, cultural, ecclesiastical, gender, race, class, pedagogical, and spiritual.[105] However, there are also common criticisms, such as, "these books seem to have a lot of repetition"; "the lessons seem much too simple"; "this approach seems to manipulate the student"; "this system seems to be the 'poor cousin' to real theological education"; "the system lacks academic discipline"; and "the system has no formal accreditation."[106] Such criticisms often come from those who are unfamiliar with the methodology and educational philosophy behind TEE.[107]

Some Scripture texts parallel TEE. Spencer compares the TEE approach with the Emmaus road encounter of the disciples and Jesus (Luke 24:13–35).[108] In the first step the disciples look back on their past journey with Jesus and gain understanding of their current context. This is a time for *taking in* (personal study). In the second step the disciples are guided by Jesus in understanding the Scriptures and interpreting events in a reflective process. This is a time for *taking stock* (group meeting). In the third step, the disciples offered hospitality

104. Van Wingerden, Green, and Aylett, *TEE in Asia*, 16–18.

105. Kinsler, "Preface," 7–10.

106. SEAN International, "How to Use SEAN Courses," 33–35.

107. Later chapters in this book address these and other criticisms.

108. Spencer, "Seminaries and Discipleship," 7–9.

to Jesus and acted on their learning. This is a time for *taking action* (practical application). This passage embodies a three-step interactive process leading to transformative learning, which parallels TEE methodology.

Other examples come from the apostle Paul (e.g. Eph 4:11–13; 2 Tim 2:2). These passages make it clear that early leadership development was primarily rooted in the local church context, and conducted by church leaders, with the aim of establishing and growing new churches. Lois McKinney explains:

> The church is in the heart of TEE. Even though TEE may be organizationally distinct from the churches, it can never function as an educational institution divorced from the church. It is created by churches and for churches. It functions best within churches. The most significant contribution that TEE has made to theological education is to return our conception of theological education to its contextual, experiential and church base.[109]

Volker Glissmann emphasizes the transformative quality of TEE. He defines TEE as "a decentralised ministry-oriented form of theological education with an emphasis on the extension of access to theological training and with an inbuilt and ongoing conversation based on reflection followed by action."[110] This definition deepens the understanding of TEE's three main components by bringing a fresh focus on spiritual formation and praxis through a reflection and application process within TEE.[111]

An alternative definition comes from McKinney: "[TEE] is the contextual experiential development of servant leaders for the church."[112] In other words, TEE has a strong developmental focus where leaders are learning and immediately applying their knowledge and skills in their local context. Leaders are learning holistically, and integrating *knowing*, *doing*, and *being* into experience. Active involvement in ministry encourages development of a servant attitude rather than a bureaucratic pattern of leadership.

109. McKinney, "How Shall We Cooperate," 30.

110. Glissmann, "What Is Theological Education by Extension?," 7–8.

111. Glissmann, "Christian Reflective Practice," 50–51.

112. McKinney, "How Shall We Cooperate," 29.

The last command of Jesus was for global disciple making (Matt 28:19). The twenty-first century church must continue to grow and mature, and respond to new mission opportunities. As one of the editors explains elsewhere: "TEE ticks all the boxes of low-cost, multi-level, quality assured, contextualized and transformative ministry training."[113] TEE is a proven and effective model of theological education that equips and empowers all God's people alongside other methods and models of transformative theological education.

Conclusion

The first section of this chapter identified challenges facing theological education. The second part of this chapter presented the case for TEE in the field of contemporary theological education. Later chapters in this book will explore these questions in greater detail, however the following summary gives an overview of how TEE can meet some of the key challenges in contemporary theological education.

Why? (Questions of purpose in theological education)
As this chapter notes, it is possible for campus-based theological training to lose connection with the mission of God through his church and with the church itself – chapter 2 will return to this theme. TEE, through its well-proven methodology, can help reconnect ministry training to the mission of God through his church and to the everyday Christian sequence of conversion–discipleship–service.

With whom? (Questions concerning the learners in theological education)
As chapter 2 discusses, there is often a significant gap between the advanced training provided to pastoral leaders and the minimal training offered to other leaders and church members, meaning that the greater part of the whole people of God are not effectively equipped for service. The grassroots church-based nature of TEE makes it an excellent vehicle for training the whole people of God in an accessible and affordable manner, and at levels varying from higher-degree level to foundational education for the life of faith and service.

113. Burke, "TEE: The New Face," 12.

Where? (Questions of location in theological education)
As noted, campus-based training may involve removing students from their home and church contexts for several years of study. This may make study inaccessible for those who cannot afford relocation to an area with higher living costs. It also runs the danger of a cultural disconnect such that a campus-educated leader is unwilling or unable to serve back in their home context. By keeping ministry training located in the local church setting, TEE maintains those community connections and facilitates a seamless link from study to service.

What? (Questions of content in theological education)
TEE methodology involves a consistent and intentional link between learning and application in service. The practical application dimension of TEE (the rail in Figure 1.2) means that every TEE learning session includes an activity designed to develop and apply the learning from the lesson and for which there is accountability at the following group meeting. This helps address the theory-practice gap which plagues much higher education, and which can produce pastors who are big-headed with cognitive learning, but low on affective and psychomotor learning.

How? (Questions of educational method in theological education)
TEE educational methodology fits well with contemporary adult education theory which focuses on the learner (rather than the teacher) and on learning (rather than teaching). The personal study activity is always the first step in a TEE learning process, which keeps the responsibility and focus of learning on the learner. Consequently, the group leader is more of a facilitator of deeper and more integrated learning rather than being the "sage on the stage," which easily becomes the default in campus-based teaching. The group learning that is integral to TEE methodology sits well with the emphasis on collaborative learning in present educational thinking. Furthermore, the church-based application component of TEE keeps field learning real in a way that is difficult to achieve in the more artificial environment of campus-based laboratories or college-centric internships.

In this book we seek to show that TEE is an alternate paradigm presenting a viable approach to theological education that has progressed from some now-outdated methods.[114] It can be fruitfully used alongside other approaches in mainstream global theological education. TEE is contemporary in its applications, established in its track record, and well-founded in its scholarship. We believe that TEE takes seriously current challenges in theological education and offers exciting ways out of the impasse.

Bibliography

Survey Respondents

Paul Clark, Education Consultant, Overseas Council.

Joanna Feliciano-Soberano, Regional Director for Southeast Asia, Overseas Council.

Robert Ferris, Executive Director, PAFTEE, 1979–1988, and Professor Emeritus, Columbia International University, Columbia, South Carolina, USA.

Tim Green, General Secretary, Increase Association.

Allan Harkness, Founding Dean, AGST Alliance, and Theological Education Consultant.

Andreas Himawan, Former Principal of Amanat Agung Theological Seminary, Jakarta, Indonesia.

John Jusu, UWM/OC Regional Director, Anglophone Africa.

Kuppusami Krishnan, Pastor, Pondicherry Grace Fellowship, Tamil Nadu, India.

Gary Millar, Principal, Queensland Theological College, Brisbane, Australia.

Samit Mishra, Pastor, Presbyterian Free Church (MP), India.

Gregory R. Perry, President, Thirdmill Seminary, Orlando, Florida, USA.

Perry Shaw, former Professor of Education, Arab Baptist Theological Seminary, Beirut, Lebanon.

Ian Smith, Principal, Christ College, Sydney, Australia.

Vijai Tagore, New Testament Lecturer, Presbyterian Theological Seminary, Dehradun, India.

Published Materials

Aylett, Graham, and Tim Green. "Theological Education by Extension (TEE) as a Tool for Twenty-First Century Mission." In *Reflecting on and Equipping for Christian*

114. In the earlier years TEE relied heavily on programmed instruction educational methods. As later chapters in the book will show, it is now characterized by alignment with contemporary educational theories.

Mission, edited by Stephen B. Bevans, Teresa Chai, J. Nelson Jennings, Knud Jørgensen, and Dietrich Werner, 59–78. Oxford: Regnum, 2015.

Buitendag, Johan. "Between the Scylla and the Charybdis: Theological Education in the 21st Century in Africa." *HTS Theological Studies* 70, no. 1 (2014): 1–5. http://dx.doi.org/10.4102/ hts.v70i1.2855.

Burke, David. "TEE: The New Face in Ministry Training." *New Life* 81, no. 1 (2018): 12.

Esterline, David, Dietrich Werner, Todd Johnson, and Peter Crossing. "Global Survey on Theological Education 2011–2013: Summary of Main Findings." Paper presented at WCC 10th Assembly, Busan, 30 October–8 November 2013. https://www.oikoumene.org/en/resources/documents/wcc-programmes/education-and-ecumenical-formation/ete/global-survey-on-theological-education.

Floding, Matthew, ed. *Welcome to Theological Field Education!* Herndon: Alban Institute, 2011.

Forster, Greg. "The Biggest Challenge for Theological Educators." 2017. https://www.thegospelcoalition.org/article/the-biggest-challenge-for-theological-educators/.

Glissmann, Volker. "Christian Reflective Practice: Prayer as a Tool for Reflection and Application in Theological Education." *InSights Journal for Global Theological Education* 2, no. 2 (2017): 35–52.

———. "What Is Theological Education by Extension?" *The Theological Educator*. 2014. https://thetheologicaleducator.net/2014/11/28/what-is-theological-education-by-extension/.

Harrison, Patricia J. "Forty Years On: The Evolution of Theological Education by Extension (TEE)." *Evangelical Review of Theology* 28, no. 4 (2004): 315–28.

ICETE. *The ICETE Manifesto on the Renewal of Evangelical Theological Education*. 3rd ed., 2002. https://icete.info/resources/manifesto/.

Kinsler, F. Ross. "Birth of a Movement: TEE." http://www.missionfrontiers.org/issue/article/birth-of-a-movement.

———. "Preface." In *Diversified Theological Education: Equipping All God's People*, edited by F. Ross Kinsler, 7–14. Pasadena: WCIU Press, 2008.

Lausanne Movement. *The Cape Town Commitment: A Confession of Faith and a Call to Action*. 2011. http://www.lausanne.org/content/ctc/ctcommitment.

Mabuluki, Kangwa. "The Relevance of TEE in African Training for Mission." In *Reflecting on and Equipping for Christian Mission*, edited by Stephen B. Bevans, Teresa Chai, J. Nelson Jennings, Knud Jørgensen, and Dietrich Werner, 79–89. Oxford: Regnum, 2015.

McKinney, Lois. "How Shall We Cooperate Internationally in TEE?" In *Cyprus: TEE Come of Age*, edited by Robert L. Youngblood, 27–39. Exeter: Paternoster, 1984.

Mulholland, Kenneth B. "TEE Come of Age: A Candid Assessment after Two Decades." In *Cyprus: Tee Come of Age*, edited by Robert L. Youngblood, 9–25. Exeter: Paternoster, 1984.

Ott, Bernard. *Understanding and Developing Theological Education*. Carlisle: Langham, 2016.

Pratt, Richard L., Jr. "Opportunities and Challenges for Theological Education at the Beginning of the Third Christian Millennium." *Reformed Perspectives Magazine* 15, no. 38 (2013): 1–12. http://reformedperspectives.org/magazine/article.asp/link/http:%5E%5Ereformedperspectives.org%5Earticles%5Eric_pratt%5Eric_pratt.ATA.html/at/Opportunities%20and%20Challenges%20for%20Theological%20Education.

Raja, Joshva, and Peniel J. R. Rajkumar. "Relevant and Effective Theological Education in the Context of Twenty-First Century South Asia." *Teaching Theology and Religion* 13, no. 3 (2010): 193–207. https://www.academia.edu/858982/Relevant_and_Effective_Theological_Education_in_the_Context_of_Twenty_First_Century_South_Asia.

Schön, Donald A. *The Reflective Practitioner: How Professionals Think in Action*. New York: Basic Books, 1983.

SEAN International. "How to Use SEAN Courses Effectively: Practical Tips on How to Set Up an Effective TEE Programme Using SEAN Courses." 2002. https://www.increaseassociation.org/images/resources-library/How%20to%20Use%20SEAN%20Courses.pdf.

Shaw, Perry. *Transforming Theological Education: A Practical Handbook for Integrative Learning*. Carlisle: Langham, 2014.

Sherlock, Charles, Mark Harding, Neil Ormerod, Robert McIver, and Gerard Moore. "Uncovering Theology: The Depth, Reach and Utility of Australian Theological Education." ALTC Report (2009): 1–9. https://www.researchgate.net/profile/Gerard_Moore3/publication/267719560_Uncovering_Theology_the_depth_reach_and_utility_of_Australian_theological_education/links/.

Spencer, Stephen. "Seminaries and Discipleship: Exploring Future Directions." *Journal of Anglican Studies* (2020): 1–15. doi:https://doi.org/10.1017/S174035532000008X.

van Wingerden, Hanna-Ruth, Tim Green, and Graham Aylett, eds. *TEE in Asia*. Carlisle: Langham Global Library, 2021.

Volf, Miroslav. "Dancing for God: Evangelical Theological Education in Global Context." Paper presented at ICETE International Consultation for Theological Educators, High Wycombe, UK, 18 August 2003. https://icete.info/wp-content/uploads/2019/04/0-03-Volf-Dancing-for-God.pdf.

Werner, Dietrich. "Challenges and Major Tasks for Ecumenical Theological Education in the 21st Century." WCC Programme on Ecumenical Theological Education. 2008. https://www.oikoumene.org/en/folder/documents-pdf/Challenges_and_major_tasks_for_theological_education_-_D._Werner.pdf.

Werner, Dietrich, David Esterline, Namsoon Kang, and Joshva Raja, eds. *Handbook of Theological Education in World Christianity*. Oxford: Regnum, 2010.

Wiggins, Grant, and Jay McTighe. *Understanding by Design*. Alexandria: ASCD, 1998.

Yu, Carver T. "Major Issues in Asian Theological Education." Paper presented at Global Theological Education Conference, World Reformed Fellowship, Jakarta, 21–22 March 2009. http://wrfnet.org/resources/2009/04/major-issues-asian-theological-education.

Part B

Multi-Disciplinary Perspectives on TEE

2

TEE in Theological Perspective – Part 1

Foundations

David Burke and Lyn Pearson

Introduction

This chapter outlines some theological foundations underpinning TEE, and is designed to be read in combination with the following chapter. Put together, they seek to give a theological foundation for TEE within the broader task of ministry training.[1] The chapter argues the case that the character and mission of God are central to the identity and mission of the church. It further argues that the mission of the church involves all of its members, that all of its members and leaders need training to fulfil their part in the mission of God, and that this training needs to be adapted for, and accessible to, the whole people of God.

1. Both writers of this chapter (Lyn Pearson in section 1 and David Burke in section 2) have cross-cultural experience but inevitably write from their theological traditions and background in Western culture. They appreciate that writers from other cultural backgrounds will approach these topics differently. For example, see the contributions in chapters 5, 7, 9 and 10 in Gener and Pardue, *Asian Christian Theology*.

Section 1: The Character and Mission of God

Jesus said, "Anyone who listens to my teaching and follows it is wise, like a person who builds a house on solid rock . . . it won't collapse because it is built on bedrock" (Matt 7:24–25 NLT).

"TEE for the twenty-first century" must be built on the bedrock of understanding the character and mission of God (section 1). This leads to understanding the identity and mission of the church (section 2). The invitation to participate in God's mission is for the whole people of God in all their diversity. The question then arises of how to equip the whole people of God. This requires a theology and practice of training (ch. 3). The methodological framework for understanding the mission and character of God and God's people is orthodoxy and biblical hermeneutics.

Orthodoxy

Orthodoxy means holding to doctrines "the faithful in the church have always believed . . . [creeds] point us to what God has led the church to see as its most important doctrines."[2] These creeds are not to be seen as an authority over Scripture, but they are derived from Scripture and are read in the community of the faithful.

Biblical hermeneutics

The interdependent disciplines of biblical theology and systematic theology[3] are adopted to explore the character and mission of God.

---

2. McKnight, *Blue Parakeet*, 31. He refers to this as the "Great Tradition." It also includes the Athanasian creed. See also Giles, "Orthodox Doctrine," 12–23. Chan, "Future of Global Theology," 5, 15, also proposes orthodoxy and sees this as "primary theology," congruent with Asian respect for ancestors. Molnar, "Karl Barth and the Importance," 153–76. Schirrmacher, *Missio Dei*, 19.

3. Goldsworthy, "Ontology and Biblical Theology." Also Gener, "Asian Evangelical Theology" emphasizes this interdisciplinary nature when considering Asian theological study. Other disciplines are included in hermeneutics, but it is beyond our scope.

Biblical theology

Biblical theology seeks an understanding of the Bible as a whole and gives full consideration to both its "unity and its diversity."[4] In *The Mission of God: Unlocking the Bible's Grand Narrative*,[5] Wright argues that the mission of God is the key to unlocking the grand story of God and creation,[6] and that "the whole Bible can be read in the light of this overarching, governing perspective."[7]

Systematic theology

A systematic[8] approach to understanding the character and the mission of God focuses on God revealed as Trinity. Furthermore, a christological lens brings in focus the personhood of God revealed in Christ.[9] "*Missio Dei*," in

---

4. Baker, "Biblical Theology," 96–99. There has been development of this discipline over time and sometimes disagreement about the definition. It is beyond the scope of this chapter to address this.

5. Wright, *Mission of God* uses a mixed approach to biblical theology as per Köstenberger, "Present and Future," 5, where he outlines four approaches to biblical theology: (1) classic approaches; (2) central theme approaches; (3) single-centre approaches; and (4) story or metanarrative approaches. A simplified understanding of these approaches identifies a uniting key which unlocks the treasures of the story of the Bible. Wright seems to use 2, 3, and 4.

6. Also Sanou, "Missio Dei," 306, writes of the development of the mission of God as a hermeneutical key "biblical interpreters will see in Scripture, as a whole missional thrust rather than having to focus only on the theme of mission in select texts. Thus, missional hermeneutics is about the triune God's redemptive activities in the world and the way he covenants with people to be part of his mission."

7. Wright, *Mission of God*, 532. In Köstenberger, "Present and Future," 15, there is significant overlap with Goldsworthy's Christ-centred metanarrative. "In understanding Christ to be at the center of Biblical theology, Goldsworthy seeks to show how the incarnation of Jesus is the link between the Testaments and at the center of God's plan begun at creation and to be completed in the new creation, epitomized by God's presence with his people." There are other biblical theological keys which are prudent to name. "Covenant" is significant even if the actual word is sometimes not mentioned (Creation, Abraham, Moses/Israel, David/Solomon and Christ – Gen 6:18; 9:8–17; 12:1–2; 15:17–21; 17:1–21; Exod 19:4–6; 2 Sam 7; Jer 31; Ezek 36; Luke 22). "Salvation through judgement" (with the accompanying mitigation demonstrating God's grace) "God's people, in God's place under God's rule." See Goldsworthy, *Gospel and Kingdom*.

8. Klooster, "Dogmatics," 350–51: "To set forth 'the whole counsel of God' . . . in an organized or systematic way," 328; Demarest, "Systematic Theology," 1162–64.

9. Thiselton, *Interpreting God*, 157. Thiselton points to Moltmann's stress on the "utter mutuality and reciprocity of communion between Father, Son and Holy Spirit in an interactive intimacy" (John 14:7, 9).

both biblical and systematic theology, is how we understand the grand story and a theme that recurs systematically.[10]

In 1991 Bosch revitalized the language of *missio Dei* to describe the mission of God as "an attribute of God. God is a missionary God."[11] This infers an "emphasis on divine ontology and the language of *missio Dei* . . . it is a contemporary assumption of mission theology that mission proceeds from the nature of God as Father, Son and Spirit."[12] One way of summarizing the mission of God could be the reconciliation of all things under the Lordship of Christ.[13]

The character of God

God's character is revealed through God's story of God's mission.[14] God's character is brought to light through a thematic study of what God says and how God acts. The names that God ascribes to himself and the names given by others describe God's character and attributes.[15]

---

10. *Missio Dei* terminology is beyond the scope of our chapter. Buys and Jansen, "With Heart and Hands and Voices," 229, refers to "little agreement" about the term because of theological and historical reasons. Sanou, "Missio Dei," 306, uses *missio Dei* as a key for understanding that "missional hermeneutics is about the triune God's redemptive activities in the world and the way he covenants with people to be part of his mission." Also see Flett, "Missio Dei," 5–18. Schirrmacher, *Missio Dei*, 19: "The concept of *missio Dei* is valid and belongs to the heart of Christianity, regardless of whether it is used to indicate that God sent himself to redeem the world or that the mission of the church is the result of God's mission."

11. Bosch, *Transforming Mission*, 390. Definition of "attribute" from the Merriam-Webster dictionary: a "quality, character, or characteristic ascribed to someone or something." https://www.merriam-webster.com/dictionary/attribute. Understanding *missio Dei* gives insight into the character of God.

12. Flett, "Missio Dei," 5.

13. Col 1:15–20; Phil 2:9–11. It follows then that any theological education must in its essence be missional.

14. Consequently, it is fitting for theological education to embrace narrative, testimony, case studies, and story.

15. Various systematic theologians have tried to classify the attributes of God. These interconnected attributes reveal who God is. Berkhof, *Systematic Theology*, 52–76, lists the attributes of God; "*incommunicable* nothing analogous in the creature and . . . *communicable*," 55. His list of incommunicable attributes includes: self-existence, immutability, infinity, perfection, eternity, immensity, unity. His list of communicable attributes includes spirituality, intellectual attributes (knowledge, wisdom, veracity), moral attributes (goodness, general benevolence, love, grace, mercy, long suffering, holiness, righteousness), attributes of sovereignty (sovereign will, sovereign power).

Exodus gives a snapshot into God's character: he discloses, he is *holy*,[16] he is the God of *covenant*,[17] and he is committed to be the *rescuer* of his people.[18] He is the God who is *with* his people,[19] revealing his name as "*I am who I am*" or YHWH (Exod 3:14); that is, "the idea that God was, is and always will be."[20] God says, "I will cause all my goodness to pass in front of you, and I will proclaim my name, the Lord, in your presence. I will have mercy on whom I will have mercy, and I will have compassion on whom I will have compassion" (Exod 33:19). When the Lord appeared the second time in Exodus 34:6–7, God described himself as "abounding in" or "filled with" *hesed*, which is translated as "love."[21] God's power and holiness are shown together with his love.[22]

Sometimes God's names are given in response to God's actions and are descriptive or prophetic.[23] Knox outlines the character of God in five ways.[24]

---

16. God's holiness is a theme through the Bible. Exod 3:5; Lev 19–20; Ezek 36; Eph 1:4; 1 Pet 1:13–15. Therefore any theological education must lead to holiness of life.

17. Exod 3:6.

18. Exod 3:9 God is their Saviour. Salvation issuing from God is who God is and what he does. In the NT *σώσω* has a broad meaning: to save, heal, make whole, preserve, rescue.

19. Exod 3:12.

20. Hemphill, "How Excellent Are Thy Names," 96; "The name *Yahweh* is not without its own theological controversies, though most biblical scholars agree that it is the closest thing we have to a proper, personal name for God."

21. Laurin, "Meaning of Chesedh," 179–82. There are various translations of *hesed*: "love and faithfulness," "unfailing love," "faithful love," "steadfast love," "mercy," and "loyal love." The core idea of this term communicates loyalty or faithfulness within a relationship. *Hesed* is closely related to God's covenant love with his people, Israel. It is important to note in 1 John 4:8 that "God is love."

22. Exod 33:20, 23.

23. In Isaiah 42:8 we read, "I am the Lord; that is my name! I will not yield my glory to another." God is described as a jealous God and consuming fire (Exod 34:14; Deut 4:24; 6:15). Commonly used names include: *Elohim* – God is creator, powerful, and mighty, Lord of lords. He is the Lord Most High (Gen 1:1; 17:7; Ps 19:1; Jer 31:33); *Yahweh-Shammah* – The Lord who is present/there (Ezek 48:35; Gen 28:15; Ezek 48:35; Pss 23:4; 46:1; 139:7–12; Jer 23:23–24; Amos 5:14); *Yahweh-Rohi* – The Lord is my shepherd. He cares for you, the way a shepherd tends his sheep (Pss 23; 80:1; 95:7; Isa 40:11; Jer 31:10; Ezek 34:12, 23); *Yahweh-Sabaoth* – The Lord of Hosts (Isa 6:1–3; 1 Sam 1:3; 17:45; 2 Sam 6:2; 7:26–27; 1 Chr 11:9; Hag 1:5). Hemphill, "How Excellent Are Thy Names," 96, notes *Elohim* is the plural of *El* (god) but usually translated in the singular. The use of *Elohim* could connate the triune nature of God. In Gen 1:26, for example, *Elohim* is used with the plural pronouns; Berkhof, *Systematic Theology*, 86.

24. Knox, *Everlasting God*.

1. The living and true God

God is dynamic, personal, self-authenticating and known through his word.[25]

2. God of infinite power, wisdom and goodness

God is the sovereign creator[26] not limited by externals, including time. He is infinite in goodness which is shown in covenant relationships of faithfulness and *steadfast love.* God is infinite in *wisdom*, knowing "possibilities as well as actualities."[27]

3. God in Trinity

Christians believe that God is one (Father Son and Spirit) and Christ is Lord.[28]

4. One Lord Jesus Christ

Jesus's friends believed him to be God. He gives self-testimony by his words and actions.[29] He is the true Israel, the true Son of Man, the son of David, the Son of God, and the suffering servant. One of the best descriptions of him is given in Colossians 1:15–20 where Christ's pre-eminence is declared.[30] He is Lord of all. If we have seen and known Christ, we have seen and known God. We know the character and attributes of God when we look upon Jesus Christ.

5. God who is rich in mercy

"But because of his great love for us, God, who is rich in mercy, made us alive with Christ even when we were dead in transgressions" (Eph 2:4).[31]

---

25. Knox, 15–16.

26. God can turn what is intended for evil to good (Gen 50:20). "God's control over His creation extends to control over the wills of men," Knox, 32 (Job 42:2).

27. Knox, 45. God's wisdom is seen in redemption and restoration. Jesus is the Wisdom of God, 46–47. "Oh, the depth of the riches of the wisdom and knowledge of God!" (Rom 11:33–36).

28. Knox, 49. Eph 4:1–16. Trinity as a term is not in the Bible but it is present in concept. Schirrmacher, *Biblical Foundations*, 54.

29. He said and did things that God alone could do. He forgave sins and calmed storms (Mark 2:1–12; 4:35–41). "Before Abraham was, I am" (John 8:58).

30. There are countless names given to Jesus, including the name above all names. It is beyond the scope of this paper to give detailed christological insight.

31. God wants all to be saved and to come to a knowledge of the truth (1 Tim 3:4).

The mission of God – the story

The story of the Bible tells the *who* and *what* about God and the reason *why* humans are in God's world. Community is a helpful lens through which the plot and trajectory of the whole Bible can be understood. Community reveals the character and mission of God as it flows from the very being of God. This is because of the perichoretic[32] relationship between the Father, Son, and Spirit. Life within the Godhead is one of mutual love, mutual grace, and mutual respect.[33]

1. Everlasting community

God who was and is and is to come,[34] is God as *Trinity*. The Bible reveals that God was present before creation. "Before the mountains were born or you brought forth the whole world, *from everlasting to everlasting* you are God" (Ps 90:2, emphasis added). God is outside of time and separate from creation. God as community has always been.[35]

From the opening lines of the Bible, we read of the creative presence of the Trinity. Even though the word "Trinity" is not used in the Bible, God was in the beginning when there was formlessness and emptiness, and the Spirit of God was hovering over the "surface of the deep" (Gen 1:1–3).[36] Into this darkness God speaks and creates by his word.[37]

2. Ideal community (Gen 1–2)

God is the *loving creator* of the world and creates humans in his image as the highpoint of creation.[38] Humans lived in harmony with God, self, each

32. Smith, "Perichoresis," 843, "means mutual indwelling, or, better, mutual interpenetration and refers to the understanding of both the Trinity and Christology."

33. Knox, *Everlasting God*, 52. "The characteristic of true relationship is other-person-centredness." Schirrmacher, *Biblical Foundations*, 23.

34. Implied in God's name YHWH.

35. Chung, "Asian Pursuit," 144–56, outlines how to help those from major Asian religions understand the Trinity, but these too are inadequate. Schirrmacher, *Biblical Foundations*, 52.

36. Bilezikian, *Community 101: Reclaiming*, 17, suggests the work of the Spirit was to protect, oversee, or sanctify.

37. John 1:1–3; 2 Cor 4:6, reminds us it is the same God who creates who gives new life in Jesus.

38. Humans are the pinnacle of creation, unlike the Babylonian creation narratives. Humans are created in God's own image and given free will. The creation of humans, man and woman, made in the image of God (Gen 1:26–27) is declared by God as "very good" (Gen 1:31).

other, and their environment. "Trinitarian understanding of God provides not only a basis for interpreting what it is to speak of God as personal, but also a foundation for respecting persons as persons in relations of love and mutuality in human society."[39]

God creates from nothing. He speaks and it comes into being. After creating each day, he declares it is "good."[40] Humans are God's vice regents, his image bearers, given dominion over all creatures and vegetation.[41] The picture from Genesis 1–2 is one where there are harmonious relationships between God and humans, and also harmony between the man and his wife. "Adam and his wife were both naked, and they felt no shame."[42] God is the source of all blessing[43] and has created humans to be in community with himself and each other.

3. Broken community (Gen 3 to Rev 20)

Humans seek to live life their way and distrust God's word and, as a result of sin, humanity and creation are no longer in harmony. It is only after the rebellion at the fall in Genesis 3 that Adam and Eve know they are naked and seek to cover themselves (Gen 3:7), and they are afraid and hide from the *holy* God (Gen 3:8). The consequence of their sin is banishment from the garden and from the tree of life. In a spiritual sense, they "certainly" died (Gen 3:4) when they rebelled. Their eyes were opened and they became "like God, knowing good and evil."[44]

Sin and judgement escalate as humans spiral further in rebellion against God. This broken community will continue until final judgement. It is always in opposition to God, but he alone is *King* and *Lord*, and any attempts to usurp his rule will be thwarted. His holiness, righteousness, and justice are also seen

39. Thiselton, *Interpreting God*, 156. James 2:9 reminds us that one must not curse other humans because they are made in God's likeness.

40. Wenham, *Word Biblical Commentary*, xlix.

41. Gen 1:29–30. The creation of humans is "very good." God has given humans the task to create and work.

42. Gen 2:25.

43. Shalom is described here. This is the fullness of blessing and life, the harmony of the relationships mentioned. It is true holism. Jayakumar, "Work of God," 227. The "work of God" can be seen as "holistic mission."

44. Gen 3:5.

in his judgement on sin. At the same time God's grace, mercy, and kindness are seen in his mitigation of judgement. He gives humans coverings, he guards the way to the tree of life so they do not stay in this broken state eternally, and he promises to send one who would "crush" the serpent's "head" (Gen 3:15). He puts a mark on Cain, provides the ark and the rainbow, scatters the people so they do not continue increasing in their sin,[45] and – most importantly – forms his community.

4. God's new community (Gen 12 to Rev 22)

After sin's escalation in Genesis,[46] God calls into being a new community. They will be God's own people. They are the ones who have the faith of Abraham, who hear God and obey. God created this new community through the particular call of Abraham and his descendants.[47] Those who followed the God of Abraham, Isaac, and Jacob were the faithful of Israel. Those like Moses, Joshua, Elijah, and the others who did not "bow the knee to Baal" (1 Kgs 19:18). God ultimately will give blessing to all peoples through Jesus Christ. Those who come to Christ are truly the children of Abraham.[48]

God's sovereign power and grace are seen in the working out of his mission. In 1 Kings 19, it is God who keeps the remnant from apostasy. God raises people to fulfil his plans;[49] his mission leads to repentance.[50] God orders historical events for his purpose and plans.[51]

---

45. Gen 4:15; 6–9; Gen 11 respectively.

46. Gen 4 – killing of Abel, Gen 6–9 – the Flood, Gen 11 – the tower of Babel.

47. Gen 12:1–3. "I will make you into a great nation, and I will bless you; I will make your name great, and you will be a blessing. I will bless those who bless you, and whoever curses you I will curse; and all peoples on earth will be blessed through you."

48. Rom 4:23–35. It was always God's plan to bless the nations, bless those not born into the children of Abraham. These gentiles were integrated. To belong they, like the children of Israel, owed allegiance to the God of Abraham. Such examples are Rahab and Ruth who are named in Jesus's genealogy in Matthew; also in Acts, Cornelius, and many others.

49. Exod 9:12; 10:20, 27; Prov 20:24; 16:9, "In their hearts humans plan their course, but the LORD establishes their steps."

50. Nathan's confrontation of David, Jonah's repentance, John 6:43–44; Rom 2:4; Eph 1:3–14; 2:8–9.

51. For example, the exodus, the fall of Jericho, the Incarnation, death and resurrection of Jesus. Schirrmacher, *Missio Dei*, 20: "God's mission and God's covenant show that Christianity is a religion of salvation history and of historical advance. The different steps and aspects of *missio Dei* do not randomly follow each other and are not exchangeable. Rather, they follow

God's new community is intertwined in God's plan of salvation in Jesus. God is the covenant-making and covenant-keeping God.[52] Through the fulfilment of God's promises, those who receive Jesus belong to God's family.[53] Those who belong include those who died in faith prior to Jesus's incarnation[54] as well as those who are still to come.[55] They are in Christ who is the Alpha and the Omega, the Lamb who was slain, who alone can open the scroll in Revelation 5. "It is in Christ crucified and risen that we find the focal point of the whole Bible's grand narrative, and therein also the focal point of the whole mission of God."[56] God's wisdom is greater than human foolishness.[57]

The vindication of Christ's finished work on the cross is his resurrection.[58] Through the resurrection God gives "living hope" to his new community. What is the purpose of this new community? Why are they redeemed? These are the people of God who live life with God as King, Christ as Lord, led by his Spirit within. They were dead, but now they are alive.[59] They live as ones who belong to God "to declare the praises of him who called you out of darkness into his wonderful light" (1 Pet 2:9). They now are united with Christ (Rom 6), and they live lives that represent Christ in them the "hope of glory" (Col 1:27). This is the mystery of God's new creation.[60] God works to transform them "into his image with ever-increasing glory, which comes from the Lord, who is the Spirit" (2 Cor 3:18). What an amazingly generous and loving God.[61] It is out of response to the generosity of God that his new community are to be involved in the things that matter to God, that are aligned to his concerns

---

God's wise design, according to which he unfolds his kingdom step by step. *Missio Dei* does not occur cyclically time and again. Rather, it points to the great goal of the entirety of history."

52. The road to Emmaus (Luke 24:13–32) shows the fulfilment of prophecy about Christ from Moses and the prophets. Also see McCarthy, "The Fulfilment."

53. John 1:12; Rom 8:15.

54. Heb 11 and John 8:56.

55. John 10:16.

56. Wright, *Mission of God*, 315. In Heb 11 and 12 the "great cloud of witnesses" exercised faith which looks to Christ.

57. 1 Cor 1:21–24.

58. 1 Cor 15; 1 Pet 1:3.

59. Col 1:13–14; Eph 2:4–10.

60. 2 Cor 5:17.

61. 2 Cor 8:9.

for creation, justice, righteousness, peace, and reconciliation amongst people, nations, and creation.[62]

5. Eternal community (Rev 21–22)

God's new community live forever in Christ now, while also living in the period of the now and not yet. The final consummated community is in the future, but this community experiences being one in Christ and a "holy people" now, while also living in their bodies of sin in a broken world.[63] They await a returning king and judge who will make all things right, all things new, who is with them now.[64] They have the gift of the Spirit as a deposit of this future.[65] Jesus's kingdom rule inaugurated at his first coming will then be experienced by all, and his rule will see the final destruction of Satan.[66]

The Shema[67] calls God's people to love the Lord our God with all our "heart, soul, mind, and strength." We are to submit to his Lordship in all things as individuals but together as the people of God, the church. This was God's plan: "His intent was that now, *through the church*, the manifold wisdom of God should be made known to the rulers and authorities in the heavenly realms, according to his eternal purpose that he accomplished in Christ Jesus our Lord" (Eph 3:10–11, emphasis added). The church belongs to God.[68]

62. Until the consummation of all things under Christ, the people of God move towards shalom to bring wholeness. If Christ is Lord of all, this means all things in heaven and earth. God's new community is not saved to focus inwardly; rather, Christians must engage in issues which stand against God, for example, against systemic racism and abuse of power, against exploitation of people and the environment (Mic 6:8; Jas 2:14–26).

63. We have union with Christ (Rom 6). 1 Pet 2:9–10 picks up on Exod 19:4–6 where the people of God are declared to be a "kingdom of priests and a holy nation." They are strangers to this world and ultimately citizens of another kingdom (Phil 3:20).

64. Matt 28:20.

65. "Set his seal of ownership on us, and put his Spirit in our hearts as a deposit, guaranteeing what is to come" (2 Cor 1:22).

66. Phil 2:9–11; Rev 20.

67. Deut 6:4–6; Mark 12:30; Matt 22:37; and Luke 10:27.

68. It has been God's plan that the church is his agent of transformation in the heavenly realms. Ecclesiology is contextual. Yung, *Mangoes or Bananas?*, critiques Western theology which itself is a "product of the histories, cultures and realities of the West. They cannot, therefore adequately address the existential realities of the rest of the world because these differ so much from those of the West." Yung identifies the Western worldview as predominantly one of individualism, empiricism, and rationalism which can lead to a division of the sacred and secular, 2–3. Franklin and Niemandt, "Polycentrism," write about the diversity in leadership and centres of influence

Summary

To summarize, section 1 of this chapter explored how God reveals his character and mission to his creation. The Father, Son, and Spirit – God in community – enables understanding of who God is and who the people of God are. "This divine 'oneness' becomes a model and pattern for a community's oneness of love and mutual regard."[69] God's intention in creating a new community is one way he chooses to restore the broken community of humanity and a "groaning" creation.[70] He invites his children to be one with him in his mission. He invites them to co-labour with him as his family, his community, his church. This has implications for theological education and reading Scripture. It is important that community plays an important component in learning. Learning should lead to transformed lives and communities.

Section 1, however, raised questions. How then can we, as the whole people of God, be better equipped for these good works that he has prepared? How can the whole people of God, "the whole church," take the "whole gospel to the whole world?"[71] How can the people of God's new community be salt, light, yeast, and peace and hope to a broken world and to the heavenlies? Section 2 of this chapter takes these themes forward as we consider the identity and mission of the church as derived from its creator.

Section 2: The Identity and Mission of the Church

The identity of the church

The divine origin of the church is key to its identity and mission.[72]

The church is a product of, and the instrument of, God's mission.[73] Its formation and growth involved human agency, but its origins lie in divine

---

especially in a globalized world. Theological education also needs to take into account rapid change in communication, growth of the church from the global south and human need.

69. Thiselton, *Interpreting God*, 156. Also, Eph 4:1–6. This oneness is what Jesus prayed for in John 17:10–14.

70. Rom 8; Rev 21, 22.

71. Eph 2:10; https://www.lausanne.org/content/twg-three-wholes.

72. Goheen comments: "Ecclesiology is about understanding our identity, who we are and why God has chosen us – whose we are." Goheen, *Light to the Nations*, 5.

73. Goheen, 174.

choice and enablement.[74] Far from being an accident, divine afterthought, or human creation, it is the new community created by God according to plan.[75]

The divine origin of the church is reflected in some common biblical metaphors that reflect its identity.[76] These metaphors are typically qualified as being "of Christ" or "of God." The consistent use of possessive genitives in the metaphors for the church reinforces that its identity lies in its origins with God, and that it belongs to him[77] and is defined by its relationship with him.[78]

Among these metaphors, the most prominent is that of the church as body, not so much in the number of occurrences,[79] but in its significance – which will be discussed below. For now, it suffices to note that the church is "*his* body" (Eph 5:30) of which Christ "is head" (Col 1:18).

At this point the identity and purpose of the church flow together.[80] The church is a recipient of grace that it might be active in witness, love, and service.[81] It is his chosen people, his royal priesthood, his holy nation – a people belonging to God "that you may declare the praises of him who called you out of darkness into his wonderful light" (1 Pet 2:9–10). The origin of the church in God's choice (the "from whence") creates its identity (the "who") and the "why" of declaring his praises.

The mission of the church

Our final glimpse of the church is a heavenly scene. People from every corner of humanity gather to sing the praise of God in his throne room (Rev 4–5;

74. Coulter, "Essence of the Church," 33.

75. Stott, *Living Church*, 19.

76. The metaphors include the church as body (Rom 12:4; 1 Cor 12:12–27; Eph 4:15–16; 5:30; Col 1:18; 2:19), bride (Eph 5:32; Rev 19:7), household (e.g. Gal 6:9–10; Eph 2:19; 1 Pet 2:5), temple (1 Cor 3:16–17; 2 Cor 6:16; Eph 2:21), dwelling place (Eph 2:22), vine (John 15:1–11), and God's fellow workers, field, and building (1 Cor 3:9). Poh refers to a study identifying 96 metaphors for the church and discusses their implications. Poh, "New Testament Metaphors," 23–31. See also Horton, *Christian Faith*, 715–37. Horton adds a wise word about not reducing church to a single metaphor and of allowing all the metaphors to interpret one another: Horton, 733–734.

77. Poh, "New Testament Metaphors," 31.

78. Coulter, "Essence of the Church," 33.

79. This metaphor is explicit in Eph 5:23 and Col 1:8 but other passages (all Pauline) assume it: 1 Cor 12:12; Eph 1:23; 3:6; 4:4, 12; Col 3:15.

80. Clowney, *The Church*, 163. Goheen, *Light to the Nations*, 21.

81. Horton, *Christian Faith*, 844–5.

7:9–17) as they enjoy the blessings of his new creation (Rev 21–22). The garden expulsion has been replaced by the garden-city gathering. The promise that all people would be blessed though Abraham (Gen 12:2) is now fulfilled. The earthly and temporal mission of the church has an instrumental aspect – it is the means by which God gathers his heavenly church. As we declare his saving praises on earth, our testimony is the means by which all peoples have the opportunity to hear and believe (Rom 10:11–15).

The origins of the church point to its mission. The Father sent the Son, and Father and Son together send the Spirit, who sends the church.[82] Wright comments that the mission of God is the connecting red thread that runs through the whole Bible.[83] The whole Bible is the story of the mission of God as he executes his mission through his church.[84] His mission of reconciling all things in Christ (Eph 1:10; Col 1:20) has a scope that is as wide as the creation and the effects of the fall. It includes reversing the effects of the fall in its spoliation of physical creation and the spoliation of his human creation which leads to tears, crying, pain, or mourning – all of which are banished in the new creation (Rev 21:4). Central to this, although not exhaustive of its scope, is the ingathering of his people.

Discussion of the church's mission must reckon with Matthew 28:16–20. Disciple-making happens under the authority of Christ (v. 18) and with his presence (v. 20). This bracketing of the disciple-making command by reference to Christ's authority and presence reinforces that the church's mission is inseparable from its origins and identity in Christ.

The text outlines the mission of the church in these words:

> 19 πορευθέντεςοὖν μαθητεύσατε πάντα τὰ ἔθνη, βαπτίζοντες
> αὐτοὺςεἰςτὸὄνομα τοῦπατρὸς καὶ τοῦυἱοῦ καὶ τοῦἁγίου πνεύματος,
> 20 διδάσκοντες αὐτοὺςτηρεῖν πάντα ὅσα ἐνετειλάμηνὑμῖν.
> (Matt 28:19–20a)

82. Wiher, "God's Mission," 68.

83. As quoted by Wiher, 83.

84. Wiher, 84–85.

This can be translated as: "Therefore, *going*, make disciples from all peoples, *baptizing* them in the name of the Father and the Son and the Holy Spirit, *teaching them to keep* all that I have commanded you"[85] (emphases added).

This translation keeps the imperative (μαθητεύσατε – make disciples) central and reads the three participles (italicized) as outlining the process of making disciples. Disciples are made as God's people go into the world to declare his praises, bearing fruit in the public commitment of baptism, followed by a process of learning and obeying, including obedience to the command to make disciples.

Mission should be something that the church *is*, not just something that it *does*.[86] It is an "ouch" moment as we consider how local and global mission is often peripheral to the theology,[87] staffing, financial budgets, and commitments of time and energy in the local church. It is also relevant to the recent trend of churches abdicating their responsibility for global mission in favour of parachurch agencies and those agencies too readily abandoning the tortoise-like church.[88]

The scope of disciple-making is *πάντα τὰ ἔθνη* (all peoples). The recent phraseology of the "missional church" is commendable if it means that churches move from a past[89] vision of missions as an "over there" task and learn from cross-cultural workers how to do mission "over here."[90] However, as Beattie observes, the phrase is often used in a restrictive sense of the local church

85. Author translation (Burke) for emphasis. Views vary on whether the opening participle should be read as having the full emphatic force of an imperative (as in many English versions) and we certainly do not want to undermine the necessity of "go" in global mission. The translation offered here is designed to highlight the central task of making disciples.

86. Goheen, *Light to the Nations*, 4; Coulter, "Essence of the Church," 37.

87. Nygaard, "Mission and Ecclesiology – Why?," 112; Ruiz and Rimkiene, "Missional Disciple," 147. Sadly, the exercise of looking over particular church budgets and websites, and of listening to weekly announcements and prayers, sometimes shows little sign of there being a world beyond this or that local church.

88. Hayes and de Carvalho, "Church and Agency Relationships," 152. Also noteworthy is the trend for some large churches to develop and implement mission activities independently of any cooperation with denominational and parachurch agencies. This can result in problems as inexperience leads to mistakes being made.

89. Goheen suggests that the church lost its missional edge as far back as the post-Constantinian period when it became an instrument of the state and adopted a Christendom mentality. Goheen, *Light to the Nations*, 9–10.

90. Nygaard, "Mission and Ecclesiology – Why?," 112.

going on mission to its local neighbourhood.[91] He calls for a shift from a church-centric sense of mission to a kingdom-centric one, a corresponding shift from a purely local to a global vision, and from a purely temporal to an eternal horizon.[92] This is more than the saving of souls from the hands of the evil one – it is about the reign of Christ over all things and all people.

This wide sense of the mission of the church is well-captured in a definition widely used in the Anglican Communion:

> The Five Marks of Mission:
>
> The mission of the church is the mission of Christ
>
> 1. to proclaim the good news of the kingdom;
> 2. to teach, baptize and nurture new believers;
> 3. to respond to human need by loving service;
> 4. to transform unjust structures of society, to challenge violence of every kind and pursue peace and reconciliation;
> 5. to strive to safeguard the integrity of creation, and sustain and renew the life of the earth.[93]

Goheen summarizes the missional church as one that participates in God's mission, continues the mission of old Israel, continues the mission of Jesus, and continues the witness of the early church.[94] Horton emphasizes the agency of regular church life in executing the mission for the Great Commission. For him, the marks of everyday church life are the means of its mission to the lost sheep.[95]

This emphasis on the church in mission reinforces the big point being made in the present argument: mission cannot be separated from the church, nor the church from mission, and neither can be separated from the character and mission of God.

---

91. Beattie, "Truly Missional Church," 120.

92. Beattie, 123.

93. https://www.anglicancommunion.org/mission/marks-of-mission.aspx.

94. Goheen, *Light to the Nations*, 184.

95. Horton, *Christian Faith*, 899, 901. He defines these marks as caring for God's people in preaching, sacraments, and discipline.

Clowney puts it well:

> Mission expresses the purpose for which Christ came into the world, and the purpose for which he sends us into the world. His purpose is the purpose of the father. We are called to mission, not only as disciples of Christ, but as children of the father . . . The heart of the gospel moves the church to mission and to deeds of mercy which have always been part the Christian mission.[96]

To summarize, mission is at the heart of the church's origins and identity. Likewise, it should lie at the heart of its activities and at the heart of theological education. Lausanne puts it clearly: "The mission of the church is to serve the mission of God, and the mission of theological education is to strengthen and accompany the mission of the church."[97]

The means of the mission

The Great Commission ends with a promise that Jesus will be with his church to the end (Matt 28:20b). With that word, Matthew ends his gospel. Luke fills the gap by giving his double account of the ascension (Luke 24:50–51; Acts 1:9). How does the now-absent Jesus keep his promise to be "with you" to the end of the age?

The answer lies in the Holy Spirit. It is significant that the first fruit of the Spirit's new presence was to enable the mission as the gospel was heard and believed in global languages.[98] Acts starts with a reference to the past work of Jesus and quickly bridges to his continuing work in and through the church by the Spirit whose agency is repeatedly stated.[99] People such as Peter, James, John, and Paul feature in the human narrative, but it is the Spirit who enables their contributions. The Spirit works through the people of God.

1 Corinthians 12 draws on the metaphor of church as "body" as it explains how the Spirit works in and through the people of the church. The Spirit enables

96. Clowney, *The Church*, 161.

97. Lausanne, *Cape Town Commitment*, Part IIF, 5. This whole section of *The Cape Town Commitment* is worth reading for its call that theological education is mission-centric.

98. To note this is not to engage with the question of whether the gift of tongues discussed in 1 Cor 14 is the same as the manifestation of the Spirit in Acts 2.

99. One count shows fifty-five mentions of the Holy Spirit in Acts.

the confession of Jesus as Lord (v. 3) and empowers its members to serve through his gifts. These gifts are of one origin (vv. 4–6, 11), for one purpose (v. 7b), universal (v. 7a), varying (vv. 4, 8–11), interdependent (vv. 12–26), and together form the one body of Christ (vv. 12, 27).[100] This attractive picture of church, which has been rediscovered in recent decades, has liberated the church from views that exaggerate the giftings and ministry of the few at the expense of the many.

However, balance is needed. An over-emphasis on every-member ministry can result in not recognizing the role of designated leaders. 1 Corinthians 12 recognizes such distinctive leadership roles as apostles, prophets, and teachers, which gives the biblical roots for the historical development of ministerial offices. These offices are further foreshadowed in Scripture by the designation of elders, overseers, and deacons in the various forms of localized church government (e.g. Phil 1:2; 1 Tim 3:1–1; Titus 1:5–9).[101] The present concern for every-member ministry has much to commend it, although it should not devalue the particular role of trained, tested, and recognized leaders.

Ephesians 4:7–16 gives a panoramic vision of leaders and members together in the church's ministry. The ascended Christ gave grace (v. 7) "to each." This grace included the leadership roles of apostles, prophets, and evangelists, along with pastors and teachers.[102] These roles each have a word ministry which is linked to the onwards life of the whole body (vv. 16–17) as every member grows from spiritual infancy to maturity in Christ (vv. 12b–16).

Translations vary in their rendition of Ephesians 4:12a and the respective emphasis on leaders and members in ministry.[103] However the passage is read,

100. The individualized and varied manifestation of the gifts of the Spirit are in sharp contrast to the fruit of the Spirit which is common to all and unvaried (Gal 5:22–23).

101. As many observe, the New Testament does not give exhaustive detail on local church leadership and ministry structures. There may be a lesson in this lack of detail!

102. We note varying views on whether each of these is an enduring office or was confined to the apostolic age, and also the varying views on whether pastor and teacher are a combined role or separate offices.

103. Views also vary among commentators. Hence Lincoln, *Word Biblical Commentary: Ephesians*, 253–4, who emphasizes the ministry of leaders, and Bruce, *Epistles*, 345, who emphasizes leaders equipping the saints.

verses 7 and 16 preserve an active role for all believers.[104] All have gifts from the Spirit and the whole body grows "as every part does its work."

It is time to connect some threads in this discussion. The mission of the church is God-given and God-enabled through the Spirit. Under God, the mission is led by the various God-given leadership roles, and it is implemented as all church members combine their individual and varied gifts.[105]

The structures of the church need to reflect its self-understanding and serve its mission.[106] The mutual nature of the church includes its leaders and members working together in its life and mission. Even Clowney, who articulates a distinction between the special and general offices of the church,[107] writes:

> Church officers . . . are coaches, who train, assist and encourage the saints who carry out the calling of the church in the world.[108]

Training for the whole people of God

The gifts of the Spirit need development to bring them to full usefulness. The New Testament has many examples of this, starting with Jesus training select followers for their role in his mission (e.g. Luke 9:1–6, 10; 10:1–20) and including Priscilla and Aquila training Apollos (e.g. Acts 18:24–28).

Paul's relationship with Timothy is a case study. Timothy was urged to "train yourself to be godly" (1 Tim 4:7), to "fan into flame the gift of God which is in you" (2 Tim 1:16), to be diligent and wholly given to his ministry "so that everyone may see your progress" (1 Tim 4:15) and "to do your best to present yourself to God as one approved, a workman who does not need to

104. Lincoln, *Word Biblical Commentary: Ephesians*, 253.

105. It is striking that Eph 4:12 refers to the ministry of the church in the singular ἔργον διακονίας. Arguably, there is only one work or ministry of the church – done as leaders and members combine.

106. Stott, *Living Church*, 57; Goheen, *Light to the Nations*, 221.

107. For example, Clowney, *The Church*, chapter 14.

108. Clowney, 114. Clowney also writes: "The model of church order is organic. The body of Christ is made up of members who are dependent on one another in the exercise of the life they have from Christ." In any case, Scripture teaches mutuality in the exercise of the gifts of the Spirit as a major principle in the ordering of the church. Clowney, 204–5. Horton has a similar sense of the distinctiveness of special office and comments: "The distinct gifts and offices that Christ has given to his church for its existence and maturity are intended to build up the whole body precisely for its varied acts of mutual service and mission." Horton, *Christian Faith*, 897.

be ashamed" (2 Tim 2:15). Timothy's time accompanying Paul as a ministry apprentice was doubtless part of developing his gifts, as was his reading of Paul's letters of pastoral instruction.

The church has long recognized the need to train its pastoral leaders and has developed various forms of theological education through its history.[109] However, it is not just these significant leaders whose gifts need to be developed to their potential. Goheen is just one who recognizes the importance of equipping the whole people of God for their service:

> It is impossible for a pastor to carry out and implement a vision for a missional church alone. Identifying and training leaders who can journey together and act as change agents is essential. But how we conceive of leadership will shape the way leaders are trained . . . Indeed, the key to a missional congregation will be leaders who are already following Christ in his mission and looking for ways to enable and equip the rest of the congregation to follow him more faithfully as well.[110]

Goheen's emphasis on church-based training for the whole people of God is commendable. However, there is a significant gap between the training typically given to leaders and that given to the whole people of God.[111]

Conclusion

This chapter has surveyed the mission of God and his church. It argues that the character and mission of God are normative for the character and mission of his church. It is emphatic that the mission of God goes beyond rescuing a few souls here and there and involves the renewal of all things in Christ and the creation of a new community within history and for eternity. The church

109. See chapter 4 of this book for a survey and discussion of the various forms this training has taken: Carey and Harrison, "TEE in Historical Perspective."

110. Goheen, *Light to the Nations*, 220–21.

111. Clergy training typically involves a three- or four-year full-time degree programme, in sharp contrast to the demanding hours and content level of what is often called "lay training." *The Cape Town Commitment* has a sharp comment on the failure of the church to take seriously the need to train the whole people of God for their distinct daily callings (let alone their callings in the church). Lausanne, *Cape Town Commitment*, Part IIA, 3, and IIF, 4.

is central to the mission of God as leaders and members together serve with the gifts given by the ascended Christ through his Spirit.

As we have also seen, the gifts of the Spirit need development to be brought to the fullness of their potential. The church has historically developed sophisticated schemes for training its leaders and has invested major resources in them. This is often not matched by a similar investment in the training of the whole body of Christ.

Can we do better? Can we develop training approaches that include both church leaders and members? Are there approaches that reinforce the mutuality and inter-dependability of leaders and members? How can we keep the church and its mission central to the form and purpose of training? That is the focus in this book.

Bibliography

Anglican Communion. "Marks of Mission." https://www.anglicancommunion.org/mission/marks-of-mission.aspx.

Baker, David L. "Biblical Theology." In *New Dictionary of Theology*, edited by Sinclair B. Ferguson, J. I. Parker, and David F. Wright, 96–99. Downers Grove: InterVarsity Press, 1988.

Beattie, Warren. "A Truly Missional Church: From Church-Centred Mission to Kingdom-Centred Mission." In *The Church in Mission: Foundations and Global Case Studies*, edited by Bertil Ekstrom, 119–24. Pasadena: William Carey Library, 2016.

Berkhof, Louis. *Systematic Theology: With a Complete Textual Index*. Grand Rapids: Eerdmans, 1959.

Bilezikian, Gilbert. *Community 101: Reclaiming the Local Church as Community of Oneness*. Grand Rapids: Zondervan, 1997.

Bosch, David. *Transforming Mission: Paradigm Shifts in the Theology of Mission*. Maryknoll: Orbis, 1991.

Bruce, F. F. *The Epistles to the Colossians, to Philemon and to the Ephesians*. Grand Rapids: Eerdmans, 1984.

Buys, Phillipus J. (Flip), and André Jansen. "'With Heart and Hands and Voices': Integral Ministry of Word and Deed from a *Missio Dei* Perspective." *Unio Cum Christo* 1, no. 1–2 (2015): 225–50.

Chan, Simon. "The Future of Global Theology: An Asian Perspective." *Journal of Asian Evangelical Theology* 18, no. 2 (September 2014): 7–20.

Chung, Paul S. "The Asian Pursuit of Trinitarian Theology in a Multireligious Context." *Journal of Reformed Theology* 3, no. 2 (2009): 144–56.

Clowney, Edmund P. *The Church: Contours of Christian Theology*. Downers Grove: InterVarsity Press, 1995.

Coulter, Paul. "The Essence of the Church: The One Holy Catholic and Apostolic Church in God's Purposes." In *The Church in Mission: Foundations and Global Case Studies*, edited by Bertil Ekstrom, 33–41. Pasadena: William Carey Library, 2016.

Demarest, Bruce A. "Systematic Theology." In *Evangelical Dictionary of Theology*, edited by Walter A Elwell, 1162–4. Grand Rapids: Baker, 2001.

Elwell, Walter A., ed. *Evangelical Dictionary of Theology*. Grand Rapids: Baker, 2001.

Erickson, Millard J. *Who's Tampering with the Trinity?: An Assessment of the Subordination Debate*. Grand Rapids: Kregel, 2009.

Ferguson, Sinclair B., J. I. Parker, and David F. Wright, eds. *New Dictionary of Theology*. Downers Grove: InterVarsity Press, 1988.

Flett, John G. "Missio Dei: A Trinitarian Envisioning of a Non-Trinitarian Theme." *Missiology* 37, no. 1 (January 2009): 5–18.

Franklin, Kirk, and Nelus Niemandt. "Polycentrism in the Missio Dei." *HTS Theological Studies* 72, no. 1 (2016): 1–9.

Gener, Timoteo D. "Asian Evangelical Theology: Theological Commitments and Interdisciplinarity." *Journal of Asian Evangelical Theology* 23, no. 2 (September 2019): 99–118.

Gener, Timoteo, and Stephen Pardue, eds. *Asian Christian Theology: Evangelical Perspectives*. Carlisle: Langham, 2019.

Giles, Kevin. "An Extended Review of One God in Three Persons: Unity of Essence, Distinction of Persons, Implications for Life." *Priscilla Papers* 30, no. 1 (2016): 21–30.

———. "The Nicene and Reformed Doctrine of the Trinity." *Priscilla Papers* 31, no. 3 (2017): 3–8.

———. "The Orthodox Doctrine of the Trinity." *Priscilla Papers* 26, no. 3 (2012): 12–23.

———. *The Rise and Fall of the Complementarian Doctrine of the Trinity*. Eugene: Cascade, 2017.

Gillett, David. "Shalom: Content for a Slogan." *Themelios* 1, no. 3 (1976): 80–84.

Goheen, Michael W. *A Light to the Nations: The Missional Church and the Biblical Story*. Grand Rapids: Baker, 2011.

Goldsworthy, Graeme. *Christ-Centered Biblical Theology: Hermeneutical Foundations and Principles*. Nottingham: Apollos, 2012.

———. *Gospel and Kingdom: A Christian Interpretation of the Old Testament*. Exeter: Paternoster, 1981.

———. "Ontology and Biblical Theology: A Response to Carl Trueman's Editorial: A Revolutionary Balancing Act." *Themelios* 28, no. 1 (2002): 37–45.

———. "The Ontological and Systematic Roots of Biblical Theology." *The Reformed Theological Review* 62, no. 3 (December 2003): 152–64.

Harris, Brian. "Beyond Bebbington: The Quest for Evangelical Identity in a Postmodern Era." *Churchman* 122, no. 3 (2008): 201–19.

Hayes, Tom, and Decio de Carvalho. "Church and Agency Relationships." In *The Church in Mission: Foundations and Global Case Studies*, edited by Bertil Ekstrom, 149–58, Pasadena: William Carey Library, 2016.

Hemphill, Kenneth S. "How Excellent Are Thy Names: What God Invites Us to Call Him Says Volumes about His Relationship to Us." *Christianity Today* 45, no. 13 (October 22, 2001): 95–97.

Horton, Michael S. *The Christian Faith: A Systematic Theology for Pilgrims on the Way*. Grand Rapids: Zondervan, 2011.

Hwa, Yung. *Mangoes or Bananas?: The Quest for an Authentic Asian Christian Theology*. Oxford: Regnum, 2014.

Jayakumar, Samuel. "The Work of God as Holistic Mission: An Asian Perspective." *Evangelical Review of Theology* 35, no. 3 (July 2011): 227–41.

Klooster, Fred H. "Dogmatics." In *Evangelical Dictionary of Theology*, edited by Walter A. Elwell, 350–1. Grand Rapids: Baker, 2001.

Knox, David Broughton. *The Everlasting God*. Homebush West: Anzea Publishers, 1988.

Konz, D. J. "The Even Greater Commission: Relating the Great Commission to the *Missio Dei*, and Human Agency to Divine Activity, in Mission." *Missiology* 46, no. 4 (2018): 333–49.

Köstenberger, Andreas J. "The Present and Future of Biblical Theology." *Southwestern Journal of Theology* 56, no. 1 (2013): 3–23.

Koyama, Kōsuke. "The Asian Approach to Christ." *Missiology* 12, no. 4 (October 1984): 435–47.

Larsen, Timothy. "Defining and Locating Evangelicalism." In *The Cambridge Companion to Evangelical Theology*, edited by Timothy Larsen and Daniel J. Treier. Cambridge: Cambridge University Press, 2007.

Laurin, Robert B. "Meaning of Chesedh." *Foundations* 7, no. 2 (April 1964): 179–82.

Lausanne Movement. *The Cape Town Commitment: A Confession of Faith and a Call to Action*. 2011. http://www.lausanne.org/content/ctc/ctcommitment.

———. "The Whole Church Taking the Whole Gospel to the Whole World." https://www.lausanne.org/content/twg-three-wholes.

Lawrence, Michael. "3 Ways to Define Biblical Theology." Crossway, 18 July 2017. https://www.crossway.org/articles/3-ways-to-define-biblical-theology/.

Lincoln, Andrew T. *Word Biblical Commentary: Ephesians: Volume 42*. Nashville: Thomas Nelson, 1990.

McCarthy, Dennis J. "The Fulfilment of the Promise." *The Way* 2, no. 4 (October 1962): 254–60.

McKnight, Scot. *The Blue Parakeet: Rethinking How You Read the Bible*. Grand Rapids: Zondervan, 2018.

Molnar, Paul D. "Karl Barth and the Importance of Thinking Theologically within the Nicene Faith." *Ecclesiology* 11, no. 2 (2015): 153–76.

Nygaard, Birger. "Mission and Ecclesiology – Why?" In *The Church in Mission: Foundations and Global Case Studies*, edited by Bertil Ekstrom, 111–7. Pasadena: William Carey Library, 2016.

Osborne, Grant R. *The Hermeneutical Spiral: A Comprehensive Introduction to Biblical Interpretation*. Wheaton: InterVarsity Press, 2006.

Poh, Eileen. "New Testament Metaphors of the Church." In *The Church in Mission: Foundations and Global Case Studies*, edited by Bertil Ekstrom, 23–31. Pasadena: William Carey Library, 2016.

Ruiz, David D., and Rita Rimkiene. "The Missional Disciple." In *The Church in Mission: Foundations and Global Case Studies*, edited by Bertil Ekstrom, 143–8. Pasadena: William Carey Library, 2016.

Sanou, Boubakar. "Missio Dei as Hermeneutical Key for Scriptural Interpretation." *Andrews University Seminary Studies* 56, no. 2 (2018): 301–16.

Schirrmacher, Thomas. *Biblical Foundations for 21st Century World Mission: 69 Theses toward an Ongoing Global Reformation*. Bonn: Verlag fur Kultur und Wissenschaft, 2018.

———. *Missio Dei: God's Missional Nature*. Bonn: Verlag fur Kultur und Wissenschaft, 2017.

Smith, Stephen M. "Perichoresis." In *Evangelical Dictionary of Theology*, edited by Walter A. Elwell, 906–7. Grand Rapids: Baker, 2001.

Stott, John. *The Living Church: Convictions of a Lifelong Pastor*. Nottingham: Inter-Varsity Press, 2007.

Thiselton, Anthony C. *Interpreting God and the Postmodern Self: On Meaning, Manipulation and Promise*. Grand Rapids: Eerdmans, 1995.

———. *New Horizons in Hermeneutics: The Theory and Practice of Transforming Biblical Reading*. Grand Rapids: Zondervan, 1997.

Wenham, Gordon J. *Word Biblical Commentary: Genesis 1-15: Volume 1*. Waco: Word Books, 1987.

Wiher, Hannes. "God's Mission and the Church's Mission." In *The Church in Mission: Foundations and Global Case Studies*, edited by Bertil Ekstrom, 67–93. Pasadena: William Carey Library, 2016.

Wright, Christopher J. H. *The Mission of God: Unlocking the Bible's Grand Narrative*. Downers Grove: InterVarsity Press, 2006.

———. *The Mission of God's People: A Biblical Theology of the Church's Mission*. Grand Rapids: Zondervan, 2010.

Yoder, Perry B. "Toward a Shalom Biblical Theology." *The Conrad Grebel Review* 1, no. 3 (1983): 39–49.

Yung, Hwa. *Mangoes or Bananas: The Quest for Authentic Asian Christian Theology*. Oxford: Regnum, 1997.

3

TEE in Theological Perspective – Part 2

TEE as an Appropriate Tool to Equip the People of God for the Mission of God

Graham Aylett and David Samuel

Introduction

The previous chapter observed that the church finds its origin, identity, and purpose in God, flowing from what he has done in Jesus Christ and through the Spirit. The mission of God birthed the people of God, and his church is now called to participate in that continuing mission.

That is the role of theological education: serving the church as it seeks to be faithful to that call. Since every believer is called to get involved with what God is doing, this chapter argues that theological education is for the whole people of God – not only the few. However, the reality is that the majority of those in church leadership – let alone those in their care – may have little or no theological education. The need is great. Churches are growing in many parts of the world.

This chapter explores TEE as one useful and appropriate tool to meet the great need for equipping the people of God for the mission of God. The chapter explores how TEE can contribute significantly to building the missional capacity of local churches and shows how the church-based methodology of TEE is well suited to provide training and equipping from the grassroots onwards. It shows how TEE methodology helps provide for holistic growth in discipleship,[1] and how TEE programmes provide pathways for growth into different areas of ministry and mission. It concludes with a call for collaboration between different forms of theological education.

Theological Education – What Is it For, and Who Is it For?

The previous chapter concluded that the church finds its origin, identity, and functions in God. Because God is who he is and has done what he has done in Jesus Christ and through the Spirit, the church is what it is. The mission of God birthed the people of God, and his church is now called to participate in his continuing mission.[2]

The call to the mission of God is a call to the whole church; the whole people of God are immersed into the life of the triune God in baptism and have the Spirit of God and are gifted by the Spirit of God; God's chosen people together are declared a royal priesthood, and therefore all are ministers.[3] All God's people, consequently, need training and equipping for their various works of ministry.

What then is the place of theological education in serving the whole people of God? *The Cape Town Commitment* expresses it in this way:

> The mission of the Church on earth is to serve the mission of God, and the mission of theological education is to strengthen and accompany the mission of the Church.[4]

1. This chapter does not regard discipleship as synonymous with foundation stages in Christian living: discipleship continues lifelong. For example, for the believer called to post-doctoral research, this also is discipleship.

2. As expressed forcefully in the Edinburgh 2010 Common Call: "We believe the church, as a sign and symbol of the reign of God, is called to witness to Christ today by sharing in God's mission of love through the transforming power of the Holy Spirit." Anonymous, "The Edinburgh 2010 Common Call."

3. "Ministers" because all are called to some kind of ministry, not because they are formally ordained to church leadership as "clergy." Compare the section, "Are we all called to ministry?" in Church of England, *Calling All God's People*, 23, which concludes a brief discussion of Eph 4:11–12 with the statement, "ministry is something done by everyone."

4. Lausanne, *Cape Town Commitment*, Part IIF, 4, https://www.lausanne.org/content/ctcommitment.

This missional-ecclesial focus for theological education is now affirmed by many authors[5] and shapes the purpose of both regional and global evangelical theological educators. One example is the Asia Theological Association (ATA), which is "a body of theological institutions . . . networking together to serve the church in equipping the people of God for the mission of the Lord Jesus Christ."[6]

Likewise, the recently approved International Council for Evangelical Theological Education (ICETE) mission statement now reads: "ICETE advances quality and collaboration in global theological education to strengthen and accompany the church in its mission."[7]

With this common commitment to the church and its God-given mission, there are surely possibilities for fruitful partnership between different modes of theological education. Since 1984, the *ICETE Manifesto* has encouraged this kind of cooperation:

> The biblical notion of mutuality needs to be much more visibly expressed and pragmatically pursued among our theological programmes. Too long we have acquiesced in an isolation of effort that denies the larger body of Christ, thus failing both ourselves and Christ's body.[8]

The *ICETE Manifesto* section 3, Strategic Flexibility, issues a call to serve the whole range of church leadership needs, at all academic levels, using a whole range of delivery modes and methods.[9] The section concludes: "Only by such flexibility in our programmes can the church's full spectrum of leadership needs begin to be met."

5. See for example the references in Shaw, *Transforming Theological Education*, ch. 1, and Werner, *Challenges and Opportunities*, 22.

6. See website of Asia Theological Association, "About Us, Our Mission," https://www.ataasia.com/%20about%20us/.

7. Email correspondence with Michael Ortiz, 21 August 2020.

8. The *ICETE Manifesto*, section 12, "Cooperation," https://icete.info/resources/manifesto/.

9. "We must learn to employ, in practical combination with others, both residential and extension systems, both formal and non-formal styles, as well, for example, as short-term courses, workshops, evening classes, holiday institutes, in-service training, travelling seminars, refresher courses, and continuing education." The *ICETE Manifesto*, section 3, "Strategic Flexibility."

But is theological education only concerned with *leadership* needs, as the *ICETE Manifesto* seems to imply? *The Cape Town Commitment* clearly includes equipping *all* God's people for mission within the task of theological education, even though there is a suggestion that this may be subordinate to leadership training:[10]

> Theological education serves *first* to train those who lead the church as pastor-teachers, equipping them to teach the truth of God's word with faithfulness, relevance and clarity; and *second*, to equip all God's people for the missional task of understanding and relevantly communicating God's truth in every cultural context[11] (italics original).

Some do understand theological education as concerned only with formal, academically recognized preparation for church leadership.[12] However, others frame a much broader definition of theological education. In this understanding, theological education aims at "developing reflective Christian identity and practice, an informed and spiritually enriched access to biblical tradition, and empowering people for participating in the mission of God in this world."[13] Therefore, theological education is "a fundamental right of every Christian adult."[14]

We can ask questions of the two positions presented here. Is theological education, by definition, concerned just with church leadership formation in the formal academy? Or is it for the whole people of God, including leaders, or at least the whole adult people of God? Which position is most coherent and best serves the people of God?

Does this matter? Everyone can agree that the church of God is a united body and different members do not all have the same functions. Different

10. Perhaps this was not intended. Chris Wright, one of the architects of *The Cape Town Commitment*, answers the question, "Who is theological education for?" with the statement: "Biblical answer – for the church, to serve the life, growth and mission of God's people, both in training its pastor [*sic*] and leaders, and in helping *all* believers to 'be transformed by the renewing of their minds' (Rom 12:1–2)," Wright, "Theological Education, Bible and Mission," 142.

11. Lausanne, *The Cape Town Commitment*, Part IIF, 4.

12. For example, Ott, *Understanding and Developing*, 196–8.

13. Werner, *Challenges and Opportunities*, 18.

14. Werner, 18.

members need different kinds and levels of training and equipping, and these different kinds of training may be given different labels. The advantage of using different labels will be to highlight the different needs and approaches of each member and encourage more relevant and effective ministry training. But the disadvantage is that the unity of the people of God, the common call to participate in the mission of God, and the necessary interconnections and interdependency of the different members, is obscured. If theological education is not understood as being for the whole people of God, then multiple disconnects can result. Joined-up learning pathways from a new believer to an active member to a leader within the congregation may be blocked. Linda Cannell asks:

> When do sheep become shepherds? What is the role of the shepherd in creating a climate wherein the sheep can become shepherds? If valid, these questions imply that theological education must be for the whole people of God.[15]

This chapter, then, argues that the whole people of God (and not only the adult members!) are called to know God, to love him, trust him, to be involved in his mission, and as a result, need theological education. Our understanding of theological education is therefore an inclusive one, such as that of Harkness:

> The processes adopted to encourage individuals and Christian faith communities to understand, appropriate, and express the Christian faith they espouse.[16]

We speak then, along with Craig Dykstra, of the whole large enterprise of "Christian theological education,"[17] or with Volker Glissmann of a "continuum of theological education"[18] for the whole people of God, allowing different methods, content and aims of training, appropriate to different groups of learners and contexts. These different groups of learners have been classified

15. Cannell, *Theological Education Matters*, 256.
16. Harkness, *From Seminary to Pew*.
17. Dykstra, "Looking Ahead," 99.
18. Glissmann, "Grassroots Theological Education," 55.

in different ways according to context and purpose,[19] and include at least "sheep," shepherds or church leaders, and scholars or academics. Perhaps the most difficult group to find an appropriate term for is the "sheep," that is, the great majority of the flock who are not currently called to be shepherds or scholars. "Laity" suggests a great divide between "clergy" and "laity"; and "ordinary church members" or "grassroots" have possible negative connotations. In this chapter we use the phrase, "the majority of God's people." Whatever classification is used, the recognition that these categories are deeply interrelated and permeable is vital.

In summary, the whole people of God, together, is priestly, ministerial, and missional. All members need to be equipped for their roles – all need theological education. Each member of the body needs the other members and looks to the one head, Jesus Christ. But members have different functions and therefore differing theological educational needs. Likewise, different modes of theological education within the whole people of God may serve different groups of learners.

Reflection: Theological Education and the Life of Local Churches

The current context of many churches includes inadequate or no theological education for either leaders or members. In November 2017, Ramesh Richards estimated that among 2.5 billion people who self-identified as Christian, there were some 2.2 million pastoral leaders. Of these, only 5 percent had training for pastoral ministry and it is said that "the rest will be doing their own thing this weekend."[20] In this situation, biblical leadership models are readily subverted by social and cultural forces, and there may be ignorance of basic biblical discipleship. The relationship between the leaders and the led can resemble

19. For example, Glissmann – grassroots, ministerial, and academic; Dykstra – (1) Educating the church and the public in Christian faith and practice; (2) Preparing ministers for church leadership; and (3) Conducting the academic study of theology.

20. Richard grounds these statistics in his correspondence with Todd Johnson, Director of the Center for the Study of Global Christianity, 8 July 2015. Re-Forma state that "Studies show that over 90% of all pastors do not have a formal theological education. According to statistics, that equates to well over 2 million Protestant pastors worldwide." See "Background/Reality Check," Re-Forma, https://www.re-forma.global.

that of a bus driver to passengers or a performer to audience more than the biblical image of interdependent members of a body.[21] Church leaders may become threatened by members' giftings and growth, and discourage rather than nurture every-member ministry.[22]

These are issues of deep concern. Where they are found, local churches fall short of their vocation: God's name is not hallowed, his will is not done, and there is little evidence of his kingly reign and rule. At their root is a lack of knowledge of God.[23]

Christ is the way to this knowledge of God, the saving truth about God, and the source of the life of God.[24] He is the door to the church, the gate for the sheep.[25] The need is therefore for theological education that leads people to Christ in fresh worship and obedience, and to God's world in fresh witness and service.

Understanding Theological Education by Extension

This book is about TEE, but this term is used to describe a number of different training methodologies. The experience of Increase Association members is that many understand TEE as some kind of distance education.[26] So a fuller description of TEE methodology and materials than that given in chapter 1

21. 1 Cor 12:12–27. Also see the discussion in chapter 2 relating to the church as a body: Burke and Pearson, "TEE in Theological Perspective – Part 1."

22. These observations are based on anecdotal evidence from Increase Association members in various Asian countries.

23. Tozer writes: "The gravest question before the Church is always God Himself, and the most portentous fact about any man is not what he at a given time may say or do, but what he in his deep heart conceives God to be like. We tend by a secret law of the soul to move toward our mental image of God. This is true not only of the individual Christian, but of the company of Christians that composes the Church. Always the most revealing thing about the Church is her idea of God, just as her most significant message is what she says about Him or leaves unsaid, for her silence is often more eloquent than her speech." Tozer, *Knowledge of the Holy*, 4.

24. Matt 11:27; John 1:14; 14:6; 15:1–5; 1 John 5:12.

25. John 10:7.

26. Some seminaries may refer to evening lecture classes, or intensive modules taught in different locations, or courses delivered at a distance to individuals, as TEE. These seminary-based TEE programmes are certainly extending the work of the seminary, but pedagogically they are very different from the church-based TEE that is the subject of this book.

is needed before exploring how TEE can support the church as it serves the mission of God.

As already described, TEE methodology involves three distinct, complementary, interconnected, and essential parts: personal study, group meetings, and practical application.

Since there are three interconnected components of a TEE course, it is important to distinguish a TEE *course* from a TEE *self-study text*. A TEE course certainly makes use of a TEE self-study text, but it involves much more. The course is the combination of the learners' use of the self-study text, their participation in group meetings arising from it, the ways that they are guided to respond in practical application and action, and the repeated opportunities for reflection that weekly group discussions provide.

Each part of a TEE course has potential to develop different skills and capacities, but it is the combination of these three elements, as they are rooted in each learner's local church context, that holds great potential to lead to growth in knowledge, skills, character, relationships, and participation in the local church and the mission of God that is the concomitant of growth in true knowledge of God.

Personal study

In this component[27] of the TEE method, each TEE learner works through a carefully prepared self-study text. In the early years of the TEE movement, programmed instruction was seen as the way to prepare TEE texts. However, a greater variety of methodologies may be incorporated into TEE texts, and TEE no longer relies on the behaviourist foundations of programmed instruction.[28]

Personal study opens pathways for interaction with God's word in relation to the subject matter and the target context of the particular course. A wide range of courses is available to contribute to a detailed knowledge of God's word. Those unfamiliar with the methodology of TEE, and who have not

27. TEE practitioners discuss the best descriptor for this component. "Personal study" does not necessarily have to be done in isolation. There are advantages to learners working together through the study text, as long as each helps the other towards greater understanding and no-one by-passes active learning by copying. Some suggest "home study," but this component does not need to be done in the home. Any suitable place is possible. Others suggest, "self-study."

28. See chapter 6, Glissmann and Green, "The Educational Efficacy of TEE – Part 2."

themselves studied or used courses with a group of learners, may be critical of what appears to be unnecessary repetition in self-study texts. In fact, the element of repetition enables deep learning, that is, a more complete and longer-lasting grasp of core content. TEE learners often comment on this.

Personal study has a basic function of providing new information. Self-study texts at all levels also raise questions of lifestyle and application; those at more advanced educational levels develop critical and theological reflection. Learners also grow in time management, study skills, and the ability to reflect on their experience and context in the light of God's word.

Evangelicals understand the Bible as God-breathed and vital for growth in true knowledge of God. Therefore, self-study texts from evangelical course developers aspire to provide a biblical basis for all their course content and to provide tools for scriptural study that help learners to interpret and apply the Bible in their context.

TEE course development teams need to include people with a range of knowledge and skills, including subject matter experts, with appropriate qualifications above the educational level of the course they are developing.[29] This will enable them to develop better quality materials for use in the personal study phase of TEE lessons.

Group meetings

Personal study is the springboard for discussion in the group meetings. In this way, TEE methodology incorporates a flipped classroom approach.[30] The group size is usually between five and ten, which allows each member opportunity for active participation. Group meetings are led by a group leader or facilitator, who is guided by a group leader's manual, another integral part of a TEE course. A good group leader's manual provides a structure for effective use of the group meeting, including questions that help to focus discussion on the learning objectives of the lesson. The group leader's main role is not to repeat the subject

29. See chapter 7 for a description of good process: Ivins and Do, "New TEE Courses"; and chapter 9 for quality assurance in relation to TEE course development: Aylett, Green, and Weymouth, "TEE and Quality Assurance."

30. The terminology "classroom flip," or "inverted classroom" seems to have been introduced in the late 1990s. See Baker, "Origins of the 'Classroom Flip.'" TEE methodology has been using this approach since the 1970s.

matter of the personal study. It is to ask questions that spark group members' discussion, helping them towards deeper and clearer understanding, providing opportunities to reflect on their personal experience in the light of the new content, to make connections with their local church, community and national contexts, and to identify and commit to relevant practical application.[31]

Well-facilitated group meetings provide a safe and hospitable place for deepening relationships, sharing, mutual support, prayer, and care.[32] In this way group discussions lead to fresh encounters with God as the Holy Spirit brings truth to life. Additionally, the group meeting provides a setting for *koinonia* – sharing with one another and sharing together in the life of the Triune God, and knowing God in the community of discipleship. In other words, the group meeting as part of the joint discipleship journey of its members may become a "fellowship within the local fellowship."

The role of the group leader is vital.[33] It is also open-ended. The role can encompass elements of tutor, guide, mentor, pastor, examiner, and spiritual director. Much depends on the personality, maturity, and vision of the individual group facilitator. In the hands of a mature, competent, and visionary facilitator, even a less well-developed course can become a dynamic, transformative experience.[34] Conversely, the most skilfully and prayerfully crafted course can be rendered ineffective and unproductive at the hands of an unimaginative and careless group leader. For this reason, the whole complex of group leader selection, training, support, and encouragement is of greatest importance for TEE programmes.[35] In addition, the relation of the group leader's ministry to the ministry of the local church(es) involved is of great importance in sustaining the group leader. Churches with a culture of every-

31. Cf. Robert Ferris's notes on the role of the facilitator in Ferris, *Ministry Education*, 51–53.

32. See Soh, *Motif of Hospitality*.

33. Cf. the saying, "Disciples make disciples," and not courses or programmes, although they may provide support. Robert Ferris writes, "The faculty is the curriculum." Ferris, *Ministry Education That Transforms*, 74. Tim Green reports an Afghan believer's observation: "When I agreed to study this course, I wasn't interested in the course. I wanted to study the group leader!" Therefore, the often-repeated TEE adage, "The text is the teacher" is at best only partially true. The text conveys new information, but the group leader's role is nevertheless vital.

34. Of course, the same also applies to courses delivered in a campus lecture room – good teachers will redeem inferior lesson material.

35. Fred Holland, TEE pioneer in Africa, wrote, "But the success of TEE depends on getting the right people to lead the seminars." Holland, *Teaching through T.E.E.*, 23.

member ministry, training, equipping, and lifelong learning give recognition and encouragement to both group leader and group members.

The element of mentoring for the group leader is especially important in helping group members in their spiritual formation, Christian character, growth in holiness, and growth in understanding of their particular gifts and callings. In the context of the small group, the different interests, passions, characters, and callings of group members begin to emerge. The hospitable small group will become a safe place for members to explore gifts and callings, and also a place from which to launch into new expressions of obedience. This brings into view the third component of TEE methodology – practical application.

Practical application

The third essential component of TEE methodology, practical application, encourages contextual responses of obedience to the word of God introduced and explained through personal study, and then discussed and explored in the group meeting. Depending on the aims of the programme, and the level of study, learners may gain practical experience in teaching, preaching, conducting worship, pastoral care, leadership, and engaging in their local church mission. Most group members carry out these kinds of practical application assignments in their own local churches, reflect on the outcomes, and learn from their participation in mission and ministry. But practical application is by no means limited to church ministry. Assignments may equally relate to ministry in the home and family, in the local community, and in the workplace and the marketplace. Obedient contextual application forms the path of discipleship, the fulfilment of the Great Commission, and is incarnational as group members enact what it means to be the body of Christ.

Robert Banks, in his influential book, *Reenvisioning Theological Education*, studies the nature and significance of groups in ministry formation in different parts of Scripture. He concludes that their purpose was not so much preparation *for* mission, but participation *in* mission – "active service or mission in furthering the kingdom."[36] And indeed, this is the aim of TEE methodology: participation in the mission of God through practical application.

36. Banks, *Reenvisioning Theological Education*, Kindle edition, Part Two, 4.C.4.

Because TEE methodology includes repeated cycles of personal study, group meetings, and practical application, there is opportunity to reflect on specific acts of intended obedience and their consequences, both hoped for and anticipated, and unforeseen and unintended. Cycles of Action – Reflection – Action are built into TEE methodology.

The Contribution of TEE to the Whole Practice of Theological Education

The role of theological education is to strengthen and accompany the mission of the church as it serves the mission of God. The need is for theological education that serves the whole people of God and equips them for participation in the mission of God. This section explores how TEE contributes to the practice of theological education by arguing that TEE methodology is church-based, supports whole-life discipleship, and is a framework for relevant learning pathways.

TEE offers a methodology that is church-based

Theological education for the whole people of God must reach to the local church. TEE supports theological education in the context of the local church. For a TEE student, there is continuing connection with the life of the local church, the issues, and the day-to-day, week-to-week, season-to-season practice of the church. The New Testament letters assume that the local church is the place for growth in knowledge and love of God, and in the obedience of faith. Reflection on the relationships, issues, and crises of local churches shaped Paul's letters.[37] The raw materials for theological education were, and still are, present in the local church. The missional-ecclesial *focus* for theological education supports an ecclesial *locus* for theological education. The *ICETE Manifesto* includes a passionate plea for the churchward orientation of theological education by saying:

37. Galatians and 1 and 2 Corinthians are clear examples.

> Our theological programmes must become manifestly of the church, through the church and for the church. This we must accomplish, by God's grace.[38]

If "the mission of theological education is to strengthen and accompany the mission of the church,"[39] then all theological education should have this ecclesial focus, and TEE is methodologically well suited. Norberto Saracco, TEE elder statesman in Latin America, comments, "The main contribution of the TEE vision was to bring the theological education to the church."[40]

Practically, theological education for the majority of God's people needs to be church-based, in the setting where they spend most of their time. Most church members cannot leave their homes, families, communities, and workplaces in order to be equipped for their callings. Nor should they. Theologically, the local church as a priestly community has the responsibility, amongst other things, of representing God to a watching world. For the majority then, their calling is both to be active members of the local church body in worship and service, and to be witnesses, salt and light, for the transformation of society as they have opportunity. Theological education will only connect with the majority of God's people if it is part of their ongoing church life and relevant to their daily experience.

TEE institutions can offer programmes for the majority of God's people. Here, group meetings take place within a specific local church, led by a member of that church, for members of that same local church. This is TEE – a tool to equip God's people for participation in the mission of God in the workplace, in the community, in the family, in society, and in and through the church. TEE assists discipleship and leadership training in the local church, by the local church, and for the local church.

TEE courses have been developed to serve the ministry needs of the *gathered* church, in preparing for and leading worship and prayer;[41] in

38. ICETE, *The ICETE Manifesto*, paragraph on "churchward orientation."

39. Lausanne, *Cape Town Commitment*, Part IIF, 4.

40. Norberto Saracco's address to the Increase Association, "Empowering Churches and Equipping Disciples: Church-Based Training in Asia Conference," Chiang Mai, Thailand, 17 November 2017.

41. For example, SEAN's course How to Prepare and Lead Services. "SEAN" is the abbreviation for Study by Extension for All Nations, a provider of TEE courses used globally. Details of SEAN

preaching;[42] in teaching children, teenagers, and adults;[43] in women's ministry;[44] pastoral care;[45] and more.

The ministry needs of the *scattered* church are also addressed by a whole range of courses on areas such as evangelism,[46] persecution,[47] issues in the workplace,[48] creation care and more. Theological education for the majority of God's people at appropriate educational levels in many contexts must be characterized by what Glissmann calls "artful simplicity."[49] Skill and hard work with repeated field testing are needed to create courses like these.[50]

A missional-ecclesial focus for theological education supports an ecclesial locus for theological education not only for the majority of God's people, but also for church leadership. Church-based TEE offers in-context learning: the challenges and issues of the neighbourhood and church members are always before the learner.[51] The crucible for application is immediately to hand, so that learning and life may be integrated effectively, leading to deep, lasting learning.

---

courses may be found on SEAN International's website, https://www.seaninternational.org.

42. For example, SEAN's How to Preach; TAFTEE's Homiletics 1 & 2. Contact details for TAFTEE may be found at https://ataindia.org/institution/the-association-for-theological-education-by-extension-taftee/.

43. For example, SEAN's course Feed My Lambs; Mongolia TEE's Ministry to Teens, and the Open Theological Seminary's series of courses for teens; PTEE's The Art of Teaching. For Mongolia TEE, see http://teemongolia.mn/en/; for the Open Theological Seminary, see https://ots-trust.org.

44. For example, Evangel Publishing House's TEXT-Africa course, Women in Ministry. See http://www.evangelpublishing.or.ke/product-category/tee-books/.

45. For example, The Open Theological Seminary's course Effective Pastoral Ministry, CCTB's The Shepherd and His Work. CCTB's contact details are at http://74.94.87.27:443/cctb.org.bd/contact.html.

46. For example, Evangel Publishing House's course, Bringing People to Jesus.

47. For example, The Open Theological Seminary's course, A Christian Response to Persecution.

48. For example, SEAN's course, Work for All, and TAFTEE's, Salt in the Marketplace.

49. Glissmann, "Grassroots Theological Education," 64.

50. Terry Barratt, part of the team involved in writing the widely used SEAN's Life of Christ series, reckons that each lesson of Book 1 took around 600 hours to complete. "After that it got easier." Personal Communication.

51. The distinction has been made between "church-based" programmes, where learners and learning are integrated into the ongoing ministry and mission of the local church, and "church-housed" programmes, which, while perhaps using a church building, have no necessary or organic connection with the life of that church. See the Global Accreditation Association for Ministries and Training (GAAMT) *Accreditation Manual*, 29. TEE programmes aspire to be church-based. Some may be vulnerable in some cases to the charge of being only "church-housed," and this is an important issue to be addressed.

Part-time study over the years builds a pattern of lifelong learning. Close and rich relationships are formed among fellow learners in the group meetings. With appropriate mentoring and supervision, well-resourced TEE programmes offer an effective and fruitful pathway for church ministry training, and many thousands have walked this path. The opportunities afforded by full-time residential theological education for a critical distance from past and future ministry locations, interaction with a scholarly community, and full-time study are, of course, recognized.[52] However, for many, it is simply not possible to leave the local context for distant, costly residential leadership training. The beginnings of TEE in Guatemala were driven by the observation that many rural church leaders had no access to theological education:

> The gifted, proven leaders of the local churches are generally older, married and with children, and employed. They cannot go to the seminary. The seminary must go to them.[53]

TEE programmes continue to provide a way of meeting this same need.

But, as argued above, TEE is also a good ministry training pathway when full-time residential training is possible. The quality of training is a different, although hugely important, question. Both TEE programmes and residential training programmes may be more or less fruitful and effective, depending on the vision, character, skills, and understanding of the individuals involved, and the level of investment and commitment of the stakeholder churches, among other significant factors.[54]

TEE institutions that offer training for church leadership may bring together local learning group members from several churches. There may be a programme entry requirement, which is that the learner should already be leading in their local church. Whether a TEE institution serves the majority of God's people, or specifically those in church leadership, there is a partnership

52. Although Bernhard Ott writes, "The church is the home of theological education," he follows this with the statement, "There are good reasons for providing theological education in institutions geographically separated from the local church." He writes about considerations of *proximity* and *distance*. Ott, *Understanding and Developing*, Kindle Edition, 197.

53. Kinsler, "Extension Center," 449.

54. See further discussion in chapter 9: Aylett, Green, and Weymouth, "TEE and Quality Assurance."

with the church whereby the TEE institution provides training materials to serve the church (developed in response to the needs of the local context) and a framework for training, while the church sets the agenda and provides oversight and accountability for practical assignments.

For the majority of God's people, and for those called to church leadership, TEE church-based training opens up access to learning pathways, a theme important from the early days of TEE.[55] By opening the door to theological education for many who were previously excluded, new possibilities for participation in the mission of God have become apparent.

TEE offers a framework that supports growth in the knowledge of God through whole-life discipleship

The first call for theological education addressed to the whole people of God is that it should help God's people to know him.[56] How can God's people participate in his mission if they do not know his character and his priorities?

One of the powerful themes of both the Old and New Testaments is that true knowledge of God is found in obedient action in response to God's word. In the New Testament, obedient action in response to Jesus, God's word incarnate, becomes the way to this knowledge. Scripture underlines powerfully the vital necessity of obedient, practical application.[57]

TEE provides repeated opportunities and requirements for this kind of response to God's word. Week by week, TEE self-study materials provide exposure to God's word, whether through the study of a particular biblical book or theme, or in relation to particular issues. Group discussion helps to connect the text with the context of the group members, which at its best, leads to self-theologizing and fine-tuned contextualization. One of the most significant roles of the group leader is to help group members reach appropriate responses. In this way, TEE is obedience- and discipleship-oriented.

55. See the ten different opportunities for access listed by Ross Kinsler given in chapter 1: Burke, Brown, and Julius, "Challenges Facing Theological Education and the Case for TEE."

56. "Now, more than ever, theology needs to be reminded of the old adage: the main thing is to keep the main thing the main thing. And the main thing for theology is God." Wolf, "Dancing for God," 2.

57. See Jer 22:15–16; Matt 7:21, 24; Luke 8:21; John 13:16–17; 14:21–23; Jas 1:22.

Some TEE courses are themselves practically oriented towards ministry skills, for example, courses in biblical counselling, teaching the Bible to children, or preaching. Other courses may have set practical assignments, and still others suggest to the group leader a range of options or provide questions that help group members to find appropriate obedient responses.

Knowledge of God arises from and leads to holistic discipleship and missional engagement. These are all parts of the same reality – the people of God called to participate in the mission of God.

One of the very encouraging signs of God at work globally is the groundswell of attention to discipleship.[58] The call of Jesus, "Follow me!," and the commitment to put his teaching into practice is sounding out loud and clear. The call to discipleship re-focuses attention on Jesus Christ who is the head of the church, the way to true knowledge of God, the key to theological education. As Jesus is Lord of all aspects of creation, the focus on discipleship not only highlights the multiple aspects of holistic mission but also brings them into proper relationship around Jesus. As church-based training, TEE provides frameworks for discipleship for all God's people.

Holistic discipleship seeks to overcome the sacred-secular divide, along with the privatization of faith, and to live under the Lordship of Jesus in all areas of life, including the public arena. That is why the vision of the church and of the TEE facilitator is so important – a facilitator who has a mindset of disciple-making will have a very different approach to one who regards the task as simply taking group members through a course.[59]

The extent to which a TEE group is discipleship- and obedience-oriented is the extent to which the group has opportunity to grow into true knowledge

58. For example, the Season of Intentional Discipleship called in 2016 by the Anglican Consultative Council, urged "every province, diocese and parish in the Anglican Communion to adopt a clear focus on intentional discipleship and to produce resources to equip and enable the whole church to be effective in making new disciples of Jesus Christ." Anglican Communion, "Season of Intentional Discipleship and Disciple-Making," https://www.anglicancommunion.org/mission/intentional-discipleship/discipleship-path/discipleship.aspx; e.g. the World Evangelical Alliance's call for 2020–2030 to be a "Decade of Disciple-making," see https://disciplemaking.worldea.org; e.g. the Faith2Share network: "The work of Faith2Share is about global discipleship for a changing world," "Discipleship," see https://faith2share.net/priorities/discipleship/.

59. Cf. a Mongolian pastor's observation: "It's important that we understand that we are not just teaching lessons, we are preparing powerful disciples, powerful ministers by means of these training materials."

of God. Conversely, if a TEE group is only focused on cognitive development, 1 Corinthians 8:1 warns that "Knowledge puffs up, but love builds up." Ultimately, knowledge without obedient response is deceptive and puffs up – that is, it leads to pride, which is perhaps the most impregnable of roadblocks to true knowledge of God.[60]

Holistic discipleship entails missional engagement and vice-versa. Paul Bendor-Samuel sees holistic discipleship as the integrative factor for mission: "Being and making disciples is the deceptively simple centre of the Christian community-in-mission."[61]

Banks proposed a missional model for theological education: "By 'missional,' I mean theological education that is wholly or partly field based, and that involves some measure of doing what is being studied."[62]

TEE provides just such a framework.[63] Steve de Gruchy begins a chapter on theological education and the mission of the church with the sub-heading, Theological Education Requires Missional Practice. He goes on to say that missional practice also requires theological education.[64] Church leaders have limited time and reach on the front line of missional opportunity; it is the majority of God's people who have multiple connections with those of other faiths and none, and reach into homes, families, work places, the arts, business, public service, local government, and so on.[65] In their practical, everyday discipleship, doing their daily tasks with God and for his glory, practising his presence, witnessing to Jesus in word and deed, and acting as salt and light

60. Scripture's thrice-repeated warning: Prov 3:34 LXX; Jas 4:6; 1 Pet 5:5. Proverbs is especially concerned: Prov 3:34; 8:13; 11:2; 13:10; 14:3; 15:25; 16:5, 18–19; 21:4, 24; 29:23.

61. Bendor-Samuel, "Discipleship: Centre of Mission," 105.

62. Banks, *Reenvisioning Theological Education*, Kindle Edition, location 1376.

63. Praise God for the example of CIPEP, Corporación Instituto para la Educación Pastoral, through whose TEE programme the number of local churches in one Colombian denomination quadrupled over a thirty-year period despite significant social unrest. This was the fruit of practical application while studying the SEAN course, Life of Christ. See Aylett and Green, "Theological Education by Extension (TEE)," 71.

64. de Gruchy, "Theological Education and Missional Practice," 42, 46.

65. See Michael Huggins's passionate plea for equipping all God's people: "There is urgent work for the churches, and every member is needed. Why cannot at least an equal investment . . . that goes into training and equipping leadership be put into training and mobilising the masses – God's tent makers, God's ants, God's partisans, God's labourers – rather than God's loiterers – all envisioned and equipped to change society for Jesus?" Huggins, "Open Russian Theological Academy," 282.

as they face injustice, God's people have daily opportunities to participate in the *missio Dei*. TEE supports and encourages them. Here is one vivid example from Pakistan. The question was put to a group of TEE students: "How have these courses helped you?" At that very moment, the Muslim call to prayer was sounding loudly from the mosque next door. One woman explained, "As we are living in a Muslim context, people ask us many questions about our faith. These courses help us to respond. They're very helpful."[66]

TEE provides a framework for joined-up learning pathways

As noted above, some TEE institutions focus on training for the majority of God's people, and others on training for church leadership. However, many TEE institutions offer courses at different educational levels, and levels of Christian maturity, and therefore provide pathways for growth from course to course, as well as a framework for growth within a particular course.

TEE as a methodology has proved effective for training church leaders at both lower and higher educational levels, as well as being a training tool for the majority of God's people who are not called to church leadership. In some contexts, only one TEE curriculum is available, and so TEE becomes identified with the courses and training in that one curriculum. But across the whole TEE movement, a great variety of courses and levels of training are available.

In Asia, TEE institutions and their programmes have developed in different ways. A "first wave" of TEE programmes began in the 1970s, some stimulated by CAMEO's Seminary Extension Workshops. These began with the aim of preparing church leaders through bachelor's level courses. Subsequently, courses at lower educational levels were added. This pattern is seen in The Association for TEE (TAFTEE) in India. The bachelor's level programme was established in the 1970s, and SEAN's Life of Christ (called Following Jesus Christ in India) was prepared in the 1980s and was eventually translated into twelve languages. Later still, the foundational SEAN course Abundant Life was contextualized and is now used widely. Courses in India at the bachelor's degree level were introduced first, and courses more widely accessible were added afterwards. But in other countries, a second wave of TEE programmes

66. Aylett and Green, "Theological Education by Extension," 67. Many more examples are given in van Wingerden, Green, and Aylett, *TEE in Asia*.

arose in response to rapid church growth, beginning with foundation level courses, often using SEAN's Abundant Life. These programmes have developed from the lowest rungs of the training pathway ladder and are now working on more demanding courses.

SEAN deliberately set out to produce leadership training courses that were simple, biblical, and practical.[67] In relation to their initial target learners, available seminary training began at too high a level educationally, and some SEAN courses aimed to supply the foundational level of the training pathway ladder. TEE courses are available to provide pathways to help new believers grow into godly leadership at basic educational levels, as well as courses to help active and mature believers grow into leadership at higher educational levels.

Some programmes have developed extensive pathways for growth. TEE Korea, for instance, offers a learning pathway with three levels – Foundation, Bible Study, and Church Leader Training – and additional practical ministry training courses at each level, a total of at least thirty-nine courses.[68] The Open Theological Seminary in Pakistan likewise offers a joined-up learning pathway beginning with foundation courses for new believers and culminating in courses at bachelor's level, accredited by the ATA.[69] Through this programme and others like it "sheep" can grow into "shepherds" in their local church contexts.

TEE institutions and methodology are often considered as "nonformal education," in that learning does not take place in a residential institution. According to the ICETE standards and guidelines (*SG-GETE*), nonformal learning is:

> Learning which is embedded in planned activities not always explicitly designated as learning (in terms of learning objectives, learning time or learning support), but which contain an

---

67. The widespread use of SEAN leadership training materials testifies to the importance of a learning pathway to godly leadership at lower educational levels. Compare this comment from an African context: "If only people would study at their appropriate level, they would be better educated. And so, I wish that trainers and bishops wouldn't push people educationally above their level of competence," Chatfield, "Topic 12: Successes," 103.

68. See the English-language brochure, "TEE KOREA Introduce," https://www.teekorea.org:492/tong/document/document_view.asp?uotc_code=4203&uotc=19442&lef=01&sublef=undefined. Note the heading, "TEECL Curriculum Discipling ALL Believers through Life-Long Study."

69. "OTS Courses," https://ots-trust.org/courses/.

> important learning element. Nonformal learning is intentional from the learner's point of view.

Formal learning, by contrast is:

> Learning that occurs in an organised and structured environment (e.g. in an education or training institution or on the job) and is explicitly designated as learning (in terms of objectives, time or resources). Formal learning is intentional from the learner's point of view. It typically leads to validation and certification.[70]

TEE institutions offering accredited programmes are able to give a full account of their programme design, and the learning framework that they offer, and should be considered as formal learning. Other TEE programmes may not have such a well-structured learning framework around the courses that they offer and could be considered nonformal. Quality assurance for TEE programmes encourages every institution to work with stakeholders and to bring clarity to the desired learning outcomes of the programme.

There are no courses for new believers written at high educational levels, but experience from many contexts shows that when well-facilitated, TEE courses at basic levels serve even highly educated professionals who are new believers very well.

TEE has yet to reach completely oral cultures, although some programmes are working on TEE courses suitable for oral learners and there is no reason why the personal study section cannot use audio or video materials. But TEE methodology can and already does help to serve oral preference learners. Pictures in the self-study text make a significant difference, and the group meetings and practical application need not require high levels of literacy, especially on the part of the group members.[71]

70. ICETE, *SG-GETE*, 37.

71. See Manley and Green, "Oral Learners," 41–55.

Conclusion

The nature of God and his mission bring an understanding of church that sees it as birthed in mission and for mission – the mission of God. Theological education's role is to help the church grow deeper in true knowledge of God as it participates in his mission. Since the whole church is called into God's mission, all its members need theological education. TEE offers a fitting methodology for this task. TEE offers church-based theological education to serve the whole people of God, providing a methodology and resources to help churches equip their members in holistic discipleship, missional engagement, and a growing knowledge of God. God is using the tool of TEE in many different contexts, and TEE methods and materials are now serving hundreds of thousands of believers globally.

But there is so much more that could be done. The 2010 pan-Asia Nepal TEE conference statement affirmed that TEE practitioners "believe TEE has the potential to equip all church members as agents of transformation, moving them from being passive receivers to active servants, salt and light where they are."[72]

The needs are immense, and TEE forms just one part of the whole practice of Christian theological education. The global church and the church in every country needs scholars. Local churches need leaders. All God's people need appropriate theological education. There is an urgent need for the various forms of theological education to work together and TEE has a vital contribution to make.

Bibliography

Anonymous. "The Edinburgh 2010 Common Call." In *Mission Today and Tomorrow*, edited by Kirsteen Kim and Andrew Anderson. Oxford: Regnum, 2011, 1–2.

Aylett, Graham, and Tim Green. "Theological Education by Extension (TEE) as a Tool for 21st Century Mission." In *Reflecting on and Equipping for Christian Mission*, edited by Steve B. Bevans, Teresa Chai, J. Nelson Jennings, Knud Jørgensen, and Dietrich Werner, 59–78. Oxford: Regnum, 2015.

72. van Wingerden, Green, and Aylett, *TEE in Asia*, 22.

Baker, J. Wesley. "The Origins of the 'Classroom Flip.'" In *Proceedings of the 1st Annual Flipped Learning Conference*, edited by Jerry Overmyer and Nissa Yestness, 15–24. Greely: University of Northern Colorado, 2016.

Banks, Robert. *Reenvisioning Theological Education: Exploring a Missional Alternative to Current Models.* Grand Rapids: Eerdmans, 1999.

Bendor-Samuel, Paul. "Discipleship: Centre of Mission." In *Discipleship: Reclaiming Mission's Strategic Focus*, edited by Melanie McNeal. Kuala Lumpur: Grassroots Mission Publications, 2014, 98–115.

Cannell, Linda. *Theological Education Matters: Leadership Education for the Church.* Newburgh: EDCOT Press, 2006.

Chatfield, Adrian. "Topic 12: Successes and Challenges of TEE in Christian Ministry in Africa: A Practitioner of TEE's Reflections." In *Understanding TEE: A Course Outline and Handbook for Students and Tutors in Residential Theological Institutions in Africa*, edited by Fareth Sendegeya and Leon Spencer, 99–110. Dar es Salaam: ANITEPAM, 2001.

Church of England, The. *Calling All God's People: A Theological Reflection on the Whole Church Serving God's Mission.* London: Church House Publishing, 2019.

de Gruchy, Steve. "Theological Education and Missional Practice: A Vital Dialogue." In *Handbook of Theological Education in World Christianity: Theological Perspectives – Regional Surveys – Ecumenical Trends*, edited by Dietrich Werner, David Esterline, Namsoon Kang and Joshva Raja, 42–50. Oxford: Regnum Books International, 2010.

Dykstra, Craig. "Looking Ahead at Theological Education." *Theological Education* 28, no. 1 (Autumn 1991): 95–105. https://www.ats.edu/uploads/resources/publications-presentations/theological-education/1991-theological-education-v28-n1.pdf.

Farley, Edward. *Theologia: The Fragmentation and Unity of Theological Education.* Philadelphia: Fortress, 1983.

Ferris, Robert W. *Ministry Education That Transforms: Modeling and Teaching the Transformed Life.* Carlisle: Langham, 2018.

Glissmann, Volker. "Grassroots Theological Education." *Insights* 5, no. 1 (2019): 53–67. https://insightsjournal.org/wp-content/uploads/2019/11/2019-Volker-Insights-Article.pdf.

Global Accreditation Association for Ministries and Training (GAAMT). *Accreditation Manual.* Colorado Springs: GAAMT, 2020. https://www.gaa-mt.com/uploads/1/9/4/0/19404491/gaamt_accreditation_manual.pdf.

Harkness, Allan. *From Seminary to Pew to Home, Workplace and Community – and Back Again: The Role of Theological Education in Asian Church Growth.* OMF International Consultation on Ecclesiology and Discipleship, Singapore, 2–5 April 2013.

Holland, Fred. *Teaching through T.E.E.* Nairobi: Evangel Publishing House, 1975.

Huggins, Michael. "The Open Russian Theological Academy." In *Diversified Theological Education: Equipping All God's People*, edited by F. Ross Kinsler, 269–95. Pasadena: WCIU Press, 2008.

ICETE. *The ICETE Manifesto on the Renewal of Evangelical Theological Education.* 3rd ed., 2002. https://icete.info/resources/manifesto/.

ICETE. *Standards and Guidelines for Global Evangelical Theological Education (SG-GETE).* 2019. https://icete.info/wp-content/uploads/2019/05/Standards-and-Guidelines-for-Global-Evangelical-Theological-Education-2019.pdf.

Kelsey, David H. *Between Athens and Berlin: The Theological Education Debate.* Grand Rapids: Eerdmans, 1993.

———. *To Understand God Truly: What's Theological about a Theological School?* Louisville: Westminster John Knox Press, 1992.

Kinsler, F. Ross. "The Extension Center: General Orientation." In *Theological Education by Extension*, edited by Ralph D. Winter, 447–74. Pasadena: William Carey Library, 1969.

Lausanne Movement. *The Cape Town Commitment: A Confession of Faith and a Call to Action.* 2011. http://www.lausanne.org/content/ctc/ctcommitment.

Manley, Regina, and Tim Green. "Oral Learners and Oral Preference Learners." In *Exploring New Horizons: Working Together for Church-Based Training in Asia*, edited by Graham Aylett, 41–55. Proceedings of a conference held in Kuala Lumpur, Malaysia, by Increase Association, 20–25 April, 2015.

Ott, Bernhard. *Understanding and Developing Theological Education.* Carlisle: Langham, 2016.

Shaw, Perry. *Transforming Theological Education: A Practical Handbook for Integrative Learning.* Carlisle: Langham, 2014.

Soh, Hui Leng Davina. *The Motif of Hospitality in Theological Education: A Critical Appraisal with Implications for Application in Theological Education.* Carlisle: Langham, 2016.

Tozer, A. W. *The Knowledge of the Holy.* New York: Harper & Row, 1961.

van Wingerden, Hanna-Ruth, Tim Green, and Graham Aylett, eds. *TEE in Asia: Empowering Churches, Equipping Disciples.* Carlisle: Langham Global Library, 2021.

Werner, Dietrich. *Challenges and Opportunities in Theological Education in the 21st Century: Pointers for a New International Debate on Theological Education*, 2009. https://www.wocati.org/wp-content/uploads/2012/12/Challenges-and-Opportunities-in-Theological-Education-in-the-21st-Century-Prospects-for-a-New-International-Debate-on-Theological-Education.pdf.

Wolf, Miroslav. "Dancing for God: Evangelical Theological Education in Global Context." Presented at the ICETE International Consultation for Theological Educators, High Wycombe, UK, 18 August 2003. https://icete.info/wp-content/uploads/2019/04/0-03-Volf-Dancing-for-God.pdf.

Wright, Christopher J. H. *The Mission of God's People: A Biblical Theology of the Church's Mission*. Grand Rapids: Zondervan, 2010.

———. "Theological Education, Bible and Mission: A Lausanne Perspective." In *Reflecting on and Equipping for Christian Mission*, edited by Steve B. Bevans, Teresa Chai, J. Nelson Jennings, Knud Jørgensen, and Dietrich Werner, 141–53. Oxford: Regnum, 2015.

4

TEE in Historical Context

Freda Carey and Patricia Harrison

Introduction

In this chapter we will use a historical perspective to survey some of the diverse ways in which churches have delivered theological education through the centuries. This variety has continued into modern times, with innovative delivery methods being adapted to circumstances. A review of the history of TEE shows that it is a ground-breaking example of past adaptation which will be described in more detail in this chapter. Some recommendations are also made for future adaptation in new programmes.

A Historical Survey of Theological Education

The term "theological education" has been applied in widely different contexts: from formal seminary training in preparation for ordained pastoral ministry to all forms of Christian religious education; from Sunday school and Bible study groups to study courses for formal qualifications. Over time, two divergent strands appeared – one focused on the formal training of clergy and recognized church leaders, the other, on the often nonformal training of the laity, the ordinary church members. In the New Testament church, the latter was very much to the fore.

Jesus's training model was typical of his day – the rabbi with a group of disciples who lived with him and learned from him. When he chose and appointed the twelve apostles, it was first, "that they might be with him," and only second, "that he might send them out to preach and to have authority to drive out demons" (Mark 3:14–15).[1] This model is seen in many places across Asia, *guru* and *chela*, *murshid* and *mureed*,[2] and the result is training which is not merely cognitive (information) but also affective and practical (formation).

The apostle Paul adopted a similar technique, gathering around himself a small team including young men with leadership potential, such as Timothy and Titus. Within the team, training was not merely passive, listening to and observing the great rabbi, but active, as Paul gave specific tasks to his young disciples, delegating to them increasing amounts of responsibility for ministry.[3] Timothy learned about mission and leadership from his master, Paul, through hands-on, on-the-job training, as an apprentice working alongside an experienced practitioner, not separated from the world out of touch with the needs and challenges of the church.

Ajith Fernando says, "During these years of Timothy's intimate contact with Paul, Timothy was able to observe Paul's life at close quarters. That life became an example for Timothy to follow . . . (2 Tim 3:10–11)."[4] Finally, Paul was confident that he could hand over responsibility for the care of the church to Timothy, and he urged him to continue the same training method of finding suitable potential leaders to train up and perpetuate the mission of the church. "And the things you have heard me say in the presence of many witnesses entrust to reliable men who will also be qualified to teach others" (2 Tim 2:2).

---

1. Bruce, *Training of the Twelve*, 29–30.

2. *Guru* (teacher) and *chela* (disciple) are common in the Hindu and Sikh tradition, while *murshid* (teacher/saint) and *mureed* (disciple) are common in the Muslim (especially Sufi) tradition of South Asia.

3. Paul sent Timothy back from Athens to check how the Christians in Thessalonica were doing (1 Thess 3:1–6). Timothy not only brought good news from there but, with Silas, brought Paul financial help from the Christians in Philippi so that Paul could turn to preaching full-time (Acts 18:5; 2 Cor 11:8–9). Timothy was with Paul in Corinth for 18 months and, along with Silas, was probably deputed to baptize the new converts there, as Paul only baptized a few people (1 Cor 1:14–16, cf. Acts 18:8). During the third missionary journey, when Paul, in Ephesus, heard disturbing reports from the church in Corinth, he sent Timothy back to Corinth as his personal representative (1 Cor 4:17). Timothy appears to have been unsuccessful, and the situation in Corinth required Paul's personal presence during a "painful visit" and a letter of strong rebuke (2 Cor 2:1–4; 7:8; 13:1–2), but Timothy's failure did not mean the end of his usefulness. By the time of Paul's first Roman imprisonment, he has no doubts about Timothy's ministry, sincerity, and commitment. Timothy has proved himself as a tried and tested fellow worker (Phil 2:19–23).

4. Fernando, *Leadership Lifestyle*, 21.

It is no coincidence that this verse became the slogan for the TEE programme SEAN (Study by Extension for All Nations).[5]

Luke describes the life of the Jerusalem church: "They devoted themselves to the apostles' teaching and to the fellowship, to the breaking of bread and to prayer" (Acts 2:42). The apostles saw this "ministry of the word of God" as of prime importance (Acts 6:2), in accordance with the often-neglected second half of Christ's Great Commission: "teaching them to obey everything I have commanded you" (Matt 28:20). The emphasis is clear throughout the New Testament epistles.

Lal Senanayake writes:

> The New Testament provides some basic but profound guidelines for understanding the ultimate purpose of theological education. One of the main themes of New Testament teaching is Christian growth and maturity . . . Paul said to Timothy – the pastor of the Ephesian church – that the numerous gifts are given to the church, such as apostles, prophets, evangelists, pastors and teachers, to equip the people for the works of service, so that the body of Christ will be mature and built up until they reach the unity of the faith and knowledge of the Son of God, and become mature, attaining to the whole measure of the fullness of Christ (Eph 4:11–13).[6]

Paul mentions the ability to teach among the requirements for episcopal or presbyteral office: "The bishop then must be . . . apt to teach (διδακτικόν)" (1 Tim 3:2 KJV).[7] However, Philip Schaff later stated that in the apostolic church,

> preaching and teaching were not confined to a particular class, but every convert could proclaim the gospel to unbelievers, and every Christian who had the gift could pray, and teach and exhort in the congregation . . . On the other hand it is equally clear that there was in the apostolic church a ministerial office, instituted by Christ, for the very purpose of raising the mass of believers from

5. The SEAN Motto, https://www.seaninternational.org.

6. Senanayake, "Imperative of Cultural Integration," 110. Ephesians 4:12 is the key verse for the Open Theological Seminary, a TEE programme in Pakistan.

7. Schaff, *History of the Christian Church, Vol. 1*, 355.

> infancy and pupillage to independent and immediate intercourse with God.[8]

Harold Rowdon says,

> At first, we find surprisingly little evidence of concern for anything like formal training for Christian leadership. One reason for this may be the charismatic gifts which outlasted the Apostolic Age. The Didache . . . gives evidence of the charismatic nature of the ministry of "apostles, prophets and teachers," a ministry which hardly called for formal training.[9]

The early church and medieval church

According to Justo Gonzalez, "the distinction that we make between theological education for the church as a whole and the training for the pastorate did not exist in the early church."[10] Later Gonzales writes: "In the ancient church, there was no difference between the biblical and theological training that the laity received and that which was required for ordination."[11]

In the early church, the need to educate new believers in the doctrines of the Christian faith led to the rise of the catechumenate, or preparation for baptism, with a systematic curriculum. The catechumenate was very important for the early church. Candidates for baptism were given special instruction under teachers called "catechists," who were generally presbyters and deacons.[12] The catechumenate was "a bridge from the world to the church, a Christian novitiate, to lead beginners forward to maturity."[13] At first, this process could last up to three years.[14]

---

8. Schaff, *History of the Christian Church, Vol. 2*, 88–89.
9. Rowdon, "Theological Education in Historical Perspective," 75.
10. Gonzalez, *History of Theological Education*, 7.
11. Gonzales, 14.
12. At first, the catechumenate preceded baptism of adults. Later, as infant baptism became the norm, it followed baptism.
13. Schaff, *History of the Christian Church, Vol. 2*, 186.
14. Young, *In the Footsteps*, 86.

The Catechetical School of Alexandria, founded at the end of the second century, grew to its greatest heights under the leadership of Origen. Its broad syllabus encompassed natural sciences, moral and religious philosophy, and Christian theology. But it was not an impersonal, coldly academic institution. As Rowdon explains:

> It revolved around the person of the Master (who was appointed by the Bishop) in whose house it met, and who provided the lion's share of the instruction. In the case of Origen, at least, it is clear that the force of his Christian character, the strength of his devotion to Christ, and the rigours of his personal standards of behaviour formed an important part of the training. Origen . . . transformed his disciples still more by his personal influence than by his scholarship. He was not a lecturer who merely appeared from time to time before an audience; he was a master and tutor who lived constantly with his disciples.[15]

The bishop came to have a similar role in the training of his clergy. Rowdon writes: "This intimate personal association of the bishop with his clergy was a source of inspiration and direction to untried clergy. The epitome of such training is to be found in the group of clergy which Augustine of Hippo gathered around him in the early fifth century."[16] Building from his own formative experiences, Augustine underscored the importance of community for theological life.[17]

During this period there was remarkable growth in the church, but the multitudes of new converts overwhelmed the catechumenate system, necessitating its reduction from two years to forty days under Gregory the Great (AD 540–604). Rapid growth, combined with the lack of a formal system of training for the clergy, contributed to growing ignorance among church leadership.[18] The decline of the old Roman Empire and the barbarian invasions

15. Rowdon, "Theological Education," 76.
16. Rowdon, 75.
17. Griffith, "History of Theological Education."
18. Griffith.

hindered thorough theological preparation. In the Latin-speaking church, few senior clergymen even knew the original languages of the Bible.

The Greek-speaking church had four theological schools: Alexandria in Egypt, Caesarea in Palestine, Antioch in Syria, and Edessa (in modern Turkey). The Latin-speaking church had no such institutions for theological instruction. Instead, there were smaller diocesan seminaries under the direction of the bishops who trained their own clergy, both in theory and in practice, as they passed through the subordinate classes of reader, sub-deacon, and deacon.[19]

Theological education for the laity was not neglected. Jerome in particular promoted the cause of monasticism in Rome among the wealthy, educated, upper classes, with great success. Most of his distinguished converts were women, such as Marcella and Paula.

> He gathered them as a select circle around him; he expounded to them the Holy Scriptures, in which some of these Roman ladies were very well read; he answered their questions of conscience; he incited them to celibate life, lavish beneficence, and enthusiastic asceticism.[20]

After her conversion, Marcella turned her palatial home into a Christian retreat where she held Bible studies and invited famous church leaders to teach, including Jerome. The Bible studies in her home were called the "Church of the Household" (Ecclesia Domestica), which became a centre for Bible study, prayer, and ministry to the poor.[21] So the practice of small group Bible study in the home for laity, which issues in practical service, is as old as Jerome.

While Western Europe was still struggling with successive waves of barbarian invasions, the rise of Islam gave another blow to the Eastern church. The most flourishing seats of patristic learning, Alexandria and Antioch, were lost to Islam. The immense library at Alexandria was burned in AD 638.[22]

---

19. Schaff, *History of the Christian Church, Vol. 3*, 165–6.

20. Schaff, 148.

21. Lutz, *Women as Risk-Takers*, 7.

22. Schaff, *History of the Christian Church, Vol. 4*, 417. Later, however, Arabic learning had a stimulating effect upon the scholarship of the church, especially on the development of scholastic philosophy.

The remnants of Roman civilization were finally overthrown by the northern barbarians and "a dark night settled over Europe."[23] Secular and sacred learning was confined to the clergy and the monks. The great mass of the laity, including the nobility, could neither read nor write. The people depended for their limited knowledge on the teaching of a poorly educated priesthood. Some priests did not know even the Lord's Prayer and the Creed.[24] One of the chief causes of prevailing ignorance was the scarcity of books. The old libraries were destroyed by ruthless barbarians and the ravages of war.[25] But monasteries, and a few secular rulers such as Charlemagne and Alfred the Great, preserved and promoted the study of ancient literature during the entire medieval period.[26]

The monastic novitiate replaced the catechumenate: "What was earlier expected of most Christians and offered to them was now reserved for a smaller group of particularly devout Christians."[27] In addition to the monasteries, cathedral schools began to develop around major urban churches. Here too basic education in the central doctrines of the faith was preserved and, in some places, resources were developed for broader dissemination. Theology was based on the Latin Bible and the Latin fathers, especially Augustine and Jerome.[28]

Universities emerged in the twelfth century. The medieval university aimed to produce mastery of the whole field of learning, with theology being the queen of the sciences. This was the period of great scholastic teachers like Thomas Aquinas. Unfortunately, theology became less and less related to the work of the ministry and became more and more the route to a life of academic scholarship.[29] The flourishing of scholasticism in the thirteenth century led

23. Schaff, 427.

24. Schaff, 428.

25. Schaff, 429.

26. Schaff, 430. Charlemagne's Palace School produced educated clergymen, noblemen, and statesmen, and was the model of similar schools throughout France and Germany. Charlemagne's grandson, Charles the Bald, followed his grandfather in zeal for learning, but after his death, "a darker night of ignorance and barbarism settled on Europe than ever before. It lasted till the middle of the eleventh century" (Schaff, 437–40).

27. Gonzales, *History of Theological Education*, 30.

28. Schaff, *History of the Christian Church, Vol. 4*, 434–5.

29. Rowdon, "Theological Education," 79.

to a growing distance between the academy and the church and, despite the theological awakening in much of the academy, little flowed into the parish church.[30]

The Protestant Reformation and later developments

One of the key emphases of the Reformation was that the Bible should be accessible to all, and that people should be instructed in it systematically. This trend first appeared at the end of the twelfth century with Peter Waldo and his followers, the "Poor Men of Lyons." Waldo had the New Testament translated from Latin into French and began preaching its message among uneducated villagers.[31]

In fourteenth-century England, John Wycliffe believed that the Bible was the final authority for all Christian teaching, so he wanted all people to be able to read and understand the Bible for themselves. Five of his friends translated the Bible from the Vulgate into English, and Wycliffe sent out preachers to read it aloud so that ordinary people could understand it. They spread the Bible's teaching in English throughout the country and prepared the way for the Reformation.[32]

As a parish priest in Switzerland, Ulrich Zwingli realized the supreme and final role of Scripture.[33] In 1518, he moved to the Great Minster in Zurich and began to preach systematically through the Bible. In 1522, he published "The Clarity and Certainty of God's Word," which expounds the fundamental Protestant principle of the final authority of Scripture that the Holy Spirit enables us to understand and for which no human interpreter is needed.[34] In 1525, Zwingli established a theological college in Zurich and organized a "school of the prophets." The school ensured an educated ministry. It was

30. Griffith, "History of Theological Education."

31. Foster, *Setback and Recovery*, 152.

32. Foster, *Setback and Recovery*, 155–58. And in fifteenth-century Bohemia, Jan Huss was influenced by Wycliffe's writings. He taught at the University of Prague and preached in the nearby Bethlehem Chapel. He emphasized the Bible and gave more importance to expository preaching in church services. He preferred to preach in the local Czech language so that the common people could understand him. After his execution as a heretic in 1415, his followers formed the Moravian Church (Foster, *Setback and Recovery*, 167–68).

33. Thomson, *New Movements*, 19.

34. Schaff, *History of the Christian Church, Vol. 8*, 124.

copied by other reformers, such as Calvin, and influenced the development of theological education until the nineteenth century when it was superseded by a full university.[35]

The main call of the Reformers was a return to the Bible as the word of God, which should be available to all people in languages they could understand. Desiderius Erasmus published the Greek text of the New Testament in 1516, which became the basis of subsequent translations into vernacular languages.[36] Like Wycliffe, he believed that the Bible should be available to everyone. He wrote: "I wish that the Scriptures might be translated into all languages . . . I long that the farm labourer might sing them as he follows his plough, the weaver hum them to the tune of his shuttle, the traveller beguile the weariness of his journey with their stories."[37]

Another rediscovery of the Reformation was the doctrine of the priesthood of all believers,[38] a New Testament concept, which gives more importance to the laity. The recognition that the laity should be theologically educated began to reappear. The Anabaptist movement in Europe moved further away from the Roman Catholic church. For the Anabaptists, the church is a "gathered community" of true believers committed to discipleship and evangelism. In matters of doctrine, the Scriptures were to be interpreted by the consensus of the local gathering in which all could speak. They called people to radical discipleship in which the believer's relationship with Christ involved a daily walk with God, Christ's teaching and example producing a transformed lifestyle.[39] All believers were committed to studying and acting upon God's word.

One result of the counter-Reformation was the establishment of seminaries by the Council of Trent, with a focus on formation rather than just information. This was the first time that the word "seminary" was used to describe institutions dedicated to the training of clergy. These "seedbeds" existed to cultivate a large number of candidates and then transplant them to the places where their

35. Schaff, 51.

36. Thomson, *New Movements*, 4.

37. McNair, "Seeds of Renewal," 359. This vision was shared by William Tyndale, who began to make a new English translation of the Bible based on Erasmus's text. Lane, "William Tyndale," 370.

38. Atkinson, "Reform," 373.

39. Yoder and Kreider, "The Anabaptists," 400.

ministry was to take place.[40] Gonzalez points out that the church managed without seminaries for fifteen centuries of its history. "For fifteen centuries the church subsisted, taught its theology, and at times flourished, without a single seminary."[41]

After the Reformation, the seventeenth century was reckoned by some to be "the age of dead orthodoxy." Many Protestants in Europe's state churches acknowledged the creeds but avoided the demands of discipleship.[42] In England in the 1650s, the spirit of the Reformation was revived by George Fox, who started the Society of Friends,[43] also known as Quakers. Fox stressed a personal experience of Christ, the forgiveness of sins, and the necessity to preach the gospel. The Quakers had no professional clergy, putting their belief in the priesthood of all believers into practice.[44] Their meetings were led by the Holy Spirit, and any believer could share the word of God, including women. George's spouse, Margaret, organized women's meetings to encourage and enable women to exercise their gifts for God's service and the edification of all. They studied Scripture and also trained in midwifery and social welfare.[45]

Pietism was an evangelical corrective to cold orthodoxy in the German Lutheran churches. It called for personal faith, regular times of prayer, fasting, and Bible study, and the demonstration of biblical truth in daily living. Pietism stressed personal Bible reading and group discussion, the illumination of the Holy Spirit in understanding Scripture, every believer's responsibility for intercession, and the application of biblical truth to everyday life. Emphasis on practical discipleship included concern and training for mission.[46] Philipp Jakob Spener, a Lutheran pastor in Frankfurt, Germany, organized his parish

---

40. Gonzales, *History of Theological Education*, 81.

41. Gonzales, xi.

42. Smeeton, *The Church*, 131.

43. The name "friends" is based on Jesus's words in John 15:14, "I no longer call you servants but friends . . . you are my friends if you obey my commands."

44. Roberts, "George Fox," 480–82.

45. Lutz, *Women as Risk-Takers*, 14–15. Fox endorsed Paul's words, "There is . . . neither male nor female, for you are all one in Christ Jesus" (Gal 3:28).

46. Smeeton, *The Church*, 131–2.

into small cell-groups in 1670, which met in homes for prayer and practical Bible study.[47]

The Church of England in the eighteenth century was not only affected by nominalism, but also by the teaching of deism, which undermined the central doctrines of the Christian faith. One clergyman who remained faithful was Samuel Wesley. He and his wife reared their nineteen children, including John Wesley and his brother Charles, in the light of the Bible. John and Charles studied at Oxford University. There they organized a club for people serious about their spiritual lives, nicknamed the "Holy Club." Others called them "Methodists" because they practiced a methodical pattern of prayer and Bible study, and a systematic programme for helping the poor and prisoners.[48]

John and Charles Wesley both went to North America as missionaries, but they returned disappointed.[49] During a prayer meeting in London in 1738, John received assurance of his salvation through faith in Christ and not through good works. He began preaching this message to the nation, first within the churches, and later in the open air. John Wesley's preaching led to a revival of religion, especially among working-class people, and many thousands joined the newly formed Methodist societies. Wesley organized the believers into fellowships, called classes, which met for prayer and Bible study and mutual accountability. He divided England into numerous circuits and trained Methodist preachers to minister in each church in the circuit.[50]

From this brief survey of the history of theological education, we can see that there has always been a variety of delivery models and approaches, of which the full-time residential seminary is only one. The periods of greatest growth and strength in the church were when the importance of adequately equipping those preparing for full-time ordained ministry was recognized, as well as that of training and equipping the laity, both men and women, "to prepare God's people for works of service, so that the body of Christ may be built up" (Eph 4:12). As Gonzalez notes, many non-traditional and church-

47. Thomson, *New Movements*, 109–10.

48. Thomson, 112.

49. Oulter, *John Wesley*, 44.

50. Thomson, *New Movements*, 114–5.

based theological training programmes have already begun returning to a discipleship model of education shaped by a profoundly biblical spirituality.[51]

The TEE Phenomenon in the History of Theological Education

A study of theological education over the previous two millennia provides ample evidence of variety and innovation. Clearly, there are many ways of delivering both pastoral training and general Christian education. The history of TEE provides several suggestions for successful implementation of new TEE programmes today.

A problem to envy

At the dawn of the 1960s, the Evangelical Presbyterian Church of Guatemala was facing a problem that would make many churches envious: their church was growing much faster than their seminary in Guatemala City could train pastors.

A problem to envy, but serious, nonetheless. And this church was not alone.

During the previous decades, Latin American Protestant churches had been growing faster than probably anywhere else in the world. In 1900, there were only about 50,000 Protestants in the whole of Latin America. By 1940, the number had grown to 1,250,000 and, by 1950, to 2,200,000. Protestant churches were growing 3.3 times faster than the population.[52]

This phenomenal growth was uneven and differed by region and denomination but, in many areas, adequate pastoral training was a challenge. Throughout Latin America at the time, there were about 15,000 Protestant pastors and 360 Bible colleges. These ranged from high-quality, prestigious seminaries, such as the Facultad Evangélica of Buenos Aires and the Seminario Bíblico of Costa Rica, to the much more numerous Bible schools, many quite small. But the disturbing reality was that, in addition to the 15,000 trained pastors, Latin America had about 100,000 "functional pastors" with no training whatsoever. Rapid church growth had not been matched with multiplication

51. Gonzales, *History of Theological Education*, 119.

52. Harrison, "Theological Education by Extension," 113–24.

of training institutions and, as a result, these thousands of leaders were functioning as pastors as best they could.[53]

Who exactly were these 100,000 functional pastors? Most were men who supported their families with secular jobs, often subsistence farming. Their pastoral work was undertaken on a voluntary, part-time basis, with proven gifts and dedication. But they still needed training to deepen their resources for teaching, preaching, and pastoring, to protect them from insidious false doctrines and often to qualify for ordination.

The Presbyterians had grown well in Guatemala, and a strong national church, evangelical in doctrine and evangelistic in outreach, had emerged. It was particularly strong in rural areas of western Guatemala, where the city of Quetzaltenango is located. However, until the early 1960s, the residential Presbyterian Seminary was located in Guatemala City, some distance from most of their churches. At the time, the seminary apparently had an average enrolment of about twenty students.[54]

A problem was that, after graduating, many students had no desire to pastor in a village and support themselves by subsistence farming. They had become accustomed to a comfortable lifestyle in the capital, and they wanted salaried jobs. Few graduates could obtain city pastorates, so many found secular employment in the city. Clearly, the seminary was not providing enough trained pastors for the many rural churches, nor could it train the numerous leaders who were functioning as pastors.

---

53. These statistics are from the above article and originate primarily from a major research project at the time, Church Growth Research in Latin America (CGRILA), in which Patricia Harrison, co-author of this chapter, participated as an editor. The study was undertaken under the auspices of the Institute of Church Growth at Fuller Theological Seminary in California. For further details and statistics, see Read, Monterroso, and Johnson, *Latin American Church Growth*. The book was also published in Spanish and Portuguese.

54. Patricia Harrison, co-author of this chapter, notes that some details in this section were sourced from her visit to the Guatemalan seminary, and from a course on TEE at Fuller Seminary taught by Ralph Winter, a pioneer of the movement. Much information in this section builds on her memories of involvement with TEE over decades, so errors are possible. If any readers can contribute corrections or additions, Patricia would be glad to communicate. With several other people, she is also collecting documents and articles on the history of TEE and would be glad to receive digital copies of such documents in any major Western European language. (Documents in other languages would require a translation.) Patricia can be contacted via the Increase Association.

In the early 1960s, the church made a bold decision. They would move their seminary to a location closer to most of their churches. Staff and students accordingly set up their seminary in the village of San Felipe, in western Guatemala. However, everyone realized it was really no easier for people with families and full-time work to attend classes in a seminary ten miles away than in a seminary two hundred miles away.

A creative solution

Church and seminary leaders knew from the biblical record and the history of theological education that a residential college was not the only way to train pastors. The Lord had often used innovative, contextual methods of training. After much prayer and deliberation, they concluded that if those needing training could not come to the seminary, the seminary must go to the students.

Several forward-looking seminary teachers, including Ralph Winter, Ross Kinsler, James Emery, and Nelly Castillo de Jacobs, decided to "move" the seminary again but this time no new buildings were needed. Village churches served as classrooms, and groups could meet at times that suited farmers. Lectures continued on the main campus for full-time students, but from 1962 the seminary extended its ministry much further, with staff making regular visits to twelve regional centres.

Before long, not twenty, but about one hundred and forty men and women were undertaking serious studies. Students now included those the church most needed to reach, namely functional pastors, elders, Sunday school teachers, youth leaders, etc. Emphasis was on training those already serving as leaders, with the intent that they would teach their own people. Nevertheless, all church members were welcomed.

But how on earth did the small faculty manage to teach in twelve centres? In pioneering TEE, they were well ahead of secular educators, who much more recently have developed a similar educational method they call the "flipped classroom."[55]

The main traditional teaching method was to present the course content in lectures. Then students were given homework to practice, apply, and extend their learning. For instance, in traditional classes a lecturer might take classes

55. See for example, https://www.adelaide.edu.au/flipped-classroom/about/.

on four evenings per week. Then students did their homework on the fifth evening. With TEE, lectures were replaced by home study on four evenings a week, leaving one evening to participate in a group session. Thus, freed from the need to lecture, a tutor (often called a facilitator) could now visit four different centres each week to conduct group sessions.[56] Students and tutors all still worked four evenings a week. All centres were located a reasonable distance from the central campus, so a small faculty could teach more students in more centres.[57] TEE can extend Christian studies geographically, numerically, demographically, and across social divides.

The original TEE programmes particularly targeted functional pastors, but also opened theological education to many who could never otherwise have had that opportunity. However, the original emphasis was not on numbers, but on reaching those leaders who most needed training, and who would then teach their congregations. Some Guatemalan extension centres had only several students, even as few as one.

Since the weight of course content is provided in home-study materials, these must be interactive and educationally sound. Originally, most TEE courses were designed as programmed instruction, which was a major educational innovation at the time.[58] Later, many writers changed to workbooks or to study guides based on textbooks. Today, we see some return to programmed (or partially programmed) materials.

Two streams

In 1968, an international, interdenominational TEE workshop was held in Medellín, Colombia. After this, the movement spread rapidly across Latin America, and eventually, globally. Interest was huge and some national TEE associations arose. In subsequent decades, a handful of practitioners and writers were invited to many countries to teach the basics of TEE and to

56. In this model, the faculty member does more travelling and marks more assignments, so should be paid accordingly. However, the students have much less travelling, an important factor in many economies. Some TEE programmes also provide supplementary short-term residential schools to boost morale and provide wider student interaction.

57. In TEE, we avoid the terms "lecturer" and even "teacher." No one lectures in the group sessions. Most course *content* is in the home-study materials. The group leader is often called a *facilitator* or a *tutor*.

58. A popular writers' guide at the time was Ward and Ward, *Programmed Instruction*.

train tutors and course designers.[59] Some programmes were denominational, others interdenominational.

Quite early, the TEE movement developed in two fairly distinct streams – the evangelical stream and the mainline ecumenical stream. Kinsler, from the evangelical seminary in Guatemala, became head of the World Council of Churches Programme on Theological Education in Geneva. He provided a link between the two streams, although each developed independently.[60]

There were several major evangelical cooperatives, whose member churches conducted their own programmes but collaborated to produce materials. Cooperative text production developed in Latin America, Africa (the TEXT-Africa project), and parts of Asia (e.g. PAFTEE in the Philippines).[61] The Association for TEE (TAFTEE) was founded in Bangalore, India, in 1971, and brought together a wide range of denominations, sharing quality materials for degree-level courses.[62]

Innovative varieties

Innovative varieties of TEE itself soon appeared,[63] often designed to address specific needs. Although forms of TEE emerged on all continents, there has been less interest in Western countries, perhaps because they have more resources for traditional training. But even in the West, strong, innovative TEE programmes appeared and flourished. In Australia, for example, the Christian and Missionary Alliance ran a TEE programme from their college in Canberra.[64]

---

59. The co-author of this chapter, Patricia Harrison, was among those who provided such training in many countries in the early decades of TEE.

60. For a description of a number of innovative programmes, both ecumenical and evangelical, at the height of the first wave of TEE, see Kinsler, *Ministry by the People*.

61. Not all these associations continue today. PAFTEE, for instance, ceased to function at some point.

62. TAFTEE, at the time of writing, has nearly 4,000 students at all levels from certificate to a doctoral programme accredited by the British Open University. For more information, see https://taftee.wordpress.com/about/.

63. Varied examples of these can be seen in Kinsler, *Ministry by the People*.

64. Christian and Missionary Alliance (C&MA) was an important pioneer in TEE and their involvement continues in a number of countries today.

An Anglican programme also arose in the Armidale Diocese of New South Wales, Australia. It was specifically designed to keep small rural churches open during the recession following a long drought. Clergy in the region were few and could only visit small churches occasionally. Congregations had the choice of closing, or of training lay people to lead worship and keep their churches open. TEE made the latter choice possible.[65]

In many countries, low literacy levels create a challenge for TEE. A programme in Thailand recorded home-study lessons in drama and story formats on cassettes. Students in a Conservative Baptist programme in Honduras were rural farmers with minimal literacy skills. But they liked reading comics. So studies in comic-book style were designed with practical assignments. Minimal reading and writing were required. Each booklet was a self-contained module with one week's work. In a flexible curriculum built around church planting, modules could be delivered whenever and wherever needed. When students were involved in personal evangelism, they could take a module to help them in this. If they were planting a new church, they could take various modules on church planting. And if a false cult came to town, creating havoc, a new module could be written quickly to meet the challenge. There was no need to say, "Sorry, we have no course on cults yet!"[66]

In northern Australia, two interdenominational training colleges developed their own versions of TEE, especially suited to the needs of Australia's indigenous people. Nungalinya College in Darwin,[67] and Wontulp-Bi-Buya College in Cairns, developed Mixed Mode TEE, which includes regional mentoring and short-term residential components on campus.[68]

Curriculum Considerations

TEE curricula were, and still are, a mixed bag. While some programmes have produced all their own courses for carefully planned curricula, others have

65. Patricia Harrison was involved in pioneering this programme, tutoring and writing TEE courses. See Harrison, "New England TEE," 274–83.

66. These mini courses were enthusiastically translated and adapted in various countries. For a fuller description of this programme, see Patterson, "Theological Extension," 52–67.

67. See https://www.nungalinya.edu.au/.

68. See https://www.wontulp.qld.edu.au.

had to rely primarily on whatever courses they could obtain from elsewhere. This means ad hoc curricula have sometimes emerged, leaving significant gaps. A number of smaller Bible colleges, including some in Papua New Guinea, have incorporated TEE courses into their campus programmes to plug gaps in their curricula.

Two waves

Rapid growth of TEE continued around the world for a number of years, but probably from about the end of the 1980s or early 1990s, the evangelical stream began to plateau, and in some areas slowly receded. Then in the early part of the present century, TEE flourished again in a second wave, particularly in Asia.[69] A snapshot of continuing diversity can be seen in Kinsler's collection of articles published in 2008.[70]

Evangelical TEE programmes have multiplied rapidly in Asia, Russia, and the Middle East in the past decade. There are now around 100,000 people studying TEE every year across this vast region.[71]

Some programmes around the world are quite large. For example, the interdenominational Christian Leaders' Training College in Papua New Guinea has about 1,000 TEE students in addition to its on-campus students. They have produced all their own TEE courses.[72] In Latin America, one example of a strong TEE programme with a long history is that of the Brazilian Assemblies of God, whose courses are also used in Portugal.[73] The TEE College in Johannesburg trains leaders and others for major denominations across five southern African nations. They have also produced their own courses and

---

69. The author is uncertain how far plateauing and resuscitation of TEE occurred on other continents.

70. Kinsler, *Diversified Theological Education*. Note that not all these programmes could be called TEE. This is a record of diversity in theological education more broadly.

71. A valuable guide to contemporary Asian programmes and innovations in TEE can be found in van Wingerden, Green, and Aylett, *TEE in Asia*.

72. https://www.cltc.ac.pg/. A history of TEE at CLTC can be found in Philip Bungo. An evaluation of the Christian Leaders' Training College's Theological Education by Extension Program and Proposals for its Future Development. Unpublished MS, Kerowagi, Papua New Guinea, 2020.

73. See http://www.eetad.com.br/v4/.

currently have over 2,200 students who are mentored by arrangement with local churches of participating denominations.[74]

In 2006 the Increase Association arose to serve multiple evangelical TEE programmes in Asia, Russia, and the Middle East.[75] In this second wave, the emphasis is a little different. There is less emphasis on training pastors and leaders to teach their own people, and more on training all church members directly. In both waves, making training available to all was a priority. The difference was about *who* would teach them – the TEE staff or the pastors that TEE had trained.

The impressive rise in TEE in the region served by Increase owes much to the adoption and translation of SEAN courses that originated with a British Anglican mission in South America[76] and which has made it much easier to start new foundational programmes in particular. TEE programmes operating at a higher academic level have usually needed to develop more of their own courses.

In recent times, a need has also been felt in some regions to write new courses that meet particular needs, which is why since 2017 Increase has been implementing an important mentoring programme, in which both authors of this chapter participate. The aim is to help writers produce courses that address local needs, such as witnessing in the context of other religions, or coping with persecution. One TEE programme in Pakistan focuses on the needs of teenagers.

Learning from History

In its early days, TEE was sometimes viewed as being in competition with traditional theological colleges. Some teachers argued for one or the other as the inherently superior form of training. This was unhelpful. As we have seen, the Lord has used many methods of delivering theological education over the centuries. Each has strengths and weaknesses. It is wise to choose appropriate

74. See http://www.tee.co.za/.
75. More information, https://increaseassociation.org.
76. https://www.seaninternational.org/.

methods, or even combinations of methods, not by default or tradition, but by purpose and circumstance.

One way of classifying delivery methods is to think of them on a continuum from *extraction* (e.g. residential colleges) to *extension* (e.g. online or correspondence courses in which students may never meet faculty or fellow students). Midway is TEE, which utilizes something of each to create a new blend.

As noted above, TEE did not initially progress, and in some regions it lost momentum for a period of time. We have learned many things from TEE's history. A few lessons may be of interest.

- TEE is a *method*, not a programme. It may be used for pastoral education, or for every-member discipleship training. It may be run independently, or by a congregation, a denomination, a college, or a mission. TEE courses may be run from an office, or as the TEE department of a college. These courses may even help provide religious instruction in secondary schools.
- TEE may be used at various educational levels and in various contexts. In the early days, TAFTEE in India was delivering degree-level courses, while elsewhere, cassettes provided home-study materials for marginal literates.[77]
- Curriculum is important. There are some great existing courses, but funds and time may need to be allocated to produce regional and contextual courses and to fill curricular gaps. Sometimes faculty need guidance in order to write the necessary courses for an adequate curriculum, not just courses that interest them.
- Quality courses are essential at different educational levels.[78] Good outcomes may be achieved at a basic level with existing courses, like those produced by SEAN and TEXT-Africa.[79]

---

77. Nonetheless, where there are very low literacy levels, TEE is not usually the best option.

78. See the appendices of this book for examples of TEE materials at foundational, middle, and higher learning levels.

79. Unlike lectures delivered within college walls, the content of TEE courses can be much more public. Lower standard courses are seen by outsiders and criticized – perhaps rightly. In the early days, some groups set standards for TEE courses, including theological and educational criteria, presentation, readability, and human interest. A good course cannot be written in a

- TEE courses often prove valuable for diaspora communities. (Note that some SEAN courses are available in many languages.)
- It may not be wise to train pastors by TEE just to cut costs. Sometimes pastors who benefitted from residential training became upset that a model perceived as inferior was being foisted on emerging leaders, apparently just to save money.[80]
- It is wise to involve national staff as much as possible and ensure that everyone supports the programme and understands why TEE is being introduced. Many first-wave programmes were initiated and conducted largely by missionaries. Normal missionary turnover sometimes left TEE programmes with few staff and little enthusiasm to continue.
- Good facilitators make or break a TEE course. Group meetings should include no lecturing, no trawling through the lesson answering every question. Group sessions need quality discussion. They should also enrich learning and address application. Every course needs a facilitator's guide with specific guidelines for conducting each session.
- Facilitators need thorough training and regular refresher courses. It is vital to plan for induction of all new facilitators, even when there is only one new recruit.

The following considerations relate specifically to theological colleges starting a TEE programme alongside their campus programme.

- If introducing TEE as an extra programme, extra staff are needed. Expecting faculty to write and teach TEE courses in addition to their campus workload is a recipe for resentment and failure.
- The TEE programme should not become an expendable extra. Run well, it may add many students and expand the college's impact on an entire nation. Consider providing the TEE programme with its

rush. On the other hand, the author of several TEXT-Africa courses explained recently how she spent 5 years revising and improving a particular course. Another factor is that programmed instruction was seen by some as indoctrination rather than education (this may be the case, but certainly *need* not be).

80. Note that TEE is not always as cheap as anticipated, when printing, travel, and staff for potentially many more students are taken into account.

own board and budget. Otherwise, endless visible campus needs ("the hole in the tank") will always take precedence. Thirty campus students may well take precedence over three hundred TEE students.

Conclusion

Our historical overview has traced some of the diverse ways theological education has been delivered since biblical times, with particular attention to the history of TEE. We believe that, if lessons from history are heeded, this method has massive untapped potential for addressing a wide range of Christian training needs today.

Bibliography

Atkinson, James. "Reform." In *The History of Christianity*, edited by Tim Dowley, 360–98. Tring: Lion, 1977.

Bruce, Alexander B. *The Training of the Twelve: How Jesus Christ Found and Taught the 12 Apostles: A Book of New Testament Biography*. 4th ed. Grand Rapids: Kregel, 1971.

Chandapilla, P. T. *The Master-Trainer*. Andhra Pradesh: OM Books, 1998.

Dowley, Tim, ed. *The History of Christianity*. Tring: Lion, 1977.

Fernando, Ajith. *Leadership Lifestyle: A Study of 1 Timothy* (Asian Edition). Singapore: Youth for Christ, 1986.

Foster, John. *Setback and Recovery: AD 500–1500: Church History 2*. London: SPCK, 1974.

Gonzalez, Justo L. *The History of Theological Education*. Nashville: Abingdon, 2015.

Griffith, C. Ryan. "The History of Theological Education." Book Review. https://trainingleadersinternational.org/jgc/41/the-history-of-theological-education.

Harrison, Patricia J. "New England TEE: A Rural Australian Experiment in Training Church Leaders." In *Ministry by the People: Theological Education by Extension*, edited by F. Ross Kinsler, 274–83. Maryknoll: Orbis, 1983.

———. "Theological Education by Extension: A Lively Evangelical Experiment in Latin America." *Journal of Christian Education* 13, no. 2 (1970): 113–24.

Kinsler, F. Ross, ed. *Ministry by the People: Theological Education by Extension*. Maryknoll: Orbis, 1983.

———, ed. *Diversified Theological Education: Equipping All God's People*. Pasadena: WCIU Press, 2008.

Lane, Tony. "William Tyndale and the English Bible." In *The History of Christianity*, edited by Tim Dowley, 370–72. Tring: Lion, 1977.

Lutz, Lorry. *Women as Risk-Takers for God*. Carlisle: Paternoster, 1997.

McNair, Philip. "Seeds of Renewal." In *The History of Christianity*, edited by Tim Dowley, 346–59. Tring: Lion, 1977.

Oulter, Albert C, ed. *John Wesley*. New York: Oxford University Press, 1964.

Patterson, George. "Theological Extension and Evangelism by Extension." In *Ministry by the People: Theological Education by Extension*, edited by F. Ross Kinsler, 52–67. Maryknoll: Orbis, 1983.

Read, William R., Victor M. Monterroso, and Harmon A. Johnson. *Latin American Church Growth*. Grand Rapids: Eerdmans, 1969.

Roberts, Arthur G. "George Fox and the Quakers." In *The History of Christianity*, edited by Tim Dowley, 480–83. Tring: Lion, 1977.

Rowdon, Harold H. "Theological Education in Historical Perspective." *Vox Evangelica* 7 (1971): 75–87. https://biblicalstudies.org.uk/pdf/vox/vol07/education_rowdon.pdf/.

Schaff, Philip. *History of the Christian Church, Vol. 1: Apostolic Christianity AD 1–100*. Grand Rapids: Christian Classics Ethereal Library, 2002. http://www.ccel.org/ccel/schaff/hcc1.toc.html.

———. *History of the Christian Church, Vol. 2: Ante-Nicene Christianity AD 100–325*. Grand Rapids: Christian Classics Ethereal Library, 2002. http://www.ccel.org/ccel/schaff/hcc2.html.

———. *History of the Christian Church, Vol. 3: Nicene and Post-Nicene Christianity AD 311–600*. Grand Rapids: Christian Classics Ethereal Library, 2002. http://www.ccel.org/ccel/schaff/hcc3.html.

———. *History of the Christian Church, Vol. 4: Mediaeval Christianity AD 590–1073*. Grand Rapids: Christian Classics Ethereal Library, 2002. http://www.ccel.org/ccel/schaff/hcc4.html.

———. *History of the Christian Church, Vol. 5: Mediaeval Christianity AD 1049–1294*. Grand Rapids: Christian Classics Ethereal Library, 2002. http://www.ccel.org/ccel/schaff/hcc5.html.

———. *History of the Christian Church, Vol. 8: Modern Christianity, The Swiss Reformation*. Grand Rapids: Christian Classics Ethereal Library, 2002. http://www.ccel.org/ccel/schaff/hcc8.html.

Senanayake, Lal. "The Imperative of Cultural Integration in Advanced Theological Studies: Perspectives from the Majority World." In *Challenging Tradition: Innovation in Advanced Theological Education*, edited by Perry Shaw and Havilah Dharamraj, 109–26. Carlisle: Langham, 2018.

Smeeton, Donald D. *The Church: From the Reformation to the Present*. Irving: ICI University Press, 1994.

Smith, David I. "The History of Theological Education – An Extended Review." *Christian Scholars Review* 47, no. 1 (2017): 51–57. https://christianscholars.com/the-history-of-theological-education-an-extended-review.

Thomson, Alan. *New Movements; Reform, Rationalism, Revolution: AD 1500–1800: Church History 3*. London: SPCK, 1976.

van Wingerden, Hanna-Ruth, Tim Green, and Graham Aylett, eds. *TEE in Asia: Empowering Churches, Equipping Disciples*. Carlisle: Langham Global Library, 2021.

Ward, Ted W., and Margaret Ward. *Programmed Instruction for Theological Education by Extension*. East Lansing: Michigan State University Press, 1970.

Yoder, John H., and Alan Kreider. "The Anabaptists." In *The History of Christianity*, edited by Tim Dowley, 399–403. Tring: Lion, 1977.

Young, William G. *In the Footsteps of the Apostles*. Lahore: Christian Publishing House, 1978.

5

The Educational Efficacy of TEE – Part 1

A Conversation with Key Learning Theories

Perry Shaw

Introduction

Education is about learning not teaching. However, learning is itself a complex and multidimensional reality. There are multiple perspectives on what "learning" is and how it takes place, and the different emphases of each learning theory can contribute meaningfully to our educational endeavours. In this chapter I will reflect on a few fairly influential models and conduct a conversation with the work of TEE, both to advocate for the learning efficacy of TEE and to challenge TEE practitioners to consider ways in which the work of TEE might better enhance and promote quality education.

The ABCs of Learning and TEE

The biblical understanding of "knowledge" stands in stark contrast to the cerebral schooling approach that dominates much of both government and church education across the world. It is noteworthy that in both Old Testament Hebrew and New Testament Greek the term "to know" is used both for sexual intercourse and for the relationship the believer should have with God – pointing to the passionate, personal, relational nature of knowledge. As such, the scriptural call to "know" God is not a call to an objective theoretical understanding but rather entry into an "intimate personal interactive relationship."[1] A recognition that quality leadership training goes beyond the mere development of our rational capacities is seen in the now ubiquitous language of "head, heart and hands." What is lesser known is that for over fifty years educationalists have been discussing and analyzing holistic learning through what have now become known as the three primary learning domains of affect, behaviour, and cognition.

Affective domain

Affective learning encompasses the values, emotions, attitudes, and motivations that shape our thinking and practice. While our traditional paradigms have focused on the cognitive domain, recent brain research has pointed to the extent to which our intellectual engagement is dependent on positive affective engagement: strong positive feelings triggered through the limbic system facilitate active thinking.[2] Affective learning is nigh on impossible to measure and consequently is often ignored in the grade-fixated environment of schools, and yet it plays a crucial catalyst role in the educational process.

The heart of affective learning is the quality of the teacher-student relationship.[3] Too often, we have forgotten that "Jesus was not so intent on teaching people religious content as he was on beckoning people into a genuine relationship with him and into compassionate relationships with one another."[4] In a wide variety of formal studies[5] it has been found that while such qualities as a passionate love for the subject, knowledge of the material, and creative teaching styles are common among exceptional teachers, even more so are warmth, genuine concern for the students' learning, even love – all characteristics which speak of personal relationship and a hospitable learning environment.[6]

1. Gorman, "There's Got to Be More," 48.
2. Nilson, *Teaching at Its Best*, 5.
3. Brookfield, *Understanding and Facilitating*, 62–64; Cranton, *Understanding and Promoting*, 112–5.
4. Schultz and Schultz, *Dirt on Learning*, 59–60.
5. Merriam, Caffarella and Baumgartner, *Learning in Adulthood*, 152–3; Stronge, *Qualities of Effective Teachers*, 23–25.
6. Shaw, "Welcome Guest," 8–26; Soh, *Motif of Hospitality*.

Repeatedly when I ask participants in workshops about the factors that have contributed to long-term learning they will talk about relationships. Often significant learning impact has come from instructors who have invited them into their homes, or talked about significant topics over meals, or given extra time out of the classroom. Learning very often emerges more from the person of the teacher than from a matter of mere content delivery.

It is precisely at this point that TEE has the potential for offering strong affective engagement: the local tutor (or group leader)[7] is generally someone from the local church or community who is already well known to the students and trusted by local leadership. Part of quality tutor training is the emphasis on out-of-class relationships with the class members. When tutors build strong connections among class members it augurs well for strong affective learning.

Behavioural domain

Our educational paradigms have been strongly shaped by Western rationalist models of schooling. The assumption has been that if we teach students the right things then they will believe and do the right things. Over the past fifty years these rationalist assumptions have been challenged by the research of social scientists. Beginning with the social-psychological research of Leon Festinger in the 1950s and continuing to the present day, a growing body of evidence points to the startling observation that the knowledge-behaviour relationship actually works the other way around – that is, people are more likely to behave their way into thinking than think their way into behaving.[8] Following research conducted among evangelical Christians in the USA, the Barna group[9] went so far as to claim that the expressed beliefs of a group of people are almost worthless in predicting how they will behave. It is for this reason that behavioural learning is such a crucial element in our education.

One of the greatest challenges for theological education is to draw experience into the learning of students. While an increasing number of institutional schools are becoming intentional in creating opportunities for

7. As other authors in this book have noted, the TEE tutor is not a "teacher" in the formal sense but rather a leader of the group of learners as they engage the text together. The tutor-led small group distinguishes TEE both from formal classroom instruction and distance education.

8. Shaw, *Transforming Theological Education*, 73.

9. Barna Group, "Born Again Christians."

a dialogue between theory and practice, TEE is particularly well-positioned to engage the behavioural domain. As has been mentioned elsewhere in these chapters, TEE is built on three key elements: (1) personal study; (2) group meeting; and (3) practical application. Unlike residential students, TEE students are engaged on a daily basis in the routines of work, family, and church life. They are practitioners seeking to inform and reflect on their ongoing experience of life and ministry engagement. Consequently, the norm for TEE courses is a regular expectation that students will seek pathways for applying the material being presented in the text in practical ways. At its best, dialogue over the applications takes place in the group meetings, further providing opportunity to learn from one another in the behavioural domain.

Cognitive domain

The cognitive domain of learning is the prime focus of most schools – from kindergarten to postgraduate. Cognitive learning is attractive in that it is easy to control, easy to plan, and easy to measure. However, even in the realm of cognitive learning, our record is mediocre at best, as the focus has too often remained on the acquisition of information – the transmission of vast quantities of data that students are required to learn and then regurgitate in the exams.[10]

At the end of the 1940s a group of educationalists under the leadership of Benjamin Bloom sought to analyze the levels and shape of cognitive learning through their seminal Taxonomy of Educational Objectives.[11] The taxonomy is a somewhat simplistic presentation of the exceedingly complex and even mysterious phenomenon of learning. Consequently, the taxonomy has been modified in later representations, and other more complex models have since been posited.[12] Nonetheless, the taxonomy's simplicity and widespread acceptance make it a good discussion partner. Bloom and his associates proposed six different levels of cognitive sophistication as follows (and Figure 5.1):

10. Shaw, *Transforming Theological Education*, 74.

11. Bloom et al., *Taxonomy of Educational Objectives*.

12. Anderson and Krathwohl, eds., *A Taxonomy for Learning*; Baxter Magolda, *Knowing and Reasoning*; Fink, *Creating Significant Learning Experiences*; Marzano and Kendall, eds., *New Taxonomy*; Perry, *Forms of Intellectual*; Shulman, "Making Differences."

- *Knowledge:* the ability to recall facts or information.
- *Comprehension:* the understanding of what is being communicated and the ability to make use of the material at a simple level.
- *Application:* the ability to use abstractions in particular concrete situations.
- *Analysis:* the ability to break material down into its constituent elements or parts.
- *Synthesis:* the ability to build a structure or pattern from diverse elements, or to put parts together to form a whole, creating a more comprehensive meaning or structure.
- *Evaluation:* the ability to make judgements about the value of ideas or materials.

Bloom's Taxonomy of Educational Objectives

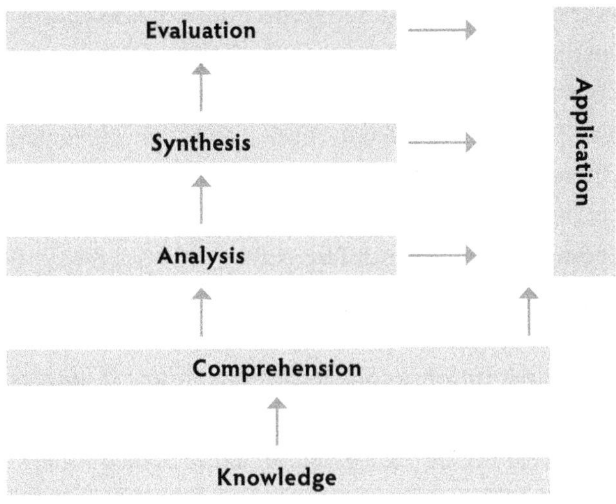

Figure 5.1. Bloom's taxonomy – a possible hierarchy[13]

While it is not completely valid, there is somewhat of a hierarchy in Bloom's taxonomy (Figure 5.1): knowledge is preliminary to comprehension;

13. Diagram by Shaw, *Transforming Theological Education*, 75.

comprehension is preliminary to analysis; analysis to synthesis; and synthesis to intelligent evaluation. Moreover, the more deeply one grasps the issues related to an idea or question, the more potentially powerful the application. Only when we challenge our students to think more deeply and step towards living and leading with theological insight can we claim to be fulfilling our holy calling of developing effective leaders for God's people.[14] It is noteworthy that accreditation standards in general promote analytic thinking at the bachelor level of study, synthetic thinking at the masters level of study, and evaluative-creative thinking at the doctoral level of study.[15] Consequently, familiarity with the taxonomy is important for the designers and developers of all programmes of theological study.

One of the most common critiques of TEE has been the claim that TEE focuses on lower order thinking. Certainly, the older style of TEE with its rigid adherence to programmed learning often erred towards an emphasis on the knowledge and understanding levels. In addition, the natural tendency of "high power distance" societies to respect the elders as authoritative[16] can lead students in much of the world to seek the "right answer" in rote-remembering the text and repeating what is given in the answers section of the course. However, as TEE has continued to develop and align with emerging educational research there has been a growing awareness of the importance of challenging students to higher-order thinking. Analytic and synthetic question design[17] is a crucial component of quality TEE texts.

Another critique of TEE is the assertion that many courses require little or no engagement with texts apart from the study guide. This limitation stands in contrast to institutional colleges, where library resources (both physical and online) are the norm, and students are trained to write critical[18] essays based on the reading of texts given on campus or online. Consequently, it is claimed that TEE lacks the analytical and synthetic components of essay

---

14. Shaw, 75–76.

15. Shaw, "Innovation and Criteria," 43–60.

16. See Hofstede and Hofstede, *Cultures and Organizations*, 61.

17. Shaw, *Transforming Theological Education*, 202–7.

18. Of course, the term "critical thinking" is an exceedingly Western concept, and perhaps a preferable term – particularly in more communal societies – is "constructive thinking." See Shaw, "Creating a Respectful Community."

writing. While the emphasis on essay writing is definitely less prevalent in TEE than in institutional approaches, the assertion that the only meaningful form of critical thinking is that generated through the critical reading of texts is questionable.

One of the great gifts of TEE is its ability to provide quality training in contexts where Christian resources in the heart language of the students may be limited to the Bible and little else. In these situations, the expectation of text-based writing is unrealistic. However, a different form of critical thinking can be nurtured through a critical engagement between theory and practice. Case studies in particular are a highly beneficial means for challenging students from oral societies to quality analytic and synthetic thinking.[19] In most TEE courses case studies are a regular feature. While the level of thinking generated is dependent on the quality of accompanying questions and on the reflective maturity of the tutor, the potential for higher level reflection is readily available through TEE methodology.

Deep Learning and TEE

The real learning is not what is remembered at the end of a course, but what is remembered five or ten years after taking the course, and even more, what shapes in the long term the character and actions of the learner. While it is beneficial to consider learning multidimensionally it is equally important to consider the factors that contribute to long-term learning – the learning that lasts and that impacts life.

Deep learning implies the long-term storage of material in the brain, which can subsequently be accessed and applied. It has been found that what we need to survive is readily recorded in long-term memory.[20] For example, you do not need to relearn every day that walking in front of a moving bus or touching a hot stove can injure you. Beyond survival, there are three elements which contribute to deep and transformative learning: emotional connection, sense, and significance.[21]

19. Zailaa, "Power of Stories."

20. Sousa, *How the Brain Learns*, 48–49.

21. Barkley, *Student Engagement Techniques*, 101.

Emotional connection

Strong emotional experiences have a high likelihood of being permanently stored in the memory.[22] We tend to remember the best and (even more) the worst things that have happened to us. If I were to ask you to recall the worst travel experience you have ever had, we would probably be here all day listening to the details. You remember these specifics precisely because of the strength of emotion that was generated at the time. As we noted above under our discussion of affective learning, thought and emotion are inseparable brain processes. In fact, a portion of the brain's emotion system called the hippocampus is in charge of transferring information into memory. This means that information associated with values and feelings will be more readily learned.[23] While recognizing the need for a level of dissonance in transformational growth, we should seek to minimize unnecessary negative emotions. Interpersonal anger and fear cause the brain to be flooded with chemicals that seriously impede the ability to retain new or call up old information. When this occurs, the brain will abandon complex thought processes and revert to more reflexive behaviours.[24]

Strong emotions lead to strong connections in our memories. In the classroom strong emotions are elicited in learners through experiential learning activities such as field trips, case studies, and role plays. By definition emotional connection entails an approach to learning that seeks integration between text and context, between theory and life. Several features place TEE in a strong position for promoting positive emotional connection. Where the relationship between tutor and class is strong, positive emotion ensues. Generally, the TEE group meeting is relaxed and relational, laughter and joy easily emerge, and stress and fear are dissipated. While most tutors naturally build a positive space for the group gathering, many tutors have been profoundly shaped by the "schooling" understanding of education. I consequently wonder whether the importance of emotional connection for long-term student learning could be more intentionally incorporated into TEE tutor training.

---

22. Willingham, *Why Don't Students Like School?*, 44–45; Barkley, *Student Engagement Techniques*, 101.

23. Davis, "Brain-Friendly Environment."

24. Davis, 6.

Sense

For deep and transformative learning to take place it is also important that the learner understand what is being said and can connect it to past experience.[25] People learn new knowledge most easily if it relates in some way to previous learning.[26] Famed educational psychologist David Ausubel once asserted, "The most important single factor influencing learning is what the learner already knows. Ascertain this and teach him accordingly."[27] Students are more likely to engage with new learning when it is presented either as an extension of or even an antithesis to previous learning, as they feel a sense of mastery in the face of new challenges that nurtures engagement and retention.

Historically, TEE has emphasized a step-by-step approach to learning. While traditional programmed learning is no longer the norm, the beneficial incremental approach to learning remains strong in TEE, and most texts incorporate constant feedback loops that ensure that students are making sense of the material. Equally the practical application component of the lesson seeks to make the sort of connection between text and context that is seen as crucial for the promotion of sense-making.

Significance

While emotional connection and sense-making are important to deep learning, ultimately the brain will only store material in long-term memory if the learner considers the material relevant and significant for life.[28] Unfortunately for most students, the only level of significance they are ever given is, "It's going to be in the exam." And so, they make the effort to engage with the material for as long as it is significant – which is until the end of the course. As soon as the examination is over, the material is no longer significant, and what has been learned quickly drops out of memory.[29] Both with institutional and TEE approaches to leadership training a focus on exams and grades can lead to deceptive assessment; we consider that passing the course is evidence of

25. Sousa, *How the Brain Learns*, 48–49.

26. Bransford, Brown, and Cocking, *How People Learn*; Ambrose et al., *How Learning Works*.

27. Ausubel, *Educational Psychology*, vi.

28. Ambrose et al., *How Learning Works*; Persellin and Daniels, *Concise Guide*; Winne and Nesbit, "Psychology of Academic Achievement."

29. Zull, *Art of Changing*, 181.

learning, but in fact the student has learned for the grade rather than learned for life, and the supposed learning does not remain.

Of course, significance can be in any mixture of the affective, behavioural, or cognitive domains, and we have limited ability to pre-determine what a particular student may consider "significant." Nonetheless two factors place TEE in a strong position to embrace significance. The first is the emphasis on practical application aligned with the theory, which enables students to see that what is being taught is not mere book learning but can have a positive impact on life. The second and more implicit factor is the "menu-driven" approach to TEE. As with many forms of distributed learning, TEE students can choose from a "menu" of courses those which best connect with an immediate felt need. While there is often a need in TEE for some level of progression from simpler to more complex course material, the norm of student choice respects the maturity of the learners, and the perceived connection between the content of the course and the felt need of the student enables a sense of significance.

Experiential Learning Theory and TEE

A number of educationalists have pointed to the significant learning that occurs through what Schön has described as "reflection-in-action,"[30] and Kolb as "experiential learning theory."[31] These influential models are built on the holistic affective, behavioural, cognitive framework mentioned earlier, seeing learning as a process that nurtures growth in knowledge, development of skills, and change in attitudes, values, and perceptions.

Drawing on Kolb's approach, this form of multidimensional learning is best nurtured through a continuous four-stage cycle of experience, reflection, conceptualization, and experimentation (Figure 5.2).[32] According to Kolb, while the cycle may be entered at any point, the stages need to be followed in sequence, thereby providing a structure for guided reflection and action. Ideally learners will pass through the cycle multiple times, hence providing a

30. Schön, *Reflective Practitioner.*

31. Kolb, *Experiential Learning.*

32. It is important to note the limitations of Kolb's experiential learning model, in particular that learning can take place without all four elements of the cycle being evident. See for example Jayson Seaman, "Experience, Reflect, Critique."

"spiral of learning."[33] Kolb's model attempts to explain how we link theory to practice. In particular the approach highlights:

1. the critical part that experience plays in learning
2. the importance of making sense of our experience through critical reflection
3. the value of feedback for the reinforcement of learning.

There are numerous pathways through which quality reflection-on-action can take place. Roth suggests the following:[34]

- questioning what, why, and how one does things and asking what, why, and how others do things
- seeking alternatives
- keeping an open mind
- comparing and contrasting
- seeking the framework, theoretical basis and/or underlying rationale
- viewing an issue from various perspectives
- asking "what if . . .?"; asking for others' ideas and viewpoints
- considering consequences
- hypothesizing
- synthesizing and testing
- seeking, identifying, and resolving problems.

33. This theoretical framework is the foundation for action research, a now respected approach to intellectual engagement through to doctoral level.

34. Roth, "Preparing the Reflective Practitioner."

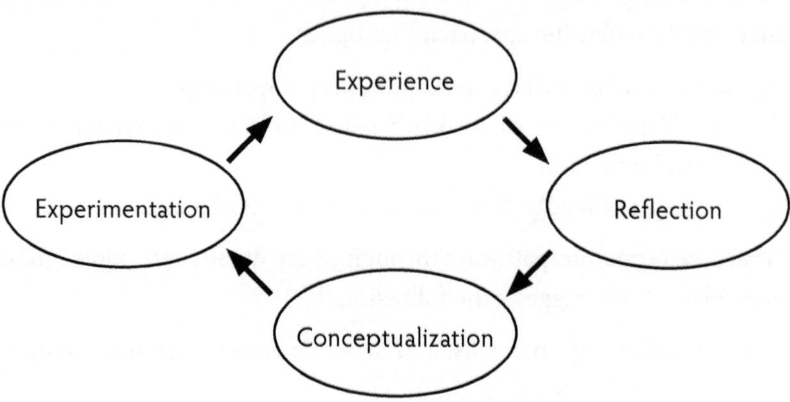

Figure 5.2. Kolb's experiential learning cycle

TEE's three-pronged approach of personal study, group meeting, and practical application places TEE in a strong position to nurture reflective practitioners through the cycle of experiential learning. Experience, reflection, conceptualization, and experimentation are all expected elements in TEE courses, and when tutors open up space for quality discussion in the group meetings, there is potential for mutual feedback and critical pathways for courageous experimentation into the future.

Adult Learning ("Andragogy") and TEE

One of the most significant educational developments has been the recognition that children and adults learn in fundamentally different ways. Spearheaded by Malcolm Knowles, the so-called "andragogical model" has had a major influence on higher education in general and theological education in particular.[35] Table 5.1 shows how Knowles contrasts pedagogy (the education of children) and andragogy (the education of adults).[36]

35. Knowles, Holton, and Swanson, *Adult Learner*.

36. As the theory developed, Knowles observed that pedagogy and andragogy "are probably most useful when seen not as dichotomous but rather as two ends of a spectrum with a realistic assumption in a given situation falling in between the two ends." See Knowles, *Modern Practice*, 43.

Table 5.1. Knowles's key distinctions between pedagogy and andragogy[37]

	Pedagogical	**Andragogical**
Concept of the learner	Dependent personality	Increasingly self-directing
Role of learner's experience	To be built on, more than used, as a resource	A rich resource for learning by self and others
Readiness to learn	Uniform by age-level and curriculum	Develops from life tasks and problems
Orientation to learning	Subject-centred	Task- or problem-centred
Motivation	By external punishments and rewards	By internal incentives and curiosity
Climate	Tense, low trust, formal, cold, aloof, authority-oriented, competitive, judgemental	Relaxed, trusting, mutually respectful, informal, warm, collaborative, supportive
Planning	Primarily by teacher	Mutually by learners and facilitator
Diagnosis of needs	Primarily by teacher	By mutual assessment
Setting of objectives	Primarily by teacher	By mutual negotiation
Designing learning plans	Teachers' content plans; course syllabus; logical sequence	Learning contracts; learning projects; sequenced by readiness
Learning activities	Transmittal techniques; assigned readings	Inquiry projects; independent study; experimental techniques
Evaluation	By teacher; norm-referenced; with grades	By learner-collected evidence validated by peers, facilitators, experts; criterion-referenced

Key elements of adult learning evident in Table 5.1 include:

- respect for the adult as a responsible and independent learner
- a focus on intrinsic motivation for learning
- the role of life experience in the learning
- contextual relevance as a learning priority
- practical applicability of the material to be learned
- the mutuality of teacher and student in the learning process
- methodology that opens a relaxed space for interactive discussion

37. Knowles, "Contributions of Malcolm Knowles."

Essential to Knowles's model is the assertion that adults are motivated to learn what they need to live life effectively.[38]

TEE students are not a captive audience. They are not required to attend, and the classes are not generally the main occupation in their lives. Most TEE students are busy with work, family, and church responsibilities. No one funds their studies, and they generally need to pay for their studies out of an often-meagre income. Because of time and cost pressures, TEE students will simply opt out of material that they deem boring, irrelevant, or too difficult. Even before the work of Knowles became widely known, the TEE movement intuitively has taken principles of andragogy seriously.

It is therefore not surprising that many of the features presented in Table 5.1 are readily seen in the typical TEE course. The adult learners' prior experiences are brought constantly into dialogue with the theoretical material of the text and shared together in the group meeting. Emphasis is placed in tutor training on the importance of an open and relaxed space for group meetings. The fact that the text merely provides the information, while the tutor plays the role of learning facilitator, creates a natural mutuality among the participants in the class. By the standards of andragogical theory, TEE performs very well indeed.

However, there can be a danger in andragogical approaches where people with less experience may lead equally less-experienced people, and where extensive sharing of experience thus takes place without adequate authoritative expertise. This can be a particular challenge in TEE where the tutor may lack the necessary expertise to guide the class to genuine reflective thinking. As a means of redressing this challenge, the TEE movement has been placing greater demands on course writers to ensure that the quality of the texts is at an appropriate level. In addition, many TEE programmes are seeking to develop quality feedback loops of expert input and provide a library of supportive resources, many of which can be accessed by tutors and students digitally.

38. Knowles, Holton, and Swanson, *Adult Learner*, 58–72.

Transformative Learning Theory and TEE

While the language used by the dominant voices in transformative learning theory[39] varies, the description of the processes involved is fairly consistent. The key is to see life crises and experiences of personal disequilibrium as potential opportunities for qualitative growth. Brookfield has suggested five stages of transformative learning.[40]

1. Trigger event that causes perplexity or discomfort
2. Appraisal phase – clarification of the issue and self-examination of what is going on
3. Exploration of explanations or of new ways of responding
4. Developing alternative perspectives, through which new ways are tried and tested
5. Integration of the new with other aspects of our lives

While stress is normal among all learners, TEE learners are particularly prone to life challenges, and consequently are in a strong position to find their studies a transformative learning experience. The normal TEE student is older, lives with multiple personal demands of work, family, and church, and on top of these is seeking to engage in studies. Add to this that TEE is particularly prevalent in contexts where political unrest, persecution, poverty, and disease are common. I stand in admiration at what so many TEE students accomplish. Where life crises are spoken of openly in TEE classes it is common for these crises to become "trigger events" for transformative learning.

While the manifold life experiences of TEE learners hold great potential for transformative learning, the local learning nature of TEE can work against transformative learning. In most residential theological institutions, both students and faculty come from a wide diversity of cultural and ecclesial backgrounds. This diversity naturally creates the sort of discomfort and tension that can catalyze transformative learning. It is common for graduates of residential schools to acknowledge that their most significant learning came through interaction with people who thought differently to themselves. In

39. Brookfield, *Developing Critical Thinkers*; Cranton, *Understanding and Promoting*; Loder, *Transforming Moment*, and *Logic of the Spirit*; Mezirow, *Transformative Dimensions*; Piaget, *Structuralism, Equilibration of Cognitive Structure.*

40. Brookfield, *Developing Critical Thinkers*, 26–28.

contrast, TEE study groups run the risk of becoming something of an "echo chamber" in which we only hear the "accepted" answers of the local community, and diverse perspectives are discouraged or dismissed. It is important for TEE course designers to ensure that TEE texts contain diverse perspectives, and that tutor guides give direction for quality openness of discussion.

Some of the key factors that have been found to be supportive for transformative learning are the learning environment, the variety of learning experiences, and reflection.

- An environment characterized by trust, empathy, care, authenticity, sincerity, and a high degree of integrity,[41] which incorporates activities that promote student autonomy, participation, and collaboration.[42] In most TEE programmes, tutors are urged to take a pastoral role within the learning group, and well-designed tutor guides generally provide a variety of options for active learning for the group meetings.
- An appreciation of the diversity of learners in the class, and the provision of a wide variety of learning experiences, so as to best meet the diverse needs of learners as they wrestle with theoretical and practical issues. Cranton observes that while some learners do well with confrontative approaches such as debate and critical analysis, others learn better through more harmonious approaches. Others find field trip experience helpful to their growth.[43] The variety of options provided in TEE tutor guides can facilitate a range of methodological approaches; the challenge is to ensure that tutors get beyond the text and open the learning space sufficiently to allow transformative learning to take place.
- Journaling and the sharing of critical incidents in a non-judgemental environment.[44] Quality guided questioning in self-reflective journals provides space for students to engage in reflective discourse. Often the process of writing and sharing their thoughts helps in a

41. Taylor, "Analyzing Research," 313.
42. Taylor, *Theory and Practice*, 48.
43. Cranton, "Teaching for Transformation."
44. Cranton.

process of perspective taking and lateral thinking. While a level of self-reflective journaling is often embedded in the personal study component of TEE courses, I do wonder if this approach could be strengthened in the world of TEE on the pathway to exploiting the unique opportunities their adult learners have for experiencing transformative learning.

Recommendations for Educational Leaders in TEE

While the philosophical framework for TEE has multiple educational qualities, we continue to live "between the already and the not yet," and in practice there is always room for improvement. Based on the discussion in this chapter I would like to conclude with some recommendations for course writers and for tutor training.

To those engaged in writing TEE courses:

- Based on previous experiences with the dominant "schooling" approach to education, there can be a tendency for you to focus on the cognitive domain of learning. There is great benefit in finding pathways to incorporate affective and behavioural elements in the questions you ask[45] and the tasks you give the students. Exercises such as case studies and personal reflective journals should not be peripheral to course design but comprise an essential component of the weekly learning.
- While recognizing the value of ensuring that knowledge and understanding have taken place, students need to be challenged to higher levels of cognition through analytic, synthetic, and evaluative questions that are not easily answered by the students or often by the tutor. The deep wrestling with these questions can facilitate cognitive growth and on occasions a level of transformative learning.
- Constantly ensure that the texts are relating to the context. While this is generally standard in TEE courses, often it can be somewhat of

45. See Shaw, *Transforming Theological Education*, 201–15.

an "add-on" rather than a core element of course design. Remember: a sense of significance is the most powerful factor in deep learning.

- In order to encourage the sort of discomfort and perplexity that are necessary foundations for promoting transformative learning, it is crucial that TEE texts provide a diversity of perspectives that are equally valued in the Christian community. Students should be challenged to wrestle with this diversity of perspective through quality analytic and synthetic questions, and tutor guides should give direction for quality openness of discussion.
- As you raise the level of questioning it is important for tutors and students to have additional resources they can turn to. Providing bibliographies of accessible texts, or even better virtual resources, can be an important supportive element to encouraging higher level thinking.
- Use case studies extensively. In situations where textual resources in your language are limited, case studies can be a highly effective means of promoting critical thinking. Well-designed case studies also provide connection between text and context, and through that the sense of significance that can support deep learning.

To those who lead tutor training:

- Tutors should see the strategic educational value of their pastoral role. When tutors can find the time to meet individually with students outside the group meetings there is great potential for providing the sort of positive emotional connection that is essential to promoting deep learning.
- Many tutors have been profoundly shaped by the "schooling" understanding of education, and the importance of emotional connection in the group meetings needs to be emphasized as critical for long-term student learning.
- It is important that tutors learn how to facilitate a mutuality of discussion with a particular emphasis on situations where the students are experiencing discomfort with the level and kind of material being discussed. Tutors should be urged not to play a dominant role in discussion but be comfortable with silence or

perplexity. Remember that discomfort and perplexity are the necessary starting points for transformative learning.

- Tutors need to be encouraged to see the sharing of life experiences as essential to adult learners. When brought into dialogue with the quality theoretical material given in the texts, this process of dialogue between text and life holds potential for deep learning and the development of expert reflective practitioners.

Conclusion

I have often heard those in traditional theological colleges critique TEE as a substandard form of education. The conversation presented in this chapter has provided a different picture demonstrating the educational efficacy of TEE. The three-pronged approach of TEE (personal study, group meeting, and practical application) is highly conducive to holistic learning in all of the cognitive, affective, and behavioural domains. The relaxed environment of group meetings provides emotional connection; this positive affect, together with the context-sensitivity of most TEE courses, has great potential for promoting deep learning. TEE places a high emphasis on practical application and reflection-in-action, key components of experiential learning. The elements of andragogical theory are readily seen in the learner-orientation, practical focus, respect for life experience, contextual relevance, and mutual learning processes that are core emphases within TEE.

There is no perfect way to develop quality leaders for the church of Jesus Christ. Each approach can contribute to God's work in the service of his kingdom mandate. Within the variety of delivery approaches that exist today, TEE is designed in such a way that holistic, deep, reflective, transformative learning can readily be supported. As the TEE movement moves forward, those involved would do well to embrace TEE's potential by taking seriously the application of the learning theories given in this chapter through course design, tutor training, and supportive structures.

Bibliography

Ambrose, S., M. Bridges, M. DiPietro, M. Lovett, and M. Norman. *How Learning Works: Seven Research-Based Principles for Smart Teaching*. San Francisco: Jossey-Bass, 2010.

Anderson, L., and D. Krathwohl, eds. *A Taxonomy for Learning, Teaching and Assessing: A Revision of Bloom's Taxonomy of Educational Objectives*. New York: Longman, 2001.

Ausubel, D. *Educational Psychology: A Cognitive View*. New York: Holt, Rinehart & Winston, 1968.

Barkley, E. *Student Engagement Techniques: A Handbook for College Faculty*. San Francisco: Jossey-Bass, 2010.

Barna Group. "Born Again Christians Just as Likely to Divorce as Are Non-Christians." Accessed 15 February 2021. https://www.barna.com/research/born-again-christians-just-as-likely-to-divorce-as-are-non-christians/.

Baxter Magolda, M. B. *Knowing and Reasoning in College: Gender-Related Patterns in Students' Intellectual Development*. San Francisco: Jossey-Bass, 1992.

Bloom, B., M. Engelhart, E. Furst, W. Hill, and D. Krathwohl. *Taxonomy of Educational Objectives. Handbook I: Cognitive Domain*. London: Longmans, 1956.

Bransford, J., A. Brown, and R. Cocking. *How People Learn: Brain, Mind, Experience, and School*. Washington, DC: National Academy Press, 1999.

Brookfield, S. *Developing Critical Thinkers: Challenging Adults to Explore Alternate Ways of Thinking and Acting*. San Francisco: Jossey-Bass, 1987.

———. *Understanding and Facilitating Adult Learning: A Comprehensive Analysis of Principles and Effective Practices*. Milton Keynes: Open University, 1986.

Cranton, P. "Teaching for Transformation." In *Contemporary Viewpoints on Teaching Adults Effectively*, edited by J. Ross-Gordon, 63–71. San Francisco: Jossey-Bass, 2002.

———. *Understanding and Promoting Transformative Learning: A Guide for Educators of Adults*. 2nd ed. San Francisco: Jossey-Bass, 2006.

Davis, D. "A Brain-Friendly Environment for Learning." *The Teaching Professor* 21, no. 4 (2007): 6.

Fink, L. *Creating Significant Learning Experiences: An Integrated Approach to Designing College Courses*. San Francisco: Jossey-Bass, 2003.

Gorman, J. "'There's Got to Be More!': Transformational Learning." *Christian Education Journal* 5, NS (2001): 23–51.

Hofstede, G., and G. Hofstede. *Cultures and Organizations: Software of the Mind*. 3rd ed. New York: McGraw-Hill, 2010.

Knowles, M. "Contributions of Malcolm Knowles." In *The Christian Educator's Handbook on Adult Education*, edited by K. Gangel and J. Wilhoit, 95–105. Grand Rapids: Baker, 1993.

———. *The Modern Practice of Adult Education*. New York: Cambridge, 1980.

Knowles, M., E. Holton, and R. Swanson. *The Adult Learner: The Definitive Classic in Adult Education and Human Resource Development*. 6th ed. Amsterdam: Elsevier, 2005.

Kolb, D. *Experiential Learning: Experience as the Source of Learning and Development*. Upper Saddle River: Prentice Hall, 1983.

Loder, J. *The Logic of the Spirit: Human Development in Theological Perspective*. San Francisco: Jossey-Bass, 1998.

———. *The Transforming Moment: Understanding Convictional Experiences*. San Francisco: Harper & Row, 1982.

Marzano, R., and J. Kendall, eds. *The New Taxonomy of Educational Objectives*. 2nd ed. Thousand Oaks: Corwin, 2006.

Merriam, S., R. Caffarella, and L. Baumgartner. *Learning in Adulthood: A Comprehensive Guide*. San Francisco: Jossey-Bass, 2007.

Mezirow, J. *Transformative Dimensions of Adult Learning*. San Francisco: Jossey-Bass, 1991.

Nilson, L. *Teaching at Its Best: A Research-Based Resource for College Instructors*. 4th ed. San Francisco: Jossey-Bass, 2016.

Perry, W. *Forms of Intellectual and Ethical Development in the College Years: A Scheme*. New York: Holt, 1985.

Persellin, D., and M. Daniels. *A Concise Guide to Improving Student Learning: Six Evidence-Based Principles and How to Apply Them*. Sterling: Stylus, 2014.

Piaget, J. *Structuralism*. New York: Harper & Row, 1970.

———. *The Equilibration of Cognitive Structures: The Central Problem of Intellectual Development*. Chicago: University of Chicago, 1985.

Roth, R. "Preparing the Reflective Practitioner: Transforming the Apprentice through the Dialectic." *Journal of Teacher Education* 40, no. 2 (1989): 31–35.

Schön, D. *The Reflective Practitioner: How Professionals Think in Action*. Aldershot: Ashgate, 1991.

Schultz, T., and J. Schultz. *The Dirt on Learning*. Loveland: Group, 1999.

Seaman, J. "Experience, Reflect, Critique: The End of the 'Learning Cycles' Era." *Journal of Experiential Education* 31 (2008): 3–18.

Shaw, P. "A Welcome Guest: Ministerial Training as an Act of Hospitality." *Christian Education Journal* 3, no. 7 (2011): 8–26.

———. "Creating a Respectful Community: Lessons from the Middle East." *The Teaching Professor*, 1 May 2018. https://www.teachingprofessor.com/topics/teaching-strategies/participation-discussion/respectful-community-lessons-from-middle-east/.

———. "Innovation and Criteria: Ensuring Standards While Promoting Innovative Approaches." In *Challenging Tradition: Innovation in Advanced Theological Education*, edited by Perry Shaw and Havilah Dharamraj, 43–60. Carlisle: Langham, 2018.

———. *Transforming Theological Education: A Practical Handbook for Integrative Learning*. Carlisle: Langham, 2014.

Shulman, L. "Making Differences: A Table of Learning." http://archive.carnegiefoundation.org/publications/elibrary/making-differences.html.

Soh, D. *The Motif of Hospitality in Theological Education: A Critical Appraisal with Implications for Application in Theological Education*. Carlisle: Langham, 2016.

Sousa, D. *How the Brain Learns*. 3rd ed. Thousand Oaks: Corwin, 2006.

Stronge, J. *Qualities of Effective Teachers*. 2nd ed. Alexandria: ASCD, 2007.

Taylor, E. "Analyzing Research on Transformative Learning Theory." In *Learning as Transformation: Critical Perspectives on a Theory in Progress*, edited by J. Mezirow, 285–328. San Francisco: Jossey-Bass, 2000.

———. *The Theory and Practice of Transformative Learning: A Critical Review*. Columbus, OH: Center on Education and Training for Employment, 1998.

Willingham, D. *Why Don't Students Like School? A Cognitive Scientist Answers Questions about How the Mind Works and What It Means for Your Classroom*. San Francisco: Jossey-Bass, 2009.

Winne, P., and J. Nesbit. "The Psychology of Academic Achievement." *Annual Review of Psychology* 61 (2010): 653–78.

Zailaa, W. "The Power of Stories." IMES blog. https://abtslebanon.org/2020/06/04/the-power-of-stories.

6

The Educational Efficacy of TEE – Part 2

Nurturing Quality Learning

Volker Glissmann and Tim Green

Introduction

Building on the previous chapter, this chapter takes a closer look at TEE methodology and course design in relation to educational theory. The educational question, "Who is being equipped for what and how?" leads on to four areas of current educational theory: reflection, memory, active learning, and the flipped classroom. Theories underpinning these four aspects of learning are brought into dialogue with the three components of TEE methodology (personal study, group discussion, and practical activities) to ask whether TEE stands up to contemporary educational scrutiny.

Three Key Educational Questions

Good educational design never begins with the question of content. It is tempting for subject experts to start by asking, "What will the students learn?" or even "What do I want to teach my students?" Better educational design asks, "*Who* will be equipped *for what* and *how*?" This question with its three constituent parts acts as a compass to set the direction and as a filter of relevance to decide the content. Without this clarity educators will teach much irrelevant content. We do well to address the question of content last, not first.

As we saw in chapter 5 and the work of Knowles, adults want to learn what is relevant to their daily lives and prior experience. This is true for all theological students but especially for those who study part-time alongside their busy lives, as with almost all TEE learners. If their studies are irrelevant to daily life and ministry, or boring, or not at their academic level, they will simply walk away. This pruning process has proved sobering but helpful in TEE history, with unpopular courses dropping out of use while the most interesting and relevant ones have spread.

WHO are our learners?

Today's theology students are extremely diverse. TEE learners are wealthy and poor, urban and rural, they come from all walks of life, and with a higher proportion of women than in traditional theological education. Some TEE students are barely literate, others have doctorates in different fields. Some grew up as Christians, while others were the first in their family to convert from another religion. Some need foundations in the faith, others are already leaders in church and society, or want to be equipped as such.

To create courses for such a huge range of learners, we cannot say "one size fits all" but instead we must analyze their situation. The following simple chart, Figure 6.1, was developed by TEE educators[1] to help in this.

By default, theological education has often connected a higher ministry responsibility with a higher educational level. Yet some highly educated people are beginners in the Christian faith, while many experienced pastors have little formal education. We may show these in Figure 6.2 at points A and B respectively, by way of example, though more types of learners could be included in different parts of the chart.

1. First presented by Tim Green at a 2006 consultation in Afghanistan, it was used later in the Increase Association and in accreditation discussions with the Asia Theological Association. The horizontal axis can be labelled either as "Ministry Involvement" or as "Christian Maturity," which are not always the same.

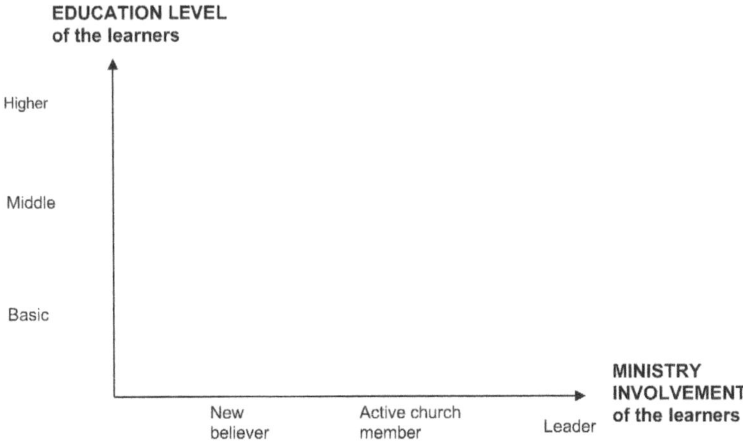

Figure 6.1 Who are our learners?

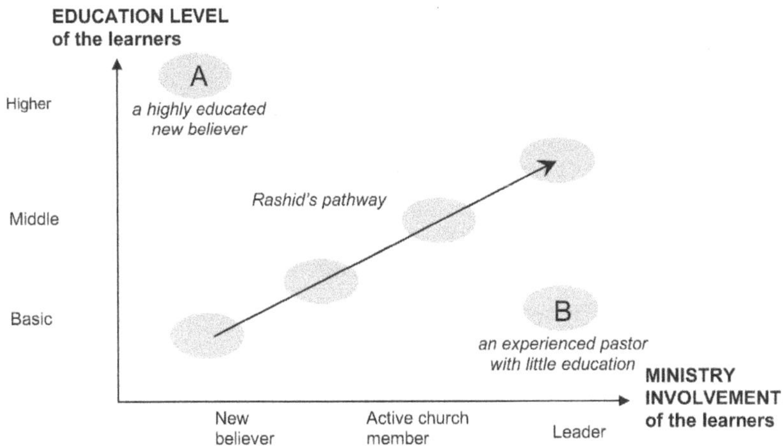

Figure 6.2 Theological Education for All

Plotting learners on the chart helps us to plan learning pathways that start with the learner's immediate needs and progress them step-by-step towards maturity and ministry. Horizontal progression along the ministry axis and vertical progress on the educational axis are not inherently linked, though in practice this often happens. For example, Rashid, a pastor in Pakistan, came from a poor family and never went to school. But coming to faith as an adult he learned to read, and then through TEE proceeded through a twenty-year pathway of part-time study which equipped him in his growing pastoral ministry responsibilities and educationally at the same time (see Figure 6.2).[2]

In addition to students' individual requirements, we must address the bigger ministry needs of rapidly growing churches in the non-Western world. Over 90 percent of all pastors have little or no formal theological education and they lead at least four million churches worldwide.[3] Most are bi-vocational pastors. Educationally they are positioned at different places on the chart. How may formal and nonformal[4] ministry education programmes work together to equip such leaders? This is an urgent task today in theological education. Equally urgent is the task of equipping God's church for missional impact in his world, for which relevant equipping is needed for learners in all sectors of the chart, whether leaders or not.[5]

FOR WHAT are our learners being equipped?

Having identified the learners, we ask "for what are they being equipped?" This includes both the end goals of a programme (i.e. the overall curricular objectives) and also the graduate profile. Whenever the objectives and profile are decided internally by an institution or by its accrediting body, it risks losing the voice of the ultimate stakeholders whom the graduates will serve. This

2. See Green, "Integrated Learning Pathways," 244. Rashid was a student of the Open Theological Seminary in Pakistan.

3. See estimates by Manfred Kohl, https://www.re-forma.global/, repeated in an online forum on 24 August 2020.

4. TEE programmes are somewhat "nonformal" and somewhat "formal" (with a curriculum, attendance requirements, frequent testing), so they bridge these categories and thereby challenge usefulness of the categories. Some TEE programmes are externally validated, others are not.

5. Theological institutions tend to focus attention and resources in the chart's top right-hand corner (see figure 6.2). This sector is greatly needed but other sectors may be treated as less important recipients of "Christian education." The TEE movement calls for church-based equipping of God's people as active ministers and is concerned for all sections of the chart.

calls for stakeholders to be at the heart of evaluating whether a programme is appropriate (fitness *of* purpose) and effective (fitness *for* purpose).

Some TEE organizations have separate programmes at different curricular levels.[6] Others, like the Open Theological Seminary in Pakistan, guide learners like Rashid along a stepwise curricular pathway whereby completion of one stage equips them to proceed to the next stage. Around 6,000 OTS students take steps along this path every year. Its educational goals progressively stretch students towards higher cognitive abilities and ministry skills as they proceed through the ATA accredited curriculum, while character development is also assessed at each level.[7]

A programme's end goals and graduate profile guide its educational objectives in the cognitive, affective, and behavioural domains. What should a person completing this programme *know* (cognitive), *be* (affective) and be able to *do* (behavioural)?[8] In the early days, TEE course design was somewhat influenced by performance-oriented behaviourists like Skinner and Mager, who argued that each objective must specify what a learner should *do* under what conditions and to what standard.[9] This approach had a value for mastery learning of key points, but has been critiqued as too prescriptive (in the

6. The Association for Theological Education by Extension (TAFTEE) in India has separate programmes at certificate, bachelor's, and master's levels.

7. The goals of OTS at each level are:

Discipleship level: Students would build a solid foundation for personal Christian living.

Certificate level: Students would be equipped to understand, articulate, share and live out their faith.

Diploma level: Students would grow in their knowledge and understanding of God's word, and in their competence to use their gifts in various local ministries.

Bachelor's level: Students would be equipped:

a) to exercise spiritual, moral, cultural, and intellectual discernment
b) to facilitate the spiritual growth and ministry of others
c) to apply principles of hermeneutics in their study of God's word
d) to use the higher thinking skills of analysis, synthesis, formulation, and evaluation
e) to pursue further studies in specific areas of Christian service

OTS, *Academic Manual*, 25–27. OTS now also offers a master's level programme, not yet accredited by the ATA.

8. These three learning domains are well established in educational circles. While "cognitive, affective, and behavioural" is their common order of representation, they can also be stated as the ABCs of learning (affective, behavioural, and cognitive).

9. "Whatever else a statement may do, if it doesn't state a performance, it isn't an objective," Mager, *Preparing Instructional Objectives*, 24.

performances it stipulates) and too constrictive (in terms of holistic learning).[10] However by combining personal study with group reflection and practical activities, the TEE method modified a narrow behaviourist approach.

Nevertheless, the traditional three domains (cognitive, affective, and behavioural) only treat individuals in isolation, not their place in community or in their contribution to society. By contrast the United Nations, the International Baccalaureate,[11] and national governments all include citizenship as an important aspect of education – thereby adding a relational domain to learning alongside the traditional trio. For both educational and theological reasons, the Increase Association adds this relational dimension as it trains new TEE course writers – "relating" is a fourth domain alongside knowing, doing, and being.[12]

Some have argued for wisdom as an additional learning domain since it is different from knowledge.[13] Wisdom is valued as a mark of maturity in many cultures, and an uneducated village elder may make wiser decisions than a young man with a doctorate. Setting specific educational objectives in this domain is difficult, but the exercise of discernment is a pointer, as in the OTS objectives at bachelor level.[14]

HOW do our learners learn best?

Having asked "Who are our learners?" and "For what are they being equipped?" we then ask, "How will they learn best?" Without repeating the material in chapter 5, further insights are here introduced from four aspects of current educational theory relevant to TEE: memory, reflection, active learning, and the flipped classroom.

---

10. Brookfield, *Understanding and Facilitating*, 141.

11. Thus, "the International Baccalaureate (IB) aims to develop inquiring, knowledgeable and caring young people who help to create a better and more peaceful world," https://www.ibo.org/about-the-ib/mission/.

12. See further in chapter 7: Ivins and Do, "New TEE Courses."

13. For example, Burgess, *Curriculum for Theological Education*, 21.

14. Space excludes a closer look at "wisdom" as an important meta-goal of theological education and human maturity; it would require an intercultural discussion on how wisdom is defined, how it grows in a person over time, and the role of educators in helping this. Cultures which value "wisdom" tend to train their members in "taking responsibility" as a way to develop moral values.

Memory – the science of remembering (and forgetting)[15]

Our experiences and understandings are stored in our memory. Even our understanding of God, which is formed in a variety of ways (not just cognitively but through emotions, community, the Holy Spirit, etc.) is ultimately stored as information in our memory. The better that theological educators understand the workings of memory, the better teaching and learning will be.

So, what is memory? "Memory is the ongoing process of information retention over time." Ultimately, "both storing and losing memories are important for selecting and holding the most relevant information."[16] Actually, we forget much of what we hear, read, see, study, think, and encounter in our lives. Learning as well as forgetting are influenced by complicated and multi-faceted factors which hugely vary between individuals and circumstances.[17]

There are two types of memory storage: short-term memory and long-term memory. The short-term memory is part of the working memory which holds the information that one is consciously thinking about at any given moment. One goal of learning is to move information from the short-term/working memory into the long-term memory where it can be retrieved later. Initially the short-term memory stores every piece of information, but only for 15 to 30 seconds.[18] Therefore, the information in the short-term memory is filtered and moved swiftly to the long-term memory for storage or else is discarded.

We might think of memory as a computer hard drive, which is also called memory. The hard drive allows the upload of vast quantities of detailed data. By contrast the brain stores information in the long-term memory in an ever changing yet connected network of synapses between brain cells. The stronger the synapses, the better one remembers. The more tasks are practiced and repeated (through experience, education, or training), the stronger the connection between brain cells grows and the better the remembering. The

15. Forgetting here does not refer to dementia or any other neurodegenerative diseases but rather the brain function that occurs in healthy individuals.

16. Wlassoff, "Why Is Forgetting Good."

17. There are no reliable generalizing statistics to predict in percentage terms how much is learned by an individual or how much is forgotten, see Thalheimer, *How Much Do People Forget*, 5.

18. "How Memory Works," Derek Bok Center for Teaching and Learning, accessed 20 February 2021, https://bokcenter.harvard.edu/how-memory-works.

brain's focus is to function effectively and so it prioritizes the instant recall of significant information (or memories with high emotional impact). The purpose of the brain is "not preserving information, but rather helping the brain make sound decisions."[19] This is why the brain filters information in the long-term memory and simplifies it by forgetting less significant details.[20]

Three processes are vital for long-term memory storage: *attention* (when information is received), *encoding and storage* (in the long-term memory), and *retrieval* (to the working memory). Initial *attention* is greatly improved when learners find it meaningful (not just cognitively but also emotionally). *Encoding and storage* improve if it is linked to existing information. The *retrieval* of information through recalling and using stored information strengthens the remembrance of information. Educational testing affords opportunity to use information, albeit an artificial one. Experiential testing in real life and ministry activities has the same (or enhanced) effect.

An important part of learning and remembering is understanding the function of forgetting. The brain not only possesses a remarkable storage ability but also an effective method to erase unnecessary information.[21] Memory deteriorates over time, starting nearly immediately after the learning experience. Yet, educators can take small and important steps to help improve the memory retention and recall through the strengthening of synapses between brain cells. This can be done by:

- (explicitly) relating new material to existing material already in the long-term memory
- actively recalling information through application (or testing) within the context of existing knowledge and skills. Regularly spaced testing (both formal and informal) helps the retention of information. Guided recall also helps the learners to evaluate which of the information in the long-term memory is significant as it will be used more frequently

19. Also Richards and Frankland, "Persistence and Transience," 1080, who propose that "the goal of memory is to guide intelligent decision making."

20. Richards and Frankland, 1078, who point out that simplification "is an essential component of adaptive memory."

21. Davis and Zhong, "Biology of Forgetting."

- actively recalling or revisiting information through strategic repetition (spaced repetition over time, also called spacing)
- reflection on information and its relevance to life and the practice of ministry.

It will be shown below how TEE methodology uses these techniques to reinforce long-term memory.

Different types of reflection

While memory is an essential building block in learning, it cannot be the whole of learning, for that would be a mere "banking" model by which instructors pour information into the minds of passive students. Reflection plays a key role, as educationalists from Paulo Freire onwards have advocated.[22] Theological educators have benefitted from this wider academic discussion and have in turn made their own contribution to it. We consider here the work of Alison Le Cornu, and of Muriel and Duane Elmer, all of whom work at the interface of secular and theological education.

Le Cornu agrees with secular theorists on the importance of *critical reflection*, with the freedom for learners to critique and speculate. But this should be balanced by *receptive reflection* and *appreciative reflection* in holistic combination. She explores how different Christian traditions[23] and different personality types affect the way individuals gravitate to these different types of reflection.[24]

For Le Cornu, receptive reflection involves learners' willing reception and pursuit of knowledge through understanding and personal acquaintance. It can be mere banking education but does not have to be. She agrees with Astley that a foundation of formative learning is "a proper – indeed essential – dimension of any education that wishes to call itself Christian."[25] As an example of appreciative

22. See chapter 5: Shaw, "The Educational Efficacy of TEE – Part 1," and the work of Stephen Brookfield, Jack Mezirow, and others.

23. Christian traditions which place an individual's judgement above external authorities will embrace critical reflection with almost no boundaries to speculation. But where authority is derived from the Scriptures or church tradition, a genuine tension arises.

24. Le Cornu, "People's Ways," and "Meaning."

25. Astley, *Learning in the Way*, 38, cited in Le Cornu, "Meaning," 287. Robert Ferris agrees that receptive reflection is genuinely reflection (not merely receptive of information) when it "explores the location of this truth with respect to other truths, and the implications of this

reflection Le Cornu describes monks and nuns whose transformational development takes place through "the gaze of admiration" as they recite the liturgy repeatedly.[26] She writes: "Whereas critical reflection rejects or modifies earlier knowledge and information, appreciative reflection digs ever deeper within the original, discovering new insights and illumination."[27]

Elmer and Elmer propose a learning cycle to integrate cognitive, affective, and behavioural domains of learning with neuroscience and educational psychology, all within a Christian framework.[28] They believe that theological educators can learn from the insights of secular transformative learning theory, provided that the learning cycle is not limited to a closed loop of reflecting and processing the learners' own experiences, but is also fed by truth from outside. Their learning cycle shown in Figure 6.3 builds on Kolb's well-known cycle while improving on it.[29]

Elmer and Elmer label each step as "recall," since each act of recalling information to working memory strengthens neural synapses. The brain functions better when key points are repeated (step 1) and reinforced through emotional engagement with what is significant (step 2), then by relating this to life (step 3). At this point learners may recognize changes needed in their lives but hesitate to push through the volitional barriers – the "barriers to change" on the diagram. Steps 4 and 5 rightly emphasize the importance of practice and forming habits, since growth into maturity is not just cognitive, but must be integrated with changed worldviews, godly habits, wise discernment, and Christian character. These are also the goals of TEE education.

---

truth for life and relationships. In this process the individual brings their own contribution to the learning, making it liberating and not domesticating" (notes from personal discussion in Oxford, UK, Feb 2012).

26. Leclerq, *Love of Learning and the Desire for God*, 226, cited in Le Cornu, "Meaning," 288.

27. Le Cornu, 289.

28. Elmer and Elmer, *The Learning Cycle*.

29. Kolb's cycle is useful but has also been critiqued from different perspectives.

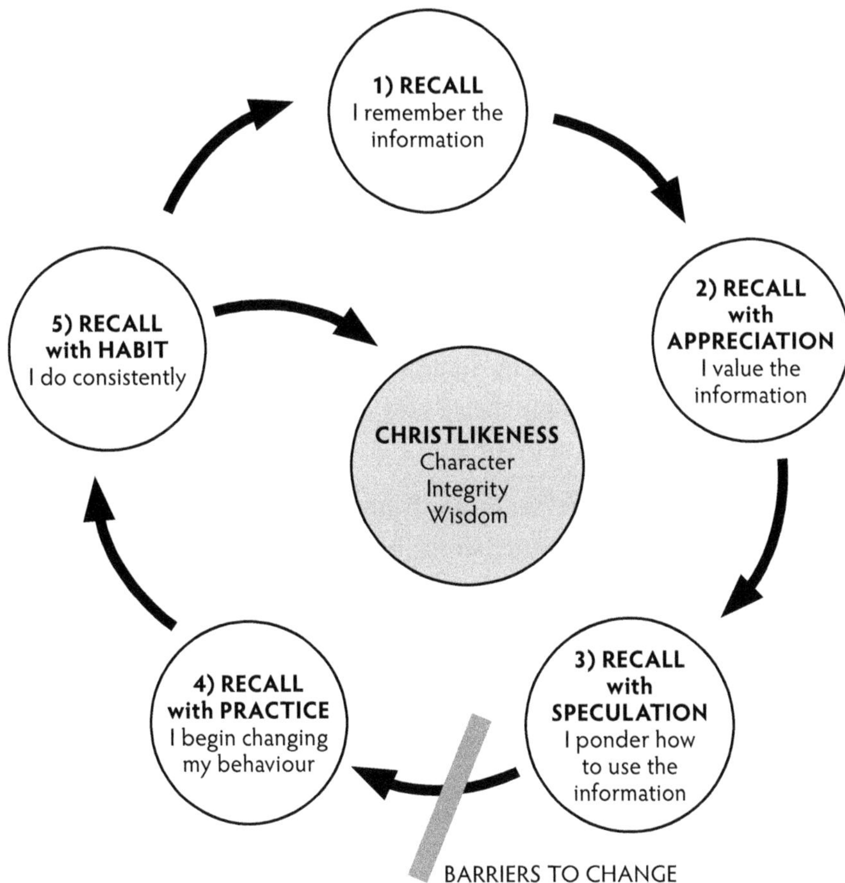

Figure 6.3 Elmer and Elmer's learning cycle[30]

Active learning

Carl Wieman is a Nobel Prize-winning professor of physics and a science educator at Stanford University who, since the 1990s, investigated different teaching methods in order to improve university science education. His research showed that those studying the lesson content on their own performed better because they were able to comprehend the content at their own learning

30. Source: Elmer and Elmer, *The Learning Cycle*, 15.

speed.[31] This allowed them to cognitively process the content better as they were able to stop and think and work out the connection between the different information (while avoiding the rapid information flow from a traditional lecture).[32]

A meta-analysis of 225 studies that compared active learning approaches to traditional lectures in science undergraduate courses,[33] found

> substantially *enhanced learning* and significant *less failure* in courses that encourage "asking rather than telling" and "doing rather than sitting." The most successful practices were those that asked students to apply their knowledge rather than merely to absorb it.[34] (emphasis original)

The studies compared learning through the traditional lecture style and active learning, or in other words between "a transmission-intensive, teacher-centric approach and a constructivist, student-centric approach."[35] Traditional or standard lectures include about 90 percent "instructor talk," while the audience passively listens without actively engaging and processing the content deeply.[36]

Active learning (sometimes called "evidence-based methods of teaching") refers here to approaches that utilize diverse active teaching methods like

31. Cognitive load refers to the brain's processing power of new information. The brain is only able to process a limited amount of information within a certain period. The main obstacle is the limited capacity of the short-term memory through which the information needs to pass in order to be considered for long-term memory. Working memory is generally overwhelmed in a lecture because of the rapid flow of information. Therefore, learning content needs to be tailored to reduce the cognitive load in order for learning to take place, see Wieman, "Why Not Try," 13. For further research see also, Wieman, "Large-Scale Comparison," and Theobald et al., "Active Learning."

32. "You give people lectures, and (some students) go away and learn the stuff. But it wasn't that they learned it from lecture[s] – they learned it from homework, from assignments. When we measure how little people learn from an actual lecture, it's just *really small*." Wieman cited in Westervelt, "Nobel Laureate's Education Plea." See also Hoellwarth and Moelter, "Implications of a Robust Curriculum," and Deslauriers, Schelew, and Wieman, "Improved Learning."

33. Freeman et al., "Active Learning."

34. Mintzes and Walter, "Preface," ix.

35. Freeman et al., "Reply to Hora."

36. Yet instructor talk that focuses on detailed and relevant feedback on learning is highly beneficial for learners.

flipped classrooms, klickers,[37] in-class discussions, etc.[38] The key idea is to improve student engagement which is vital for learning and especially for developing "higher-order thinking skills that lead to better understanding and improved ability to transfer knowledge to other applications."[39]

Based on the above findings, Wieman adjusted the delivery by assigning pre-class readings that covered the class content. The idea was to move

> the simple transfer of factual knowledge outside of class as much as possible and creating tasks and feedback that motivate students to become fully engaged. As the students work through these tasks, they receive feedback from fellow students and from the instructor.[40]

An important part of the contact (class) time is answering questions, working together on applying the content, and guiding the students to a deeper engagement with the content.[41] What is important is that, although contact time is filled with diverse instructional practices, yet "the educational benefit does not come primarily from any particular practice but rather from the integration into the overall deliberate practice framework."[42]

Flipped classroom

Flipped classroom or flipped learning, sometimes referred to as inverted classroom, is not a new concept, but it is gaining popularity among educators.[43]

---

37. Klickers are individual response units (like a remote control) which allow students to respond quickly and anonymously to active learning tasks in class.

38. Active Learning is defined as "a model of instruction that encourages meaningful learning and knowledge construction through collaborative activities that support thinking and doing: 'hands-on, minds-on teaching.'" See Mintzes and Walter, *Active Learning*, xiii.

39. Coleman, Smith, and Miller, "Catalysts," 36.

40. Deslauriers, Schelew, and Wieman, "Improved Learning," 862.

41. In a way the class room becomes the tutorial, which is why TEE could also be described as "tutorial-based theological education." See Glissmann, "Fragmentation of Theological Education."

42. Deslauriers, Schelew, and Wieman, "Improved Learning," 862.

43. The difference between flipped classroom and active learning is that active learning is not always defined with the pre-class engagement but instead focuses on active learner engagement. For a good discussion of the history of the terminology, see Bäcklund and Hugo, "Paradox of Flipped Classroom," 451–2; Abeysekera and Dawson, "Motivation and Cognitive Load"; and Johnson and Renner, "Effect of the Flipped Classroom," 3–7. Two studies that did not find significant improvements in the flipped classroom approach should be highlighted: Jensen,

Basically, the flipped or inverted classroom highlights two changes to a traditional classroom setting. First, the main learning content is given as self-study or homework prior to the class, instead of class followed by homework (this is also a deliberate shift from teacher-centred to learner-centred education). Second, the class time is mostly used for active learning activities, especially problem solving, application of learning activities to new areas, and collaborative learning.

The flipped classroom gives teachers more opportunities to engage with individual learners, including one-on-one engagements, to support their learning. The learning content is delivered through pre-recorded video lectures or through assigned readings.[44] The popularity of this approach rests on the significantly improved class time available for guiding learners to comprehend the learning content. Even the sequencing of content delivery allows learners to ask clarifying questions during class time after they have already actively engaged the pre-assigned learning content. One of the key advantages of the flipped classroom approach from a teacher perspective is the constant quality feedback on the learners' comprehension and engagement of learning content compared to the more passive lecture style.[45] However, the approach does require learners to be highly motivated and capable of self-direction, with good tools for self-study, and teachers able to adapt to becoming facilitators of learning.

The flipped classroom uses many active learning techniques (but also often some elements of teacher talk) during its contact time, in order to promote deep learning.[46] Some have defined the flipped classroom as based on technology, especially instructional videos for content delivery as popularized by Jonathan

Kummer, and Godoy, "Improvements from a Flipped Classroom," and Johnson and Renner, "Effect of the Flipped Classroom."

44. DeLozier and Rhodes, "Flipped Classrooms."

45. This is even more important in adult theological education where learners often bring a more fully-formed theological worldview to class based on previous reflection. Adult learners may have strong feelings about learning content that they disagree with.

46. Learning is always dynamic and dependent on a variety of contextual learning activities and the same is true for flipped classroom approaches which also use a variety of learning activity including active learning. Research is still ongoing to determine how the individual active-learning elements contribute to the whole: see DeLozier and Rhodes, "Flipped Classrooms."

Bergmann and Aaron Sams.[47] However, in this technologically fast-changing world, a preferable approach is to define the flipped classroom predominantly based on its set of pedagogical approaches as Abeysekera and Dawson have done. They identified the following three characteristics:

1. move most information-transmission teaching out of class
2. use class time for learning activities that are active and social
3. require students to complete pre- and/or post-class activities to fully benefit from in-class work[48]

The TEE method is a good example of the Abeysekera and Dawson description of the flipped classroom, with its threefold method of *personal study* (for information-transmission), the *group meeting* (for active social learning), and *practical activities* – all of these including aspects of active learning. So we now examine each element of the TEE method in more detail.

TEE Personal Study in Conversation with Educational Theory

The pedagogical value of personal study

The twentieth and twenty-first centuries have seen an unprecedented rise in theological knowledge, understanding, and content. This exceptional growth has also fuelled specializations of theological content in a way that previously did not exist within theology. All of this raises foundational questions about the direction of theological education in preparing theologically informed individuals for a rapidly changing and globally connected world of new ideas, philosophies, and worldviews that require mature, theologically informed responses. "Unfortunately, traditional schooling processes teach us to be taught, but they do not teach us to learn."[49] Essential for both lifelong learning and independent professional theological reflection is the skill to learn in an active and self-directed way. This is why pedagogical learner-centred approaches emphasize strongly the need for learners to engage actively with their learning

47. Popularized by Bergmann and Sams, *Flip Your Classroom*, and *Flipped Learning*.
48. Abeysekera and Dawson, "Motivation and Cognitive Load," 3.
49. Ferris, "Future of Theological Education," 45.

material. Traditionally in TEE, this is done through the personal study[50] step, which consists of any kind of preparatory engagement with learning content, either through guided workbooks or initial research through individual or community learning tasks. This is conceptually linked to independent learning, self-directed learning, or self-initiated learning as part of lifelong growth, development, and learning.[51] Freire observed long ago that no one can be liberated by someone else.[52] This is true for learning – no one can "learn" for someone else. Learning is always an individual's reformulation of learning content, through mentally processing the material in some way.

Knowles defined adult education essentially as the process of helping learners to become increasingly self-directed by moving from teacher-directed learning to self-directed learning.[53] TEE's self-study follows this conceptual process of self-direction, moving the student towards higher-order thinking and learning. The advantages of self-study are the active engagement with the learning content and learning at one's own speed and (where applicable and options are given) learners can investigate projects of their own interest.

Effective personal study material

TEE originated before the advent of contemporary adult learning theories so it did not always use the same terminology. Nevertheless, nearly sixty years ago the pioneers of TEE built their methodology on principles which are now being clearly confirmed by the research described above. Ross Kinsler wrote:

> We strongly resisted the behaviourist psychology which is behind much of the early literature in this field. But we adopted certain basic empirical principles: learning proceeds best from the known to the unknown; learning depends on prompt use of newly acquired information, concepts or skills; learning increases when appropriate use of the new material is confirmed; and learning

50. Personal study is also called self-study or home study.

51. There is insufficient space to discuss thoroughly the differences between these terms and their nuances. See van der Walt, "Self-Directed Learning," Merriam, "Andragogy," and Brookfield, "Self-Directed Learning."

52. Freire, *Pedagogy of the Oppressed*, 53.

53. See Knowles, "Adult Learning Processes."

effectiveness is directly related to the perceived relevance of the material in the life of the learner.[54]

When learners have merely superficial exposure to a mass of material, little of it is retained in long-term memory. By contrast, an approach called mastery learning[55] aims to teach thoroughly a smaller amount of key material. TEE personal study materials typically use short-step learning sequences whereby the learner responds actively to a small amount of information which is then repeated in different ways and tested frequently. This strengthens brain synapses in the ways described above and is highly effective at the lower levels of Bloom's taxonomy described in chapter 5.[56] Admittedly it can become a domesticating "repeat after me" form of education. But this need not be the case if augmented by the types of reflection that extend learning into Bloom's higher levels. Contemporary TEE course design incorporates individual reflection into the personal study step and becomes the springboard for further shared reflection in the group meeting. This extends short-step learning sequences far beyond TEE's earlier use of programmed instruction, critiqued by educationalists such as Patricia Harrison and Robert Ferris,[57] who nevertheless remain supportive of TEE as a whole.

Thus, effective TEE personal study, while retaining the use of logical sequences leading to key learning points, also stretches the learning *upward* towards Bloom's higher levels, *backward* by reflecting on prior experience, *inward* by touching the heart, *outward* by stimulating group discussion and *forward* by prompting changed behaviour.

Such courses have been tried and tested by several million TEE students over sixty years, in many cultures and with mixed educational backgrounds.

54. Kinsler, *Extension Movement*, 50–1.

55. Developed by Benjamin Bloom from 1968. See for example, Bloom, "Mastery Learning."

56. See chapter 5: Shaw, "The Educational Efficacy of TEE – Part 1."

57. Harrison believes that programmed instruction textbooks are hard to write well and recommends a mix of styles: Harrison, "Forty Years On," 322. Ferris supports the principle of focused learning goals and short learning steps, combined with reflection, but objects to use of "programmed instruction" with its origins in the behaviourist educational philosophy of B. F. Skinner (1904–1990). Skinner assumed humans could be "programmed" like computers and were psychologically equivalent to the pigeons with which he conducted experiments. Ferris points out that behaviourist philosophy is sub-biblical for it demeans the image of God in reflective human learners (email correspondence with Tim Green, 4 January 2021).

In Asia today, around ten thousand learning groups meet each week in homes or local churches, led by facilitators who believe strongly enough in TEE's effectiveness to give their own time to it as unpaid volunteers. Almost all of them are nationals, not missionaries. The same is true of TEE practitioners in Africa and Latin America.

Many adult learners in Asia are first generation Christians from other faith backgrounds. TEE courses are being written to combine the formative education needed for people new in the faith, with reflection exercises to help catalyze worldview transformation. For example, the TEE course Come Follow Me is designed for first generation Christian believers from Muslim backgrounds (also known as BMB).[58] It combines short-step active learning sequences for formative education with critical reflection catalyzed not through long, written assignments but through stories, pictures, and case studies to compare old and new worldviews. It begins in the personal study phase and is strengthened in the group meeting, leading to worldview transformation.

Students of this course have often highlighted the lesson on forgiving persecutors as impacting their attitudes and behaviour. The lesson (similar to the one in Appendix 1) begins with this picture:

Figure 6.4 A clash of worldviews

58. Green, Come Follow Me. https://come-follow-me.org/ explains the educational design, combining an inductive study of 1 Peter with issues relevant for the learners.

Such pictures are not mere decorative extras but an integral part of the learning sequence, a mini-case study where the learner is asked to make discerning choices between options. Pictures also lodge in the memory, trigger emotion, and provide a visual focal point for group discussion by learners of all education levels. In our visual age, graphics cannot be ignored in theological education.

The picture of two men is designed to engage learners in the worldview clash of revenge versus forgiveness. When old and new worldviews are deliberately brought to collide and crunch with each other in the learner's mind, it prompts personal reflection which is where deep-level transformation begins. Even if such reflection uncovers painful memories and emotions, it can be processed in a supportive group atmosphere and harnessed for transformative growth. As Mezirow and others have shown, cognitive dissonance need not be destructive if it goes on to trigger transformative learning.[59] In contrast to Mezirow, however, biblical educators do not treat all adult choices as equally valid but instead teach Scripture as authoritative for being "transformed through the renewal of your mind" (Rom 12:2 ESV). Therefore this Come Follow Me lesson emphasizes Christ's teaching and example on forgiving enemies. It concludes with challenging the learners to think of one person who hurt them, and as a practical activity, to go through the steps of forgiving that person – if they so choose.[60]

Not all TEE courses use short-step sequencing, especially at higher curricular levels. Thus, in the Open Theological Seminary's stepwise curriculum, at the early stages learners gain confidence through short-step active learning sequences, but proceeding to middle and higher stages, they are cognitively stretched through incrementally longer reading and writing assignments, until finally they complete a 30,000 word independent research project to gain their bachelor degree. In other words, TEE self-study materials are not inherently linked to short-step learning design. TEE stretches to higher educational levels as well as serving the grassroots.

59. See chapter 5: Shaw, "The Educational Efficacy of TEE – Part 1."

60. Critical reflection can help someone discern what the new path of discipleship involves, but it is that person's own choice whether or not to follow that path with God's help. Hence the "barriers to change" between steps 3 and 4 in Elmer and Elmer's cycle.

TEE Group Learning and Educational Theory

TEE is not a form of distance learning. Rather, it is rooted in the local learning group. This marks it as distinct from the classroom lecture (where the teacher speaks, and students listen) and also from any kind of education where students learn in isolation. "Adults learn best when they are in collaborative groups," writes Stephen Brookfield, and "the discussion method is uniquely suited to facilitating critical adult learning."[61] Jane Vella believes that in this kind of dialogue education, "the teacher discovers herself to be a learner among learners, learning with her adult colleagues."[62] For these educationalists, small group interaction lies at the heart of transformative learning.

Typically, a TEE learning group comprises five to ten members, drawn from one or more local churches, meeting face-to-face each week and led by a trained facilitator. Because the cognitive material is already covered beforehand, precious class time is freed up for discussion, questions, and life application. As Kinsler wrote of the first TEE programme in Guatemala:

> Having studied the basic content of the courses before coming to class and being able to relate the ideas and skills they were studying to a living situation, the weekly sessions of professor and students came alive. Again and again the professors were surprised and inspired by the spontaneous discussion and grappling with real issues that occurred almost constantly in the extension centers.[63]

When well led by a competent group leader (a vital element in TEE), some key elements of transformative learning take place in the group meeting. Adult learners reflect on their reservoir of life experience, evaluate their opinions in the light of material taught through homework, critique this material, articulate their viewpoints through expressing them to others, reflect in turn on others' expressed opinions, and develop a supportive group culture of mutual respect. Here "theology in context" emerges as members bring biblical truth to bear on earthed realities. It is here too that members express their joys and struggles, and enter into the emotions of other members, and together bring all of these

61. Brookfield, *Understanding and Facilitating*, 113–4.

62. Vella, *Learning to Listen*.

63. Kinsler, *Extension Movement*, 5.

to God. It is here that they are energized for their practical ministry assignment and for the next week's self-study.

The TEE method combines home study with group discussion, but which of these is more helpful in learning, or is it both in combination? This question was put to twenty-eight first time TEE students in Malawi.[64] Table 6.5 shows the results of responses in self-evaluation questionnaires.

Table 6.5. Malawi TEE students' views of home study and discussion

"Which element of TEE is more helpful?"	Students in Urban Groups	Students in a Rural Group	Total
Home study was the most helpful element	0	0	0
Group discussion was the most helpful element	1	1	2
The combination of both elements was the most helpful	21	5	26

Interviews clarified that the self-study material actually was very helpful, but the combination was even more powerful. The results were consistent between urban and rural students despite the big difference in their educational background. Overall, there are strong indicators that the combination of self-study and group discussion significantly improved the likelihood of students' learning.[65]

The group meeting is vital for sustaining engagement and motivation. Much depends on the group leader to facilitate discussion, give a godly example and help members apply the teaching in their lives. Sometimes this person is called a "tutor," but their task is not primarily to provide teaching content, since TEE is a flipped classroom method whereby learners have already engaged with the core teaching beforehand. The group leader's role is more that of a learning facilitator than teacher-tutor. Instead, the experienced group leader selects some of that prior individual engagement as a springboard to deeper group reflection leading to changed lives. This range of skills comes naturally to some, but for most group leaders it is greatly helped by careful training

64. These research findings are part of an ongoing new course evaluation by Volker Glissmann. For a similar finding, see O'Donovan, "Doing It Differently."

65. For a similar conclusion that "the combination of personalised pre-class learning and peer-learning classroom activities facilitated deeper learning," but in a higher education setting, see Goedhart et al., "Flipped Classroom," 297.

and monitoring from the TEE programme, along with prior experience of the method and a well-designed leader guide for each session. Chapter 3 of this book explains further the vital role played by TEE group leaders.

TEE Practical Activities in Conversation with Educational Theory

A concern that TEE practitioners share with the wider church and theological educators in general is the need to balance cognitive input with practical, vocational, and spiritual application. This is driven by a theological concern for learners to be "doers of the Word and not hearers only" (Jas 1:22 ESV), and also by a pedagogical necessity to strengthen memory retention by applying learned content to new situations. Kinsler wrote: "The third component (of TEE) . . . was ongoing, practical testing or application of the substance and issues of the course material in the students' local ecclesial and social contexts."[66]

Often TEE practitioners have called this third component "practical application." However, the word "application" is also used in a cognitive sense in Bloom's taxonomy for using information from one setting and applying it a new setting. This cognitive skill, though essential, is different from the kind of practical learning task used in the third part of the TEE method. Therefore, we here use "activity" to encompass active learning tasks before and after personal study as well as before and after the group discussion. Geoff Petty comments that "students need *activities which encourage them to process new material.* Activities that make students use . . . the ideas you are trying to teach them will make them learn more efficiently than passive activities such as listening" (emphasis original).[67]

While learning tasks may be woven into all components of the TEE method, there is also typically a separate practical activity to reinforce what is learned from the personal study and group discussion components. It may be an individual activity to strengthen a learner's relationship with God[68] or with

66. Kinsler, "Equipping All God's People," 27.

67. Petty, *Teaching Today*, 3.

68. For example, to start a daily devotional habit or to keep a reflective journal.

family members[69] and others, or practicing a ministry skill,[70] or explaining newly acquired knowledge to others. Or it may be a group activity in serving the community.[71] Some TEE courses specify practical activities as an integral part of the course, while others leave it to the students or group leader to choose an activity. However, if the activity is left too vague it can be neglected altogether, so accountability should be hard-wired into the system by the facilitator asking at the next group meeting what students actually did as a result of the previous lesson. TEE best practice gives credit for completing these assignments, but best practice is, of course, not always followed.

Activities are essential to move learners towards deep learning, but it is reflection upon these activities that is so vital for higher-order thinking. Praxis-oriented education centres on the interplay between action and reflection, whether through a Reflection – Action – Reflection sequence[72] or Action – Reflection – Action, for both have their place.

An Action – Reflection – Action (ARA) strategy has been used by the organization More Than a Mile Deep to equip African Christians as agents of transformation in their societies.[73] Richard Morris describes the design:

> An ARA learning response incorporates a continuous cycle of action followed by reflection upon each action. The aim of this cycle is to steadily build competence in learners as they are being transformed and effecting transformation in their societies. Good reflection leads to the development of insights that will benefit the next action. Notice that the starting point in the cycle is action

69. For example, to do something in the coming week to make one's spouse happy.

70. For example, to preach a sermon and receive feedback on it from two listeners or prepare a Sunday school lesson.

71. For example, in Pakistan, a group activity in the young people's course Me and My Environment is to go out together one time to pick up litter. In Nepal, students of Mission, Mercy and Me went together to give blood at the blood bank.

72. Snook's version was that "the first component part (self-study material) involves reflection. Students reflect cognitively on a biblical lesson. The second component part (service to God) involves action – the participants act in response to their previous reflection. In the third component part (group discussion), they bring the results of their service to the discussion seminar and reflect on the consequences of action to refine and better their ministry." Snook, *Developing Leaders*, 7–8.

73. MMD was established in Africa by Dr. John Jusu and other Africans to address situations faced by the church in Africa.

> (within the situation and context) and not the input of content. Content, for example biblical content, enters the cycle during the reflection phase.[74]

For example, their course designed to change attitudes to HIV/AIDS requires the student first to go on a discovery visit to meet a patient, sit with them and their family, and experience their own reaction, and then reflect on that while engaging in the personal study and group discussion.[75]

So, the "activity" part of learning may include a mix of post-class reinforcement learning, which is how TEE has normally used it, and pre-class discovery learning through hands-on immersion prior to the study phase. Chapter 7 explains how Increase has sought to combine transformative learning design[76] with classic TEE methodology to equip new TEE course writers to develop transformative courses. A particular strength of this approach is the focus on specific contexts. Instead of taking courses from the West and contextualizing them for other settings, this approach starts within those very settings, with questions arising from the context and guiding the shape of the course.

Conclusion

Educationally, we live in exciting times. There has never been so much scientific research about best practices in education than in our times. This is especially the case where neurological research, cognitive psychology, and pedagogical research come together to address the questions of how memory works in the brain, how we learn and how best pedagogical practices enhance teaching and learning.

74. "MMD ARA Training System," Richard Morris: https://withcommunity.org/resources/foundations.

75. This course, Pastoral Guidance and Counselling in HIV and AIDS, by Dr. Elesinah Chauke is in MMD's Bachelor of Theology programme, accredited through the South African Theological Seminary.

76. Specifically, it used the Situation Response Development (SRD) framework based on the action-reflection-action approach and developed by the same educators. See chapter 7: Ivins and Do, "New TEE Courses."

TEE has been cognizant of educational theories from the start of its conceptualization. Overall, the movement has continued to engage and be challenged by new pedagogical theories and understanding of learning. This has proven vital for delivering sound transformative learning independent of the academic level of training offered. TEE as an educational approach is based on solid adult learning theories that are designed around learner-centred approaches that seek to provide relevant, contextual, and appropriate theological engagement with the learners' surroundings. This chapter presents the underlying theories and challenges TEE practitioners to assess their own understanding and compliance with best educational practices in TEE. The theories also offer creative approaches for theological institutions, following the closure of classrooms by a global pandemic,[77] that have pushed them into the same educational space as TEE – that of needing to design content delivery for flipped classrooms in an interesting, relevant, active, and memorable ways.

Overall, TEE stands up well to educational theories discussed in this chapter including the science of memorization, the importance of active learning, flipped classroom approaches, a balance of formative and critical learning, the importance of appropriate reflection on learning objectives, and the ongoing need for contextual relevance across the three essential components of TEE: personal study, group learning, and practical activities. However, TEE educators would benefit from deeper engagement with evolving educational theories and a willingness to keep refining their courses and methods accordingly.

Bibliography

Abeysekera, Lakmal, and Phillip Dawson. "Motivation and Cognitive Load in the Flipped Classroom: Definition, Rationale and a Call for Research." *Higher Education Research & Development* 34, no. 1 (2 January 2015): 1–14.

Astley, Jeff. *The Philosophy of Christian Religious Education*. Birmingham: Religious Education Press, 1994.

Bäcklund, Johan, and Martin Hugo. "The Paradox of the Flipped Classroom: One Method, Many Intentions." *Problems of Education in the 21st Century* 76, no. 4 (2018): 451–64.

77. The COVID-19 pandemic was still raging in August 2021 when this book was finalised. Even after it comes under control the educational implications will be ongoing.

Banda, Stephen. *Dialogue Education in Adult Education Enhancing Environmental Sustainability*. Saarbrücken: LAP LAMBERT Academic Publishing, 2014.

Bergmann, Jonathan, and Aaron Sams. *Flipped Learning: Gateway to Student Engagement*. Eugene: International Society for Technology in Education, 2014.

———. *Flip Your Classroom: Reach Every Student in Every Class Every Day*. Eugene: International Society for Technology in Education, 2012.

Bloom, Benjamin S. "Mastery Learning." In *Mastery Learning: Theory and Practice*, edited by J. H. Block, 47–63. New York: Holt, Rinehart & Winston, 1971.

Brookfield, Stephen. "Self-Directed Learning." Informal Education Archives. Accessed 8 August 2020. https://infed.org/mobi/self-directed-learning/.

———. *Understanding and Facilitating Adult Learning: A Comprehensive Analysis of Principles and Effective Practices*. Milton Keynes: Open University Press, 1986.

Burgess, Paul, ed. *Curriculum for Theological Education: Towards a Theology of Training Methods*. Pakistan: Gujrawala Theological Seminary, 2003.

Coleman, Mary S., Tobin L. Smith, and Emily R. Miller. "Catalysts for Achieving Sustained Improvement in the Quality of Undergraduate STEM Education." *Daedalus* 148, no. 4 (October 2019): 29–46.

Davis, Ronald L., and Yi Zhong. "The Biology of Forgetting – A Perspective." *Neuron* 95, no. 3 (2017): 490–503.

DeLozier, Sarah J., and Matthew G. Rhodes. "Flipped Classrooms: A Review of Key Ideas and Recommendations for Practice." *Educational Psychology Review* 29, no. 1 (March 2017): 141–51.

Deslauriers, Louis, Ellen Schelew, and Carl Wieman. "Improved Learning in a Large-Enrollment Physics Class." *Science* 332, no. 6031 (13 May 2011): 862–64.

Elmer, Muriel I., and Duane H. Elmer. *The Learning Cycle: Insights for Faithful Teaching from Neuroscience and the Social Sciences*. Downers Grove: IVP Academic, 2020.

Ferris, Robert W. "The Future of Theological Education." In *Cyprus: TEE Come of Age*, edited by Robert L. Youngblood, 27–39. Exeter: Paternoster, 1986.

Ferris, Robert W., John R. Lillis and Ralph E. Enlow. *Ministry Education That Transforms: Modelling and Teaching the Transformed Life*. Carlisle: Langham, 2018.

Freeman, Scott, Sarah L. Eddy, Hannah Jordt, Michelle K. Smith, and Mary P. Wenderoth. "Reply to Hora: Meta-Analytic Techniques Are Designed to Accommodate Variation in Implementation." *Proceedings of the National Academy of Sciences* 111, no. 30 (29 July 2014): E3025.

Freeman, Scott, Sarah L. Eddy, Miles McDonough, Michelle K. Smith, Nnadozie Okoroafor, Hannah Jordt, and Mary P. Wenderoth. "Active Learning Increases

Student Performance in Science, Engineering, and Mathematics." *Proceedings of the National Academy of Sciences* 111, no. 23 (10 June 2014): 8410–15.

Freire, Paulo. *Pedagogy of the Oppressed.* New York: Continuum, 1970.

Glissmann, Volker. "The Fragmentation of Theological Education and Its Effect on the Church, Grassroots Theological Education in Malawi and TEE." In *Towards a Malawian Theology of Laity*, edited by Volker Glissmann, 169–98. Mzuzu: Luviri Press, 2020.

Goedhart, N. S., N. Blignaut-van Westrhenen, C. Moser, and M. B. M. Zweekhorst. "The Flipped Classroom: Supporting a Diverse Group of Students in Their Learning." *Learning Environments Research* 22, no. 2 (July 2019): 297–310.

Green, Tim. "Integrated Learning Pathways." In *TEE in Asia: Empowering Churches, Equipping Disciples*, edited by Hanna-Ruth van Wingerden, Tim Green and Graham Aylett, 239–44. Carlisle: Langham Global Library, 2021.

———. *Come Follow Me.* Durham: Lulu Press, 2013.

Harrison, Patricia. "Forty Years On: The Evolution of Theological Education by Extension (TEE)." *Evangelical Review of Theology* 28, no. 4 (2004): 315–28.

Hoellwarth, Chance, and Matthew J. Moelter. "The Implications of a Robust Curriculum in Introductory Mechanics." *American Journal of Physics* 79, no. 5 (May 2011): 540–45.

Jensen, Jamie L., Tyler A. Kummer, and Patricia D. d. M. Godoy. "Improvements from a Flipped Classroom May Simply Be the Fruits of Active Learning." *CBE Life Sciences Education* 14 (2015): 1–12.

Johnson, Lisa W., and Jeremy D. Renner. "Effect of the Flipped Classroom Model on a Secondary Computer Applications Course: Student and Teacher Perceptions, Questions and Student Achievement." EdD, University of Louisville, 2012.

Kinsler, F. Ross. *The Extension Movement in Theological Education: A Call to the Renewal of the Ministry.* Pasadena: William Carey Library, 1978.

———, ed. *Ministry by the People: Theological Education by Extension.* Maryknoll: Orbis, 1983.

———. "Equipping All God's People for God's Mission." In *Diversified Theological Education: Equipping All God's People*, edited by F. Ross Kinsler, 15–32. Pasadena: WCIU Press, 2008.

Knowles, Malcolm S. "Adult Learning Processes: Pedagogy and Andragogy." *Religious Education* 72, no. 2 (1977): 202–11.

Le Cornu, Alison. "Meaning, Internalization, and Externalization: Toward a Fuller Understanding of the Process of Reflection and Its Role in the Construction of the Self." *Adult Education Quarterly* 59, no. 4 (2009): 279–97.

———. "People's Ways of Believing: Learning Processes and Faith Outcomes." PhD, University of Surrey, 2004.

Mager, Robert F. *Preparing Instructional Objectives: A Critical Tool in the Development of Effective Instruction*. 3rd ed. Atlanta: Center for Effective Performance, 1997.

Merriam, Sharan B. "Andragogy and Self-Directed Learning: Pillars of Adult Learning Theory." *New Directions for Adult and Continuing Education* 89 (2001): 3–14.

Mezirow, Jack. "How Critical Reflection Triggers Transformative Learning." In *Fostering Critical Reflection in Adulthood: A Guide to Transformative and Emancipatory Learning*, edited by Jack Mezirow and Associates, 1–20. San Fancisco: Jossey-Bass, 1990.

Mintzes, Joel J., and Emily M. Walter, eds. *Active Learning in College Science: The Case for Evidence-Based Practice*. Cham: Springer International Publishing, 2020.

———, eds. "Preface." In *Active Learning in College Science: The Case for Evidence-Based Practice*, ix–xi. Cham: Springer International Publishing, 2020.

O'Donovan, Theresa. "Doing It Differently: Unleashing Student Creativity." *Teaching Theology & Religion* 6, no. 3 (2003): 159–63.

Open Theological Seminary. *Academic Manual*. Lahore, Pakistan: Open Theological Seminary, 2020.

Petty, Geoffrey. *Teaching Today: A Practical Guide*. 4th ed. Cheltenham: Nelson Thornes, 2009.

Richards, Blake A., and Paul W. Frankland. "The Persistence and Transience of Memory." *Neuron* 94, no. 6 (2017): 1071–84.

Snook, Stewart G. *Developing Leaders through Theological Education by Extension: Case Studies from Africa*. BGC Monograph. Wheaton: Billy Graham Centre, 1992.

Thalheimer, Will. *How Much Do People Forget?* Somerville, MA: Work-Learning Research, Inc., 2010. http://www.willatworklearning.com/files/how-much-do-people-forget-v12-14-2010-2.pdf.

Theobald, Elli J., Mariah J. Hill, Elisa Tran, Sweta Agrawal, E. Nicole Arroyo, Shawn Behling, and Nyasha Chambwe. "Active Learning Narrows Achievement Gaps for Underrepresented Students in Undergraduate Science, Technology, Engineering, and Math." *Proceedings of the National Academy of Sciences* 117, no. 12 (24 March 2020): 6476–83.

van der Walt, Johannes L. "The Term 'Self-Directed Learning' – Back to Knowles, or Another Way to Forge Ahead?" *Journal of Research on Christian Education* 28, no. 1 (2019): 1–20.

van Wingerden, Hanna-Ruth, Tim Green, and Graham Aylett, eds. *TEE in Asia: Empowering Churches, Equipping Disciples.* Carlisle: Langham Global Library, 2021.

Vella, Jane K. *Learning to Listen, Learning to Teach: The Power of Dialogue in Educating Adults*. Rev. ed. San Francisco: Jossey-Bass, 2002.

Westervelt, Eric. "A Nobel Laureate's Education Plea: Revolutionize Teaching." Accessed 8 August 2020. https://www.npr.org/sections/ed/2016/04/14/465729968/a-nobel-laureates-education-plea-revolutionize-teaching.

Wieman, Carl. "From the National Academies: Overview of the National Research Council's Board on Science Education and Personal Reflections as a Science Teacher." *Cell Biology Education* 4, no. 2 (June 2005): 118–20.

———. "Large-Scale Comparison of Science Teaching Methods Sends Clear Message." *Proceedings of the National Academy of Sciences* 111, no. 23 (10 June 2014): 8319–20.

———. "Why Not Try a Scientific Approach to Science Education?" *Change: The Magazine of Higher Learning* 39, no. 5 (January 2007): 9–15.

Wlassoff, Viatcheslav. "Why Is Forgetting Good for Your Brain and Health?" Blog. http://www.brainblogger.com/2017/09/20/why-forgetting-is-important-for-the-brain-functions/.

7

New TEE Courses

Nicholas Ivins and Miyung Do

Introduction

In this chapter we show how the transformative learning principles presented in chapter 5[1] and chapter 6[2] were translated into practice using the Situation Response Development (SRD) model. First, Ivins explains how both the principles and the model were applied to the design of training for new TEE course writers across Asia through Increase Association's course-writing programme.[3] Then, Do describes the transformative learning experience of one of the course-writing groups in Central Asia for both the writers and the students. The case study presented in this chapter demonstrates how the TEE movement continues to mature, embracing quality developments in educational theory and practice. Increase's programme is an example of innovation to help develop a new suite of "Tools to Equip and Empower" that will help to equip the church for the mission of God in the twenty-first century.[4]

1. Chapter 5: Shaw, "The Educational Efficacy of TEE – Part 1."
2. Chapter 6: Glissmann and Green, "The Educational Efficacy of TEE – Part 2."
3. See: Increase, "Course Writers in Asia."
4. "Tools to Equip and Empower" is an alternative rendering of the term "Theological Education by Extension," bringing a fresh emphasis on TEE as valuable tools and resources to equip the church for God's mission.

Why New Courses?

The reach of the gospel has advanced to the extent that the presence of new believers in places where Christ has not been known has created a need for theologically sound training in these contexts.

The original TEE courses were written for rural pastors with low education in South America who were leading churches but had no theological training. Of course, TEE is now used around the world not just for pastors, but also in church-based training for lay members. New courses are being written for believers in situations that are both local and challenging.

The church has grown tremendously in many countries across Asia in recent decades. Mongolia, for example, had only a handful of believers in the early 1990s, but numbered well over 40,000 by 2010.[5] Mature believers in these countries know better than anyone what challenges the local churches face and they are ready to take the opportunity to develop courses appropriate to their situations.[6]

In April 2015, over forty people from twenty TEE national programmes in Asia and the Middle East came together for an Increase Association consultation called Exploring New Horizons.[7] Consultation participants were asked: "What are the most widespread and important social issues to be addressed by new courses?" Through small group discussions, a consolidated list was compiled (Figure 7.1).

---

5. Operation World: https://www.operationworld.org/country/mong/owtext.html. A report by SEAN International in 2010 indicated a higher figure of 50,000 Christians in Mongolia. See: https://www.seaninternational.org.

6. The writing of new TEE courses is not a new quest in the world of TEE. For example, Kangwa Mabuluki describes the commitment of the All Africa TEE conference held in Zambia in 2006 to encourage new course writing: Mabuluki, "Diversified Theological Education," 258–61; Sendegeya and Spencer wrote a TEE manual which included a chapter on developing new courses in an African context: Sendegeya and Spencer, *Understanding TEE*, 67–79; other examples of course writer training manuals include: Harms, *Writing for T.E.E.*, and Gatimu et al., *Manual for Writers and Designers*.

7. For a discussion of transformative aspects of training, see section 4.1 of conference proceedings from the 2015 Kuala Lumpur Increase consultation: Flores et al., "Exploring New Horizons," 21–31. This is downloadable from: https://www.increaseassociation.org/resources/new-horizons.

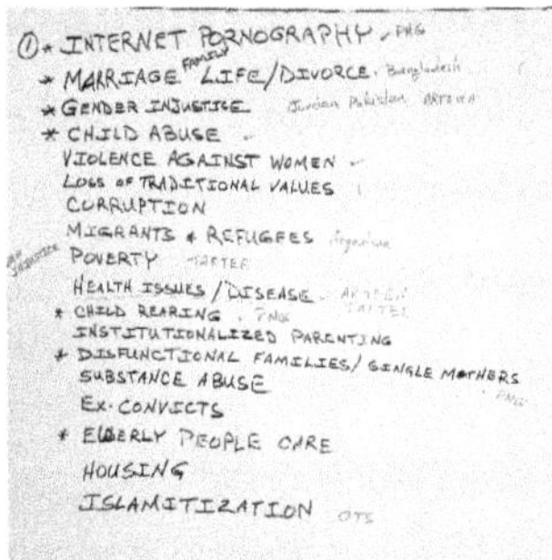

Figure 7.1. List of burning issues in Asia

Either TEE courses did not exist on these topics or they were written for different contexts. For many years, Asian TEE programmes had been translating other courses from English and adapting them for use in their own countries. There is a growing desire for believers in Asia to write their own new courses on their own issues in their own contexts and languages. For example, both the Pakistani and Bangladeshi TEE programmes chose to write on Christian responses to persecution in Urdu and Bengali. Other national programmes wanted to develop courses according to their needs: ministry to teens in Mongolia, family life in Nepal, the spirit world in Cambodia, pre-marital relationships in one Central Asian country, and discipleship challenges in another.[8]

But who was to write the new courses to address these issues? Increase invited TEE directors from around the region to form writing teams that would take up the cause. But how would these women and men who were not necessarily trained educators learn the art and science of course writing?

8. These indigenous TEE programmes are all led and governed within their own countries. They are core member organizations of the Increase Association. The definition of a core member, and contact details for these organizations where security allows, are found in: https://www.increaseassociation.org/members/core-members.

The Course Writer Training Programme – Design

The need for new courses focusing on local, contextual needs provided the impetus for twelve writing teams from nine countries[9] to commit to writing new courses.[10] To equip these writers (eleven women and ten men), Increase developed the Course Writer Training programme in 2016 that would eventually be implemented over three years. Richard Morris,[11] who guided Increase through the initial years as chair of the board, introduced the Situation Response Development (SRD) model upon which the course writer training would be based.

1. Developing a vision for transformative TEE

The course-writer training team – Freda Carey, Tim Green, Patricia Harrison, and Nicholas Ivins[12] – developed a concise statement that would act as a guide for the writers.

> GUIDING STATEMENT
>
> We plan to develop TEE courses which help learners in community to:
>
> - shine God's word on issues arising from specific situations in local contexts,
> - integrate action and reflection intentionally,

9. The countries were Bangladesh, Cambodia, Mongolia, Nepal, Pakistan, Jordan, Kazakhstan, Kyrgyzstan, and Uzbekistan. A first-generation church is growing in most of these countries despite poverty and persecution. One of the writing teams was from SEAN International which is a global provider of TEE courses.

10. The significance of context as a driving force in curriculum development is a growing emphasis in contemporary theological education. In particular, see: Das, *Connecting Curriculum with Context.*

11. Richard Morris and Nicholas Ivins serve on the WITH International Community team. See: https://withcommunity.org/.

12. This team has much expertise in education and experience in writing courses and training writers. Dr. Patricia Harrison was among the first to train TEE course writers in the 1970s; with a doctorate and several master's degrees in theology and education, and five decades of experience, she is widely acknowledged in the field. Freda Carey has taught at the Open Theological Seminary in Pakistan for over twenty years, writing and editing many courses and helping to train the course-writing team there. Nicholas Ivins has fifteen years teaching experience in China and a further ten years in equipping writers. For thirty years Tim Green has been developing TEE and other courses, which have been used in seventy languages and countries. Volker Glissmann and Allan Harkness also contributed to workshop 1.

- grow in Christlike knowledge, attitudes, abilities, and relationships, and
- be transformed themselves and help bring transformation in their circles of influence.

Each phrase was carefully constructed to reflect the priorities for twenty-first-century, transformative TEE courses. The rationale for each phrase is explained more fully below.

Develop TEE courses which help learners in community

TEE course writers are encouraged from the start to think of their students not as individuals but as a group learning together. By focusing on their group as a learning community, they are able to implement relevant and improved transformational learning theory elements such as building relationships, acting together, sharing reflections, asking questions, building emotional connections, making sense, and finding significance through the group.[13]

Shine God's word on issues arising from specific situations in local contexts

To encourage the local TEE organizations to develop courses for their own contexts, we made the starting point the specific situations in their locations. Because the courses respond to and address the situations that learners are emotionally, relationally, and intellectually connected to, they will resonate with the TEE groups who take the courses. As the writers deepen their understanding of the local situation through research, they also consider how God's word might bring his light into those situations in contextually appropriate ways. Student engagement is heightened as the course is written with them in mind and is directed towards their personal engagement to bring change to that situation.

13. See chapter 5: Shaw, "The Educational Efficacy of TEE – Part 1."

Integrate action and reflection intentionally

This phrase reminds course writers and developers to include Action – Reflection – Action[14] in the course, including for home assignments and group discussion. Action is not simply application of a lesson. Action and reflection are related to each student's growing competence in their role in bringing about change. Action – Reflection – Action emphasizes the growth process that is designed into the course.

Grow in Christlike knowledge, attitudes, abilities, and relationships

This phrase reminds writers and course developers that the purpose of the course they write is for the participants to grow in Christ. Such a course will not merely instil knowledge in the learners (cognitive domain) but will also build in opportunities to reflect on attitudes and feelings about the issues and their involvement in them (the affective domain) and develop their abilities (behavioural domain).[15] Adding *relationships* as a fourth domain acknowledges that the course will affect the way students interact with people in their situations. The course writers and developers should be aware of those relationships and direct the course in ways that help the students competently relate in more Christlike ways.

Be transformed themselves and help bring transformation in their circles of influence

The group of students is encouraged to bring transformation to the people in their lives. In this way, the course writers are challenged to write a course that is not satisfied with addressing an issue topically but that provides the framework for the students to actively engage with the situation and the people in it while they are taking the course. This naturally increases the emotional

---

14. Consistent with Kolb's learning cycle explained in chapter 5: Shaw, "The Educational Efficacy of TEE – Part 1."

15. For further details see the section on the ABCs of Learning in chapter 5: Shaw, "The Educational Efficacy of TEE – Part 1."

connection, the connection to what they already know and have experienced, and the personal significance of their involvement.[16]

The guiding statement for writers proved to be an accessible way for them to implement transformative learning theories, although the courses will vary in the degree of implementation.

2. Using the SRD framework

One challenge for the training team was that the course writers would not necessarily be educators. How could we present the transformative learning priorities in ways that would be useful for them to gain confidence and competence in writing their courses? We chose to use the SRD model[17] as the core of the training because of its focus on a particular local situation that a course will be developed to address and change. The learning activities built into each course are given deep meaning because the outcomes focus on transformation in the learners and in their local community. As such, students will be personally challenged to initiate the changes that the course prepares them for.

The SRD framework focuses on the transformation intended in both the learners and their situations. The course writer training leads the writers and developers through a process that puts the context at the centre of course development. Course writers are equipped to thoroughly research the situation and the learners within their own context by following the SRD course design sequence (Figure 7.2). Only after adequately profiling the situation and the learners do they begin the writing process. This is why it is called Situation Response Development – the course is a response to the situation, equipping students to bring about transformation in their local communities. As group leaders and students implement the course in their local context, this contextual transformative effect is enhanced.

16. Emotional connection, sense, and significance are three key factors in deep learning. See chapter 5: Shaw, "The Educational Efficacy of TEE – Part 1."

17. The framework used in the course writer training is called Situation Response Development (SRD). SRD is based on a methodology used in Africa called Action Reflection Action (ARA) that was developed by Dr. John Jusu. The ARA methodology was used to develop the curriculum for More than a Mile Deep (MMD). For a short explanation of SRD, see, "Situational Response Development." For an explanation of ARA, see Jusu, "More Than a Mile Deep."

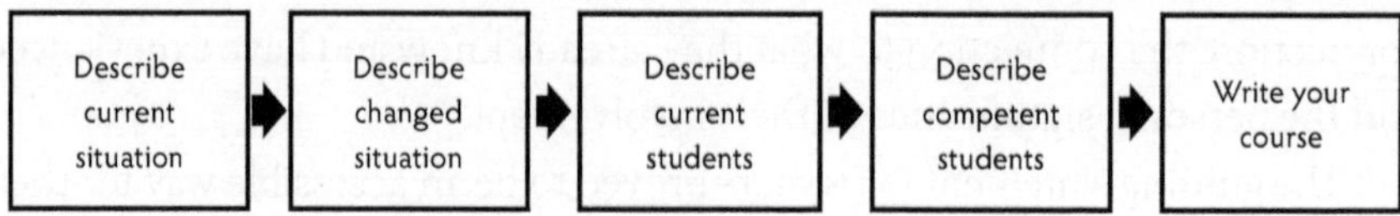

Figure 7.2. SRD course design sequence

Through the SRD framework, writers:

- deepen their understanding of their own context through research that engages the local community
- reflect on local, contextually relevant opportunities for students to engage their local situation
- can write courses that are biblically and educationally sound, contextually relevant, and impact their communities without having to become subject matter experts first
- can implement transformative learning principles without having to become experts in educational theory.

One of the most dynamic aspects of the SRD framework is that from the start the writers are placed in a position of contextual expertise. They know their own situations. They are the ones who deepen their knowledge of those situations through the research process. They are the ones who develop the response to those situations.[18]

Writing teams in Bangladesh, Nepal, Cambodia, Mongolia, Pakistan, Jordan, and Central Asian countries are challenged but strengthened as they develop courses to address their local issues using the SRD process.

The Course Writer Training Programme: Implementation

TEE programme directors from around Asia and the Middle East were invited to choose writers within their own organizations who would commit to developing new courses based on situations that they had identified as a

18. Writers are empowered and motivated because the SRD process starts and ends with their context. It should be noted, however, that the collaborative nature of each stage includes the expertise that content and education experts bring as mentors so that a comprehensive response can be developed.

need that a course in the programme could address. Twelve TEE organizations committed to take part in the full training programme by participating in a series of three workshops, with each workshop followed by a period of course development in their contexts (see Figure 7.3). The participating organizations all had a high sense of ownership and commitment that resulted in all twelve writing teams participating in the workshops and continuing towards completion of their courses.

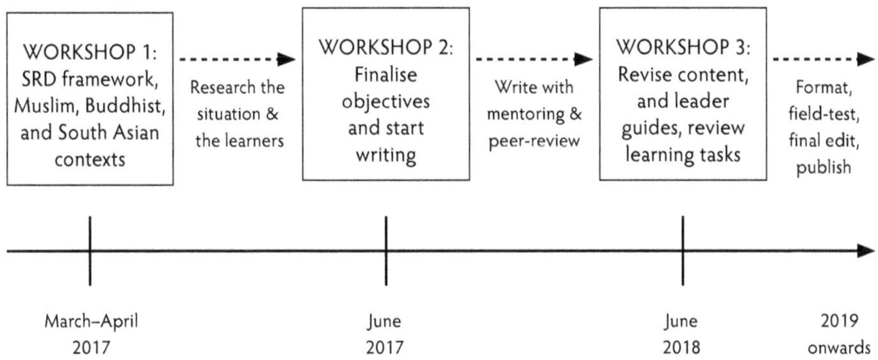

Figure 7.3. Timeline of Course Writer Training

Course writer training: Workshop 1 (followed by research)

International collaboration was evident as educational experts and TEE practitioners from England, Pakistan, Germany, Australia, and the USA worked together to design and deliver the first workshop. The three-day workshop followed the structure of the SRD framework.

The first day centred on deepening understanding of the situation their team wanted to address, using the following activity as a guide.

> *Activity*
>
> It is now time for you to practice writing a description of the situation you want to write a course on. With your course-writing team, do the following activity.

> Task 1: Identify a local situation that you may want to address. Describe it as well as you can, including the following: Describe how believers are not engaging well with the situation you identified. Here you will describe something that is negative and that needs improvement or transformation.
>
> At this point, do not worry about writing a course, just describe the current situation. Be prepared to report your descriptions to the larger group.

A similar activity was carried out on the second day, which described the learners who would be involved in addressing that situation. On day three, each TEE programme developed a research plan for the months between workshops 1 and 2. The research was not to be about the topic; it was not about collecting materials to form the content of the course. It was to deepen the writers' understanding of local situations and the people engaged in those situations, to strengthen the contextual relevance of their courses. It was this deeper understanding of the local context that gave the writers the confidence their courses would, in fact, have a transformational outcome. The research also provided opportunities to collect local stories, case studies, quotes, and other anecdotal material to include in their courses.

To direct their research, the writers were encouraged to use as a guide the following seven areas[19] which connect the research to the four learning objective types: know, be, do, relate.

- **Decide:** How do people make decisions? What decisions are they making that contribute to the bad situation that they want to address? What decisions are made by people who are currently doing well?
- **Do:** What are people doing now?
- **Create:** What do competent people create that helps them be successful in this area?
- **Knowledge:** What do people know or not know that gets in the way of acting competently in the situation? What knowledge would help them overcome current barriers?

19. The research list is a modification of the six types of objectives presented in Horton, *E-learning by Design*, 14.

- **Belief:** What do people believe that prevents them from acting competently in the situation? Why do people make the decisions they do?
- **Feeling:** What are people feeling? (Fear, resentment, shame, pride?) What are they not feeling? (Compassion, contentment, security, confidence?)
- **Relationships:** What are the relationships that will help bring about the change you hope for? What are relational aspects of the people involved that prevent change?

The writing teams developed surveys, questionnaires, and interviews to help them develop a broader and deeper understanding of the issues within their context. The first stage was finished when the writers completed their research, analyzed the data they had collected, and developed profiles of the situation and of the learners. These profiles would then form the basis for the objectives, content, and activities of the courses to be written. In this way, months of discovery work prepared them for the second stage, writing their twenty-first-century transformative TEE course.

Course writer training: Workshop 2 (followed by writing with mentors)

From the start, it was recognized that each writing team would benefit from an experienced mentor who could coach them through the writing process. When the teams gathered for the second workshop, an international team of mentors joined them and became an integral part of the writing process for each team.[20]

At the second workshop, which was nine working days, each team developed learning objectives in the areas of know, be, do, and relate, based on their profiles of the situation and of the students. Presentations on the practical aspects of course writing were followed by writing teams working

20. In addition to the course writer training team, mentors included: Perry Shaw, widely recognized for his work in transforming theological education; Allan Harkness, with important contributions to theological education in Asia and now a consultant with Lea Dev-Langham New Zealand and Overseas Council Australia; David Burke, with much experience in theological education in different continents; and Rosemary Dewerse, who has written and delivered many online and blended theological courses.

on those aspects. Mentors were available to guide the work but most of the interaction was among team members.

Sessions by the mentors included educational priorities, such as the course and lesson objectives, outlines, assessments, questions for discussion and reflection, the group leader guide, writing styles, how students could apply their learning, field testing of the draft course materials, and revision. All sessions were followed by ample time for each team to work on their course. This emphasis on development proved to be one of the best outcomes of the workshop because it provided a space for the writers to focus on their courses and to practice the principles they were learning. Writing teams reported that they were greatly encouraged by being with others who were attempting the same thing. New course writers living in isolated situations were especially encouraged.

The second workshop was followed by a whole year of writing, field testing, and revising. The success of the writing effort was largely a result of the mentors who worked with their teams from afar to encourage, guide, provide feedback, and pray. Programme directors also played a key role in that they participated in the first workshop, approved the budgets, and where possible allowed time for the writers to focus on completing their course.

Course writer training: Workshop 3 (followed by field testing and completion)

The five days that comprised workshop 3 equipped writers to create the group leader guide, to arrange effective field testing of their lessons, and to understand publishing issues like format and images. In the ensuing months, writers persevered with these stages. This took longer than originally expected, but after two years, seven courses were completed in a form that could be used, with two more nearly completed and three more making slower progress. This more than satisfactory output is attributed to the workshop format and the support of co-writers, mentors, and programme directors.[21]

21. Patricia Harrison, who has been involved in TEE course writer training for decades, comments: It's not so much that the ingredients of the Increase Association programme were new in writers' training, but that Increase was able to bring them all together so effectively. It helped a lot that Increase already had an established, committed network of active TEE programmes and was able to resource three workshops plus ongoing mentoring over a wider

Summary of implementation

Using the SRD process for writing courses encourages programme directors and writing teams to complete contextually relevant TEE courses structured on sound educational theory. The SRD framework provides a process for course developers to follow that is accessible and incorporates transformative learning principles, and which has resulted in seven completed transformative TEE courses to date. Some of these have now been translated from their original language into English, a welcome change from the normal flow of translation from English to other languages. Moreover, experienced course writers are now coaches for a second cohort of writers in Russia.

In this section we described the process from the perspective of a course-writing trainer. In the next section, we explain how the writer training programme impacted course writers and their students.

Writing a TEE Discipleship Course for Muslim Background Central Asian Believers [22]

For me (Do), developing a new TEE discipleship course for believers from Muslim backgrounds (BMBs) in Central Asia alongside two mature Central Asian BMB women has been a daunting yet deeply rewarding experience. We have touched the sacred together as we asked, "How can the word of God be deeply understood, truthfully interpreted, effectively and relevantly communicated, and practically applied in the everyday life of Christ followers, here and now, in Central Asia?"

As we developed the course, called "Men and Women of God in the Old Testament," we grappled with learning to ask, analyze, and dig deeper into our own contexts as well as the word of God. We then laboured through an iterative process of writing, testing, and rewriting. During the development process,

---

area of this part of the world. It has been possible to use both local and international mentors, providing all teams with ongoing help. It should be noted that the internet and more affordable international travel have provided huge advantages that earlier training programmes did not enjoy. All this has combined to create an important breakthrough in course writers' training for this part of the world.

22. Inspiration and some of the content of this section comes out of a presentation given at a When Women Speak (WWS) conference held August 2018 in Melbourne, Australia. For more information about WWS see: https://whenwomenspeak.net/.

BMB men and women of Central Asia told their stories first-hand, echoing the voices of men and women of God in the Old Testament.

Central Asia and TEE

Following the collapse of the Soviet Union in 1991, new independent Central Asian republics were formed. From virtually no believers at that time, thousands of Central Asian Muslim background people came to Christ in the following decade. Today, the Central Asian church continues to grow and there is a great need for accessible and relevant discipleship tools to nurture the first generation church.

The TEE work in Kazakhstan and Kyrgyzstan began in the mid-1990s with limited success. It was not until the mid-2000s that the work became more established and included the training of local facilitators. In 2006, the Kyrgyz national team was formed, followed by Kazakhstan in 2012. In 2017, as a joint project of these two Central Asian TEE national teams, my two co-writers, Juldiz and Nuria,[23] and I began writing a new course.

Our shared vision was to create a new TEE course born in the soil of Central Asia, addressing relevant and specific issues that BMBs face in the light of God's transforming Word. Our aim was to design a group study-based TEE course to fill gaps that were not covered by existing courses.

Course-writing steps

1. Training

Since early 2017, as new course writers, we received training and mentoring by experienced course writers and educators through participation in the three "New TEE Course Writers Training" workshops organized by Increase. The workshops provided useful guidelines for researching the context, doing field interviews, developing course objectives, and writing lessons, and also included a tutor guide for group discussions and conducting field testing.

23. All names changed to preserve anonymity.

2. Preparing for the research

Along with other team members from both the Kazakh and Kyrgyz TEE national teams, we took part in the first course writer workshop in March 2017. With the help of our colleagues, we brainstormed the general context and the state of believers in Central Asia. Conflicts, fears, pressures, selfishness, family issues including high divorce rates, nationalism, Islamization, and ethnic tension in the region were among the issues noted. Through this process, a general profile of the Central Asian situation was created.

Then we focused on the current situation of Christians in Central Asia and began to build up a learner profile. This focused on the BMBs in Central Asia as our target learners, covering areas of difficulty they face, emotions they feel, and their educational and family backgrounds. After that we developed a plan for field interviews. Together we drafted interview questions and prepared a list of interviewees from among our contacts.

3. Field interviews

In the months following the first workshop, we conducted field interviews with thirty-five BMBs aged in their mid-20s to mid-60s. Interviewees varied in gender, marital status, education level, and vocational background. We interviewed people we knew from our own local faith community, including our own TEE national team members. Some interviews happened after Sunday services and others after TEE group meetings. A number of conversations also took place at an unrelated event attended by young and mature women leaders. The purpose of the interview was first explained to the participants. We assured interviewees that their personal information and what they shared would be sensitively handled and kept confidential. Interviewees were asked to share their faith journeys as believers in Jesus.

The following questions were used as prompts: How did you come to God?; What were the reasons for repentance?; What difficulties of life and inner life did you face before your conversion?; How did your family members, friends, and community react to your conversion?; What barriers and difficulties have you faced that prevents your faith in Jesus from growing stronger?; What helped you to grow?; What challenges do you have in sharing the gospel with others?

Through this process we heard the faith journey stories of our brothers and sisters. They told of God's work in and through their lives, and of their heart-breaking challenges, struggles, and difficulties. The interviews were recorded as audio files or in written notes. Their voices speak clearly in these quotations from some of the different people who were interviewed.

> I was searching for the meaning of life and true love. When I came to Jesus, I found what I had desperately been looking for!
>
> When I became a believer, I was rejected by my classmates and friends. People from my village came to my parents to ask me to leave the village because their son had sold his religion.
>
> Of course, it is hard to hear their strong words against you. But the truth keeps us going and prevents us being swayed by others.

4. Analyzing the interview data

During the second workshop held in June 2017 we listened to recordings and read written reports of interviews. Together, we arranged the stories thematically. We identified themes in repeated and unique stories or information shared in the interviews. Through this process, the following themes were identified – identity, fear, shame and honour, suffering and persecution, worshipping other gods, magic and curses, offence, conflict, faith and obedience, God's love, wisdom, forgiveness, and repentance. These themes then shaped the course outline.

5. Crafting the course objectives and outline

The process to put together course objectives and draft the course outline was demanding; however, it helped us to sharpen our thoughts and direction. The overall purpose of the course was clarified as being "to strengthen the new believers from a Muslim background from Central Asia in their faith walk in Christ."

After that, we applied the four main learning outcomes of "know, do, be, and relate" (discussed earlier in this chapter) in order to clarify general objectives for the course (see Figure 7.4) based on the themes identified through the field research.

<table>
<tr><td colspan="2">TOPIC: Heroes and heroines of Old Testament (Men and women of God in the Old Testament)
MAIN PURPOSE: To strengthen the new BMBs from Central Asia in their faith walk in Christ.
Through life examples of OT heroes and heroines, learners will:</td></tr>
<tr><td>KNOW
• Understand who God is as creator and our Father.
• Strengthen their identity as honoured members of God's family.
• Have a strong/confident sense of belonging as covenant descendants of Abraham.
• Know how to respond to the traditional and cultural obstacles/barriers/difficulties that prevent growth in faith.</td><td>BE
• Confident in their own identity in Christ.
• Strengthened and deepened faith in God.
• Courageous to share the good news.
• Overcome feelings of fear and shame and feel valued, honoured, and loved.</td></tr>
<tr><td>DO
• Worship and obey only him by turning away from old practices of worshipping other gods; ancestor worship, visiting of folk healers, fortune tellers.
• Stand strong in the midst of persecution and pressure.
• Live righteous lives worthy of the calling as chosen people of God.</td><td>RELATE
• Be committed to meet with other believers.
• Relate with love and compassion to non-believing members of family and community.</td></tr>
</table>

Figure 7.4. Original draft of course objectives

Next, the themes were matched with Old Testament characters. For example, "fear/courage" was matched with Gideon and David; "identity" with Moses, Daniel, and Ruth. In addition, we discussed and compared Old Testament characters who are familiar to Muslims such as Adam and Eve, Noah, Abraham and Sarah, Hagar, Solomon, Job, Elijah, and Daniel. We then sequenced these Old Testament characters chronologically as a course skeleton. In the following months of working together, with input from our mentor, we continued to discuss and amend the list. The objectives and outline were considered a "work in progress," a guiding framework as the writing advanced.

6. Writing lessons

The following is a specific example of how the lesson on Gideon was developed. This was the first lesson we three wrote together.

When it came to the point of writing, after the analysis and the initial mapping of draft course objectives and outline, we were all feeling anxious and unsure, afraid and lost. Where would we start? Which issue should we choose? And which character? We also felt under pressure because we were progressing more slowly than our course-writing peers. We were unsure how to make decisions and work together as a multicultural writing team. We speak different languages (I speak English, fairly fluent Kazakh, and intermediate Russian; Nuria speaks fluent English, Kyrgyz, and Russian; Juldiz speaks Kyrgyz and Russian). It was agreed the course would be written in Kazakh, Kyrgyz, Russian, and English as the main languages. After many trials, we established a pattern of translation in the writing process. For example, in the Gideon lesson, Juldiz wrote her first draft in Kyrgyz. Then it was translated into Russian and English for feedback from the co-writers and a mentor. Any feedback was incorporated into the second draft if relevant.

Juldiz and Nuria are from the same country and work together in the same team, while I am an expatriate cross-cultural worker. We had previously met one another at occasional meetings and events and had some level of mutual respect and trust to begin with. However, we still felt as if we had been thrown in the deep end to grow together as a team. We had to not only learn how to write a lesson together but also to find ways to operate, communicate, relate to, and understand each other.

We benefitted from having an experienced team mentor who was also an experienced TEE course writer as well as having first-hand experience of Muslim people and contexts. He understood our team dynamics and suggested that we should start our course writing with the issue of "fear." This was a good suggestion as fear was one of our shared emotions at the time. In fact, our mentor suggested Judges 6:23 as a memory verse for the lesson, "But the LORD said to him, 'Peace! Do not be afraid. You are not going to die.'" When we read it together, we all laughed and even became teary. We recognized how much this verse spoke to our own feelings and situation in the writing process. This whole experience cemented us together as a team. We all memorized the verse and constantly reminded one another: "Peace! Do not be afraid. You are not going to die."

We reviewed the research findings on fear, looking for examples of fears, causes of fear, and interviewees' responses to fear. We also asked ourselves the same questions and shared our own experiences.

Then we moved our focus onto what the Bible says about fear. We considered which biblical characters' experience could speak to this theme. We agreed that Gideon's story might be a good match. We prayed earnestly together and started studying Judges chapters 6, 7, and 8. At first, we read and studied individually. Then we came together to share what we had found. We studied who Gideon was, his context and issues, and how God dealt with him and his people. We really enjoyed this part of the process of studying the text together. We recognized that many good and useful lessons could be drawn from Gideon's story but quickly realized that we could not possibly cover them all. We had to select which passages and parts of the passage to focus on. Looking at Gideon's story through the lens of fear, the following points stood out to us: opinions of others, worshipping other gods, and Gideon's own understanding of who he was – his identity. It was exciting to gain new insights on this ancient text through contemplating it from the perspective of Central Asian believers.

As a result of this process, we agreed together on the objectives for a lesson on Gideon (Figure 7.5).

Aims of Lesson

By the end of this lesson each learner will:

- understand steps to overcome fears by believing and putting into practice God's words of truth.
- be assured of who God says he/she is and be strengthened by the community of Isa's followers.
- be committed to worship and serve only God and get rid of any false gods.
- memorize Judges 6:23.

Figure 7.5. Objectives for TEE lesson on Gideon

We divided the lesson into sections for each of us to develop. Then we came together to make it more coherent. We suggested different wording, examples, types of questions, and suitable real-life stories to be used for the teaching points and to enhance learners' reflection and application. At the start of the lesson, we drew our learners' attention to the real issues of their own context, using examples drawn from the interviews. Then we invited them to look at their own life situation and experiences,[24] as the following excerpt from the lesson illustrates (Figure 7.6).

We have learned in our previous Lessons that we are God's chosen people and God Most High is our father. He promised that He will be with us and never forsake us. Yet we often find ourselves fearful of many things in our daily life.

Anar: "None of my family members know that I have decided to follow Isa. If they find out, it will bring such shame on them and they may even want to kill me. For sure my friends will leave me. It's better to keep it as secret."

Nurlan: "When I pray, I pray to God the Almighty in Isa's name. But I also call out to the spirit of Manas and the spirits of my ancestors so that I may not offend nor upset them."

1. Which of the following do you think Anar and Nurlan are afraid of? (Tick more than one)

   a. Rejection
   b. Power of other spirits
   c. Shame
   d. Opinions of others
   e. Death
   f. Curse

2. In your own life, have you experienced these feelings? Have you had any similar experiences? Be prepared to share in the group discussion.

Figure 7.6. Draft introduction for Gideon lesson

Question 2 is further explored in the group leader's guide as part of the group discussion time when people share their experiences. Wherever possible, we used reflective questions with real-life examples that the learners could relate to. Learners are encouraged to reflect and act on each teaching point from the biblical text, as the following excerpt from the lesson demonstrates (Figure 7.7):

24. For a discussion on how TEE course design can intentionally incorporate such reflection into the self-study materials and leader guides, see chapter 6: Glissmann and Green, "The Educational Efficacy of TEE – Part 2."

10. This is a real story of Kanishai who became a follower of Isa. This is a good example of how false gods influence people.

> When I was 2 years old, my mum passed away. I grew up with my mum's sister's (auntie) family. When I was a child I was very sick, they took me to chief molda. They said that they would train me to become a folk healer and fortune teller (козу ачык). Since I was a child, I healed children who were sick (using bread, salt, a knife or feather). People came to me and I told their fortune. At night, I was visited by a ghost and was choked by it and I heard its voice. The ghost commanded me to say things to certain people and I had to obey it. I didn't want to go and tell them because it was always about the death of a person. But the ghost forced me to do it. Otherwise I was tormented by it. Once it came to me and told me about my sister's husband and I didn't tell him. But it turned out my brother-in-law died after one month, just like I was told by the ghost. And then I felt guilty more than before. And I was captured by a great fear. When I got married, even my husband was afraid of me, because he thought I could kill him if I wanted to. There was no peace in my family life. Because my mum passed away of cancer at a young age, I also had fear of dying young.

What kind of feelings did you observe from Kanishai? ______________________________

> Kanishai said: 'I heard about Isa Masih and the Good news that he could set me free from false gods and evil spirits. I realized that only he could help me, and I accepted him into my heart. I was set free from the feelings of guilt and from the evil spirits that used to control me and from my fear of death. Isa brought peace into my family. And my husband also became a believer.'

11. Until we turn away from worshiping false gods, we cannot overcome our fears and difficulties. We cannot see victory in our spiritual life until we tear down the altars of false gods in our hearts. We can learn from Gideon's example. Are you ready to obey God's commands, get rid of false gods and worship only Him? If so, how? ____

Figure 7.7. Reflection and Action example

7. Writing the group leader's guide

Once the whole lesson was drafted, we worked on the group leader's guide. This aspect of course design was covered during the third writers' workshop in June 2018. In order to achieve lesson objectives as well as the overall course aims, we tried to include various learning activities that would aid further learning in a group context. Group sharing of individual learners' reflections from the personal study was one of the key elements included. Where possible, group activities such as role plays, drawing, and completing a problem tree were also used to help consolidate learning and expand application. These activities were tested, modified, and adjusted through feedback from the field testing.

8. Field testing the lessons

Once lessons were written and internally reviewed between the three of us and our mentor, we gathered different groups to field test the material. Primarily, we gathered Central Asian BMBs for the purpose. Some were new to TEE courses and others were trained TEE group leaders. Sometimes, we had a group from a local BMB fellowship that had not used TEE materials before. The size of the groups varied in number anywhere between three and ten people. We prepared printed copies of lessons in the relevant language for each group. When possible, participants completed the personal study component at home prior to the group meeting. At other times, participants were given time to study the material before the group discussion.

The group discussion was facilitated by a trained group leader. The aim was to see if the group leader guide was self-explanatory and clear to follow. If a trained group leader was not available, one of the writers facilitated the discussion. At the end of the session, we asked prepared questions to gather the group's feedback. Questions focused on gauging the appropriateness of the level, relevance and clarity of the content, examples and illustrations used, and length of the lessons.

When doing the field testing, we writers were encouraged as various lessons came alive during the group discussion. Group members shared rich personal stories of their past and current experience and made relevant applications in the light of teaching points from their personal study. These were the sacred moments when the voices of men and women of Central Asia echoed the voices of men and women of biblical times. On occasions, real and raw pain resulted in shared tears. Yet tears of gratitude and celebration also welled up. We all felt the beauty and courage of God's people here and now, and how God has been faithful and real to us. Here are representative comments from two participants about the lessons on Abraham and Ruth:

> Well done! This lesson on Abraham really helps us (Central Asian BMBs) see where we fit in the plan of our creator God! We are chosen and blessed through Jesus to be a blessing to nations.
>
> It was not easy to be shamed and disowned by my own family. Just like the story of Bakhitgul and Ruth in the lesson, I literally

> lost my entire life support, status and security . . . (tears) . . . Yet, Isa lifted me up, as I followed him, as you know.

We made notes about the activities and questions we used to achieve each intended learning outcome. Any comments and suggestions about uncertain or ambiguous points, activities, and questions were also noted. The collected feedback from field testing was then shared among the three writers before revising the draft lesson. In this way, the cycle of writing, testing, revising, and editing, then writing again was repeated.

Due to each of us living great distances from one another, we established a pattern of periodic intensive writing weeks together. At the time of writing, we have come together six times for writing, studying, and field testing. We still have much to do in order to complete the course, but we are much more confident now, compared to when we first started this journey.

Reflections on course writing

At first, the three of us wondered, "How are we to write a course? If we write, will anyone take us seriously? Will it be accepted and used at all?" Generally, women have only a limited voice in Central Asian society. As one of my co-writers commented, "We (women) are not allowed to speak, ask or give opinions. But we began to speak and have our voices when we became followers of Jesus."

Certainly, we, as three women writers, have been struck by how God has nurtured and transformed us through this collaborative process. We are encouraged by the fact that over half of the new course writers in the Increase writers training programme are also women. We have been empowered by the training we have received and supported by both brothers and sisters from our TEE national teams and families. We have dug deeper into God's word and seen his Spirit open our eyes, ears, and minds, speaking first to us individually and collectively, then to our brothers and sisters in Central Asia. We have grown in our relationships as sisters in Christ beyond our backgrounds and differences. Together we observed how God has knit us together to love and nurture each other. Sharing our lives together is one of the greatest fruits. And the new course will be a by-product of this transforming fellowship.

Conclusion

This chapter has shown how TEE educational theory, as explained in chapters 5 and 6, has been made practical in an innovative training programme to equip new course writers in Asia. Increase pioneered an integrated process with three workshops and ongoing support by mentors leading to a high completion rate of courses written. Participants were empowered to create transformative courses by a hands-on process in which they learned educational principles by actively applying them. They researched local needs in their own contexts and wrote in local languages. The writing process exemplified partnership between women and men, Asians and Westerners, the Increase Association and national TEE organizations. The training initiative is presently[25] being adapted as a series of modules that will be available for download through the Increase website.

The development and writing of a new TEE course for use in Central Asia that was described in this chapter is part of the drive by Increase to develop new "Tools to Equip and Empower" and is typical of the innovation and change that is part of the ethos of contemporary global TEE.

Bibliography

Aylett, Graham, ed. *Exploring New Horizons: Working Together for Church-Based Training in Asia.* Increase Association. Proceedings of a conference held in Kuala Lumpur, Malaysia, 20–25 April, 2015.

Das, Rupen. *Connecting Curriculum with Context: A Handbook for Context Relevant Curriculum Development in Theological Education.* Carlisle: Langham, 2015.

Flores, Philip, Paul Cornelius, Terrick Barratt, and Graham Aylett. "Exploring New Horizons: Training for Transformation." In *Exploring New Horizons: Working Together for Church-Based Training in Asia*, edited by Graham Aylett, 21–31. Proceedings of a conference held in Kuala Lumpur, Malaysia, by Increase Association, 20–25 April, 2015.

Gatimu, Kiranga, Juliet Gachegoh, Karen Oyiengo, Lucy Kithome, and Bernard Suwa. *Manual for Writers and Designers of TEE Study Materials.* Nairobi: Uzima Press, 1997.

Harms, Hartwig F. *Writing for T.E.E.: A Handbook for Training Authors.* Unpublished work, 2003.

25. At the time of writing, in 2020.

Horton, William. *E-Learning by Design*. 2nd ed. San Francisco: Pfeiffer, 2012.

Increase Association. "Course Writers in Asia." 2018. https://www.increaseassociation.org/about/news-events/98-course-writers-in-asia.

Ivins, Nicholas. "Situational Response Development." *WITH International Community Blog* 2017. https://withcommunity.org/situational-response-development/.

Jusu, John. "More Than a Mile Deep: Education Strategy and Processes." 2020. Forthcoming publication at https://withcommunity.org/resources/.

Mabuluki, Kangwa. "Diversified Theological Education: Genesis, Development and Ecumenical Potential of Theological Education by Extension (TEE)." In *Handbook of Theological Education in World Christianity*, edited by Dietrich Werner, David Esterline, Namsoon Kang and Joshva Raja, 251–62. Oxford: Regnum, 2010.

SEAN International. "Mongolia." SPREAD Newsletter, March 2010. https://www.seaninternational.org/newsletter-archive.

Sendegeya, Fareth, and Leon Spencer, eds. *Understanding TEE: A Course Outline and Handbook for Students and Tutors in Residential Theological Institutions in Africa*. Dar es Salaam: ANITEPAM, 2001.

8

TEE and Transformation in the Digital Age

Rick Weymouth

Introduction

The TEE movement has so many strengths to build upon for the future . . . but significant change is coming. I believe that the future of transformative TEE is online.[1] In this chapter I explore the opportunities that online learning offers TEE and key principles for effective online course delivery. It considers how to preserve TEE's crucial partnership with the local church and the benefits of blended (online and face-to-face) learning, while also addressing potential challenges, including the future of TEE group discourse. Encouragement is offered to TEE and theological educators to embrace the future presented.

Why Online?

Why must the movement embrace online learning[2] and digital technologies? Global higher education trends are rapidly evolving, with mobile learning

1. The term "online" here refers to the use of digital technologies and media, and the systems that connect switched-on digital devices and their users, which include (but are not limited to) the internet and mobile (phone) networks; "online" thus embraces both internet- and *non*-internet-based possibilities.

2. This author prefers the phrase "online learning" as an all-embracing term incorporating various forms of intentional learning using online media and digital technologies (cf. footnote above). It thus includes both e-Learning (electronic learning enabled or supported via internet delivery using desktop computers and laptops) and m-Learning (tools and content delivered via

(m-Learning) advancing far beyond the realms of the e-Learning seen in the first digital revolution of the early 2000s, creating a narrowing of the digital divide in which countries are now leapfrogging straight from face-to-face (F2F) learning to m-Learning. However, TEE programmes, for the most part, have not yet embraced even the first learning revolution. Younger adult learners in the countries served by TEE programmes will expect this situation to change as they increasingly seek accessible, flexible learning using the digital tools they hold in their hands every day.[3] Education reformer John Dewey is attributed as having said, a century ago, "If we teach today's students as we taught yesterday's, we rob them of tomorrow."[4] Without twenty-first century learning, theological education faces irrelevancy in this changing landscape.

Online education offers the incredible potentiality of multiple digital technologies to assist in delivering more effective, more engaging, and more enjoyable transformative learning for TEE students. At the same time, increased access and expanded reach will result, including serving and connecting diaspora communities more effectively. Online is not part of our future; it *is* our future.

Responding to the Digital World and Learners of the Twenty-First Century

For many, the COVID-19-shaped world of 2020 forced F2F educators, including TEE group facilitators, to engage in emergency remote learning video conferencing for the first time. Understandably, video meeting platforms created genuine excitement about the possibilities of online learning among

---

mobile or smart phones and handheld electronic devices, such as tablets). Alternatives, such as "digital learning" or "technology-enhanced learning" (TEL), are often used interchangeably but have their limitations ("digital" appropriately links with *technology*, yet in relation to *learning* connotes a focus on data delivery) and critics (Bayne, "What's the Matter").

3. At risk of appearing to detract from the emphasis upon *online* learning, it is noted that many everyday devices and apps are capable of functioning "off-line" (i.e. without internet or cell-network access). In this chapter "online" embraces such functionality, for which switched-*on* devices are still necessary; cf. fn. 1 above.

4. Alleged sources for this quotation were examined closely, but the quote could not be corroborated as Dewey's.

both educators and students. While this raises pedagogical issues,[5] this excitement is worth building upon.

Responding to the digital world requires grappling with new terminology: Edu–tech or EdTech (educational technology) terms are commonly used for educational delivery platforms, instructional design models, learning delivery modes, discourse modes, and for learners themselves.[6]

Another critical need then is to understand the generations of younger adult learners who are now or soon will become our students in the coming years.[7] Who are they? What are their educational needs and learning preferences? A majority of younger adult learners today are Millennials or Gen Ys,[8] while the first batches of Post-Millennial (Gen Z) Christians are beginning to enter theological education programmes.[9] These generations of believers grow up with technology integrated into their lives.

The very different and changing educational needs and preferences, and learning styles, of Gen Y and Gen Z learners clearly need to be well understood before tailoring programmes of learning to them. For example, Gen Z learners presently use their smart mobile devices almost exclusively for social media connections and networking, and for viewing videos.[10] They rarely read books or emails and will often turn to online peers and social media forums for advice and knowledge.[11] Videos are preferred sources of information over and above online (static) written sources.[12] While many educational implications arise,

5. Unfortunately, emergency remote learning has not always been implemented with appropriate pedagogical intentionality or design.

6. For a helpful list with definitions, see the "Education Technology Dictionary" (https://edshelf.com/education-technology-dictionary).

7. Widely accepted generational definitions are provided by the Pew Research Center; see Dimock, "Defining Generations." A growing literature of generational research is developing; for an overview, see McCrindle, *ABC of XYZ*. However, care is needed since significant variations will naturally exist from country to country, culture to culture, and according to social and economic factors.

8. Gen Y adults are aged between 25 and 40 years in 2021; see McCrindle, "Understanding Generation Y."

9. In 2021, Gen Z will be aged between 9 and 24 years; see McCrindle and Fell, "Understanding Generation Z."

10. Cf. McCrindle and Fell, 10–12.

11. McCrindle, *ABC of XYZ*, 75.

12. Apparently on average over 3.5 billion Google searches are made per day worldwide (https://www.internetlivestats.com/google-search-statistics/, accessed 5 September 2020), yet nearly 5.0

let us mention one to illustrate the path ahead. TEE course delivery that will engage and appeal to Gen Z learners must therefore incorporate frequent, short (3–5 minute) videos, which enhance the learning process.

And one short decade from now, the first of those known as the Alpha Generation will reach adulthood.[13] Alpha Gen learners will become the largest, most educated, and most globally connected generation ever.[14] They will expect almost all cognitive learning to be offered virtually or online. Will we be ready to serve them?

TEE will only remain relevant to such learners if we begin now to embrace the everyday information and communication technologies of their world.

Finally, to do that, we need to respond to the pedagogical challenges of the digital age. A first challenge, then, is to understand the medium and tools of digital learning delivery pedagogically. A second challenge is that within the TEE movement there are very real concerns about the adoption of digital technology and how it might compromise the proven methodologies of historic TEE.[15]

TEE's Head Start into Online Learning

It is worth mentioning that the TEE movement already has a good head start into the online learning journey. There are four clear advantages. First, the provision of instructional materials already very well designed for student self-study (although they will need adaptation for online media delivery – the instructional design gap between print-media TEE course books and online versions is relatively small). Second, learner and facilitator (tutor) roles are very

billion YouTube videos are watched every day, more than half of them on mobile devices, and in the last two years, the annual growth rate in hours of YouTube videos watched per day has been 60 percent (MerchDope, "YouTube Statistics 2020," https://merchdope.com/youtube-stats/, 26 February 2020).

13. In 2021 the Alpha Gen are all those up to 8 years of age; on this generation, see McCrindle and Fell, "Understanding Generation Alpha"; McCrindle Research, "Generation Alpha Explained" (2020).

14. McCrindle and Fell, "Understanding Generation Alpha," 7, 12.

15. As described elsewhere in this book (See: "TEE at a Glance"), the traditional three-fold formulation of TEE has been (i) self-study materials, (ii) group discussion or local learning groups, and (iii) practical application or ministry.

similar in traditional TEE course delivery and online course delivery. Third, part-time education, situating TEE learners in their local contexts, often makes for more effective transformative, holistic formation.[16] A fourth advantage is TEE's holistic educational model and rootedness in local churches, for it is through partnership with local churches that much intentional discipleship, spiritual formation, and ministry training needs to take place alongside online course delivery.

The Potentiality of Online for the TEE Movement

Online learning offers many enhancements and opportunities, especially in relation to content delivery, with new creative pedagogical possibilities for course writers and designers. Mary Hess describes the potential for "providing a richer, more multiply intelligent environment within which to learn."[17] Multimedia possibilities are endless, including static, dynamic, and interactive images, video, and sound. Static media may include full colour photos, charts, maps, diagrams, infographics and PDFs; dynamic media could be animations, short films and video clips, audio clips, or slide presentations.

Yet other learning enhancements also arise as the following examples demonstrate:

- student construction of their own learning experiences,[18] as access to learning resources potentially increases exponentially
- the ability to accommodate a variety of learning styles
- e-tivities (from e-activities)[19] for enabling active, participative, and collaborative online learning for individuals and groups

16. Cf., for example, the study of Nichols, "Comparison," 198–99.

17. Hess, "What Difference?," 83. It is worth noting that such creative pedagogies will usually stretch the abilities and skills of most face-to-face educators, and that the input of experienced online instructional designers is usually necessary for online course development.

18. This potentiality offers a confronting challenge to the TEE movement whose learning resources are generally predetermined by course writers, allowing little opportunity for students to discover new learning resources for themselves or to create their own learning experiences. With careful design and implementation, online learning can and should be used to help students in TEE programmes become *self-directed*, lifelong learners.

19. The term has been popularized by Gilly Salmon, "E-tivities – Introduction"; see especially her *E-tivities: The Key*.

- enhanced participation through online synchronous and asynchronous group discussion forums
- realistic and complex case studies for scenario- or story-based learning
- participation of international experts in online classes
- secure digital delivery of course information and readings
- instant student access to the latest version of a course.

Understanding the Online Medium and Tools for Content Delivery

If we are preparing to engage the newer generations of learners and have begun to understand their educational needs, the next most important thing is to appreciate their preferred means of receiving information and learning. Yet online technology is not only ubiquitous but also very diverse. It is crucial that we gain a deep understanding of both the online medium or environment and the various tools available for content delivery, and their suitability and applicability, first for the different groups of learners we are attempting to reach, and second to the holistic learning programme we are offering. We begin with some critical principles.

Critical principles for effective online learning

The three most important principles for successful online learning (within TEE) are the following:

1. Pedagogy comes before technology.
2. Pedagogy comes before technology.
3. Constantly remind yourself of principles 1 and 2.

In other words, *how* you use the technology for effective pedagogical purposes is more important than *what* technology you use. One of the ways we intentionally remind ourselves of this is always to write e-Learning or m-Learning with a lower case "e" or "m" and a capital "L." Effective student learning is the ultimate aim, not the precise methodology or tools employed.

The next important principle is fundamental as TEE moves online:

4. Transformative online learning requires an intentional commitment to holistic pedagogy.

We will further develop this key principle below. For any theological education, we should look at online learning as enhancing what we already do, rather than replacing it. Online learning is not always better, yet it can offer many enhancements, which will indeed lift the effectiveness of TEE to new heights.

With that in mind, the next principle may initially cause unease for some TEE practitioners:

5. Flexibility and adaptability is essential in applying TEE methodologies.

Some aspects, even of TEE's core methodological elements, as explained in earlier parts of this book,[20] need to be adapted for various types of online delivery and learning. And instructional design in TEE course writing will certainly need rethinking, while at the same time protecting what is important to the TEE movement. However, here, the first four principles guide and frame the implementation of our fifth principle. Our pedagogical needs and goals are the starting place, and the new tools we use to deliver online learning must support those pedagogical objectives.

This is the reason, for example, why one should not start with a Learning Management System (or LMS) for e-Learning, or a mobile platform or app(lication) for m-Learning, and then merely display one's content using those tools. From a management point of view, they may be starting places; however, exposing students to content on a new delivery tool does not mean learning is going to happen.[21] We need to *understand* how various new tools and platforms can be used to enable learning, *identify* which tools need to be selected and which will best and most appropriately serve the culture of the learners, *determine* the most effective ways these tools will help facilitate learning, *ensure* that the whole online learning approach is built upon biblical principles, and then *re-design* the presentation and delivery of content, reflection, discussion, and application accordingly. The plural "tools" is deliberate, for no one tool will meet all our needs. Furthermore, our several chosen tools will need integration and connection for effective online delivery of TEE courses.

20. See "TEE at a Glance" on pp11-15 of this book. TEE methodology is further illustrated in the appendices.

21. See Siemens, "Learning Management Systems."

e-Learning

The possibilities offered by multimedia-rich online learning are so significant that e-Learning appears to younger adult learners as vastly more preferable and attractive than print-media, and easily has the potential to surpass the learning value of print-media courses. How well the e-Learning is done, of course, is crucial. Greater variety in the presentation of content, greater use of multimedia tools, higher degrees of student interactivity and participation, and excellent online facilitation will be needed.

e-Learning courses are usually designed to be provided on an LMS or an equivalent, and delivered to students via their computers (PCs) and laptops. Ideally, though, the LMS should be mobile responsive.[22] Running an LMS can be costly and usually requires internal or out-sourced technical administration. Less costly, less technical options are also worth considering. As mentioned above, TEE institutions should consider the possibility of using multiple edu-tech tools to serve their educational and pedagogical needs, integrating them wherever possible.

An LMS is especially appropriate for bachelor and master's level courses, since it offers superb features and functionality for the academic needs of those degree levels, including the provision for extended reading of texts and the writing and submission of lengthier assignments and forum postings, for which larger screens are preferable and mobile phones are less ideal. An LMS can also be used with certificate and diploma level courses, but with care, as its complexity could be overwhelming for some users. More mobile friendly educational apps are recommended for lower academic levels and for m-Learning rather than e-Learning.

A key need is the utilization of instructional design appropriate for the e-Learning platform used. Print-media, self-instructional materials will still need to be adapted for online delivery via an LMS. Understanding the delivery medium, with great pedagogical care and insight into how learners will use the online tools, is necessary here.

---

22. "Mobile responsive" refers to e-Learning instructional design primarily intended for course delivery via computers and laptops yet designed to allow for mobile device access and display as well.

Depending on the learning elements being redesigned, different tools will require different adaptions. For TEE content creators, for example, the online medium requires rethinking the learning connections between mind/brain and hand/pen (for expected written responses to questions in printed workbooks) to mind-to-digital-text answers. For online learners, especially younger ones, there will be a temptation not to type answers (which reinforce learning connections in the brain), but rather merely to copy and paste the answer. Such learners are likely to find the repetitiveness of programmed learning texts boring, exacerbating their use of short-cuts, despite the pedagogical intentionality behind the original written texts, and the reduced brain-learning taking place online. Programmed learning texts, therefore, need to be rethought and redesigned for online delivery.

m-Learning and microlearning

m-Learning offers similar potential for enhancing learning through multimedia additions as for e-Learning,[23] though arguably with greater possible accessibility, since many if not most adults in our world possess mobile devices (especially smart phones), even if they do not have computers or laptops. m-Learning may be regarded as a second revolution in online learning (following e-Learning as a first and continuing one),[24] though other technologies are also looming on the educational horizon. Yet, as for e-Learning, pedagogical instructional design for delivery of course materials via mobile devices must understand the medium, the technology, and the way in which learners typically interact with their mobile devices.

A crucial difference, of course, is the screen size. This presents an immediate limitation and disadvantage for those wanting to engage in m-Learning for bachelor and higher levels of study. While external keyboards can be electronically connected to the mobile devices for typing purposes, the smaller devices are generally less suitable for extended reading and writing, and for the

23. On the differences between e-Learning and m-Learning, see SH!FT Disruptive Learning, "Understanding the Difference"; Chan, "mLearning"; Clothier, "Right Time"; Brown, "Role of m-Learning"; see also Behera, "E- and M-learning"; and Basak, Wotto, and Belanger, "E-learning, M-learning."

24. M-Learning is not, however, replacing e-Learning; both will have continued relevancy for many years to come, though each with many new technological developments expected.

critical engagements required for more academic study. Small text size may also create difficulties for some. Mobile devices should be considered for those higher academic levels, but probably mainly as supplemental or complementary tools to computers and laptops, including specific tasks, such as class messaging and reporting back via audio, video, or digital photograph.[25]

On the other hand, for discipleship, certificate and diploma levels of study, mobile devices may prove to be ideal learning tools. Yet, their courses must be designed for delivery on mobile devices.

An important difference exists between "mobile responsive" instructional design and "mobile first" design.[26] The former tends to be courses that are designed for larger screens, but which still work on mobile devices. For example, most modern LMS now have mobile apps that (mostly) allow their content to be displayed well on smaller devices. To take m-Learning seriously, one should explore mobile first instructional design.[27] This means completely re-thinking the instructional design and presentation of content and other learning elements and activities, and designing learning specifically to be delivered on a mobile device, with all the limitations and potentiality of such devices.[28] It also means responding to the ways in which mobile device users typically interact with their devices.

This is where microlearning is important.[29] Microlearning acknowledges the reality that most mobile users concentrate for learning purposes (of any

---

25. Even so, younger adult learners will surprise by choosing to tackle e-Learning courses on their mobile devices, including extended readings.

26. In contrast to "mobile responsive" (see fn. 22 above), "mobile first" refers to m-Learning instructional design, intended primarily for delivery via mobile devices, but which can also be made accessible for computer and laptop users. On mobile first instructional design, in relation to mobile responsive/adaptive/friendly design, see Pandey, "Mobile First Designs"; Bourne, "2.6 Billion Reasons"; So-Young Kang, "Digital Christianity" and "Upskilling Billions."

27. An excellent commercial mobile app, specifically designed for m-Learning and mobile first instructional design (but also web-responsive for computer access) is Gnowbe (https://www.gnowbe.com/; for demonstrations, see: https://www.youtube.com/watch?v=B1Dld7nI35g, and https://www.youtube.com/watch?v=JL55Xl-G72w).

28. For a video overview of some of the possibilities, see EIDesign, "10 Ways" and "15 Types."

29. "Microlearning" is m-Learning where the instructional design breaks learning units down into 3–15 minute "chunks" of varied but integrated learning activities (a "chunk," in this usage, is a small, manageable unit or section of shareable information; many such chunks make a whole) with this timeframe representing the typical usage or concentration span limits of mobile phone users. For initial *reading*, see LeClair, "Technologies with Potential"; and his "Mobile Microlearning" interview; Pandey, "10 Ways" and "Why Adopt Microlearning"; and for initial

kind) for periods ranging between three to fifteen minutes. And usually fifteen minutes is the maximum time spent on one learning unit; less may be better in some cases. Good m-Learning pedagogy, then, will break up course delivery into small, bite-size "learning chunks" of up to a maximum of fifteen minutes of several connected learning activities, which convey a maximum of one learning concept per "chunk."

If a TEE course requires an average, say, of four hours of learning activity per week, that will mean a minimum of sixteen "learning chunks" (microlearning) to present that week's lessons and perhaps more. A typical certificate-level TEE print-media course may have two or three lessons per week. These two or three lessons need to be redesigned into many more learning "chunks" for m-Learning. Although a TEE course needs to be creatively adapted for e-Learning, it needs to be completely reimagined for m-Learning.

Online oral-literacy learning

Online learning offers tremendous potential for the TEE movement (and others) to serve oral-literacy learners[30] better through visual media and audio-video communication tools. Most internet browsers and operating systems today support text-to-speech (TTS) apps (including handwriting recognition) and speech-to-text (STT) apps, with voice/speech recognition software. Optical character recognition (OCR) software can also recognize "inaccessible text" in pictures and locked PDFs, which can then be read with TTS software. Video and audio presentations and posts can be made by both facilitators and learners. Visual media allows for video case studies and animated stories, and game-based learning, and role-playing software allows for learning experiences to be created within online virtual worlds (such as Second Life). There are also, as one would expect, many online phonics-based tools to teach literacy and ICT skills. Audio books are growing in availability, while online dictionaries

viewing on microlearning, watch the Gnowbe demonstration videos (see fn. 27); Kang, "5 Biggest Misconceptions"; and ElDesign, "15 Types."

30. Oral-literacy learners are those who are either non-literate or weak with respect to reading and writing (in whatever language) and prefer to communicate and learn verbally or orally (and aurally). The visually impaired may also fit this category but cannot, of course, be served with any visual online media. *The Cape Town Commitment* asserts that a majority of the world's population are oral communicators, "who cannot or do not learn through literate means," more than half of whom are presently "unreached." Lausanne, *Cape Town Commitment*, Part IID, 2.

can provide audio definitions. Synchronous video conferencing is a major tool to be exploited for these learners, who may be capable of short text responses on social media. The future is promising.

However, not all oral-literacy learners will be able to use the available technologies. Lack of internet access and poverty may create significant obstacles, and older learners simply may not be capable enough with the technology.[31] Generally speaking, technology for oral learners should not be used to replace F2F instruction for these learners, but rather to complement or supplement it.[32] While aware of the particular educational needs of oral communicators, the TEE movement has much still to do to begin meeting them.

Consideration of the educational abilities and internet access of today's learners

Yet some caveats are necessary. Not all TEE students will have the same access to the internet or to mobile data. For some it may not be available, for others it may be unaffordable. Some simply may not be digitally literate enough to participate in online learning. Cultural factors may require specific interventions prior to the participation of some learners and to remove barriers to their success. We need to identify such learners in our target countries and ensure that they may receive every care and practical help possible. Older learners should not be forced to move away from traditional print-media learning materials and local learning groups. Similarly, not all forms of online study will be suited for everyone. Asynchronous online discussion forums, for example, are well suited to the critical, higher-order thinking skills required at bachelor level and above, but are probably less appropriate for those with strong preferences for oral communication[33] or for lower academic levels. Who our learners are must also determine how we serve them with our learning programmes.

31. So UNESCO, "Harnessing the Potential," 7, 9.

32. UNESCO, for example, reports that there is not yet enough evidence to show that mobile technology by itself leads to better learning success (for literacy-challenged learners), despite the high expectations it has created for the future ("Harnessing the Potential," 9–10). There is here a clear case for blended-learning, discussed further below.

33. However, here, allowing students to post video or audio responses to an asynchronous forum could alleviate some difficulties.

The Future of TEE Group Discourse

Group discourse represents the second element of TEE's traditional educational methodology; however, the twenty-first century has brought about sufficient change that this element no longer implies or requires a local learning group that is situated in a local church or community. Online discussion possibilities[34] mean TEE class groups can function with students who are geographically remote from each other. This brings with it both strengths and weaknesses.

Three group discourse methods

Without an expanded discussion, it will be worthwhile noting the comparative advantages and disadvantages of three possible group discourse methods: (i) F2F discussion within weekly seminars or local learning groups; (ii) synchronous online video-conference discussion; and (iii) asynchronous online forum discussion. Table 8.1 presents these three alternatives.

Table 8.1. Three alternative group discourse methods

Traditional TEE Learning	Online TEE Learning	
Face-to-Face Discussion	Video-Conference Discussion[35]	Threaded Forum Discussion[36]
Discussion is synchronous (at the same time).		Usually asynchronous (not same time).
Sharing of immediate thoughts; responsive and interactive; shallower thoughts and responses (only reflective if preparation is required and completed beforehand).		Sharing following reflection; considered, deeper, more thoughtful responses.
Learner thinking processes hidden.		Learner thinking-in-process revealed.
Lower order thinking skills (LOTS) focused upon.		Higher-order thinking skills (HOTS) developed: analyzing, evaluating, synthesizing.

34. For an excellent, detailed overview of the field of online discourse, see Nichols, "Online Discourse."

35. For the purposes of this table, video-conferencing for Emergency Remote Learning has been excluded, since it is a temporary substitute for F2F learning and discussion.

36. "Threaded" forum discussion refers to extended group discussion of the same topic, using the same subject heading (or "thread") in an online forum, with an initial post and multiple responses within that "thread" of discussion.

<table>
<tr><th>Traditional TEE Learning</th><th colspan="2">Online TEE Learning</th></tr>
<tr><th>Face-to-Face Discussion</th><th>Video-Conference Discussion</th><th>Threaded Forum Discussion</th></tr>
<tr><td colspan="2">Suitable for all levels of study, including discipleship, certificate, and diploma levels.</td><td>More suitable for bachelor and higher academic study.</td></tr>
<tr><td colspan="2">Not equal participation: extroverts dominate and introverts tend to be quiet or do not participate.</td><td>Equal participation: introverts share as equals in the class; everyone "hears" (reads) each other's thoughts.</td></tr>
<tr><td colspan="2">Regular weekly meetings on set day of the week, time-limited.</td><td>Weekly discussions throughout the period of a whole week; can be more time-consuming.</td></tr>
<tr><td>Less accessible; limited to learners in same local town or area.</td><td colspan="2">Accessible to larger numbers of learners who can live anywhere in the world, including in mega-cities.[37]</td></tr>
<tr><td>Learners only experience the limited, narrow backgrounds of fellow believers from their town or city.</td><td colspan="2">Much greater diversity in the backgrounds of learners is possible, leading to richer, horizon-expanding discussion, and courses can bridge or link those learners across the world (or a country or region), including diaspora learners.</td></tr>
<tr><td>Courses limited by availability of local facilitator and what they are willing to lead.</td><td colspan="2">Allows access to larger variety of courses (including those a local facilitator is not able to offer).</td></tr>
<tr><td>Limited number of courses per year</td><td colspan="2">Relatively unlimited number of courses per year are available.</td></tr>
<tr><td>No access to subject matter experts;[38] local facilitator may not be able to answer difficult subject-related questions.</td><td colspan="2">Participation of subject matter experts is possible, and can be called upon if needed (if they agree to be available through prior arrangement).</td></tr>
<tr><td>Limited to learners in one local community or area.</td><td>Accessible to most adults who possess smartphones (or computers with web-cameras).</td><td>Limited only to initial access and capability of learner with the needed technology.</td></tr>
</table>

37. A practical reality for learners in mega-cities is the transport time required to cross from one side of a city to the other in order to attend weekly meetings – with online class meetings, this is averted.

38. However, a subject matter expert could be brought to a F2F class through one-off or occasional video-conferencing, if a large smart TV or computer screen with camera and microphone was available.

Traditional TEE Learning	**Online TEE Learning**	
Face-to-Face Discussion	**Video-Conference Discussion**	**Threaded Forum Discussion**
Meetings not technology dependent (though learners can study online or in print).	Technology and internet bandwidth dependent for meeting success.	Internet access is necessary, but not 100 percent of the time.
Local church-based.	Geographically remote students, not from the same church.	
TEE educational philosophy remains fully intact.	Temptations to move away from church-based training, which now requires significant intentionality and commitment.	
Learners have knowledge of each other's needs/lives/families/work/ministries.	Learners do not easily know each other very well, and (without significant effort) do not know each other's backgrounds and contexts.	
A very supportive learning community is possible; personal sharing is possible.	Community building is possible, but limited, and requires significant effort, without which personal sharing is reduced or inhibited.	
Relationality and learner "connectedness" between learners enhanced through physical presence, visual facial cues, and body language.	Relationality and learner "connectedness" enhanced through visual facial cues only.	Impersonal relationships between fellow learners and facilitator; learners may feel less "connected" to each other.
Learners are more motivated for home self-study through their weekly class connections.	Learners receive some motivation from the group for home self-study.	Learners are less motivated by the group for home self-study, and require high personal discipline to keep going.
Facilitator can reinforce learning and, crucially, can support the application of learning.	Difficult to facilitate or monitor practical application of course materials.	
Facilitator can mentor and disciple learners.	More difficult and time-consuming to mentor or disciple learners.[39]	
Group leader can easily facilitate practical ministry requirements.	Practical ministry requirements must be arranged through intentional partnership with local churches of learners, which is possible, but more difficult to do.	

39. However, with an agreed, intentional partnership with local churches, mentoring and discipleship can be supplied, though not by the group leader or facilitator. On this see further below.

What is clear from Table 8.1 is that each of the three kinds of group discussion have strengths and are superior in certain respects, while each has deficiencies in comparison to the other methods. It is useful to note that video-conference discussion sometimes shares strengths and weaknesses with F2F discussion and at other times with online forum discussion. A combination of methods is likely to lead to better learning outcomes for students compared to that possible with only one kind of group discourse.[40] This certainly suggests the possibility that a macro-blend of course delivery methods may allow learners to benefit from the strengths of each, while remedying any deficiencies.[41] It is strongly recommended that TEE programmes considering threaded-forum discussions for bachelor and higher studies also include some synchronous video conferencing discussion for class groups.

What about local learning groups?

TEE practitioners considering online learning are naturally concerned about the potential loss of F2F local learning groups and the benefits accruing from a traditional weekly seminar that is hosted by local churches. Here we must ask, what is fundamental to TEE? Is it group discussion or local learning groups? While each has been described as a second element of traditional TEE methodology, in fact neither by itself does justice to twenty-first century TEE. Group discourse is essential, but by itself could lead to a situation in which church-based training is totally dropped in favour of so-called "fully online" theological education.[42] On the other hand, the demands and needs of twenty-first century TEE include the need for flexible delivery of learning programmes, which may not always involve local learning groups.

---

40. This is precisely the conclusion of a large meta-analysis of online learning studies by the US Department of Education (Means et al., *Evidence-Based Practices*, 6, 53), drawn with respect to a combination of both synchronous and asynchronous discourse in online learning against purely one form of online discourse or the other.

41. Deficiencies are not always insurmountable obstacles, but will usually require significant effort and intentionality, and excellent facilitation skills, to remedy or overcome. Awareness of potential deficiencies is the first step toward overcoming them.

42. The term "fully online" theological education is, in fact, a misnomer since, if practical ministry or application is required for holistic theological education, then almost certainly some aspects of the holistic learning experience are not going to be "online," but rather in a real-world context.

What is the primary function of local learning groups for TEE? It is *not* to allow instructors to have F2F contact with students. Rather they have two purposes: first, to facilitate group discussion and subsequent application of the learning materials; and second, to root the learning in a local church context and community. With appropriate care in online learning the first function can readily be met through online discourse. The question is, how can the second function of the local learning group be met if a class group does not meet as a local learning group? We return to this critical issue again below.

To be sure, local learning groups should not be dropped entirely by TEE programmes and especially not by those who are committed to TEE's vision of church-based training. Local learning groups remain an integral part of a quality TEE programme.

From a holistic learning point of view, the local-context, local-church-based communities of learners provided through F2F groups offer many benefits and facilitate not only growth in individual learners, but local church growth, which is especially significant for TEE. From a student point of view, experience reveals that motivation for disciplined homebased self-study and the successful completion of all course requirements is much stronger within F2F discussion groups than in online class groups.

Facilitating online classes

The task of facilitating online classes using video conferencing has many similarities to regular TEE F2F group facilitation,[43] and the training gap between F2F facilitation and video-conference facilitation is not large.

Facilitation of e-Learning classes hosted on an LMS, which includes online forum discussion, is however more complex and undoubtedly requires advanced tutor training. Ideally, trainees should be presented with excellent models of course and forum facilitation by the online trainers. It is highly recommended that TEE programmes considering online learning put their

43. Online synchronous group discussion, for example, works best with between five to ten (with a maximum of fourteen) students in the class. Online video-conference group dynamics have clear similarities to F2F group dynamics. With larger numbers, "breakout rooms" might be considered to divide the class into groups small enough to allow for every person participation.

senior educators through a proven course in effective online teaching,[44] though later they will need to design their own training course(s) for online facilitation based on the chosen LMS, desired facilitator role, and educational needs.

Forum discussion, of course, is a different kind of discourse to F2F discourse, and a special skill set is needed to facilitate it well.[45] Forum discussion must be well designed to be successful,[46] and will typically require more time for both the online tutor and the learners, week by week. As with F2F discussion, online forum discussion functions best with class sizes of between five to fourteen students. Too few and the group dynamics become awkward; too many and students become overwhelmed with the number of posts to read.[47]

While practical knowledge of such things is essential, the principles of teaching, facilitating, and learning online need to be well understood also.[48] Note the "and learning": effective online facilitators must understand how online learners learn and what will make their learning more effective. While many resources are available,[49] online facilitators should be familiar with, for example, Gilly Salmon's Five Stage Model,[50] the Garrison, Anderson, and Archer Community of Inquiry Model,[51] and the related concepts of "teaching presence," "social presence," and "cognitive presence."[52] However, while

---

44. An excellent set of online tutor training courses (in English) is offered by the Horizon Education Network (https://horizoneducationnetwork.org), who provide superb modelling of best practice in online course and forum facilitation.

45. Among other possible resources at this point (including those mentioned in fns. 49–51 below), see Akin and Neal, "CREST+ Model"; Rovai, "Facilitating Online Discussions"; and Maddix, "Generating."

46. Nichols, "Online Discourse," 46.

47. For larger class sizes, it is necessary to divide the online class into smaller groups for forum discussion, and a good LMS will allow for this possibility, but this will increase facilitator workload.

48. The models mentioned below are purpose-specific to online learning but complement the broader educational models discussed in chapter 5: Shaw, "The Educational Efficacy of TEE – Part 1."

49. An online tutor training course is one of the best ways to prepare TEE online facilitators (see fn. 44 above); however, see also Nichols, "Online Discourse"; Chickering and Gamson, "Seven Principles"; and those listed in the following two notes.

50. Salmon, "Five Stage Model."

51. These models are purpose-specific to online learning and complement the broader educational models discussed in chapter 5: Shaw, "The Educational Efficacy of TEE – Part 1."

52. Briefly, "teaching presence" refers to facilitator engagement regarding teaching/learning goals; "social presence" to engagement with the learners themselves; and "cognitive presence"

some basic theory will be helpful, practical knowledge built upon first-hand experience of excellent online facilitation models will best prepare them for online TEE.

Remaining Church-Rooted in Online TEE

The cruciality of the local church

The Cape Town Commitment states that "the mission of theological education is to strengthen and accompany the mission of the church," which itself is "to serve the mission of God in the world."[53] The Increase Association states its purpose as being "to connect and strengthen church-based training movements across Asia and beyond."[54] Norberto Saracco has recently reminded Increase that the most significant contribution of TEE is not TEE study materials, nor even "TEE methodology," but that it brought theological education to the local church.[55] TEE pioneer, Lois McKinney, perhaps stated it best in 1984:

> The church is in the heart of TEE. Even though TEE may be organizationally distinct from the churches, it can never function as an educational institution divorced from the church. It is created by churches and for churches. It functions best within churches. The most significant contribution that TEE has made to theological education is to return our conception of theological education to its contextual, experiential and *church* base.[56]

Similarly, to extend a previous comment, the *most* significant aspect of local learning groups for TEE is *not* that they provide a F2F encounter with students,

---

to engagement with course content. See Garrison, Anderson, and Archer, "Critical Inquiry"; early development of their three elements is summarized and expanded in Garrison, *E-Learning*; but see also Anderson, "Teaching"; and the Community of Inquiry (CoI) website (https://coi.athabascau.ca/) run by Garrison and other educators. While important, space does not permit fuller explication of this model here.

53. Lausanne, *Cape Town Commitment*, Part IIF, 4.

54. Increase, "Vision and Purpose."

55. Saracco, "TEE in Latin America"; and "Main Contribution of TEE," unpublished comments made to the 2017 Increase Association Conference in Chiang Mai, Thailand. Cf. also the concern of Robert Banks to situate a missional theological education in the context of the local church, *Reenvisioning Theological Education*, especially, 122–26, 135–36, 218–222.

56. McKinney, "How Shall We Cooperate?" 30, emphasis added.

which is alleged to be essential for the personal formation of learners,[57] nor their provision for group discourse, which is important but can be met by alternate means (as we have seen, in the form of online discourse); it is that student participation in a local learning group helps root their theological education in the local church, and this precisely becomes the essential element in holistic personal formation.

As we are seeing, though, if we have online self-study materials (a good thing for TEE) and can have online group discourse (which has both strengths and weaknesses) and can thereby eliminate the absolute necessity for local learning groups, this opens the possibility for international online classes, better connecting diaspora believers with those in home countries and enabling even more students to be reached (a noble goal).

In a weaker or merely pragmatic moment, we may then be tempted to eliminate practical ministry requirements and other aspects of holistic formation, as they will be much more difficult to implement, and this may lead to the temptation to move away from church-based training and local church connections and partnerships altogether. This is a key danger for the TEE movement and would be a tragic mistake if we allowed it to happen.

As we reimagine TEE for the twenty-first century, this then is a pivotal moment in our history. To be true to the TEE vision, it is crucial that online TEE keeps theological education rooted in the local church.[58]

Keeping online TEE holistic

We may be willing to pay lip-service to the importance of the church in theological education, but unless we apply it and move beyond that, to active, intentional, and practical partnership, then we face the danger of diminishing

57. So Nichols, "Comparison," 219. Situated learning studies are showing that local churches are typically more significant for spiritual, character, and ministry formation of learners than campus-based colleges or seminaries; and, I would add, than the weekly face-to-face seminars of TEE.

58. Cf. the extended discussion of Cannell, *Theological Education Matters*, 247–348 and note her conclusion that "the future of theological education in its several modes is found in a commitment to lifelong learning *for the whole people of God*" (317; emphasis added); and Nichols, "Comparison," 189, 191–223, who writes (210), "the church is the most authentic context for discipleship and Christian formation," and therefore "the church and theological education ought to be inseparable, intertwined and mutually beneficial" and notes (220) that "'situated theological distance education' places the curriculum in the congregation."

the holistic nature of TEE. Among other losses, we will also diminish prospects for external accreditation, since evangelical theological education accreditation is very concerned to ensure that theological education remains holistic.[59] And more than mere inclusion and supervision of practical ministry is involved in this. Providers of online distance education or so-called "fully online" education are simply not able to achieve holistic integration by themselves.[60] Holistic learning will always be collaborative and require partnership.

My contention, therefore, is that TEE must add an explicit fourth element to its traditional threefold methodological formulation, which, I argue, is an intentional commitment to church-based training (CBT). Without this, TEE risks embracing online learning, as it must do to remain relevant in the twenty-first century, while losing a core element of its significance within theological education.[61] Adding this fourth element to the explicit methodology of TEE will allow it to retain the cruciality of the church in its vision and practices, even as these practices are being adapted for the realities and needs of the digital age.

We must intentionally commit to a holistic education partnership triangle. The aim for the overall formation of each student is a three-way learning partnership between the TEE programme, the student, and their local church,[62] as shown in Figure 8.1.

---

59. Note the new *SG-GETE* published by ICETE (April 2019), which titles a major section on programme standards and guidelines with "B1. Holistic Integration" (20–21) and its "Appendix F: Standards and Guidelines for Online Evangelical Theological Education" (39–56), which in a section titled "Holistic Educational Programme" takes a strong stand against those who "do not give adequate consideration [to]" or, worse, "deliberately sacrifice" holistic learning outcomes in online programmes (47, but see also 39–40, 42–43, 47–49). The ICETE standards are already being adopted by ICETE member accrediting agencies, such as the ATA, who serve the region in which most Increase Association members serve.

60. So ICETE, *SG-GETE*, 47.

61. Jaison has already lamented the fact that "the essential reciprocity between church and theology school is increasingly diminishing in spite of the literature produced on the issue" (*Towards Vital Wholeness*, 2); online learning clearly has the potential to exacerbate this relationship deficiency further – if we are not careful. On the other hand an advocate of online (non-TEE) distance education such as Mark Nichols is fully convinced that through intentional "situated" engagement with local churches, online theological education can provide significant personal transformation (see his "Comparison," 218–23).

62. See chapter 2: Burke and Pearson, "TEE in Theological Perspective – Part 1," and chapter 3: Aylett and Samuel, "TEE in Theological Perspective – Part 2." These provide an extended discussion of how TEE relates to the identity and mission of the church and its training needs within the broader mission of God.

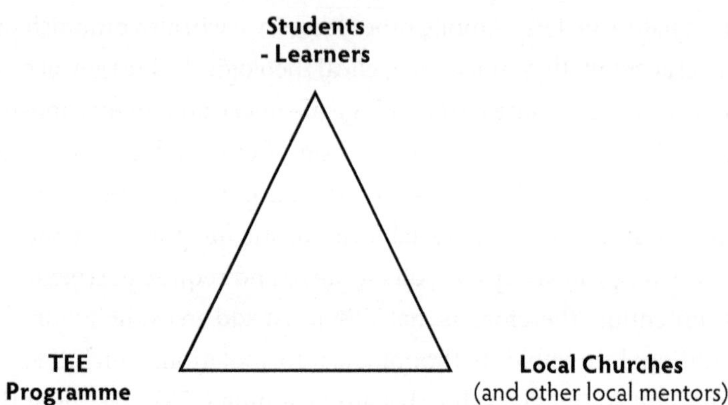

Figure 8.1. Holistic education partnership triangle

What this means in practice is the recognition that whole-life discipleship, including the areas of character and spiritual formation,[63] and ministry formation, takes place in the real-world situated learning circles of students,[64] of which the local church is typically the most significant.[65]

Where participation in a local learning group is possible, that also enables the learning processes of discourse, reflection, and application to take place in a supportive local learning community who know each other and their

63. I sense that for TEE, as for any theological education where a commitment to holistic learning and growth is maintained, the areas of character and spiritual formation are a challenge for intentionality and practical implementation. TEE specifies practical application and ministry as a core third element of its traditional methodology but does not explicitly emphasize these other aspects of holistic formation. Further efforts are needed in the movement to add intentionality for learner growth in these areas.

64. "Situated learning" refers to learning that takes places in the various spheres of normal life situations of students, usually outside their formal education programmes. While not in itself a form of online learning, situated learning is an appropriate and often essential complement to various forms of online study for the creation of blended learning opportunities. The most significant situated learning sphere for theological students is often the church or believing community that they belong to. This is often true, even for campus-based college students, over and above the learning sphere of the college. Situated learning, then, is significant for all modes of educational delivery, but becomes especially important for online programmes where students are geographically remote from each other. For an introduction to the topic, see Kemp, "Situated Learning"; Lowe and Lowe, "Spiritual Formation" (2010); Nichols, "Comparison," especially 53–54, 61, 72–85, 101–3, 191–223.

65. Locally situated learning spheres also include the family, local community, parachurch organization, or place of work; see the previous note, and further, Lowe, "Spiritual Formation" (2012).

respective life situations well, and who know the surrounding context, culture, and environment well, too. The mutual support, encouragement, and learning potential resulting from such participation is not to be underestimated. Even students who take "fully online" courses (with online group discussion) should, where possible, be encouraged to participate in a local learning group. If they are the only student from their local area, they are encouraged to recruit new students and thus form the nucleus of a new local learning group.

On top of this, a TEE programme can intentionally reinforce the learning partnership with the local church in a number of ways. This partnership and engagement together should commence from the beginning of the student's relationship with the programme. Applications to enter the programme should only be accepted when it is clear they have the support of their local church or believing community,[66] and have identified one, though preferably more, local leaders (or peers, if the student is already a leader) who potentially could mentor them and/or be a source of accountability and/or be a willing dialogue partner. Once identified, the local leaders should be contacted to formally initiate a partnership relationship in connection with each student. The TEE programme will probably need a church partnerships (or liaison) officer to facilitate all this, and a partnership department, as the online student body grows. It should not be forgotten that the relationship between programme and church needs to be two-way.[67]

Naturally, for greatest impact, students should themselves be active members in their local church.[68] If they are members of a regular home group or home church, that relationship will provide a supportive local reference group outside of the TEE programme, where the student can share their learning experiences and connect them naturally and regularly with the context of their local church.[69]

Finally, online TEE courses need to be designed to maximize practical applications of learning materials in local church contexts and settings (not to

66. Nichols, "Comparison," 206.

67. Practically, this means the TEE programme should invite church input into not only the student's personal growth, development, and assessment, but also into the development of the programme and curriculum.

68. Nichols, "Comparison," 218–19.

69. Nichols, 197.

mention in the wider community). Course learning outcomes need to include regular and frequent cognitive, affective, and behavioural outcomes, where practical engagement with the local church is required.[70] Practical application assignments or projects need to be creatively and imaginatively designed for this purpose, and students should be required to report back, with reflection, on these local church engagements. Group collaboration should be encouraged or expected where possible.

Not to be neglected in our discussion is the major area of practical application for TEE. Without this element, TEE is no longer TEE, and that is true for online or regular TEE. While practical application needs to be fully integrated within each course offered, practical ministry or fieldwork in the local church and community must also be planned for.[71] With local learning groups and local facilitators, it is of course easier to facilitate practical ministry assignments, mentoring, reflection, and evaluation through the local church. At a distance, with geographically remote online students, this requires greater effort and intentionality. A church partnerships department, mentioned above, will be a necessity, together with a written implementation plan.

Practical ministry expectations and requirements need to be clearly communicated to all students and to their local church leaders. As with regular TEE, practical ministry needs to happen alongside taking courses. Appropriate local mentors need to be identified and brought into regular contact with the partnership department. Ministry unit planning tools should be developed, as well as student self-evaluation and mentor student-evaluation tools. It is likely that both students and mentors will need to be coached in their use (this is an opportunity for some short online videos).

70. cf. Nichols, 215. Examples might include: (i) asking students to interview their pastor or church members about their understanding of the kingdom of God, share their new learning about it from the course, and report back to the online class group about what was discussed; (ii) surveying church members about their personal devotional practices, and summarizing this for the class group; (iii) presenting a summary of a learning unit to a local church group, discussing issues that arise and, again, reporting back to the class; (iv) helping to lead a local church group in a community engagement activity; and so on.

71. This is also known by other names such as ministry action learning, service learning, in-ministry formation, or experiential learning.

A Blended Future: Options for Online Course Delivery[72]

So, as we put all of this together, what are the preferred options for TEE course and programme delivery in the digital age? While variations are possible, and course delivery could be via e-Learning or m-Learning, four main options exist for holistic TEE online course delivery as shown in Figure 8.2, and as subsequently explained.

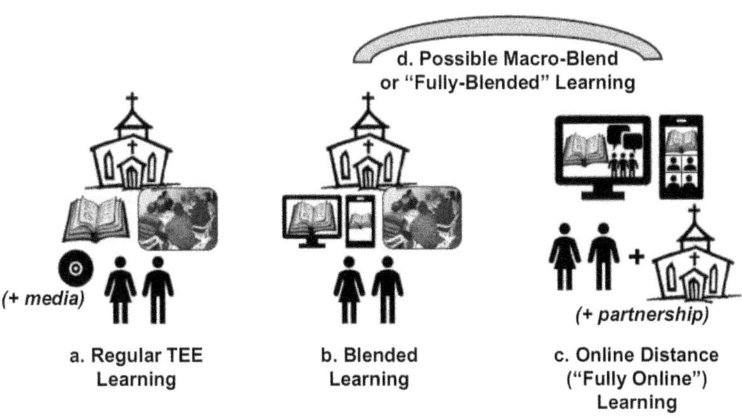

Figure 8.2. TEE educational delivery options[73]

Regular F2F course delivery

The F2F option a, in Figure 8.2, includes print-media courses plus F2F group discussions in local learning groups. Regular F2F delivery will continue to be preferred by older learners, among others, and should not be eliminated in the move towards online learning. However, once a TEE programme has begun to develop online versions of its print-media courses, any multimedia files prepared to enhance the learning materials should be made available to print-media readers on portable storage media such as a CD-ROM, USB drive or an SD-card. Not all will choose, or be able, to use this media, but since it should

72. The word "blended" is used deliberately in a broader, non-technical sense here; see below for an explication of that.

73. Source: R. J. Weymouth, used by permission, © 2020.

enhance learning effectiveness, help may be offered to digitally challenged learners to make use of it. Regular course delivery offers all the benefits of F2F group discourse mentioned above, and an immediate connection with the local church, which of course still needs to be built upon.

Blended or hybrid course delivery

Blended or hybrid learning notionally combines online learning elements with F2F learning elements, usually both offered by the same educational provider, but now with blending being understood in broader ways.[74] Blended learning (b, in Figure 8.2), then, could involve learner participation in local learning groups and F2F group discussion, while receiving learning materials online via computers and laptops and/or mobile devices. The same advantages as for regular TEE delivery are apparent, including natural church-rootedness, plus the benefits of online learning materials, which will make courses more attractive for younger adult learners. As we have already discussed, online courses have the potential to make learning more effective, engaging, and enjoyable.

It is further possible that some learners in a local learning group may study with print-media and others study online (though clearly without any online discussion in this case). Theoretically it is also possible to film a live F2F group discussion, enabling participation of remote learners with a F2F class through video conferencing and a large screen in the meeting room. With good technology it may work well, provided there is access to quality internet services, otherwise it is probably not a satisfactory option.

One thing that should be highlighted here is that online learning experts are generally convinced of the superiority of blended learning options (which encompass a huge variety and range of designs)[75] over either fully F2F or "fully online" options.[76] This is not surprising since it allows the strengths

74. As will be seen in option d. Significantly, one important form of blended learning, the flipped classroom, has been part of the TEE movement since the 1960s.

75. This chapter certainly over-simplifies the complex field that is blended or hybrid learning, but for present purposes this limited discussion is adequate.

76. See the conclusions of Means et al., *Evidence-Based Practices*, which highlight the greater empirical effectiveness of blended learning over face-to-face learning (ix, xiv–xv, xviii, 6, 19, 51–53). They note the possibility that blended learning is more effective because it generally involves more learning time, offers additional instructional resources, and includes group discourse and

of each, while reducing the overall impact of the weaknesses of each. TEE's methodologies mean it can have consistently excellent holistic learning outcomes when well implemented. It follows that, if well designed and delivered online, multimedia courses offer significant learning enhancements over print-media courses, then blended learning within TEE will lead to better learning outcomes than regular F2F TEE. Yet further blending is possible when we include the possibility of macro-blends, which we discuss below.

Online distance ("fully online") course delivery

Our third main option (c, in Figure 8.2) is online distance education or so-called "fully online" course delivery, where students and their facilitator are geographically remote from each other, and they engage with both content and group discussion (synchronous and/or asynchronous) online. As already mentioned, where asynchronous forum discussion is included, we recommend combining it with synchronous video conferencing, perhaps with alternating modes week on week. Middle Eastern and Asian students tend to relate better when they can see each other.

This method offers great strengths for a TEE programme and to learners. For example, diaspora communities can be linked with local, national communities, or believers linked between multiple towns or cities within a country, and subject matter experts (SMEs) can be included (for at least part of course) for group discussion or question and answer, even with possible translation to and from another language, both enriching the group discussion considerably. In addition, students can take more courses, or different courses, from those the local tutor is able to offer each year. Greater flexibility and accessibility to courses is guaranteed for those with the needed technology and digital literacy. There are many benefits.

As mentioned before, though, for online TEE to remain true to the TEE vision, this method of online learning needs to be combined with an active, intentional commitment to partnership with the local church. Without that we are betraying our TEE roots. Thus, TEE programmes including online distance

learner interactions (52). The 2017 *Horizon Report* notes that blended learning topped the list of key trends in higher education for six years in a row from 2012 to 2017 (Adams Becker et al., 18–19); however, many tertiary institutions are still catching on. Cf. also Delamarter and Brunner, "Theological Education," 145–64 (esp. 153–55) and Nichols, "Comparison," 46–52.

courses in their delivery methods, need to add a higher level of engagement with the local churches of each of their online students. And if you have one hundred "fully online" students, then you will need one hundred partnership relationships to be developed (and so on). This quickly reinforces the need to create a church partnership department.

In this respect, as noted above,[77] "fully online" is really a misnomer for the TEE world, since we are expecting significant learning elements to continue to take place in the situated, real world contexts of the local church and community, outside of the online learning environment. Personally, then, I strongly encourage an emphasis away from "fully online" learning to what could be called "fully-blended" online learning, which draws together multiple delivery modes *and*, at the same time, includes a vital partnership with the local church of each student.

Macro-blends and fully-blended learning

A fourth programme delivery option (d, in Figure 8.2) arises for us – the possibility of creating "macro-blends" of learning, where students may take some courses as blended or hybrid learning and some as online distance learning. What would be a good balance in doing this? If students have access to local learning groups (and facilitators), one suggestion is that they are asked to take at least two-thirds or three-quarters of their courses through local learning groups (and blended or hybrid learning), and not more than between one-quarter to one-third as "fully online" courses.

Exceptions would need to be made, for "fully online" courses will readily attract students from all around the world, and many will not have access to local learning groups in their town or city. Where possible, then, geographically remote students who enrol in "fully online" courses should be encouraged to invite others from their local communities to become fellow learners. This recruitment can be incentivized through rewards such as a discounted fee for the next course. In this way the nucleus of a new local learning group can be created, offering the potential for future blended learning.

Prior to such a local learning group being created, plans to implement a holistic education partnership with each student's local church need to be

77. See fn. 43.

actioned. Hopefully, then, the larger "macro-blending" of different modes of online learning (i.e. both "fully online" and blended learning courses) may become "fully-blended" through intentional local church engagement, and will continue well past the formation of a new local learning group.

Explorations in Online TEE

While the TEE movement has generally been slow to move forward into online learning, several are now making encouraging and positive efforts in different directions.

The Programme for Theological Education by Extension (PTEE), serving the Arab world in the Arabic language, began developing bachelor level e-Learning courses hosted on Moodle in 2017, following a decade of pedagogical preparation.[78] Within a few years of this book's publication it plans to host almost fifty e-courses for its Bachelor of Theology. However, in late 2020, the PTEE also committed itself to m-Learning delivery for Certificate of Ministry courses, mostly from the organization Study by Extension for All Nations (SEAN) and began early m-Learning development work.

The Institute for TEE in Nepal (ITEEN) has explored the possibility of m-Learning using Schoology as an LMS, with a couple of SEAN courses already available.[79] Similarly, Word of Life has developed an m-Learning app for TEE courses in partnership with SEAN.[80] The "Come Follow Me" and "Abundant Life" courses were being field-tested in four countries in 2020, with plans to add more courses and in different languages.[81] The Relay Trust, in partnership with SEAN, are working with this and other apps to offer m-Learning for church-based training in West Africa. While the early courses have not yet been designed for microlearning, the app holds great promise. In Latin America,

78. An extended case-study of the PTEE's efforts in online learning may be found on the Increase Association website.

79. ITEEN initially tried the Moodle LMS but found it to be an inappropriate tool for certificate and diploma courses and students.

80. The m-Learning app uses coding which allows content to be displayed on devices of any size.

81. It is expected that the Come Follow Me course (and related curricular materials) will eventually be available and deliverable in sixteen languages. Languages so far being used include Arabic, Farsi, Russian, German, Somali, and English.

TEE programmes in Costa Rica and Panama are experimenting putting SEAN courses online, while the Christian and Missionary Alliance (C&MA) denomination in the USA is developing its own LMS to deliver SEAN courses. With SEAN being a common denominator in many of these efforts, it is not surprising that it has already developed its own document, titled "Guidelines for Producing Digital Versions of SEAN Courses."[82]

The vision for online learning is growing within the TEE movement – and that prospect is exciting!

Conclusion

The twenty-first century has brought with it innumerable new possibilities and new opportunities. These must be welcomed. It has also brought a new generation of learners who are expecting their education to be online and integrated into the technological world they daily inhabit. The TEE movement must understand these younger adult learners, their needs, learning styles, and technological preferences. These learners must be served.

Challenges exist for the TEE movement as it embraces online learning, especially with respect to being church-rooted and remaining truly church-based training. There are good reasons why the movement has so far been rather cautious with respect to the digital age. While risks and difficulties may be encountered, none of them are insurmountable. The early reticence of the TEE community must change.

Learning in the online medium is not the same as learning with printed media and F2F discourse. The digital medium needs to be deeply understood and instructional designs appropriate for various kinds of online media need to be applied. Student learning must remain a priority. Yet online multimedia content, together with excellent facilitation of online and F2F group discourse, deliberate community building, and mentored practical ministry, can and must be combined with an intentional commitment to the local church to create deeply holistic situated learning experiences that are "fully-blended."

82. Ball, SEAN International, 25 July 2019.

The local church must remain central for TEE and indeed for all theological education. But it is time for the TEE world to take the plunge, for the future of TEE is online.

Bibliography

Adams Becker, S., M. Cummins, A. Davis, A. Freeman, C. Hall Giesinger, and V. Ananthanarayanan. *NMC Horizon Report: 2017 Higher Education Edition*. Austin: New Media Consortium, 2017. https://library.educause.edu/resources/2017/2/2017-horizon-report.

Akin, Lynn, and Diane Neal. "CREST+ Model: Writing Effective Online Discussion Questions." *MERLOT Journal of Online Learning and Teaching* 3, no. 2 (June 2007): 191–202.

Anderson, Terry. "Teaching in an Online Learning Context." In *The Theory and Practice of Online Learning*, 2nd ed., edited by Terry Anderson, 343–65. Edmonton: AU Press, 2008.

Ascough, Richard S. "Designing for Online Distance Education: Putting Pedagogy before Technology." *Teaching Theology and Religion* 5, no. 1 (2002): 17–29.

Asia Theological Association. *Manual for Accreditation*. Manila, January 2017.

———. *Manual for Accreditation*. Manila, January 2021.

Ball, David. "Guidelines for Producing Digital Versions of SEAN Courses." SEAN International, 25 July 2019.

Banks, Robert. *Reenvisioning Theological Education: Exploring a Missional Alternative to Current Models*. Grand Rapids: Eerdmans, 1999.

Basak, Sujit K., Marguerite Wotto, and Paul Belanger. "E-learning, M-learning and D-learning: Conceptual Definition and Comparative Analysis." *E-Learning and Digital Media* 15, no. 4 (2018): 191–216.

Bates, A. W. (Tony). *Teaching in a Digital Age – Second Edition: Guidelines for Designing Teaching and Learning*. Vancouver: Tony Bates Associates, 2019. https://pressbooks.bccampus.ca/teachinginadigitalagev2/.

Bayne, Sian. "What's the Matter with 'Technology Enhanced Learning'?" *Learning, Media and Technology* 40, no. 1 (2015): 5–20. https://doi.org/10.1080/17439884.2014.915851.

Behera, Santosh K. "E- and M-learning: A Comparative Study." *International Journal on New Trends in Education and Their Implications* 4, no. 3 (July 2013): 65–78.

Bourne, Alan. "2.6 Billion Reasons for Thinking Mobile First in eLearning." 22 February 2016. https://elearningindustry.com/mobile-first-in-elearning-2-6-billion-reasons-thinking.

Brown, Tom H. "The Role of M-learning in the Future of E-learning in Africa?" Presentation to the 21st ICDE World Conference, Hong Kong. June 2003. Accessed 14 July 2020. https://www.researchgate.net/publication/237221533_The_role_of_m-learning_in_the_future_of_e-learning_in_Africa.

Cannell, Linda. *Theological Education Matters: Leadership Education for the Church*. Newburgh: EDCOT, 2006.

Chan, Joanne. "mLearning: The Way of Learning Tomorrow." 28 May 2014. https://elearningindustry.com/mlearning-the-way-of-Learning-tomorrow.

Chickering, Arthur W., and Zelda F. Gamson. "Seven Principles for Good Practice in Undergraduate Education." *AAHE Bulletin* 39 (March 1987): 3–7.

Clothier, Paul. "Right Time and Place: mLearning Use Cases." 12 May 2014. https://learningsolutionsmag.com/articles/1420/right-time-and-place-mlearning-use-cases.

Conceição, Simone C. O. "Understanding the Environment for Online Teaching." *New Directions for Adult and Continuing Education* 113 (Spring 2007): 5–11.

Debergue, Yvette, and James R. Harrison, eds. *Teaching Theology in a Technological Age*. Newcastle upon Tyne: Cambridge Scholars, 2015.

Delamarter, Steve, and Daniel L. Brunner. "Theological Education and Hybrid Models of Distance Learning." *Theological Education* 40, no. 2 (2005): 145–64.

Dimock, Michael. "Defining Generations: Where Millennials End and Generation Z Begins." Pew Research Center. Date published, 17 January 2019. https://www.pewresearch.org/fact-tank/2019/01/17/where-millennials-end-and-generation-z-begins/.

EIDesign. "10 Ways to Use Microlearning for Making Corporate Training Effective." 23 March 2017. https://www.youtube.com/watch?v=4JUInzT3oDY.

———. "15 Types of Microlearning for Formal and Informal Learning in the Workplace." 21 March 2018. https://www.youtube.com/watch?v=nLFAUVnA8IA.

Garrison, D. Randy. *E-Learning in the 21st Century: A Community of Inquiry Framework for Research and Practice*. 3rd ed. New York: Routledge, 2017.

Garrison, D. Randy, et. al. "The Community of Inquiry." Accessed 9 September 2020. https://coi.athabascau.ca/.

Garrison, D. Randy, Terry Anderson, and Walter Archer. "Critical Inquiry in a Text-Based Environment: Computer Conferencing in Higher Education." *Internet and Higher Education* 2, no. 2–3 (2000): 87–105.

Gnowbe. "Experience Gnowbe: A Walkthrough of the Mobile Microlearning App." 6 May 2019. https://www.youtube.com/watch?v=B1Dld7nI35g.

———. "This Is Gnowbe: Demo Video." 4 September 2020. https://www.youtube.com/watch?v=JL55Xl-G72w.

Hess, Mary E. *Engaging Technology in Theological Education: All That We Can't Leave Behind*. Oxford: Rowman & Littlefield, 2005.

———. "What Difference Does It Make? Digital Technology in the Theological Classroom." *Theological Education* 41, no. 1 (2005): 77–91.

ICETE. *Standards and Guidelines for Global Evangelical Theological Education (SG-GETE)*. 2019. https://icete.info/wp-content/uploads/2019/05/Standards-and-Guidelines-for-Global-Evangelical-Theological-Education-2019.pdf.

Increase Association. "Vision and Purpose." Accessed 25 September 2020. https://increaseassociation.org/about/vision-purpose.

Jaison, Jessy. *Towards Vital Wholeness in Theological Education: Framing Areas for Assessment*. Carlisle: Langham, 2017.

Jung, Joanne J. *Character Formation in Online Education: A Guide for Instructors, Administrators, and Accrediting Agencies*. Grand Rapids: Zondervan, 2015.

Kang, So-Young. "5 Biggest Misconceptions about Mobile Learning." 4 July 2017. https://www.youtube.com/watch?v=h8zkh9sRoU0.

———. "Digital Christianity." Plenary Session 2, ATA Triennial General Assembly, Singapore, 13 August 2019.

———. "Upskilling Billions through Smartphones." Open Learning Campus. Disruptive Technology Learning Series. 18 May 2018. https://olc.worldbank.org/content/disruptive-technology-Learning-series-upskilling-billions-through-smartphones.

Kemp, Stephen J. "Situated Learning: Optimizing Experiential Learning through God-Given Learning Community." *Christian Education Journal* Ser. 3, 7, no. 1 (2010): 118–43.

Lausanne Movement. *The Cape Town Commitment: A Confession of Faith and a Call to Action*. 2011. http://www.lausanne.org/content/ctc/ctcommitment.

LeClair, Dan. "Mobile Micro-Learning: Course Design for Mobile First." Interview with So-Young Kang, CEO of Gnowbe. 23 April 2018. https://www.aacsb.edu/videos/aacsb-explores/2018/mobile-micro-Learning-course-design-for-mobile-first#gsc.tab=0.

———. "Technologies with Potential to Transform Business and Business Education: Mobile and Micro-Learning." AACSB Business Education Intelligence. September

2018. https://www.aacsb.edu/publications/researchreports/mobile-and-micro-Learning.

Lehman, Rosemary M., and Simone C. O. Conceição. *Creating a Sense of Presence in Online Teaching: How to "Be There" for Distance Learners*. San Francisco: Jossey-Bass, 2010.

———. *Motivating and Retaining Online Students: Research-Based Strategies That Work*. San Francisco: Jossey-Bass, 2014.

Levy, Dan. *Teaching Effectively with Zoom: A Practical Guide to Engage Your Students and Help Them Learn*. E-book. Dan Levy: July 2020.

Lowe, Mary E. "Spiritual Formation as Whole-Person Development in Online Education." In *Best Practices of Online Education: A Guide for Christian Higher Education*, edited by Mark A. Maddix, James R. Estep, and Mary E. Lowe, 55–63. Charlotte: Information Age Publishing, 2012.

Lowe, Stephen D., and Mary E. Lowe. "Spiritual Formation in Theological Distance Education: An Ecosystems Model as Paradigm." *Christian Education Journal* Ser. 3, 7, no. 1 (2010): 85–102.

Maddix, Mark A. "Generating and Facilitating Effective Online Discussion." In *Best Practices of Online Education: A Guide for Christian Higher Education*, edited by Mark A. Maddix, James R. Estep, and Mary E. Lowe, 105–19. Charlotte: Information Age Publishing, 2012.

Maddix, Mark A., James R. Estep, Mary E. Lowe, eds. *Best Practices of Online Education: A Guide for Christian Higher Education*. Charlotte: Information Age Publishing, 2012.

McCrindle, Mark. *The ABC of XYZ: Understanding the Global Generations*. 3rd ed. Sydney: McCrindle Research, 2014.

———. "Understanding Generation Y." Sydney: Australian Leadership Foundation, June 2003. http://www.emoneco.com/wp-content/uploads/2014/12/UnderstandingGenY.pdf.

McCrindle, Mark, and Ashley Fell. "Understanding Generation Alpha." Sydney: McCrindle Research, 2020. https://generationalpha.com/wp-content/uploads/2020/02/Understanding-Generation-Alpha-McCrindle.pdf.

———. "Understanding Generation Z: Recruiting, Training and Leading the Next Generation." Sydney: McCrindle Research, 2019. https://generationz.com.au/wp-content/uploads/2019/12/Understanding_Generation_Z_report_McCrindle.pdf.

McCrindle Research. "Generation Alpha Explained." 2020. Accessed 3 September 2020. https://generationalpha.com/#article-grid.

McKinney, Lois. "How Shall We Cooperate Internationally in TEE?" In *Cyprus: TEE Come of Age*, edited by Robert L. Youngblood, 27–39. Exeter: Paternoster, 1984.

Means, Barbara, Yukie Toyama, Robert Murphy, Marianne Bakia, and Karla Jones. *Evaluation of Evidence-Based Practices in Online Learning: A Meta-Analysis and Review of Online Learning Studies*. Washington, DC: US Department of Education, September 2010. https://www2.ed.gov/rschstat/eval/tech/evidence-based-practices/finalreport.pdf.

Nichols, Mark B. "A Comparison of Spiritual Formation Experiences between On-Campus and Distance Evangelical Theological Education Students." PhD, University of Otago, 2014. https://ourarchive.otago.ac.nz/handle/10523/4943.

———. "E-Primer Series No. 1: E-Learning in Context." Auckland, August 2008. http://akoaotearoa.ac.nz/project/eprimer-series/resources/files/e-Learning-context-1-eprimer-series.

———. "E-Primer Series No. 4: Online Discourse." Auckland, May 2009. http://akoaotearoa.ac.nz/project/eprimer-series/resources/files/online-discourse-4-eprimer-series-pdf.

Pandey, Asha. "10 Ways to Use Microlearning to Make Your Corporate Training More Effective." 11 April 2017. https://www.eidesign.net/use-microlearning-to-make-your-corporate-training-more-effective-10-ways/.

———. "Mobile First Designs in eLearning: A Mobile Learning Case Study." 7 May 2018. https://elearningindustry.com/mobile-first-designs-in-elearning-mobile-Learning-case-study.

———. "Why Adopt Microlearning – 15 Questions Answered." 22 June 2017. https://www.eidesign.net/adopt-microlearning-15-questions-answered/.

Rovai, Alfred P. "Facilitating Online Discussions Effectively." *Internet and Higher Education* 10 (2007): 77–88.

Salmon, Gilly. *E-moderating: The Key to Teaching and Learning Online*. 3rd ed. New York: Routledge, 2011.

———. "E-tivities – Introduction." Accessed 7 September 2020. https://www.gillysalmon.com/e-tivities.html.

———. *E-tivities: The Key to Active Online Learning*. 2nd ed. New York: Routledge, 2013.

———. "The Five Stage Model." Accessed 7 September 2020. https://www.gillysalmon.com/five-stage-model.html.

Saracco, Norberto. "TEE in Latin America: History, Present and Challenges." In *Exploring New Horizons: Working Together for Church-Based Training in Asia*, edited by Graham Aylett, 21–31. Proceedings of a conference held in Kuala Lumpur,

Malaysia, by Increase Association, 20–25 April, 2015. https://increaseassociation.org/resources/new-horizons.

———. "The Main Contribution of TEE." Unpublished comments made to the Increase Association *Empowering Churches and Equipping Disciples: Church-Based Training in Asia 2017* Conference, Chiang Mai, Thailand, 13–17 November 2017. Session 1, 17 November 2017.

SH!FT Disruptive Learning. "Understanding the Difference between eLearning and mLearning." 13 March 2018. https://www.shiftelearning.com/blog/difference-between-elearning-and-mlearning.

Siemens, George. "Learning Management Systems: The Wrong Place to Start Learning." elearnspace. November 22, 2004. http://www.elearnspace.org/Articles/lms.htm.

UNESCO. "Harnessing the Potential of ICTs for Literacy Teaching and Learning: Effective Literacy and Numeracy Programmes Using Radio, TV, Mobile Phones, Tablets, and Computers." Hamburg: UNESCO Institute for Lifelong Learning, 2014.

Weymouth, Richard J., and Paul J. Branch. "Appendix F: Standards and Guidelines for Online Evangelical Theological Education." In *ICETE Standards and Guidelines for Global Evangelical Theological Education (SG-GETE)*, 39–56. ICETE, 2019. https://icete.info/wp-content/uploads/2019/05/Standards-and-Guidelines-for-Global-Evangelical-Theological-Education-2019.pdf.

9

TEE and Quality Assurance
Contributions from Asia to a Global Discussion

Graham Aylett, Tim Green, and Rick Weymouth

Introduction

This chapter aims to present a well-grounded quality-assurance framework for TEE programmes. From a discussion of quality and quality assurance in relation to TEE it proceeds to tell the story of quality assurance in Asia, then discusses significant quality-assurance issues relevant to wider theological educators and accreditation agencies. Quality assurance may be linked to academic accreditation but does not need to be. This chapter discusses alternative options and possible interconnections between them. Finally, it contributes a suggested framework for TEE quality assurance as a foundation for these various options.

Quality and Quality Assurance in Theological Education and TEE

Quality in theological education and TEE

"Quality" expresses a thing's degree of excellence, but this requires us to know what that thing is intended to be (its identity) and to do (its purpose), and how well it achieves that purpose (its outcomes, impact, or product). Further, evaluation of quality presupposes a value system, and values are received, recognized, and promoted by a community of use. "Quality" then, becomes established in connection with identity, purpose, product, and those involved in evaluation.

We believe that the purpose of theological education is to equip the whole people of God for the mission of God.[1] Therefore, quality for theological education should be understood in terms of how effectively and fruitfully it contributes to missional training for all God's people.

However the *missio Dei* is defined, Jesus Christ plays the central role: the church is his church, his bride, his body, and he is its head. All things were created by him and for him. Jesus said, "I am the vine, you are the branches. Those who abide in me and I in them bear much fruit, because apart from me you can do nothing" (John 15:5 NRSV), so maintaining the centrality of Christ is vital for fruitfulness. John 15:1–17 further explains fruitfulness as creating a community of obedient followers, connected to Christ, who demonstrate love within that community (vv. 10, 12, 17). Therefore, quality assurance for theological education will expect institutions to demonstrate these marks of vital connection with Christ in their processes, structures, and people. And since the quality of a tree will be known from the quality of its fruit,[2] quality assurance will pay close attention to an institution's products and impact.

In the wider educational world, the European Bologna Process[3] has crystallized two helpful concepts: *fitness of purpose* and *fitness for purpose*. In these terms, effective and fruitful theological education institutions will show both:

> *Fitness of purpose*: a clearly articulated purpose, appropriate and relevant to God's mission through his church in their context,
>
> and

---

1. "The mission of the Church on earth is to serve the mission of God, and the mission of theological education is to strengthen and accompany the mission of the Church." Lausanne, *Cape Town Commitment*, Part IIF, 4. "Theological education" has been understood as for pastoral leadership only, but now a broader definition encompassing all believers is widely accepted. See chapter 2: Burke and Pearson, "TEE in Theological Perspective - Part 1," along with chapter 3: Aylett and Samuel, "TEE in Theological Perspective – Part 2."

2. Matt 7:16, 20.

3. ENQA, *Standards and Guidelines*.

> *Fitness for purpose*: personnel, courses, programmes, structures, processes, and resources that combine effectively towards fulfilling this good purpose.

Theological education providers need evaluation in such areas as governance, leadership and administration, sustainability, programme design, and development. TEE is one particular methodology of theological education, with its own characteristics, while other delivery methods have their distinctive characteristics. No one would think of applying the particular characteristics of oranges as criteria for excellence in apples. Oranges and apples share some similarities of identity, purpose, and outcomes, but have clear differences. Likewise, different theological education methodologies need different criteria for excellence. But too often TEE "apples" have been measured against the quality characteristics of campus-based "oranges." Hence, this chapter focuses on appropriate quality measures specifically for TEE as a tool for equipping all God's people for his mission.

Appropriate quality assurance for TEE

Quality assurance evaluates whether agreed expectations and standards are being met. Thus, in a TEE institution, quality assurance evaluates whether its aims, structures, processes, programmes, personnel, students, graduates, and impact meet agreed quality standards of good practice, effectiveness, and fruitfulness.

In a TEE institution, quality assurance is valuable for its governing body and personnel who desire long-term fruitfulness in serving the Lord and his church. It also gives confidence to present and prospective students, user churches, and other stakeholders that this institution is fulfilling its publicly stated purpose.

If the purpose of theological education is to equip all God's people for his mission, then theological education (including TEE) should be evaluated accordingly: is it effective and fruitful missional training for every church member? Does the programme listen and respond creatively to the context, to the church, and above all to the Lord, in pursuit of this great purpose? Who should determine quality-assurance measures for TEE and assess specific TEE programmes? These are critical questions.

For an individual TEE institution, at least six groups of stakeholders[4] can evaluate its effectiveness in equipping the people of God for the mission of God. These different stakeholder groups focus on the TEE programme's context, bringing their own values and evaluation perspectives concerning its effectiveness. Relevant stakeholder groups might include:

- Leaders and educators currently running the programme
- Investors
- Current students, who may have been studying for many years, and recent graduates[5]
- Churches and families impacted by the programme
- Local communities impacted by learners or graduates and their churches[6]
- Theological educators from non-TEE programmes in the same context.

External agencies play a role in working with TEE institutions to appraise them in relation to a bigger picture. Four broad groups of external agencies may help in setting regional quality measures:

- National or regional denominations which may set standards for ordination or licensed ministry within their families of churches
- National, regional, or government agencies which set secular educational standards; they might not share theological education's values and purposes but are sometimes needed for national recognition
- Regional TEE networks (such as the Increase Association) and wider TEE practitioners who have good understanding and experience of TEE
- International or regional theological quality-assurance agencies, such as the Asia Theological Association (ATA), with standards

4. Stakeholders are groups having an interest or "stake" in the success of the institution.

5. Recent graduates offer especially valuable evidence, having experienced the whole programme and knowing its effectiveness in equipping them.

6. Assessment of programme impact through its graduates is rightly receiving attention. See ICETE's 2015 conference resources (http://theologicaleducation.net/articles/index.htm?category_id=77); Brooking, *Is It Working?*, and Das, *Connecting Curriculum with Context.*

recognized over a wide region and across different modes of theological education.

External quality-assurance agencies need mechanisms to hear various stakeholder voices and perspectives, and to involve these stakeholders rigorously in quality assurance of TEE programmes. Stakeholder feedback contributes to the ongoing improvement cycles shown in Figure 9.1 – the first, to improve the quality standards used in assessment, and the second, to improve effectiveness of the programme.

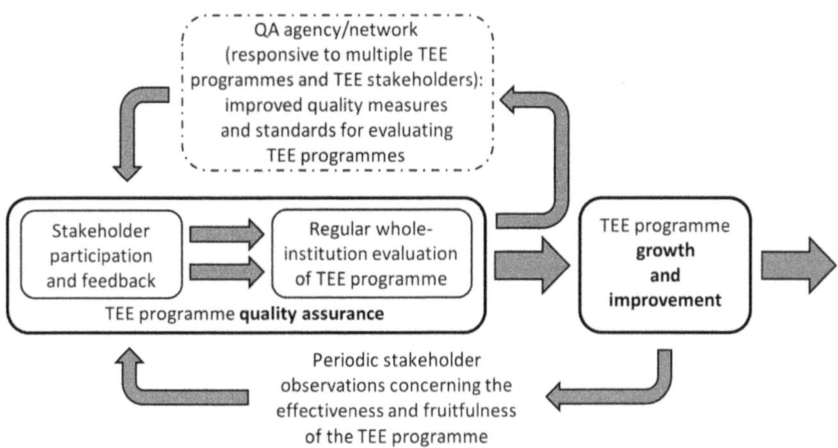

Figure 9.1. Quality measure and institutional improvement cycles

In evaluating TEE programmes, TEE practitioners and their networks are especially significant since they understand TEE's identity, purpose, and vision. Wise theological quality-assurance bodies will involve these networks in providing more relevant quality assurance for their TEE member institutions.[7]

Where a quality-assurance agency understands TEE and offers appropriate service, there will be great benefit in membership. But if it does not provide a suitable framework for TEE quality assurance, a regional TEE network or

7. For example, by including them in the improvement cycles mentioned and involving TEE practitioners in visiting evaluation teams to help in institutional evaluation and development.

an alternative may need to fill the gap. This may be avoided if all parties work together with good mutual understanding.

The Story of Quality Assurance for TEE in Asia

No common ground?

Should TEE submit to an external framework for quality assurance? In the 1970s and 1980s some TEE practitioners argued that to seek accreditation would deny TEE's nature as a renewal movement within theological education, since accreditation processes seemed overly rigid and entrenched.[8] Others saw unacceptable and insufficient reasons for seeking accreditation.[9] They believed that submitting to an accreditation process founded on values inimical to TEE would not serve the new things God was doing through this movement.

Breaking new ground

However, in the mid-1980s, the ATA began to develop a TEE-specific accreditation approach since it was required by Indonesian TEE programmes for government recognition.[10] A group under Robert Ferris researched TEE's nature and identity, asking practitioners what TEE values were important to them.[11] They also explored various philosophies of accreditation, combining insights from Robert Stake's responsive evaluation, Esterline's community-based evaluation, and Ferris's emphasis on renewal values analysis.[12]

Their ground-breaking work produced the first TEE *Accreditation Manual and Self-Study Guide* in 1986, approved by the ATA in 1987.[13] This framework required a TEE institution to work closely with stakeholders to see the programme through their eyes and report the findings. It also required

8. "TEE associations should avoid developing accrediting functions. TEE is, above all else, a dynamic developmental process; it is a spirit and an attitude and a stance." McKinney, "How Shall We Cooperate," 38.

9. For example, Ferris, *Accrediting TEE*, 3–4.

10. Hart, *TEE Stakeholder Roles*, 4.

11. Ferris, "Strategic Flexibility," 6. These values are listed in note 42 below.

12. Hart, *TEE Stakeholder Roles*, 6–7. Esterline, *Evaluation of Theological Education*; Stufflebeam and Coryn, *Evaluation Theory*, 373–402.

13. See Ferris, *Accrediting TEE*; ATA, *Accreditation Manual* (1987); Ferris, "Accreditation and TEE"; Ferris, "Strategic Flexibility."

the institution to explain how the values agreed widely by TEE educators were being expressed through their programme. Finally, an ATA visiting evaluation team would visit to verify that the reports were accurate and to make a recommendation concerning accreditation.

For the first time, TEE institutions in Asia had a quality-assurance framework tailored to their needs. It was sensitive to their identity in the wider theological education world and to the values they cherished. By assigning such a significant role to stakeholders' contributions, it affirmed the institution's context and purpose, and included the range of stakeholders in deciding about quality. In addition, it was outcomes-based. It did not specify volumes of learning in terms of credit hours, but defined programme levels in terms of general competencies.

In a separate development, the World Council of Churches (WCC) sponsored a consultation on the evaluation of TEE in Costa Rica in 1990, which led to the publication of *Opting for Change* in 1991.[14] This WCC quality-assurance framework was similar to ATA's, with a strong emphasis on stakeholder participation.

Later, in 1995, the ATA's TEE accreditation framework was reviewed and revised, amplifying some sections while retaining the same general approach.

Shifting ground?

In 1998, the ATA decided to produce one new accreditation manual to serve both campus-based and TEE institutions. Completed in 1999, it was based on the theoretical foundation of responsive evaluation used for the ATA's 1995 *TEE Accreditation Manual*. However, it gave less prominence to participatory evaluation. Subsequently, the 2004 *Manual for Accreditation* introduced Carnegie credit hours[15] alongside learning outcomes in award definitions. This manual did not embrace all the TEE values of the earlier *TEE Accreditation Manual* and gave less attention to the particular characteristics of TEE institutions. Unfortunately, the new manual's terminology, appropriate

14. Kinsler and Emery, *Opting for Change*.

15. The Carnegie unit specifies an amount of time spent studying a subject (see https://www.carnegiefoundation.org/faqs/carnegie-unit/), but with varying formulations.

for campus-based seminaries, gave some TEE institutions the impression that it was not intended for them.[16]

Finding fresh common ground

In 2014 a very constructive, collaborative process addressed the issue, with a working group including TEE practitioners from Increase and members of ATA's Commission for Accreditation and Educational Development. ATA's revised accreditation manual that resulted from this process in 2016[17] used more inclusive terminology, allowed for a "flexible Carnegie credit hour" based on a variety of learning activities and contexts, and addressed elements critical for TEE and other non-traditional programmes. It showed how different quality measures were appropriate when the same ATA values were expressed in different educational settings (see Figure 9.2).

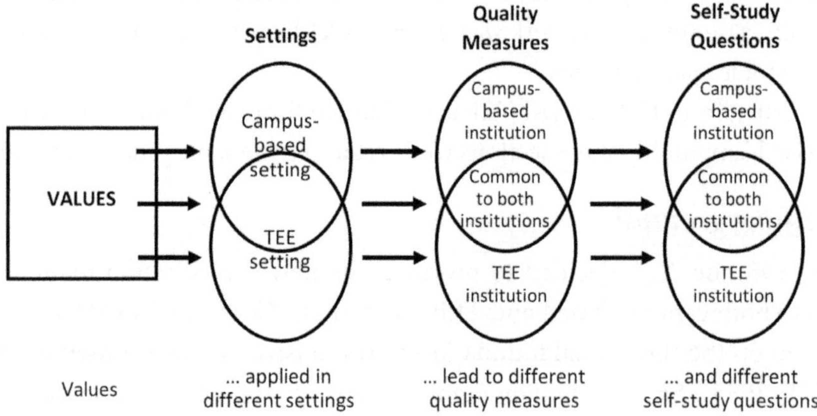

Figure 9.2. Values applied to different settings for quality-assurance purposes[18]

16. While stating that, "because of the differences in educational delivery systems, some guidelines will logically be interpreted differently" (12), the rest of the 2004 *Manual for Accreditation* clearly had campus-based institutions in focus.

17. With minor improvements, this was re-published in 2017 and remained current to late 2020; it has now been replaced by the 2021 revision.

18. Source: Adapted from ATA, *Manual for Accreditation* (2017), 23.

Meanwhile, on the global stage, the International Council for Evangelical Theological Education (ICETE) Manifesto (first published in 1984) had continued to challenge theological educators with values widely acknowledged and agreed, but inadequately actioned.[19] In 2019 ICETE, making a significant effort to globalize quality assurance for evangelical theological education, published its *Standards and Guidelines for Global Evangelical Theological Education (SG-GETE).* The ATA's 2021 *Manual for Accreditation* represents a major revision, incorporating many of the ICETE standards and guidelines, while continuing the previous inclusivity for extension (and similar) programmes.

This chapter gratefully acknowledges the prayers and labours of many over the years and reaffirms their emphasis on values-based and participatory evaluation.

Global Issues for TEE in Relation to Quality Assurance

TEE within the broader theological education world

TEE shares the goal of theological education in general, to equip the people of God for the mission of God, making a distinctive contribution through its own values, emphases, and concerns. TEE programmes may face in two directions: towards the church as it serves God's mission, and towards the academy for award recognition and/or quality assurance. These directions are sometimes aligned, sometimes divergent.

The first direction should be the core concern of every TEE programme. As servant and partner to the church, it must seek feedback from the church, the premier stakeholder, and from outside observers and evaluators. The core criteria are effectiveness and fruitfulness in equipping the whole people of God for the mission of God. It is vital to maintain the ecclesiological-missional purpose of TEE programmes.

The second direction, however, requires comparability to external standards and quality measures, raising issues about the academic aspects of theological education. Does a TEE programme need accredited academic qualifications?

19. ICETE, *ICETE Manifesto*. ICETE (https://icete.info/) serves as an umbrella agency for eight regional evangelical accrediting agencies (including the ATA), with global coverage.

Will evaluation processes help or hinder in fulfilling the programme's purpose? Not all TEE providers require academic recognition, but for those that do, how can academic comparability with other delivery methods be ensured? What is more important, credit counting or holistic competency-based learning outcomes? And what criteria should be most important for validation of TEE programmes?

Below, we affirm two potential quality-assurance pathways and suggest possible interconnections between them. One pathway is for TEE programmes that require academic accreditation and awards, and the other for TEE programmes where specific holistic competencies are most important. In each case, we seek mutually beneficial partnerships between TEE programmes and quality-assurance providers.

Moreover, how can TEE learners progress to campus-based institutions for higher qualifications or fast-track their training? How can learners unable to remain in their urban, residential institution, complete their primary awards through a TEE programme back in their rural sending context? And how can church leaders be trained to equip the whole people of God in learner-centred ways? Other important matters are transferability of credit and mutual recognition of church-based and campus-based partners for kingdom ministry.

Integrated learning pathways, nested programmes, and stepwise progressions

Integrated or connected learning pathways are proving fruitful for equipping God's people for his mission of God through TEE, and they hold great promise. TEE practitioners see the importance of their recognition within the wider theological education world.[20] Recognition is needed of the discipleship journey that many millions of grassroots believers take from brand new disciple to mature and fruitful participation in God's mission. Possible pathways are illustrated in Figure 9.3.[21]

20. The basic concept and need is developed well by Tim Green in his chapter "Integrated Learning Pathways" in *TEE in Asia*, 239–44; alternative names for integrated learning pathways are connected, joined-up, or intentional learning pathways.

21. Note that pathways to church leadership do not always also lead to higher formal educational attainment, and not all believers are called to church leadership; however, such pathways as

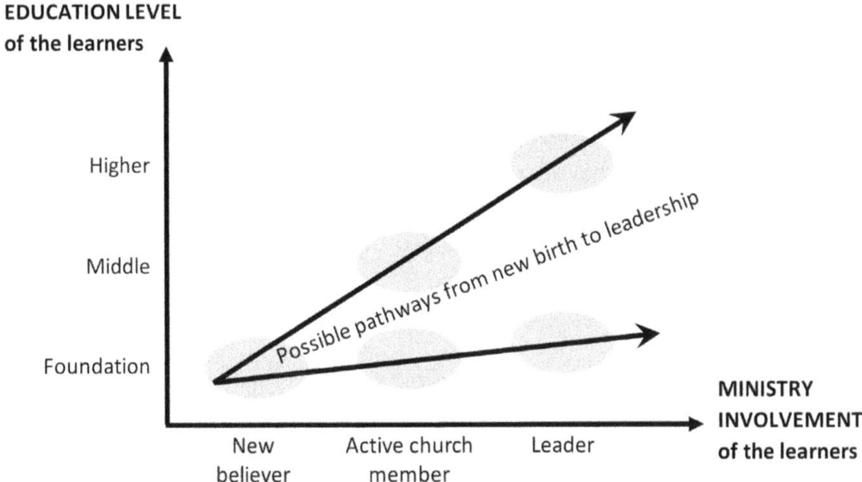

Figure 9.3. Integrated learning pathways possible within TEE[22]

The discipleship journey begins at the first level of training with foundational materials, leading on to certificate level courses, diploma courses, up to bachelor level, and even to master's degrees. As learners progress through the various levels, they grow holistically – in personal and spiritual maturity, in knowledge and cognitive skills as courses become more demanding, and in ministry ability and effectiveness.[23] With TEE methodology, all of these are crucially provided in a local church (or believing community) context, where learning materials lead into group discussion and practical application and are supported by personal face-to-face nurturing.

An example is the Open Theological Seminary in Pakistan, a TEE institution that offers five levels in a stepwise progression from foundation courses up to a master's degree.[24] Not all TEE programmes offer a complete

shown in Figure 9.3 need to be available to new believers and recognized by churches and theological education leaders and agencies.

22. Source: Adapted from Green, "Integrated Learning Pathways," 244.

23. So Green, "Integrated Learning Pathways," 244.

24. The five levels offered by OTS are discipleship, certificate, diploma, bachelor, and master's. The first four levels are delivered through TEE, with the certificate, diploma, and bachelor programmes accredited by the ATA. Not all OTS students progress through every level. Other examples of ATA-accredited TEE programmes offering nested programmes are the College of

pathway like this. Others serve local churches with a holistic programme for grassroots believers, helping them to lay good foundations of discipleship and ministry among their members. Further steps on the pathway could come through partnership with other theological education providers, and with parachurch ministries that offer occasional workshops and seminars.[25] For such intentional learning pathways,[26] "nested" or "stepwise"[27] programmes can be very beneficial by having earlier stages of discipleship development "nested" inside later stages and progressively so.

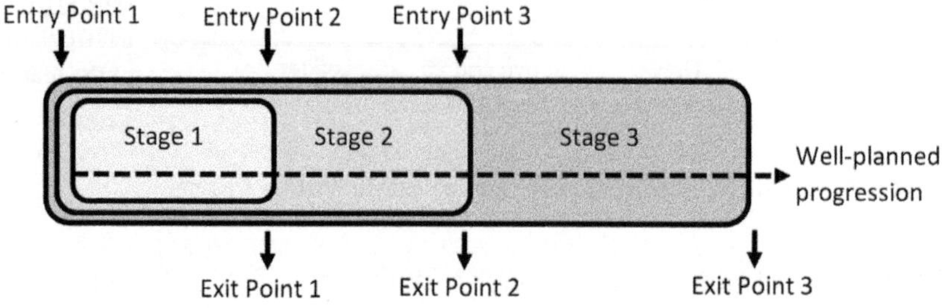

Figure 9.4. Nested learning programme

In such a programme, there are planned entry and exit points. At stage 1 a student could choose to exit with a qualification, or to enter stage 2, and so on. Credits gained in the earlier stages of the programme contribute to the total number of credits required for later stages of the programme and to its final award.[28]

Christian Theology Bangladesh (CCTB) and the Kingdom Leadership Training Center (KLTC) in Mongolia.

25. Parachurch ministries may offer excellent training led by specialists in various fields. If they are from outside local contexts, while still valuable, they may lack contextual sensitivity. For further discussion, see Green, "Integrated Learning Pathways," 245–46.

26. For general principles of integration of formal, informal, and nonformal theological education, see ICETE, *SG-GETE*, 37–38; ECTE, *Manual* (2018), 49–59. The key in integration is intentionality. One-off, otherwise "nonformal" trainings, become formal when planned as parts of a whole curriculum, with appropriate assessment of defined learning outcomes.

27. In one or two Asian countries the term "ladderized" is used for nested or stepwise programmes.

28. We recognize that for some accreditation agencies difficulties may arise if stage 1 certificate level courses contribute credits toward a stage 3 bachelor level award. We believe that provided

Depicted stepwise, the same nested learning programme is shown in Figure 9.5.

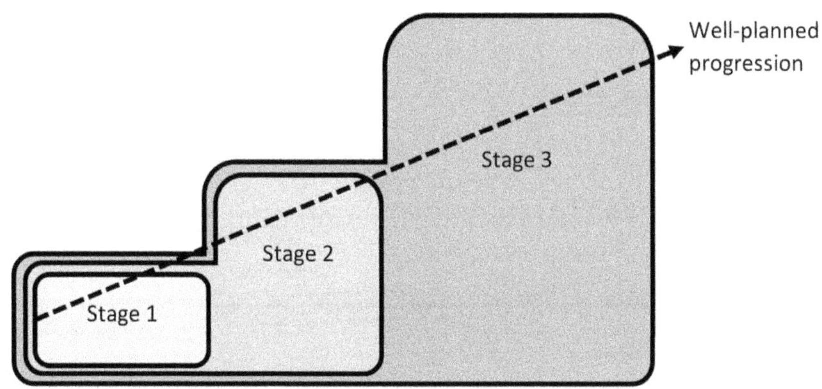

Figure 9.5. Stepwise progression in a nested learning programme

As shown in Figure 9.5, alongside progression in time we may expect holistic progression in knowledge, skills, and abilities. The three stages depicted might refer to certificate, diploma and bachelor awards, or alternatively to growing levels of competence as, for example, a village evangelist, church planter, pastor, counsellor, or workplace minister.

An individual TEE programme may offer all stages on the pathway itself, or it might partner with other learning providers. Such a pathway, with input from outside providers, might look like Figure 9.6 for example.[29]

appropriate progression is demonstrated through suitable measurement of exit parameters, the principle of a three-stage, stepwise, nested programme should not be rejected. See also notes 30 and 40 below.

29. Instead of using academic designations like certificate, diploma, and bachelor studies, a TEE programme could refer to foundation, intermediate, and advanced studies; the principle of recognized stages and progression is important, not the precise designations.

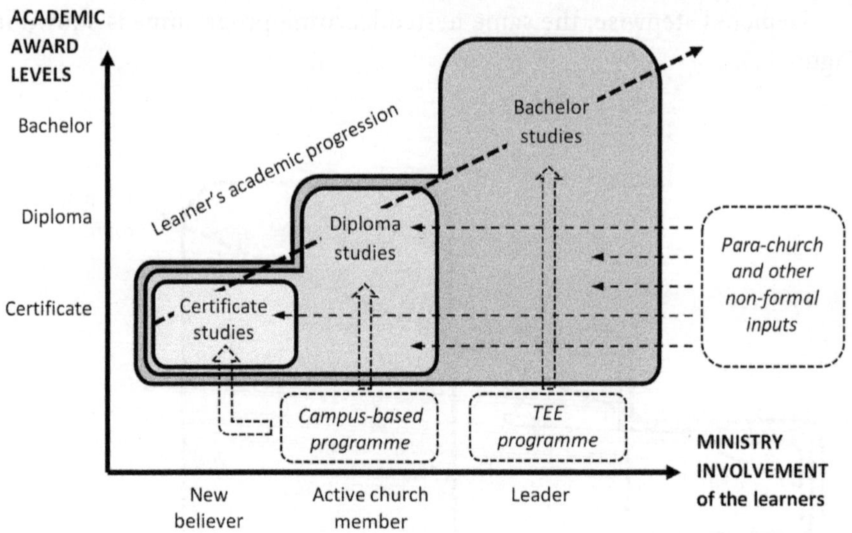

Figure 9.6. Potential integrated learning pathway with partnered nested programmes[30]

If the graduate outcomes are achieved at the end of each award, it does not necessarily matter that the early stages of study were at lower academic levels, since lower stages can be designed to lift learners sufficiently to be ready for learning at the next level.[31]

This acknowledges the accepted principle of recognition of prior learning (RPL) and the granting of advanced standing for entry into higher award study. Indeed, "prior learning" for the higher-level TEE awards can be intentionally planned into the earlier levels of a stepwise programme. Such planning avoids careless provision of "previous ministry experience" credits of dubious value – a common form of RPL abuse in the past.

30. Figure 9.6, as drawn, depicts the scenario of a student attending a campus-based institution and completing a certificate and diploma, but then returning home for church responsibilities, and completing a bachelor's degree via TEE, alongside ongoing ministry. However, alternatively, the three stages could occur with different combinations of educational providers.

31. The New Zealand Qualifications Authority, offering ten levels of tertiary education in its Qualifications Framework, allows completion of a 120 credit (one-year full-time equivalent) level 5 diploma with 48 credits (40%) from a level 4 certificate, and a 360 credit level 7 bachelor degree, with up to 288 credits (80%) from level 5, 6, or 7 diploma studies, with an expected spread across levels, so that "*the qualification demonstrates progression*," and only 72 credits (20%) required from level 7 bachelor studies. So NZQA, *New Zealand Qualifications Framework* (2016), 12, 15.

When an integrated learning pathway is intentionally planned,[32] it may include not only TEE courses but also inputs from other educational providers (for example, campus-based intensive courses) or from parachurch organizations, such as a workshop, online course, or preaching seminar. Each relevant intentional input is counted as a valid contribution to fulfilling the graduate profile and achieving the award.

Intentionally connected or integrated learning pathways offer huge promise for TEE programmes (and others) to serve grassroots learners globally, and credible pathways to recognized awards, including academic awards where needed.[33] Quality-assurance and internationally recognized frameworks for good practice could help such programmes to even greater fruitfulness.[34]

Encouragingly, international agencies such as ICETE, the ATA, and the Overseas Council are already engaging in serious conversations toward recognition of intentionally integrated learning pathways. More work remains to be done.

Academic comparability, credits and competencies, and other related issues

How may TEE programmes be compared academically with other theological education programmes? This question is important in its own right and also

32. Programme intentionality for an integrated learning pathway involves more complexity than we can describe here. For quality-assurance purposes an educational case for stepwise programme decisions must be clear.

33. The ATA's 2021 *Manual for Accreditation* (Part I: 4.4, 88–89) includes the following as factors to be considered for accreditation evaluation and approval of nested learning programmes: (i) the aims of the programme; (ii) the formational contexts of the students; (iii) the ministry contexts of students after graduation; (iv) the requirements for entry into each stage of the overall programme; (v) the mechanisms for demonstrating students' readiness to study at each stage; (vi) whether the curriculum displays well-planned progression from one stage to the next; (vii) whether the requirements for completion of each stage contribute adequately to the requirements for completion of more advanced stages; (viii) the proportion of credits gained at previous stages that contribute to the credit requirement for successful graduation at each exit point; (ix) the role of supplementary, bridging modules at the transition from one stage to the next; and (x) the quality of evidence showing that students have achieved the outcomes for successful completion of each stage.

34. It is believed that ATA member schools serve approximately 59,000 students (across 226 institutions in 2019). This includes six ATA-accredited TEE programmes, also Increase Association members, which together serve about 9,500 learners at tertiary level, and an additional 7,000 at foundation levels (all part-time).

to enable integrated learning pathways linking TEE institutions and others. For such pathways and partnerships to flourish, the institutions involved need to have confidence in the academic credibility of each other's contribution, however the various contributions are configured. External validation of each component will be important.

Who should provide that validation service, and *how* should quality be measured? An accreditation agency such as the ATA offers internationally recognized certification of awards, measured by achievement of holistic learning outcomes listed in graduate profiles, linked to specified volumes of learning measured by learning hours and credit allocations. Additionally, two recently formed international agencies now provide alternative approaches to certification, one based on achievement of specific holistic competencies,[35] and the other on a combination of competencies and credit hours.[36]

Debate continues about the respective merits of credit counting in fulfilment of holistic learning outcomes versus competency achievement for assessing students and granting awards.[37] Perhaps these are not so far apart as sometimes presented. Achievement of holistic learning outcomes can be accompanied by credit counting, which show where a student has reached and how long it took to get there. Similarly, demonstration of specific holistic competencies by various means can also show student achievement without necessarily counting credits (though a programme could still measure the learning hours taken to demonstrate those competencies).

In both cases, it is the demonstrable achievement of learning outcomes or competencies that serves the great vision of equipping the people of God. A credible evangelical theological education framework insists that student

35. Re-Forma offers an assessment tool with thirty-five specific competency outcomes for church leader training (see https://www.re-forma.global/ and their "Outcomes" document).

36. The newly created Global Accreditation Association for Ministries and Training (GAAMT) allows for church-based development of curricula and offers comprehensive, ministry-oriented competency-based evaluations, nevertheless with credit counting, leading to accredited bachelor degrees (see their website, https://www.gaa-mt.com/ and *Accreditation Manual*).

37. A summary of the debate, discussed in TEE circles at least since 1969 (Winter, "Essential Elements," 416–17), is beyond the scope of this chapter. Each approach has strengths and weaknesses.

learning must necessarily be holistic and expressed as whole-life discipleship, resulting in holistic graduate profiles and learning outcomes.[38]

For TEE programmes needing to demonstrate academic comparability, counting credit hours may also be necessary, whereas for those who want primarily to equip students with specific competencies for mission and ministry, competency-based assessment may be adequate. Hence, quality-assurance pathways for various kinds of TEE programmes are needed.

Within a holistic evangelical training programme, academic achievement forms only one aspect of an integrated curriculum that combines intellectual formation, ministry skills formation, and spiritual, relational, and personal formation.[39] Likewise, ministry training includes the aspect of intellectual formation but is by no means limited to it.[40]

An individual TEE programme may need to decide which body or association to join for quality-assurance purposes. Each will naturally have its own strengths and emphases, and indeed it can be beneficial to take part in two or more quality-assurance networks simultaneously.

Some TEE programmes may need regional recognition and certification for partnerships in integrated learning pathways, for denominational ordination programmes, or simply due to stakeholder demand. For TEE programmes a suitable quality-assurance agency will accredit or validate multiple awards, at least at certificate and diploma levels, if not also foundational studies.[41]

---

38. Such a holistic approach includes elements aimed at intellectual formation or development, ministry skills formation, and spiritual, relational, personal, and character formation, sometimes described as development of the cognitive, affective, and psychomotor or behavioural learning domains (for example, Shaw, *Transforming Theological Education*, 67–77; cf. Brynjolfson and Lewis, eds., *Integral Ministry Training*, 5–6, 8, 23–24, 29–36; Cannell, *Theological Education Matters*, 281–317), and often described popularly as "head, heart, and hands." This is not always well-understood by government accrediting bodies.

39. A majority of ICETE member agencies offering accredited degrees at all levels now strongly emphasize holistic formation.

40. We understand, GAAMT, *Accreditation Manual*, 3, 34 when it speaks of a paradigm shift "from academic excellence to ministry-oriented [training]," to mean "from over-emphasis on intellectual formation to properly holistic ministry-oriented training." We agree in resisting academic approaches where cognitive or intellectual formation is indeed the main goal.

41. Some agencies only accredit bachelor degrees and higher: those agencies may not serve a multi-level or multi-stage TEE programme. And in some countries, awards with titles from a national qualifications framework, such as certificate, diploma, and bachelor degrees, cannot be granted legally without national government accreditation.

Bachelor (and higher) award levels may or may not be mandated; however, validation of "lower" academic awards recognizes learners' efforts to grow as Christ's disciples serving God's mission in the world.

All TEE organizations will definitely benefit from competency-based quality assurance, whether or not they also need accredited academic qualifications. Competency assessments may include portfolio assessments, self-reflection upon praxis, oral interviews, testimonials from those impacted by a student's ministry, and expert or mentor evaluations. They must necessarily include active partnerships with local churches and their leaders.

Competency-based approaches will suit TEE programmes serving local church communities where whole-life discipleship of believers and development of skills for ministry and service are the greatest perceived needs. In such cases the highest "level" needed may be equipping individuals to be effective village pastors, rural evangelists, or church planters. Academic education at tertiary level may not be relevant for such institutions and those they serve. A quality-assurance agency that helps such TEE programmes fulfil their mission and vision will be more appropriate than one aiming primarily to maintain academic standards.

Whichever quality-assurance approach is preferred (alone or in combination), we need an appropriate quality-assurance framework that will evaluate the effectiveness of a TEE institution *as TEE* and help it to become even more fruitful in its efforts. To this task we now turn.[42]

A Quality-Assurance Framework for TEE

Quality assurance for all TEE programmes

The ATA's approach to accreditation faces towards both church and academy. To accommodate the latter, it must show that its awards match comparable university standards. For some TEE programmes this is welcome, but formal accreditation may not be desired by all.

The Increase Association supports relevant quality assurance for all TEE programmes, including those without formal academic awards. Therefore,

42. Our contribution builds on discussions within both the Increase Association and the ATA, and with various educational experts. We are grateful for their contributions.

alongside its commitment to the ATA accreditation framework, Increase has also been exploring with the ATA, Overseas Council, and others a quality-assurance framework that could certify quality and help programme improvement without requiring academic accreditation. The following proposals draw on these discussions.

Important priorities, values, and educational factors for TEE practitioners

TEE practitioners, in the years up to 2012, have produced key documents that identify important priorities, values, and educational factors to guide TEE programmes.

- Robert Ferris's research in the 1980s, leading to the 1987 and 1995 ATA TEE Accreditation Manuals[43]
- TEE commitments in Kinsler and Emery's 1991 *Opting for Change*[44]
- Jim Lo's "Seven Ingredients" from his 2002 TEE research in Southern Africa[45]
- Patricia Harrison's 2004 evaluation of the TEE movement[46]
- SEAN's user handbook (2005), which gives expression to both values and aspects of good practice in running a TEE programme[47]

43. The ATA's list of TEE values included: (i) priority on training; (ii) integration of learning and ministry; (iii) programme accessibility; (iv) church relatedness; (v) focus on Bible-in-context; and (vi) service orientation. ATA, *Accreditation Manual* (1987), 8–11.

44. Introducing a section on community-based evaluation, Kinsler and Emery (*Opting for Change*, 16) list four commitments: "The same basic commitments exist in virtually every [TEE] programme – commitments to training in context, to the selection of students by local churches, to dialogue between students and tutors, and to providing service to a particular community."

45. Lo, "Seven Ingredients." These are: (i) relevant spiritual issues; (ii) sociopolitical involvement leading to community transformation; (iii) adequate administrative provision; (iv) practical ministry assignments in the local church context; (v) modelling of evangelism and church planting; (vi) appropriate TEE curriculum providing learning pathways from foundation onwards; and (vii) importance of both clergy and laity in ministry.

46. Harrison, "Forty Years On." Harrison mentions four key factors: (i) the key stakeholders in the TEE programme understand it, are convinced of its value, and are keen to implement and promote it; (ii) the TEE programme has clear objectives and caters appropriately for a well-defined target group; (iii) the administration is well organized, fits the local context, functions with integrity, and is adequately funded; and (iv) quality self-instructional materials are used, with all or most designed for the context.

47. Factors in SEAN's handbook include (i) organized curriculum; (ii) relevant; (iii) clear objectives; (iv) student learns in context; (v) emphasis on training and equipping; (vi) for the

- Increase's 2010 "Kathmandu Conference Statement"[48]
- Increase's 2012 "Priorities for Fruitful Practice."[49] These priorities combined contributions from contemporary TEE practitioners in Asia and previous written materials.

Building upon these various statements and with explicit gratitude for them, we propose the following five clusters of related values and educational factors as crucial for effective, fruitful TEE programmes.

1. Theological

- The centrality of Christ, and thus of the gospel of Christ
- Faithfulness to the Scriptures

2. Missional

- Serving the whole people of God for the mission of God
- Practical training and equipping for the mission of God
- Growth in lived-out, everyday discipleship[50]
- Individual, community, and context transformation

3. Ecclesiological

- Local church-connected, in-context training
- Learning pathways for all God's people

---

whole people of God; (vii) selection and training of small group leaders; (viii) clear administrative structures; (ix) competent leadership. SEAN, *How to Use SEAN*, 17–25.

48. van Wingerden, Green, and Aylett, *TEE in Asia*, 21–22. Factors emerging include (i) transformation; (ii) immediate application; (iii) holistic growth; (iv) integration of learning and living; (v) equipping with a variety of skills; (vi) faithful to the Scriptures; (vii) interdenominational; (viii) providing pathways for growth; (ix) flexible and adaptable; (x) accessible; (xi) in-context training; (xii) discipleship, leadership and church planting all resourced by TEE; (xiii) local church-related or -based; (xiv) equipping all church members; (xv) equipping as agents of transformation.

49. Increase Association, *Priorities for Fruitful Practice* (unpublished, 2012) lists at least twenty-two factors, which are explicit or implicit in the "priorities"; it may be found on the Increase website.

50. This factor could be placed in the educational cluster (iv); there are several overlaps across our five categories.

4. Holistic educational

- Sound pedagogical understanding of the TEE method
- A commitment to relevant, well-designed TEE courses and curricula
- Focus on small group leader selection, training, support, and affirmation
- Effective utilization of small group interactions
- Intentional and accountable practical application

5. Administrative

- Well-led and well-organized programme administration
- Ongoing evaluation and programme improvement

TEE educators agree on these areas as vital for effective and fruitful ministry, and a quality-assurance framework for TEE institutions must put the spotlight on them.

A process for TEE quality assurance

The evaluation process proposed here builds on the experience of TEE institutions in Asia over four decades and involves four stages.[51]

1. Stakeholder survey and impact assessment

The TEE institution carries out a stakeholder survey and some kind of impact assessment. How do the institution's stakeholders evaluate the programme? What evidence is there of desired impacts in churches and communities served by the programme?

2. Institutional self-study and self-evaluation

Drawing on the findings of the stakeholder survey and impact assessment, the institution prepares a report responding to a detailed self-study questionnaire. This questionnaire leads the institution in a process of self-evaluation against clear criteria, which may include the agreed standards and values of an external quality-assurance agency, for effective and fruitful practice for TEE institutions.

51. The four stages described are implicit in the institutional improvement cycle depicted in Figure 9.1.

3. Quality-assurance agency evaluation

The institution then hosts a visit from representatives of an external quality-assurance agency, meeting with stakeholders including institution staff to verify the process and follow up on issues arising from the stakeholder survey and the self-study report. Representatives have a clear grasp of TEE methods and values, and at least one has extensive personal experience in TEE ministry. The representatives observe TEE groups in action in more than one location.

4. Reporting back

These representatives report to the TEE institution with suggestions and recommendations for improvement, required actions where necessary to meet baseline standards, and, hopefully, assurance that the required quality standards have been met. The institution then reports the agency's findings back to the stakeholders involved in the first stage; this is important for accountability and continuing improvement.

Standards and guidelines for TEE

Here we explore standards and guidelines arising from values held in common by TEE educators. These would form the basis of the self-study questionnaire in the second stage of the process for TEE quality assurance described above.

1. In relation to the purpose of TEE

A fruitful quality-assurance system fits the contours of the institution. How fruitful is the programme in fulfilling *this* purpose, in training *these* people, for *this* ministry, in *this* context? If an institution or programme has not clearly articulated what it is trying to do, quality assurance becomes impossible.

i. Institutional vision

Effective and fruitful institutions have a clear vision relating to churches as they serve the mission of God. They recognize and celebrate the centrality of Christ in all they do and seek in all their courses and curriculum to be faithful to Scripture.

ii. Who, What For, and Where?

Effective and fruitful institutions have a clear statement of *who* their programmes are aiming to equip, *what* their programmes are aiming to equip them for, and *where* their learners are serving and intend to serve.

They produce purpose statements through a participative process involving their main stakeholders. Institutional leadership, staff, local mentors and group leaders, church leaders and other stakeholders, therefore, know and own these aims.

2. In relation to the preparation for fruitful TEE

i. Understanding TEE methodology
Effective and fruitful TEE institutions have a deep and thorough understanding of TEE methodology and have developed contextually relevant ways of communicating it.

ii. Graduate profile and curriculum design
Effective and fruitful TEE institutions know the needs of the communities and contexts they are seeking to impact, what ministries they are intending to equip their learners for, and how they intend to equip them. They research the entry strengths and weaknesses of their learners.

With prayerful research and stakeholder participation, they produce a Graduate Profile describing holistic learning outcomes including the knowledge and understanding, ministry skills, character, and relational qualities the programme intends learners to develop. These learning outcomes include foundational outcomes, such as growth as a disciple of Jesus and in knowledge and love of God and neighbour. Institutions can demonstrate how each course contributes to the learners' journey from entry to fulfilment of the Graduate Profile. Curricular design may also encourage training and ministry multiplication.[52]

iii. Preparation of courses
When writing new courses for their context, effective and fruitful TEE institutions use teams of course writers, involving suitably qualified people who between them know the subject matter, the context, characteristics of adult learners in their context, instructional design, and the technicalities

52. For example, a programme may require students to facilitate one or more courses they have already taken before graduation.

of TEE course writing.[53] They research their context and its specific needs before selecting content for their courses and have access to a wealth of relevant materials.

They develop TEE courses that help learners in community to shine the light of the Bible on specific situations in local contexts; integrate action and reflection intentionally; grow more Christ-like in knowledge, attitudes, abilities and relationships; be transformed themselves, and to help bring transformation in their circles of influence.[54]

They also follow best practices when using TEE courses that were written outside their context. This involves well-documented pathways for selection, analysis, contextualization and translation, editing, and field testing.

TEE courses comprise attractively presented student self-study materials and group leaders' guides. Full documentation of course design provides learning outcomes, detailed guidelines for group meetings, practical application and ministry assignments, and holistic assessment frameworks. A student workbook for practical application may be included separately.

iv. Selection and preparation of TEE group leaders

Effective and fruitful TEE institutions understand the critical importance of those who lead the learning groups.

They partner with stakeholders, especially church leaders, in establishing clear and appropriate criteria to select new group leaders at each level of their programme.

Their training for new group leaders demonstrates how to lead group discussions well, includes adequate opportunity for practice with feedback, and gives solid grounding in TEE methodology.[55] As far as possible, training uses participative, interactive methods to model dynamics expected in good group discussions.

They bring together group leaders for mutual sharing, learning and support, and for continued training in areas such as:

53. This should include semi-programmed and non-programmed writing alongside programmed writing.

54. See chapter 7: Ivins and Do, "New TEE Courses."

55. SEAN's suggested principles for group leader training are provided in van Wingerden, Green, and Aylett, *TEE in Asia*, 223–26.

- Creating a safe and hospitable group environment, including establishing good "group rules"
- Adult learning
- Group dynamics – handling diversions and distractions, and dominant and dormant members
- Coaching and mentoring, identifying and encouraging group members' giftings
- The art of facilitation through skillful questioning
- Mistakes to avoid in TEE group facilitation
- Intentional creative variety in group meetings
- The importance of practical application and assessment of learners in relation to holistic learning outcomes.

v. Local church/user organization relationships

Effective and fruitful TEE institutions maintain good communication with churches and other users of their programmes. They listen to church leaders and their needs and respond with servant-hearts as they seek together to equip the whole people of God. They affirm and encourage churches in their missional life, and ensure church leaders understand what TEE is and how it can be used effectively and fruitfully. They help churches discern how best to embed TEE in their life.[56] They will also arrange "TEE-taster" sessions for potential new user churches and ensure good representation of church leadership in TEE governance structures.

vi. Local mentors and coaches for practical ministry and spiritual formation

Effective and fruitful TEE institutions work to create good local support for growth towards holistic learning outcomes. This may include equipping group leaders with coaching and mentoring skills, and/or helping local churches identify appropriate mentors and coaches. When courses develop particular skills, proficient local supervisors are involved.

---

56. There is encouraging, increasing acknowledgement of the crucial place of the church in theological education quality-assurance circles. See the discussion in chapter 3: Aylett and Samuel, "TEE in Theological Perspective – Part 2"; cf., for example, Cannell, *Theological Education Matters*, 248–80; Banks, *Reenvisioning Theological Education*, especially 218–222.

vii. Educational resources

Effective and fruitful TEE institutions ensure that group leaders and members know how to access relevant educational resources. These could include physical books and journals in public, personal, or theological libraries, and internet and other digital resources.

3. In relation to the practice of fruitful TEE

i. Course materials and delivery methods

Effective and fruitful TEE institutions ensure timely provision of courses and appropriate technical support where delivery is online. They have good mechanisms for gathering students' and group leaders' feedback on course content for ongoing course revision.

ii. Group meetings and group leader support

Effective and fruitful TEE institutions understand the central importance of the group in sustaining, with God's help, the continuing discipleship journey of each learner. They ensure that group leaders understand why each person should participate in group discourse for learning and transformation, with an ideal group size between five and ten students.

They connect regularly with group leaders and visit TEE groups for encouragement and coaching. They celebrate learner milestones towards programme completion and honour appropriately the service of volunteer group leaders. They encourage local church leaders to sustain TEE groups and leaders by prayer, sharing testimonies, marking progress, and creating opportunities for practical application and ministry assignments, including local missional activities.

Effective and fruitful TEE institutions encourage group leaders to connect group members for group discussion. While acknowledging that learners grow best when meeting face to face, they also use online discussion forums, video conferencing, and other technologies to supplement in-person engagement, or to replace it when circumstances make that impossible.[57]

57. Moving beyond "emergency remote learning" to best practices in the use of such technologies.

iii. Practical application, reflection, and mentoring/coaching
Effective and fruitful TEE institutions see TEE courses as equipping *for* ministry and mission, and also equipping *in* ministry and mission. Their assessment frameworks recognize the vital importance of practical application, the educational benefit of repeated cycles of action and reflection, and the need for well-prepared group leader guides or manuals.

In all, they work hard to integrate student self-study, group discourse, and practical application.

The Future of Quality Assurance for TEE

Appropriate quality assurance may include but is not limited to academic accreditation. It can result in recognition of a wide range of awards and student achievements, and it should always lead to institutional and programme improvement. Programmes that invest the necessary time and effort become more fit for purpose, to the benefit of those they serve. In recent years, Increase member TEE programmes have generally had a very positive experience in quality assurance with the ATA.

TEE institutions are strongly encouraged to identify their needs and then to find one or more appropriate external quality-assurance agencies or networks that understand TEE well, including its mission, vision, values, educational philosophy, and methodologies.

Various kinds of quality-assurance agency are now available. We encourage TEE institutions to explore possibilities for recognition both of academically comparable qualifications, such as certificate, diploma, and bachelor awards, and of other kinds of equipping awards that are based on progressive, specific competencies.

TEE programmes that participate in TEE-friendly quality assurance will find it helps them offer more effective and fruitful service to churches and to individual disciples who make up the whole people of God. They will also be better equipped to collaborate with other training providers in building integrated learning pathways for God's people, and they will discover more opportunities for such collaboration because quality-assurance agencies usually foster networking and mutual encouragement.

Although academic and non-academic frameworks may appear very different, the world of theological education is shifting. The old categories of "formal" and "nonformal" are breaking down, leading to interconnections between the two and thus new possibilities for integrated learning pathways. We anticipate creative new conversations in the coming years, to which the TEE movement is well placed to contribute, precisely because it bridges both approaches.

Conclusion

This chapter has sought to provide a framework for comprehensive self-evaluation and external quality assurance of TEE. Fleshing out this framework requires further work, though hopefully we have pointed interested parties in the right direction. Similarly, we urge and invite quality-assurance agencies to take a closer look at the services they offer extension education and church-based training providers by re-examining standards and quality measures, policies and procedures, stakeholder and self-study questions, and assessment methods and criteria, so that they too might grow in fitness for purpose to the glory of God.

Bibliography

Aleshire, Daniel O. *Earthen Vessels: Hopeful Reflections on the Work and Future of Theological Schools*. Grand Rapids: Eerdmans, 2008.

Asia Theological Association. *Accreditation Manual for Extension Education and TEE Self-Study Guide*. Taichung: Asia Theological Association, 1987.

———. *Theological Education by Extension (TEE) Accreditation Manual: Revised and Updated July 18, 1995*. Vernon Hills: Asia Theological Association, 1995.

———. *Manual for Accreditation*. Revised July 2004. Quezon City: Asia Theological Association, 2004.

———. *Manual for Accreditation*. Revised January 2017. Quezon City: Asia Theological Association, 2017.

———. *Manual for Accreditation*. Revised January 2021. Quezon City: Asia Theological Association, 2021.

Banks, Robert J. *Reenivisioning Theological Education: Exploring a Missional Alternative to Current Models*. Grand Rapids: Eerdmans, 1999.

Brooking, Stuart, ed. *Is It Working? Researching Context to Improve Curriculum: A Resource Book for Theological Schools*. Carlisle: Langham, 2018.

Brynjolfson, Robert, and Jonathan Lewis, eds. *Integral Ministry Training: Design and Evaluation*. Pasadena: William Carey Library, 2006.

Cannell, Linda. *Theological Education Matters: Leadership Education for the Church*. Newburgh: EDCOT, 2006.

Das, Rupen. *Connecting Curriculum with Context: A Handbook for Context Relevant Curriculum Development in Theological Education*. Carlisle: Langham, 2015.

ECTE. *Manual with Visitation Guidelines of the European Council for Theological Education*. 6th ed. Sutri: ECTE, 2018.

ENQA. *Standards and Guidelines for Quality Assurance in the European Higher Education Area (ESG)*. Brussels: European Association for Quality Assurance in Higher Education, 2015. https://enqa.eu/wp-content/uploads/2015/11/ESG_2015.pdf.

Esterline, David V. "A Proposal for the Evaluation of Theological Education by Extension." PhD diss., Graduate Theological Union, Berkeley, California, 1985.

Ferris, Robert, in cooperation with David Esterline, Jeff Gulleson, Richard K. Hart, and G. David Samuel. *Accrediting TEE: Steps towards Understanding and Practice*. Asian Perspectives Series 34. Taichung: Asia Theological Association, 1986.

———. "Accreditation and TEE." In *Excellence and Renewal: Goals for the Accreditation of Theological Education*, edited by Robert L. Youngblood, 59–79. Exeter: Paternoster, 1989.

———. ed. *Establishing Ministry Training: A Manual for Programme Developers*. Pasadena: William Carey Library, 1995.

———, with John R. Lillis, and Ralph E. Enlow Jr. *Ministry Education That Transforms: Modeling and Teaching the Transformed Life*. Carlisle: Langham, 2018.

———. "Strategic Flexibility in Accreditation Programmes." An address presented to the 1993 Conference of the International Council of Accrediting Agencies meeting in Bangkok, Thailand, 19–22 July 1993.

Global Accreditation Association for Ministries and Training (GAAMT). *Accreditation Manual*. Colorado Springs: GAAMT, 2020. Accessed 23 November 2020. https://www.gaa-mt.com/uploads/1/9/4/0/19404491/gaamt_accreditation_manual.pdf.

Green, Tim. "Integrated Learning Pathways." In *TEE in Asia: Empowering Churches, Equipping Disciples*, edited by Hanna-Ruth van Wingerden, Tim Green, and Graham Aylett, 239–44. Carlisle: Langham Global Library, 2021.

Harrison, Patricia J. "Forty Years On: The Evolution of Theological Education by Extension (TEE)." *Evangelical Review of Theology* 28, no. 4 (2004): 315–28.

Hart, Richard K. "TEE Stakeholder Roles in Educational Evaluation and Renewal: A Study of the Evaluation Beliefs of TAFTEE Stakeholders in the 1987–1988 Asia Theological Association sponsored Responsive Accreditation Evaluation." PhD, Trinity International University, 1999.

Holland, Fred. *Teaching through T.E.E.* Nairobi: Evangel Publishing House, 1975.

ICETE. *The ICETE Manifesto on the Renewal of Evangelical Theological Education*. 3rd ed., 2002. https://icete.info/resources/manifesto/.

———. *Standards and Guidelines for Global Evangelical Theological Education (SG-GETE)*. https://icete.info/wp-content/uploads/2019/05/Standards-and-Guidelines-for-Global-Evangelical-Theological-Education-2019.pdf.

Jaison, Jessy. *Towards Vital Wholeness in Theological Education: Framing Areas for Assessment*. Carlisle: Langham, 2017.

Jung, Joanne J. *Character Formation in Online Education: A Guide for Instructors, Administrators, and Accrediting Agencies*. Grand Rapids: Zondervan, 2015.

Kinsler, F. Ross, and James H. Emery, eds. *Opting for Change: A Handbook on Evaluation and Planning for Theological Education by Extension*. Pasadena: William Carey Library, 1991.

Kohl, Manfred W., and A. N. Lal Senanayake, eds. *Educating for Tomorrow: Theological Leadership for the Asian Context*. Bangalore: SAIACS, 2002.

Lo, Jim. "Seven Ingredients of Successful TEE Programs." *Evangelical Missions Quarterly* 38, no. 3 (July 2002): 338–41.

McKinney, Lois. "How Shall We Cooperate Internationally in TEE?" In *Cyprus: TEE Come of Age*, edited by Robert L. Youngblood, 27–39. Exeter: Paternoster, 1984.

Ott, Bernhard. "Accreditation: Importance and Benefits for the Institution." In *Foundations for Academic Leadership*, edited by Fritz Deininger and Orbelina Eguizabal, 181–214. Nürnberg: ICETE/VTR Publications, 2013.

———. *Understanding and Developing Theological Education*. Carlisle: Langham, 2016.

Oyco-Bunyi, Joy. *Beyond Accreditation: Value Commitments and Asian Seminaries*. Bangalore: Theological Book Trust, 2001.

Re-Forma. "Developing Global Ministry Outcomes." Accessed 23 November 2020. https://www.re-forma.global/.

———. "Outcomes." Accessed 23 November 2020. https://www.re-forma.global/outcomes.

Ro, Bong Rin, Ken Gnanakan, and Joseph Shao. *New Era, New Vision: Celebrating 40 Years of the Asia Theological Association*. Manila: Asia Theological Association, 2010.

SEAN International. "How to Use SEAN Courses Effectively: Practical Tips on How to Set up an Effective TEE Programme Using SEAN Courses." 2005. https://www.increaseassociation.org/images/resources-library/How%20to%20Use%20SEAN%20Courses.pdf.

Shaw, Perry. *Transforming Theological Education: A Practical Handbook for Integrative Learning*. Carlisle: Langham, 2014.

Stufflebeam, Daniel L., and Chris L. S. Coryn. *Evaluation Theory, Models and Applications*. 2nd ed. San Francisco: Jossey-Bass, 2014.

van Wingerden, Hanna-Ruth, Tim Green, and Graham Aylett, eds. *TEE in Asia: Empowering Churches, Equipping Disciples*. Carlisle: Langham Global Library, 2021.

Winter, Ralph D. "Keep the Essential Elements in Mind." In *Theological Education by Extension*, edited by Ralph D. Winter, 401–26. Pasadena: William Carey Library, 1969.

10

TEE and Campus-Based Training in Partnership

Qaiser Julius

Introduction

The Cape Town Commitment's statement that "The mission of the Church on earth is to serve the mission of God, and the mission of theological education is to strengthen and accompany the mission of the Church,"[1] is finding wide agreement. Different providers of theological education share a common vision for equipping the whole people of God for the mission of God through his church.

The common vision encourages "the recognition that 'formal' and 'nonformal,' residential and church-based theological education can and should be partners in the twenty-first century, to serve the whole people of God."[2] This chapter is written out of that strong conviction. The first part of the chapter explores possibilities for collaboration between residential training institutions and TEE to mutual and shared advantage, and the second gives a more detailed account of such partnership in action in Pakistan, namely its challenges, barriers, and successes.

1. Lausanne, *Cape Town Commitment*, Part IIF, 4, https://www.lausanne.org/content/ctcommitment.

2. Paul Sanders, International Director of ICETE 2006–2012, email correspondence, 6 November 2020. See fn. 6 for definitions of formal and nonformal education.

Part 1. Possibilities for Partnership

Partnership as TEE prepares learners for campus-based training

With changing student patterns of study, lifestyle, and expectations, some campus-based institutions training for Christian leadership are experiencing declining student numbers. They face pressure to accept students without firm foundations in discipleship and Christian maturity. *The Cape Town Commitment* warns that:

> Biblically, only those whose lives already display basic qualities of mature discipleship should be appointed to leadership in the first place.

The *Commitment* then goes on to express a longing to see "greatly intensified efforts in disciple-making, through the long-term work of teaching and nurturing new believers, so that those whom God calls and gives to the Church as leaders are qualified according to biblical criteria of maturity and servanthood."[3]

Church-based training such as TEE can resource this long-term work of teaching, nurturing, and equipping new believers. Those who have already demonstrated commitment and ability to manage their TEE studies alongside the demands of daily living are better prepared to make use of further opportunities for learning and transformation through residential study. For example, the Anglican diocese of St. Albans in England takes this approach with some of its candidates for ordination training.[4]

One TEE institution in Asia utilizes TEE study in preparation for residential study within its own Bachelor of Theology programme, which is accredited by the Asia Theological Association (ATA). The College of Christian

3. Lausanne, *Cape Town Commitment*, Part IID, 3, https://www.lausanne.org/content/ctcommitment.

4. "St. Albans Diocese requires that all those in the discernment process for ministry should demonstrate that they are able to engage with theological learning. Candidates who come forward for vocational discernment and who have no prior evidence of theological learning are encouraged to join recognised courses for which they will need a theological education reference. GOLD Project Level 3 [TEE] courses are recognised by the Diocese for this purpose." David Ball, GOLD Project Director, email correspondence, 10 November 2020.

Theology Bangladesh (CCTB)[5] offers the equivalent of the first two years of a three-year Bachelor of Theology programme solely by extension. Students all over Bangladesh study this part of the curriculum in small groups, often facilitated by those who have themselves completed those courses as students. The third year is then completed in campus-based study at CCTB just outside Dhaka. This example shows a close partnership between a TEE and a campus-based institution.

Partnership through credit transfer between TEE and campus-based institutions

The variety of TEE institutions and programmes globally spans the formal and nonformal divide.[6] Where TEE institutions give an account of their courses in terms of learning objectives and their assessment, and the time and resources involved in learning through TEE, this can more simply lead to advanced standing in a residential programme. Such partnership is found in Mongolia between Mongolia TEE and the Union Bible Training College (UBTC). Mongolia TEE offers a Certificate in Christian Ministry accredited by the ATA which requires a minimum of four years part-time study. UBTC offers two different three-year Bachelor of Theology programmes, both also ATA accredited. Graduates of the Mongolia TEE certificate programme are able to enter these programmes at the start of the second year.

Relevant considerations for this kind of partnership include:

i. Shared vision and values: In the example from Mongolia, both institutions are members of, and accredited by, the ATA with a good foundation of agreed values.

5. CCTB, http://bengalcreativemedia.com/cctb/.

6. "Formal learning. Learning that occurs in an organized and structured environment (e.g. in an education or training institution or on the job) and is explicitly designated as learning (in terms of objectives, time or resources). Formal learning is intentional from the learner's point of view. It typically leads to validation and certification. Nonformal learning. Learning which is embedded in planned activities not always explicitly designated as learning (in terms of learning objectives, learning time or learning support), but which contain an important learning element. Nonformal learning is intentional from the learner's point of view." ICETE, *SG-GETE*, Appendix E, 37.

ii. Similar training objectives and learning outcomes: When learning outcomes and graduate profiles for the programmes show substantial agreement, there is good reason for credit transfer.
iii. Clear measurement of the volume of learning involved: Accrediting agencies are encouraged by the ICETE Standards and Guidelines to give credit for time spent in all intentional learning activities.[7] Thus, TEE programmes assess the volume of learning in relation to time spent in personal study, group meetings, practical application, and reflection on practical application.

Partnership as TEE courses are used in the campus-based training programme's curriculum

1. TEE courses can help fill gaps in the campus-based programme's curriculum

In some contexts, a campus-based programme may not have a suitably qualified member of the faculty to teach a particular course. Where there is a TEE course available at the relevant level, prepared by qualified subject experts, the course may provide the means for students to fulfil that course's learning objectives. The TEE course should be facilitated by suitably trained people, whether faculty, staff of the TEE programme, or others.

2. TEE courses intentionally integrated into the campus-based programme's curriculum

TEE courses are available for most subjects usually found in a campus-based curriculum, whether studies of biblical books, church history, systematic theology, or pastoral ministry (e.g. Christian response to persecution, laying Christian foundations in prayer, understanding the Bible, teaching the Bible to children, working with teenagers, and much more).[8]

7. "Contact hours (face-to-face instruction) constitute one of many possible learning activities but are not an essential requirement for assigning course credit." "Credits are awarded for all learning activities that match learning outcomes and institutions make provision for allocation of credit for prior learning, nonformal and informal learning." ICETE, *SG-GETE*, B2.6, 22, 23..

8. For examples of the subjects covered by TEE courses, see the Increase Association website, https://courses.increaseassociation.org; the SEAN International website, https://

There are three reasons for incorporating TEE courses into the curriculum.

i. Increasing instructional variety in the curriculum – beneficial for students
The *ICETE Manifesto* urges that "our programmes of theological education must vigorously pursue the use of a variety of educational teaching methodologies, evaluated and promoted in terms of their demonstrated effectiveness, especially with respect to the particular cultural context."[9] Different students have different learning preferences, and the introduction of a range of teaching and learning methodologies through TEE courses gives more students opportunities to flourish and grow in their learning.

Note the phrase "evaluated and promoted in terms of their demonstrated effectiveness." TEE programmes may be included in the curriculum because of their effectiveness in leading to deep learning.[10] Students often appreciate TEE as reflected in this student's comment:

> As a student I really liked the method of teaching. First, it is easy to handle. Repetitions of key ideas help me to remember the material well.[11]

ii. Increasing instructional variety in the curriculum – helpful for faculty
The *ICETE Manifesto* states that "our programmes need to take practical steps to introduce and train their staff in new methods of instruction."[12] Introducing TEE courses into the curriculum exposes faculty to a range of skills very different from those used in the traditional (and commonly adopted) lecturing method. Skills needed for effective facilitation of TEE group discussion include asking good questions,[13] listening well, and involving every member of the group in a

---

seaninternational.org; Evangel Publishing House, Kenya for TEXT Africa courses, https://www.facebook.com/Evangelpublishing/.

9. *The ICETE Manifesto*, Section 9, Instructional Variety, https://icete.info/resources/manifesto/.

10. See the exploration of the educational basis for the effectiveness of TEE methodology in chapter 5: Shaw, "The Educational Efficacy of TEE – Part 1," and chapter 6: Glissmann and Green, "The Educational Efficacy of TEE – Part 2."

11. From the testimony of a student in a Central Asian Bible college.

12. *The ICETE Manifesto*, Section 9, Instructional Variety, https://icete.info/resources/manifesto/.

13. Indeed, learning the skill, or perhaps the art, of discerning what constitutes a "good question" for this particular topic and these particular group members at this particular time.

balanced way. Developing these skills may not come easily for some facilitators who are more used to lecturing. The TEE group facilitator seeks to create a space for group members to contribute their understanding and experience, with all group members sharing and learning together. In some contexts, this is deeply countercultural. However, the joy of seeing group members engaging together with God's word greatly outweighs the necessary effort.

Accrediting agencies increasingly stress lifelong learning: by embracing new possibilities for learning in the classroom through TEE, faculty can model their own commitment to lifelong learning. One faculty member of a campus-based organization who joined a TEE class as a learner reported:

> I found it to be very good and helpful. It looked very simple, yet the knowledge is deep. After going through the six books [of SEAN's "Life of Christ" series], I have a clear picture of Jesus's life and ministry and more.[14]

iii. Providing a context for strengthening and deepening faculty – student relationships

A hospitable environment in the classroom has been identified as an important factor for transformational learning.[15] Good facilitation of TEE group discussion helps create that environment and provides opportunities for faculty to discover much, much more about their students than is possible in a typical lecture. The need for holistic assessment, including assessment of spiritual and character formation, is becoming increasingly emphasized. Group discussion provides more than superficial relationships, so this kind of assessment is possible. TEE groups can provide opportunity for significant growth in the personal relationship between faculty and students.

3. TEE courses integrated into the campus-based training's curriculum

Integrating TEE courses into the campus-based curriculum is beneficial. But far greater benefit comes from equipping students to lead TEE groups themselves,

14. Former Associate Dean at Malaysia Baptist Theological Seminary, Sai Mooi Lim, email correspondence, 20 July 2016.

15. Soh, *Motif of Hospitality*.

and therefore enabling them to use TEE courses to equip their church members for service.

The ICETE 2018 Triennial Assembly, "The Sacred-Secular Divide in Theological Education," asked: "Are we equipping our students with the right worldview and tools in order for them to truly equip their church members for an effective service in all areas of life?"[16] TEE is one such tool for equipping the people of God. Intentional inclusion of TEE courses, followed by training to use them, can help campus-based institutions to fulfil the "mission critical" objective of preparing future church leaders to become equippers of God's people for their ministries in all their diverse callings in church and in society. TEE is a tool to serve this vision.

Many voices are critical of traditional patterns of ministry training and call for more relevant, practical approaches. To quote one recent example: "We need good doctors in this [2020] pandemic, able military people to fight our battles. Likewise, we need theological schools like medical and military schools rather than research universities."[17]

Teaching and learning methodologies often used in traditional campus-based institutions may not help their graduates to equip God's people for their ministries. Powerful messages are communicated to learners when predominantly lecture-based instruction is offered. Perry Shaw tells the true story of "Gregory," who attempted to reproduce the materials and methods of his seminary training in his church after graduation. The attempt was a dismal failure, and Gregory, disillusioned, left that ministry, and went to study for a doctorate in theology.[18] This story shows that lecture-based cognitive instruction may not be helpful for equipping the church ministry workers at the grass-root level.

Programmes for training for church leadership can model and commend truly transferable materials and methods for church-based training. When

16. ICETE, "ICETE Current Newsletter, April 2018," https://icete.info/wp-content/uploads/2019/04/Spring-2018.pdf.

17. Dr. David Sang-Bok Kim, former ATA Chairperson 2001–2007, in his address for the 50th anniversary celebrations of the ATA on 30 October 2020. ATA, "Towards a Mature Church: Celebrating God's Faithfulness," https://www.facebook.com/300305729999393/videos/1009290202867795.

18. Shaw, "Hidden Curriculum," 23–24.

training introduces future pastors to TEE in such a way that they experience the power of God at work through the group study of his word, they will be better prepared as equippers of the saints for ministry.[19] The powerful vision of those who intentionally introduce TEE courses into their training curriculum is reflected in the following comments.

> When I heard about the [TEE] course the "Life of Christ," I was very interested in it because I would like my students to study Bible courses in seminary which they can teach in the church.[20]
>
> Our students study systematic theology and acquire a lot of knowledge which I believe helps them grow and prepare them for ministry. But they also need some practical tools which they can take and use right away when they graduate from the seminary and begin as full-time ministers in their churches.[21]
>
> [The] ORTA [Russian language TEE] program trains the seminary students for ministry in local churches, makes for personal spiritual growth of ministers, develops qualities needed to communicate with people.[22]

In each of these cases, as the following comments show, there has been good fruit:

> Yes, many of our students (some are pastors) started classes at their church and some helped other churches to teach their members.[23]

19. As Ephesians 4:12.

20. Former Associate Dean at Malaysia Baptist Theological Seminary, Sai Mooi Lim, email correspondence, 20 July 2016.

21. Academic Dean, a Central Asian seminary, in personal communication to Increase Association leadership, July 2016.

22. Former Principal, Vladivostok Presbyterian Theological Seminary, Lee Young Hoon, in personal communication to ORTA staff members.

23. Former Associate Dean at Malaysia Baptist Theological Seminary, Sai Mooi Lim, email correspondence, 20 July 2016.

> It has been four years since we started using SEAN materials in the seminary. Our students have given a good feedback.[24]

> Studying in ORTA [TEE] groups our church members loved the Bible. They had a desire to study the Scriptures diligently. Thanks to group discussions and studying the same subjects, church members got united.[25]

Most campus-based seminaries include a course on homiletics to prepare graduates to rightly handle the word of God from the pulpit. But many seminaries give less thought to preparing graduates to rightly handle the word of God in small groups, or to helping them equip their future congregations to do so.

Equipping students as effective TEE group leaders requires at least two steps. First, there needs to be good modelling. Students need experiential immersion in the TEE method so that they have more than head knowledge of good group dynamics and the outcomes possible when a group is well-facilitated. Second, and crucially, students need to have at least two opportunities to practice leading TEE group discussions, followed by evaluation (self-evaluation, group-evaluation, and evaluation by an experienced TEE coach).

i. Modelling

When TEE courses are integrated into a residential institution's curriculum, it is vital that those facilitating are themselves well-trained and present an appropriate model. It is helpful if the faculty is involved in leading some of the model groups, but whereas one lecturer can present material to a class of forty, four or five group leaders will be needed to facilitate four TEE groups for the same number.[26] This may be an excellent opportunity for drawing in suitably qualified members or leaders of local churches,[27] or TEE programme staff.

---

24. Academic Dean of a Central Asian seminary, in personal communication to Increase Association leadership, July 2016.

25. A graduate of Vladivostok Presbyterian Theological Seminary in personal communication to ORTA staff members.

26. It is so important that each member of the group has opportunity to be involved in discussion. With more than ten in a group, some members may remain silent, passive, and less engaged. The learning experience for them will not be so positive.

27. Especially alumni who are using TEE materials fruitfully in their churches.

ii. Reflection with practice

After the vital stage of modelling, additional training is needed to use TEE materials well. Trained TEE group leaders need to understand the TEE method, know how to use the group leader's manual, and have mastered key facilitation skills.

Two opportunities to practice leading TEE group discussions are very important. Often, in the first practice session, despite modelling and explanation, trainee group leaders – especially teachers and preachers – revert to their default setting of lecturing or preaching. But many are able to correct their approach on the second attempt, with a marked improvement in the group dynamics. Wide experience suggests that both teachers and preachers need an intentional change of mindset when approaching TEE small group facilitation, because different skill sets are needed.

In addition to participation in TEE group meetings, and then training as TEE group facilitators, for a fuller introduction to TEE, learners may study other subjects:

- TEE course design – TEE methodology as a combination of different teaching and learning events
- Student workbook design – the structure and content of the personal study materials; learning objectives, frequency of different frame types, function of questions involving personal and critical reflection in courses at different levels
- The significance of small groups – the role of the facilitator and the importance of the facilitator's handbook; opportunities and possibilities for learning in group discussion and in lecture and preaching
- Adult learning theory – its relevance for adult learners in the students' likely ministry contexts; contrasting opportunities for learning in the lecture and the small group discussion
- Transformational learning – the importance of obedience and practical application for transformation

- The role of ministers as equippers – providing teaching and learning, training, and equipping pathways for every member of their future congregations, for their participation in the mission of God.[28]

Partnership as campus-based learners trained as TEE facilitators lead TEE groups as part of their fieldwork

Newly trained TEE group leaders grow in their competence as they put the TEE group facilitation skills that they have gained into practice in a local church context. For "learners know they know because they have chosen to do what they are learning."[29] For many students, the opportunity for practice may only come after graduation. But some campus-based training institutions provide the opportunity for students to gain this experience as part of their field education programme. For example, Bethany Global University trains students in its BA in Intercultural Ministry Studies programme to use foundation level TEE courses with a view to the students starting groups during their sixteen months of field experience.[30]

Partnership by using TEE courses as a springboard to online courses

As campus-based institutions shift to online learning, they may draw on the principles and approaches of church-based training. For example, the Teach-Learn project in the Arab world adopted and adapted church-based training courses developed by the Program for Theological Education by Extension (PTEE) for use in its online program. Interactive study texts can be adapted for online learning courses much more easily than lecture notes.

28. See good resources in van Wingerden, Green, and Aylett, *TEE in Asia*; also SEAN's practical handbook: SEAN International, *How to Use SEAN Courses Effectively*, https://www.increaseassociation.org/images/resources-library/How%20to%20Use%20SEAN%20Courses.pdf, and also the range of possibilities in the excellent workbook produced by ANITEPAM "to conscientize and educate residential theological students to the principles, theories and practice of distance education and TEE." Sendegeya and Spencer, *Understanding TEE.*

29. Vella, *Learning to Listen*, 17.

30. Freeman, personal communication, November 2020. See https://bethanygu.edu/programs/undergraduate/Intercultural-Ministry/.

Partnership between seminary faculty and TEE staff to develop new TEE courses

This kind of partnership has led to many new courses in TEE programmes across Asia. Campus-based faculty as subject experts can give very helpful contributions as members of course-writing teams. Educationally, a seminary teacher's lecture notes written as a book are not suitable for church-based training programmes. The good content needs skilful arrangement and processing to produce an interactive self-study text.

Part 2. TEE Complementing Campus-Based Theological Education: The Perspective of the Open Theological Seminary (OTS), Pakistan

The second part of this chapter explores partnership and complementarity between TEE and campus-based institutions from the perspective of the Open Theological Seminary (OTS) in Pakistan.

OTS uses TEE methodology for equipping God's people in Pakistan (and beyond). OTS has a vision to see each member of Christ's body grow in their knowledge of Scripture, their relationship with God, and their use of their gifts in building up God's kingdom.

OTS aims not only to instruct the minds of students but also to change their hearts and to equip them practically for a wide range of Christian service. OTS courses are designed around an extension learning approach, whereby students undertake a combination of guided self-study and group discussion, self-reflection, projects, and practical ministry assignments.

Awards at various levels are offered. Each level has a defined aim, and courses are carefully graded for learner progression.

- Discipleship level provides a balanced foundation for the Christian life, giving students confidence in their faith.
- Certificate level engages the students in systematic Bible study and helps them to influence their neighbours and families for Christ.
- Diploma level focuses on training lay leaders to play an active part in their churches in various ministries, such as preaching, evangelism, and Sunday school teaching.

- Bachelor level provides more in-depth training for full-time Christian workers.
- Master's level helps pastors to address contemporary social issues theologically and biblically and to equip lay Christian leaders and workers to apply biblical principles in their daily life and work, engaging with society in a Christlike manner.

The interactive self-study texts make increasing demands as learners progress from one level to the next. At earlier levels, the texts are fully programmed, but by degree level, there are longer sections of reading material, less repetition, and more searching questions requiring longer answers. Higher-level cognitive skills will be expected, moving from comprehension and analysis to evaluation and synthesis, through to expression and formulation.

In addition, OTS has developed a separate programme for teenagers. The Christian Education Curriculum for Teenagers is an age-appropriate, culturally relevant, systematic curriculum for teenagers. Interactive courses have been designed with flexibility so that they can be used in schools as well as church youth groups.[31]

The purpose of this part of the chapter is to show that TEE has many features that complement campus-based theological training, and likewise campus-based theological education has the potential to support church-based TEE in many ways. TEE has spread to almost all areas of the world, and rather than being a substitute for residential theological education, it is definitely a needed complement.[32] How these two modes of education can work together for achieving their shared purpose is explored below with special reference to OTS in Pakistan.

A comprehensive methodology

As already outlined in this book,[33] TEE is a unique method of learning combining three elements: personal study, group meetings, and practical application. The first step especially serves cognitive learning, the "head"; the second step, affective learning, the "heart"; and the third step, psychomotor

31. OTS, *Academic Manual*, 46.
32. Anderson, "Theological Education by Extension," 944.
33. See Green and Aylett, "TEE at a Glance" following the Introduction to this book.

and skill development, the "hands." These three steps are linked together in each learning cycle. "None of these three strands is exceptional on its own, but the TEE method weaves them together into a stronger cord."[34]

In the first step, personal study, a participant completes the relevant section of an interactive study book. It is different from simple reading because TEE lessons engage the reader in different activities such as brainstorming, Bible passages, and personal or theoretical questions. Personal, reflective questions impact students' lives as they begin to connect the learning of the TEE lesson with their own circumstances. The book serves as an instructor leading towards achievement of specific objectives. "All this becomes a springboard to the next learning step,"[35] the group meeting.

The second step of the TEE method is the group meeting, the centre of all activities. The major component of this group meeting is discussion in which the learners reflect on the lesson and their personal experience. The group leader or tutor does not give a lecture, but rather, facilitates the discussion. The group time does not revolve around one person only, and members learn from the diverse experiences and perspectives of the different group members. Here, at this point, theology is seen in context, relevant to the life and situation of the learners. The group leader asks open-ended questions encouraging each participant to speak and share. This discussion challenges and leads towards transformative learning.

The third step is practical application. What the learners have learned from the previous two steps must now be applied in their daily lives at home, work, church, or in the wider community because "practical application is the goal of TEE courses."[36] Mindsets, behaviours, habits, deeds, speech, all areas of practical living are challenged at this point. If practical application is missing, then there is doubt as to whether real learning has occurred. So TEE activity leads towards practical application with the help of personal study and group meetings.

34. Green, "Equipping Disciples," 17.

35. Green, 16.

36. Green, 17.

Comprehensive assessment

TEE is a process that leads towards practical application and life transformation. Accordingly, OTS has many assessment components. Generally, in campus-based theological colleges assessment may take place only at the end of the course or semester, but in OTS, assessment is an ongoing process using different means and resources. OTS students are required to prove their competence and progress in each of the areas of knowledge, Christian character, and ministry skills. OTS has developed an assessment scheme for testing in all these areas (Table 10.1).

Table 10.1. Open Theological Seminary assessments of students' competence and progress[37]

Training Aspect	Method of Testing
Knowledge	1. Weekly test 2. In-course written assignments 3. Final exams 4. End-of-level written assignments
Christian Character	1. Class Participation 2. Character assessment (self-reflection) 3. End-of-level interview
Ministry Skills	1. In-course practical assignments 2. End-of-level practical assignments 3. Practical ministry

TEE programmes are often included under the general heading of nonformal education. That may prove a barrier to partnership with formal programmes. But in fact, some TEE programmes, the ones OTS included, put great emphasis on assessment and evaluation, and are in fact more formal than some explicitly formal residential institutions.[38]

37. Source: OTS Academic Manual, 15.

38. See Green, "Pakistan," for examples of transformation.

Provision of effective TEE courses to supplement the training capacity of Bible colleges

The OTS's TEE courses are well designed and developed by scholars who keep the learners and their contexts in view. Courses are prepared with specific learning objectives, which include the traditional domains of knowing (cognitive), being (affective) and doing (psychomotor) domains of learning. However, "most TEE learners . . . are members of collectivist societies . . . So, in addition to the three traditional domains, we add a fourth: relating."[39] Courses are designed with these four types of objectives and these objectives are achieved with different techniques. Moreover, OTS's TEE courses are designed so that knowledge is transferred in small chunks (equivalent to the microlearning discussed in chapter 8)[40] with questions and other activities.

The OTS has more than forty courses designed to be holistic in this way. Some courses have been taken from other TEE movements, others from SEAN International, while still others were written by Pakistani writers. Courses taken from other TEE organizations are first translated, adapted and contextualized, and printed only after thorough field testing. Courses written by local writers are written specifically for the Pakistani context. The value of OTS courses is widely recognized within Pakistan by campus-based institutions. OTS courses such as Church History, Pastoral Ministry, Folk Religion, Bible Survey, Expository Preaching, Poverty Elimination, Caring for the Environment, and Biblical Languages form part of the curriculum of a number of Pakistan's Bible colleges. User institutions include the Full Gospel Assemblies (FGA) Bible College in Lahore, the Zarephath Bible Seminary (ZBS) in Rawalpindi, the Assemblies of God Bible School (AoGBS) in Quetta, and the Brethren Institute of Theological Education (BITE) in Lahore. Other more recently established Bible colleges also use OTS courses and may invite OTS tutors to lead them to model TEE methodology. In the Pakistan context, as in other Asian settings, many campus-based colleges do not have enough local faculty members, therefore, OTS courses can be useful when there are insufficient faculty for a particular subject.

39. Green, "Intelligent TEE Course Design," 26.

40. See chapter 8: Weymouth, "TEE and Transformation in the Digital Age."

Students appreciate these courses. For example, one BITE student commented, "I find OTS classes very interesting and relevant to my situation. I always enjoy OTS classes and look forward when next OTS class will be."

Partnership to provide instructional variety

Even though campus-based theological colleges are working towards innovation in teaching methodology, still the lecture method is dominant which, no doubt, reduces transformative learning. As highlighted above, TEE's hybrid learning approach and methodology is tried and tested, leading towards transformation and practical application.

In Pakistan, TEE's three-in-one educational methodology has motivated theological educators in campus-based training programmes to bring innovation to their traditional lecture method. At the past two conferences of the Theological Educators' Forum (TEF) in Pakistan great emphasis was laid on using learner-centred methodologies in theological education. One of the highlights of the TEF Conference in 2020 came when participants prepared and demonstrated lesson plans designed with various creative teaching-learning strategies.[41] Participants highlighted the value of this exercise in bringing diversity and innovation to their teaching.

Partnership to fulfil a vision – Equipping all of God's people for God's mission

The whole Bible tells the story of the mission of God,[42] and theological education is to be in tune with the mission of God, "fleshing out the gospel of the kingdom of God and equipping people to live as citizens and soldiers of that kingdom."[43] Theological education is to equip people for the mission of God. Unfortunately, "when missional focus is lost, theological education is reduced to an academic exercise in God-talk."[44] In campus-based institutions, training people for full-time ministry as clergy, the laity may have fewer opportunities

41. OTS, *TEF Annual Conference Report 2020*, 8.

42. Wright, "Mission of God's People," 26–32. See also chapter 2: Burke and Pearson, "TEE in Theological Perspective – Part 1."

43. Wanak, "Developing an Operational Philosophy," 38.

44. Wanak, 38.

for receiving theological education. Clergy may be trained within a limited and closed system which makes going out missionally difficult for them. But OTS works directly with church members who are living and working in a non-Christian environment and are strategically placed to be used by God in mission and evangelism. Christian mission is first of all God's mission, therefore "every church member who is part of the family of God through faith in Jesus – is called to be involved in the family business, the mission of God."[45]

TEE, as church-based training, can equip and empower everyone in the church family to play their part in the mission of God. The range of OTS students includes people from all different walks of life: government employees, medical staff, businessmen, farmers, educators, and students. These people are already placed as indigenous missionaries in a difficult and adverse situation. One OTS student commented, "I started forgiving and loving my enemies who made false accusations against us."[46]

The heart and vision of a theological college is vital: an enthusiastic heart and spirit that communicates to theological students the importance of the Great Commission, and the understanding that mission is for all and includes all aspects of life. If a college succeeds in impacting its students in this way, then as graduates they will integrate the work of mission into their ministries. If they are pastors, they will equip their church members as gospel witnesses on the job, at home, or in their community, living testimonies who grasp the opportunity for mission. If they are involved in teaching or parachurch ministry, they will be preparing others for this great task of mission with understanding and insight.

TEE is a tool to fulfil the vision of every church member equipped for active participation in the mission of God. If a residential college has this vision, and ignites this vision in its students, the door is open for fruitful partnership with OTS, which exists for this vision.

Partnership to further contextual and practical theology

OTS serves the church at the grassroots level with courses designed and written for the Pakistani context. Group discussions take place in context, and as a

45. Vinden and Aylett, "God's Mission and Ours," 5.

46. *Cup of Tee*, Issue no. 34, 2019, 4.

result theology is understood in that context in the light of knowledge gained from the study materials and the experience of the group members. The subject matter is therefore relevant at the grassroots. According to SEAN International "[TEE] is a highly mobile and effective system of training within the local context based on Home and Group Study led by trained tutors (facilitators)."[47] TEE strongly supports contextual theology.

Faculty in campus-based theological institutions in Pakistan are sometimes isolated from the realities of life for the grassroots communities. They may be expert in relation to texts and theory, but distant from ordinary people, and this same distance may also characterize their graduates. In the context of post-colonial third-world countries, this is quite normal. It is understandable that some theological leaders may behave like the colonial masters, seeking to rule and suppress the common people. With this same mentality, theologians attempt to show that theology is a serious business and not child's play. "There is a great phenomenon in Pakistan that there is a huge gap between the Christian Theology and its applicability."[48] This gap needs to be filled in the light of the challenge of Narendra John and Ken Gnanakan:

> Are we training men and women to communicate within these contexts? Courses need to be taught that will equip our students to understand and be ministers in today's context. We seem to be training students to face yesterday's problems with yesterday's answers, rather than shaping them in today's context to face tomorrow's challenges.[49]

Jesus Christ was at home among grassroots people and used their language and communication patterns to teach theology. TEE is also at home among grassroots people, serving them with relevant materials with application to all areas of their lives. TEE provides tools that can help connect the theology of the campus with the everyday challenges of life for the grassroots. TEE can help bring theology out of the campus, so that it will serve as a guiding star for the common people.

47. "What Is 'TEE'?" SEAN International, https://www.seaninternational.org.

48. Julius, "Importance of Contextual Sensitivity," 31.

49. John and Gnanakan, "Theological Education and Contextualization," 71.

Partnership in equipping seminary graduates as TEE tutors (group leaders)

Some campus-based institutions have welcomed partnership with OTS. Zarephath Bible Seminary has been using OTS courses for many years, as its former principal Ashkenaz Asif explains:

> OTS courses are well-structured, and the students learn a new method of learning as well as teaching. Our students are qualified to teach TEE as soon as they leave the seminary. This makes them better equipped for ministry in the city or town. We are doing what is best for our students and what helps the kingdom cause. The graduates become cutting-edge workers all over the country offering viable teaching tools. This is a win-win partnership for the glory of our Master, Jesus Christ.[50]

The OTS field department holds tutor training workshops for the second- and third- year students of campus-based institutions using OTS courses. When graduates begin church ministry, they are ready to offer OTS courses as part of their ministry.

Partnership in writing contextually relevant theological materials

Members of several campus-based institutions have collaborated with OTS in developing new TEE courses relevant for the Pakistani context.[51] The OTS Course Development Department has taken lecture notes from subject matter experts and re-worked them as interactive self-study texts. This type of partnership strengthens the relationship between theological educators and demonstrates how they can help to strengthen each other.

Producing new courses in context and for context is of great importance in Pakistan. Almost everything used in seminaries comes from the West. Majid Abel reflects on this: "We have inherited the same theology that missionaries

50. Green, "Pakistan," 149.

51. For example, a TEE course in Christian theology was recently developed in partnership with a seminary faculty member. Campus-based faculty assist OTS course development department in reviewing TEE self-study texts and serve on the Academic Commission of OTS.

brought to us decades ago and we have adopted it with rigidity."[52] This dependency continues, so that living in an Islamic context, Christians in Pakistan have a stamp of being Western – our identity as Pakistanis is distorted. The church is the only hope for Pakistani Christians, but when the church's way of life and religious code is alien to the culture, bridge-building between Christians and the majority is difficult. Abel reflects on the role of the barber in Pakistani village life: involved in every event, keeping the genealogies of the village families, always there for their people, and there not to dominate and control, but to serve. Abel concludes:

> Doing theology in such a way will help to illuminate the history of the church in Pakistan. However . . . both . . . theology and history are at a premature stage. Much work lies ahead for the church in Pakistan to be able to articulate its theology adequately and gain maturity in understanding its history.[53]

With its experience of developing contextually relevant materials, OTS is encouraging local writers and theologians of campus-based theological institutions to produce literature in Urdu and in English for the global scholarly community. OTS has prepared a contextualized, holistic, ten-course Urdu-language curriculum for teenagers, recognizing an urgent need in our community for young Christian people to discover their identity in Christ. Now this programme is being translated into English and Dutch, an example of how local writers' work can contribute towards global training needs. And from the platform of the TEF (see next paragraph), OTS is helping faculty members of campus-based theological institutions to write books on topics that are not so curriculum-oriented and will be accessible to meet the needs of the wider Christian community, those who are unlikely to attend such institutions as students.

52. Abel, "Theology in Context," 19.

53. Abel, 29.

Partnership through the Theological Educators' Forum in Pakistan

OTS has the privilege of playing a leading role in the Theological Educators' Forum (TEF), which brings together the main theological colleges of Pakistan. TEF was formed in 1993 with OTS as a founding member to provide a platform for theological educators to come together and discuss their challenges in the context of Pakistan. Other than the OTS, all the members are campus-based institutions. In 2018 a TEF Consortium was initiated, co-ordinated from the OTS office. Seven core theological institutions are supported in developing their systems, curriculum development, course writing, administration, church and community mobilization, leadership development, and financial management. Members of the consortium aim to learn from each other, stimulating innovation and a culture of collaborative learning. Annual conferences organized by OTS under the umbrella of TEF have created an environment of mutual acceptance and growing friendship.[54] Denominational biases are being set aside, and member institutions have started to acknowledge each other's strengths. OTS has become a stimulating example for other theological institutions in Pakistan in terms of financial and human resource management, team building, capacity building, and promotion of interdenominational harmony.

Being the first accredited theological seminary in Pakistan, the OTS motivates other theological institutions to seek accreditation. As a result, in recent years the first residential seminary received accreditation with the Asia Theological Association. OTS is providing consultancy and guidance to other colleges in the accreditation process.

It has not been easy for the OTS as a TEE programme in Pakistan to reach this level of collaboration. However, we praise God that the development of strong relationships between different churches and Bible colleges is bearing good fruit for the kingdom of God.

54. The first TEF Annual Conference was organized on 25–28 February 2019 with the theme of "Transforming Theological Education in Pakistan." The second TEF conference was held on 26–28 February 2020 with the theme of "Enhancing Learning Centered Methodologies for Theological Education."

Conclusion

This chapter has explored and given examples of possibilities for partnership between TEE institutions and campus-based training institutions. Broader partnership considerations include intentional, integrated learning pathways that will serve the whole church and involve a range of training providers. Such pathways would provide resources for growth and development for God's people who are called to be salt and light with a ministry focus in their homes, families, communities, and work places, and also those called to church leadership, as well as those called to explore, expound, and defend the faith at the highest academic levels.

May the Lord of the whole church give a heart and passion for partnership that paves the way for more integrated pathways for all his people involving all kinds of theological training institutions. We end where we began, with "the recognition that 'formal' and 'nonformal,' residential and church-based theological education can and should be partners in the twenty-first century, to serve the whole people of God."[55]

Bibliography

Abel, Majid. "Theology in Context." In *Reader in Contextualization for Pakistan*, 14–29. Lahore: Open Theological Seminary, 2013.

Anderson, Justice C. "Theological Education by Extension." In *Evangelical Dictionary of World Mission*, edited by Scott A. Moreau, Harold Netland, and Charles Van Engen, 944. Grand Rapids: Baker, 2000.

Asia Theological Association. *Manual for Accreditation*. Manila: Asia Theological Association, 2017.

Green, Tim. "Equipping Disciples and Leaders through TEE." In *TEE in Asia*, edited by Hanna-Ruth van Wingerden, Tim Green, and Graham Aylett, 13–20. Carlisle: Langham Global Library, 2021.

———. "Intelligent TEE Course Design." In *TEE in Asia*, edited by Hanna-Ruth van Wingerden, Tim Green, and Graham Aylett, 23–28. Carlisle: Langham Global Library, 2021.

55. Paul Sanders, International Director of ICETE 2006–2012, email correspondence, 6 November 2020.

———. "Pakistan: Thriving under Pressure." In *TEE in Asia*, edited by Hanna-Ruth van Wingerden, Tim Green, and Graham Aylett, 143–49. Carlisle: Langham Global Library, 2021.

Hardy, Steve. "Factors That Contribute to Excellence in Theological Education." In *Leadership in Theological Education, Volume 1: Foundations for Academic Leadership*, edited by Fritz Deininger and Orbelina Eguizabal, 83–103. Carlisle: Langham, 2017.

ICETE. *The ICETE Manifesto on the Renewal of Evangelical Theological Education*, 3rd ed. 2002. https://icete.info/resources/manifesto/.

———. *Standards and Guidelines for Global Evangelical Theological Education (SG-GETE).* 2019. https://icete.info/wp-content/uploads/2019/05/Standards-and-Guidelines-for-Global-Evangelical-Theological-Education-2019.pdf.

John, Narendra, and Ken Gnanakan. "Theological Education and Contextualization." In *Reader in Contextualization for Pakistan*, 66–77. Lahore: Open Theological Seminary, 2013.

Julius, Qaiser. "The Importance of Contextual Sensitivity for the Church in the Islamic Context with Special Reference to Pakistan." In *Reader in Contextualization for Pakistan*, 30–40. Lahore: Open Theological Seminary, 2013.

OTS. *Academic Manual*. Lahore: Open Theological Seminary, 2020.

———. *Annual Report 2020*. Lahore: Open Theological Seminary, 2020.

———. *Cup of Tee*, Issue no. 34, Lahore: Open Theological Seminary, 2019.

———. *TEF Annual Report 2020*. Lahore: Open Theological Seminary, 2020.

SEAN International. "How to Use SEAN Courses Effectively: Practical Tips on How to Set up an Effective TEE Programme Using SEAN Courses." https://www.increaseassociation.org/images/resources-library/How%20to%20Use%20SEAN%20Courses.pdf.

Sendegeya, Fareth, and Leon Spencer, eds. *Understanding TEE: A Course Outline and Handbook for Students and Tutors in Residential Theological Institutions in Africa*. Dar es Salaam: ANITEPAM, 2001.

Shaw, Perry W. H. "The Hidden Curriculum of Seminary Education." *Journal of Asian Mission* 8, no. 1–2 (2006): 23–51.

Soh, Hui Leng Davina. *The Motif of Hospitality in Theological Education: A Critical Appraisal with Implications for Theological Education*. Carlisle: Langham, 2016.

van Wingerden, Hanna-Ruth, Tim Green, and Graham Aylett, eds. *TEE in Asia*. Carlisle: Langham Global Library, 2021.

Vella, Jane. *Learning to Listen, Learning to Teach: The Power of Dialogue in Educating Adults*. San Francisco: Jossey-Bass, 2002.

Vinden, Penny, and Graham Aylett. "God's Mission and Ours." In *TEE in Asia*, edited by Hanna-Ruth van Wingerden, Tim Green, and Graham Aylett, 3–7. Carlisle: Langham Global Library, 2021.

Wanak, Lee. "Developing an Operational Philosophy of Theological Education: A Primer on Moving from Philosophy to Strategy." In *Leadership in Theological Education, Volume 1: Foundations for Academic Leadership*, edited by Fritz Deininger and Orbelina Eguizabal, 33–64. Carlisle: Langham, 2017.

Wright, Christopher J. H. *The Mission of God's People: A Biblical Theology of the Church's Mission*. Grand Rapids: Zondervan, 2010.

11

TEE for Discipleship of People on the Move

David Ball and Rina Robinson

Introduction

Global migration is nothing new,[1] yet the pace of migration in the twenty-first century means it is one of the most pressing issues of our time. The UNHCR suggests that in 2020 there were 79.5 million forcibly displaced people worldwide,[2] while the UN report on global migration estimates that "there were around 272 million international migrants in the world in 2019, which equates to 3.5 percent of the global population."[3]

This chapter examines the issue of discipling different diaspora[4] groups using Theological Education by Extension (TEE) and considers its effectiveness. The question is whether TEE may provide one significant way to disciple diaspora believers in order to strengthen their faith and witness in, through,

1. See Holter, "My Father Was a Migrant Aramean," 57. See also, Woods, *Theologising Migration*, 2.

2. UNHCR, "Global Trends," 2.

3. IOM World Migration Report 2020.

4. For this paper, we are particularly focusing on those people and communities living outside their homeland. We use the term "diaspora," in its singular form, in line with Medeiros et al., *Scattered to Gather*, 10: "We are referring to the fact of leaving one's homeland and being on the move (voluntary or involuntary migration/immigration of an individual or people group e.g., Filipino diaspora, the Brazilian diaspora)." Woods, *Theologising Migration*, 58, distinguishes between "migrants" and "diasporas" suggesting that "the latter has connotations of settlement." For this paper, we suggest that migrants are a category within diaspora.

and beyond their own communities. Here, the call from Cape Town 2010 remains highly significant:

> We long to see greatly intensified efforts in disciple-making, through the long-term work of teaching and nurturing new believers, so that those whom God calls and gives to the Church as leaders are qualified according to biblical criteria of maturity and servanthood.[5]

Beginning with a brief overview of the motif of migration in the Bible, we then consider some recent missiological thinking on diaspora. We show how TEE is being used globally among different categories of diaspora communities before we reflect on specific issues of using TEE amongst refugees and migrant workers in Malaysia. In conclusion, we reflect on key challenges and lessons to be learned from TEE among diaspora groups around the world.

Global Migration

A biblical perspective

The phenomenon of global migration may seem to be a newcomer to theological debate. However, when we turn to the Christian Scriptures, we find that migration with all its complexities has been part of the history of God's dealings with his people from the earliest times.[6] We could start with the exile from Eden in Genesis 3:23, or with the scattering of the peoples at Babel (Gen 11:9). Alternatively, we could see the beginnings of diaspora in the command to be fruitful and multiply and fill the earth (Gen 1:28).[7] Certainly, God's call to Abram (later to be called Abraham) to leave his country, his people, and his

5. Lausanne, *Cape Town Commitment*, Part IID: "Discerning the Will of Christ for World Evangelization," 3: "Christ-Centred Leaders."

6. For example, Maruskin, "The 'Biblical Case' for Caring for Migrants," states: "From the opening chapter of Genesis, 'migration' is a continuous thread in the biblical narrative."

7. Andrew Walls draws a distinction in the biblical theology of migration between "voluntary, hope-driven migration" (e.g. Abraham on the way to the promised land), and "involuntary, punitive migration" (e.g. Adam and Eve being expelled from the garden of Eden). Such a distinction enables us to understand migration in a nuanced way, recognizing that God's purposes in scattering the nations may be for multiple reasons. In the case of the Israelites in exile, it ended up being both punitive and a cause for hope. See Walls, "Towards a Theology of Migration," 407–17, and referred to in Holter, "My Father Was a Migrant Aramean," 63.

father's household and go to the land that God would show him (Gen 12:1) sets the mission of God to bless the world in the context of migration.[8]

The theme of migration continues as God's people spent time as aliens and strangers in Egypt before wandering for forty years as refugees in the wilderness without a home (Exod–Deut). The theological identity of the people of God as a migrant community is highlighted in Deuteronomy 26:5–9. Even as the people find their home in the promised land, their identity is still linked to Abraham the wandering Aramean[9] and to their treatment as foreign slaves in Egypt.[10] The Ten Commandments are prefaced by the statement that God is the one who brought them out of slavery in Egypt (Exod 20:2; Deut 5:6).[11] From Deuteronomy through to the end of Kings, exile is threatened as a punishment for covenant unfaithfulness and the latter part of the Old Testament sees God's people seeking to come to terms with what it means to live in exile or in a world dominated by hostile nations.[12]

When we turn to the New Testament, this theme of migration remains. Matthew describes Jesus's own experience as a refugee, fleeing persecution by Herod the Great (2:13), and recounts the fear of living under his son Archelaus (2:22). Jesus's ministry begins with echoes of the wilderness wanderings (e.g. Matt 4:1–11). The Son of Man has nowhere to lay his head (Luke 9:58). Luke even describes Jesus's death in Jerusalem as accomplishing a new exodus (Luke 9:31). When we come to the beginnings of the new community of believers at Pentecost the theme of diaspora comes to the forefront:

8. It would be possible to go further and suggest that mission, certainly cross-cultural mission, always involves some form of migration: sending or going to another culture as part of God's plan to redeem humanity.

9. This is an annual declaration to be made as the people bring the first fruits of their crops as an offering before the Lord.

10. For a more detailed discussion of Deut 26:5–9 in terms of a theological understanding of the people of God, see Holter, "My Father Was a Migrant Aramean," 64–67.

11. See Holter, 66.

12. See especially, Holter, 67: "A possible third aspect of Israel's experience and understanding of migration – as reflected in the Credo in Deut 26:5–9 – is the Babylonian exile in the sixth century BC" and, 68, 69, "Israel is portrayed in the OT as having gone through a series of what we today would call migrant experiences, but they are all read through the interpretive experiences of the Babylonian exile. As such, when later readers of the OT – through 2,500 years of interpretive history – perceive their own experiences of migration in light of OT texts and motifs, they follow an interpretive strategy that is developed within the OT itself."

> Now there were staying in Jerusalem God-fearing Jews from every nation under heaven . . . Parthians, Medes and Elamites; residents of Mesopotamia, Judea and Cappadocia, Pontus and Asia, Phrygia and Pamphylia, Egypt and the parts of Libya near Cyrene; visitors from Rome (both Jews and converts to Judaism); Cretans and Arabs. (Acts 2:5, 9–11 NIV)

In other words, the church was born in the context of the diaspora. God was at work in bringing Jews from every part of the world to the feast of Pentecost. It was possibly through some of these diaspora believers that the gospel reached distant parts of the known world.[13] In the context of a church formed by persecuted migrants in Antioch (Acts 11:19–21),[14] Paul and Barnabas are set apart for God's mission (Acts 13:1–3). Paul's epistles address issues arising from multi-ethnic, multicultural communities seeking to work out what it means to live as Christians in the context of a world on the move (e.g. 1 Cor 9:19–23).[15] Diaspora believers are specifically addressed in 1 Peter and the church itself is identified as a diaspora community.[16] Much more needs to be done by way of recognizing the diaspora context as important to the biblical background of the people of God. Nevertheless, this brief overview shows that God has always been at work in and through the complexities of migration and the movement of people to fulfil his sovereign purpose.[17]

---

13. Compare, for example, the places listed in Acts 2 with the places listed at the beginning of 1 Peter, where Peter refers to his readers as "God's elect, exiles scattered throughout the provinces of Pontus, Galatia, Cappadocia, Asia and Bithynia" (Acts 1:1). Certainly, tradition suggests that the church originally came to Ethiopia through the witness of the Ethiopian eunuch returning after his pilgrimage to Jerusalem (Acts 8:26–40). For example, Irenaus, *Adversus Haereses*, 3:12:8: "This man was also sent into the regions of Ethiopia, to preach what he had himself believed."

14. See Kahl, "Migrants as Instruments," 71–86. For example, 71, "The dissemination of the Christian faith did not unfold in a systematic and organized manner. It was rather due to the forced and impromptu migration of some of the Jews who shared this belief, and who wanted to escape persecution and a possible premature death. On their journeys and at their various destinations, some were able to communicate their faith and their interpretations of the meaning of Christ in intelligible ways to audiences of different cultures, languages, and beliefs."

15. See Kahl, 80–81.

16. For example, 1 Pet 1:1; 2:11 (also Phil 3:20). See Ball, "Foreigners and Exiles."

17. Woods, *Theologising Migration*, devotes two chapters to the biblical materials on migration and seeks to develop from these and other writings a theology for migration. See especially chapter 4: "Migration and the Ancient Faith Community," and chapter 5: "Migration and the Expanding Faith Community," 84–152.

Contemporary missiological perspectives

Having briefly surveyed the significant motif of diaspora in the biblical narrative, we turn to some recent missiological thinking about migration in our present context. In 2010, the evangelical community recognized the worldwide phenomenon of diaspora communities as both an opportunity and a challenge to the proclamation of the Christian gospel worldwide.

> Christians live in diaspora conditions . . . We are convinced that contemporary migrations are within the sovereign missional purpose of God, without ignoring the evil and suffering that can be involved.[18]

In the same year, the pivotal Edinburgh conference recognized that in a world of diversity, there was a need for new forms of theological education.[19] In the decade following, the pace of migration has progressed so fast that the UNHCR is able to speak of 2010–2019 as a decade of global displacement.[20]

Reflecting on the sovereign missional purpose of God, missiologists have recognized four significant ways in which God has been working in the context of global migration.[21] First, mission *to* the diaspora,[22] where deliberate attempts are made by churches, organizations and individuals in host countries to reach out to diaspora communities with the love of Christ in word and action.[23] Second, mission *in* the diaspora, where diaspora believers share the love of Christ with their own diaspora communities. Third, mission *by* the

18. *Cape Town Commitment*, Part IIC: "Living the Love of Christ among people of other faiths," 5. "Love reaches out to scattered people." The idea of opportunity and challenge is echoed by T. V. Thomas: "I believe the global Church stands at an exciting Kairos moment of opportunity and challenge." In the foreword to Medeiros et al., *Scattered to Gather*, 3.

19. Im and Yong, *Global Diasporas and Mission*, viii, quote the Common Call from Edinburgh 2010 where theological education is addressed in point 6.

20. UNHCR, "Global Trends 2019," 4.

21. Zafar Ismail first brought this missiological thinking to the attention of TEE leaders in 2015. See Increase Association, *Exploring New Horizons*, 66–69.

22. Woods, *Theologising Migration*, 182–84, refers to this as "Ministry to Migrants in the Host Nations."

23. For example, outreach among international students has been highly effective in many places, see Chinn, "Diaspora Missions on Campuses," 235–43. For example, "International students who come from a context that is resistant to or ignorant about Christianity may appreciate the freedom to explore the Bible and learn of Jesus Christ," 236.

diaspora, where believers return to their countries of origin to share the love of Christ which they have received in the diaspora.[24] Finally, mission *beyond* the diaspora, where displaced people share the love of Christ cross-culturally, including evangelizing the people in the host country.[25]

Perhaps more than anything else, migration has enabled Christians worldwide to recognize that mission is no longer just a question of the Christians leaving their own countries to share the gospel in other nations. Because of global migration, opportunities have arisen for mission on our own doorstep, even to people groups that have traditionally been closed to the gospel.[26]

Categories of Diaspora Communities

We now turn our attention to different categories of diaspora communities.[27] We also give some examples of where TEE is being used among each of these categories. It is, however, important to recognize that the categories are not watertight compartments. People may exist in more than one category and may also move between different categories as their situation changes. For example, Believers from a Muslim Background (BMBs)[28] may exist in any of these categories but are important enough to be considered as a separate category in their own right.

24. For example, Chinn, 235, "Many church and mission leaders have become Christians and were discipled while studying in another country and have returned home to contribute to the expansion of God's kingdom in their homeland and region."

25. These models of diaspora mission are seen for example in the Lausanne booklet, Medeiros et al., *Scattered to Gather*. See also, Tira, "Ministering to Scattered Peoples."

26. For example, Woods, *Theologising Migration*, 174, "Many migrants in East Asia come from countries where the church cannot minister freely or where there could be consequences for those who become Christians."

27. It is possible to categorize diaspora communities differently. For example, see Ismail and Ball, who categorize the diaspora into three groups: temporary workers, first generation migrants, and later generation communities (Ismail and Ball, *Exploring New Horizons*, 69). Here, we have instead chosen to categorize diaspora communities according to economic status, although it can be seen that there is some similarity between these different ways of categorization. The migrant workers tend to be temporary, while the professional or skilled migrants tend to be more settled.

28. Commonly also referred to as Muslim Background Believers (MBBs).

Refugees

The UNHCR defines a refugee as:

> someone who has been forced to flee his or her country because of persecution, war or violence. A refugee has a well-founded fear of persecution for reasons of race, religion, nationality, political opinion or membership in a particular social group. Most likely, they cannot return home or are afraid to do so. War and ethnic, tribal and religious violence are leading causes of refugees fleeing their countries.[29]

While the refugee crisis is often seen in negative terms, it can also be seen within the divine purposes of God.[30] Refugees are not only receivers of the gospel, they can also be agents of the gospel in the host country.[31] The refugee crisis brings a tremendous opportunity to fulfil the Great Commission to disciple the nations (Matt 28:19–20) not only as "mission to" but also as "mission by" and "mission beyond" refugees. TEE can be a useful tool in discipling refugees and in enabling them to disciple others in their community in the host country and also back in their country of origin.

Perhaps one of the most remarkable stories of diaspora TEE has been in the Christian and Missionary Alliance (C&MA) churches, especially among the people of South East Asia. As an example of mission *to* the diaspora, the C&MA started using the Life of Christ courses from SEAN International[32] to train leaders for Vietnamese churches in the USA. These churches, initially made up

29. UNHCR, "What Is a Refugee?" See also UNHCR, "Migrants and Refugees," "A "refugee" is strictly defined in international law as a person who is fleeing persecution or conflict in his/her country of origin."

30. This was a constant theme of a virtual summit hosted by the Lausanne Diaspora Network on 26–27 August 2020. See https://www.lausanne.org/gatherings/lausanne-diaspora-summit.

31. Sam George, the Director of Wheaton College's Global Diaspora Center, goes as far as to believe that God is reviving Christianity in Europe through refugees. See George and Adeney, *Refugee Diaspora*.

32. SEAN International (https://www.seaninternational.org) has been providing TEE courses to national and local TEE organizations around the world since its inception in 1971. Many organizations have translated or adapted the six-book course Life of Christ to train people for pastoral and lay ministry. The basic discipleship courses, Abundant Life and The Big Picture (a biblical survey course also known as Abundant Light or Pure Gold), have been used as effective discipleship courses in many contexts.

of refugees from Vietnam, then became an example of mission *by* the diaspora as they took TEE back to Vietnam in 1992. What started as the training of disciples and leaders in the refugee community became a programme used by the same refugees to train disciples and leaders in their country of origin so that since then "this TEE programme has trained more than one thousand new pastors!"[33]

More recently, with increasing numbers of refugees in Europe, churches have begun reaching out in various ways to provide help and support as well as sharing the good news.[34] Discipling these refugee believers has become a key issue and, even in the light of COVID-19, organizations are seeking innovative ways to strengthen discipleship.[35] The discipleship course Come Follow Me, which uses the TEE method, has been translated into at least sixteen languages and has started to become a key tool for discipling such refugees.[36] This course aimed specifically at BMBs has been taken up as a key discipleship tool among many refugee groups. At the same time, the Program for Theological Education by Extension (PTEE)[37] has started Sudanese Arabic groups using SEAN courses among refugees including those fleeing from South Sudan and those in Ugandan refugee camps.

The flexible nature of TEE and the availability of courses in more than seventy languages means that local groups can disciple believers in situations where there are limited resources. However, because TEE organizations have tended to focus on the majority populations of their particular country, those who wish to disciple refugees often do not know these resources exist. Even when they do, it is not always possible to obtain courses easily. Furthermore, the printing and distribution costs can mean that churches and organizations

---

33. Aylett and van Wingerden,"Vietnam: God Can Work," 131.

34. For example, The How Will They Hear network as a partnership of various evangelical mission agencies seeking to serve refugees.

35. "Many online discipleship groups were started amongst Arab migrants soon after the onset of COVID-19 and are still going strong." How Will They Hear 10:14 prayers for refugees, 14 August 2020.

36. According to the Come Follow Me website (https://www.come-follow-me.org), the following languages are available: Arabic, Azeri, Bengali, Dutch, Farsi, French, German, Kurdish Sorani, Dari, English, French, Norwegian, Tajik, Russian for Central Asia, Somali, and Urdu. The following languages are in translation, Amharic, Pashtu, Russian (Standard), Swahili, Uighur, and African English Edition.

37. PTEE (http://ptee.org/eng/) is the Arabic TEE organization based in Jordan.

are unable to make use of TEE resources. Additionally, there is the constant need to train group leaders to be able to lead interactive discussions in cultures where this is not the normal way of learning. Training leaders for such groups in a refugee setting is an issue that still needs to be overcome if TEE is to be used more effectively in this context.[38]

Migrant workers

According to the UNHCR, "there is no legal definition of 'migrant.'"[39] However, to distinguish migrants from refugees, migrants can be seen as those who leave their own country and move voluntarily to another country to better themselves economically.[40] The first category of such migrants are low-paid workers whom we categorize as "migrant workers."[41] Such people are often employed in factories, construction, or seasonal labour (such as agriculture or tourism). Their working conditions are often poor, and their legal status is precarious.[42] A second category of migration is that of international students. A third category of migration are those we will identify as "professional" or "skilled" migrants who seek employment in countries where there is a need for their skills and where they may be offered higher wages than in their country of origin.

We turn first to migrant workers. This group is the focus of our later discussion where we consider the use of TEE amongst migrant workers in Malaysia. For now, it is enough to note that TEE has been effectively used among migrant workers in the Gulf countries where, because churches often

38. Word of Life (https://word.org.uk/) have begun to run regular online workshops to train leaders for Come Follow Me. ORTA (The Open Russian Theological Academy) and TEE Malaysia also runs training sessions for leaders via Zoom.

39. UNHCR, "Migrants and Refugees." However, as Alison Eldridge states: "Migrant and refugee . . . in particular have become hot topics in the media and political discourse owing to large numbers of people fleeing countries in Africa and the Middle East for better and safer prospects in Europe." See Eldridge "What Is the Difference." https://www.britannica.com/story/whats-the-difference-between-a-migrant-and-a-refugee.

40. "Simply speaking, a migrant is someone who chooses to move, and a refugee is someone who has been forced from their home." From Eldridge, "What Is the Difference?"

41. Woods, *Theologising Migration*, 42–45, separates this category into "Foreign Domestic Labourers" (FDWs) and "Contract Labourers."

42. See for example, Woods, 44–45.

exist as separate linguistic entities,[43] they are usually served by TEE programmes in their country of origin. Thus, Nepali communities are served directly by the Institute for Theological Education by Extension, Nepal (ITEEN), Indian believers by The Association for Theological Education by Extension (TAFTEE), and Pakistani believers by the Open Theological Seminary (OTS). Over the years, many students have been trained in the Gulf and many have returned to serve the Lord in their country of origin. While these organizations have focused mainly on lay education, there has been some impact even among untrained pastors of such churches.[44] However, the need and opportunities for systematic theological education in such churches are evidently far more than is being met.[45]

Another example of the use of TEE with migrant workers is amongst Central Asians in Russia and the former Soviet Union. The story of Ben and Una is documented in the recent book, *TEE in Asia*:

> The couple use TEE materials to serve migrants because the courses are so easy to understand and because they are a helpful discipleship tool. Many of the migrants they encounter have very basic or no education. There are examples of people who have learned to read and write through the TEE courses![46]

In this context, the availability of TEE courses in different ethnic languages means that groups can each study in their own heart language, but when they meet together, they can discuss in Russian.[47]

43. See Thomas, "South Asian Diaspora Christianity," 117–129, especially 122.

44. Thomas, 124, "A tiny percentage is seeking to upgrade and enhance their ministry competence by enrolling in distance learning avenues like theological education by extension courses offered modularly onsite or through the internet."

45. Thomas, 129, "The gospel preached is sometimes watered down and people embrace an easy believism. The result is that believers do not receive solid biblical instruction or pursue serious discipleship or training."

46. van Wingerden, "Migrant Mission," 93.

47. van Wingerden, 93.

International students

International students leave their country voluntarily to better their education. Away from home they are often receptive to the gospel[48] and can take the gospel with them wherever they go. Among international students, there are examples of groups from a wide variety of countries meeting and studying in English in Malaysia.[49] There are also examples of people in Cambridge in the UK who have studied TEE courses and have returned to their own countries where they have continued to study courses.[50] In one case, a student based in the UK has returned to Czechia, where she is involved in translating courses into Czech.

Professional or skilled migrants

As indicated above, professional or skilled migrants comprise educated and wealthy migrants who move to another country for work. In America more than a third of migrants are such professionals, while in Canada and Australia professional migrants form the majority of the foreign-born population.[51] In terms of the take-up of TEE, the global Chinese Christian community is significant. TEE is now used significantly among the Chinese diaspora in the USA, UK, Australia, New Zealand, and Malaysia, and there are smaller groups adopting TEE as discipleship programmes in their churches in many other countries. Chinese groups have tended to adopt a very regimented form of TEE. The courses are used extensively among highly educated business people. From these people, the use of TEE in mainland China as well as other countries in South East Asia has also increased in another example of "mission by" the diaspora.[52]

48. "International students who come from a context that is resistant to or ignorant about Christianity may appreciate the freedom to explore the Bible and learn of Jesus Christ," Chinn, "Diaspora Missions on Campuses," 236.

49. In conversation with Tim and Rachel Green, who have used the courses among international students in the context of a church in Malaysia.

50. In conversation with Cecilia Brassett, who has used the courses amongst students of various nationalities.

51. Connor and Ruiz, "Majority of U.S. Public."

52. TEE Movers for the Chinese Church (TMCC) and Friends of Grace (FoG) are both involved in "mission among the diaspora" in the USA and elsewhere and "mission by the diaspora" in the mainland.

Immigrants (long-term diaspora)

As noted above, Vietnamese refugees in the USA formed churches and many of them remained in the USA. In the USA, there are C&MA churches among Vietnamese, Hmong, Cambodian (Khmer), and Jurai-Montagnard ethnic communities. Most of these groups use TEE as part of their leadership training programmes. The C&MA Church Leadership Academy has also adapted the TEE method to provide an online programme of study for students.[53]

One challenge facing immigrant churches is how different generations connect with their ethnic identity. Often the younger generations, who have been born in the host country, are more at ease with the host country's culture and language. They often want to study in the language of their peers and either prefer the language of the host country or English. Again, the Chinese churches have found that they are able to offer TEE courses in both Chinese and English, which enables children to study the same course as their parents and allows churches to offer a programme to suit the needs of both generations.[54]

Believers from Muslim Backgrounds (BMBs)

In recent years there has been an increased turning to Christ of Muslims from different ethnic backgrounds.

> Leaving Islam can sometimes bring shame on the BMBs, rejection from their birth community and intimidation by, and expulsion from, their relations. Can the church community they have joined become their new, chosen family, to take the place of the one they have lost? Is the church able to help them navigate life between their previous and new lives? What sort of relationship should

53. The Basic Training Program of the C&MA Leadership Academy uses the SEAN Life of Christ course as a key part of the training. https://www.cmalliance.org/ministries/basic-training-program.

54. A challenging feature of TEE in the context of multi-cultural or multi-language groups is that over the years several courses have been revised and updated. This is especially true for the Life of Christ course offered by SEAN International. Sometimes the translated course reflects an earlier version of the materials. Sometimes the translated courses have also been adapted to suit a particular culture. The bigger the difference between different versions of courses, the bigger the challenge of holding multi-ethnic groups. It is precisely because of this issue, that SEAN International has commissioned a new Chinese version of its courses so that they will be brought into line with the latest English and Spanish versions.

> the BMB maintain with their birth family? When should they announce their conversion to the faith community they are seen to have deserted?[55]

Such issues, among many others, mean that discipling BMBs is often more challenging than other groups.[56]

Three key TEE programmes have been involved in discipling and training people from Muslim backgrounds for many years. The first is the Open Theological Seminary (OTS) in Pakistan, which has developed its own curriculum over many years in the context of a Muslim country.[57] The second is the Program for Theological Education by Extension (PTEE) based in Jordan.[58] Both these organizations seek to develop disciples and leaders for the church but also have an interest in serving the majority community in their countries. The third organization, Shikkha Kalyan Trust (SKT) in Bangladesh, focuses on equipping believers of Muslim background.[59] Their TEE courses use language and terms that are familiar to Muslims.

More recently there has been a renewed interest in developing TEE courses for believers of Muslim background. For example, Word of Life "is committed to equip and provide relevant discipleship resources to enable this, and plans to produce a curriculum of courses over the coming years."[60] This looks to be a significant step for TEE in the years to come and several TEE organizations as well as mission agencies have begun to use the Come Follow Me course to this end.

---

55. Mahabba Network, Karamat, Lovefast. Day 30.

56. For example, Woods, *Theologising Migration*, 182, "Indonesians need to read the Bible in Bahasa Indonesia and many *would approach it from an Islamic perspective*" (emphasis added).

57. Chapter 10: Julius, "TEE and Campus-Based Training in Partnership," gives more details of OTS and its campus TEE partnership.

58. PTEE is probably the leading organization in terms of adapting TEE for online learning. Other organizations that have developed online versions of TEE courses include ITEEN (Nepal), SEAN Costa Rica, and the C&MA Leadership Academy.

59. There is a larger TEE organization in Bangladesh, College of Christian Theology Bangladesh, which focuses on courses for the Christian community.

60. https://word.org.uk/word-of-life-curriculum/.

Issues Encountered in Discipling the Diaspora Using TEE

Having considered how TEE is being used among different types of diaspora communities globally, we turn to the use of TEE among refugees and migrant workers in Malaysia. By focusing on these groups as an example of diaspora TEE, we can analyze some challenges as well as successes that have been discovered in using TEE for discipleship in this context. The discussion is based on the first-hand experiences of the Malaysian national TEE team.[61] In Malaysia, as in many parts of the world, refugees and migrant workers are a significantly disadvantaged and marginalized community due to their educational and economic background, current living conditions, language, culture, and other factors that affect their life and spirituality.[62] With TEE, as with any other discipleship tool, discipleship is a process.[63] Those who serve migrants and refugees need to understand the factors that influence the diaspora ministry in order for this process of discipleship to succeed.[64]

Some of the common issues and challenges for discipling refugees and migrant workers in Malaysian context are:

1. their low educational level
2. the transient nature of the community, the frequent turnover of migrant workers and especially of those who can lead groups
3. the limited time they have for their study
4. language
5. financial limitations
6. access and skill to use technology

61. Rina Robinson, along with her spouse Martin, has been involved in setting up discipleship groups using TEE courses in Malaysia amongst Nepali, Myanmari, and Pakistani migrants and refugees. The reflections in this section are from Rina's own experience of this process.

62. This is seen for example in the recent treatment of refugees and migrant workers during the COVID-19 lockdown: Latiff and Ananthalakshmi, "Malaysia Detains Hundreds of Refugees and Migrants during Virus Lockdown: Rights Groups." See also Kaur, "Refugees and Refugee Policy in Malaysia." See also Woods, *Theologising Migration*, 18.

63. Rittenhouse, *Challenges to Discipleship*, 11, "The discipleship process is not complete until the disciples we make are making other disciples. Disciples are not disciples and aren't fully obedient until they are making disciples."

64. See Woods, *Theologising Migration*, 182–84.

Educational level

Most migrant workers and refugees in transition are not highly educated. Should this be a disadvantage in enabling them to be disciples of Jesus Christ? Peter, Andrew, James, and John were fishermen. They received on-the-job training with Jesus and they turned the world upside down (Acts 17:6). So limited education should be no disqualification for discipleship.[65]

TEE offers simple methods – simple yet in-depth courses and training that make it possible to overcome the challenge of the educational level of the migrants and refugees. In Malaysia a Nepali sister, who was educated in school for two classes only, has studied TEE courses with such passion, even though it took her much longer to do the self-study than others. People with limited education can even be trained to become group leaders.[66] Many TEE students are becoming leaders in their ethnic church in Malaysia.

Transient community

Refugees and migrants are on the move.[67] Discipling a community that is on the move poses challenges and also creates opportunities.[68] Refugees and migrant

65. Cf. Acts 4:13: "When 'the religious leaders' saw the courage of Peter and John and realised that they were unschooled, ordinary men, they were astonished" (Bible quotation from Wallace, "Were the Disciples?"). While this verse does not necessarily mean that Jesus's disciples had no education, it does indicate that they did not have a "professional" religious/theological education as would be expected of teachers. See also 1 Cor 1:26–29. For a brief discussion of the varied educational backgrounds of Jesus's earliest disciples, see: Wallace, "Were the Disciples?"

66. The TEE method of personal study, group meetings, and practical application has been tried in more than one hundred countries and has been found particularly effective amongst those with little or no formal education. For example, SEAN's basic Abundant Life course was written in South America with such people in mind. Canon Geoffrey Dixon, (on using SEAN's Abundant Life course in Uganda) states: "Five years ago we began a Christian Discipleship programme . . . We have been teaching church leaders, using SEAN materials. They have been a marvellous tool for the Discipleship ministry. The people we teach go back to their villages and teach their people. We began with twenty-four students, this expanded to two more small groups. To date over four hundred people have studied Abundant Life. The SEAN studies are a marvellous teaching resource for new Christians and any Christian who wants to grow in their faith and understand what it means to be a 21st-century Christian" (https://goldproject.org/sean-worldwide).

67. Here we can see some similarities with the patriarchs in the Old Testament and the people of God wandering in the wilderness. The identity of a transient community is often not in where it is, but in where it has come from or where it is going to.

68. Some of the specific challenges faced in setting up TEE for diaspora communities in Malaysia are documented in the booklet published by the Increase Association, "Discipling the Nations in

workers are not permanent in the new country. Disciple-makers therefore have to make best use of a limited period to disciple the migrants and refugees as well as to raise leaders among them. In Malaysia, most migrant workers are in a three to five-year contract after which they return to their country of origin. Therefore a process of discipleship training has to be completed during this limited period before they go back to their own country.[69] During this time, sufficient training must also be given to group leaders who can then make disciples whenever they move on.

Through TEE, people are being raised both to be disciples and to be disciple-makers wherever they go (Matt 28:19–20). Abhishek was working in Malaysia for three years as a construction worker. While in Malaysia he completed the six course books on the Life of Christ and showed leadership potential. He trained as a TEE group leader.[70] For two years Abhishek led two TEE groups. On returning to Nepal, he introduced TEE to his church and started TEE classes in his village. Today Abhishek has four TEE classes in Nepal. The example of Abishek shows us that sometimes God allows scattering that more may be gathered. In such examples, being a transient community helps to take the disciple-making process further. By enabling migrant students to become leaders, we see disciples who make disciples of all nations and teach them everything Jesus has commanded.

Since contract workers frequently have to return to their country, leadership of TEE groups among migrants often changes hands. TEE groups must find another leader to replace the one that leaves. Since TEE requires leaders to be trained before they facilitate a class, group leader training must be repeated regularly to enable new leaders to carry on groups that have already started. In Malaysia, a system has been developed in which a leader finds their successor before their time to return to their home country has come. If we want to see consistent progress and growth, we need continually to train group leaders.

---

the Diaspora: Using TEE Courses in Multiple Languages." This booklet is available for download from https://www.increaseassociation.org/.

69. We recognize that the discipleship process should be lifelong. Nevertheless, there needs to be a clear process that can be completed within the timeframe they have in the country where they are working.

70. Such training is required for all TEE tutors/facilitators.

Time limitations

Migrants and refugees have limited time available because they follow a work schedule that their employers decide. Most of them work long hours. For some Sunday is free but for others even Sunday is a workday.[71] So time is limited in which they can study God's word and be discipled. In Malaysia, we have found that these migrants and refugees have hungry hearts. They seek the Lord and study his word in the limited time they have. The flexibility of TEE means that we can work around their time schedule. Sometimes their classes are held at night (e.g. 9:00 p.m. to 12:00 midnight) because they are not free any other time.

Language

In diaspora ministry, we are working with varied language groups. Language is important in every culture.[72] In previous generations, missionaries went to another country to minister and at least the first six months were spent learning the language of those they were going to minister to. Similarly, when working with diaspora communities, it is often necessary to learn their language or have someone who understands and speaks their language.[73]

One advantage of using TEE in discipleship is that course materials have been translated into more than one hundred languages and the work is still going on.[74] Furthermore, the groups are able to have their discussions in the language of their choice.[75] This makes the task of discipleship easier, especially among refugees and migrant workers, since in most cases it is possible to find the TEE courses in the language of the new community. In this way, it is possible to work with different language groups. Furthermore, leaders from

71. Woods, *Theologising Migration*, 44. "Similar to FDWs (Foreign Domestic Workers), foreign workers often work in difficult conditions and for long hours without overtime pay, some even seven days per week."

72. For example, Woods, 182. "Cultural and linguistic differences require that gospel ministry be contextualized for the migrants' situation and needs."

73. Woods, 183–84, highlights the significant issues involved in ministering among diaspora groups.

74. In Malaysia, SEAN International has been the main supplier of TEE courses through its partners in Nepal, Pakistan, and Myanmar.

75. There are many examples of TEE groups around the world doing the study in their workbooks in one language (e.g. the national or state language), but discussing the lesson and its application in another language (e.g. their own mother tongue) when they meet.

the community can be trained and these are the ones that will disciple their friends. In Malaysia, the Chinese churches use TEE courses in their language. Likewise, Nepalese, Burmese, and Pakistanis are all using courses in their own language. However, second generation Burmese have problems understanding Burmese, as they grew up outside their parents' country of origin. They prefer to study in English.

Financial limitations

Most refugees and migrants have a limited income, which they must utilize to meet their needs and their families' needs.[76] TEE does not want to add to the burden of people who are already hard pressed financially. Consequently, Malaysia TEE seeks to mobilize local believers who can help support the costs of TEE course books, training and other expenses. We intentionally keep the books reasonably priced so that migrants and refugees can afford their course books.[77]

Access to technology

In the face of the COVID-19 pandemic, meeting together to study together in a group became even more challenging. Having knowledge of and access to technology has helped many believers continue to study God's word as part of a local discussion group. Those with smartphones, laptops, and Wi-Fi were able to carry on with their classes. However, due to lack of technical knowledge, non-availability of the internet, or long hours of work, there are other people who could not continue their studies in TEE groups. As with other forms of discipleship, we need to change our methods according to the needs or current situation. Some TEE organizations are planning online group leader training.[78]

76. Interestingly, Woods, *Theologising Migration*, 44, points out that it is not only a case of low wages, but also the fact that "it is common for almost half of a foreign worker's time in a richer country to be spent paying off his debt" (i.e. fees to brokers who find them the work).

77. One challenge of supplying courses around the world is for TEE organizations to find a financial model to enable courses to be studied at a cost that can be affordable in each setting. SEAN International has a system of providing courses to national TEE programmes in return for a "royalty fee." This fee is set in conjunction with the local TEE provider to ensure that courses remain affordable while TEE programmes seek to be financially sustainable.

78. Examples of online group leader training that have taken place in lockdown include webinars for new group leaders in Georgia, training for Come Follow Me facilitators in multiple countries,

Others are experimenting with various online methods of delivering courses using various platforms to allow group discussion.[79] Irrespective of the times or situation, the work of discipling must go on and new forms of enabling TEE groups to continue are emerging. Yet, we must ensure that we do not exclude those who do not have access to technology.

Important Considerations in Discipling the Diaspora Using TEE

Having considered specific issues encountered in using TEE among migrants and refugees in the Malaysian context, we turn to some general considerations for using TEE to disciple the diaspora, along with some suggested solutions gathered from those who have been engaged in diaspora TEE around the world.[80]

The value of cooperation and partnership

An important factor in discipling the diaspora is to connect to partners in the country of origin and also between churches in the host country. If the national TEE organization of the country of origin has a signed agreement with the diaspora TEE group, it is possible for sharing of resources and course books to be ethical, legal, simple, and affordable.[81]

This cooperation has been happening in Malaysia. In 2015 an Increase Association conference in Malaysia provided an opportunity for me (Rina) and my spouse to meet Tanka Subedi, the director of ITEEN. For the first time we

---

and training for group leaders on the GOLD Programme in the UK. For other examples or online group leader training, see footnote 39.

79. South American TEE organizations have used WhatsApp and Facebook. Others have used conferencing platforms such as Zoom.

80. In 2015, the Increase Association set up a Diaspora Task Group to look at the issues faced in enabling diaspora TEE. Much of this section is based on the work of that group which comprises various TEE practitioners connected with TEE in Asia: Anneta Vysotskaya (Russia, Central Asia, former Soviet countries, and New Zealand), Lyn Pearson (Central Asia, South East Asia, and Australia), Rachel Green (Malaysia), Rina Robinson (Malaysia) and David Ball (South Asia and UK). This group has been collecting stories and examples of diaspora TEE around the world and seeking to find models of best practice.

81. SEAN International and Increase Association have worked on model templates for TEE organizations across Asia to enter into Partner-to-Partner agreements for this purpose.

saw the Abundant Life, Abundant Light, and other TEE courses in Nepali. We were overjoyed, as we were always looking for resources to systematically train Nepali believers in Malaysia. Subedi then helped us by training thirty Nepali believers. This help included providing resources in the Nepali language. Since then, Nepali TEE has thrived in Malaysia, having more than forty discipleship classes at the time of writing (2021) – more than two hundred group leaders have been trained. In November 2019, in an Increase gathering in Turkey, TEE Malaysia signed a memoranda of understanding with ITEEN, TEE Myanmar, and TEE Pakistan. There are several Pakistani TEE classes going on led by a Pakistani believer.[82]

Having made the connections with national TEE organizations of host countries, TEE course books, certificates of completion, and examination papers can become readily available to support diaspora TEE ministries.[83]

In addition to making connections between different TEE organizations, it is important to make links with the many churches or fellowships in the host country. The experience in Malaysia suggests that TEE thrives when there is a network of believers or churches working with the same diaspora community. For this reason, TEE Malaysia has sought to make connections with a wide variety of church leaders in order to promote the TEE discipleship tool among the churches who are serving the diaspora communities. It is important to work through local churches in the host country for TEE to be a successful discipleship tool.

Availability of TEE courses

In Malaysia, as in many countries, when diaspora TEE started among different ethnic groups, the availability of courses was a significant challenge. As mentioned, this involved developing good relationships with various organizations. Formal links with SEAN were needed to reproduce courses in various languages. However, since SEAN works through national TEE partners for translation and distribution of its courses, it was necessary to link with

82. These are Rina's own reflections on what has happened in Malaysia.

83. There are situations where such cooperation has been more difficult. Sometimes this is because of lack of clarity or lack of trust. One TEE organization in South Asia, for example, had shared courses with an organization many years ago, but that organization had apparently claimed those courses as their own. Rebuilding trust between such organizations becomes difficult.

individual national TEE organizations who had translated the courses in order to access courses in the languages needed in Malaysia. With the help of SEAN and Increase, TEE Malaysia was able to make the necessary connections with national TEE organizations from the countries of origin of the diaspora community.[84]

These connections have led to the signing of printing and distribution agreements between TEE Malaysia and host countries in order to make TEE courses readily available for diaspora TEE ministry.[85] These agreements not only allow the courses to be printed locally but make clear arrangements for the payment of royalties to SEAN and to the national TEE programmes providing the courses. Malaysia TEE has in many ways been a pioneer for such agreements. In just a few years, systems and procedures for obtaining courses have become smoother. Courses are now readily available to groups who want to study TEE courses in Nepali, Burmese, and Urdu, as well as English and Chinese.

In Australia, a different model has been developed. There, the recently established national TEE programme[86] was specifically set up with a vision for diaspora TEE. TEE Australia entered into an agreement with SEAN to provide courses in multiple languages for use in Australia.[87] To print courses in Chinese, Farsi, Turkish, and Urdu, each course has been uploaded to a print-

84. The reality is that building these connections depends on the help, support, and perseverance of particular individuals who believe in the vision of diaspora discipleship using TEE. In the case of the Nepali TEE work in Malaysia, the vision and support of the Director of ITEEN, Tanka Subedi, along with the encouragement and wisdom of the General Secretary of Increase Association, Tim Green along with Rachel (who were on the ground in Malaysia), enabled the courses to be made available easily. In the case of diaspora work among the Myanmari community, SEAN's Regional Coordinator for Asia, David Ball, was able to make links with the Director of Joshua Mission, Young Saeng Cho, in Myanmar to make Burmese materials available. In other words, the complex relationships between organizations was eased by those who had a vision for the effectiveness of diaspora TEE.

85. Printing books is never cheap, neither is transporting books from another country. One solution is for the TEE course books to be printed locally. This requires an understanding as well as signing an MOU between the national TEE organizations of the two countries. In the case of SEAN courses, these MOU's take the form of a "partner-to-partner" agreement encompassing the different aspects needed for the smooth sharing of courses.

86. TEE Australia: see https://tee.org.au.

87. TEE Australia accesses most courses directly through SEAN International. An exception to this was the Center for Leadership Development (CLD) in Thailand, who have worked out an agreement with TEE Australia for the supply of courses in Thai.

on-demand website and the links for ordering course materials provided to TEE Australia. This system opens up new opportunities for diaspora students around the world. It means that courses in these languages will be available for any country via a link provided by SEAN. What started as an experiment to serve diaspora believers in Australia, is also being used to serve Farsi and Turkish groups in Europe.

Training of group leaders

Training group leaders is one of the keys to the effectiveness of TEE as a discipleship tool.[88] In 2015 Increase gave special focus to training and supporting group leaders.[89] A task group was formed to explore group leader training further. In 2016 the group identified the need for a group leader training package. In 2017 Increase redesigned the group leader's manual for Abundant Life. This updating provided the key to running effective group leader training for new diaspora TEE group leaders.[90] SEAN and Increase then worked jointly on the development of an online resource to run a group leader training workshop.[91]

For diaspora TEE, group leader training is more complicated due to training being required in diaspora languages. In Malaysia, the first training of leaders for diaspora groups was conducted by inviting leaders from national TEE organizations in host countries to travel to Malaysia to conduct the training.[92] As the work developed, it was possible for those based in Malaysia to train people from the diaspora groups. Now those from the diaspora language groups have themselves reached a level of experience where they can conduct training themselves, in their own mother tongue. It is now possible to conduct several training sessions a year in diaspora languages, depending on need.

As indicated, TEE has a unique way of training group leaders who in turn can lead discipleship courses among their own communities and, in turn,

88. See Aylett, "Equipping and Supporting," 223.

89. See Increase Association, *Exploring New Horizons*, 91–93.

90. Aylett, "Equipping and Supporting," 225–26.

91. This online resource is presently available on the Crosswire platform and can be accessed from anywhere in the world (https://connect.crosswired.com/web/c2927223/overview). Future downloadable versions of the resource are planned and are expected to be available in 2021.

92. ITEEN, in Nepal, and OTS, in Pakistan, sent resource people to conduct training in Malaysia.

enable others to become leaders. It does not require any theological background or high level of education. As long as they can read and write their language and understand the TEE method, they are able to provide the continuity of studies to their groups. It is truly marvellous to see how semi-educated migrants are able to run TEE classes so consistently and successfully. As discussed already, whenever a leader is transferred to another city or returns to their country, another leader must be ready to take their place. Therefore, preparation and foresight as to when and where to conduct training is needed.

Local church and its support

Finally, we consider the role of the local church for the effectiveness of TEE as a tool for discipleship among diaspora communities. Local churches, in the country where migrants and refugees have come to dwell, are called to love foreigners (e.g. Lev 19:33–34). Loving foreigners means sharing the gospel as well as resources. This calling includes sharing in the lifelong process of discipleship.

Migrants and refugees do not usually have their own buildings or facilities in the country in which they are residing.[93] Local churches can help by providing a place of worship for migrants and refugees.[94] In terms of TEE, migrants and refugees do not normally have access to spaces for TEE group meetings. Local churches are therefore a key component to enable TEE groups to meet.[95] Local churches and individuals can also contribute towards the costs of producing

93. More established diaspora communities such as the Chinese churches in Europe and some Mar Thoma churches in the UK are able to purchase their own buildings.

94. Many churches in Malaysia have taken up this responsibility and provided a place within their church premises for the worship service of foreigners. This fits with Scripture – Isa 54:2. Many churches have not only provided a place of worship for the foreigners living among them but have also provided "mission houses" or "drop-in centres." These drop-in centres provide a place where Christian migrants can meet for prayer, fellowship, bonding, and meals.

95. This could be in church premises or in members' homes. Local churches can also provide transport to enable migrants and refugees to come to the church or the study group. Quite often in a foreign country, migrants and refugees do not find it safe to move around by themselves especially when their services or TEE groups are in a far-off church. See e.g. Woods, *Theologising Migration*, 18, "Malaysia has shown some intolerance toward foreign workers, often associating them with health problems and crime."

courses for migrants and refugees.[96] For example, scholarships or bursaries can be set up by local churches to help diaspora groups with costs.

An important factor for effective discipleship using TEE is to find those in the local church who are committed to discipling others.[97] In the context of diaspora TEE, these are people with a missional, serving attitude who are willing to come alongside the TEE students and support them, not only in their studies, but in living as fellow believers in the host country. Courses such as Come Follow Me and Abundant Life are now often being used in multilingual groups facilitated by ordinary believers from local churches who want to see migrants grow as disciples of Jesus.

Conclusion

The question this chapter examines is whether TEE may provide one significant way to disciple diaspora believers in order to strengthen their faith and witness in, through, and beyond their own communities. Having looked at the theme of migration in the Bible and some current missiological thinking about diaspora, we showed how TEE is being used for discipleship amongst different categories of diaspora. Then we considered key issues for TEE coming from experiences of TEE in the Malaysian context. We then gave consideration to the global effectiveness of TEE among diaspora groups and concluded that the local church has a key role to play if diaspora TEE is to be effective.

We hinted that TEE needs to adapt to the realities of living in a global pandemic. TEE will need to adapt to these challenges and possibilities without excluding those who do not have access to technology. TEE amongst diaspora peoples is not new. Yet, TEE is only now recognizing it can be a significant global resource for discipleship among diaspora communities. How far TEE develops to serve this need will depend on the availability of courses, the cooperation of TEE organizations around the globe, the effective training of TEE leaders in the local community, and the awareness of the global church to this resource

96. Sometimes support from local churches can enable larger print runs and provide storage spaces that reduce the cost of producing each book.

97. "TEE works best when local churches use it as the core of their intentional discipleship and training," Green, "Equipping Disciples and Leaders," 14.

available in so many languages. Whether TEE is effective in discipleship will, as with any other discipleship resource, depend on faithful followers of Jesus in the local church committed to fulfilling the Great Commission to make disciples of all nations (Matt 28:20).

Bibliography

Aylett, Graham. "Equipping and Supporting TEE Group Leaders." In *TEE in Asia: Empowering Churches, Equipping Disciples*, edited by Hanna-Ruth van Wingerden, Tim Green, and Graham Aylett, 219–23. Carlisle: Langham Global Library, 2021.

———, ed. *Exploring New Horizons: Working Together for Church-Based Training in Asia*. Proceedings of a conference held in Kuala Lumpur, Malaysia, 20–25 April 2015. https://www.increaseassociation.org/images/downloads/exploring-new-horizons.pdf.

Aylett, Graham, and Hanna-Ruth van Wingerden. "Vietnam: God Can Work in Any Circumstance." In *TEE in Asia: Empowering Churches, Equipping Disciples*, edited by Hanna-Ruth van Wingerden, Tim Green, and Graham Aylett, 129–35. Carlisle: Langham Global Library, 2021.

Ball, David. "Foreigners and Exiles: Reflecting on the Nature of the Church as a Diaspora Community and Some Implications for Mission and Discipleship." 2016. Accessed 21 October 2020. https://www.increaseassociation.org/resources/diaspora/95-foreigners-and-exiles.

Bonhoeffer, Dietrich. *The Cost of Discipleship*. Translated by R. H. Fuller. London: SCM Press, 1937/1959.

Chinn, Leiton E. "Diaspora Missions on Campuses: John R. Mott and a Centennial Overview of the International Student Ministry in North America." In *Global Diasporas and Mission*, edited by Chandler H. Im and Amos Yong, 236–43. Oxford: Regnum, 2014.

Christian and Missionary Alliance Leadership Academy. Accessed 3 September 2020. https://www.cmalliance.org/ministries/.

Connor, Phillip, and Neil G. Ruiz. "Majority of US Public Supports High-Skilled Immigration." 2019. Accessed 1 September 2020. https://www.pewresearch.org/global/2019/01/22/majority-of-u-s-public-supports-high-skilled-immigration/.

Dixon, Geoffrey. "Discipleship in Non-Book Cultures." Accessed 3 September 2020. https://goldproject.org/sean-worldwide.

Eldridge, Alison. "What Is the Difference between a Migrant and a Refugee?" Accessed 3 September 2020. https://www.britannica.com/story/whats-the-difference-between-a-migrant-and-a-refugee.

George, Sam, and Miriam Adeney, eds. *Refugee Diaspora: Missions amid the Greatest Humanitarian Crisis of Our Times*. Littleton: William Carey Publishing, 2018.

Green, Tim. *Come Follow Me*. Accessed 21 August 2020. https://www.come-follow-me.org.

———. "Equipping Disciples and Leaders through TEE." In *TEE in Asia: Empowering Churches, Equipping Disciples*, edited by Hanna-Ruth van Wingerden, Tim Green, and Graham Aylett, 13–20. Carlisle: Langham Global Library, 2021.

Holter, Knut. "My Father Was a Migrant Aramean: Old Testament Motifs for a Theology of Migration." In *Global Diasporas and Mission*, edited by Chandler H. Im and Amos Yong, 57–70. Oxford: Regnum, 2014.

How Will They Hear, 10:14 Prayers for Refugees, 14 August 2020 (email circulation).

Im, Chandler H., and Amos Yong, eds. *Global Diasporas and Mission*. Oxford: Regnum, 2014.

Increase Association. "Discipling the Nations in the Diaspora: Using TEE Courses in Multiple Languages." 2020. Accessed 14 October 2020. https://www.increaseassociation.org/images/Discipling_the_Nations_Booklet.pdf.

IOM. "World Migration Report 2020," accessed 17 August 2020. https://www.iom.int/wmr/.

Ishmail, Zafar, and David Ball. "Working with Diaspora in Multicultural Contexts." In *Exploring New Horizons: Working Together for Church-Based Training in Asia*, edited by Graham Aylett, 66-69. Proceedings of an international conference held in Kuala Lumpur, Malaysia, 20–25 April, 2015. https://www.increaseassociation.org/resources/new-horizons.

Kahl, Werner. "Migrants as Instruments of Evangelization: In Early Christianity and in Contemporary Christianity." In *Global Diasporas and Mission*, edited by Chandler H. Im and Amos Yong, 71–86. Oxford: Regnum, 2014.

Kaur, Amarjit. "Refugees and Refugee Policy in Malaysia." Accessed 3 September 2020. https://www.researchgate.net/profile/Amarjit_Kaur3/publication/240640927_Refugees_and_Refugee_Policy_in_Malaysia/links/544708c70cf22b3c14e0bc05.pdf.

Latiff, Rozanna, and A. Ananthalakshmi. "Malaysia Detains Hundreds of Refugees and Migrants during Virus Lockdown: Rights Groups." Reuters. Accessed 3 September 2020. https://www.reuters.com/article/us-health-coronavirus-malaysia-migrants/

malaysia-detains-hundreds-of-refugees-and-migrants-during-virus-lockdown-rights-groups-idUSKBN22D5JU.

Lausanne Movement. *The Cape Town Commitment: A Confession of Faith and a Call to Action*. 2011. http://www.lausanne.org/content/ctc/ctcommitment.

Mahabba Network, "Lovefast. Day 30." Accessed 1 September 2020. https://www.mahabbanetwork.com/blog/lovefast.

Maruskin, Joan. "The 'Biblical Case' for Caring for Migrants." CWS, 28 November 2012. https://cwsglobal.org/news-features/the-biblical-case-for-caring-for-migrants/.

Medeiros Elias, Greg Woon Young Paek, Vergil Schmidt, Sadiri Joy Tira, Enoch Wan, Tetsunao Yamamori, and T. V. Thomas. *Scattered to Gather: Embracing the Global Trend of Diaspora, Revised Edition*. Quezon City: Global Diaspora Network, 2017.

Rittenhouse, Ralph. "Challenges to Discipleship." Camarillo Community Church, Camarillo, CA, 2015. https://www.theglobaldiscipleshipinitiative.org/images/newsletters/gdi-news-november-2015.pdf.

Thomas, T. V. "South Asian Diaspora Christianity in the Persian Gulf." In *Global Diasporas and Mission*, edited by Chandler H. Im and Amos Yong, 117–25. Oxford: Regnum, 2014.

Tira, Sadiri Joy. "Ministering to Scattered Peoples – Diaspora." Accessed 18 August 2020. https://www.lausanne.org/content/ministering-to-scattered-peoples-diaspora.

UNHCR. "Differentiation between Migrants and Refugees." Accessed 3 September 2020. https://www.ohchr.org/Documents/Issues/Migration/GlobalCompactMigration/MigrantsAndRefugees.pdf.

———. "Global Trends: Forced Displacement in 2019." Accessed 17 August 2020. https://www.unhcr.org/uk/statistics/unhcrstats/5ee200e37/unhcr-global-trends-2019.html.

———. "What Is a Refugee?" Accessed 3 September 2020. https://www.unhcr.org/uk/what-is-a-refugee.html.

van Wingerden, Hanna-Ruth. "Central Asia 3: Migrant Mission." In *TEE in Asia: Empowering Churches, Equipping Disciples*, edited by Hanna-Ruth van Wingerden, Tim Green, and Graham Aylett, 91–95. Carlisle: Langham Global Library, 2021.

van Wingerden, Hanna-Ruth, Tim Green, and Graham Aylett, eds. *TEE in Asia: Empowering Churches, Equipping Disciples*. Carlisle: Langham Global Library, 2021.

Wallace, Gail. "Were the Disciples of Jesus Unschooled, Ordinary Men?" Accessed 8 September 2020. https://www.huffpost.com/entry/were-the-disciples-of-jes_b_9508024.

Walls, Andrew F. "Towards a Theology of Migration." In *New Immigrant Congregations and Transnational Networks in North America and Europe*, edited by F. Ludwig and J. K. Asamoah-Gyadu, 407–17. Trenton: African World Press, 2011.

Woods, Paul. *Theologising Migration: Otherness and Liminality in East Asia*. Oxford: Regnum, 2015.

Word of Life. Accessed 21 August 2020. https://word.org.uk/word-of-life-curriculum/.

12

TEE as a Tool for Providing Theological Education to Churches Facing Persecution and Poverty

Anneta Vysotskaya and Tanka Subedi

Introduction

In this chapter we reflect on how TEE serves the churches under persecution. In the first section we reflect on theological education in the context of persecution in the early church. Then an overview of contemporary persecution and human rights is discussed drawing on recent statistics, including the related issue of poverty which often accompanies persecution. We then discuss what TEE offers as a theological education tool for churches that are facing persecution. Finally, we illustrate how TEE works practically in two situations of persecution: South Asia and the former Soviet region.

Theological Education in the Early Church

John Stott in his book, *What Christ Thinks of the Church: An Exposition of Revelation 1–3*, names persecution together with error and sin as three main elements in the devil's tactics to attack the church.[1] Much teaching in the early

1. Stott, *What Christ Thinks*, 102.

church was focused on confronting these three tactics. Good knowledge of the word of God and all the elements of Christ's teaching could help God's people to stay strong under persecution and protect them from falling into heresies and sin.

When Jesus gave the Great Commission to his followers to go and make disciples of all nations, teaching them to obey everything he commanded them, he knew they would face opposition and persecution when fulfilling that task. In Luke 21:12–13, Jesus warned his disciples, "But before all this, they will seize you and persecute you. They will hand you over to synagogues and put you in prison, and you will be brought before kings and governors, and all on account of my name. And so you will bear testimony to me" (NIV). From the book of Acts and the letters of the apostles, it is clear that the apostles and other believers in the early church lived and did their ministry under enormous persecution, often risking their freedom and life. Acts 4:1–3 tells how the apostles Peter and John were arrested when teaching people. Acts 8:1 speaks about a great persecution that broke out against the church in Jerusalem, and all believers except the apostles were scattered throughout Judea and Samaria. The persecution did not stop the apostles and other believers from evangelism, planting new churches and teaching the people of God to obey everything Jesus commanded them. As a result of persecution, the scattered church continued to bear testimony to Jesus to a much wider community of people than before. Many people turned to their teaching in search of truth and found salvation. However, as the teaching spread, persecution increased.

Acts 2:41–47 presents a profound glimpse into the life of the early church. About three thousand people who were converted on the day of Pentecost devoted themselves to the teaching of the apostles, prayer, and daily fellowship. As we can see, the church in Jerusalem initially did not face extreme persecution but this relatively peaceful time was the calm before the storm. Studying the word of God was an essential part of life of the early Christians who were all first-generation believers living in a predominantly hostile world, facing tremendous persecution. It helped them to stay strong and be the salt of the earth and the light of the world despite all the false accusations of their oppressors, and they enjoyed much favour. As a result, the Lord regularly added new converts to the church.

An important daily task of the early church leaders was to devote themselves to the "public reading of Scripture, to preaching and to teaching" (1 Tim 4:13 NIV). The early church leaders were not only preachers, but were also disciples who trained other disciples.

In the early church, theological education, in a simple form, was available not just to a limited number of potential church leaders but to all believers. It did not require special buildings and just took place where the people of God gathered. Acts 11 tells us about Barnabas and Saul in Antioch: "So for a whole year Barnabas and Saul met with the church and taught great numbers of people" (Acts 11:26).

As we can see, theological education was very simple but at the same time very effective in those early days of the church. It was available to all believers, based on the apostles' teaching and very practical. They lived what they learned.

Persecution of Christians in the Modern World

The persecution of Christians has never ceased and is escalating in the modern world. The Bad Urach Statement, issued by religious freedom experts at a consultation in Germany in 2009 on the theology of persecution, states,

> Due to the massive rise of the population and the explosion in the number of Christians, never before in the history of the church have so many of Christ's followers experienced persecution as they do in today's contemporary world.[2]

However, as in the times of the apostles, the growth of persecution also results in increased opportunities to bear testimony to Jesus and the growth of the kingdom. In "Dangerous Faith," a study resource on the book of Acts by Open Doors, the link between persecution and the growth of the kingdom of God is emphasized:

> Here's the thing: without this persecution, the gospel would never have spread in the way it did. It is precisely because of the persecution, because of the pains and the chains and the floggings

2. Sauer, *Bad Urach Statement*, 4.

> and the martyrdoms that the gospel spreads to the ends of the earth. And today the same thing is happening around the world. Today, Christians are being persecuted and attacked, and still the Kingdom of God of growing.[3]

Persecution can happen in many different forms and its severity can vary from mild to very strong. Although traditionally it is believed that persecution mainly affects minority Christians in predominantly Muslim, Buddhist, and Hindu countries, and countries with dictatorial regimes, persecution can also happen to the converts of different diaspora groups in Western countries. Based on a survey conducted by Pew Research Centre in April–August 2017 in fifteen European countries, "Western Europe, where Protestant Christianity originated and Catholicism has been based for most of its history, has become one of the world's most secular regions."[4] It can be expected that growing secularization will inevitably result in an increase of intolerance to traditional Christian values and persecution of Christian churches and believers in those countries as well.

While there are many different definitions of Christian persecution, for this chapter we chose the definition used in the Open Doors Complete World Watch List based on the book by Ronald Boyd-MacMillan, *Faith That Endures: The Essential Guide to the Persecuted Church.*[5] Persecution is

> any hostility experienced as a result of one's identification with Christ. This can include hostile attitudes, words and actions towards Christians. This broad definition includes (but is not limited to) restrictions, pressure, discrimination, opposition, disinformation, injustice, intimidation, mistreatment, marginalization, oppression, intolerance, infringement, violation, ostracism, hostilities, harassment, abuse, violence, ethnic cleansing and genocide.[6]

With this definition, Open Doors annually prepares and publishes the World Watch List of the top fifty countries where it is most dangerous to be

3. Boyd-MacMillan, "About."
4. Pew Research Center, *Being Christian.*
5. Boyd-MacMillan, *Faith That Endures.*
6. Open Doors WWR, *Complete World Watch List Methodology.*

a Christian.[7] According to World Watch List 2021, more than 340 million Christians suffer high levels of persecution and discrimination for their faith, a ratio of one in eight Christians worldwide.[8]

Persecution affects different areas of the life of Christians including their access to secular and religious education, and the publication, importation, and dissemination of religious literature.

Human Rights and Theological Education

The United Nations Universal Declaration of Human Rights,[9] when speaking about the human right to freedom of thought, conscience, and religion, includes everyone's freedom to manifest their religion or belief in teaching as an integral part of that freedom, and states unequivocally:

> Everyone has the right to freedom of thought, conscience and religion; this right includes freedom to change his religion or belief, and freedom, either alone or in community with others and in public or private, to manifest his religion or belief in teaching, practice, worship and observance.[10]

While every Christian has the human right to theological education, in practice this right is often violated in countries where Christians are a minority and are persecuted. In dictatorial regimes the education of Christians is often restricted. Even if the laws of a country allow churches to establish theological education institutions, in practice it is difficult and often impossible to obtain registration and an educational licence from the state. Those realities explain

7. Open Doors, *World Watch List 2021*.

8. Open Doors, *World Watch List 2021*. Accessed 18 February 2021, https://www.opendoorsusa.org/2021-world-watch-list-report/.

9. In addition to the UDHR there are other conventions that address the issue of religious freedom, namely, the International Covenant on Civil and Political Rights (ICCPR), the Convention on the Rights of the Child (CRC), the International Covenant on Economic, Social and Cultural Rights (ICESCR), the International Convention on the Elimination of All Forms of Racial Discrimination (ICERD) and the International Convention on the Protection of the Rights of All Migrant Workers and Members of Their Families. Becoming a signatory or party to these conventions does not necessarily mean that a country respects their terms, and in practice, there are many issues beyond signing a document.

10. United Nations, *Universal Declaration of Human Rights*, Article 18.

why there are insufficient theological education institutions to meet fully the need for theological education and training of church leaders and pastors in contexts of persecution.[11]

In many pluralistic nations of the world, especially in Asia, religious freedom is defined vaguely and with an inbuilt bias towards the majority religion and associated cultural practices and festivals. Any activities of evangelism and conversion may be regarded as an offence or threat to the predominant religion, culture, and national traditions, and are often used as the reason for restricting Christian activities and theological education. Recent efforts to pass and implement anti-conversion (apostasy) laws in many countries are another way of persecuting Christians and their institutions.[12]

Religious nationalism and secular intolerance have become very much the basis of trying to curb what is commonly referred to as Christian expansionism and westernization of national cultures. Secular governments and their state instruments frequently turn an unseeing eye to those who drive and perpetuate anti-Christian propaganda, social media attacks, and legal restrictions.[13]

State authorities may interpret charity work and community care initiatives as the means of coercing people to convert and then treat such initiatives of compassion as undesirable, illegal, and anti-national. Such community initiatives can lead to Christians being taken to court and prosecuted. Persecution affects Christians and their efforts to serve the society at large, and their contribution to national development in sectors including education, health services, and emancipation of the under-privileged and marginalized.

In many countries, money is seen as something that Christians use to induce conversion,[14] and so governments investigate all kinds of financial transactions, especially from Christian organizations worldwide. The printing

---

11. In some cases, the state establishes a quota for the number of students and a requirement for an approval for each student from a state religious committee or another controlling agency.

12. USCIRF, *Limitations*; There are anti-conversion laws in various Indian states, though the degree to which they are implemented varies. Ostensibly, these laws are aimed only at conversions carried out by "forcible" or "fraudulent" means, but these categories are defined vaguely and very broadly, and can include "any temptation in the form of any gift or gratification . . . or any benefit either pecuniary or otherwise," which could include peace of mind or forgiveness of sins. Claims to any spiritual benefit could be illegal.

13. Veerman, "Religious Persecution and Violence," 130.

14. Pattisson, "They Use Money."

of Bibles has been affected in countries where foreign funding for Christian work has been made illegal.[15]

Persecution, such as the above, greatly affects the ability to offer and deliver theological education programmes. Additionally, refusal to register theological institutions and training legally is another form of harassment of Christians and their training programmes by authorities.

Another area of persecution that impedes theological education is the ability to print and distribute Christian materials. In order to import and distribute Christian literature, approval from the state is required, which is often difficult or impossible to obtain. The officers of the government agencies that have the authority to make decisions and grant approvals regarding Christian and other religious literature often belong to the country's majority religion. In some countries, Christians can be heavily fined for possessing and distributing Christian books and other materials. Printing Christian books without state permission can be considered a serious crime, punishable by imprisonment.

The 2019 report by the Pew Research Center, *A Closer Look at How Religious Restrictions Have Risen around the World*, states that in the period 2007–2017 "government restrictions on religion – laws, policies and actions by state officials that restrict religious beliefs and practices – increased markedly around the world. And social hostilities involving religion – including violence and harassment by private individuals, organizations or groups – also have risen since 2007."[16]

Persecution and Economic Hardship

When speaking about persecution we must mention poverty.[17] The persecution of Christians is often accompanied by economic hardship due to generally poor economic conditions in the country. Discrimination means that Christians often find it even more difficult than others to find good jobs or to receive promotions, and they also face a higher risk of being dismissed from their

15. United States Department of State, *Nepal 2017*, 7.

16. Pew Research Center, *Closer Look*.

17. Poverty is a fact of life in many Majority World countries and is too big a topic to address in detail here. As the paragraph notes, it has particular force in contexts where poverty can increase when a minority religion is targeted for persecution and economic means used.

jobs. Many have more than one low-paid job in order to provide for their families. Sometimes they leave their families to work in other countries as labour migrants.

Economic hardship also makes it difficult for believers to attend residential institutions that offer theological education. Churches and denominations do not have enough funds to construct or buy buildings and equip residential institutions for training church leaders and believers.

As the few existing residential institutions cannot meet the needs of Christians in theological education, other forms of education and training are needed for Christians living under persecution and economic hardship. In such situations TEE provides a solution for quality theological education that is affordable even to the very poor and is also suitable for people who cannot leave their jobs and who must study while still working full time.

The Importance of Theological Education for Persecuted Believers

The importance of theological education for all church members is expressed in *The Cape Town Commitment* of the 2010 Lausanne Congress on World Evangelization.

> Theological education serves *first* to train those who lead the church as pastor-teachers, equipping them to teach the truth of God's word with faithfulness, relevance and clarity; and *second*, to equip all God's people for the missional task of understanding and relevantly communicating God's truth in every cultural context.[18]

Where Christians are a religious minority and suffer persecution, the task of providing theological education to all church members is of strategic importance because every believer is a potential target of persecution. Many believers do not have a Christian background or knowledge of the Bible. As first generation believers they were brought up as atheists or in the beliefs and practices of another religion, and their daily environment still remains predominantly non-Christian. Knowledge and understanding of the Scriptures

18. Lausanne, *Cape Town Commitment*, Part IIF, 4.

and key Christian doctrines, fellowship with other believers, and the practical application of Christ's teaching in their daily lives are of high importance for their perseverance under persecution and their witness to the world.

TEE is more a radical alternate approach to theological education than just a method for training more people.[19] TEE methodology reflects the biblical model of theological education used by the early church in times of persecution, of teaching by the apostles, regular meetings and practicing Jesus's teaching in daily life, a model that is expressed in the three main components of TEE: self-study, group discussion, and practical application.

Using TEE in the Context of Persecution and Economic Hardship

For many years, TEE has been an effective tool for strengthening believers of churches of different denominations where Christians experience persecution. In some countries where TEE has been available for decades national TEE programmes have been established, such as India, Nepal, and Pakistan. In other countries TEE programmes are much younger. Table 12.1 shows the 2021 World Watch List of fifty countries where Christians experience different forms of persecution and discrimination and the thirty-one countries where TEE programmes and groups were active as at January 2021.[20] Many of these countries also suffer from poverty and so the conjunction of persecution and poverty is a situational factor.

The success and growing popularity of TEE among the persecuted churches can be explained by several factors. One factor is TEE's low-profile presence compared with residential institutions: "Leaders can learn on location in small groups and remain 'under the radar' in places where a visible theological college would attract attention."[21] Another factor is mobility, since groups can easily move and meet in different locations. An additional factor is that TEE courses are low-cost and affordable for believers in situations of economic hardship.

19. Harrison, "Forty Years On," 316.

20. Personal communication.

21. Aylett, "A Fresh Look," 1–2.

Table 12.1. Active TEE in top fifty countries where it is most difficult to follow Jesus[22]

Top Fifty Countries (*Active TEE programmes and groups)									
1	N. Korea	11	Iraq	21	* Uzbekistan	31	* Bangladesh	41	* Kazakhstan
2	Afghanistan	12	* Syria	22	* Laos	32	Burkina Faso	42	* Cameroon
3	* Somalia	13	* Sudan	23	* Turkmenistan	33	* Tajikistan	43	Bhutan
4	Libya	14	* Saudi Arabia	24	* Algeria	34	* Nepal	44	Oman
5	* Pakistan	15	Maldives	25	* Turkey	35	C. African Rep	45	Mozambique
6	* Eritrea	16	* Egypt	26	Tunisia	36	* Ethiopia	46	* Malaysia
7	Yemen	17	* China	27	Morocco	37	* Mexico	47	* Indonesia
8	* Iran	18	* Myanmar	28	Mali	38	* Jordan	48	* Kuwait
9	* Nigeria	19	* Vietnam	29	Qatar	39	Brunei	49	* Kenya
10	* India	20	Mauritania	30	* Colombia	40	DR Congo	50	Comoros

TEE in South Asia and the Former Soviet Region

The effectiveness of TEE in countries where churches face persecution and economic hardship can be illustrated from the experience of South Asia and post-Soviet countries.

South Asia

South Asia is the southern region of Asia and includes Afghanistan, Bangladesh, Bhutan, India, the Maldives, Nepal, Pakistan, and Sri Lanka. Christians are a minority in these countries where Hindus, Muslims, Sikhs, Jains, and Zoroastrians are in the majority. In this region TEE is widely used, and some countries have highly developed national TEE programmes (e.g. Nepal, Pakistan, India) and other countries have TEE programs that are just starting.

The traditional religions of South Asia were passive and tolerant towards other beliefs and ways of life for centuries. But things have changed in recent decades. Missionaries who brought education and healthcare were sometimes suspected of using their ministries of compassion as a means of proselytization.

22. Source: *Open Doors, World Watch List 2021.*

The recent formation of fundamentalist religious groups within the traditional religions has aggravated the situation by influencing public opinion which has prompted governments to introduce harsh laws and restrictions on Christians and Christian work. Governments in much of South Asia regard evangelism as being opposed to traditional religious practices, culture, and nationalism.

If opponents of Christians are unable to oppose them on philosophical and practical grounds, they may turn to activities of hate, spreading false and misleading information, attacking church property, and physically harming individuals and families.

Christians regard regular and systematic teaching from the Bible and fellowship for care and nurturing as vital aspects of faith. However, these aspects of faith are unavailable to Christians where persecution restricts their access to open gatherings, conferences, and other means of training, and where church leaders are not always well-educated and biblically trained. Bible schools and training centres are mostly limited to cities and only a few can leave their homes, families, and farms to study in expensive residential programmes. Furthermore, too many of those who undertake residential training do not return to their villages, but continue self-development or church positions with secure financial income. In fact the very existence of residential institutions in restricted countries is threatened by an increase of persecution.

Recently in Uttar Pradesh, India, the state government banned many Christian activities such as Bible schools and church gatherings. The residential discipling facility in a major town had to cease operating and ongoing government restrictions curtailed the use of facilities, funding, and travel of Christians from villages.

Such persecution deprives churches of sound biblical and theological teaching and makes them vulnerable to false teachings, cults, syncretism, and immoral practices. The leaders usually struggle to keep believers growing in the truth and adhering to a basic level of Christian living and practice. Such a situation is a challenge to the quality of Christian witness and the mandate to be the salt of the earth and light of the world.

Here we see the necessity and relevance of TEE, particularly for South Asia. It is available to all and does not require students to be highly educated, nor does it require teachers or lecturers with high educational qualifications. TEE does not need to be located in an institution, but can be delivered in houses or churches, for example. TEE opens up an opportunity for anyone who wants to gain biblical understanding. It helps to develop core Christian values in individual students, their families, and churches. All that is required is access to TEE materials and training through national TEE programmes.

Many TEE learners in South Asia are village church leaders and believers with minimal education whom God has used to start churches. However, while some may be poorly educated, they are usually mature adults with good mental ability and insights.

The South Asian experience is that students who decide to learn and commit themselves to a TEE course are motivated to learn when the teaching methods and materials have been adapted to their local context. Such TEE programmes and materials are planned and implemented in an adaptable, approachable, and achievable way, leading the students from the known to unknown with methods of learning that are relevant to their living context and work situations. Problem solving and discussion methods are integrated into the learning process to make group discussions lively and applicable to their own social situations. Such discussions also prepare students for change and transformation in their lives. TEE programmes can function safely in these hostile conditions through interactive small groups where the people of God learn together and encourage one another. Discussion of case studies and relevant contemporary issues in South Asia makes the learning process appealing and useful. It is a process that facilitates learning in times of challenges and helps redefine faith and life. This is especially vital in the present hostile situations that exist in South Asia where residential training centres and churches are commonly restricted in their activities and discipleship.

TEE programmes in South Asia are able to address local needs because learning groups can operate in a low-profile manner and receive course materials, guidance, and support from the national TEE programmes.

TEE programmes in South Asia maintain contact with learners – individuals, families, and leaders – through various forms of communication that take into account security risks in these environments of hostility toward Christians. A concern is the risk associated with transferring digital materials. Therefore, various online and digital strategies are actively being developed.

TEE learning groups in South Asia are made up of members from one family or from a number of families and individuals. Usually, learners undertake self-study at home, then come together to discuss what they have learned, led by a group leader. During the group meetings they are encouraged and directed towards immediate implementation of their learning from the materials and group meeting. Most of the materials are simple, and use repetition and understandable concepts and language. It is difficult for outsiders to stop this kind of learning process since it takes place at home in privacy and is not seen in public. There are multi-level and well-prepared TEE study materials available for families, youth, and leaders. Learners can continue studying from one course to another at their own pace and convenience. In addition, it is easy to train group leaders. To do this training, one resource person from the national TEE team can go to homes and provide on-site training using the actual TEE materials the new group leaders want to use.

It is remarkable that in just over sixty years (to the time of writing in 2020) 3 percent of the population of Nepal have become followers of Christ. Unprecedented growth has been seen in this predominantly Hindu nation, particularly in the last thirty years. The growth was made possible by a short time of freedom of religion that came about after multi-party democracy began in 1990. In 2008, there were estimated to be around 700,000 Christians in Nepal.[23] *Operation World* gives a figure of just over 850,000 Christians in 2010, and states that "there is a church planted in every one of the seventy-five districts of Nepal, and there are at least some believers in almost every people and caste group."[24] More recent estimates state that there are over 1.5 million believers.[25]

The programme of the Institute for TEE in Nepal (ITEEN) is a refreshing example of what can be achieved for the kingdom of God through a carefully planned and realistically funded TEE programme that is forced to operate with the constant threat of persecution.[26] An anti-conversion law is a new tool for persecution and the constitution of Nepal is unclear on the matter of religious freedom.[27]

23. Bisset, "Institute for TEE," 109.

24. Mandryk, *Operation World*, "Nepal."

25. van Wingerden, "Nepal: Moving Mountains," 124.

26. For more stories from ITEEN, see van Wingerden, "Nepal: Moving Mountains."

27. United States Department of State, *Nepal 2017*, 2–5.

To see Christians living in poverty benefiting by being able to take TEE courses is encouraging. Poor churches are often unable to send their leaders for residential training due to lack of finance, but they are able to afford TEE courses which provide "on-the-job" training. The vision of ITEEN is to provide contextualized TEE courses to equip lay members and leaders of the church adequately.[28]

Former Soviet region

The collapse of the Soviet Union and the dissolution of its former fifteen republics into independent states was followed by spiritual revival and massive church growth across that vast territory in the early 1990s. After the seventy years of the communist regime, the rule of atheist ideology, and the persecution of all religions, there was a short period of religious freedom, which is concisely described by Sauer and Schirrmacher:

> First, in the successor states of the Soviet Union, particularly, in the Islamic states but also in some of the Orthodox states, initial enthusiasm about democracy, freedom and religious freedom has given way to increasingly restrictive religious laws. After several years of freedom, the religious persecution and/or persecution of Christians once practiced by Communists in these former states of the USSR has returned; Christians are being oppressed by the respective majority religion or by the control of the religion by the government.[29]

The former Soviet countries affected by the restrictions of religious freedom and persecution are represented by two large groups: the predominantly Orthodox Christian countries of Russia and Belarus, and the predominantly Muslim countries of Central Asia and Azerbaijan.

The countries of the former Soviet region are regularly included in the World Watch List top fifty most persecuted countries. Five of these countries are included in the World Watch List 2021 (Table 12.1): Uzbekistan (21st), Turkmenistan (23rd), Tajikistan (33rd), and Kazakhstan (41st). The Russian

28. Bisset, "Institute for TEE," 107.

29. Sauer and Schirrmacher, "Global Survey."

Federation, Kyrgyzstan, and Azerbaijan are not in the top fifty list, but Protestant churches are vulnerable: religious freedom is uncertain. These churches face risks of search, refusal of registration, closure of registered churches, punishment for illegal church meetings, and detention and fines for church leaders.[30] Central Asia is a region where poverty is widespread. In 2020, due to the COVID-19 pandemic, many people lost their jobs and Central Asian economies became significantly worse.

Persecution seriously affects religious education in post-Soviet countries, which results in an insufficient number or absence of educational institutions or programmes that are permitted, approved, registered, or licensed by the state. The lack of recognition by the state has resulted in widespread unregistered, unlicensed, underground Bible schools and seminaries. At the same time, some authorities make it a requirement for pastors and other church workers to have an approved diploma or certificate of professional religious education.

The printing, importation, and distribution of Christian literature is important for theological education but that is also strongly affected by restrictions on religious freedom and persecution in former Soviet countries. Censorship, the requirement of approval by a religious committee, raids, confiscations, fines, and other forms of harassment are common occurrences. Such pressures on churches make it difficult to provide theological education across the former Soviet region. An additional problem is that the churches in Central Asia have insufficient study materials in national languages. Furthermore, many discipleship and leadership training materials are only available in the Russian language.

To deal with the pressures of persecution, many churches and denominations in the region have turned to TEE. At present, there are around 2,600 registered TEE students in the Russian Federation and over 2,000 students in Central Asia and Azerbaijan.[31]

In the former Soviet countries, foreign missionaries first attempted to introduce TEE in the late 1980s and early 1990s but quickly stopped because of the lack of interest from national church leaders, who were not yet prepared

30. For more information about religious freedom in Central Asian countries until 2014 see Vysotskaya, "Is the Silk Road Still Open?"

31. Personal communication, 2020.

to take on the ownership and leading role for the work of TEE. One reason for the lack of interest could be due to not understanding TEE methodology and how TEE works. However, the work resumed in the early 2000s after the national church leaders became familiar with TEE methods and the benefits TEE could bring to their churches. TEE was first established in Russia in 2004 and later in Kyrgyzstan, Tajikistan, Kazakhstan, Uzbekistan, Turkmenistan, and Azerbaijan. The newly formed young national teams began their programmes with SEAN[32] courses, which have been tried and tested in many contexts over decades. The work of establishing TEE national programmes includes translation of study materials to national languages, introducing the programme to the churches, training group leaders, and printing and distributing study resources to churches. A big help and support in different aspects of TEE work to the national teams in the Central Asian region is offered by the Increase Association, SEAN International, the Central Asia Vision Group (CAVG),[33] GZB,[34] Hilfe für Brüder International,[35] and other Christian organizations. However, the main contribution is made by the national churches and hundreds of volunteers who participate in this ministry.[36]

Although TEE does not fully solve the issue of security – because the study materials need to be printed – its advantages still make TEE attractive to the churches. As a result, the recognition and popularity of TEE is growing in the region. Some but not all of the obvious TEE advantages are: (1) it provides a solid and practical theological education to believers in their natural environment without interrupting their ministry, work, and family life; (2) it is aimed at all church members regardless of their previous academic background; (3) it is based on small groups and can be easily moved to different places without attracting attention, which allows it to be safely used by churches

32. SEAN International is a major global provider of TEE courses. SEAN stands for Study by Extension for All Nations. See www.seaninternational.org.

33. The Central Asia Vision Group is a group of mission practitioners assisting TEE development in Central Asia.

34. GZB, Gereformeerde Zendings Bond, or Reformed Mission League, is a church-based mission organization based in the Netherlands. See www.gzb.nl.

35. Hilfe für Brüder International is a German-based Christian organization. See www.gottes-liebe-weltweit.de/aktuelles/aktuelle-berichte.

36. For more information about an earlier period of TEE development in Central Asian countries until 2012, see Vyssotskaia, "Theological Education."

in the context of persecution; (4) it is low-cost and affordable to believers who live in situations of economic hardship; and (5) it is available in the national languages and is contextualized.

The national TEE teams in the former Soviet region use creative approaches to apply TEE. As an example, one national team used the SEAN course, Life of Christ, which has six books, as a foundation for a two-year leadership school combining TEE with blocks of seminary lectures. The graduates of that school are now involved in different ministries of the church. Some national teams established working relationships with registered seminaries resulting in TEE being used as part of their curriculum. TEE helps students in their studies and equips them with a tool they can use in their future ministry to disciple and train others. All national TEE teams in the region are members of the Increase Association. One national team, the Open Russian Theological Academy (ORTA) in Russia, became a full member of the Euro-Asian Accrediting Agency (EEAA) in 2019.[37]

In recent years, national TEE teams joined Increase's TEE course-writing programme, and new courses are being developed based on the needs and lessons from churches in the region, including how to overcome fear, stay strong, and persevere in times of persecution.

From the beginning the national TEE teams in the former Soviet region have worked in partnership, shared their knowledge and study resources, organized joint meetings and conferences, visited and learned from each other, and helped to start TEE in other former Soviet countries and diaspora churches. The unity among the national TEE teams in post-Soviet countries is strengthening. This is confirmed by the formation of a regional TEE partnership following the "Empowering Churches, Equipping Disciples," Increase conference in October 2017. Partnership is a great blessing and achievement because in the former Soviet region, churches and national TEE teams face similar problems. Together, the teams feel much stronger and have a heightened sense of responsibility. They are motivated to help each other improve and see each other's programmes progress.

37. For the story of the early years of ORTA, see Huggins, "Open Russian Theological Academy."

Conclusion

In this chapter we provided an overview of the persecution and economic hardships faced by the church in South and Central Asia. We then discussed how and where TEE is being used to serve persecuted churches with theological education and training. The final section draws from experiences of TEE programmes in South Asia (Nepal) and the former Soviet region where Christians are a religious minority and live under daily persecution and restrictions of religious freedom.

We conclude that TEE is a well-proven solution to empower and equip God's people for the missional task of understanding and relevantly communicating God's truth, despite their religious freedom being restricted, persecution, and economic hardship.

Bibliography

Aylett, Graham. "A Fresh Look at Theological Education by Extension." *ATA News* (July-September 2012): 1–2. http://www.ataasia.com/wp-content/uploads/2016/04/ATA-Newsletter-July-Sept-2012.pdf.

Bisset, Peter. "The Institute for TEE in Nepal." In *Diversified Theological Education: Equipping All God's People*, edited by F. Ross Kinsler, 107–132. Pasadena, WCIU Press, 2008.

Boyd-MacMillan, Ronald. "About." Dangerous Faith. 2018. https://dangerousfaith.org/about/.

———. *Faith That Endures: The Essential Guide to the Persecuted Church.* Grand Rapids: Revell, 2006.

Harrison, Patricia J. "Forty Years On: The Evolution of Theological Education by Extension (TEE)." *Evangelical Review of Theology* 28, no. 4 (2004): 315–28.

Huggins, Michael. "The Open Russian Theological Academy." In *Diversified Theological Education: Equipping All God's People*, edited by F. Ross Kinsler, 269–94. Pasadena: WCIU Press, 2008.

Lausanne Movement. *The Cape Town Commitment: A Confession of Faith and a Call to Action.* 2011. http://www.lausanne.org/content/ctc/ctcommitment.

Mandryk, Jason. *Operation World: The Definitive Prayer Guide for Every Nation.* 7th ed. Downers Grove: IVP, 2010. "Nepal." https://www.operationworld.org/country/nepa/owtext.html.

Marshall, Paul, Lela Gilbert, and Nina Shea. *Persecuted: The Global Assault on Christians*. Nashville: Thomas Nelson, 2013.

Open Doors. *Dangerous Faith. A 9-Week Study through the Book of Acts*. https://dangerousfaith.org/about/.

———. *World Watch List 2021: The Top 50 Countries Where It's Most Difficult to Follow Jesus*. Santa Ana: Open Doors USA, 2021. https://www.opendoorsusa.org/christian-persecution/world-watch-list/.

Open Doors WWR. *Complete World Watch List Methodology*. Harderwijk: Open Doors International. 2020. http://opendoorsanalytical.org/wp-content/uploads/2020/04/Complete-WWL-methodology-revised-April-2020.pdf.

Pattisson, Pete. "'They Use Money to Promote Christianity': Nepal's Battle for Souls." *The Guardian*, 15 August 2017. https://www.theguardian.com/global-development/2017/aug/15/they-use-money-to-promote-christianity-nepal-battle-for-souls.

Pew Research Center. *Being Christian in Western Europe*. Washington, DC: May 29, 2018. https://www.pewforum.org/2018/05/29/being-christian-in-western-europe/.

———. *A Closer Look at How Religious Restrictions Have Arisen around the World*. Washington, DC, 2019. https://www.pewforum.org/2019/07/15/a-closer-look-at-how-religious-restrictions-have-risen-around-the-world/.

Sauer, Christof, ed. *Bad Urach Statement: Towards an Evangelical Theology of Suffering, Persecution and Martyrdom for the Global Church in Mission*. The WEA Global Issues Series 9. Bonn: VKW, 2012. https://www.iirf.eu/site/assets/files/92913/wea_gis_9-christof_sauer-bad_urach_statement.pdf.

Sauer, Christof, and Thomas Schirrmacher. "A Global Survey: Religious Freedom and the Persecution of Christians." In *Sorrow and Blood: Christian Mission in Contexts of Suffering, Persecution, and Martyrdom*, edited by William D. Taylor, Antonia van der Meer, and Reg Reimer, 11–15. Pasadena: William Carey Library, 2012.

Stott, John R. W. *What Christ Thinks of the Church: An Exposition of Revelation 1–3*. London: Monarch Books, 1990.

United Nations. *Universal Declaration of Human Rights*. 1948. http://www.ohchr.org/EN/UDHR/Documents/UDHR_Translations/eng.pdf.

United States Department of State. *Nepal 2017 International Religious Freedom Report*. https://np.usembassy.gov/wp-content/uploads/sites/79/International-Religious-Freedom-Report-for-2017.pdf.

USCIRF Special Report. *Limitations on Minorities' Religious Freedom in South Asia.* November 2018. https://www.uscirf.gov/publications/limitations-minorities-religious-freedom-south-asia.

van Wingerden, Hanna-Ruth. "Nepal: Moving Mountains." In *TEE in Asia: Empowering Churches, Equipping Disciples*, edited by Hanna-Ruth van Wingerden, Tim Green, and Graham Aylett, 119–25. Carlisle: Langham Global Library, 2021.

Veerman, Frans. "Religious Persecution and Violence in the 21st Century: A Global Survey Based on the World Watch List." In *Freedom of Belief and Christian Mission*, edited by Hans Aage Gravaas, Christof Sauer, Tormod Engelsviken, Maqsood Kamil, and Knud Jørgensen, 127–48. Oxford: Regnum, 2015.

Vysotskaya, Anneta. "Is the Silk Road Still Open? Central Asia: Christian Mission under Growing Restrictions on Religious Freedom." In *Freedom of Belief and Christian Mission*, edited by Hans Aage Gravaas, Christof Sauer, Tormod Engelsviken, Maqsood Kamil, and Knud Jørgensen, 309–19. Oxford: Regnum, 2015.

Vyssotskaia, Anneta. "Theological Education in the Context of Persecution and Economic Hardship: Focus on TEE in Central Asia." *International Journal for Religious Freedom* 5, no. 2 (2012): 111–22.

13

TEE in Central Asia

An Evaluation of Recent Trends and Future Trajectories Using a Religious Market Framework

Richard Brown

> Christianity . . . has throughout its history spread outwards, across cultural frontiers, so that each new point on the Christian circumference is a new potential Christian centre. And the very survival of Christianity as a separate faith has evidently been linked to the process of cross-cultural transmission.
>
> *Andrew Walls (1996)*[1]

Introduction

When the Soviet Union collapsed in 1991, the remarkable phenomenon of religious revivals, particularly Christian and Muslim, swept across the post-Soviet landscape for a decade.[2] Andrew Greeley, in the aftermath of the collapse,

1. Walls, *Missionary Movement*, 22.

2. Borbieva, "Foreign Faiths and National Renewal"; Bourdeaux, "Religion Revives in All Its Variety"; Collins, "Faith and Reason"; Froese, *The Plot to Kill God*; Hoskins, "Russification"; Peyrouse, "Christians as the Main Religious Minority"; Radford, "Contesting and Negotiating."

summed up the situation in Russia: "Despite seventy years of socialism, God seems to be alive and well and living in all Russia."[3]

Interestingly, Christian revivals also took place in the Muslim lands of Central Asia including Kyrgyzstan, Kazakhstan, Uzbekistan, Tajikistan, and Turkmenistan. As well as revitalizing existing Christian churches, the revivals led to thousands of new churches, mainly Protestant, being established. In the post-revival period after the year 2000, churches sought ways to systematically disciple and equip new members for Christian life and ministry. One of the promising theological education options to achieve this was Theological Education by Extension (TEE).

In this chapter I evaluate the TEE movement in Central Asia using data that I gathered in informal interviews with Central Asian TEE national team leaders in May 2016 and November 2017. The data, combined with observations from experiences in Central Asia,[4] is evaluated using a religious market framework which is described below.

This discussion examines three main areas: (1) reasons behind the strong TEE growth trend in Central Asia since it was introduced; (2) features of the Central Asian TEE movement including the dominance of Russian language-based TEE groups and the concentration of TEE groups in urban centres; and (3) future trajectories of the TEE movement in the light of factors affecting the religious market. In the short-term these include market share and product availability. In the longer-term they include the Russian factor, the nation-building factor, the globalization factor, and the Islamization factor.

This study of the burgeoning TEE movement in Central Asia will be of interest to TEE practitioners, church leaders, and theological educators exploring the value and relevance of TEE as a potential theological education option.

Inclusion of data over a longer time frame would add further confidence to the findings, but this was beyond the scope of the present study.[5] However, the findings are supported by observation data gathered by the author through

3. Greeley, "A Religious Revival in Russia?," 255.

4. The author helped pioneer TEE in one of the Central Asian republics and was involved in the Central Asian Vision Group that was set up to strengthen national TEE teams in Central Asia.

5. Informal conversations with TEE leaders suggest that TEE has not grown significantly in Central Asia during 2020. One of the main reasons is the global Corona virus pandemic which led authorities to heavily restrict church activities.

informal relationship building and direct involvement in TEE in Central Asia over a period of more than ten years.

This chapter adds to the understanding of TEE in Central Asia provided in chapter 12[6] which focuses on issues of persecution and economic hardship, and also to chapter 7[7] which presents the experiences of a TEE course-writing team based in Central Asia.

Background to the TEE Movement in Central Asia

TEE arose in the early 1960s in Guatemala in response to rapid church growth and the need for church-based theological education to equip church leaders, a need beyond the capacity of existing residential seminary programmes.[8] TEE's popularity soon spread across Latin America, then to Africa, Asia, and beyond.[9] TEE experienced both successes and failures in the early decades, and today the movement continues to grow, particularly across Asia.[10]

One of the major global providers of TEE courses is SEAN International, founded in 1971 through work in Latin America. SEAN's TEE courses are designed to be interdenominational and are predominantly used by Protestant churches and seminaries as part of their programmes to disciple and equip church members and leaders for life and ministry.[11] SEAN's courses form the bedrock of the TEE movement in Central Asia.

Reasons for the attraction of TEE as a training option for churches include its affordability, effective methodology, and systematic, biblically based curriculum from foundational to leadership level.[12] Typically, courses run on a weekly basis for ten weeks in a small group format. Each lesson has three

---

6. Chapter 12: Vysotskaya and Subedi, "TEE as a Tool for Providing Theological Education to Churches Facing Persecution and Poverty."

7. Chapter 7: Ivins and Do, "New TEE Courses."

8. Mulholland, "TEE Come of Age," 1–2.

9. Carey, "Theological Education by Extension in Pakistan," 160–62; Harrison, "Forty Years On," 315–16; Mabuluki, "Diversified Theological Education," 251; Sendegeya and Spencer, *Understanding TEE*, 30–35.

10. Aylett and Green, "Theological Education by Extension (TEE)," 68–71; Increase Association, "Conference Press Release."

11. SEAN operates in more than 100 countries and 80 languages and claims to have over 160,000 students using courses annually. See: https://www.seaninternational.org.

12. Aylett and Green, "Theological Education by Extension (TEE)," 59–63.

components: personal study, group meeting, and practical application.[13] As a form of theological education, the TEE method promotes formative learning through reflective practice.[14]

The TEE movement in Central Asia began in response to the religious revivals in those countries in the 1990s. The new churches, mainly Protestant, have a growing need to provide systematic theological education for church members and leaders.

Each Central Asian republic today has a TEE national team that oversees and facilitates the TEE programme in their country. Kyrgyzstan was the first republic to form a TEE national team in 2006, followed by Tajikistan, Kazakhstan, Uzbekistan, and Turkmenistan in 2012.[15]

Data gathered from the informal interviews with TEE national team leaders indicates strong growth of TEE in the Central Asia region, though not uniformly. The findings related to this growth are presented below followed by a discussion of factors that will influence future trajectories of the TEE movement. Due to the sensitivity of the information, individual Central Asian republics are not identified but rather labelled randomly as republics A, B, C, D, and E.[16]

Background to the Religious Market Framework

This study uses a "religious market" framework to evaluate the TEE movement in Central Asia, a concept derived from the theory of religious markets (or economic theory of religion) attributed to American sociologists including Stark, Finke, and Iannaccone.[17] The theory argues that religious pluralism

13. See: van Wingerden, Green and Aylett, *TEE in Asia*, 13.

14. Glissmann, "Christian Reflective Practice," 50–51. Sometimes TEE courses vary in their effectiveness of achieving formative learning.

15. Vyssotskaia, "Theological Education in the Context of Persecution," 120–21. It is also important to note earlier TEE efforts in Central Asia in the 1990s including translations to Central Asian languages and some TEE groups operating.

16. In Central Asia freedom of religion is restricted and this includes theological education. See chapter 12, Table 12.1 which shows a list of the top 50 countries in the world for Christian persecution. In this table four Central Asian republics are listed: Uzbekistan – 21st; Turkmenistan – 23rd; Tajikistan – 33rd; and Kazakhstan – 41st.

17. Iannaccone, "The Consequences"; Iannaccone, Finke, and Stark, "Deregulating Religion"; Stark, "Secularization, R.I.P."; Stark and Iannaccone, "A Supply-Side Reinterpretation"; Stark and Finke, *Acts of Faith*.

increases religious participation in society.[18] This challenges the traditional secularization thesis, which claims that modernization brings decline and irrelevance of religion in society.[19]

The religious market consists of religious suppliers who offer religious products to religious consumers in the religious marketplace. In the marketplace there are competitors and regulators. Froese has applied the theory in his study of Russia, Central Asia, and Eastern Europe.[20] He claims the Soviet Union represents seventy years of forced secularization. In Central Asia where the majority of the population are Muslim, Soviet antireligious propaganda and repression were severe but failed to quash religion completely.[21] Using religious market terms, Froese explains that

> the secularisation experiment essentially shut off religious supply but failed to undermine the persisting religious demand. As religious knowledge and participation declined in the absence of religious supply, deep-seated beliefs in God and the supernatural continued to provide Soviet citizens with a vague sense of something beyond the confines of their proscribed lives.[22]

The religious markets theory has been applied in other contexts including Hungary,[23] Sweden,[24] China,[25] and Latin America.[26] The theory has been critiqued by various sociologists[27] who argue the theory does not adequately account for the irrational side of religion and that data used to support the positive relationship between religious pluralism and religious participation is tenuous.

---

18. The American experience of ongoing religious vitality is sometimes referred to as "American exceptionalism." See: Tiryakian, "American Religious Exceptionalism."

19. See: Berger, *The Sacred Canopy*; Wilson, "Aspects of Secularization"; Dobbelaere, *Secularization: An Analysis.*

20. Froese, *Plot to Kill God.*

21. Froese, 11.

22. Froese, 121.

23. Froese, "Hungary for Religion."

24. Hamberg and Pettersson, "The Religious Market."

25. Yang, "Red, Black and Gray Markets."

26. Chesnut, *Competitive Spirits.*

27. Alles, "Religious Economies"; Breault, "New Evidence"; Beyer, "Religious Vitality in Canada"; Chaves and Gorski, "Religious Pluralism and Religious Participation."

The study reported in this chapter does not seek to test or validate the religious markets theory in Central Asia, already attempted by Froese. Rather, it draws on a religious market framework as a novel approach to describe and explain the TEE movement in Central Asia. The movement is a direct outcome of religious vitality in Central Asia resulting from post-Soviet religious revivals.

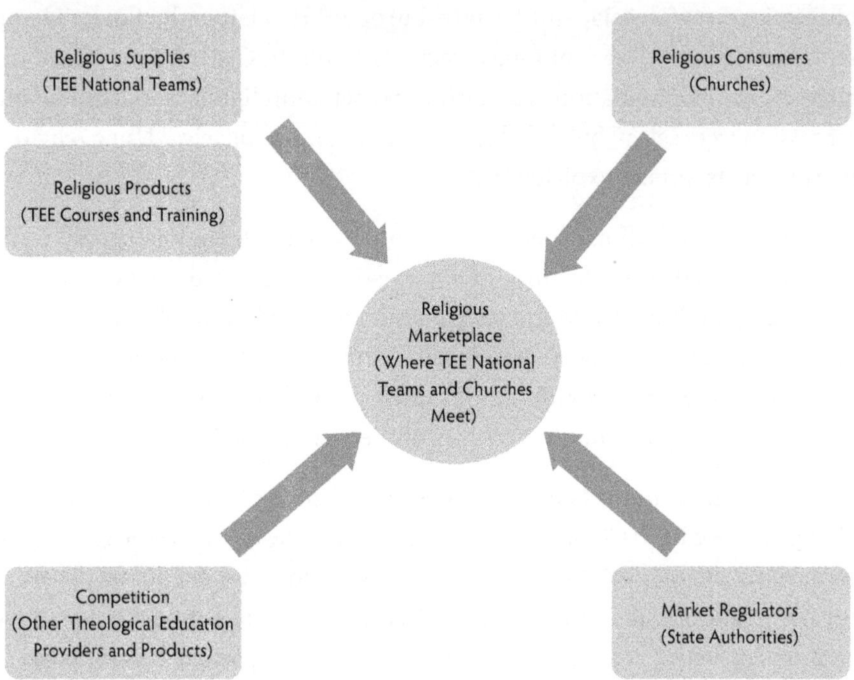

Figure 13.1. A Religious Market Framework for the TEE movement in Central Asia

When the religious markets framework is applied to the TEE movement in Central Asia (see Figure 13.1) the suppliers are the TEE national teams, the products are the TEE courses and facilitator training, and the consumers are the churches that are seeking theological education and training options for their members and leaders.[28] In some cases consumers include seminaries seeking

28. The "consumers" are churches (and sometimes seminaries) seeking to set-up TEE groups within their structure, not individuals seeking theological education.

new training approaches. The religious marketplace has competitors and regulators that influence the development of TEE. Competitors include other theological education products competing for market share.[29] The regulators include state authorities who implement controls and restrictions, all of which affect the size and operation of the marketplace.

Discussion of Findings

Finding 1: The TEE movement in Central Asia has grown strongly

Data from informal interviews with TEE national team leaders from the five Central Asian republics on two separate occasions (May 2016 and Nov 2017) indicates the TEE movement in Central Asia has grown strongly since TEE arrived in Central Asia. Tables 13.1 and 13.2 reveal two different growth aspects of the movement: the number of churches using TEE and the number of students using TEE.

Table 13.1 shows that ninety-four churches in Central Asia were using TEE by November 2017, and between May 2016 and November 2017 the number of churches increased from eighty-five to ninety-four (11 percent increase).

Table 13.1. Number of churches using TEE in Central Asia (May 2016 and Nov 2017)

Central Asian Republic	Number of Churches Using TEE (May 2016)	Number of Churches Using TEE (Nov 2017)	Total % Change
Republic A	15	18	
Republic B	32	40	
Republic C	29	30	
Republic D	3	2	
Republic E	6	4	
TOTAL	**85**	**94**	**+11%**

29. Other training options that may be viewed as "competition" with TEE include denominational curricula, ICI courses, CPM/DMM materials, and other courses.

Table 13.2 shows that the number of active TEE students in Central Asia reached 2,211 by November 2017, and a sharp increase from 1,258 to 2,211 students took place between May 2016 and November 2017 (76 percent increase).

The term "active student" in this context refers to enrolled and participating TEE students. It does not include students who are no longer enrolled. Most TEE students are part of church-based TEE small groups with typically six to ten members that are progressing through a series of TEE courses. Sometimes TEE groups are seminary-based.[30]

Table 13.2. Number of active TEE students in Central Asia (May 2016 and Nov 2017)

Central Asian Republic	Number of Active TEE Students (May 2016)	Number of Active TEE Students (Nov 2017)	Total % Change
Republic A	280	522	
Republic B	468	1,000	
Republic C	390	500	
Republic D	70	64	
Republic E	50	125	
TOTAL	**1,258**	**2,211**	**+76%**

Closer examination of tables 13.1 and 13.2 shows that the strongest TEE growth took place in republics A, B, and C. This data combined with my own observation and experience indicate that the TEE national teams (the suppliers) in these republics have grown in effective leadership, administration, technical, and marketing skills which have helped build a strong network of churches (the consumers) for their TEE courses (the products). In contrast, the two TEE programmes in republics D and E are currently the smallest and show a small drop in the number of churches participating between May 2016 and November 2017. Both programmes are less established and face issues related

30. At an annual Central Asian prayer conference in late 2020, a TEE leader reported that church pastors highlighted the importance of home groups and studying the Bible during the pandemic. It is worth noting that both priorities can be met by TEE.

to team structure and government restrictions (market regulation). In republic E, although the number of participating churches has dropped from 6 to 4, the number of TEE students increased, which indicates that these churches have expanded their use of TEE to more church members.

A comparison of tables 13.1 and 13.2 data also raises the question of what accounts for the large increase in the number of TEE students between the two data points relative to the more modest increase in the number of churches participating in TEE. This is mainly explained by the fact that churches generally begin using TEE on a small scale. If TEE proves successful in the church, the programme is then made available to more church members.

Another factor contributing to the growth of TEE in Central Asia is the simple not-for-profit financial model. This model consists of TEE national teams raising seed funds from donor organizations to translate and print TEE courses and to cover running costs. The course books are sold to churches and students at affordable prices, with the proceeds used for further translation, printing, running costs, salaries (if any), and royalty payments (if required).[31] TEE national teams consist mainly of volunteers from local churches. The financial model aims towards self-sustainability. However, reliance on donors is likely to continue for the foreseeable future, primarily to keep the price of the TEE course books affordable for local churches.

A product-related factor that is helping to propel the growth of TEE in Central Asia is the availability of ORTA's Russian translations of SEAN courses. Russian is widely spoken across Central Asia by Slavic, European, and Korean populations, as well as a large proportion of indigenous populations. The availability of these courses provided a springboard for new TEE national teams to launch quickly while indigenous language translations were initiated. One notable exception is republic C where the TEE national team began the movement with indigenous language translations of TEE courses rather than Russian versions.[32] Interestingly, both approaches have led to strong TEE

31. Most TEE courses used in Central Asia are SEAN courses. SEAN International and ORTA (who provides the Russian translations of courses) have required minimal or no royalty payments. The main reason for waiving royalty rights is to support the Central Asian TEE national teams in their early stages of development.

32. Recent observation shows that the TEE national team in republic C has increased its TEE ministry among Russian-speaking churches. Growth in this area will depend on factors such as

growth. Also, one of the strengths of the TEE courses is that they are strongly Bible-based and have been adapted and contextualized, which makes these materials appealing to local churches, compared to many other training products that are not contextualized. For example, local names and illustrations are incorporated into translations of TEE courses.

However, regulation issues affect the religious marketplace and the growth of TEE. In Central Asia strict government regulations hamper accessibility to all theological education options. Most seminaries are prohibited from operating, though many continue unofficially. An advantage of TEE is that its small group format can continue to operate even in challenging situations. Only in severe persecution would TEE not be able to function. Advances in digital technology have also been able to meet some of the challenges. While TEE in Central Asia has grown strongly, the impact of strict government regulation has still been felt.

Finding 2: The majority of TEE groups in Central Asia are Russian language groups rather than indigenous language groups

A second finding from my informal interviews with TEE national team leaders is that Russian is the dominant language for TEE small groups in Central Asia. The data in Table 13.3 shows that around 60 percent of TEE groups in Central Asia operate in Russian language compared to 40 percent using indigenous languages, and this level stayed relatively constant between May 2016 and November 2017.

On the surface this finding may seem surprising given that 77 percent of the Central Asian population are indigenous people (Table 13.4).

---

team structure and cross-cultural dynamics. In rural areas, the TEE team in republic C also uses TEE in combination with community development projects which helps to build relationships in the local community.

Table 13.3. Number of TEE small groups in Central Asia using Russian / Indigenous languages (May 2016 and Nov 2017)[33]

Central Asian Republic	No. of Russian Language TEE Groups (May 2016)	No. of Indigenous Language TEE Groups (May 2016)	No. of Russian Language TEE Groups (Nov 2017)	No. of Indigenous Language TEE Groups (Nov 2017)
Republic A	55	15	82	20
Republic B	41	11	92	8
Republic C	15	49	7	83
Republic D	1	4	4	5
Republic E	4	3	7	8
TOTAL	**116**	**82**	**192**	**124**
TOTAL %	**59%**	**41%**	**61%**	**39%**

Table 13.4. Percentage of indigenous population in the five Central Asian republics[34]

Central Asian Republic	Percent of Total Population Which Is Indigenous
Kyrgyzstan	71% Kyrgyz
Tajikistan	84% Tajik
Kazakhstan	63% Kazakh
Uzbekistan	80% Uzbek
Turkmenistan	85% Turkmen
TOTAL %	**77% Indigenous**

Four reasons explain the dominance of the Russian language in TEE groups. The first reason is related to the consumer base of churches. Most members of churches in Central Asia are Russian-speaking Christians from Slavic, European, and Korean backgrounds. Widespread preference for the Russian language also extends to indigenous populations because of Soviet and

33. Note: for sensitivity reasons the order of republics in this table (and other tables with general statistics) does not correspond to the A to E listing of republics in other tables and figures.

34. Source: IndexMundi 2017.

Czarist "Russification,"[35] particularly during Soviet years when Russian became the dominant language and pushed indigenous languages to the periphery. The use of Russian dominated the spheres of education, health, economics, and politics because Russian language fluency was essential to be a productive Soviet citizen. Today, most Christians from Slavic, European, and Korean populations, and a large proportion of converts from indigenous populations, continue to speak Russian as their preferred language.[36] Looking towards the future with continuing emigration of Slavic and European populations combined with immigration of indigenous populations, it is predictable that the consumer base of churches using TEE will gradually shift from Russian to an indigenous language preference. However, that will depend heavily on the availability and supply of indigenous language courses to indigenous churches and congregations in the marketplace.

The second reason is supplier related. Currently most TEE national teams are majority non-indigenous members (see Figure 13.2) and function primarily in the Russian language. According to social network theory, network ties tend to be homophilous,[37] that is, people in a network tend to develop relational ties with those similar to themselves, including cultural and language commonalities. It is therefore unsurprising that the TEE consumer base in Central Asia is largely made up of Russian-speaking churches.

One exception to the dominance of the Russian language in TEE groups is republic C where eighty-three out of ninety TEE groups operated in the indigenous language in November 2017 (Table 13.3). As explained above, indigenous leaders who initiated the TEE programme in republic C have a preference for indigenous language use. In this case also, it appears that the principle of homophily has been at work and led the TEE national team to "naturally" build a strong consumer base among indigenous churches.

The third reason relates to product availability. The TEE movement in Russia was established in 2004[38] and SEAN courses translated into Russian

35. Hoskins, "Russification," 430–31.

36. During Soviet times, the Russian language was particularly dominant in cities and indigenous populations in cities developed a preference for the Russian language.

37. McPherson, Smith-Lovin, and Cook, "Birds of a Feather," 416.

38. Huggins, "Open Russian Theological Academy," 269.

were made readily available to Central Asian TEE national teams.[39] However, the slow progress in translation to indigenous language versions created limited opportunity to penetrate the potential consumer base of indigenous language churches.

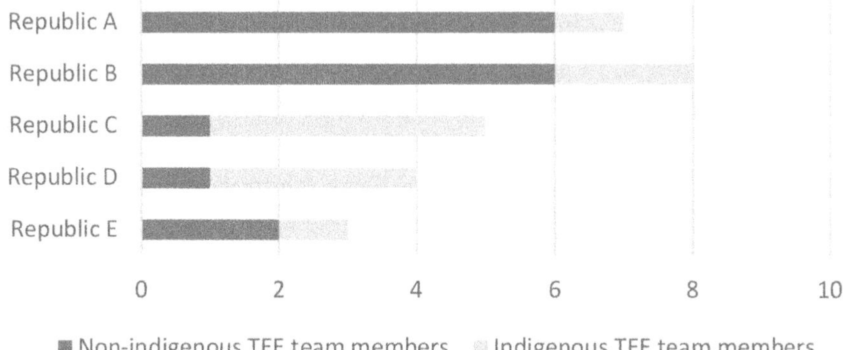

Figure 13.2. Number of non-indigenous and indigenous TEE national team members (Nov 2017)

Once again, the exception is republic C. The TEE national team there began TEE groups with indigenous language versions of SEAN courses, and today there are more indigenous language courses available there than for any other national teams (Table 13.5).

Table 13.5. Number of TEE courses available in indigenous and Russian languages (Nov 2017)

Central Asian Republic	TEE Courses Available in Indigenous Languages (Nov 2017)	TEE Courses Available in Russian Language (Nov 2017)
Republic A	3	13
Republic B	3	13
Republic C	8	13
Republic D	3	13
Republic E	3	13

39. Vyssotskaia, "Theological Education in the Context of Persecution," 118–19.

The fourth reason relates to regulation of the religious marketplace by state authorities. Officially, the Central Asian ruling elites claim that religious freedom and separation of religion and state are fundamental to their national identity building programmes; however, the reality in the religious marketplace tells a different story, related particularly to the issue of conversion to Protestant Christianity which is seen as a foreign religion. Authorities seek to control and limit the growth of churches through strict management of religion. Conversion for Slavic and European populations is not as contentious as for indigenous Muslim populations. Muslim-background converts to Christianity sometimes experience intense pressures from family, community, and the state.[40] Furthermore, indigenous-language churches often face strict scrutiny in their ministry activities and struggle to gain legal registration. For these reasons, many indigenous-language churches operate underground as small house churches. As previously mentioned, TEE can operate in strict conditions, but strict regulations still limit the scope of TEE among indigenous churches.

Given that religious market conditions continue to be restrictive, particularly the targeting of indigenous-language churches, it is all the more remarkable that 40 percent of TEE groups in Central Asia operate in indigenous languages (Table 13.3). This perhaps reflects the intentionality of TEE national teams to attract indigenous churches to TEE, realizing that the longer-term future of TEE as an effective discipleship tool for indigenous churches depends on it. This high percentage of indigenous language TEE groups also indicates that, even with strict regulation, indigenous churches are willing to take risks in order to provide theological education to their members.

Finding 3: Most TEE Groups in Central Asia are urban based rather than rural based

The third finding from this study is that most TEE groups (58 percent) in Central Asia are urban based (Figure 13.3), which is in contrast to where the majority of the Central Asian population live as shown in Table 13.6 (61 percent live in rural settings).

---

40. Vysotskaya, "Is the Silk Road Still Open?," 317. Further insights into persecution in Central Asia are provided by Vysotskaya and Subedi in chapter 12: "TEE as a Tool for Providing Theological Education to Churches Facing Persecution and Poverty."

A closer look at the data in Figure 13.3 reveals a variation of results between different Central Asian republics that reflects the character of the church network each TEE national team has developed. Notably, TEE groups in republics B, D, and E are strongly urban based. A key reason for this is that national teams are based in major cities, allowing easier access to TEE courses and training, compared to village churches.

Another reason for the prevalence of urban based TEE groups is that many church networks focus church-planting efforts in cities rather than villages, which leads to larger numbers of urban-based Christians. However, this is not always the case. For example, rural churches located near major cities often have easier access to TEE than churches in small regional cities.

A major exception to the general trend is, once again, republic C where two thirds of TEE groups are rural based. The primary reason for this exception is that the TEE national team in republic C not only has mostly indigenous leaders and a large selection of courses in the indigenous language but also has an intentional rural focus, where there is a high concentration of the indigenous population.

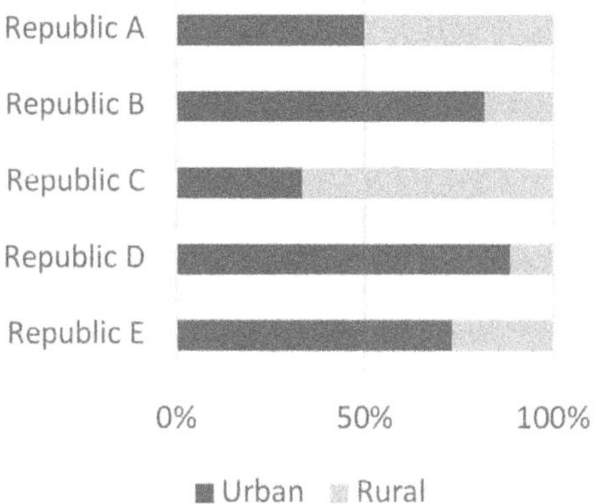

Figure 13.3. Percentage of urban based / rural based TEE groups in Central Asia (Nov 2017)

Table 13.6. Percentage of population living in urban / rural locations in Central Asia[41]

Central Asian Republic	% Population Urban	% Population Rural
Kyrgyzstan	35%	65%
Tajikistan	27%	73%
Kazakhstan	50%	50%
Uzbekistan	35%	65%
Turkmenistan	48%	52%
TOTAL %	**39%**	**61%**

Factors Affecting Future Trajectories of the TEE Movement in Central Asia

Looking to the future, continued growth of the TEE movement in Central Asia depends on both supply-side and demand-side factors affecting the religious marketplace.

Supply-side factors

Particularly in the short-term, growth in the Central Asian TEE movement depends on the supply-side, namely, the effectiveness of the TEE national teams (the suppliers) to deliver the TEE courses and training (the products) to both Russian-speaking and indigenous-language churches (the consumers). Two areas need to be addressed:

1. Market share

First, TEE national teams need to be effective in expanding their market share among existing church networks. TEE in Central Asia is still at an early stage of development with currently around 100 Protestant churches using TEE, out of several thousand churches (registered and unregistered). This market share

41. Source: Worldometers 2017.

represents a fraction of the potential market share which could be gained from engaging with more Protestant church networks in Central Asia.[42]

Part of this expansion will depend on the ability of each team to grow indigenous-leadership capacity that will facilitate access to the networks of indigenous-language churches and congregations. Indigenous-leadership capacity will be particularly important at management and board levels to help shape vision, strategy, and goals. One of the challenges of growing indigenous-leadership capacity in Central Asia is the smaller pool of candidates to draw from, compared to the pool of Slavic and European Christian populations.

2. Product availability

Second, TEE national teams need to be effective in enlarging their product availability. Further translation of existing courses and the writing of new courses in indigenous languages relevant to Central Asian culture and traditions, and drawing on modern adult educational theory, will help meet the felt needs of indigenous churches.[43] Towards this goal, several national teams are writing new TEE courses through a course-writing programme developed by the Increase Association.[44]

Demand-side factors

Longer-term, the growth of the TEE movement depends on demand-side religious marketplace factors. If churches continue to grow and multiply, then demand for theological education products such as TEE will also grow, but if churches decline in number then the demand for training products will also wane.

Further insight into longer-term future trajectories of the TEE movement in Central Asia is possible by examining the sociopolitical and religious context

42. In comparison, the TEE movement in Mongolia was established in the mid-1990s and by 2014 it was estimated that over 4,300 students had studied TEE courses – see: Aylett and Green, "Theological Education by Extension (TEE)," 69. In addition, personal correspondence with one of the founders of TEE in Mongolia suggests that TEE was used as a theological education tool by 30 percent of all evangelical churches in Mongolia in the early years of the TEE programme.

43. See chapters 5 and 6 in this book for discussion of adult education theory relevant to TEE.

44. The Increase Association's course-writing programme is producing new courses relevant to local cultures. Details of this programme are provided in chapter 7: Ivins and Do, "New TEE Courses." Also see: Increase, "Course Writers in Asia."

of the region. There are four major factors that are likely to affect future church growth and subsequent demand for theological training products such as TEE.

1. The Russian factor

Russia continues to be a major influence on Central Asia in the areas of politics, economics, and religion. Russia's influence is stronger and more enduring than that from the West, China, India, Turkey, and other countries. The reason for this influence is connected to the fact that ruling elites in Central Asia once held positions of power during Soviet times and their preferred language is Russian.[45]

As mentioned previously, Russia's model of management of religion leads the way in the post-Soviet landscape and since 1997 has chosen a path of increasing repression. The target of this repression is first, Islamic extremists who threaten state security and second, religious sects, particularly Protestant churches who are seen as a threat to peace and stability due to their "proselytizing"[46] activity.

The methods of religion management and regulation used by Russia and followed by the Central Asian republics are drawn from earlier Soviet tactics, with the key difference being that few alternatives are offered as an ideological replacement. Whereas the Soviets had the highly engineered programme of scientific atheism to replace religion, contemporary Russian and Central Asian regimes have nothing in comparison apart from state-sponsored "traditional religions." For Central Asian indigenous Muslim populations, the "traditional religion" offered is a tailored version of moderate Sunni Islam, and for the dwindling Slavic and European Christian populations, it is Russian Orthodoxy. Both options are tightly managed by the state, which is unattractive for a burgeoning modern society that would prefer a religious market with a variety of religious choices to cater for individual preferences.

In the future, it is conceivable that if Russia eases its regulation of the religious marketplace then Central Asian states will follow the same direction.

45. Atkin, "Central Asia and the Caucasus," 538.

46. Authorities in Central Asia commonly use the term proselytism rather than the preferred terms evangelism and witnessing used by churches and Christian organizations. Proselytism carries a sense of manipulation and coercion, which churches consider morally wrong.

An atmosphere of greater religious freedom is likely to stimulate church growth and result in an increased demand for theological education training products such as TEE. However, if Russia follows an increasingly repressive trajectory, then church growth and training programmes such as TEE face an uncertain future.[47]

2. The nation-building factor

One of the failings of the Soviet Union was not recognizing the power of nationalism in the modern era. Benedict Anderson argues that "the reality is quite plain: the 'end of the era of nationalism,' so long prophesied, is not remotely in sight. Indeed nation-ness is the most universally legitimate value in the political life of our time."[48]

Each Central Asian republic is developing its own nation-building strategy, with varying degrees of "de-Russification" taking place. One of the elements of nation-building that is particularly visible is language management. As already mentioned, from the Soviet and Czarist periods the use of the Russian language in Central Asia today appears, on the surface, to be unusually high given the large percentages of indigenous populations. Following the collapse of the Soviet Union in 1991, the Central Asian republics reacted in different ways to language issues. For example, Uzbekistan and Turkmenistan moved quickly to change their scripts from Cyrillic to Roman as part of their new national identity building programmes. Other states like Kazakhstan were more cautious about the politics of language.

Though the influence of the Russian language remains strong in Central Asia, its dominance is gradually waning as republics form their new national identities around which indigenous languages are an integral element. Kazakhstan, for example, plans to transition to Latin script by 2025 as a move towards making Kazakh the dominant language, while maintaining Russian and English as part of a trilingualism policy.[49]

47. The repression of Protestant evangelical churches in Russia continues. In the 2020 Open Doors World Watch List, Russia is ranked as a high persecution context. See: https://www.opendoorsusa.org/christian-persecution/world-watch-list/.

48. Anderson, *Imagined Communities*, 3.

49. Linn, "Kazakhstan Is Changing Its Alphabet."

A second significant element driving nation-building forward is population change. Since the collapse of the Soviet Union, the region has witnessed mass emigration, particularly of Slavic and European populations moving back to their "homelands." For example, in Kazakhstan during the 1990s nearly three million non-Kazakh ethnicities emigrated, mainly Russians, Ukrainians, and Germans.[50] On the eve of independence in 1991 approximately 38 percent of the population was ethnic Russian but dropped to 23.7 percent by 2020.[51] Furthermore, to counteract these massive emigration flows the state authorities introduced repatriation programmes to attract *oralmans* (returning Kazakhs) from mainly neighbouring Central Asian states, China, and Mongolia. Immigration of returning Kazakhs, combined with a recovery of fertility rates, has resulted in net population growth.[52] Other Central Asian states have experienced similar population trends.

A further major element influencing nation-building in Central Asia is political instability reflected in events since the collapse of the Soviet Union in 1991. Tajikistan experienced a civil war (1992–1997); three popular revolutions occurred in Kyrgyzstan (2005, 2010 and 2020); an Islamic uprising took place in the Andijon province of Uzbekistan (2005); and tense transitions of power from authoritarian presidents occurred in three republics – Turkmenistan, Uzbekistan,[53] and Kazakhstan.[54] The next thirty years may be just as dramatic, influenced by foreign political powers, and particularly Russia, the West, and China.

The impact of these elements on nation-building will impact the growth potential of churches in Central Asia in various ways. For example, changes in language policy or political instability may result in further waves of emigration among Russian-speaking Christian populations who see more of a future for their families in their homelands. A continuing emigration trend will decrease the size and influence of existing churches and will consequently lead to a lower demand for theological education options such as TEE. As these nation-

50. Tolesh, "Population History of Kazakhstan."

51. World Population Review, "Kazakhstan Population."

52. Kazakhstan's population was 18.9 million in 2020. See: Worldometers.info. "Population: Central Asia."

53. Atkin, "Central Asia and the Caucasus," 532–39.

54. Kazakhstan's president stepped down in early 2019 resulting in intense political tensions.

building trends continue, the growth of indigenous churches is vital for the survival of Christianity. TEE offers the potential to contribute to this growth through effective church-based discipleship programmes.

3. The globalization factor

The post-Soviet environment in Central Asia quickly ushered in the powerful forces of globalization chiefly driven by Western business enterprise. Central Asia was fertile ground for new opportunities with a market that had been locked up for seventy years.

The impact of globalization has been felt across different sectors – business, health, education, entertainment, and religion. The forces of consumerism and secularization might be expected to have a detrimental impact on religiosity. However, as Castells has observed in America, the presence of Christianity and other religions continues alongside the powerhouse of globalization: "Christian fundamentalism . . . is a major force in shaping the values and social practices of American society. The strength of religion in America shows that scientific and technological development, supposedly the harvest of rationalism, can expand in a highly religious context."[55]

The occurrence in recent decades of the revitalization of religion in many parts of the world including the post-Soviet bloc, Africa, Latin America, and Asia suggests that despite opposing elements, globalization is not halting growth of religion but contributing to it. For example, digitalization and the internet are driving the development of digital religion, which is dramatically increasing access to religious products.[56] New digital approaches including online courses and online group leader training are being developed for TEE and these have potential to attract increasing numbers of learners and churches in the future.[57] A potent contemporary example is the response of TEE to the COVID-19 virus pandemic which swept the globe from early 2020. Despite the

55. Castells, *Information Age*, xxi.

56. Helland, "Digital Religion," 178–81.

57. See chapter 8 for a discussion of new learning technologies within TEE: Weymouth, "TEE and Transformation in the Digital Age."

pandemic, TEE leaders have reported that many TEE groups have successfully switched to meeting online by using Zoom and other software programmes.[58]

Another aspect of globalization is urbanization. In Central Asia there is a strong trend for large numbers of people, particularly the young, to flock to cities for education and employment opportunities. The flow of these people to the cities increases access to Christian churches, which are concentrated in urban centres.

Based on these observations it is likely that globalization will continue to contribute to the vitality of Christianity in Central Asia which in turn will benefit theological education including TEE. However, other powerful forces remain potential threats to the religious marketplace, the most significant of which is Islamization.

4. The Islamization factor

Islam is gaining momentum in the post-Soviet landscape of Central Asia and is bringing about a re-Islamization of the region. Islamic influences come from foreign sources such as Turkey, the Middle East, and Iran and have led to mosque-building programmes as well as the establishment of schools, universities, hospitals, and businesses.[59] Some Islamic groups have been restricted by authorities because of their extremist ideology and activities, for example, Hisbut-Tahrir, IMU (Islamic Movement of Uzbekistan), and Tablighi Jamaat.[60]

Another major contributor to re-Islamization is from Central Asian ruling elites who are active in the instrumentalization of Islam to develop their preferred version of "traditional" moderate Sunni Islam as part of their nation-building programmes.[61] Instrumentalization has had mixed success among indigenous Muslim populations due to competition from alternative forms of Islam and a desire for more religious choice.

58. This information about TEE groups using online approaches during the Corona virus pandemic comes from correspondence between the Increase Association and Central Asian TEE leaders in mid 2020.

59. Balci, "Fethullah Gülen's Missionary Schools," 153–57.

60. Balci, "Rise of the Jama'at al Tabligh," 72–74; International Crisis Group, "Kyrgyzstan: State Fragility and Radicalisation," 13–15.

61. Omelicheva, "Islam and Power Legitimation," 145–54.

The impact of Islamization on churches as an aspect of religious market competition is becoming increasingly evident. Persistent intolerance to Christian conversion exists at all levels – family, community, and state. Intolerance brings challenges for churches reaching out to indigenous Muslim populations.[62]

Sebastien Peyrouse points out that "missionary movements are . . . driven by the doctrine of Christian universality to target the local population, whom they see as vital to the long-term survival of Christianity in Central Asia. This view has provoked conflict with Muslim leaders, who see all non-European locals as *de facto* Muslims rather than potential Christians."[63] Further analysis of the challenges for Christianity has been provided by David Radford who examines discursive strategies employed by Kyrgyz Christians who converted from Islam.[64]

With continuing religious marketplace competition from Islamization in Central Asia, combined with emigration flows of Slavic and European populations from the region, the future survival of the church in Central Asia depends on its ability to become rooted in the indigenous populations. Put simply, to survive longer-term, the Protestant church in Central Asia must increase its religious market share by overcoming barriers to evangelism and effectively passing the baton to succeeding generations. TEE is positioning itself to offer a viable approach to effective discipleship in the midst of these challenges.

Conclusion

The TEE movement in Central Asia has been gathering pace since the mid-2000s. In this chapter I have highlighted three significant findings about the TEE movement from informal interviews with TEE national team leaders in May 2016 and November 2017. The chapter discusses future trends and trajectories for TEE in the light of major social forces at work in Central Asia.

62. Montgomery, "Namaz, Wishing Trees, and Vodka," 366.
63. Peyrouse, "Christians as the Main Religious Minority," 373–74.
64. Radford, "Contesting and Negotiating," 19–24.

The first finding is that the TEE movement in Central Asia is growing strongly. After starting in the mid-2000s, there were over 2,200 active students in 2017.[65] This remarkable growth in TEE has taken place to meet the training needs of churches following the religious revivals of the 1990s. The second finding is that the majority of TEE groups (60 percent) in Central Asia use the Russian language despite majority indigenous populations. This is mainly due to the legacy of Russification that took place in Central Asia during the Czarist and Soviet periods. The third finding is that the majority of TEE groups are urban based despite a predominantly rural population. The concentration of TEE groups in cities relates to the fact that most churches and TEE national teams are located in major cities making accessibility easier for urban populations compared to rural populations. However, rural churches near major cities also benefit from easy access to TEE.

An exception to the latter two findings is noted in one of the Central Asian republics where the TEE national team is comprised mostly of indigenous leadership and has an intentional strategy to operate in rural areas where indigenous populations predominate.

The future trajectory of the TEE movement in Central Asia depends on supplier, product, consumer, competition, and regulation factors. In the short-term, supply-side factors are most significant, including the ability of the TEE national teams to increase their market share through expanding and tapping into existing church networks, and also through enlarging and strengthening their product availability.

In the longer-term, demand-side factors become increasingly important for the survival of TEE in Central Asia. These include the ability of churches to be strongly rooted in the midst of powerful sociopolitical and religious influences. Four major social influences are identified. First, the Russian factor: the continuing influence of Russia in all major spheres of life in Central Asia. Second, the nation-building factor: the ongoing agenda of Central Asian ruling elites to construct national identities through their interpretations of history, culture, language, and religion. Third, the globalization factor: the

65. Informal conversations with TEE leaders in 2020 suggests that the number of active TEE students in Central Asia has dropped significantly though programmes remain strong. One of the main reasons for the drop is the global Corona virus pandemic.

forces that continue to be a powerful influence through international business, secularization, and digitalization. Fourth, the Islamization factor: the influence of Islamization among the majority Muslim indigenous populations, which will continue to harden attitudes towards Christian conversion and bring challenges for church growth.

As Andrew Walls points out in his classic treatment of Christian history (highlighted in the quote at the beginning of this chapter), the long-term survival of Christianity depends on how firmly it is rooted among indigenous populations and languages. The TEE movement in Central Asia seeks to respond to the challenges this raises and to provide quality theological education to help local churches become firmly established in this first generation and succeeding generations. The evaluation of TEE in Central Asia that has been presented here demonstrates the agility of TEE to serve the theological education needs of churches in varied and changing contexts.

Bibliography

Alles, Gregory D. "Religious Economies and Rational Choice: On Rodney Stark and Roger Finke, Acts of Faith (2000)." In *Contemporary Theories of Religion: A Critical Companion*, edited by Michael Stausberg, 83–98. Abingdon: Routledge, 2009.

Anderson, Benedict. *Imagined Communities: Reflections on the Origin and Spread of Nationalism*. Revised ed. London: Verso, 2006.

Atkin, Muriel. "Central Asia and the Caucasus from the First World War." In *The New Cambridge History of Islam: Volume 5: The Islamic World in the Age of Western Dominance*, edited by Francis Robinson. The New Cambridge History of Islam, 517–41. Cambridge: Cambridge University Press, 2010.

Aylett, Graham, and Tim Green. "Theological Education by Extension (TEE) as a Tool for Twenty-First Century Mission." In *Reflecting on and Equipping for Christian Mission*, edited by Stephen B. Bevans, Teresa Chai, J. Nelson Jennings, Knud Jørgensen, and Dietrich Werner, 59–78. Oxford: Regnum, 2015.

Balci, Bayram. "Fethullah Gülen's Missionary Schools in Central Asia and Their Role in the Spreading of Turkism and Islam." *Religion, State and Society* 31, no. 2 (2003): 151–77.

———. "The Rise of the Jama'at Al Tabligh in Kyrgyzstan: The Revival of Islamic Ties between the Indian Subcontinent and Central Asia?" *Central Asian Survey* 31, no. 1 (2012): 61–76.

Berger, Peter. *The Sacred Canopy: Elements of a Sociological Theory of Religion*. New York: Doubleday, 1967.

Beyer, Peter. "Religious Vitality in Canada: The Complementarity of Religious Market and Secularization Perspectives." *Journal for the Scientific Study of Religion* 36, no. 2 (1997): 272–88.

Borbieva, Noor. "Foreign Faiths and National Renewal: Christian Conversion among Kyrgyz Youth." *Culture and Religion* 13, no. 1 (2012): 41–63.

Bourdeaux, Michael. "Religion Revives in All Its Variety: Russia's Regions Today." *Religion, State and Society* 28, no. 1 (2000): 9–21.

Breault, Kevin D. "New Evidence on Religious Pluralism, Urbanism, and Religious Participation." *American Sociological Review* 54, no. 6 (1989): 1048–53.

Carey, Freda. "Theological Education by Extension in Pakistan." *Ecumenical Review* 64, no. 2 (2012): 160–68.

Castells, Manuel. *The Information Age: Economy, Society, and Culture: Vol 2: The Power of Identity*. 2nd ed. Chichester: Wiley-Blackwell, 2010.

Chaves, Mark, and Philip S. Gorski. "Religious Pluralism and Religious Participation." *Annual Review of Sociology* 27, no. 1 (2001): 261–81.

Chesnut, R. Andrew. *Competitive Spirits: Latin America's New Religious Economy*. New York: Oxford University Press, 2003.

Collins, Kathleen. "Faith and Reason: Christian Strategies under Post-Soviet Repression in Central Asia." *The Review of Faith & International Affairs* 15, no. 1 (2017): 43–55.

Dobbelaere, Karel. *Secularization: An Analysis at Three Levels*. Brussels: Peter Lang, 2002.

Froese, Paul. "Hungary for Religion: A Supply-Side Interpretation of the Hungarian Religious Revival." *Journal for the Scientific Study of Religion* 40, no. 2 (2001): 251–68.

———. *The Plot to Kill God: Findings from the Soviet Experiment in Secularization*. Berkeley: University of California Press, 2008.

Glissmann, Volker. "Christian Reflective Practice: Prayer as a Tool for Reflection and Application in Theological Education." *InSights Journal for Global Theological Education* 2, no. 2 (2017): 35–52.

Greeley, Andrew. "A Religious Revival in Russia?" *Journal for the Scientific Study of Religion* 33, no. 3 (1994): 253–72.

Hamberg, Eva M., and Thorleif Pettersson. "The Religious Market: Denominational Competition and Religious Participation in Contemporary Sweden." *Journal for the Scientific Study of Religion* 33, no. 3 (1994): 205–16.

Harrison, Patricia J. "Forty Years On: The Evolution of Theological Education by Extension (TEE)." *Evangelical Review of Theology* 28, no. 4 (2004): 315–28.

Helland, Christopher. "Digital Religion." In *Handbook of Religion and Society*, edited by David Yamane, 177–96. Basel: Springer, 2016.

Hoskins, Daniel G. "Russification as a Factor in Religious Conversion: Making Lenin Roll over in His Grave." *Culture and Religion* 16, no. 4 (2015): 430–44.

Huggins, Michael. "The Open Russian Theological Academy." In *Diversified Theological Education: Equipping All God's People*, edited by F. Ross Kinsler, 269–94. Pasadena, WCIU Press, 2008.

Iannaccone, Laurence R. "The Consequences of Religious Market Structure: Adam Smith and the Economics of Religion." *Rationality and Society* 3, no. 2 (1991): 156–77.

Iannaccone, Laurence R., Roger Finke, and Rodney Stark. "Deregulating Religion: The Economics of Church and State." *Economic Inquiry* 35, no. 2 (1997): 350–64.

Increase Association. "Conference Press Release." Empowering Churches and Equipping Disciples: Church-Based Training in Asia, 2017.

———. "Course Writers in Asia." 2018. https://www.increaseassociation.org/about/news-events/98-course-writers-in-asia.

Indexmundi.com. "Asia Region Statistics." 2017. https://www.indexmundi.com/asia.html.

International Crisis Group. "Kyrgyzstan: State Fragility and Radicalisation." *Crisis Group Europe and Central Asia Briefing No. 83* (2016). https://www.crisisgroup.org/europe-central-asia/central-asia/kyrgyzstan/kyrgyzstan-state-fragility-and-radicalisation.

Linn, Andrew. "Kazakhstan Is Changing Its Alphabet – Here's Why." *The Conversation*. 2017. https://theconversation.com/kazakhstan-is-changing-its-alphabet-heres-why-87466.

Mabuluki, Kangwa. "Diversified Theological Education: Genesis, Development and Ecumenical Potential of Theological Education by Extension (TEE)." In *Handbook of Theological Education in World Christianity*, edited by Dietrich Werner, David Esterline, Namsoon Kang, and Joshva Raja, 251–62. Oxford: Regnum, 2010.

McPherson, Miller, Lynn Smith-Lovin, and James M. Cook. "Birds of a Feather: Homophily in Social Networks." *Annual Review of Sociology* 27, no. 1 (2001): 415–44.

Montgomery, David W. "Namaz, Wishing Trees, and Vodka: The Diversity of Everyday Religious Life in Central Asia." In *Everyday Life in Central Asia: Past and Present*, edited by Jeff Sahadeo and Russell Zanca, 355–70. Bloomington: Indiana University Press, 2007.

Mulholland, Kenneth B. "TEE Come of Age: A Candid Assessment after Two Decades." In *Cyprus: TEE Come of Age*, edited by Robert L. Youngblood, 9–25. Exeter: Paternoster, 1984.

Omelicheva, Mariya Y. "Islam and Power Legitimation: Instrumentalisation of Religion in Central Asian States." *Contemporary Politics* 22, no. 2 (2016): 144–63.

Open Doors WWR. *World Watch List 2020: The 50 Countries Where It's Most Dangerous to Follow Jesus.* Santa Ana: Open Doors USA, 2020. https://www.opendoorsusa.org/christian-persecution/world-watch-list/.

Peyrouse, Sebastien. "Christians as the Main Religious Minority in Central Asia." In *Everyday Life in Central Asia: Past and Present*, edited by Jeff Sahadeo and Russell Zanca, 371–84. Bloomington: Indiana University Press, 2007.

Radford, David P. "Contesting and Negotiating Religion and Ethnic Identity in Post-Soviet Kyrgyzstan." *Central Asian Survey* 33, no. 1 (2014): 15–28.

SEAN International. "43rd Anniversary News: Day of Prayer, Celebration and Challenge." *SPREAD Newsletter, July* (2014). https://www.seaninternational.org.

Sendegeya, Fareth, and Leon Spencer, eds. *Understanding TEE: A Course Outline and Handbook for Students and Tutors in Residential Theological Institutions in Africa.* Dar es Salaam: ANITEPAM, 2001. http://www.increaseassociation.org/images/resources-library/ANITEPAM%20-%20Understanding%20TEE%20(2001).pdf.

Stark, Rodney. "Secularization, R.I.P." *Sociology of Religion* 60, no. 3 (1999): 249–73.

Stark, Rodney, and Roger Finke. *Acts of Faith: Explaining the Human Side of Religion.* Berkeley: University of California Press, 2000.

Stark, Rodney, and Laurence R. Iannaccone. "A Supply-Side Reinterpretation of the 'Secularization' of Europe." *Journal for the Scientific Study of Religion* 33, no. 3 (1994): 230–52.

Tiryakian, Edward A. "American Religious Exceptionalism: A Reconsideration." *The Annals of the American Academy of Political and Social Science* 527, no. 1 (1993): 40–54.

Tolesh, Fariza A. "The Population History of Kazakhstan." European Population Conference 2012, Stockholm, EAPS, 13–16 June 2012.

van Wingerden, Hanna-Ruth, Tim Green, and Graham Aylett, eds. *TEE in Asia: Empowering Churches, Equipping Disciples.* Carlisle: Langham Global Library, 2021.

Vysotskaya, Anneta. "Is the Silk Road Still Open? Central Asia: Christian Mission under Growing Restrictions on Religious Freedom." In *Freedom of Belief and*

Christian Mission, edited by Hans A. Gravaas, Christof Sauer, Tormod Engelsviken, Maqsood Kamil, and Knud Jørgensen, 309–19. Oxford: Regnum, 2015.

Vyssotskaia, Anneta. "Theological Education in the Context of Persecution and Economic Hardship: Focus on TEE in Central Asia." *International Journal for Religious Freedom* 5, no. 2 (2012): 111–22.

Walls, Andrew F. *The Missionary Movement in Christian History: Studies in the Transmission of Faith.* Maryknoll: Orbis Books, 1996.

Wilson, Bryan. "Aspects of Secularization in the West." *Japanese Journal of Religious Studies* 3, no. 4 (1976): 259–76.

worldometers.info. "Population: Central Asia." 2020. http://www.worldometers.info/population/asia/central-asia/.

worldpopulationreview.com. "Kazakhstan Population." 2021. http://worldpopulationreview.com/countries/kazakhstan-population/.

Yang, Fenggang. "The Red, Black and Gray Markets of Religion in China." *The Sociological Quarterly* 47, no. 1 (2006): 93–122.

14

The Increase Association

A Theological Education Movement and Collaborative Network Strengthening TEE across Asia and Beyond

Richard Brown, Tim Green, and Graham Aylett

Introduction

The Increase Association,[1] also known as Increase, exists to connect and strengthen church-based training in Asia and among its diaspora peoples worldwide. Increase's vision is "to see churches equipping all Christ's followers in their contexts so that many millions are discipled and empowered for mission, ministry and leadership."[2] Among theological educators, Increase also contributes to discourse on church-based training in general and TEE in particular, as evidenced in this present book.

This chapter tells the story of Increase's development with reflections from a sociological perspective, so it has alternating sections of narrative and analysis. Some readers may prefer to focus on the former. To include a sociological perspective in a book on theological education is unusual and somewhat experimental, but this cross-disciplinary approach helps in understanding an organization that is social, human, and fallible – while also led by God. As

1. https://www.increaseassociation.org.
2. Both statements are in https://www.increaseassociation.org/about/vision-purpose.

authors who are also actors[3] in Increase's story, we face the embarrassment of having to write about ourselves among others. Above all we want God to have the credit, and we will give evidences of his work even where this steps beyond sociological explanations.

The chapter begins by introducing relevant sociological theory, then continues with the story of Increase's development in three periods: 2006 to 2008, 2009 to 2014, and 2015 to 2020.

A Sociological Lens: Social Movements and Networks

Social movements

Scholarly interest in social movements has grown particularly since the 1990s.[4] Social movements often start as a small group of friends gathering together around a common cause which may then develop into a full-blown movement. Contemporary social movements are often a response to social issues, concerns, and grievances.[5] Social movements produce collective action and mobilization for bringing about desired change. Social movement research on "value-oriented" religious movements is important but less well established. However, some studies have been made in relation to Islamic activism:[6] Wiktorowicz evaluates factors affecting mobilization of individuals including religious seeking, religious authority, commitment, and solidarity between members of the movement.[7]

Snow and colleagues explain that when social movements grow over time "the activities with which they are associated . . . become an increasingly

---

3. The word "actor" is used in its sociological sense, meaning participant. Tim Green was Increase Association General Secretary until March 2021 when Graham Aylett assumed that role. Richard Brown is an Increase Equipper. The narrative sections of this chapter are written by Green and Aylett, and analysis by Brown and Green.

4. della Porta, *Social Movements*; Diani and McAdam, *Social Movements and Networks*; Snow, Soule, and Kriesi, *Blackwell Companion*; Diani, "Social Movements and Collective Action."

5. Snow, Soule, and Kriesi, "Mapping the Terrain," 3. Large-scale movements attract media attention on such issues as human rights, abortion, and environmental movements. Small-scale movements typically develop around less newsworthy local issues, such as protests against building plans or public amenity closure.

6. Bekele, "Islamist Activism"; Wiktorowicz, *Islamic Activism*; Vertigans, *Militant Islam*; Sutton and Vertigans, "Militant Islam."

7. Wiktorowicz, "Introduction: Islamic Activism."

conspicuous feature of the social landscape."[8] In the landscape of theological education, Increase began as a small inconspicuous group of like-minded theological educators with a shared vision, which in time developed into a large transnational movement.

Development of social movements depends on characteristics including organizational form, collective identity, leadership, tactics, innovation, participant mobilization, diffusion, and framing.[9] Social movements may experience divisions and factions. Benford observed for nuclear disarmament movements that "while a movement's organizations typically share an overarching goal, disagreements frequently erupt . . . regarding specific objectives, strategies and tactics."[10] These intra-movement divisions can be both detrimental and facilitative,[11] as confirmed by other studies.[12] The analysis sections of this chapter discuss Increase as a social movement including a positive outcome that resulted despite an early divergence of vision.

Social networks

A second sociological lens providing valuable insights into Increase's emergence and development is social network theory. Whereas social movements provide a framework for understanding Increase's progressive growth, social networks focus on the characteristics and dynamics of relationships within the movement. Social network research has continued to grow prolifically since it emerged in 1970s.[13] There are four concepts integral to social networks and useful for analysis of Increase.

---

8. Snow, Soule, and Kriesi, "Mapping the Terrain," 4.

9. Snow, Soule, and Kriesi, 12.

10. Benford, "Frame Disputes," 678.

11. Benford, 677.

12. Other social movements with intra-movement frame disputes include the American labour movement (Clemens, "Organizational Form as Frame"), the US anti-death penalty movement (Haines, *Against Capital Punishment*), and a study of a Black feminist movement (White, "Talking Feminist, Talking Black").

13. Burt, *Structural Holes*; Burt, "Contingent Value"; Granovetter, "Strength of Weak Ties"; McPherson, Smith-Lovin, and Cook, "Birds of a Feather"; Borgatti and Lopez-Kidwell, "Network Theory"; Lin, *Social Capital*; Everton, "Networks and Religion"; Wood and Gray, "Toward a Comprehensive Theory."

1. Strength of "Weak Ties"

In his Strength of Weak Ties concept, Granovetter showed that a local community can mobilize and coordinate resources and action when it has a broad structure of weak ties (relationships with acquaintances) rather than a smaller dense network of strong ties (with close friends and colleagues).[14] In other words, if many weak ties exist in a network they represent rich untapped resources with potential to be activated to achieve its aims and goals. The analysis below will highlight Increase's intentional strategy to build a broad network of weak ties to serve its purposes.

2. Homophily

The building of a diverse transnational network such as Increase does not come naturally. The concept of homophily helps in understanding the dynamics. Borgatti and Lopez-Kidwell argue that "people tend to be *homophilous*, meaning that they naturally gravitate to people similar to themselves."[15] Lin explains that in a network, homophily tends to result in strong ties between actors with similar social positions, locations, and resources.[16] McPherson and colleagues argue that "contact between similar people occurs at a higher rate than among dissimilar people. The pervasiveness of homophily means that cultural, behavioural, genetic, or material information that flows through networks will tend to be localized."[17]

For Increase as a transnational network, homophily helps to forge relationships between similar people from a wide range of contexts. However, there is also a risk of cliques forming within the network along educational, cultural, linguistic, age, and gender lines. Potential negative impacts of homophily are counteracted through strong cross-cultural communication skills and investment in relationships between people from different backgrounds. The benefits of these efforts are evident from Increase's rapid growth and diverse nature.

---

14. Granovetter also showed that people with a wide network of "weak ties" were more effective in finding jobs than those with a small network of "strong ties."

15. Borgatti and Lopez-Kidwell, "Network Theory," 40.

16. Lin, *Social Capital*, 39.

17. McPherson, Smith-Lovin, and Cook, "Birds of a Feather," 416.

3. Social capital

A third relevant concept is social capital.[18] Burt explains that

> the player has social capital: relationships with other players. You have friends, colleagues, and more general contacts through whom you receive opportunities to use your financial capital and human capital . . . The social capital of people aggregates into the social capital of organizations.[19]

A network's success is related more to social capital than individual capital, bringing access and timing of information, innovation, efficiency, and effectiveness.[20] Lin describes social capital in a network context as "resources embedded in a social structure that are accessed and/or mobilized in purposive actions."[21] Increase's network structure is wide and diverse, and the aggregate social capital forms a rich structure of social resources that can be mobilized towards achieving the goals.

4. Collaboration

Definitions of collaboration vary widely, and Wood and Gray describe it as "an interactive process between autonomous stakeholders who bring action and decisions to a problem domain."[22] In the Increase network the stakeholders are individuals and organizations, and the problem domain is the task of promoting and strengthening church-based training across Asia and beyond. The stakeholders are autonomous in their individual decision-making powers but abide by a common commitment to the goals of Increase and to Christ's Great Commission to "go and make disciples of all nations."[23]

18. Lin, *Social Capital*; Burt, *Structural Holes*; Burt, "Contingent Value"; Bourdieu, "Forms of Capital"; Coleman, "Social Capital," 95–120; Putnam, "Bowling Alone," 65–78; Fukuyama, "Social Capital," 89–103.

19. Burt, Structural Holes, 8–9.

20. Burt, 13–25.

21. Lin, *Social Capital*, 40.

22. Wood and Gray, "Toward a Comprehensive Theory," 146. See also Nooteboom, "Collaboration, Trust, and the Structure of Relationships"; Schilling and Phelps, "Interfirm Collaboration Networks"; Wellman et al., "Networking Scholars"; Uzzi and Spiro, "Collaboration and Creativity."

23. Matt 28:18–20.

However, for collaboration to yield collective benefit, stakeholders must also "derive some benefit" argue Wood and Gray.[24] Moreover, they comment that a convener plays an important role in establishing, legitimizing and guiding a collaborative network[25] and should have four key attributes. First, a convener's legitimacy comes from being considered open-minded and fair. Second, the person must be seen as trustworthy since no formal authority exists to enforce shared rules. Third, a convener uses resources to proactively encourage actors to collaborate. Fourth, they draw on their own credibility, knowledge, relational ties, influence, and charisma to persuade stakeholders to participate.[26] In Increase, the executive team and other leaders have an influential convener role that fosters collaboration.

Increase Association – Period One (2006–2008): Forming and Storming

Narrative

Because Increase is a transnational movement and network where members generally keep in touch through electronic communication, they treasure rare opportunities to meet face to face. These occasions have generated vision, direction, energy, and relational warmth to sustain the movement. Unsurprisingly, therefore, Increase's gatherings have triggered pivotal moments in its story, and they feature prominently in the narrative. For ease of reference, the main gatherings are listed in Table 14.1.

In February 2006, Entrust[27] board member Graham Hibbert brought together in Atlanta, USA, some twenty people active in nonformal education in different regions of the world. Entrust's concern was the millions of untrained Christian leaders, thus discussion centred on how to increase access to leadership training globally. The name Increase was agreed for a network to further this aim.[28]

24. Wood and Gray, "Toward a Comprehensive Theory," 160–61.
25. Wood and Gray, 149–50.
26. Wood and Gray, 152–53.
27. Formerly Biblical Education by Extension, International, or BEE International.
28. The name "Increase" was suggested by conference participant Johan Boekhout of Entrust.

Table 14.1. Main Increase gatherings until 2020

Month/Year	Location	Event
January 2006	Atlanta	Initial consultation
February 2008	London	Conference
October 2010	Kathmandu	Conference "Twenty-First Century TEE in Asia: Challenges and Opportunities"
October 2012	Central Asia	Training conference (jointly with GZB[29] and Central Asia Vision Group) "Laying a Good Foundation"
March 2013	Seoul	Consultation "New Directions: TEE Curricula for the Twenty-First Century"
May 2013	Oxford	Committee gathering, planning next steps
April 2015	Kuala Lumpur	Consultation "Exploring New Horizons – Working Together for Church-Based Training in Asia"
April 2016	Kuala Lumpur	Increase Teams Gathering "Moving Forward Together"
November 2017	Chiang Mai	Conference "Empowering Churches and Equipping Disciples: Church-Based Training in Asia"
November 2019	Istanbul	Increase Teams Gathering "Reflect and Envision"

Attendees at Atlanta 2006 had differing though related interests. Michael Huggins had a passion "that God could still raise up, disciple and multiply the Peters, James, Johns, Simons and Matthews and change society through humble, ordinary, working people."[30] Qaiser Julius[31] was excited that, while campus-based institutions already had a place to discuss their concerns, now in Atlanta providers of church-based and extension education could have their own

29. GZB, Gereformeerde Zendings Bond, or Reformed Mission League is a church-based mission organization based in the Netherlands. See www.gzb.nl.

30. Michael Huggins to Graham Aylett, email correspondence, 22 September 2020. Huggins is a former sheep farmer, SEAN course writer and illustrator, and TEE pioneer in Russia. He was inspired by Tony Barratt, Anglican minister and missionary who with others founded SEAN (Study by Extension for All Nations). https://www.seaninternational.org/courses#foundation.

31. Then and now Director of the Open Theological Seminary, Pakistan.

forum.[32] Richard Morris[33] was highly motivated by the theme of access[34] and a desire to see more transformative practice in theological education. Anneta Vysotskaya[35] was excited to see "like-minded people from different countries with the same passion of helping all God's people to grow in their knowledge of the word of God."[36] Another key participant was Zafar Ismail,[37] a TEE veteran since its earliest days in Asia, who later became Increase's chairperson.

In this first phase of Increase, its mission was defined as providing "increasing access to church training through distance learning in order to help meet the global need of untrained leaders." Its purpose would be to promote cooperation and mutual support and to encourage fresh thinking globally in "contextual theological education."[38] So in those early days Increase focused on the *global* issue of *leadership training*, and on *distance learning*[39] for *contextual* theological education. At this stage, the network included organizations using a wide range of training delivery methods. Aiming for fresh thinking they launched five groups to explore different areas, though only the group tasked with innovation[40] continued.

At Increase's next gathering in London in February 2008, thirty-four participants gathered from all continents. Participants shared a vision for contextual learning,[41] but were deeply polarized between the TEE advocates

---

32. Qaiser Julius to Graham Aylett, WhatsApp voicemail, 8 October 2020.

33. Then with MAF Learning Technologies, now serving as part of WITH International Community. https://withcommunity.org/about-with/.

34. MAF Learning Technologies aimed to use technology to provide access to training for "the least of the least, and the remotest of the remote." Richard Morris, personal communication.

35. Then International Director of ORTA in Russia, now General Director of ORTA and Chair of the Increase Committee.

36. Anneta Vysotskaya to Graham Aylett, email correspondence, 22 September 2020.

37. Former Director of the Open Theological Seminary (a national TEE movement in Pakistan), and later Director of Deir Mar Thoma.

38. These statements, reached in January 2007 meetings, are quoted from Graham Hibbert's email correspondence with Anneta Vysotskaya, 16 February 2007.

39. TEE practitioners would now not usually describe TEE methodology as "distance learning," in recognition that it is better regarded as a locally located and church-based form of training where distance largely collapses.

40. Zafar Ismail, Richard Morris and Johan Boekhout, concerned to develop and promote more transformative pedagogies.

41. Including TEE pioneers Fred and Grace Holland, and Terry Barratt.

(more than half the total) and those who saw the future in Action – Reflection – Action models and competency-based training.

TEE practitioner Tim Green writes: "It took a deliberate peace-building and consensus-seeking initiative. I invited Richard Morris to meet up . . . we talked and talked and got to know each other better. As we did so, we found we had more in common . . . than we had realized."[42] As a result Morris stayed with Increase even though the active majority were now TEE practitioners, so they continued to benefit from his drive towards innovation and renewal. In this reconciliation there was a sense of God's guiding hand.

Analysis

Invitees to the initial Atlanta gathering were selected not through any systematic survey or nomination process, but through informal use of social networks. Hibbert reached beyond his strong ties within Entrust, to use weak ties of acquaintance with individuals in other organizations. They in turn drew on their own connections beyond Hibbert's circle.[43] This leverage of weak ties brought together in Atlanta people who had never met each other before, thus facilitating a wider network and a stronger base of social capital and social resources than if Hibbert had attempted to work through his own organization alone. That relational process perhaps overlooked some important contributors, but overall proved sufficient to launch the new movement. The Atlanta participants had the homophily of a shared general vision and the shared language of English. Most were Westerners but there was some ethnic diversity, which was to grow greatly in Increase's later membership.

As with other social movements, initially the actors came together with a generally shared vision for change. But as actual collaboration began, two things happened. First, they uncovered differences of approach that were further exposed in the London conference. Second, London 2008 expanded the circle to new actors who had their own ideas of what Increase should do.

As a social movement gets underway, differing approaches and factions (known as dispute frames) are not uncommon; they can be detrimental or

42. Tim Green to Graham Aylett and Richie Brown, email correspondence, 9 October 2020.

43. For instance, Michael Huggins had already developed a weak ties network of TEE practitioners sharing news and prayer needs by email.

facilitative. Thankfully, the divisions unveiled in the 2008 London conference were ultimately facilitative for the Increase movement. By listening to each other, the main actors[44] could identify sufficient common ground for Increase to move forward without a radical split. Their God-guided decision to work together bore fruit in many ways, including the later programme to develop a new generation of transformative TEE courses.[45]

Increase Association – Period Two (2009–2014): A New Focus

Narrative

After London 2008, Increase's leadership changed to reflect its active membership. The new committee invited Increase-connected individuals to advise on where it should focus. Guided by this discussion and fuelled by their own background and ministry vision,[46] the committee decided to focus on Asia and on TEE within church-based training approaches. However, the scope was also broadened: "Our vision is not just restricted to pastors and missionaries, but to equipping all Christ's followers for active growth and service . . . ordinary working people in all walks of life."[47]

The committee planned for relationship, reform, and renewal in the TEE movement. Relationship was needed first to build confidence and capacity for subsequent reform and renewal. With these aims, planning began for a pan-Asia conference built around three training tracks. But who could lead this

44. Richard Morris and Tim Green were not officially commissioned to start this mutual listening process, it was their own initiative.

45. Green's background in TEE and Morris's in transformative learning were combined in this programme. See chapter 7: Ivins and Do, "New TEE Courses."

46. The new Committee to lead the Increase Association intentionally comprised a greater proportion of non-Westerners. Several were Asian and all except one had personal involvement with TEE in Asia. The members were Richard Morris, Michael Huggins, Anneta Vysotskaya, Sungrae (Stephen) Cho, Tim Green, and Zafar Ismail. After the May 2009 meeting, Richard Morris took over as chair from Graham Hibbert, and in turn stepped down in 2015 to make way for Zafar Ismail.

47. Because Increase holds together *both* leadership training *and* equipping all God's people, and sees them as organically connected under the general head of discipleship, integrated learning pathways are significant for Increase. Leaders (in church and society) emerge from churches focused on being and making disciples, and tracks are needed to facilitate this natural process.

training? Instead of relying on outside experts, thirteen people were selected within Increase's own circles,[48] all of them having significant TEE experience in their own countries. Equipping themselves through a structured combination of three face-to-face gatherings in 2010–2011[49] and assignments between each gathering, they became a vanguard of reflective practitioners to equip others. They forged strong interpersonal relationships, acquired a collective identity as "TEE Equippers" and developed capacity to lead the three training tracks of the upcoming pan-Asia conference.

The conference, "Twenty-First Century TEE in Asia: Challenges and Opportunities," took place in Kathmandu in October 2010, hosted by the Nepali TEE organization, ITEEN.[50] Conference preparation was bathed in prayer; it proved to be a pivotal event, marking a "second birth" for Increase. Of the seventy-five participants, sixty came from over twenty countries in Asia.[51] Most had never met before, and new friendships led to new initiatives. Previously isolated TEE practitioners found much in common and much to celebrate, share, and learn together. The conference modelled a highly participative style and an emphasis on capacity building which would characterize all subsequent Increase gatherings.

The energy and excitement in this conference came from a sense that God was at work in and through the Increase movement. On arrival participants were greeted by the question "What excites you about TEE?" Their written answers, pasted up on a huge banner in the hall, were afterwards summarized in the conference statement. A similarly participative process led to this vision statement:

> that in the [twenty-first century], the Lord would use the TEE movement in Asia powerfully to strengthen churches, helping

48. These were Qaiser Julius, David Samuel, Jackson and Janeffer Lee, Sungrae (Stephen) Cho, Graham Aylett, Siebe Meindertsma, Rick Weymouth, Anneta Vysotskaya, Tim Green, Lyn Pearson, and Matthew Jeong.

49. In different Asian countries with help from educationalists Robert Ferris, Patricia Harrison, Richard Hart, and Perry Shaw.

50. The first such conference in more than twenty-five years, for almost all participants their first international TEE gathering. Thomas Schirrmacher (Secretary General of the World Evangelical Alliance as from March 2021) addressed the conference.

51. "News: Kathmandu 2010 Press Release," Increase, https://www.increaseassociation.org/news-archive/32-kathmandu-2010-press-release.

> them to multiply, equipping all believers to bring transformation in all areas of society for the growth of His kingdom and the glory of His Name.[52]

From this conference, we may highlight the focus on church, equipping for all believers, transformation of believers and society, kingdom orientation and growth, and God's glory. These values were woven into Increase's DNA, along with discipleship under the Lordship of Jesus, local ownership, indigenous leadership, attention to the context, relationship, reform, renewal, prayer, learning from one another, sharing, mutual service, becoming reflective practitioners, giving time free of charge, and decentralized networking across Asia.

For the next four years Increase developed as an informal network based on these values. Starting in 2011, the Equippers made country visits either to strengthen existing TEE programmes (at their invitation) or to help catalyze the formation of new ones. For example, they helped in Central Asia, where steady groundwork over the years led to a dramatically fruitful training conference in 2012. From all five "-stan" countries and Russia, indigenous leaders with a vision for discipleship came together for a week's training, "Laying a Good Foundation."[53] This aptly named event sought both to raise vision and to offer practical tools towards fulfilling that vision. Within that one week, four new TEE national teams were born. All of them continue to this day.[54]

A 2013 workshop in Turkey guided these Central Asian programmes in effective translation and contextualization of the SEAN courses,[55] which formed the backbone of their curricula and are widely effective across Asia. However,

52. For both statements see Increase, "News: Kathmandu 2010 Conference Statement," Increase https://www.increaseassociation.org/news-archive/31-kathmandu-2010-conference-statement, and in the Introduction to TEE in this present book. The idea originated from Zafar Ismail's proposal for a "TEE Manifesto," made at a conference planning session in Oxford in June 2010.

53. The Increase Association, GZB, and the Central Asia Vision Group jointly organized it. TEE Equippers led the training, helped by leaders from the national TEE programmes ITEEN, ORTA, and KuCH.

54. Chapter 13 analyzes their subsequent growth over time in relation to sociological theory of religious markets; one additional TEE programme in the region had started back in 2006.

55. SEAN is a major global provider of TEE courses. The name SEAN is derived from "Study by Extension for All Nations" and pronounced "say-an." See further in https://www.seaninternational.org.

every TEE national body decides its own curriculum for its own context, whether by adapting courses from other providers or by creating its own.[56] To help twelve of these national programmes learn from each other, Increase ran a 2013 consultation on curriculum planning, hosted as so often by a member body, this time TEE Korea led by Sungrae (Stephen) Cho. It exemplified the value Increase places on collaboration, as a space for TEE educators to learn from each other, sharing expertise within the movement while also receiving input from others where appropriate.[57]

Except for occasional gatherings, participants in the Increase network were mostly separated by thousands of miles and many time zones. It is somewhat surprising that the movement could survive and grow despite having no bank account, no employed staff, no office, no vehicle, not even a single computer or mobile phone. Yet Increase did survive and even flourished. Morris comments: "We did much out of love for the Lord and our love for each other that grew over time."[58]

This working model required only lightweight administrative processes and modest funding. Most income could therefore be invested directly in airfares for Increase leadership and Equippers to visit countries, since maintaining warm relationships (strong ties) and developing strategic new relationships (through weak ties) remained a top priority. An era of cheap air fares and wide visa availability helped in sustaining connection. In the long gaps between face-to-face meetings technology helped hugely, not just email but especially videoconferencing[59] which did much to foster the relational warmth important in Asian cultures. Also, Increase began to produce occasional newsletters to keep network members informed and attract the interest of potential new

56. External TEE course providers include SEAN and to a lesser extent TEXT-AFRICA. Courses within Asia were written by the long-established TEE programmes in India, Pakistan, Bangladesh, Papua New Guinea, and the Arab world. Newer TEE organizations have been equipped by Increase to write their own courses, as described in Chapter 7: Ivins and Do, "New TEE Courses."

57. Participating organizations shared their experience in curriculum development; invited expert Patricia Harrison provided focused presentations and wise comment.

58. Personal communication, December 2020.

59. Teleconferencing was just becoming available in the early days of the Increase Association; the internet was making it ever more accessible as Increase was growing after 2010.

stakeholders. Strategic connections started to develop, especially with the Asia Theological Association.

Above all there was a sense of God's provision, guidance, empowerment, and blessing of relationships. Increase committee members experienced this when they met face-to-face in 2013, their only such opportunity in nearly five years though they met regularly online.[60] With the incisive help of an organizational consultant, Denise Pavey,[61] they decided that Increase should maintain its focus on Asia while also having a global voice. It should foster fresh thinking for twenty-first century TEE and expand gradually from its TEE core to engage also with other forms of church-based training. Furthermore, Increase would shift to a more structured network while retaining an organic style, and register a supporting UK charity while keeping Increase's "heart and head" in Asia.[62]

To implement these decisions the committee authorized Tim and Rachel Green, and Graham and Nicola Aylett, to establish in Asia a serving base for the work. Their October 2014 move to Kuala Lumpur in Malaysia set the stage for Increase's next period of development.

Analysis

Restarting in early 2009 as a group of like-minded friends with a vision for TEE in Asia, Increase emerged into a growing social movement galvanized by its 2010 conference. Social movements theory points to actors coming together either from a shared sense of exclusion or from a shared vision. Both were evident in Increase's relaunch. The sense of exclusion from mainstream theological education, and the polarized tone of London 2008, were quickly forgotten in the confidence created in Kathmandu 2010. The question, "What excites you about TEE?," united and motivated participants. It assured them that this was *their* safe space with others who understood them. Moreover, as with other value-oriented social movements, the participants expressed

60. The members of the Committee at this time were Richard Morris (chair), Zafar Ismail, Michael Huggins, Anneta Vysotskaya, Sungrae (Stephen) Cho, Tim Green, and Graham Aylett.

61. A business professional with long experience as a consultant, programme manager and business manager, and a good friend to Increase.

62. "Increase Network News June 2013," Increase Committee, https://www.increaseassociation.org/news-archive/55-increase-network-news-june-2013.

commitment and solidarity around their shared vision. They used the same theological training methodology and mostly the same SEAN courses. This gave them a common meeting point and language and helped to build social capital between them.

Kathmandu 2010 also demonstrated that Increase could draw on its own social resources through a strong sense of collaboration. Everyone working for the conference did so at their own expense and on their own computers. Most participants covered their own travel expenses and fees, ITEEN took care of the logistics, the Equippers ran the training tracks. Stakeholders' commitment to collaboration and the voluntary contribution of skills, time, and resources still persist as important values of Increase.[63] Increase members share not only a sense of God-given vision for TEE but also a strong trust in the leadership and a belief that involvement would also benefit their own vision, goals, and interests.[64]

After Atlanta 2006 it had proved hard to sustain Increase's forward movement. By contrast it did not slump after Kathmandu 2010. What sustained the commitment by busy volunteers who seldom met face-to-face? Here the twin factors of leadership and participant mobilization proved important in Increase as in other social movements.

Leadership was initially exercised by the committee, better described as a working group since there was no organizational structure requiring a governing body. All members played an active part, with capacity extended through the Equippers as a second circle of volunteer leaders.[65] Since these trainer-consultants were also leaders in their national TEE organizations as their prime responsibility, they kept close to the issues on the ground. Leadership was also provided by Green and Aylett, seconded part-time by a mission organization, Interserve, which covered their salaries without seeking any control over Increase.

63. The volunteer principle in TEE at a local level, where weekly TEE learning groups are nearly all led by unpaid group leaders, finds transnational expression in the Increase Association.

64. As discussed earlier in the chapter, Wood and Gray point out various aspects of collaboration and the convener role which are characteristic in collaborative networks.

65. Note that nearly all of the committee were also Equippers and formed about half of their total number.

Participants in Kathmandu 2010 were from a wide range of national, ethnic, and linguistic backgrounds but found a homophilous identity as fellow marginals in the theological scene in Asia who had something to celebrate with a shared vision. But when participant numbers doubled in Increase's next major conference in 2017, there was some tendency in such a large event for culturally and linguistically homophilous groups of participants to spend a lot of time together, especially if they could not easily communicate in English with other groups. This reduced the development of strong or even weak ties beyond their own cliques. Increase leadership is aware of these risks and conference programmes are intentionally designed to encourage healthy intermingling and interaction across cultural, language, and interest domains.

At local and national levels, TEE in Asia is almost entirely run by Asians. This is reflected in Increase with majority Asian membership. The committee and Equippers have a balance of Asians and of Westerners with long experience in Asia. However, Increase's reliance on individuals with discretionary time to give to the work, while proving successful for financial sustainability and participant mobilization, also brought an unintended consequence. Those with more time available, fluency in English and a love of computer work, often tended to be Westerners. So, by default and not by intention, over the next decade an undue proportion of Increase's work was being led by Westerners despite the membership being majority Asian. Increase is currently seeking to address this imbalance.

Increase Association – Period Three (2015–2020): Expanding Work, Evolving Structures

Narrative

As soon as Increase's small serving base was established in Malaysia with the arrival of the Ayletts and Greens, preparation began for Increase's next gathering. By now the TEE movement in Asia had its own space and voice, giving it confidence to start looking outwards and forwards. Relationships were established, and the movement was ready to move forward into reform and renewal. Hence the title, "Exploring New Horizons," which was held in Kuala Lumpur in April 2015, proved highly significant for Increase's growth.

Kuala Lumpur 2015 was significant in four respects. First, Increase took the decision to move from being a loose network to a constituted association with a structure and membership. The following core statements (Figure 14.1) were reached by a consultative process before and during the gathering:

The **vision** of Increase is to see Churches equipping all Christ's followers in their contexts, so that many millions are discipled and empowered for mission, ministry and leadership.

The **purpose** of Increase is to connect and strengthen church-based training movements across Asia and beyond. It does this in the following ways:

- build a network of good relationships
- encourage collaborative projects and partnerships
- initiate and catalyze innovative approaches
- identify and share fruitful practice
- provide support, resources, advice and training
- make a global contribution to theological education and adult learning
- connect with other church-based training associations and accrediting associations
- communicate widely the news and stories from Increase members.

The work of Increase is guided by the following core **values**:

- Sharing – through relationships and networking
- Inclusive – of all people, cultures and denominations
- Servant-hearted – in leadership and with each other
- Learning and changing – together and from each other
- Relevant – to local cultures and contexts
- Biblical – in how we work and act.

Figure 14.1. Increase vision, purpose, and values adopted in Kuala Lumpur 2015

Second, participants discussed categories of membership in the new association. Should core membership be only for TEE organizations, or extended to other church-based training programmes that fulfilled relevant criteria? The latter was agreed,[66] a mark of the TEE movement's newfound confidence, and this was important for positioning it to enrich and be enriched

66. See the Increase Association website for these criteria for core membership: https://increaseassociation.org.

by other forms of church-based theological education.[67] Crucially, core membership was restricted to national church-based training organizations within the countries of "greater Asia," a loose term allowing for spill-over to some countries bordering the region. Western organizations could affiliate as fellowship members but would not have a vote. This positioned Increase as a self-governing association of Asian organizations, which were also themselves self-governing within their own countries, accountable to their own national boards, and deciding their own curricula.[68] The voice of these national organizations had hitherto been overlooked but now, joined as an association, their corporate voice would be heard better. Thus, Increase as a transnational movement and network had coalesced and matured into something to be taken seriously.

A third significant feature of "Exploring New Horizons" is revealed by its title. How could Increase stakeholders explore new horizons, such as the ever-expanding Asian diaspora, intentionally transformative courses, digital possibilities, and interactive ways to train local TEE group leaders? Task groups were launched to work on these topics.[69]

Fourth, this gathering of Increase members from so many countries gave an opportunity to present the vision to Malaysian church leaders at a celebration dinner. At that event, Tanka Subedi, director of Nepal's TEE movement, met local Christians Martin Victor and his spouse Rina Robinson. They were already seeking a regular, reproducible, mother-tongue way to disciple Nepali migrant believers in Malaysia. This weak tie connection, meeting once at a dinner, catalyzed the rapid expansion of Nepali diaspora TEE in Malaysia which in three years grew to 380 students in sixty-three groups led by their own trained facilitators.[70] Diaspora TEE experience gained in Malaysia and

67. As of November 2020, twenty-five of Increase's twenty-eight core members are TEE organizations, but the association anticipates growing membership of other kinds of church-based training providers.

68. For other categories of membership, see the Increase website.

69. See Aylett, *Exploring New Horizons*, for the full conference proceedings.

70. Remarkable, as both TEE students and group leaders work up to twelve hours a day, seven days a week in factories or as security guards. See also Green and van Wingerden, "Diaspora," 113–14, and chapter 11 of this book: Ball and Robinson, "TEE for Discipleship of People on the Move."

elsewhere[71] was used by Equippers in Australasia, and the Diaspora TEE Task Group created guidelines now available for worldwide use.[72] This example shows how a servant network can link organizations and individuals towards achieving far-reaching goals for God's kingdom.

Thus, Kuala Lumpur 2015 was significant for Increase in moving from a network to an association. But how would the work be sustained? Increase adopted a flat organizational model with different volunteer teams empowered to carry out much of the needed work themselves but remaining accountable to the committee. An organizational diagram (Figure 14.2), deliberately non-hierarchical,[73] was approved in December 2015 and enacted in a teams' gathering the following year: "Moving Forward Together."

The teams-based structure has served the association well. The committee gives oversight and a steering hand to the ministry.[74] The Increase Equippers function as the hands and feet of Increase,[75] volunteering some time each year to help train and advise existing member organizations and also visiting new countries to encourage formation of national programmes.[76] In parallel,

71. For example, Increase Equippers Anneta Vysotskaya and Maria Vdovina, together with Central Asian and other Russian TEE workers, have helped Russian-speakers in South Korea to begin using TEE.

72. See Increase Association, *Discipling the Nations*, and chapter 11: Ball and Robinson, "TEE for Discipleship of People on the Move." The Diaspora Task Group consists of Anneta Vysotskaya, Lyn Pearson, Rina Robinson, Rachel Green, and David Ball. They found solutions to problems such as course book supply and group leader training in different countries and developed this resource to encourage TEE initiatives among diaspora.

73. This representation of Increase's structure grew out of Sungrae (Stephen) Cho's seminal suggestion in Oxford, 2013.

74. Currently (2021) the committee comprises Anneta Vysotskaya (chair, Russia), Jiries Habash (Jordan), Qaiser Julius (Pakistan), and Tanka Subedi (Nepal), with Graham Aylett and Miyung Do as coopted members.

75. The Equippers Team was renewed and expanded during the "Moving Forward Together" gathering. The Team then comprised Graham Aylett, David Ball, Richard Brown, Freda Carey, Sungrae (Stephen) Cho, Miyung Do, Tim Green, Jiries Habash, Qaiser Julius, Jackson and Janeffer Lee, Siebe Meindertsma, Lyn Pearson, Tanka Subedi, Anneta Vysotskaya, and Rick Weymouth. Since 2016, Rachel Green, Nicholas Ivins, N. D. Lama, Rosana Longgat, Wailes Rangsa, Lewis Varley, Maria Vdovina, and Rina Robinson have joined the Team, and Sungrae (Stephen) Cho, Jiries Habash, and Jackson and Janeffer Lee have left. Ewen Kitto, while not formally an Equipper, has given invaluable service. The acronym, PAGES (suggested by Rick Weymouth), summarizes Equippers' attitudes and values: Prayerful preparation; Appropriate expertise; Good listening; Encouraging; Servant heart.

76. Examples include visits to Myanmar (initially Qaiser Julius and Graham Aylett, and later Sungrae (Stephen) Cho and Siebe Meindertsma separately); Vietnam (Lyn Pearson, Graham

the Task Groups work to discern trends and create practical resources for contemporary issues such as training TEE group leaders, serving diaspora TEE, and writing transformative TEE courses. Their focus on specific projects in specific timeframes has led to tangible outputs to serve member organizations. Other teams include the Increase Trust UK, providing a registered charity and financial support, and the Intercessors team,[77] which has been of inestimable importance in providing weekly prayer updates and undergirding the whole work in prayer. God has used this team at particularly key moments to push through spiritual obstacles.[78] Increase Advisers are wise individuals who advise on matters of organizational development or educational expertise. They have also played an unplanned but pivotal role as advocates for Increase in senior circles of theological education.

Increase's next major milestone came with its 2017 Chiang Mai conference, "Empowering Churches, Equipping Disciples." With 168 participants from nearly forty countries, including a large Russian-speaking contingent, this was by far the largest conference Increase had organized. Most participants were from national TEE programmes. Non-TEE partners were also well represented but functioned on the margin as visitors or observers. Teaching in the plenaries and workshops came from Increase's own members. The sense of shared purpose and unity was strengthened by a tangible sense of the Lord's presence, especially at the closing communion service.

Aylett, and Rosana Longgat); Laos (Lyn Pearson); Japan, where Sungrae (Stephen) Cho worked hard to launch TEE; then in 2019 Graham Aylett brought different users together for a TEE consultation. Sungrae (Stephen) Cho also re-ignited TEE ministry in Indonesia after it had fallen into disuse. All visits were valuable – formation of national teams is a continuing goal.

77. As of November 2020, two teams of intercessors meet monthly by Zoom, praying in English and Korean. Jolyon Trickey has been a great encouragement as coordinator.

78. For example, prayer changed the approach to seeking a new General Secretary; and when a key Equipper was about to miss the Increase Teams' Gathering in November 2019 with crippling back pain, the Lord answered prayers. He came, with many fruitful results.

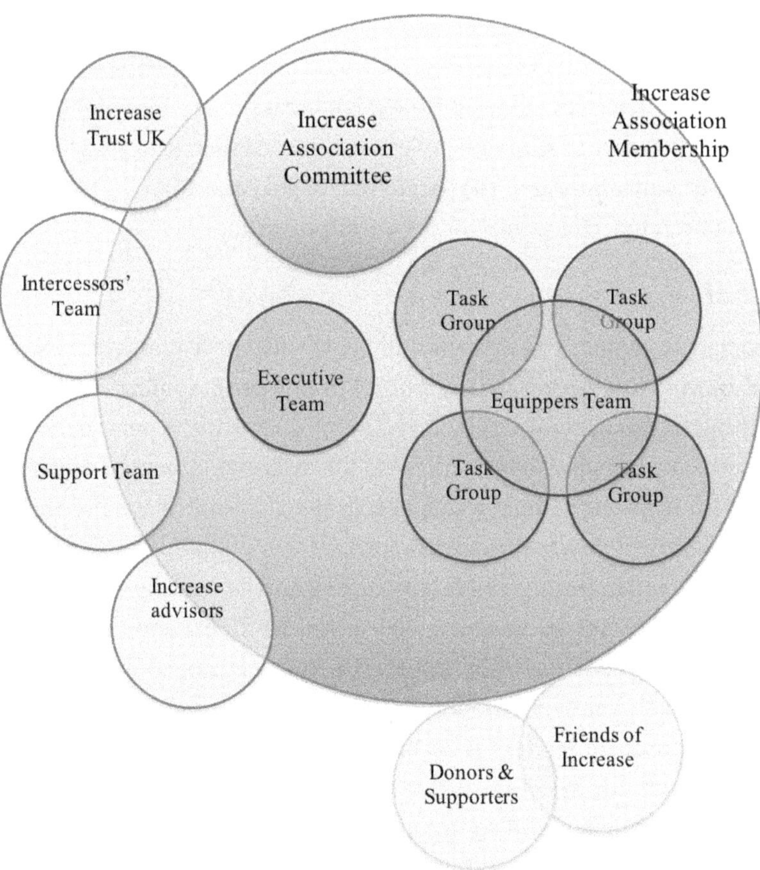

Figure 14.2. Structure of Increase teams adopted in 2016

At the conference, a writing team interviewed participants about what God was doing through TEE in Asia. Written up afterwards with further material, and published in 2018 as *TEE in Asia: Empowering Churches, Equipping Disciples*, this book attracted attention from theological educators around the world. It serves Increase's aims to "communicate widely the news and stories from Increase members" and "make a global contribution to theological education and adult learning."

In November 2019, the various Increase teams met in Istanbul and sought God's direction for the next steps. Following several years of rapid expansion, Increase needed time for consolidation. New leadership would also be needed to take over from Green and to build an executive team with a greater proportion of Asians.[79] The year 2020, with a global pandemic shutting down travel and conferences, allowed time for Increase to appoint a new executive team to be headed by Graham Aylett. It was a challenging year for Increase member organizations, but the pandemic forced experiments in online group learning both for TEE groups and for training group leaders.

Analysis

No social movement can emerge and grow without leadership. Historically, social movements have typically started in one geographical location before spreading transnationally. They owed much to a leader's personal charisma, influence, and persuasiveness. Increase was unusual in being a transnational movement from the start. It had no geographical power base and the leaders had no authority, so a hierarchical approach was implausible. The movement could only happen through wide networking and generating a sense of shared vision. What kind of leadership style was needed to expand the network and make wider connections while still serving the needs of core members?

As discussed above, Wood and Gray found that collaborative networks commonly require leaders who are open-minded, fair, and trustworthy convenors, who draw on resources to promote collaboration and use their credibility, knowledge, and communication skills to persuade stakeholders to participate.[80] Increase leadership has aspired to these qualities, along with a pastoral concern for members and dependence on God. Others must evaluate to what extent these aspirations have been realized.

Increase's executive leadership and other teams drew on their relational ties and social capital in existing networks to serve the movement. For example, Vysotskaya expanded the influence of Increase beyond Russia, drawing on her network of weak ties across the ex-Soviet bloc in an entrepreneurial way and building these into the strong ties that underlie the TEE work in Central Asia.[81] Lyn Pearson did similarly in South East Asia. Equippers used their

79. By the end of 2020, the four team members included two Asians and one more of Asian heritage. The fourth was British with years of ministry experience in Asia.

80. Wood and Gray, "Towards a Comprehensive Theory," 152–53.

81. See chapter 12: Vysotskaya and Subedi, "TEE as a Tool for Providing Theological Education to Churches Facing Persecution and Poverty," and chapter 13: Brown, "TEE in Central Asia."

influence and expertise to provide training and consultancy for national programmes, extending into pioneering contexts.[82] All exercised leadership through influence, not control, serving without financial return.[83]

Small locally based social movements attract little attention from other organizations or the media. As they grow in scope and influence this attracts more interest. Brokered connections can help in this, as described by Diani and others.[84] Increase as a social movement greatly benefitted from brokered connections. In 2012, when Increase leaders began attending conferences of the theological associations, ICETE and ATA,[85] they had no influence. But in those associations, they had pre-existing weak ties with several influential theological educators[86] who then brokered connections with other influential leaders, thus expanding the network of weak ties. This led to opportunities to give seminars, which Increase did at successive ICETE and ATA conferences.[87] Also through brokered invitations, three Increase leaders were included into ATA's accreditation commission, leading to strengthened trust and eventually to an opportunity to help make the accreditation system more relevant to TEE organizations.[88] In these ways respected educationalists[89] acted as informal patrons of Increase in extending wider connections.

However, such connections only lead to something significant if there is a sense of synergy and relevance for the concerns of both parties. As described

82. For example, Sungrae (Stephen) Cho in Japan, Indonesia, India, Myanmar, and the Philippines.

83. The Increase Association has received modest (but vital) grants; other income has come from membership fees. Increase operates on a relatively small budget, total expenditure was under US$60,000 in 2019.

84. See Diani, "'Leaders' or Brokers?" Also see Fleming, Mingo, and Chen, "Collaborative Brokerage"; Long, Cunningham, and Braithwaite, "Bridges, Brokers and Boundary Spanners."

85. ICETE (International Council for Evangelical Theological Education) is a global umbrella body for the self-governing regional bodies such as the Asia Theological Association (ATA).

86. Richard Hart, Perry Shaw, and Paul Sanders. Tim Green had met them while working in Jordan.

87. Including the ICETE conferences of 2012, 2015, and 2018, and the ATA conferences of 2016 and 2019.

88. Rick Weymouth, Graham Aylett, and Qaiser Julius are members of ATA's Commission for Accreditation and Educational Development. They were introduced by Richard Hart who had represented the TEE movement in ATA since the 1980s.

89. Patricia Harrison, with forty years of experience in TEE, has helped in many ways, including connecting the Increase Association with the ICETE Academy.

above, collaboration requires both individual interests and collective interests to be met.[90] Theological educators had tended to see TEE as largely irrelevant, but Increase's growing connections and collaborative approach enabled it to make a case for church-based theological education for all, and for seminaries to equip pastors as equippers. This case was helped by a growing awareness among senior theological educators that changes were needed in global theological education. This greater sense of felt need has drawn their attention to the alternative forms of church-based theological education espoused by Increase, resulting for instance in their helpful contributions to chapters 15–21 of this book.

Looking Ahead

Any social movement that consolidates into an organization faces the risk of stagnation. Just because it was needed at an earlier stage, is its existence still justified? If Increase disbanded tomorrow, what difference would this make to its member bodies? By 2020 Increase had grown to a membership of thirty-nine organizations and eight additional individuals. They are much better interconnected than ten years ago, and this could continue at a bilateral level if Increase disbanded, but with a loss of multilateral connections and flow of news. They would continue to benefit from the reflective thinking and training resources developed through Increase in the previous decade, but without the interconnection would find it harder to keep moving ahead in new ways.[91] Also their collective voice to the wider theological education world would be reduced were Increase to disband.

Looking forward in early 2021, and looking outwards beyond Increase's own circle, new opportunities are coming into view. First, the COVID-19 global pandemic has accelerated the self-questioning already underway in the world of theological education. This has led to growing interest in the work of Increase and new invitations to contribute to constructive discussion on the future of theological education.

90. Wood and Gray, "Toward a Comprehensive Theory," 160–61.

91. For instance, interconnections help members serve each other's diasporas effectively and share their learning from experimentation with TEE group facilitation and group leader training by Zoom following Corona virus restrictions.

Second, Increase's defined purpose is "to connect and strengthen church-based training movements across Asia and beyond." Non-TEE church-based training providers are welcome in Increase, whether by membership or by partnership. The need is becoming ever more apparent for different and disconnected providers of church-based training to work together. Together, they may offer a more effective and integrated way to equip God's people.

Third, the phrase "Asia and beyond" in Increase's purpose statement already includes diaspora TEE for Asians beyond Asia. In 2020 national TEE teams became established in Australia and New Zealand to serve both the diaspora and indigenous Christians, expanding Increase's already generous understanding of greater Asia to include the Asia-Pacific region. The 2020s could well see new national TEE teams established in Europe to serve both nationals and Asian diaspora. How should Increase relate to these? Should Increase shift to becoming a worldwide organization? Or should it remain Asia-focused but helping to foster similar church-based training associations in other continents? Exciting times!

Conclusion

Studies in relation to Christian movements often focus on theological, missiological, leadership, and organizational development dimensions. This chapter has chosen to draw on less well known yet valuable sociological lenses. It has presented the story of Increase from inception to early 2021 with analysis using concepts from social movement and social network theory.

However, a sociological lens can only describe actors on the visible stage of human activity. It cannot perceive the divine director behind the scenes. The authors of this chapter are convinced that God's hand has been evident in helping Increase to strengthen the body of Christ in Asia and beyond, through TEE and other forms of church-based discipling and leadership training. "Not to us, LORD, not to us but to your name be the glory, because of your love and faithfulness" (Ps 115:1 NIV).[92]

92. Happily, this psalm includes (in the NRSV) the verses, "May the LORD give you increase, both you and your children. May you be blessed by the LORD, who made heaven and earth." The psalm is precious to us, and these verses are our prayer for you, the reader (Ps 115:14–15 NRSV).

Bibliography

Aylett, Graham, ed. *Exploring New Horizons: Working Together for Church-Based Training in Asia.* Proceedings of a conference held in Kuala Lumpur, Malaysia, by Increase Association, 20–25 April 2015. https://www.increaseassociation.org/images/downloads/exploring-new-horizons.pdf.

Aylett, Graham, and Tim Green. "Theological Education by Extension (TEE) as a Tool for Twenty-First Century Mission." In *Reflecting on and Equipping for Christian Mission*, edited by Stephen Bevans, Teresa Chai, J. Nelson Jennings, Knud Jørgensen, and Dietrich Werner, 59–78. Oxford: Regnum, 2015.

Bekele, Anna. "Islamist Activism through the Lens of Social Science." In *Meeting the Ideological Challenge of Islamism: How to Combat Modern Radical Islam*, edited by Anna Bekele and Patrick Sookhdeo, 113–34. McClean: Isaac Publishing, 2015.

Benford, Robert D. "Frame Disputes within the Nuclear Disarmament Movement." *Social Forces* 71, no. 3 (1993): 677–701.

Borgatti, Stephen P., and Virginie Lopez-Kidwell. "Network Theory." In *The Sage Handbook of Social Network Analysis*, edited by John P. Scott and Peter Carrington, 40–54. London: SAGE, 2011.

Bourdieu, Pierre. "The Forms of Capital." In *Readings in Economic Sociology*, edited by Nicole W. Biggart, translated by R. Nice, 280–91. Malden: Blackwell, 1983; repr. 2002.

Burt, Ronald S. "The Contingent Value of Social Capital." *Administrative Science Quarterly* (1997): 339–65.

———. *Structural Holes: The Social Structure of Competition.* Cambridge: Harvard University Press, 1992.

Clemens, Elisabeth S. "Organizational Form as Frame: Collective Identity and Political Strategy in the American Labor Movement, 1880–1920." In *Comparative Perspectives on Social Movements: Political Opportunities, Mobilizing Structures, and Cultural Framings*, edited by Doug McAdam, John D. McCarthy and Mayer N. Zald, 205–26. Cambridge: Cambridge University Press, 1996.

Coleman, James S. "Social Capital in the Creation of Human Capital." *American Journal of Sociology* 94 (1988): S95–S120.

Committee on Bible Translation (CBT), ed. *Holy Bible: New International Version.* London: Hodder & Stoughton, 2011.

della Porta, Donatella. *Social Movements, Political Violence, and the State: A Comparative Analysis of Italy and Germany.* New York: Cambridge University Press, 1995.

Diani, Mario. "Social Movements and Collective Action." In *The Sage Handbook of Social Network Analysis*, edited by John P. Scott and Peter Carrington, 223–35. London: SAGE, 2011.

———. "'Leaders' or Brokers? Positions and Influence in Social Movement Networks." In *Social Movements and Networks: Relational Approaches to Collective Action*, edited by Mario Diani and Doug McAdam, 105–22. Oxford: Oxford University Press, 2003.

Diani, Mario, and Doug McAdam, eds. *Social Movements and Networks: Relational Approaches to Collective Action*. Oxford: Oxford University Press, 2003.

Everton, Sean F. "Networks and Religion: Ties That Bind, Loose, Build-Up, and Tear Down." *Journal of Social Structure* 16 (2015): 1–34. https://www.cmu.edu/joss/content/articles/volume16/Everton.pdf.

Fleming, Lee, Santiago Mingo, and David Chen. "Collaborative Brokerage, Generative Creativity, and Creative Success." *Administrative Science Quarterly* 52, no. 3 (2007): 443–75.

Fukuyama, Francis. "Social Capital and the Global Economy." *Foreign Affairs* 74, no. 5 (1995): 89–103.

Granovetter, Mark S. "The Strength of Weak Ties." *The American Journal of Sociology* 78, no. 6 (1973): 1360–80.

Green, Tim, and Hanna-Ruth van Wingerden. "Diaspora: Discipling the Nations." In *TEE in Asia: Empowering Churches, Equipping Disciples*, edited by Hanna-Ruth van Wingerden, Tim Green, and Graham Aylett, 111–16. Carlisle: Langham Global Library, 2021.

Haines, Herbert H. *Against Capital Punishment: The Anti-Death Penalty Movement in America, 1972–1994*. New York: Oxford University Press, 1996.

Increase Association. "Discipling the Nations in the Diaspora: Using TEE Courses in Multiple Languages." 2020. https://www.increaseassociation.org/images/Discipling_the_Nations_Booklet.pdf.

Lin, Nan. *Social Capital: A Theory of Social Structure and Action*. New York: Cambridge University Press, 2001.

Long, Janet C., Frances C. Cunningham, and Jeffrey Braithwaite. "Bridges, Brokers and Boundary Spanners in Collaborative Networks: A Systematic Review." *BMC Health Services Research* 13, no. 1 (2013): 1–13.

McPherson, Miller, Lynn Smith-Lovin, and James M. Cook. "Birds of a Feather: Homophily in Social Networks." *Annual Review of Sociology* 27, no. 1 (2001): 415–44.

Nooteboom, Bart. "Collaboration, Trust, and the Structure of Relationships." In *Micro-Foundations for Innovation Policy*, edited by Bart Nooteboom and E. Stam, 199–218. Amsterdam: Amsterdam University Press, 2008.

Putnam, Robert D. "Bowling Alone: America's Declining Social Capital." *Journal of Democracy* 6, no. 1 (1995): 65–78.

Schilling, Melissa A., and Corey C. Phelps. "Interfirm Collaboration Networks: The Impact of Large-Scale Network Structure on Firm Innovation." *Management Science* 53, no. 7 (2007): 1113–26.

Snow, David A., Sarah A. Soule, and Hanspeter Kriesi, eds. *The Blackwell Companion to Social Movements*. Malden: Blackwell, 2004.

———. "Mapping the Terrain." In *The Blackwell Companion to Social Movements*, edited by David A. Snow, Sarah A. Soule, and Hanspeter Kriesi, 3–16. Malden: Blackwell, 2004.

Spencer, Stephen. "Seminaries and Discipleship: Exploring Future Directions." *Journal of Anglican Studies* (2020): 1–15. https://www.cambridge.org/core/journals/journal-of-anglican-studies.

Sutton, Philip W., and Stephen Vertigans. "Militant Islam in Local, National and Transnational Networks." In *Militant Islam: A Sociology of Characteristics, Causes and Consequences*, edited by Stephen Vertigans, 35–54. Abingdon: Routledge, 2009.

Uzzi, Brian, and Jarrett Spiro. "Collaboration and Creativity: The Small World Problem." *American Journal of Sociology* 111, no. 2 (2005): 447–504.

van Wingerden, Hanna-Ruth, Tim Green, and Graham Aylett, eds. *TEE in Asia: Empowering Churches, Equipping Disciples*. Carlisle: Langham Global Library, 2021.

Vertigans, Stephen, ed. *Militant Islam: A Sociology of Characteristics, Causes and Consequences*. Abingdon: Routledge, 2009.

Vyssotskaia, Anneta. "Theological Education in the Context of Persecution and Economic Hardship: Focus on TEE in Central Asia." *International Journal for Religious Freedom* 5, no. 2 (2012): 111–22.

Wellman, Barry, Dimitrina Dimitrova, Zack Hayat, Ying Mo Guang, and Lilia Smale. "Networking Scholars in a Networked Organization." In *Contemporary Perspectives on Organizational Social Networks*, edited by Daniel J. Brass, Giuseppe (Joe) Labianca, Ajay Mehra, Daniel S. Halgin, and Stephen P. Borgatti. Research in the Sociology of Organizations, 479–97. Bingley: Emerald, 2014.

White, Aaronette M. "Talking Feminist, Talking Black: Micromobilization Processes in a Collective Protest against Rape." *Gender & Society* 13, no. 1 (1999): 77–100.

Wiktorowicz, Quintan. "Introduction: Islamic Activism and Social Movement Theory." In *Islamic Activism: A Social Movement Theory Approach*, edited by Wiktorowicz Quintan, 1–33. Bloomington: Indiana University Press, 2004.

———, ed. *Islamic Activism: A Social Movement Theory Approach*. Bloomington: Indiana University Press, 2004.

Wood, Donna J., and Barbara Gray. "Toward a Comprehensive Theory of Collaboration." *The Journal of Applied Behavioral Science* 27, no. 2 (1991): 139–62.

Part C

Church Leadership and Theological Education Perspectives on TEE

15

Reflections on TEE from the World Evangelical Alliance

Thomas Schirrmacher[1]

Introduction

This chapter offers a reflective comment on TEE from the perspective of the global church as represented by the World Evangelical Alliance (WEA).

In the Theological Commission of the WEA, we often discuss TEE. Vast numbers of people are being baptized in Christian churches each year, with no Christian background, and the number of trained leaders is not growing in proportion. The result is that many new converts are not discipled and leave our churches again. And this does not mean they lose their faith, but they often move away from orthodox Christian faith towards heresy. When we do not train good leaders, bad leaders arise.

The WEA sees TEE training as one response to this challenge and as an integral part of the evangelical world. Without the work of TEE starting in the late 1960s and 1970s, there would be an absence of thousands of evangelical leaders today.

1. Secretary General, Secretary General of the World Evangelical Alliance. Some material in this chapter was given by Dr. Schirrmacher as a special address in Kathmandu 2010. https://www.increaseassociation.org/news-archive/35-dr-thomas-schirrmacher-s-address-in-kathmandu-october-2010.

Theological Education Was Made for Man, Not Man for Theological Education[2]

The COVID-19 crisis struck the world of schooling, education, and academia. At Harvard University and other elite universities, there have been two delivery systems, the traditional campus-based and the online system. The online programmes have their own deans and their degrees have been regarded as inferior. But with the restrictions of COVID-19, on-campus students have had to transition to the online programme only to find that they have to work harder to keep up! In India, school programmes are now broadcast on television, and unexpectedly millions of parents are watching and learning things they could not learn as children. Hybrid education, mixing all kinds of ways to learn, has suddenly become possible. In many countries "homeschooling" has lost its negative meaning.

As evangelicals we should not be confined to public and politically correct categories of education. We need to use any and every means to overcome biblical illiteracy at every level and to help future leaders grow spiritually and in knowledge so that they can guide God's flock and disciple and educate the next generation of leaders. I like to apply Jesus's saying about the Sabbath[3] to theological education: "Theological education was made for man, not man for theological education." All believers willing to learn should be offered a wealth of ways to learn so that they find something that fits their contexts, their personalities, their personal situations, the situations of their local churches, and the churches in their ethnic or national surroundings.

Thus, I especially love chapter 10, "TEE and Campus-Based Training in Partnership." To start with, the chapter sounds somewhat lacking in self-confidence, but then it moves forward towards real partnership and becomes more and more bold. TEE needs to be convinced of its proven three pillars of personal study, group meeting, and practical application, and yet for the sake of its students to offer any cooperation and partnership to other means of education. These partnerships will improve TEE, and they will also, even more, open new doors for traditional educators to learn from TEE's global experience.

2. This first section was written over Christmas 2020, in response to chapters 1–14.

3. Mark 2:27, "Then he said to them, 'The Sabbath was made for man, not man for the Sabbath.'"

The same is true of chapter 8, "TEE and Transformation in the Digital Age," which includes the section, "The Future Generation Is Here Already." I think it would be ironic if TEE, which began as a renewal movement for theological education, failed to take up the challenges and the advantages of new technology and the new habits of the younger generation and became "traditional." This chapter sets out possibilities carefully and thoroughly.

Out of the wealth of chapters from 1 to 14, let me underline three further elements I find especially heartening.

Chapter 2 speaks about "The Character and Mission of God." In my books, *Missio Dei*,[4] and *Biblical Foundations for 21st Century World Mission: 69 Theses*,[5] I emphasize that God himself is the first missionary. He does not wait for human invitation but sends himself anywhere people and their problems are to be found. Following God's own character, we are not called only to the nice places of this world, and to well-paying customers, but into any situation, no matter how problematic it is. Wherever the Holy Spirit goes and convinces men and women to submit their lives to our Lord Jesus Christ, church, mission, and theological education have to follow. TEE as a flexible, agile form of theological education may be especially suitable.

This becomes relevant in two chapters that are close to my heart.

Chapter 11 highlights "TEE for Discipleship of People on the Move," and chapter 12 highlights TEE for "Churches Facing Persecution and Poverty." Mission, church, theological education, and thus TEE have to follow people where they are. We cannot expect them to leave their situation and get trained in a nice campus in a rich and persecution-free country. If they are on the move, we have to be on the move. If they are persecuted, we have to provide tools that fit their bitter reality and adapt to what is possible. And believers and churches in poverty-stricken contexts need Bible knowledge, growth, and leadership skills as much as anyone else. The Holy Spirit does not depend on

4. Thomas Schirrmacher, *Missio Dei: God's Missional Nature*, World of Theology Series 10 (Bonn: Verlag für Kultur und Wissenschaft, 2017), https://www.bucer.de/fileadmin/dateien/Dokumente/Buecher/WoT_10-Thomas_Schirrmacher-Missio_Dei.pdf.

5. Thomas Schirrmacher, *Biblical Foundations for 21st Century World Mission: 69 Theses toward an Ongoing Global Reformation*, World of Theology Series 11 (Bonn: Verlag für Kultur und Wissenschaft, 2018), https://www.bucer.de/fileadmin/dateien/Dokumente/Buecher/WoT_11_ThSchirrmacher_-_Biblical_Foundations_-_69_Biblical_Theses.pdf.

the income of a person – the gospel is given free of charge – and thus discipling and education must be adapted and available in situations where believers struggle to survive physically.

As bishop I represent the *Communio Messianica*, a global communion of people from seventy countries who found their way from Islam to Christ under indigenous leadership. Therefore, I know by experience how important TEE is to provide training to them wherever political pressure and turmoil scatters them.

Reflections on TEE from My Experience[6]

Introduction

My father became a Christian at the age of thirty-four from an atheistic background. At that age, he was said to be "too old" for the ministry, although nobody could really tell you why. However, the general understanding was that by that age you should stay in your secular profession. So my father prayed that his children would go into the pastoral ministry. When my father was sixty-three, he retired as professor of engineering and started to develop Christian schools. He retired from this job twenty-five years later when he was 88! He always told me that he would have loved a theological training programme to study while teaching at university.

My senior pastor was fifty-five years old when he became a pastor. He became one of the most successful evangelical pastors we ever had in Germany. His call to pastoral ministry came after a high-salaried career in industry, but the first church he served with hesitated to hire him because he had no theological training, nor a means of getting one. When I was already a professor of theology, I became his junior pastor, and I learned a lot. He always urged me, "Thomas, someone like me, starting church ministry at fifty-five, needs some way to get training on the job. I have run big businesses. Does that mean I shouldn't become a leader in the church?"

I myself went to study theology for four years. Most of the teachers I had while training had not been in active church ministry for twenty to thirty years.

6. From an address to the Increase Association Conference, "Twenty-First Century TEE in Asia: Challenges and Opportunities," Kathmandu, Nepal, 5 October 2010.

They were seminary professors. Later I was invited to speak at one of the best residential schools in Germany. I had been in pastoral ministry for twelve years, and they invited me to give a guest lecture. The eleven faculty members there had a total of only ten years' pastoral ministry experience! Looking back, I realized that during my training I had been taught by "medical doctors" who had never actually practiced themselves. Their teaching was theoretical.

During the socialist era, the church in East Germany was virtually wiped out. Everyone, including theological students, wanted to move from East Germany to West Germany because of economic hardship. The seminary I was involved with, Martin Bucer Seminary (officially Martin Bucer European School of Theology and Research Institutes) planted several of our TEE centres in East Germany. There was much debate about this. But when the best students go to big seminaries in the West, they do not return. Before long even the state church thanked us for helping top leaders to stay in the region.

During my time in the Theological Commission, I was aware that our biggest theological problem is not to define our theology, but to make sure that every new believer has opportunity to understand the basics of our Christian faith. If only the best-educated and affluent people know their theology, they will become more and more knowledgeable. But we will lose millions, even while we may rejoice at the huge numbers apparently coming to Christian faith. We must not let this happen! We are passionate that all believers should read their Bible, study the world around them, and become solid, mature, world Christians.

I have also served on the WEA's Religious Liberty Commission, founded to fight persecution and work for religious freedom in the political realm. This is an integral part of WEA's history. For example, in 1849, a high-ranking commission of the newly founded WEA visited the Sultan of Turkey on behalf of Christians there. The topic of persecution becomes more important year by year and TEE provides a means of theological education under persecution.

Traditional reasons for TEE

I see three kinds of reasons for TEE that were evident from its beginnings. The first could be called theological reasons. Consider Jesus's calling and training of his disciples, the foundation of his church. Jesus prayed, and called them "that they might be with him and that he might send them out" (Mark 3:14

NIV). They lived together with Jesus, they had private lectures, public lectures, personal experience, counselling, and practical experience – they had it all! In terms of skills training, take preaching as an example. First, Jesus preached, and they watched him. The next time, Jesus and the twelve were preaching. Then Jesus was not preaching, but the twelve were sent out and later reported back. At this stage they went out for just a short time. We had power over the bad spirits! they said. Jesus, the theological teacher, told them, That's true. Not wrong, but you have your priorities in the wrong order.[7] In Jesus's programme of education for the twelve, there is a theological basis for TEE: the content of the teaching and the demonstration of how to live and how to serve belong together. We do not teach theory, but we teach and model how we want to live and minister together. TEE is a great way to do this.

Then there are practical reasons for TEE. Many potential leaders are too old for traditional campus-based training. Where I trained, there were fifty students aged eighteen to nineteen, all from Christian families, none of them new converts. This did not really work when I was a student, and it does not work today. In addition, we need to make sure that we are training those who will be people of influence. When I taught in a residential setting, I discovered I was not training future leaders. I thought, "Why not train those in the church who are already leading, who will immediately use what I am teaching them?" And in many global contexts, those already leading churches are desperately needed in those leadership roles. It should not be the case, but sometimes a church has just one key leader. TEE offers a pathway to enable training in context, on the job.

Financial considerations also point towards TEE and similar kinds of training, since the cost of campus-based facilities for leadership training is prohibitive. Quality TEE is not cheap, but the investment required for a single residential campus could provide support for a national TEE programme with a wide reach.

7. Luke 10:17–20.

Conclusion

Beyond the relevance and scope of TEE as outlined above, there are further reasons for using TEE as we seek to respond to theological education challenges in the twenty-first century. TEE as it developed in Guatemala was not a response to persecution. Thank God for free countries! But because TEE is not so high profile, it is suitable for difficult situations. Studying part-time means you do not have to leave your work. This is a major reason for TEE. Persecution is a basic theological topic – it was promised from the beginning. The New Testament reminds us again and again that persecution should not be something we look for, and certainly should not be something we deserve because we have done wrong, but the New Testament and the experience of the church through the centuries shows that it is a normal thing to be persecuted. Jesus was, and he promised we would be also. I urge you to see TEE as a much-needed answer for theological training under persecution.

And finally, we need context-based training in today's globalized world where extremism and violence stemming from fundamentalism are grievous realities. Globally, Christianity has become more peaceful over the last fifty years. We will not use force to propagate the faith, and we have an Ethics Code for Mission, which is vital as other religions may use more violence. But this creates theological and practical questions we have to discuss. What if the state does not protect you as a Christian? Does a church usually teach its members how to defend themselves against a machine gun attack? Not usually, so Christians may be easy targets. We now live in a world where just telling others what we believe is considered as fundamentalism, even though we use no violence. My experience is that this kind of problem can only be solved by those encountering this reality.

We need leaders who are able to lead their churches in these situations, and that means we need training in their own context. I am convinced that the issues arising from living with different religious communities is one of the major tasks we face.

16

Reflections on TEE from the Anglican Communion

Stephen Spencer[1]

Introduction

This chapter offers reflection on the capacity of TEE to help the church in its task of training and forming an adequate number of suitably equipped people for ministry leadership, and it highlights things that can be learned from theological colleges and seminaries.

The Challenges and Opportunities of Theological Education for the Church

In an earlier role it was my privilege to pay several visits to a rural diocese in northwest Tanzania. At the diocesan headquarters there were a few offices, some clergy houses, a multi-purpose hall, and a small theological college. With one resident staff member and a handful of students, this was a struggling institution. The compound lacked a safe water supply and water had to be fetched from a distant well in drums on the back of a truck. The college library, such as it was, was kept in a bookcase in the principal's office. There was no access to online resources except through mobile phones. Transport to placements was expensive and therefore limited. Before each of my visits I

1. Director for Theological Education in the Anglican Communion.

wondered if the college would still be functioning when I got there. Somehow it managed to keep going but appeared less and less viable.

But this was not the only theological education taking place in the diocese. One of the ordained pastors was running a TEE programme across a dozen local churches. He took me to visit some of the TEE groups. Using handbooks that had been published in Swahili a decade earlier, he was guiding the learning of Christians who were clearly committed, disciplined, energized, and empowered by the experience. It was inspiring to witness these local church groups being gradually transformed by meeting together, sharing stories of their daily lives, working through the handbooks, praying, and then putting into practice an aspect of their learning in the week ahead. Furthermore, for a poor rural diocese it had proved to be a sustainable form of education. The only financial investment was support for part of the pastor's time and the costs of copying the handbooks.

I came away from my visits more worried than ever about the future of its residential theological education and, by contrast, increasingly enthused about the potential of TEE to transform the life of that diocese.

Since then, I have become aware that this is only one (fairly extreme) expression of wider trends in theological education across the world. When I took up my current role of supporting theological education across the Anglican Communion, I quickly became aware of the pressures that many theological colleges and seminaries are under. Between 2018 and the start of the COVID-19 lockdown in March 2020, I was able to visit colleges and seminaries in Kenya, Uganda, the USA, Egypt, Sudan, South Sudan, South Africa, Australia, Hong Kong, and Malaysia, as well as a number of colleges in England and Ireland. Colleagues in the Anglican Communion office also have contact with colleges and courses in South Asia and Latin America.[2] From these visits and contacts it has become clear that in general, as one colleague in Malaysia put it, theological colleges and seminaries are at a crossroads. As mentioned in earlier chapters, their inherited pattern of working is becoming less and less sustainable: churches, dioceses, and districts are no longer sending students in sufficient numbers to sustain the life of many of the institutions. This is partly because the cost of sending a student and

2. For information on TEAC (the department for Theological Education in the Anglican Communion) see https://www.anglicancommunion.org/theology/theological-education.aspx.

their dependents to full-time residential training is increasingly prohibitive, and also because students themselves in many parts of the world are unable or unwilling to relocate to a college for two or three years of study. Instead, dioceses and large churches are often setting up their own non-residential and part-time training schemes to compensate, some of good quality and others less so. Colleges, on the other hand, are needing to diversify their business in order to remain solvent, sometimes setting up extension study programmes, or letting out their accommodation for rental income, or offering a range of non-theological programmes. While these are creative responses, many have the effect of distancing the college from its core constituency, the sending churches and dioceses, which makes the latter even less inclined to send them their students for training.[3] Long-term viability is in question.

Second, though, I have also become aware of a growing, innovative and promising movement in theological education. As with the TEE course in rural Tanzania, this is context-based theological education, where students are primarily located in church and home settings rather than within theological institutions. A precursor of this has been in existence in the UK since the 1980s and is now responsible for training over half of Anglican ordination candidates. The institutions doing this used to be called non-residential part-time courses but are better described as context-based programmes whose students, either full-time or part-time, are located in churches, workplaces, and homes and only go to their college one day or one evening a week for lectures and workshops, and attend three residential weekends per term for more classes, worship, and work in small groups. The content of the education, especially in the assignments, is related to the student's context, making it more relevant and engaged than that in many residential institutions. Also, the level of commitment required from students for this form of education is huge, for they must balance their studies with home and work life. As someone who was a tutor on such context-based programmes for many years, I can attest to their quality, often producing ministers of resilience and imagination.

But these programmes still remove the student from their home church community for classroom learning, so are only partially context-based. A more

3. The generic nature of financial pressures on colleges and seminaries across the Anglican Communion is also discussed by Martyn Percy. See Percy, "Context, Character and Challenges," 500–501.

thoroughgoing approach is found in the growth of church-based TEE in many parts of the Majority World, beginning in Guatemala in the 1960s and spreading through Latin America, Africa, and Asia in subsequent decades, as described in chapter 4. The clear and engaging account in the book, *TEE in Asia*, tells this story in much greater detail for one continent.[4] The richly informative chapters in this present book, furthermore, provide academic commentary on all this, also showing that it can operate at higher as well as lower academic levels. All these writings show how context-based theological education is becoming increasingly available to God's people whatever their age, background, and educational level. The spread and development of TEE's reach across Asia, the most populous continent on earth, including in regions where Christians are persecuted (see ch. 12), is a wonder to behold. The translations of SEAN TEE courses, the bedrock of this movement in many places, into more than seventy languages is an extraordinary achievement (see ch. 11). Its "agility to serve the theological education needs of churches in varied and changing contexts" is another (ch. 13). The role of Increase Association in the movement has been a great boon (ch. 14). One story from chapter 11 beautifully illustrates the fruits of all this:

> Abhishek [from Nepal] was working in Malaysia for three years as a construction worker. While in Malaysia he completed [SEAN's] six course books on the Life of Christ as a student and showed leadership potential. He trained as a TEE group leader. For two years Abhishek led two TEE groups. On returning to Nepal, he introduced TEE to his church and started TEE classes in his village. Today Abhishek has four TEE classes in Nepal.[5]

What, then, can theological education in general learn from this grounded and promising movement?

A Gift to Theological Education

It is clear from the previous chapters that the heart of church-based TEE is a simple but transformative educational pedagogy (ch. 3), or "andragogy" (as

4. van Wingerden, Green and Aylett, eds., *TEE in Asia*.

5. See chapter 11: Ball and Robinson, "TEE for Discipleship of People on the Move," 310.

Shaw describes it in ch. 5, reflecting terminology current in adult education literature), involving three basic steps. It is an approach that can be replicated in different places, which explains its growth. I have already begun to reflect on its significance elsewhere.[6] In the following paragraphs I want to highlight and applaud its effectiveness for the learner and draw out its innate consonance with Scripture. It is, I believe, an approach that theological education in general should emulate. In the final section I turn to a couple of lessons the theological education sector could offer the TEE movement.

From the outset we should recognize how the three-step approach flips the relationship between classroom learning and personal study. An earlier chapter quotes Abeysekera and Dawson on what is meant by flipping the classroom, describing three characteristics: "(1) move most information-transmission teaching out of class; (2) use class time for learning activities that are active and social; and (3) require students to complete pre- and/or post-class activities to fully benefit from in-class work"[7] (ch. 6). This is seen in the three steps of TEE.

- The first step of personal study is usually a learner working through a carefully prepared worksheet, using active learning, often in a question and answer format, rather than just passive reading, in order to engage with Scripture, gain new knowledge, and start connecting it with their own life experience, which then becomes a springboard to the next learning step.
- This is the group meeting in which members share what they learned in the first step, reflect on their own experience, and learn from each other. They study Scripture together, which a group leader facilitates (rather than giving a lecture). Members also prepare for the third step by discussing how they will put the lesson into practice.
- The third step is practical application, which is all about finding a way to practically express what was learned in steps 1 and 2. This happens in a member's daily life at home, church, work, or in the wider community. Practical application is the goal of TEE. In this kind of way, the student undertakes a specific assignment, whether for personal life or for ministry.

6. Spencer, "Seminaries and Discipleship."

7. Abeysekera and Dawson, "Motivation and Cognitive Load," 3.

The great merit of this approach is that it engages four dimensions of learning (as Shaw in ch. 5 argues). It is concerned with the learning of the mind, from the handbook-based study of the first step, and so is about *knowing*. It is concerned with who the learner becomes, with changes within their own person, especially through the interaction of the group meetings, and so is all about their *being*. It is concerned with enhancing how the learner connects with strangers and friends, again through the meetings, and so is all about their *relating*. Finally it is concerned with how they live, in particular with what they do as a result of their learning, through the practical application, and so is all about their *doing*. In these ways it is formative in a whole-of-life or "holistic" way. Shaw elaborates on this helpfully:

> The three-pronged approach of TEE (personal study, group meeting, and practical application) is highly conducive to holistic learning in all of the cognitive, affective, and behavioural domains. The relaxed environment of group meetings provides emotional connection; this positive affect together with the context-sensitivity of most TEE courses has great potential for promoting deep learning. TEE places a high emphasis on practical application and reflection-in-action, key components of experiential learning. The elements of andragogical theory [as distinct from pedagogical theory of children's education] are readily seen in the learner-orientation, practical focus, respect for life experience, contextual relevance, and mutual learning processes that are core emphases within TEE (ch. 5, 141).

Furthermore, such andragogy has important consonance with the kind of learning we see in Scripture. One of the best examples is the account of the resurrected Jesus walking with Cleopas and his companion on the road to Emmaus (Luke 24:13–35), already briefly mentioned in chapter 1. It is a pivotal passage, coming between Luke's account of Jesus's life and death in his gospel and his account of the birth and growth of the church in the book of Acts. It has also become a paradigmatic passage for Christian learning in many different contexts (e.g. the Emmaus learning resources produced by the Church of England[8]). When we ask how the two disciples were educated and formed

8. See the series: *Emmaus: The Way of Faith* (London: Church House Publishing, 2003–2012).

as they walked with the stranger to the village of Emmaus, we can identify an interactive process with the same three steps.

The first step is seen in the way they discussed "all these things that have happened," which was repeated and expanded in response to the stranger's initial question to them. This also included taking in where they were, the third day after the events, being their context on the road as they approached the village and entered the home; and it included sharing their hopes and disappointments with the stranger. This first element can be described as one of "taking in" – taking in where they are, taking in their context, a kind of "seeing" as described within the threefold pedagogical process of Roman Catholic social teaching.

The second step is the way they were sharply challenged ("How foolish you are . . .") and then guided by someone who knew Scripture and tradition and helped them to interpret and understand what had happened through that. This was a reflective step in which their feelings as well as their understanding were caught up in the interaction, as they later admitted after their guest had gone ("Were not our hearts burning within us?"). This can be summed up as a "taking stock" of the ways Scripture and tradition spoke into their contextual realities, described as "judging" within the threefold pedagogical process of Roman Catholic social teaching.

A third step is seen in the way they extended hospitality to the stranger who was walking with them, through sharing a meal, and after he left, through acting immediately on what they had learned by returning to Jerusalem and telling others what had happened, a widening of the net of learning. This third step can be described as one of "taking action," of working with God to bring about God's will in that place, the "acting" stage within Roman Catholic social teaching (hence the name of this process as "See, Judge, Act").[9]

Here, then, is a great gift from TEE to all those engaged in educating and equipping the people of God for his mission; a three-step holistic and scriptural approach that can be used across the board, not only for designated TEE programmes but within all adult theological education, from discipleship formation and lay ministry training through to ordination training, at higher as well as lower academic levels. It is tried and tested, it is growing in many parts of the world, it is economically sustainable, and it is increasingly available for the church as a whole.

9. See, for example, Cuff, *Love in Action*, chapter 8.

Lessons From Institutional Theological Education

If the weakness of many established colleges and seminaries has been their disconnection from the life of the local church, one of their strengths has been their connection with the community of international scholarship. With teaching staff trained in the different disciplines of theology and often with well-stocked libraries and access to online resources, they offer their students rich opportunities for positive critical engagement with Scripture and tradition. Such opportunities can provide those students with strong foundations for dealing with challenges to faith from secularism and other worldviews. They can make valuable contributions to the church, challenging complacency and presenting the Christian faith in a structured and academically rigorous way. Jesus himself, after all, sharply challenged Cleopas and his companion, as we have already seen, before "beginning with Moses and all the prophets" and interpreting "to them the things about himself in all the Scriptures" (Luke 24:27 NRSV).

In his chapter in this book, Shaw helpfully describes how one of the most common critiques of TEE has been the claim that it focuses just on lower order thinking:

> Certainly, the older style of TEE with its rigid adherence to programmed learning often erred towards an emphasis on the knowledge and understanding levels. In addition, the natural tendency of "high power distance" societies to respect the elders as authoritative[10] can lead students in much of the world to seek the "right answer" in rote-remembering the text and repeating what is given in the answers section of the course.[11]

But he then adds that:

> However, as TEE has continued to develop and align with emerging educational research there has been a growing awareness of the importance of challenging students to higher-order thinking.

10. See Hofstede and Hofstede, *Cultures and Organizations: Software of the Mind*, 3rd ed., 61.
11. Chapter 5: Shaw, "The Educational Efficacy of TEE – Part 1," 128.

> Analytic and synthetic question design[12] is a crucial component of quality TEE texts.[13]

It is in this area that the TEE movement can learn from institutional colleges that have deep experience of providing environments where analytic and synthetic thinking can happen in a constructive way. This has often been through bringing students into residential settings, where such support can happen intensively and in the context of daily prayer and worship. But this does not have to be through long-term residence, as in traditional patterns of residential training: it can be in a series of short intensive periods of residence, as in the weekend conference programmes provided by many colleges across the Anglican Communion.

The TEE movement can also learn from the discipline-based approaches of these institutions. They often facilitate in-depth study of Scripture, Christian history, liturgy, doctrine, pastoral care and ministry with their respective methodologies. These allow critical understanding of the different ingredients of Christian faith and life which make up the rich and complex phenomenon of Christian mission. There have, of course, been issues with students only gaining understanding of various disciplines and not being able to see how they fit together in the big picture. Discipline-based studies need to be supplemented with integrative studies, which allow students to grasp how the different elements of Christian Scripture, tradition, and practice are part of one movement, the mission of God in which the church is privileged to participate. But as in cooking, there needs to be understanding of the nature and properties of these individual ingredients before there can be a full and rich understanding of the dish as a whole, in this case the *missio Dei*. Colleges and seminaries have extensive and valuable resources to offer the TEE movement in this task. There is, then, a need for a new partnership between these two parties, the theological colleges and seminaries on the one hand and the TEE movement located in church-based training programmes on the other, so that the aspiration of the *Cape Town Commitment* can be fulfilled, namely: "The mission of the church

12. Shaw, *Transforming Theological Education*, 202–207.

13. Chapter 5: Shaw, "The Educational Efficacy of TEE – Part 1," 128.

is to serve the mission of God, and the mission of theological education is to strengthen and accompany the mission of the church."[14]

Conclusion

This chapter has reviewed the challenges of providing the kind of theological education that can rise to the needs of the contemporary church. It has suggested that TEE can be a strong contributor in this task, offering an approach that can inspire and equip God's people at different educational levels. It has also suggested ways that TEE can learn from and benefit from working more closely with institutional theological education. The potential for fruitful partnership is strong.

Bibliography

Abeysekera, Lakmal, and Phillip Dawson. "Motivation and Cognitive Load in the Flipped Classroom: Definition, Rationale and a Call for Research." *Higher Education Research & Development* 34, no. 1 (2 January 2015): 1–14.

Cuff, Simon. *Love in Action: Catholic Social Teaching for Every Church*. London: SCM Press, 2019.

Lausanne Movement. *The Cape Town Commitment: A Confession of Faith and a Call to Action*. 2011. http://www.lausanne.org/content/ctc/ctcommitment.

Percy, Martyn. "Context, Character and Challenges: The Shaping of Ordination Training." In *The Oxford Handbook of Anglican Studies*, edited by Mark D. Chapman, Sathianathan Clarke, and Martyn Percy, 490–503. Oxford: Oxford University Press, 2015.

Shaw, Perry. *Transforming Theological Education: A Practical Handbook for Integrative Learning*. Carlisle: Langham, 2014

Spencer, Stephen. "Seminaries and Discipleship: Exploring Future Directions." *Journal of Anglican Studies* 18, no. 1 (2020): 1–15. doi: https://doi.org/10.1017/S174035532000008X.

van Wingerden, Hanna-Ruth, Tim Green, and Graham Aylett, eds. *TEE in Asia: Empowering Churches, Equipping Disciples*. Carlisle: Langham Global Library, 2021.

14. Lausanne, *Cape Town Commitment*, Part IIF, 4.

17

Reflections on TEE from the Asia Theological Association

Paul Cornelius[1]

Introduction

Over the last three decades a greater understanding in both educational theory and theological education as the formation of the people of God has emerged. This book addresses both of these issues admirably well. The various chapters present a critique of traditional approaches to theological education while at the same time forcefully arguing for the efficacy of the TEE approach to training.

Readers may wonder if it is a choice between the typical residential approach or the TEE method. My own sense is that the writers do not intend to evoke an either/or response. Rather, the intent, I may suggest, is to present carefully and articulately the history and development of TEE as a very viable model to effectively train the whole people of God. Therefore, the purpose of this brief response is to reflect on and affirm the fundamental aspects of transformative learning. In particular, it will highlight some key take-aways from TEE as well as suggest areas for growth.

1. Regional Secretary (India) for Asia Theological Association (ATA).

TEE Aims to Be Rooted in Biblical Patterns of Learning[2]

The strength of TEE, if done well, is its deep rootedness in biblical patterns of learning. The integrated nature of the training offers a wholesome learning and transformative experience. Two aspects, in particular, are key to TEE philosophy and practice and I would like to expand on those here.

Whole person formation

Several of the contributions have highlighted the focus on "whole person" formation. Whole person formation has strong biblical foundations with the goal of learning and education in Scripture as a whole. In the Old Testament we note that religious and life education went hand in hand. Education took place by means of both *informal* and *formal* instruction.[3] It is evident that most of the instruction in early Israel was informal. The locus of early Israelite education was the home and family. The *Shema* in Deuteronomy 6 enunciates this very clearly.[4] Here, learning is at its best. Parents were entrusted with the responsibility of nurturing their children to walk in the ways of the Lord. It is likely that much of this training was oral, with the "older generation passing along to the youth a wealth of insights it had gained through wide experience."[5] Gangel and Benson add:

> Hebrew parents were continually to whet the intellectual appetites of their children . . . They were to sharpen their minds,

---

2. Some of the material in this section is from my dissertation titled "Bridging the Expectation-Reality Gap: Exploring a Transformational Model for Theological Education in India" (PhD dissertation, Fuller Theological Seminary, 2014).

3. The first is my own phrasing, whereas the second is borrowed from Golka, *The Leopard's Spots*, 10–11. Other scholars such as Eavey, and Gangel and Benson, writing on the history and philosophy of Christian Education have categorized early Jewish education thus: (a) education in the family; (b) the law and education; (c) the priests and education; (d) education and the wise men; (e) the prophets and education.

4. "Hear, O Israel: The LORD our God, the LORD is one. You shall love the LORD your God with all your heart and with all your soul and with all your might. And these words that I command you today shall be on your heart. You shall teach them diligently to your children, and shall talk of them when you sit in your house, and when you walk by the way, and when you lie down, and when you rise. You shall bind them as a sign on your hand, and they shall be as frontlets between your eyes. You shall write them on the doorposts of your house and on your gates" (Deut 6:4–9 ESV).

5. Crenshaw, *Education in Ancient Israel*, 86.

> prompting questions which would create teachable moments so that instruction in the faith of Israel might be given.[6]

Instruction was passed on by the priestly tribe. Obviously such instruction was concerned with the law and commandments.[7] Deuteronomy 31:10–13 is indicative of the role the priests played in both direct and indirect education of the community. We cannot ignore the fact that in all this instruction there was integration of ethical rules, civil law, and duty to God.[8]

Another channel of instruction was provided by "wise men." Eavey points out that "every nation of the ancient East had its wise men, whose functions had to do with education along with other matters."[9] Proverbs 1:2–6 offers us a glimpse of the type of teaching the wise men were to provide. They were to give prudence to the simple and knowledge and discretion to the youth. It is evident that the wise men of Israel were to teach wisdom that was not only intellectual but that which involved the whole person, dealing with the whole of life.

Even the more *formalized* aspect of instruction focused on whole person formation. An example of this is Daniel and his three friends who were given Babylonian learning (Dan 1:3–5). They were chosen from all the Israelite youth and were from the nobility, "without blemish, of good appearance and *skillful in all wisdom, endowed with knowledge, understanding learning, and competent to stand in the king's palace*" (Dan 1:4 ESV, emphasis added) indicating that they already had received some formal education but in a well-rounded manner.

In the New Testament, learning through engagement in the ministry was the focus of Jesus's teaching methodology. The master-disciple relationship was not worked out in isolation, but rather in the midst of total involvement in the lives of people and the circumstances they found themselves in. Theology was learned in the midst of dialogue both with the master and happenings around. It was taught as Jesus interacted with the scribes and Pharisees. They learned as he healed the sick, provided food for the hungry, and helped the needy. As Banks succinctly observes, "mostly his association with, and formation of, his

6. Gangel and Benson, *Christian Education*, 60.
7. Eavey, *History of Christian Education*, 55.
8. Eavey, 56.
9. Eavey, 56.

disciples took place 'on the job' and following Jesus involved them in a kind of a mobile 'seminary.'"[10]

Here are some noteworthy aspects in relation to TEE. First, learning took place in multiple ways and with a variety of people involved. This is evident in TEE's approach as it employs different people from content creators, to facilitators, to small group leaders, to collaborative learning and so on. There is a clear awareness that learning takes place in multiple levels of relationships. Second, such a method of learning and communicating presupposes that personal experiences and lifestyle are integrated into the whole learning experience.

Integration of learning

Consider Paul as the teacher who was focused on the renewal of the mind, leading to change in attitude and behaviour based on truth and the knowledge that it brings.[11] Victor Cole points out that Paul's teaching simultaneously "touched the cognitive, the affective and the psychomotor domains" of those around him.[12] Unlike the Greeks who constantly dabbled in new ideas and exercised the intellect, Paul sought to effect *behavioural change* with the propositional truths that he laid out for his hearers.

The cognitive aspect was accompanied by lessons from his personal experience, thus augmenting knowledge with *affective* information. Cole observes that at least 89 percent of what Paul lists in 2 Timothy 3:10–11 in terms of what Timothy knew and learned, concerned the areas of character and spiritual values. However, the content had to do with what Paul learned through his own experience and lifestyle and thinking. It was knowledge born out of personal experience and a sharing of that experience with the student mostly taking place in informal settings.

In the *psychomotor* domain, Cole maintains that Paul focused on doing and used the practical hands-on approach in the context of his ministry. Cole distinguishes this from what is commonly termed *application*. Application for Cole is possible in the cognitive level too, where principles might be applied

10. Banks, *Reenvisioning Theological Education*, 106.

11. Lawson, "Education in the Epistles," 229.

12. Cole, *Training of the Ministry*, 46.

to a hypothetical situation. Rather, Paul instructs Timothy to "preach the word . . . correct, rebuke and encourage" and to "do the work of an evangelist, discharging all the duties of your ministry" (2 Tim 4:2, 5 NIV). These are all action words, implying doing and thereby applying.[13]

The "head," "heart," and "hands" approach of TEE attempts to bring the "cognitive," "affective," and "psychomotor" domains into good balance. This is accomplished by the "in context" training and focus on coaching and mentoring that are essential to an integrated learning experience. TEE helps us understand that education must impact people's lives and provide them with the resources to "grapple with the practical consequences of those truths studied and discerned."[14] This simply means that an education devoted solely to the theoretical and academic agenda and that is divorced from "affections and action" is suspect.

TEE Embraces Good Educational Philosophy and Practice

As much as TEE seeks to be rooted in biblical models of education, emphasis is also given to a proper understanding and implementing of current educational philosophy and practice. TEE uses the solid theoretical frameworks of education that lead to best practices in training.[15] Here are some ways by which this is manifest.

Focus on the learner and their contexts

In the area of theological education, TEE has led the way in "flipping" things around. The chapters of this book have highlighted the crucial differences between *pedagogy* and *andragogy* in two important ways.

First, it has helped shift the focus to the learner, with the teacher taking on the role of one who facilitates and designs the learning experience. In

13. Cole, 49.

14. Pazmino, *Foundational Issues in Christian Education*.

15. Notably Malcolm Knowles, Benjamin Bloom, David Kolb and Jane Vella. Other noteworthy theological educators that have already been referred to are Duane Elmer and Perry Shaw.

this scheme, as Knowles[16] points out, students, as adults, are self-starters and learners who participate actively in their learning experience. Typically, in many seminaries, especially in the non-western Majority World, learners are not viewed through the lens of andragogical methods and so are considered individuals who do not need to participate in the learning experience. What TEE does is to turn this notion on its head and offer a more constructive approach to education.

Second, along with affording importance to the learner, TEE takes into consideration the varied contexts the students come from. So, the locus and starting point of theological education is not the centralized campus, away from the reality of life situations, rather it is embedded in the multi-varied contexts of human existence and experience. This is where "theologizing" or "doing theology in context" can be at its best. The danger however is that it may readily be assumed that theologizing is happening in TEE simply because training is in context.

Focus on outcome-based learning

Reflecting from an Indian and South Asian context, up until very recently, content-based education was the norm. This was exacerbated by the importance given to getting a degree and not necessarily building competencies that made one "fit for purpose." What gives TEE an edge is its emphasis on outcome-based learning. Four aspects come to mind.

First is the focus on clearly intended outcomes for each course of study enabling the course designer and facilitator to create both content and process to ensure that these are met. This is an extremely creative effort, but well worth the while. Second, a further benefit to this approach is that learning is intentionally "bite-sized," chewable and digestible. It is crucial to appreciate the fact that transformation too, for the most part, takes place in increments and not in one large chunk.

Third, as adult learning methods remind us, there is an immediacy of application. Learning is appreciated when the student is able to put to practical use the knowledge gained.

16. Knowles, *Modern Practice.*

Fourth, assessment is also designed to be bite-sized with more importance given to formative learning tasks and assessments than the all-in-all summative exam at the end of the semester. Learning here is realistically conceived of and easily measurable.

Generally speaking, this approach to making learning meaningful and transformative is not practiced in many of the training programmes I am aware of. What we are left with then is a hurriedly put together course outline, with little or no attention paid to outcomes, processes, assessment criteria, and learning tasks. Students are expected to master large portions of content in a limited amount of time without time to digest and comprehend, making the learning experience a stunted one.

Given our current circumstances, the four aspects of learning highlighted above are even more critical when one considers the huge shift towards online or hybrid modes of theological education. As institutions begin to embrace technology for the purposes of education, TEE's methodology is bound to gain traction. This bodes well for theological education in general.

Conclusion

As much as traditional approaches to theological education present significant gaps, we would do well to remember that we must not throw out the proverbial baby with the bath water. Allow me to highlight three areas of traditional, residential education that lend strength to argue for this mode to continue to exist alongside other methods and approaches.

First, while the learner is not in his or her specific context, what the campus community provides is accessibility to the many contexts and experiences that are represented in microcosm. Learning that comes from exposure to the realities of one's peers and colleagues is immensely valuable. This is a reality that institutions often neglect much to their detriment. Here is where embracing good educational practice, such as TEE offers, will benefit traditional seminaries.

Second, the positives of setting aside sustained time for study, reflection, and growth in a guided mentoring process, is often undermined. There are many, who once in the ministry, will find little time for such training or mentoring. Such training is especially beneficial for those who enter ministry at a younger age and need a regimen that is disciplined and focused.

Third, we must appreciate that much seminal thinking and reflection occurs in a learning community that is dialoguing within itself and with other learning communities. Such learning contributes widely to theological understanding and contributes to right belief and practice. Content generation also takes place here, so others do not have to reinvent the wheel. And, as we all well know, reflection and practice do not take place in a vacuum but are dependent on good, solid content.

It is imperative therefore to affirm that multiple approaches to learning enrich one another and in the long run will prove beneficial to the faith, life, practice, and witness of the church. Partnership and acknowledgement of the richness of the various modes of learning is vital to the effective training of the whole people of God. Mutually enriching and collaborative efforts will ensure the vitality and growth of the church in the days ahead.

Bibliography

Banks, Robert. *Reenvisioning Theological Education: Exploring a Missional Alternative to Current Models*. Grand Rapids: Eerdmans, 1999.

Cole, Victor B. *Training of the Ministry: A Macro-Curricular Approach*. Bangalore: Theological Book Trust, 2001.

Cornelius, Paul P. "Bridging the Expectation-Reality Gap: Exploring a Transformational Model for Theological Education in India." PhD, Fuller Theological Seminary, 2014.

Crenshaw, James L. *Education in Ancient Israel*. New York: Doubleday, 1998.

Eavey, Charles B. *History of Christian Education*. Chicago: Moody Press, 1964.

Gangel, Kenneth O., and Warren S. Benson. *Christian Education: It's History and Philosophy*. Chicago: Moody Press, 1983.

Golka, Friedmann W. *The Leopard's Spots*. Edinburgh: T&T Clark, 1993.

Knowles, Malcolm S. *The Modern Practice of Adult Education: From Pedagogy to Andragogy*. Cambridge, NY: Adult Education Co, 1980.

Lawson, Michael S. "Education in the Epistles." In *Evangelical Dictionary of Christian Education*, edited by Michael J. Antony. Grand Rapids: Baker, 2001.

Pazmino, Robert. *Foundational Issues in Christian Education: An Introduction in Evangelical Perspective*. Grand Rapids: Baker, 1988.

18

Reflections on TEE from Overseas Council in Africa

John Jusu[1]

> *It is counterproductive for TEE to be compared to traditional residential theological education which has been historically dominant. Each approach to theological education has its own niche and its own contribution. (John Jusu)*

Introduction

The church is facing existential challenges in the twenty-first century that require attention from theologians and ministry practitioners. In one region is a dwindling church with more than adequate resources, and in another a growing church with inadequate resources. This situation debilitates the church in carrying out her mission. Leaders in regions where churches are dwindling need to reassess their training modes and perhaps their ecclesiology and align them with leadership that can reverse the trend and resuscitate a once vibrant church. Regions in which churches are growing need to re-pace their training models and strategies to provide adequate leadership that will shepherd the growing flock.

1. African Regional Director, United World Mission / Overseas Council.

When leadership is mentioned in terms of building or rebuilding a vibrant church that is positioned to carry out its divine mandate, fingers point at theological education. This is because, according to Dietrich Werner,

> theological education is vital for the transmission of Christian tradition from one generation to the other. Theological education is essential for the renewal and continuity of the church and its leadership. Theological education is a matter of survival for an authentic and contextual mission of the church in contemporary contexts. Theological education is crucial for the interaction between church and society where many issues demand for a sharpened stand and position of Christianity.[2]

Theological education plays a role in sustaining the mission of the church embedded in the mission of God. These roles have in the last few decades thrown theological education into the global limelight as the global church, irrespective of what region one looks at, struggles with continuity, renewal, relevance, and survival in different ways. The question of how theological education systems can position themselves to undertake this herculean task is a global question in vogue. Definitely, no one theological education model or approach can provide the relief we need in global theological education. It is time the different models start to talk to each other as equal and critical partners in leadership development.

Trends in Theological Education

The earliest explicit and intentional theological education came when God justified his choice of Abraham as the father of nations. God said, "I have singled him out so that he will direct his sons and their families to keep the way of the Lord by doing what is right and just."[3] The full components of theological education – content, teacher/student, aim, and method – are embedded in that statement. Thus, the earliest hint on the place of theological education was the home (Deut 6:1–9). During the exile, the synagogues became the

2. Werner, "Challenges and Major Tasks," 1.
3. Genesis 18:19 (NLT, Africa Study Bible).

place of theological education and after the exile, specialized teachers like Ezra and Nehemiah emerged. At Pentecost, with the Christian message reaching non-Jewish nations, Paul initiated the practice of writing "education letters" to build, live, and preserve the faith. Paul's strategy may have initiated what we may today call Theological Education by Extension (TEE).

Though Paul wrote several letters to personal individuals, most of his letters were written to churches where both leaders and congregations worshipped together. Paul was developing the whole body of Christ and not only its leaders from a distance. By the late eighth century, the level of training for church leaders was appalling, being at the same level of those they led. The Carolingian renaissance[4] of the late eighth century, sanctioned by Charlemagne, demanded that priests be trained "severely" in matters of doctrine and language. Consequently, special learning institutions with highly trained scholars were deployed. Theological education became education for the clergy offered in specific places (court, monastic and cathedral schools) at specific times. This trend continued into our contemporary times where theological education has become education for the professional clergy offered in specialized places called seminaries or Bible schools by professors who may not necessarily be "church people."

Putting theological education into specialized institutions beyond the reach of the populace and their immediate leaders can create a theologically illiterate population, whether in church of the past or in the present. A theologically untrained population is prone to manipulation, abuse, and exploitation. It was in that context that Martin Luther tried to reform the church by democratizing theological education. His ideas spread in regions far away from Wittenberg where he first posted his ninety-five theses. The dissemination of learning was made possible by the Gutenberg printing press. Through the press, writings and instructional materials developed by Luther and other reformers reached the extremes of Europe, entrenching the Protestant reformation. In fact, this constituted another form of global theological education by extension aided by technology.

4. Summary notes on the Carolingian renaissance can be found at https://www.britannica.com/topic/education/The-Carolingian-renaissance-and-its-aftermath.

Technology has contributed to liberalizing education. The development and spread of railways facilitated correspondence theological education through the mail system. The advent of the transistor radio decentralized learning and the television tube put a face to the instructor who taught from a distance. Today, the worldwide web has contributed to completely decentralize, liberalize, and democratize education. Technology enables seminaries and similar institutions to extend their curriculum beyond the walls of what they had called "school." Through technology, theological education at a distance has emerged, whether through seminary extension activities or through the TEE model.

This summary of trends in theological education suggests that any time theological education is entrenched in selective residential modes, a counter movement will arise to provide unfettered access. Dynamics within these trends have shaped the various perspectives many have about global theological education in view of TEE.

Global Perspectives on TEE

For the past two hundred years, classical and traditional models of developing leaders for the church continued in seminaries that were accessible to only very few people. At the advent of the last century, that model of doing theological education became inadequate for addressing the contextual needs of the church. Foremost, the church was growing very fast and the output of leaders from the seminaries could not match the pace of the growth, mainly because of lack of funds and personnel to train the required leaders for the growing churches. Second, the era of the professional clergy was closing as many bi-vocational and multichurch ministers emerged in church leadership. Third, the majority of those trained in the seminaries did not return to their churches, especially those who migrated from rural areas to seek seminary education in urban areas. Fourth, it was becoming increasingly difficult for gifted working adult leaders in the church to put their life on hold for four years or more to seek seminary education. Fifth, most of those who graduated from seminary could not integrate their education with the realities of the church.

The issues were not localized. The capacity of residential theological education to meet the needs of the global church was a global issue especially in regions of Africa, Asia, and South America where Christianity was exploding.

Global problems require global solutions. A critical solution to the global issues threatening the church was to be found in the extension activities of seminaries, distance education movements, and models such as TEE.

There is consensus among scholars and practitioners that TEE carries the potential to address many of the inadequacies of residential theological education, however, there are concerns about what product TEE offers, how it is offered, and the quality of what is offered. Past versions of TEE have been open to just criticism around these issues. The present book shows a willingness to recognize the problems and engage with them.

Changing Perspectives on Theological Education

Perspective transformation starts with having the facts of what is to be transformed. Perspectives are often held uncritically. Perhaps the starting point in our discussion about theological education is to ascertain the purpose of theological education. Noelliste believes that,

> essential to the renewal of theological education is the retrieval and the maintaining of its uniqueness and distinctiveness . . . Theologically understood then, theological education consists in the formation of the people of God in the truth and wisdom of God for the purpose of personal renewal and meaningful participation in the fulfilment of the purpose of God in the church and the world.[5]

Considering this purpose of life and societal transformation, theological education should not be preoccupied only with the question of ignorance – what should I know? Rather questions of *who I must be* and *what I must do* should also be at the fore of our engagements. Farley lamented the displacement of the purpose of theological education from a "way of living" (*what should I be* and *what should I do*) to an academic discourse (*what should I know*). Consequently, in Farley's thinking, contemporary theological schools can no

5. Noelliste, "Toward a Theology of Theological Education," 299.

longer provide theological education.[6] Farley's point is endorsed by Kinsler when he asserts:

> History teaches us that the Western academic-professional system of clergy tends to be static, incapable of responding to the needs of the masses, preoccupied with position and privilege at the expense of dynamic, corporate ministry. Theological education can in fact be a major obstacle to the growth of the church and fulfilment of her ministry.[7]

This is indeed a scathing attack on institutionalized theological education which has a definite niche in the formation of God's people. Foremost, almost all major players in the extension movement had their formation through institutionalized theological education. Second, our faith and the dogma and praxis that had upheld it throughout the centuries had their preservation and definitions in institutionalized theological education that produced both the "churchman" and the "schoolman." Understanding the role institutionalized theological education plays in the preservation and propagation of our faith is critical. In building the people of God, academic excellence is equally important as character development and ministry efficiency. One should not be held in higher esteem than the other.

Trading accusations is not helpful, especially for TEE which has struggled to find acceptance in global theological education. What will be helpful in changing perspectives on both sides of the divide is a definition of the role of the church leader in context. My experience in Africa puts a four-fold role that sees the individual as a counsellor, a disciple-maker, a preacher/teacher, and a leader. In these roles, the leader functions as a pioneer, a problem-solver, a peacemaker, and implementer. Also, understanding the levels and complex situations in which these roles are performed will give an idea of what type of theological education is required. This will lay to rest the superiority battle as each mode will find its critical niche in training of leaders.

6. Farley, *Theologia*, 14.

7. Kinsler, *Extension Movement*, 11–12.

Bridging the Gap

Several attempts have been made to bridge the gap, the most recent one being the September 2019 consultation hosted by the Association of Evangelicals in Africa[8] on upscaling nonformal theological education. About three hundred individuals representing various providers of theological education came into meaningful dialogue that aimed at seeing the two modes, institutionalized theological education and extension programmes, as complementing rather than conflicting with each other in the mutual task of preparing the whole people of God for various tasks. The dialogue facilitated an understanding of each player's role and how the strengths of both modes can be harnessed for the good of the church.

Kinsler has compiled a diverse group of theological training programmes introducing new paradigms that do not necessarily use the traditional TEE method and are not linked to seminaries.[9] Quite recently, groups like the Increase Association, More Than a Mile Deep (MMD), and many more have revolutionized theological education by not simply extending seminary training but by bringing theological education to where it belongs – the church. This is not seminary extension nor distance education, but a relocation of theological education to the local community and the local church. While the early expressions of TEE were about contextualizing theological education, these more recent groups and movements are about contextual theological education. These groups have contributed immensely to changing the perspectives of global theological education as they significantly scaled up nonformal education to be not only an alternative to residential theological education but also to complement and renew residential modes of training, its philosophical foundations, and practice.

MMD[10] has found its philosophical basis in mainstream constructivism and with sound, defensible and explicable training pedagogy that moved away

8. Association of Evangelicals in Africa, *Scaling Up*.

9. Kinsler, *Diversified Theological Education*.

10. MMD is a homegrown approach to doing theological education that fits the epistemologies of Africans. The conceptual framework of the approach has not been published, and the model and design are still in process. Notwithstanding, the approach has been field-tested with astounding success as its graduates are accepted in a major seminary in South Africa. Those interested in the approach can reach the designer of the model at jkjusu@yahoo.com.

from Reflection – Action – Reflection inherent in traditional TEE to a more transformative approach of Action – Reflection – Action (ARA). Whereas TEE self-consciously starts with self-study materials, MMD starts with the perennial activities of the leader and then uses self-study materials to help the leader to reflect on those activities. Such deviations from the original TEE and the justifications therein for such pedagogies, as also evident in approaches of Increase, have helped to build a robust stature of non-seminary-based training in global theological education. It is because of models and approaches like these that Kinsler asserted some TEE programmes are as good as residential seminary programmes.[11]

Another extraordinary phenomenon that has blurred the divide is the pandemic of COVID-19. The pandemic forced all residential theological education providers to migrate to distance learning. Although the self-study materials and community learning are in most cases mediated by technology, the seminal idea of learning at a distance was highlighted. This has given the opportunity to many institutions to break barriers of access and professional training. With the intrusion of seminaries into the space of distance learning and TEE, non-seminary providers must also pay attention to quality and embrace technology as a delivery means. With the advent of COVID-19, all modes must learn to work together if they are to survive.

Conclusion

Global theological education perspectives on TEE have traditionally not been encouraging partly because of the ambiguous nature of the TEE approach that many think lacks a strong philosophical and pedagogical framework. Global theological education demands order, certainty, and quality which some believed could not be found in TEE. TEE also has had its own negative perceptions about institutionalized theological education that they consider irrelevant and elitist. These perspectives are antagonistic, not helpful to either side. Rather than build a case on the demerits of another mode, both modes must endeavour to showcase their strengths and how they can be used in the overall development of leaders for the global church and its training institutions.

11. Kinsler, *Extension Movement*, 16.

TEE practitioners should not concentrate on the shortcomings of residential theological training, but they must improve their own stature in global theological education. TEE needs sound philosophical, pedagogical, and practical reasons and frameworks for the essence of TEE on the global stage – and that is exactly the intent of this present book. They must have group leaders and course writers who are reflective practitioners as discussed in chapter 7 of this present book. Such people should exhibit both academic excellence *and* efficiency in ministry, not one against or above the other. The duel is no longer between academic excellence and ministry efficiency. Many more programmes have been developed that combine both.[12] It is no longer an issue of either/or, but which is the most appropriate tool to use in a given situation. TEE must present itself as the tool of choice when vocational hands-on training is required, when decentralized training is needed, and when reflective practice is required in the formation of individuals for ministry. Kinsler[13] asserted that TEE is a new methodology of ministerial training. What Kinsler may not have considered is that the seminal ideas embedded in TEE were envisaged as early as the advent of the four-fold[14] division of theological education in the early nineteenth century, where the outcomes of intellectual discourse, stemming from research-oriented theological, historical, and biblical studies, may find their way into the congregations through the practical theologies. TEE has been a hidden tool within the practical theologies that have now been awakened by circumstances beyond the scope of institutionalized theological education.

This present book shows a healthy awareness of the past problems within the TEE movement, that are noted above, and a readiness to engage with them. The book is written by reflective TEE practitioners and contributes to the need, identified above, for a solid, theological, philosophical, and education framework for contemporary church-based TEE. It also shows that there is a new openness to collaborative partnerships with campus-based theological education within the TEE movement, and a willingness to engage with contemporary thinking in adult education. These shifts help to position TEE as a positive partner, alongside other approaches, in the earlier-noted herculean

12. Kinsler, *Diversified Theological Education.*

13. Kinsler, *Extension Movement*, 1–2.

14. Farley, *Theologia*, 99–141.

task facing theological education within the global church. As noted at the top of this chapter, "Each approach to theological education has its own niche and its own contribution." This book shows that TEE makes such a contribution.

Bibliography

Association of Evangelicals in Africa. *Scaling Up Theological Education in Africa.* Nairobi, 2020. https://aeafrica.org/free-ebook-scaling-up-theological-training-in-africa/.

Farley, Edward. *Theologia: The Fragmentation and Unity of Theological Education.* Philadelphia: Fortress Press, 1983.

Harrison, Patricia J. "Forty Years On: The Evolution of Theological Education by Extension (TEE)." *Evangelical Review of Theology* 28, no. 4 (2004): 315–28.

Hogarth Jonathan, Kiranga Gatimu, and David Barrett. *Theological Education in Context: 100 Extension Programs in Africa.* Nairobi: Uzima Press, 1983.

Kinsler, F. Ross. *The Extension Movement in Theological Education: A Call to the Renewal of the Ministry*. Pasadena: William Carey Library, 1978.

———, ed. *Diversified Theological Education: Equipping All God's People.* Pasadena: WCIU Press, 2008.

———, ed. *Ministry by the People: Theological Education by Extension*. Maryknoll: Orbis Books, 1983.

Noelliste, Dieumeme. "Toward a Theology of Theological Education." *Evangelical Review of Theology* 19, no. 3 (1995): 299–306.

Wagner, Peter C. "A Pattern for Evangelical Cooperation in Seminary Extension Training." In *Theological Education by Extension*, edited by Ralph D. Winter, 282–94. Pasadena: William Carey Library, 1969.

Werner, Dietrich. "Challenges and Major Tasks for Ecumenical Theological Education in the 21st Century." 2008. https://www.oikoumene.org/en/folder/documents-pdf/Challenges_and_major_tasks_for_theological_education_-_D._Werner.pdf.

19

Reflections from an African TEE Perspective

Kangwa Mabuluki[1]

Introduction

This chapter seeks to bring an African perspective on TEE, because TEE is presented and discussed from an Asian perspective in chapters 1–14 of this book.

The start of TEE is well described in this book and elsewhere.[2] It does not require repeating except to stress that when TEE spread from Guatemala to other parts of Latin America and on to other developing countries particularly in Africa and Asia, it did not present as a rigid approach. Instead, it is a flexible programme, "able to adjust to the needs and abilities of the students, and can be developed and adapted to the local situation meeting particular needs."[3]

Because this reflection is from our experience of TEE in Africa, it will help if I give a brief introduction of how it was introduced, its development, and the formation of the All-Africa Theological Education by Extension Association (AATEEA), which is a counterpart and collaborative member of Increase.

1. General Secretary, All Africa Theological Education by Extension Association (AATEEA).

2. See Mabuluki, "Diversified." And see also Sendegeya and Spencer, *Understanding TEE*, 33.

3. Bontrager, "Theological Education by Extension." https://gameo.org/index.php?title=Theological_Education_by_Extension&oldid=122808.

TEE in Africa

TEE was introduced in Africa at a workshop of church leaders and theological educators organized by the World Council of Churches (WCC), held in Limuru, Kenya, in 1969. Following this workshop TEE programmes were started simultaneously in Ethiopia and Zambia.[4]

In its early years, TEE developed into two fairly distinct streams – the evangelical stream and the mainline ecumenical stream.[5] The two streams were also evident in the introduction of TEE to Africa. Ross Kinsler, then head of the WCC-ETE, is credited with providing a link between the two streams, although each developed independently.[6]

The reflections here are based on TEE programmes present in over twenty-five African countries that are members of the AATEEA.

Moving Forward Together – The Formation of AATEEA

TEE in Africa grew rapidly, so that by 1983 there were more than one hundred TEE programmes, and by 1995, there were 341.[7] But this growth was not sustained. There was a noticeable slowdown in progress, in some cases total collapse, especially for those programmes that were not institutionalized, and those that were denominational rather than ecumenical.[8] That fluctuating situation continued into the current period.

One of the key developments in the current state of TEE programmes in Africa has been the formation of the AATEEA, a support and collaborative network of TEE programmes in over twenty-five African countries.[9] This is somehow comparable to Increase, which is well presented in chapter 14.

The AATEEA was formally launched at a conference in Livingstone, Zambia, in 2006, bringing together TEE practitioners from different countries in Africa. It was not the first such conference. Before this, TEE practitioners

4. Sendegeya and Spencer, *Understanding TEE*, 32–33.

5. Sendegeya and Spencer, 32–33.

6. Sendegeya and Spencer, 32–33.

7. Sendegeya and Spencer, 33.

8. Mabuluki, "Diversified," 252.

9. This number is rapidly growing as new programmes are started and/or revived in various African countries.

from some TEE programmes[10] who had been invited to the WCC Conference in 2002,[11] realized that they were not aware of the existence of each other's TEE programmes. This realization made them resolve to bring as many as possible of the existing TEE programmes in Africa together in a conference. The resolve culminated in an All-Africa TEE conference in 2003 in Mukono, Uganda. Participants at this conference realized that most of the TEE programmes had slowed down drastically, existed only in name, or had collapsed altogether. But TEE was still needed because churches were growing rapidly, while resources to fund theological colleges, seminaries, and theological facilities were drastically reducing.[12]

Participants resolved to work towards a similar conference during which they would, among other things, "start a TEE Association which would serve as a forum for jointly addressing some of the issues affecting TEE in Africa."[13] That was the conference in Zambia in 2006, attended by thirty-four TEE practitioners from fifteen countries. Besides the formation of AATEEA, another outcome of the conference was a resolution to hold such a conference every four years. The All-Africa TEE conference has become one of the key activities of AATEEA.[14] Conferences have been successfully held in Dodua, Ghana, in 2010, Addis Ababa, Ethiopia, in 2014, and Nairobi, Kenya, in 2018.

Some Reflections on Chapters 1–14

This book has raised and addressed many issues that are also critical to TEE in Africa.

10. Namely TEE programmes in Mozambique, Angola, Zambia, Botswana, Kenya, South Africa, and Uganda.

11. The conference brought together different key players in theological institutions and organizations. One of the objectives of the conference was to review the whole process of theological education in Africa.

12. Mabuluki, "Diversified," 258–59.

13. Mabuluki, 259.

14. The conference is normally in two parts. The first part, which lasts for three days, is a thematic conference where input directed towards addressing issues of concern for TEE is given. The second, lasting two days, is a General Meeting where reports from the General Secretary and the treasurer are received and policy and operational matters of AATEEA are discussed.

The need to prove the educational efficacy of TEE

The challenge of proving that TEE is a method that meets general educational standards and requirements is one issue that has faced TEE right from its inception. As clearly stated in the opening chapter of this book, where TEE is introduced, those not conversant with the methodology and educational philosophy of TEE treat it casually without a careful in-depth study of the method. They regard it as "a poor cousin" to real theological education, lacking academic discipline, with no formal accreditation.[15] That is why this book addresses a challenge that has faced TEE in general, and in Africa perhaps more than other regions, by presenting TEE "as a viable approach to theological education that is contemporary in its applications, established in its track record and well-founded in its scholarship."[16]

In Africa, just as in the case of Asia, the TEE method caters for different categories of Christians needing theological education. This includes the less formally educated who have no academic qualification with which to enter the residential seminary. Most of the TEE students in Africa fall into this latter category, but as has been well discussed, argued, and proved in this book, this does not indicate any inferiority.

For many years TEE practitioners in Africa have struggled to dispel the notion of TEE being sub-standard, narrow, and severely limited, and efforts to respond to this challenge have in some cases led to a departure from some of the principles underlying TEE.[17]

---

15. See Chapter 1: Burke, Brown, and Julius, "Challenges Facing Theological Education and the Case for TEE."

16. See the "*Why* this Book?" section in the introduction of this book, "Introduction."

17. Such as "accessibility" even for the less educated. Some TEE programmes, in a bid to upgrade TEE, resort to affiliations with a university. The university, with its academic and administrative demands, stops the needed emphasis on courses that cater for less-educated church-based groups. Raising the level of TEE courses is not a bad or negative idea in itself, but this has to be done for the right reason of also making TEE available to those who already have higher academic qualifications. It also has to be done remembering that TEE is intended to reach out and offer theological education to "all God's people," and no one, educated or uneducated in the conventional sense, must be left out because of the limitation in the level of courses offered. So Ross Kinsler has advised that in TEE when you upgrade, you must also downgrade, but not in the negative sense. In a way this also relates to the observation made in chapter 1 of this book where the challenges arising from the "with *whom*?" of theological education are discussed, namely that "high academic entry standards and the academic nature of courses may be a barrier to those who are rich in life experience but low in academic orientation and experience. The

Of special relevance to TEE in Africa is how this book brings TEE into conversation with key educational principles and attests that "TEE is a proven and effective model of theological education that equips and empowers all God's people alongside other methods and models of transformative theological education."[18]

TEE equipping all God's people for Christian mission

The task of theological education is to prepare for the fulfilment of the mission of the church which should be God's mission, as argued in the first part of chapter 2.[19] Developing such theological education is a task as big as an elephant.[20] No one theological training method (for our purposes formal, informal, or nonformal) can do the task completely on its own. All the different methods are needed. TEE has an important part in the theological education enterprise of addressing the challenges, especially in making theological education accessible to all God's people. Let me just touch on two areas in this regard.

1. Bridging the theological training gap between ordained and lay

Green's response to the challenges arising from the "why?" of theological education, that "professionalization of the ministry is tragically unbiblical, crushes the full-time pastors, and fails to release the ministry of all believers,"[21] rings true for the African church. As Ben Y. Quarshie posits: "Theological education in Africa is often understood only in terms of formation for the ordained ministry."[22] Most African churches however believe in the priesthood

tragedy is that such people have immediate potential for mature church leadership as opposed to younger students," 22.

18. Chapter 1: Burke, Brown, and Julius, "Challenges Facing Theological Education and the Case for TEE," 38.

19. See discussion in chapter 2: Burke and Pearson, "TEE in Theological Perspective – Part 1." See also Bosch, *Transforming Mission*, 389–92.

20. The Indian story of the six blind men who went to feel an elephant – each touched a part and thought that constituted the elephant not realizing that the elephant was made up of all the parts that each one touched put together. In some cases, you need all options put together to get the full picture or effect.

21. Chapter 1: Burke, Brown, and Julius, "Challenges Facing Theological Education and the Case for TEE."

22. Quarshie, "African Perspectives."

of all believers.[23] But this belief cannot be seen in reality. There is an evident dominance of ordained clergy in the ministry and work of the local church, and a "significant gap between the training typically given to leaders and that given to the whole people of God."[24]

There is certainly room and need for specialized clergy training, but this should not be at the expense of or to the neglect of making proper and sound theological training accessible to the laity. The mission of the church should essentially derive from God's mission, and God's mission is to all and for all (Matt 28:19; Mark 16:15). So when the church is selective in its theological education by focusing on full-time clergy and neglecting other members, it is not true to God's calling and mission.

The focus of TEE is "to prepare all God's people for the work of Christian service, in order to build up the body of Christ" (Eph 4:12 GNT). In staying true to its commitment of preparing "all," TEE has responded to the existence of poor-quality theological training programmes for lay church members and leaders by providing proven sound theological education, thus improving the effectiveness of lay leaders, and relieving the excessive demand on the time and service of the ordained minister. Drawing from the example of Zambia, an ecumenical TEE programme was started by church leaders from the United Church of Zambia and the Anglican Church. One of the main reasons they gave for the need to start the ecumenical TEE programme was a realization that "even in churches where there is a full-time pastor or clergy, the bulk of the work is carried out by voluntary unpaid lay members, yet the training of these lay members is not as well defined and resourced as that of ordained pastors."[25] To ensure holistic and sound theological training for lay people, a TEE programme was started. Its relevance and success is seen in the increased number of beneficiary denominations from two in 1979 to the current nine, and from being present only in urban districts along the railway line to covering

23. For example, Presbyterian Church in Ghana, and The United Church of Zambia.

24. Chapter 2: Burke and Pearson, "TEE in Theological Perspective – Part 1."

25. Mabuluki, "Theological Education by Extension in Zambia." And also in UCZ archives, notes on early efforts to start TEE in Zambia.

all the districts of the nation including the rural ones.[26] Similar stories can be shared in many countries where there are TEE programmes.

2. Reaching out to those who missed out in the delivery of sound theological education

TEE serves to bring sound theological education to all God's people by reaching out to those who missed out on the regular delivery of theological education for one reason or another. These could even be church leaders who have no academic qualification to enter a seminary, or the people in prison or correctional facilities, which is the group I wish to share about as an example from Africa.

People in prison represent some of God's people who can easily be neglected in the delivery of theological education. Two TEE programmes in Africa, Zambia TEE (TEEZ), and Presbyterian Church of East Africa in Kenya (PCEA-Kenya) have robust prison TEE ministries. The motivation for such programmes is that not everyone in prison is a criminal or is in prison for a crime they committed. The many times Paul was in prison (Acts 16:16–40; 24:27), and the words of our Lord Jesus Christ "I was in prison" (Matt 25:36), emphasize this fact. But even if they are in prison because of crime, they are the people for whom Christ came (Luke 5:32).

It is possible to visit prison merely for evangelism. Many churches do this from time to time, which is good and important. But we are talking here about theological education, which is sustained over some time, aimed at converting of course, but also teaching in the sense of making real disciples.[27] At a graduation ceremony in Kenya at a maximum-security prison, a death sentence convict who graduated with a diploma in theology testified how Christ changed his life. Having gone through TEE and seeing the change in his life he now understood the purpose of going to prison – "it was not the police who arrested me, it was Christ who arrested me, and even with the high wall and the bars, I am more free than the people outside." In a maximum-security prison in Zambia, at a graduation ceremony of TEE students who had been trained

26. Mabuluki, "Theological Education by Extension in Zambia."

27. Matt 28:19, "baptizing them in my name and teaching them to obey all that I have commended you."

in agriculture, the top prison official who was officiating testified that there are more TEEZ students on parole because of the very evident change in their behaviour, which can only be attributed to the work of Christ in their lives.

Testimonies like these as a result of the work of these two TEE programmes demonstrate that theological education is also for the transformation of lives with the aim of "presenting everyone mature in Christ" (Col 1:28).

The impact of limitations with course materials

A key factor in the effectiveness of one of the pillars of TEE, namely the pillar of "personal study," is appropriate and effective course material.[28]

The challenge of course material for some TEE groups is real in our African context. Some cases of continuous use of the same materials, sometimes old and outdated, may not be out of choice but due to lack of new and relevant material for the changing context. This lack results from not having enough resources for proper reviews and for writing new courses, or there could be a lack of competent writers with sufficient time to commit to this task.

Most TEE programmes no longer use the common materials developed by early, mostly European, missionary TEE practitioners printed by Evangel Publishing House. In the current situation, each TEE programme produces its own material according to context. This situation has made it difficult for TEE groups to share study materials because it is not easy to revise and adapt existing course material. Sometimes, even when the material is good quality, there is the issue of relevance to context as in the case of Mozambique.[29] Another problem could also be the limitation in course availability due to the language, as is the current case of Guinea.[30] The question of language is an

28. Chapter 3: Aylett and Samuel, "TEE in Theological Perspective – Part 2."

29. The TEE programme in Mozambique started by using the course material from TEE College – South Africa. The material was well translated into Portuguese; they are still using the material with minimal complaint. The one complaint that came up often when we visited the TEE groups was that of the South African context coming through the course material, especially but not only in the examples of illustrations. Even though the two countries are neighbours, their contexts are different.

30. The latest TEE programme to be established is in Guinea, and as usual we had to look for already existing TEE course material for them to start using before they could develop their own. Being a French speaking country, we immediately requested material from Rwanda TEE, only to discover that the good and relevant material Rwanda TEE has is all in the local Rwandese language. We then had to turn to Mauritius whose soft copies are still in Word Perfect. Thanks

important factor that has severely hindered the growth of TEE in Portuguese-speaking and French-speaking countries and regions.

The training of writers aggressively embarked on by AATEEA seeks to address some of these challenges. Having a clear process for training writers is a point of collaboration between Increase and AATEEA, as well as the sharing of experiences for effective use of resources.

The partnership between residential schools and TEE programmes

The issue of residential theological school versus TEE was a vicious but silent battle for some time, even though for a long time there were TEE programmes based at seminaries or university theological faculties. In some cases, at the centre of the animosity was the issue of the relative availability of resources to the seminary and the associated TEE programme.[31] Tremendous progress has been made in resolving this even though some misgivings continue to simmer here and there. In the current situation most TEE programmes, including institutional TEE programmes like Malawi and Zambia, work closely in partnerships with seminaries. These partnerships facilitate the training of pastors who are about to graduate so that they can go and train leaders who become TEE tutors in their congregations or parishes.

The key issue is that having residential theological institutions and TEE programmes is not an either/or but a both/and. In this regard, the matters raised in chapter 10 are helpful, in particular the identified points of possible collaboration. Matters raised in the second part of the chapter likewise resonate with experiences in the African context especially: "Partnership to fulfil a vision – Equipping all of God's people for God's mission." This is something I have earlier reflected on under a similar title.

to advantages of the digital age, we were able to download a programme to convert files into Microsoft Word with a few manageable challenges.

31. Example of Tanzania Mennonite College, whose campus also hosted the TEE programme. The TEE programme had to be discontinued because supporting partners preferred to support only TEE because more people were trained at minimal cost.

Equipping leaders to respond to social, political, and economic challenges

The numerous sociopolitical challenges Africa faces demand African church leaders who are competent to lead the church to the required level of maturity and who are able to meet these challenges. New educational tools are required for this task of equipping church leaders. Drawing from theological education literature, Wahl identifies six models of theological education that can contribute to the task of raising appropriate church leaders to help address the challenges facing Africa. Among these models is TEE, also sometimes referred to as Diversified Theological Education.[32] Among the advantages of TEE, Wahl notes that its contextualized curricula make the model meaningful in addressing the sociopolitical and, especially, socioeconomic challenges of Africa. In this regard, Kinsler claims that professional Western models of healthcare in the foreseeable future will fail to provide adequate services among the expanding poor populations of Africa, where 15,000 children die daily for lack of clean water, basic nutrition, and preventive healthcare. Kinsler proposes that grassroots health education and community development in partnership with TEE might transform that situation with a new holistic vision of God's mission, which could bring together these movements and their local leaders.[33]

Sociopolitical and socioeconomic challenges are mentioned in other chapters, including discussion of the persecuted and poor, people on the move (refugees and the displaced in the African context), victims of tightly controlled religious markets, and the digital age. These challenges require a Christian response.

Conclusion

Much of what is discussed and raised in this book, though representing the perspective of TEE in Asia, also applies to TEE in Africa, although in different ways. These similarities emphasize the need for collaboration and mutual support for maximized utilization of resources, especially human resources.

32. Wahl, "Towards Relevant Theological Education in Africa."

33. Kinsler, "Equipping All God's People."

Bibliography

Amanze, James N. "Paradigm Shift in Theological Education in Southern and Central Africa and Its Relevance to Ministerial Formation." *International Review of Mission* 98, no. 1 (2009): 120–31. https://onlinelibrary.wiley.com/doi/full/10.1111/j.1758-6631.2009.00010.x.

Aylett, Graham, and Tim Green. "Theological Education by Extension (TEE) as a Tool for Twenty-First Century Mission." In *Reflecting on and Equipping for Christian Mission*, edited by Stephen B. Bevans, Teresa Chai, J. Nelson Jennings, Knud Jørgensen, and Dietrich Werner, 59–78. Oxford: Regnum, 2015.

Bevans, Stephen B. "Theological Education as Missionary Formation." In *Reflecting on and Equipping for Christian Mission*, edited by Stephen B. Bevans, Teresa Chai, J. Nelson Jennings, Knud Jørgensen, and Dietrich Werner, 93–105. Oxford: Regnum, 2015.

Bontrager, Joseph. "Theological Education by Extension." *Global Anabaptist Mennonite Encyclopedia Online*. 1989. Accessed 11 February 2021. https://gameo.org/index.php?title=Theological_Education_by_Extension&oldid=122808.

Bosch, David J. *Transforming Mission: Paradigm Shifts in Theology of Mission*. Maryknoll: Orbis, 1991.

Glissmann, Volker. "What Is Theological Education by Extension?" *The Theological Educator*. 2014. https://thetheologicaleducator.net/2014/11/28/what-is-theological-education-by-extension/.

Kinsler, F. Ross. "Equipping All God's People for God's Mission." In *Diversified Theological Education: Equipping All God's People*, edited by F. Ross Kinsler, 15–32. Pasadena, WCIU Press, 2008.

Kinsler, F. Ross, and James H. Emery, eds. *Opting for Change: A Handbook on Evaluation and Planning for Theological Education by Extension*. Pasadena: William Carey Library, 1991.

Mabuluki, Kangwa. "Diversified Theological Education: Genesis, Development, and Ecumenical Potential of Theological Education by Extension (TEE)." In *Handbook of Theological Education in World Christianity*, edited by Dietrich Werner, David Esterline, Namsoon Kang, and Joshva Raja, 251–62. Oxford: Regnum, 2010.

———. "The Relevance of TEE in African Training for Mission." In *Reflecting on and Equipping for Christian Mission*, edited by Stephen B. Bevans, Teresa Chai, J. Nelson Jennings, Knud Jørgensen, and Dietrich Werner, 79–89. Oxford: Regnum, 2015.

———. "Theological Education by Extension in Zambia." In *Diversified Theological Education: Equipping All God's People*, edited by F. Ross Kinsler, 33–46. Pasadena: WCIU Press, 2008.

———. "Theological Education for All God's People: Theological Education by Extension (TEE) in Africa." In *Handbook of Theological Education in Africa*, edited by Isabel A. Phiri and Dietrich Werner, 832–40. South Africa: Cluster Publications, 2013.

Mgeyekwa, Gabriel E. "The Historical Development of Theological Education by Extension (TEE) in the Evangelical Lutheran Church of Tanzania, Southern Diocese, 1990–1997." MTh, University of Natal, 1998.

Quarshie, Ben Y. "African Perspectives on Theological Education for Mission." In *Reflecting on and Equipping for Christian Mission*, edited by Stephen B. Bevans, Teresa Chai, J. Nelson Jennings, Knud Jørgensen, and Dietrich Werner, 258–67. Oxford: Regnum, 2015.

Selvanayagam, Donald S. "Theological Education by Extension for Parishioners: Developing a Curriculum." MTh, University of South Africa, 1995.

Sendegeya, Fareth, and Leon Spencer, eds. *Understanding TEE: A Course Outline and Handbook for Students and Tutors in Residential Theological Institutions in Africa*. Dar es Salaam: ANITEPAM, 2001.

Wahl, Willem P. "Towards Relevant Theological Education in Africa: Comparing the International Discourse with Contextual Challenges." *Acta Theologica* 33, no. 1 (2013): 266–93. http://www.scielo.org.za/pdf/at/v33n1/14.pdf.

Werner, Dietrich. "Theological Education in the Changing Context of World Christianity: An Unfinished Agenda." *International Bulletin of Missionary Research* 35, no. 2 (2011): 92–100.

20

Reflections from a Latin American TEE Perspective

Norberto Saracco[1]

Introduction

It was a little over fifty years ago when Theological Education by Extension (TEE) was born in Central America. Indeed, its founders never dreamed of the scope that this model of theological education would have, based on a renewed vision of ministerial preparation and a methodological revolution, fruit of the new philosophical currents in education in the 1960s.

Much has been done since then, and today this movement has a wide experience and has been studied in depth. Proof is in this book; its first fourteen chapters are an in-depth look at the history, development, and possibilities of TEE in a global perspective.

Personally, I have been part of this history. My first contact with the TEE movement was in Guatemala in 1972. Then I participated in the formation of PRODIADIS[2] (Programa Diversificado a Distancia) at the Seminario Bíblico Latinoamericano (today Universidad Bíblica) and forty-four years ago I founded FIET,[3] a seminary that from its origins belonged to the TEE model. But at the same time, and in parallel, I have developed a pastoral ministry that

1. J. Norberto Saracco. Rector Emeritus of the International Faculty of Theological Studies (FIET).

2. Diversified Distance Program.

3. Facultad Internacional de Educación Teológica (International Faculty of Theological Education).

I have exercised for fifty-two years. I mention this biographical data in order to frame my reflection, which stems from the close relationship between TEE and the church, and my leadership role in both.

Given the brief space available to me, I simply mention three lessons learned, three challenges for TEE, and three challenges for the church.

Lessons Learned

Lesson 1 – TEE was not born to "save" seminaries but as an instrument for the church to fulfil its mission

The original challenge was how to create a theological education programme to meet the ministerial needs of a church that was beginning to grow. In Guatemala, the concern was to reach out especially to the indigenous world, the majority in that country, who because of their own culture and limitations could not access traditional training. When Rubén Lores returned from his sabbatical at Seminario Bíblico Latinoamericano in 1974, he posed the challenge: "In the next ten years there will be more than ten thousand pastors in Latin America, and we will be unable to prepare them with the current models of ministerial training." The response was the creation of PRODIADIS. However, the seminaries saw in this model an opportunity to "extend" their institutions, so the challenge was how to make the seminary go to where the student was, rather than provide the training that the ministries needed.

Thus, structures were created that could only function with missionaries, that could only be paid for with funds from abroad, and that did not listen to the churches' needs. In the first fifteen years over four hundred programmes were opened and closed in Central America alone. The problem was not financial resources, because millions of dollars had been invested. Nor were human resources the problem, since hundreds of missionaries were working in TEE. The problem was to understand that TEE was not born to save the seminaries but to empower the church in the fulfilment of its mission.

Lesson 2 – Theological education must be relevant and grounded in the church and its mission

This statement applies not only to TEE but to all theological education. According to this philosophy of education, the local church occupies a central role – it is the starting point. Therefore, theological education is not an end in itself, but a response to the needs of the church and its leadership. In this sense theological education should be dynamic, not static; flexible, not rigid; and remain open to new realities. TEE is in a better position than traditional models to fulfil this philosophy. Traditional models in Latin America have been imported, both in methodology and content, and therefore respond to different realities.

A church-based model recognizes that the church defines the ministerial formation agenda which is an instrument for the goal of the church's mission.

Lesson 3 – Educational materials are only a means to mission

One of the most common mistakes we have encountered in TEE is the excessive faith placed in materials. We have had an almost magical hope in the power that the materials we use in TEE can have. It is true that they allow us to get where we want to go, but the big question is, "What are we getting there for?" In other words, what is the purpose? TEE has often fallen into the trap of being a movement focused on materials and pedagogical resources and not on vision. Over the years TEE has been at the forefront in the use of new media: programmed texts, recordings, VHS, CD, DVD, internet, digital and online courses. When we only use these instruments, we experience the frustration of seeing thousands registering and only a few completing their studies. Today we live the great illusion and the great frustration of the digital age. We have learned that the greatest value of a programme is not in the tools it uses, but in the process it generates.

Challenges for TEE

Challenge 1 – Maintain academic quality

From its inception, TEE was considered a second-class education in theological institutions, an alternative for those who could not access traditional training. It is true that TEE reached where others did not and incorporated thousands who were outside the system. The mistake was to believe that to achieve this it had to move in a level of academic poverty, leaving higher and quality education in the hands of the traditional seminaries.

It is interesting to look at some of the accreditation requirements of accrediting agencies to see how far they are from measuring genuine quality. In this field, TEE has been fighting a long battle and will have to show with facts and results that it is capable of meeting the highest quality standards. For this to be possible, the responsibility falls first and foremost on TEE's protagonists. They are the first who must be convinced that it is possible to provide training of the highest quality, and act accordingly.

Challenge 2 – Develop a solid structure

We have learned that for TEE to be effective it needs a solid administrative and academic structure. One of the most common mistakes at the beginning of the outreach movement was to think that just by putting certain materials in the hands of the church, the education process would work by itself. The frustration has been enormous since countless financial and human resources have been invested in getting the right materials to the students without achieving significant results. In the 1980s, there were seminaries in Latin America that bought buildings only for recording studios and cassette duplication but without paying attention to programme implementation. Again, as we have mentioned, the energy was put into the production of materials and not in the process.

To be successful, a TEE programme needs a structure that ensures the development of a quality church-centred curriculum, provides up-to-date materials, and closely monitors regional centres and study groups.

Challenge 3 – Create self-sustaining programmes

Traditional theological education, as it is conceived, is very expensive and impossible to sustain through student fees. TEE has the possibility to break with this model of dependency that conditions ministerial formation so strongly.

Unfortunately, TEE has developed with great dependence on the financial and human resources of mission agencies. The great challenge posed by the possibility of thousands of pastors and leaders being trained in their own context meant that significant financial and personnel resources were poured into TEE, repeating the cycle of dependency that had occurred in traditional models. With the same goodwill to make the courses accessible, they were offered for free or at a minimal cost, far removed from reality.

TEE is in a position to reverse this situation. If fees are charged fairly and appropriately, the number of students who generally participate makes it possible for the programme to be self-financing, including staff salaries. If we think of self-financing the programmes as they are today, it is an impossible venture. But if we assume self-financing as an unavoidable challenge, this principle forces the institution to work with realistic budgets according to its context. Management of resources will be more careful and closer to the lived reality of the students and their churches.

The idea is not to refuse all external aid, but this aid should be used in the advancement of certain areas and not in the regular development of the programme. Financial independence is possible in TEE and achieving it opens up endless possibilities.

Challenges for the Church

Challenge 1 – Open spaces for ministerial formation

The divorce between theological education and the church is a growing phenomenon, especially in contexts where the church is growing and alive. The reasons are manifold, and this is not the space to address them fully.

Basically, the problem has been that what seminaries offer, beyond their academic value, does not meet the needs of a church committed to mission and its full development. The church has not found in the seminaries a space that accompanies it, based on theological reflection, in its pastoral and missionary task.

For their part, seminaries feel that the churches do not sufficiently value their contribution to the construction of a theological framework that protects them from deviations, gives meaning to their actions and alerts them to mistakes already made in history.

The result of this divide is that the church has become impoverished in its reflection and the seminaries have become isolated from the life of the church. Both have lost. Today's church in Latin America, and certainly in other latitudes, faces the challenge of revaluing theological reflection and the contribution that a ministerial formation programme can make.

The TEE model offers a unique opportunity to re-establish a mutually beneficial relationship. TEE is flexible and seeks to be church-based and mission-driven. It is incumbent upon the church to take seriously this opportunity to be equipped with useful tools for a more effective and robust ministry.

Challenge 2 – Actively participate in shaping the curriculum

It is particularly important that churches take a proactive role in their relationship with TEE programmes. Churches are in the best position to define an agenda for action and set academic priorities.

The issues that emerge from pastoral action and insertion into the world should become the challenges for a relevant curriculum. In the New Testament church, theological reflection was theology made out of the conflicts and problems faced by the churches. It was not theology in a vacuum, but theology incarnate. Hence its great value. It is true that this will require a humble attitude on the part of theological institutions, but it is indispensable. TEE can be transformed into a truly revolutionary movement leading to a paradigm shift in the church-theological education relationship.

It will also be important for TEE to change the way it perceives itself as a mere methodological option and to assume a leadership attitude in theological work. The great challenge is to break with mental structures and paradigms on the part of both churches and TEE programmes and unleash the potential that would arise from a close relationship between both.

Challenge 3 – Make room for a new, broader and more inclusive model of leadership

Over the centuries the church has strengthened its structures and consolidated a style of functioning centred on pastoral leadership. This model has entered into crisis in contemporary society.

On the one hand, institutions as such are in crisis. Society prefers models that are more flexible and able to respond to multiple challenges. On the other hand, leadership is also in crisis. Imposed leadership that concentrates the sum of power and decisions is no longer easily accepted. This has led to another crisis, which is that of ministerial vocations.

Increasingly, those who dedicate themselves to a ministry, be it pastoral or any other, do so in a bi-vocational way. In other words, ministry is one more vocation, perhaps the most important, in the midst of other vocations for life. The traditional model of a student spending four or five years of their life in a seminary to develop a theological or ministerial career is on its way to extinction in the Latin American context. In fact, some traditional institutions have already closed.

TEE can make a huge contribution in preparing a new type of leadership and helping to bring about a more democratic and diverse church model. The priesthood of every believer has been one of the strongest affirmations of the Reformation, yet in practice this affirmation has not always been lived out.

Churches can find in TEE an important ally in empowering a diverse and pluralistic leadership.

Conclusion

The lessons learned and the challenges we face are many more than those briefly mentioned here. What is really important is that the TEE movement moves beyond the idea that it is a resource for basic levels of leadership. TEE is a different paradigm in ministry formation that goes beyond mere methodological issues or the production of materials. TEE begins where those who serve the Lord are, but its end has no boundaries. TEE is not materials, but a vision.

As I said in my presentation on TEE in Kuala Lumpur, a solid ministerial training will be one that is able to articulate the word of God with theological reflection and the *missio Dei*.[4] When the study of the word of God only deals with the biblical text, when theology only satisfies theologians and mission is neglected, theological education becomes useless. Conversely, if we manage to integrate Bible, theology, and mission, then theological education will make sense for the seminaries themselves, the students and the church.

It is time for us to learn from our own history, to correct our mistakes and to become protagonists of an innovative theological education in the twenty-first century.

4. Saracco, "TEE in Latin America," 131.

Bibliography

Saracco, Norberto. "TEE in Latin America: History, Present and Challenges." In *Exploring New Horizons: Working Together for Church-Based Training in Asia*, edited by Graham Aylett, 127-132. Proceedings of a conference held in Kuala Lumpur, Malaysia, by Increase Association, 20–25 April, 2015.

21

Lessons from TEE That Invite ICETE Reflection

Michael A. Ortiz[1]

Introduction

In February of 2008, I found myself visiting Cuba on a short-term mission trip. Our group decided we would split up into different parts of the country. I was assigned to travel to a small hillside village along the northern coast of the country. The village was remote and required complicated travel. Once there, a pastor named Obdiel who led the only church in the village greeted me and gave me a brief tour, including that of his tiny apartment which also served as the church for the community. Obdiel knew I had studied at a seminary in the United States, and as his tour drew to a close, he told me he wanted to sit and talk. He pulled out two white plastic chairs normally used on Sunday for congregants, and we walked towards the edge of the village and sat under trees looking down the hillside. Once settled into our spot, the pastor paused for a few moments, not saying a word but rather intently looking at me. Obdiel opened a Bible, leaned closer to me, and requested, "Will you please tell me something?"

Obdiel, located in a remote village in Cuba, had not received any pastoral training. He was a man who earnestly desired to know the word of God and faithfully communicate its truths to his small congregation. In essence, Obdiel was asking me to extend some insight about the Scriptures that he could share

1. International Director, International Council for Evangelical Theological Education (ICETE).

with others. This moment began to shape my appreciation of the tremendous need for pastoral and leadership training in churches outside the West.

For those of us who have had the remarkable privilege to study under scholars and the luxury of time to reflect on our own biblical and theological development, it is incumbent upon us to come alongside those who might have little to no training. My encounter with Obdiel launched me into a journey concerned over adequate and appropriate theological education to prepare leaders to fulfil the church's role in God's mission, no matter the context.

Within this essay, I continue to explore that journey, considering global lessons from TEE as related to ICETE.[2] In doing so, I suggest how TEE is an important contributor towards the global task of educating and equipping the whole people of God for his mission, including leaders like Obdiel.[3] The essay specifically addresses recent refinements in ICETE's mission and vision, and how TEE, especially as expressed within this book, corresponds with ICETE's anticipated future.

An ICETE Core Value

My role as International Director for ICETE began in November 2019. Soon after taking on that position, an initial task was to carefully understand the history of ICETE and develop a sense of where it might go moving forward. To an extent, that task was a continuation of the journey that had begun years prior in Cuba. For example, I discovered that ICETE, throughout its history and particularly through its Manifesto on the Renewal of Evangelical Theological Education, first published in 1981, always contemplated a sincere interconnectedness between theological education and the local church. Not only does this important document advocate for that nexus, but it also suggests that a renewal for evangelical theological education should include varied

2. ICETE is the abbreviation for the International Council for Evangelical Theological Education, founded in 1980 to foster and support community and collaboration between those involved globally in theological education, particularly regional accreditation agencies. See https://icete.info/.

3. TEE may be defined in a number of ways, and within the present publication one can glean varied definitions and aspects. For purposes of this chapter, the focus rests in TEE's value which seeks to promote theological education programmes closely connected to the needs of local church contexts, regardless of the form.

forms of education to more fully serve the global body of Christ. In part, the Manifesto states:

> We must learn to employ, in practical combination with others, both residential and extension systems, both formal and nonformal styles, as well, for example, as short-term courses, workshops, evening classes, holiday institutes, in-service training, travelling seminars, refresher courses, and continuing education programmes. Only by such flexibility in our programmes can the church's full spectrum of leadership needs begin to be met, and we ourselves become true to our full mandate. This we must accomplish, by God's grace.[4]

Even a cursory reading of this excerpt makes it evident that for forty years ICETE has intended to interrelate globally with all forms of theological education. Certainly, TEE falls well within the scope of ICETE's global purpose and Manifesto, and in that sense a kinship exists that should be encouraged as we mutually advance church-centred theological education.

In addition to the Manifesto, interviews with key present and past leaders, along with a review of other ICETE historical documents, further assured me of ICETE's significant value to advocate for global theological education that precisely serves the mission of the church. Consequently, all this affirmed that ICETE's future must not only align with my own personal convictions on theological education initiated in Cuba, but also with the whole of ICETE as developed over the previous forty years.

ICETE's Refined Mission and TEE

ICETE has undertaken to refine how it expresses both its mission and vision. The new expressions not only capture ICETE's history and Manifesto, but also succinctly highlight its high value for global theological education that serves the church in its mission.

4. ICETE, *ICETE Manifesto on the Renewal of Evangelical Theological Education*, 3rd ed., Part 3, Strategic Flexibility, 2002. https://icete.info/resources/manifesto/.

TEE initially developed within the context of Latin America to address the need for trained pastors.[5] But the challenges and needs of training pastors is global in nature. As expressed in chapter 3, recent studies suggest that there may be about 2.2 million pastoral leaders globally, but only 5 percent have had pastoral training.[6] That is, there are roughly over two million pastors in the world, including Obdiel, who have not had training. Lausanne's *Cape Town Commitment* states in the relevant part that "the mission of theological education is to strengthen and accompany the mission of the Church."[7] As we considered ICETE's history, the Manifesto, the global need for trained pastors, TEE programmes and others, and Lausanne, the ICETE leadership committed to give the church a prominent position within our renewed mission statement.

Accordingly, as of June 2020, ICETE's mission statement became: ICETE advances quality and collaboration in global theological education to *strengthen and accompany the church in its mission* (emphasis added). The mission statement's expressed focus on the church's mission aligns with TEE's influence and work over the years, and certainly as represented within this book by numerous authors. The church-centred focus is especially represented by Rick Weymouth in chapter 8 on the future of TEE in the digital age:

> My contention, therefore, is that TEE must add an explicit fourth element to its traditional threefold methodological formulation, which, I argue, is an intentional commitment to church-based training. Without this, TEE risks embracing online learning, as it must do to remain relevant in the twenty-first century, while losing a core element of its significance within theological education.[8]

TEE projects an intended future, including through online programmes, that will intentionally sustain it as closely connected with the local church.

5. Chapter 4, section on "The TEE Phenomenon in the History of Theological Education," 110-115. The authors, Carey and Harrison state, "In 1968, an international, interdenominational TEE workshop was held in Medellín, Colombia. After this, the movement spread rapidly across Latin America."

6. These numbers come from a presentation submitted by Dr. Ramesh Richard to the Leadership Development Consultation, Chiang Mai, Thailand, 25 May 2017.

7. Lausanne Movement, *The Cape Town Commitment: A Confession of Faith and a Call to Action*, Part IIF, 4, 2011. https://www.lausanne.org/content/ctcommitment.

8. Chapter 8: Weymouth, "TEE and Transformation in the Digital Age," 221.

Likewise, ICETE has embraced this as a crucial value, especially as now declared in its mission statement.

Suffice it to say that TEE and ICETE each maintains a global expectation that theological education will have an ecclesial and missiological focus. Within the next section, that mutual focus is further considered through specific lessons from TEE which are helpful for reflecting upon ICETE's refined vision and anticipated work.

ICETE's Envisioned Future and TEE's Contributing Lessons

Following the development of a new mission statement for ICETE, the leadership set out to consider what might be its vision to help realize that mission. ICETE concluded that as the global hub for evangelical theological education, it should envision three primary functions:

- Develop, promulgate, and mutually validate quality in theological education
- Cultivate worldwide relationships for reflection, mutuality, and practice in support of the church's mission
- Train, consult, and provide resources for theological education leaders marked by relevance, accessibility, and collaborative effectiveness.

As ICETE examines its work and ministry in the future, these three vision objectives will guide its activity.

The global hub serves as a metaphor intended to communicate the confluent role that ICETE will continue to represent. As we understand, there are numerous organizations operating regionally and some globally that have significant interests in various aspects of theological education. ICETE intends to continue to provide space for these ministries to develop community and collaboration for the sake of the church. As we consider which organizations might participate in ICETE's hub, certainly TEE holds an important spot. Some TEE global lessons are pertinent to ICETE's refined vision.

TEE places a high value on group meetings as part of its educational process. Moreover, it regularly considers ways to collaborate and even potentially create pathways for further educational opportunities.[9] A similar collaborative and innovative value is seen when we consider the history of TEE. Within this book, we can read about how TEE expanded globally and often made adjustments to better coincide with specific needs within local church communities and particular regions.[10] As an example, Carey and Harrison state in chapter 4: "As we have seen, the Lord has used many methods of delivering theological education over the centuries. Each has strengths and weaknesses. It is wise to choose appropriate methods, or even combinations of methods, not by default or tradition, but by purpose and circumstance."[11] TEE has had important global lessons centred on community, exploring ways to collaborate, and developing training distinctly fit for varied purposes. These are lessons that contribute to ICETE's own global vision for theological education, particularly as related to cultivating mutuality, practice, and collaborative effectiveness in support of the church's mission.

Another lesson from TEE that contributes to ICETE's vision is the way it has navigated through the formal versus nonformal theological education distinction. As most understand, this has been an ongoing debate for some time in theological education, and currently the lines between the two are more blurred than ever. ICETE's cultivation of "worldwide relationships for reflection, mutuality, and practice" purposefully includes all forms of theological education. TEE illustrates this value in practice in a number of ways, including campus-based institutions providing opportunities for students to be TEE facilitators and – especially relevant today – campus-based programmes using TEE courses as a springboard for online courses.[12] TEE has even blended various teaching methods to minister to migrants and

9. Chapter 3: Aylett and Samuel, "TEE in Theological Perspective – Part 2." The authors state, "However, many TEE institutions offer theological education at different educational levels, and levels of Christian maturity, and therefore provide pathways for growth from course to course, as well as a framework for growth within a particular course. TEE as a methodology has proved effective for training church leaders at both lower and higher educational levels, as well as a training tool for the majority of God's people who are not called to church leadership" 91.

10. Chapter 4: Carey and Harrison, "TEE in Historical Perspective," section on "The TEE Phenomenon in the History of Theological Education."

11. Chapter 4: Carey and Harrison, "TEE in Historical Perspective," 117-118.

12. Chapter 10: Julius, "TEE and Campus-Based Training in Partnership." The author appropriately states, "TEE has spread to almost all areas of the world, and rather than being a substitute for campus-based theological education, it is definitely a needed complement," 281.

refugees through training in the Malaysian context.[13] ICETE looks forward to TEE's continued global contribution as a collaborative model for theological education, regardless of the labels assigned to programmes.

Lastly, we may all glean from global lessons of TEE related to contextualization. TEE offers illustrations of how ICETE's aspired vision for "practice" that supports the mission of the church and "relevance [and] accessibility" in training might be actualized. This book explains how TEE developed a course writer training programme that specifically focused on local needs through twelve writing teams from nine countries.[14] For years, TEE has worked on developing training programmes for people with Muslim backgrounds, some of which are now accredited.[15] TEE has also worked diligently to develop materials intended to serve those who are persecuted and in economic hardship.[16] Unfortunately, these are the ones most often underrepresented when we think of theological education. Through creativity and an earnest focus on contextual needs, TEE has given us much to reflect on when it comes to relevancy, accessibility, and meaningful educational practices that serve particular churches, leaders, and contexts.

Conclusion

We began listening to a remotely located pastor in Cuba with no training attempting to serve his local congregation. Obdiel serves as a literal case of the continued global demand for theological education programmes that well equip church leaders in diverse contexts. As mentioned earlier, credible data exist to support the statement that Obdiel's circumstance is not an isolated one.

As we consider organizations like ICETE, serving as the global hub for evangelical theological education, its mission and vision must take into account

13. Chapter 11: Ball and Robinson, "TEE for Discipleship of People on the Move."

14. Chapter 7: Ivins and Do, "New TEE Courses."

15. Chapter 11: Ball and Robinson, "TEE for Discipleship of People on the Move."

16. Chapter 12: Vysotskaya and Subedi, "TEE as a Tool for Providing Theological Education to Churches Facing Persecution and Poverty." The authors highlight how TEE is a good solution to providing theological education to churches in the context of persecution and economic hardship. They further emphasize how TEE naturally reflects the biblical model of providing theological education for all believers used by the early church in times of persecution, which is expressed in the three main components of TEE: self-study, group discussion, and practical application.

the realities faced by churches globally. And so I have presented ICETE's new mission and vision and have noted a number of global lessons from TEE on theological education that can advance aspects of ICETE's envisioned future.

Looking ahead, we must continue to learn from one another, and we ought to do so through real-life educational examples such as those experienced through TEE. Doing so might move us closer to realizing theological education globally that indeed strengthens and accompanies the church in its mission.

About the Contributors

Graham Aylett became General Secretary of the Increase Association in March 2021. He studied Natural Sciences at Cambridge University, specialising in Botany, and earned his PhD for research in high altitude rain forests in Jamaica. He then trained as an Anglican minister and met his wife, Nicola, at theological college in Durham. They served with churches in three very different parts of England, before doing further studies at All Nations Christian College. In 1998 they moved to Mongolia, with their two small children, as Mission Partners with Interserve. Graham served with the Mongolian national TEE programme for fourteen years. He joined the Increase Committee in 2010, and in 2014 he and Nicola moved to Malaysia to work alongside Tim and Rachel Green in setting up an Increase support base there. Since returning to England in 2016, Graham has continued to serve with Increase as an Increase Equipper and as part of the Executive Team, becoming General Secretary in 2021. He is Vice-Chair of the Trustees of SEAN International, and a member of the Asia Theological Association's Commission on Accreditation and Educational Development. His publications include parts of *TEE in Asia* and other writings on TEE, specialising in interactive ways to equip leaders of local TEE groups. He continues to enjoy plants, especially growing cacti from seed!

David Ball is Director of the Group-based Open Learning Discipleship (GOLD) Project. He also works part-time for SEAN International where he links with church-based training organizations across Asia. Born in Kenya, David studied Biblical Studies at Sheffield University where he met his spouse, Angie. His PhD in New Testament was specifically on the "I am" sayings in John's gospel. Since 1994, he has been involved in training Christians in their context of ministry. He and Angie spent fifteen years in India working with The Association For Theological Education by Extension (TAFTEE) as Crosslinks mission partners before returning to the UK. David is an Increase Equipper and chair of Increase's Task Group for the diaspora; he has written in this area and was co-creator of an online resource to equip TEE local group leaders. He and Angie are actively involved in their local church in Bristol.

David believes that the strength of the church's life and witness depends on the equipping of all God's people for mission and ministry in the world. A motorcycle enthusiast since he was 16, David is also actively involved in the Christian Motorcyclists' Association.

Richard Brown grew up in Northern Ireland and moved to Australia after completing his bachelor's degree in geology. Together with his family he has worked in Central Asia for the past twenty years as a mission partner with Interserve. He became an Assemblies of God minister in 2003 and has served in various areas including international church leadership, discipleship and mission training, and managing community projects. He and his spouse, Miyung, helped pioneer TEE in one of the Central Asian republics and were part of the Central Asia Vision Group (CAVG) assisting the development of TEE across the Central Asian region. He continues to be involved in TEE as an Increase Equipper. In 2007 he completed an MA in Contemporary Mission Studies at All Nations Christian College, England. Currently he is a PhD candidate with the University of South Australia, with a sociological research focus on second-generation faith journeys of Central Asians. Richard and his family currently live in Perth, Australia.

David Burke became a minister of the Presbyterian Church of Australia in 1979 and has served as Moderator of the Presbyterian Church in New South Wales. He has led churches in rural and suburban Australia and city-central Singapore, and he was denominational Director of Christian Education for ten years. David has taught in theological colleges in Australia, Southeast Asia, and the Pacific since 1981 and recently completed a nine-year term as a full-time lecturer at Christ College Sydney, where he remains as an adjunct lecturer and research fellow in cross-cultural studies. He has been involved in ministry education for the Majority World over many years, including coordinating ministry training for the Evangelical Presbyterian Church of Timor-Leste and for South Sudanese pastors serving churches in Ethiopian refugee camps. His present research and writing interests are in Majority World ministry training and he is an Individual Member of the Increase Association. David and his spouse live in regional Australia and have an adult family.

Freda Carey, hailing from England, has spent over thirty years in Pakistan working in the field of theological education, the last twenty in the TEE Course Development department of the Open Theological Seminary (OTS), Lahore, which has over 6,000 students studying from basic discipleship courses to master's level. She also teaches the Bible, Christian doctrine and church history in various residential theological education institutions around Pakistan. Freda first went to Pakistan as a volunteer librarian at a women's college in Lahore. After completing the Cambridge Diploma in Religious Studies in 1985 through All Nations Christian College, England, Freda returned to teach at the United Bible Training Centre for women in Gujranwala. In 1999, after gaining her Master of Theology in the Study of World Christianity in Edinburgh, she took up a new post in Lahore with the OTS in 2000 and is currently serving as a theological education consultant. She has written one complete course, co-authored another, revised several others, and trained and supervised other course writers for OTS, particularly for the teenagers' curriculum courses. She is an Increase Equipper and has helped to shape and facilitate the Increase Association's course writers training workshops.

Paul Cornelius currently serves as the Regional Secretary in India for the Asia Theological Association (ATA). He is involved mainly with accreditation and providing value-added services to member institutions. He also helps in an ATA partnership with Scholar Leaders International on vital sustainability in theological institutions. Over the years, Paul has developed a passion for training "thinking practitioners" for the church and her witness in society. Formerly, Paul and his spouse, Mary, served with Youth for Christ in the city of New Delhi, before furthering his theological studies and engaging with theological education in India. After completing his Master of Theology in New Testament Studies from the South Asia Institute of Advanced Christian Studies (SAIACS) in Bangalore and teaching for a while, he obtained a doctorate in intercultural studies from Fuller Theological Seminary. His spouse, Mary, works in the residential life department at the Kodaikanal International School in South India. They have three adult children.

Miyung Do is originally from South Korea. After university she served in the Middle East, working mainly with women and children. Since 2003, with her family, she has been in Central Asia as an Interserve mission partner.

The main focus of her ministry over many years is equipping and training in discipleship and cross-cultural mission. Along with her spouse, Richard, she has served on one of the TEE national teams in Central Asia and contributed to developing TEE national teams across the Central Asian region. She completed an MA in Contemporary Mission Studies in 2007 from All Nations Christian College, England. She has served as an Increase Equipper since 2016 and in 2021 became an Increase Committee member. As a reflective practitioner, her research and writing interests include discipleship, culture, women, and mission. Together with her Central Asian colleagues, she is currently writing a new TEE course for Central Asian believers from a Muslim background.

Volker Glissmann, originally from Germany, has a PhD in Old Testament studies from Queen's University in Belfast and an MA in Theological Education from London School of Theology. He was the Executive Director of TEE in Malawi (TEEM) from 2010 to 2018. He is a course writer for the All Africa Theological Education by Extension Association (AATEEA) and an educational consultant for TEEM in Malawi and the TEE College in Johannesburg, South Africa. He facilitates a course on "Designing and Delivering Effective Theological Education" for the MA in Theological Education programme at the London School of Theology. He has written grassroots TEE courses for the Malawian context. He is a theological educator and Old Testament biblical scholar with an interest in grassroots theological education. He has written on TEE, theological education and diaspora theology. He is an Individual Member of the Increase Association.

Tim Green grew up in the UK. After graduating in natural sciences from Cambridge University he worked in the textile industry, and then with his spouse, Rachel, trained at All Nations Christian College (England) before arriving in Pakistan in 1988 to serve in the national TEE organization, the Open Theological Seminary. After fifteen years, his TEE experience continued in Jordan, then part-time with Increase from 2008 and helping support the new TEE work in Central Asia. He moved to Malaysia in 2014 and was General Secretary of the Increase Association from 2015 to 2021. He is a trustee of SEAN International which published his TEE courses Abundant Light and Feed My Lambs. Tim's other published courses include Friendship First, Joining the Family and Come Follow Me as well as parts of *TEE in Asia* and other writings on TEE. In his capacity as an Increase Equipper, he also trains TEE course writers. Tim holds a Diploma in Religious Studies from Cambridge University, a master's in Islamic Societies and Cultures, and a PhD on issues of identity for former Muslims following Jesus (both degrees from the School of Oriental and African Studies, University of London). He is currently Director of Word of Life which helps the worldwide church to welcome, disciple, and learn from Christ's followers of Muslim background. He has three children and three grandchildren.

Patricia J. Harrison is an Australian who has been involved in education all her life, and with TEE since studying under Dr. Ralph Winter and visiting the original TEE programme in Guatemala. During an initial career teaching in schools and in training teachers for an Australian university, Patricia also helped pioneer TEE in a rural area, designing a number of courses and serving as a group facilitator. While employed with theological colleges in Australia, she has also taught intensive courses at Fuller Seminary and at theological colleges in other countries. For a number of years Patricia served with the World Evangelical Alliance Theological Commission as a consultant in theological education, and in that capacity has often conducted seminars in curriculum design, teaching methods, and various aspects of TEE for theological colleges and TEE programmes on all continents. She helped to design and deliver Increase's training for TEE course writers. She has studied at Oxford University, Fuller Seminary, and several Australian universities, and holds graduate degrees in education, theology, missiology, teaching English to speakers of other languages (TESOL), and ethics. Her PhD was on cross-cultural theological education. Currently semi-retired, she teaches online and supervises dissertations for several theological colleges, including the London School of Theology, in conjunction with Middlesex University.

Nicholas Ivins. Armed with a bachelor's degree in education, a master's degree in biblical studies and pastoral ministry, and half-empty suitcases, Nicholas and his spouse, Denele, arrived in southern China in 1987. Nicholas spent eighteen years within the Chinese education system studying Chinese, teaching English, and delivering his children by bicycle to local schools. In 2006, he joined MAF Learning Technologies where he served for a decade coaching international ministries to develop training with increased impact. Currently,

Nicholas is part of the WITH International Community team serving several organizations that have a focus on transformative learning, including the Increase Association, the Asia Theological Association, Entrust4, More Than a Mile Deep, and the Union Baptist Church of Mozambique. As an Increase Equipper he currently leads Increase's programme to train course writers. He is thankful to God for the ministry he has given him.

Qaiser Julius has been Director of the Open Theological Seminary, Lahore, Pakistan since 2003. He received an MA in theological studies at Trinity College, Bristol (England) and a PhD in practical theology from the Australian College of Theology, as well as an MDiv from Gujranwala Theological Seminary, Pakistan. He is the General Secretary of the Theological Educators' Forum (TEF) in Pakistan and Country Coordinator for the Langham Expository Preaching Programme. He is also a member of the Commission for Accreditation and Educational Development (CAED) of the Asia Theological Association (ATA). His studies and writing have focused on the Christian response to suffering and persecution, particularly in the context of Pakistan. He has also served as a member of a visiting evaluation team of the Asia Theological Association for accreditation evaluation of theological institutions in Asia and the Middle East. He serves as Equipper and committee member in the Increase Association.

John Jusu is a missionary of the Association of Evangelicals in Africa, seconded to the Africa International University (AIU) in Nairobi, Kenya. He is an ordained minister of the Church of the United Brethren in Christ – Sierra Leone. He has a PhD and is currently on extended leave of absence from the AIU, serving with the United World Mission/Overseas Council International as Africa Regional Director. He works extensively on transformational curriculum issues in response to African formal and nonformal educational contexts. His interest is in understanding the epistemological frameworks of Africans seeking to enter pastoral and teaching ministries of the church in Africa, and how they influence educational practices. In light of this expertise, John serves as curriculum consultant for the More Than a Mile Deep-Global, Supervising Editor for the Africa Study Bible, Senior Researcher for the Africa Leadership Study, and member of the Global Associates for Transformational Education. John is also involved in faculty development for many educational initiatives in Africa. John is married to Tity, and they have three children.

Kangwa Mabuluki is a native of Zambia and an ordained minister of the United Church of Zambia. He has been a pastor in various local congregations, Chaplain of the University of Zambia (1986–1989), Africa Regional Secretary (1990–1994) and General Secretary (1995–1999) of the World Student Christian Federation. Currently he is General Secretary of the All Africa Theological Education by Extension Association (AATEEA). His involvement in TEE began in his student days when he volunteered to translate TEE courses into one of the Zambian local languages. Later as Executive Director of TEE in Zambia (TEEZ) from 2002–2014, he was also one of the founders of the All Africa Theological Education by Extension Association (AATEEA), in which he served as volunteer General Secretary from 2006–2014, becoming full-time in 2015. He holds a graduate diploma in theology from Makerere University (Uganda), a master's degree in applied theology from Oxford University (England), and a PhD in Christian education from the University of KwaZulu Natal (South Africa). Passionate about the biblically mandated "priesthood of all believers," he sees TEE as one effective way of "preparing all God's people for works of Christian service" (Eph 4:12) and effective ministry.

Michael A. Ortiz was born in New York City to Cuban immigrants. After receiving a law degree from Southern Methodist University in 1988 and practicing in Florida, he submitted his life to Christ and developed a hunger for biblical and theological studies. Following his ThM in New Testament from Dallas Theological Seminary (DTS) in 2008, he obtained a PhD in theological education from Seminario Teológico Centroamericano (SETECA) in 2015. Michael is currently chair of the Department of World Missions and Intercultural Studies at DTS. Prior to this he was involved in theological education leadership and teaching in Spanish-speaking countries, especially Cuba. While at DTS, he served as the initial director of DTS enEspañol, a department offering master's level programmes to the Spanish world. His primary academic interests relate to global theological education and contextualization. He also currently serves as International Director for the International Council for Evangelical Theological Education and Interim Vice President for the South Central Region of the Evangelical Missiological Society. He often speaks at conferences and churches, and has published many articles.

He has been married to Kathy for over thirty years, and they have two married children. He also maintains a law practice in Florida.

Lyn Pearson is an ABC (Australian Born Chinese) currently living with her family in Australia. She trained in medicine and development and has a master's degree in theology; she is currently enrolled in the Peace Studies programme of AGST (Asia Graduate School of Theology). Until recently Lyn worked with the International Leadership Team of Interserve. She continues to serve with Interserve and works part-time as a family practice doctor. She is an ordained Anglican minister in the Diocese of Melbourne, Australia. While living overseas, Lyn worked in community development and theological education. In the late 2000s, she served in a national team that helped pioneer TEE in Central Asia. From 2010, she has worked as an Increase Equipper with national TEE programmes in SE Asia and diaspora TEE development in Australia and New Zealand. In the Increase Association she also serves on the Executive Team as Partnerships Coordinator and on the Diaspora Task Group.

Rina Robinson lives in Malaysia with her family. Along with her spouse, Martin, she serves in a leadership and training capacity in diaspora TEE ministry with TEE Malaysia. She has worked with the Nepali diaspora in Malaysia since 2001 through Migrant Ministry Klang (MMK) and helped pioneer diaspora TEE ministry among the Nepali community. She has a master's degree in Christian studies from the Malaysia Bible Seminary. She is an Increase Equipper and serves on the Diaspora Task Group.

David Samuel is from Tamil Nadu, India. Ordained a Presbyter of the Church of South India, he worked in the Kanyakumari Diocese. He obtained a BSc in physics and an MA in English, before completing a BD from Union Biblical Seminary, Pune (India), an MTh from the United Theological College, Bangalore (India), and a PhD from Kings College, London (England). He has been serving as Director of TAFTEE (The Association For Theological Education by Extension) since 1984. He also serves as President of the Union Biblical Seminary Society and as a Trustee of the South Asia Institute of Advanced Christian Studies. He has also served as Chairman of the Evangelical Fellowship of India, Secretary of the Evangelical Fellowship of India Theological Commission, Chairman of the Christian Institute of Management (Bangalore), and member of the boards of Theological Education of the Senate of Serampore and the Asia Theological Association, India.

J. Norberto Saracco is a pastor, educator, and theologian. He has master's degrees in theology (Universidad Bíblica Latinoamericana) and religious sciences (Universidad Nacional de Costa Rica), and a PhD in theology (University of Birmingham, England). He became a Pentecostal pastor in 1969 and pastor of Good News Church (1985 to the present). He was a founder and co-president of the Buenos Aires Council of Pastors. He is a member of the Bible Society and of the Argentine Evangelical National Alliance (ACIERA). He was a member of the International Council of the World Evangelical Alliance and International Deputy Director of the Lausanne Movement from 2004 to 2011. Since 1973 he has been involved in TEE. He founded in 1977 the Instituto Teológico FIET (International Faculty of Theological Studies), of which he is currently Rector Emeritus. FIET offers programmes from certificates to doctorate level. From 1981 to 1984 he was co-founder and International Director of the Latin American Faculty of Theological Education which has sponsored TEE programmes in twenty-two countries across the continents of North and South America, Africa, Asia, Australia, and Europe. From 2001 to 2018, he was a member of the Latin American Doctoral Programme (PRODOLA) and continues to direct the Latin American Network of Doctoral Programmes.

Thomas Schirrmacher, author, pastor, and scholar, is Secretary General of the World Evangelical Alliance after having previously been responsible for theology and education within the alliance for a long period. He has four earned doctorates, ranging from studies in missiology and ecumenism, to cultural anthropology and ethics, and comparative sociology of religion. He founded the Martin Bucer Seminary (Bonn, Germany) and has taught and lectured on several continents, including in the advanced programme on "Human Rights and Religious Freedom" at Regent's Park College, Oxford University. He is also Director of the International Institute for Religious Freedom. He is married and interacts directly with many global leaders in other religious traditions.

Perry Shaw is Researcher in Residence at Morling College, Sydney, Australia, and author of *Transforming Theological Education*. Prior to moving to Australia,

Perry and his family served from 1990 to 2019 in the Middle East. During the 1990s, he helped to establish extension centres in Syria for the PTEE (the Programme for Theological Education by Extension). He then taught at the Near East School of Theology (Beirut) during the early years of the millennium, joining the Faculty of the Arab Baptist Theological Seminary (ABTS, Beirut) in 2007, where he served as Professor of Education. While at ABTS, Perry was closely involved in the development of their highly innovative curriculum, while also becoming increasingly involved in international consultancy for theological education. Perry has authored two TEE texts, The Acts of the Apostles and The Art of Teaching and co-edited the collection *Challenging Tradition: Innovation in Advanced Theological Education*. He has also published numerous articles in the fields of theological education, intercultural studies, and Christian leadership.

Stephen Spencer studied theology at Oxford University, achieving a doctorate on the social thought of Archbishop William Temple. He has tutored in theological education in the north of England, most recently as Vice Principal of St. Hild College in Yorkshire, UK. He has published books on William Temple, Anglican social theology and a study of church growth in Tanzania and England. He has also published study guides on Christian mission, Anglicanism and church history, and a book on seasonal retreats. He has worked as a parish priest in England and Zimbabwe, in urban, suburban, and rural parishes, and for six years was the Diocesan Link Officer between Leeds and the Mara Region in Tanzania (where he saw TEE in action). In 2018 he became Director for Theological Education in the Anglican Communion, based at the Anglican Communion Office in London, working to build up links between theological colleges and courses across the world and commissioning learning resources for online publication. His spouse, Sally, is a Methodist minister and they have three adult children.

Tanka Subedi was born into a Christian family in 1971 and grew up in the western part of Nepal. In college days he became active as a disciple-maker among fellow students. While engaged with the student movement he caught a vision for the growing church in Nepal and its need for grassroots level teaching and training for its self-appointed and least educated church leaders. This led him to take up the translation of SEAN TEE materials. With the help of some like-minded people, this programme, known as ITEEN (Institute for TEE in Nepal), was warmly welcomed and used by hundreds of village pastors. They in turn used it as a tool for discipling in their churches. Many who completed ITEEN courses pioneered new churches and facilitated the needs of the fast-growing churches. Tanka has also promoted ITEEN among Nepali diaspora. After democracy was introduced to Nepal, there were opportunities to promote religious freedom, but in the light of more recent restrictions and persecution against religious minorities, fighting for equality and freedom continues to be a part of Tanka's mission. He serves as Equipper and committee member in the Increase Association.

Anneta Vysotskaya was born in Russia in 1960 and has lived in New Zealand since 2004. She holds an MA in philology and a BA in religious studies from the Far Eastern Federal University in Vladivostok (Russia); and she gained a Certificate in Christian Ministry and a Diploma in Christian Studies from Faith Bible College, Tauranga (New Zealand). Anneta was awarded an honorary Doctor of Divinity by Vision International University (USA). Although brought up as an atheist, she became a believer in 1992 and has been actively involved in Christian ministry ever since. She was a pastor in the Evangelical Christian Church of Vladivostok, Russia from 1997–2004, and is a religious liberty journalist, researcher, and theological educator. Her ministry focus is on Russia, Central Asia, Azerbaijan, and other former soviet countries, and she makes regular visits to the region. She was International Director of the Open Russian Theological Academy (ORTA) from 2005 to 2017 and has been General Director since 2017. She has been a TEE consultant for Central Asia since 2006, a member of the Increase Committee since 2008, and chair since 2017. She is a member of TEE Aotearoa, New Zealand, a member of the Central Asia Vision Group (CAVG), and was a member of the Religious Liberty Commission of the World Evangelical Alliance from 2005 to 2018. She has authored many publications on issues of religious freedom and Christian persecution.

Rick Weymouth is the e-Learning Director for the Arabic language Program for Theological Education by Extension (PTEE), based in Jordan, where he has served since 2005. Rick holds a PhD in theology (Otago University, NZ), building on two earlier theology degrees, and a bachelor's in chemical engineering. Originally from Australia, Rick is married with two older teenage sons. He has been a mission partner with Middle East Christian Outreach (MECO) and the New Zealand Church Missionary Society (NZCMS), serving in both the Middle East and Asia since 1996. In 2018 his family relocated to New Zealand, with Rick now working for the PTEE at a distance. He has also been a member of the Asia Theological Association (ATA)'s Commission for Accreditation and Educational Development (CAED) since 2010, and is a co-editor of the ATA's "Manual for Accreditation." For nine years he had a similar role in the Middle East and North Africa Association for Theological Education (MENATE). Since 2010, Rick has been an Increase Equipper and co-authored *Standards and Guidelines for Online Evangelical Theological Education* published by ICETE in 2019 as part of its larger *Standards and Guidelines for Global Evangelical Theological* Education *(SG-GETE).*

Introduction to Appendices

Dear Reader,

The compilers of this book anticipate that you may have come to the Appendices for one or more of the following reasons. You may be:

- looking for a weekly small group discipleship programme to complement your church's or seminary's programme or to introduce into your church denomination or network
- seeking to raise up leaders in your church or among the churches in your denomination or network
- desiring a way to provide long-term systematic discipleship from new believer to leadership level
- wanting to disciple diaspora groups in your church and community and looking for discipling materials in different languages
- looking for a discipleship programme which has a strong, practical component built into study of the Bible
- wanting to understand more about TEE by looking at its lesson materials

In these appendices you will find three examples of lessons from TEE courses at different levels.

They need some introduction, because it is not possible to experience the impact of TEE from a reading of sample lessons. An interested enquirer may be unimpressed when they glance through sample lessons, especially if they only see the personal study materials. They may appear mechanistic and repetitive, perhaps even simplistic. But the interested enquirer may well not realize that they are only looking at the "raw ingredients" of TEE. The raw ingredients of a wonderful cake or a delicious meal may not look or taste particularly attractive. They need to be combined and cooked. In the same way the ingredients of a TEE course, when combined and "cooked" become very powerful. The same interested enquirer, when given a "taste of TEE," would be able to grasp the full benefits of TEE. That is, they would have the opportunity to complete the stimulating personal study materials, experience a lively group discussion led by an able facilitator, and be empowered for practical application. TEE practitioners have often seen this.

Perhaps another analogy would be to compare the difference between reading the printed notes of a musical score and hearing the soul-stirring music when these notes are played on a grand piano. There is a world of difference! What you can read in these appendices is like the printed notes of a TEE score. TEE music is very different and combines the general and specific contexts of the group members, the directions of the Group Leader's Manual and above all, the master musicianship of the Holy Spirit.

However, these sample lessons are included here so that you can gain an initial impression of the method. This will involve writing your answers, either in the book or on a separate piece of paper, and not just skim-reading. When you have completed the personal study test, turn to the Group Leader's Guide and the Practical Application, analyzing why they are designed this way and how you might use them in a group.

So ideally, the best way to grasp the meaning and methodology of TEE is to participate as a learner in at least one cycle of personal study followed by a well-led group discussion and practical application. Please contact the Increase Association, increaseassociationoffice@gmail.com, for information about a local TEE organization in your context or the possibility of an online TEE taster group.

Appendix 1 is a lesson from Come Follow Me, a foundation level TEE course described in chapter 6 of this book. It was written specifically for believers in Jesus from a Muslim background. The course follows the letter of 1 Peter, and lesson 13, "Giving Witness," explores principles from

1 Peter 3:14–15.[1] More information about Come Follow Me can be found at https://www.come-follow-me.org.

Appendix 2 is a lesson from Book 1 of the middle-level Life of Christ TEE series from Study by Extension for All Nations, or SEAN.[2] The series is based on Matthew's gospel, and is also described as a Compendium of Pastoral Theology. Life of Christ has been used to equip many thousands around the world for practical pastoral leadership. Book 1 gives an introduction to the gospel and covers the infancy narratives; lesson 6A from unit 6 of Book 1 introduces three basic techniques of Bible study – observing, explaining, and applying.[3] Unit 6 comprises Lessons 6A, 6B, and 6C, and the whole unit may be found on the Increase website at https://www.increaseassociation.org/resources/LOC1-Unit6.

Appendix 3 is a lesson from the higher-level TEE course, The Art of Teaching. This course was written by Perry Shaw for inclusion in the curriculum offered by the Program for Theological Education by Extension, the PTEE, which serves Arabic-speaking Christians and church leaders. Week 5 gives a framework for effective lesson planning, "Hook," "Book," "Look," and "Took," and Week 5 Day 1 deals with the "Hook."[4] The whole of the personal study for Week 5, that is Days 1, 2, 3 and 4, may be found on the Increase website at https://www.increaseassociation.org/resources/Art-Week5. In this TEE lesson, expected responses are printed underneath the questions, and students are asked to cover these up, only revealing them after writing their own responses.

1. Reproduced here with permission from the author Tim Green.
2. Pronounced "say-an," an indicator of SEAN's origins in Spanish-speaking South America.
3. Reproduced here by permission of SEAN International, www. seaninternational.org.
4. Reproduced here by permission of the author and the Program for Theological Education by Extension, ptee.org.

Appendix 1

A Lesson from "Come Follow Me"

(Foundation Level TEE Course)

Come Follow Me is a foundation level TEE course described in chapter 6 of this book. It was written specifically for believers in Jesus from a Muslim background. The course follows the letter of 1 Peter, and lesson 13, "Giving Witness," explores principles from 1 Peter 3:14–15.[1] More information about Come Follow Me can be found at https://www.come-follow-me.org.

1. Reproduced here with permission from the author Tim Green.

Excerpt from Student Book

Lesson 13 Giving Witness

Mehdi Dibaj was a pastor in Iran. The government put him in prison for nine long years. Finally, in December 1993, they brought him to trial on the charge of apostasy.

- ***If you were an old man, after nine years in prison, wouldn't you long to be free? This would be so easy – just by disowning Christ and returning to your old religion.***

Medhi Dibaj gave courageous testimony in front of the whole court. Here are some extracts from his actual speech:

"I have been charged with 'apostasy' [rejecting my faith] . . . I would rather have the whole world against me, but know the Almighty God is with me; be called an apostate, but know I have the approval of the God of glory.

They tell me, 'Return!' [to my former religion]. But from the arms of my God, who can I return to? . . . It is now 45 years that I am walking with the God of miracles, and his kindness upon me is like a shadow . . . The love of Jesus has filled all my being and I feel the warmth of his love in every part of my body.

Life for me is an opportunity to serve Christ, and death is a better opportunity to be with him. Therefore, I am not only satisfied to be in prison for the honour of his Holy Name, but am ready to give my life for the sake of Jesus my Lord and enter his kingdom sooner.

With respect,
Your Christian prisoner, Mehdi Dibaj"

Do you want to know what the outcome of Mehdi Dibaj's trial was? You will have to wait until the group meeting! But now, let's learn how we can give witness for Christ.

Giving Witness for Christ

1. 1 Peter 3:14–15 tells us three important guidelines for our witness. Read the verses and fill the blanks:
A) "Do not be ___________. But in your hearts revere Christ as Lord."
B) "Always be _____________ to give an answer to everyone who asks you."
C) "But do this with __________________ and respect."

2. Come, let's learn about each of these guidelines.

A) 'Do Not Be Frightened'

We are naturally frightened about how our friends and relatives will react when they discover we are Christ's followers. Have you personally felt that fear?

____

3. God says:

> "Do not be frightened." (1 Peter 3:14)

Fear holds us back from making spiritual progress. But when we break through the barrier of fear, it sets us free.

> In a country in North Africa, some young people had become Christ's followers but they kept this a secret. They feared that their parents would find out. But later the police heard about these young people and threatened them, "If you persist in your new religion, we will tell your parents."
>
> The young believers remained faithful to Jesus, and the police told their parents. They suffered some persecution after that. But they grew much stronger in trusting their Lord, because they had survived the very thing that they had feared the most!

What guideline of giving witness did these young believers learn through experience?
"Do not be _____________."

4. 1 Peter 3:14–15 continues, "Do not be frightened. But in your hearts revere Christ as Lord." To revere Christ as Lord means honouring him as our Ruler, not anyone else.

If we revere Christ as Lord, should we deny we are his followers? [Yes / No]

5. In principle, we should openly give witness for Christ. But sometimes our circumstances make this very difficult. Perhaps you feel the time is not yet right to tell your loved ones about your faith in Jesus Christ.

This may be wise for a period of time. But it should only be a temporary stage, on the path towards giving open witness. We should not remain secret forever! Those who do so, almost always grow weaker spiritually.

Therefore, which of the prayers below is better, A or B? ______

6. In John's gospel we read about a man called "Joseph of Arimathea." He was Jesus's follower. At first he remained a secret believer because of his circumstances. But later, at the time of testing, he publicly proved loyal to Christ (John 19:38).

By contrast, the apostle Peter boasted of his loyalty to Jesus. But at his time of testing, out of fear he publicly denied being Christ's follower. Afterwards he deeply regretted this and "wept bitterly" (Luke 22:62).

So, when we face our time of testing, should we be like Joseph or Peter?

____

7. Some of us are still secret believers, but in due time we too will face the test. At that time, we will take strength from this promise of our Lord Jesus:

> "On account of me you will stand before governors and kings as witnesses to them . . . Whenever you are arrested and brought to trial, do not worry beforehand about what to say. Just say whatever is given you at the time, for it is not you speaking, but the Holy Spirit." (Mark 13:9, 11)

This reminds us of the first guideline for giving witness, from 1 Peter 3:14–15. What is it?
"Do not be ________________."

If you are still a secret follower of Christ, talk about it with your advisor. Above all talk with God, for by his Spirit he will guide you what to do.

B) "Be Prepared to Give an Answer"

8. The apostle Peter wrote "be prepared to give an answer." People might ask us questions like these:

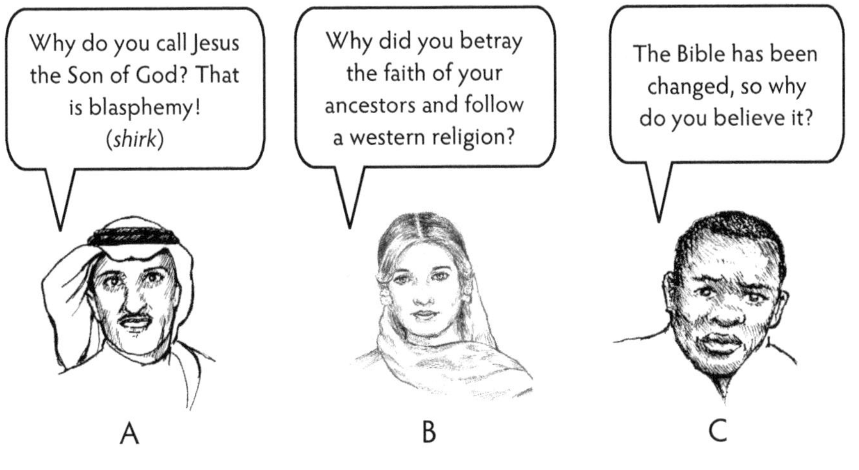

Pick <u>one</u> of these questions, whichever one you like; think about how you would answer it.

Which person's question have you chosen? ______ *(write the letter)*

What answer would you give? ____

____

____

____

____

(Just note down a few ideas, they need not be perfect. We will discuss this more together.)

9. Some people are spiritually closed. They ask questions merely to attack our beliefs and to trip us up. We should be careful in speaking with those people and not say too much.

But other people are more open. They genuinely want us to "give the reason for the hope that you have," like the lady in this picture:

What answer would you give her? ____

____

10. We should "be prepared to give an answer" to those who have genuine questions. We should be ready to explain the good news of Christ in a simple way. Some key points of our message come in 1 Peter 3:18:

> "For Christ also suffered once for sins, the righteous for the unrighteous, to bring you to God." (1 Peter 3:18)

Repeat this verse until it is firm in your memory.

11. Our non-Christian friends think that Jesus Christ came to this earth only to give "right guidance." But we long for them to know his real purpose! What was it? ". . . to bring you to ________." *(see the verse above)*

12. Write the verse again from memory:

"For Christ ____

__________, ____

__________" (1 Peter ___:___)

13. Suppose your friend or family member asks you this question:

What did Jesus Christ do for human beings?

Are you "prepared to give an answer"?

Note your answer here, including some points from Peter 3:18, and be ready to explain it to others in the discussion time.

____

____

____

____

C) "With Gentleness and Respect"

14. Let's read 1 Peter 3:14–15 once more:

> "Do not be frightened. But in your hearts revere Christ as Lord. Always be prepared to give an answer to everyone who asks you to give the reason for the hope that you have. But do this with gentleness and respect." (1 Peter 3:14–15)

According to this verse, which of the following is the best way to speak about Christ to our relatives and friends? *(tick one)*

___ a) Speak openly about Jesus but in a disrespectful way.

___ b) Be ready to speak about Jesus, with gentleness and respect.

___ c) Don't speak at all about Jesus even when we are asked.

15. As "God's chosen people," we should show gentleness and respect. If we argue and quarrel with non-Christians, we will only build up bigger barriers.

Therefore, how should we give witness? With gentleness and ______________.

16. Read this true account:

Saleem was a young man when he received Christ. His non-Christian brothers were very angry with him. They tried to persuade him to return to his old religion but he carefully explained his reasons for following Christ. Saleem's brothers set fire to his house, but he managed to escape. Then they gave him poison and he nearly died.

After this he moved to another city, but he kept in contact with his brothers and sisters. He sent greetings at Eid and helped financially when they were sick. Seeing his love, their attitude gradually began to change. Today they are still not followers of Jesus, but they trust and respect Saleem. But this change took 20 years!

Which one answer below describes how Saleem gave witness to his loved ones?

___ a) Saleem was "prepared to give an answer" but not "with gentleness and respect."

___ b) Saleem showed "gentleness and respect" but was not "prepared to give an answer."

___ c) Saleem showed "gentleness and respect" and also was "prepared to give an answer."

17. Yes, Saleem followed the guidelines of 1 Peter 3:15. He was bold in his witness but also gentle and respectful. This is hard to do, especially for those who live at home under their parents. We wonder how far should we compromise and go along with their wishes.

For instance, what would you do in the following circumstances?

- Suppose your father commands you to throw away your Bible . . .
- Or your mother pleads, with tears, that you stop meeting with Christians . . .
- Or your parents want you to marry your non-Christian cousin?

Think about what you would do in these difficult situations, and be ready for discussion.

18. If at all possible, it is best not to run away from our families. We should try to stay, respect our parents, and earn money to contribute to the household. By our actions as well as our words, what will we show? *(tick two answers)*

___ a) gentleness ___ b) respect ___ c) pride ___ d) rebellion

The Bread of Life

19. In telling other people about the Lord Jesus Christ, we don't have to be experts. As someone said, it's just like "one beggar telling another beggar where to find bread." Any beggar knows how to do that!

Jesus Christ is the Bread of Life. He has satisfied our spiritual hunger. But how will our loved ones also have this opportunity? *(tick one)*

___ a) if we remain secret believers

___ b) if we give witness for Christ only through our deeds not through our words

___ c) if we give witness for Christ in our words as well as our deeds

20. Read this true account:

> An Afghan man was Christ's follower for many years but did not tell his wife. Later she received Christ herself through the witness of her friend. Afterwards she was astonished to find her husband too was a believer. "Why didn't you tell me earlier?" she exclaimed.

If we have the "bread of life," should we deny it to our loved ones? [Yes / No]

How can we refuse the "bread of life" to hungry people? Our Lord Jesus Christ offers to satisfy their hunger eternally. Let's ask God to guide us to those who have genuine spiritual hunger and let's have the courage to tell them.

> **LESSON 13 PRACTICAL TASK**
>
> Think of one person you want to tell about the good news of Jesus Christ. Ask God to make that person ready to listen. Then look out for an opportunity to show or tell him/her just a little of what Christ has done for you.

LESSON 13 REVIEW

1. 1 Peter 3:14–15 gives three guidelines on how to witness for Christ. What are they?

a) "Do not be ____________."

b) "Always be ______________ to give an answer."

c) "But do this with ____________________ and _______________."

2. Look at these two believers:

- ***Nadia***'s sister asks her why she has accepted Jesus. Nadia replies "I don't really know. I can't tell you."
- ***Anwar*** says to his father, "If you don't become a follower of Jesus you will go to hell."

a) Which guideline for witness has Nadia forgotten?

"Be ______________ to give an ______________________."

b) Which guideline for witness has Anwar forgotten?

"With ________________ and ________________."

3. Write the memory verse:

"For Christ ________________________________

________________________, ______________________________,

____________________________." (1 Peter ___:___)

LESSON 13 ANSWERS

1. read the verses to find the answer
2. personal answer
3. frightened
4. no
5. B
6. Joseph
7. frightened
8. be ready for discussion
9. personal answer
10. memorize the verse
11. God
12. write the verse from memory
13. be ready for discussion
14. b)
15. respect
16. c)
17. for discussion
18. a) and b) are correct
19. c)
20. no

Study tip: Head knowledge is not enough. Ask God to change your heart too.

Excerpt from Group Leader's Guide

Lesson 13: Giving Witness

Aims for each learner:	**Cultural clues:**
a. Want to tell others about Christ	• Muslims and witness (*shahada*)
b. Be wise in knowing whom to tell and when	• Boldness or caution?
c. Be able to explain what Jesus Christ has done for us	• The "bridge" diagram
d. Memorize 1 Peter 3:18	**Prepare:** Optional video clip for q.13

Opening

Review the practical task: Were you able to solve a dispute with someone, or are you still praying for the right opportunity? What happened?
Praise God for what he has done for us, then pray for this lesson.

Lesson 13 home study review:
Question 1: a) frightened; b) prepared; c) gentleness, respect
Question 2: a) prepared, answer; b) gentleness, respect
Question 3: see q.10 (1 Peter 3:18)

Introduce today's topic: Who told you about new life in Christ? *Ask each person to share.* We have new life because someone told us about it. In the same way we need to share about our new life and tell others where to find it. Giving witness (*shahada*) is a duty for all Christ's followers.

Discussion

Giving witness for Christ (question 1)

Read 1 Peter 3:14–18

• What three important guidelines for witness did we learn from 1 Peter 3:14–15?	*"Do not be frightened," "Be prepared to give an answer," "Speak with gentleness and respect."*

Do not be frightened (questions 2–7)

Question 5: Read the question.

- Which of your family members know that you are Christ's follower?
- Do you usually pray more like the man in this picture or like the lady?

Question 6: Read the question. What answer did you write here?

- Have you faced the "time of testing" when your Muslim relatives found out you are Christ's follower? If so, what happened and what was the result? *An important discussion, don't rush it.*
- If you have not yet faced this, can you choose when you tell others or might it happen outside your control? *We should be prepared in case it happens at an unexpected time.*

Be prepared to give an answer (Questions 8–13)

Question 8: Ask learners to share what they might say for A, B, and C. *Possible answers:*

A. *The son shows the father's authority and character. We use "son of" as a metaphor, not literally. For example, in Arabic "son of the road" means a traveller, and in Farsi "son of Kabul" means a person from Kabul.*

B. *We love our ancestors and tribe and family. I follow Jesus Christ who was an Easterner not a Westerner. For the first thousand years most Christians in the world were not Westerners, and the same is true again today!*

C. *It is not true that the Christians changed the Bible. In the world's museums today are thousands of old manuscripts of the Bible. By comparing them we can have great confidence about the original text of the Bible.*

Question 9: Read the speech bubble. What answer would you give this lady?

Question 10: Read the question and practice the memory verse.

Practice: Telling people our good news

Question 13: Divide everyone in pairs. They should use their answers for q.13.

- The first person takes three minutes to explain what Jesus Christ did for humans.
- Then swap around, and the second person takes three minutes for their explanation.
- Come together again. Did this exercise help you "be prepared to give an answer"?
- Did you find 1 Peter 3:18 helpful in explaining what the Lord Jesus has done for humans?

Telling our story from the prophets:

- We need not start straight away with Jesus and the New Testament. How could you use the Old Testament prophets as a journey to lead us towards Jesus the Messiah?

Our Muslim friends are very familiar with prophets such as Adam, Noah (Nuh), Abraham (Ibrahim), Joseph (Yusuf), Moses (Musa) and David (Daud). But the Qur'an does not give much detail about them. We can tell our friends that there is much interesting information in the Tawrat about these prophets. Then, using these stories we can show how they point us towards Christ the perfect sacrifice and the solution for Adam's curse.

If time allows, watch the beginning of the *Jesus film* ***(the version which starts at creation), or*** *"the prophets' story"* ***on YouTube. Both are about 8 minutes long and available in many languages.***

With gentleness and respect (Questions 14–18)

Questions 16–17: Read the questions.

- In question 17, what would you do in each of those difficult situations? *The first two situations might change over time, but the third is more serious because it has permanent consequences.*
- In a situation where you have to refuse your Muslim relatives for Christ's sake, how can you do it "with gentleness and respect"? *Speak with respect, not in anger. Support the family in lots of practical ways and show you love them. Do not do things to embarrass them. Choose the right time.*

The bread of life (Questions 19–20)

Question 19:

- Why is our task like "one beggar telling another beggar how to find bread"?

Mehdi Dibaj at his trial made the same point with a Persian proverb. He said, "They object to my evangelizing. But 'if you find a blind person near a well and keep silent then you have sinned'." Six months later he was martyred. His courageous witness cost him his life. The witness (shahid) became a martyr (shaheed).

- Was Mehdi Dibaj's boldness worth it? What do you think?

Question 20: Read the story and the question.

- How can we find a balance between rushing to tell our family about Jesus Christ and waiting too long?

Advice from experienced believers includes the following:

- ▶ Let your life show positive changes to your family;
- ▶ Don't harshly criticize your family's religion;
- ▶ Don't say immediately that you have "become a Christian";
- ▶ Gradually hint that you find helpful teaching in the Bible;
- ▶ If your family directly asks if you are Christ's follower, do not deny it;
- ▶ Pray a lot for God to prepare their hearts;
- ▶ Tell a more sympathetic family member first;
- ▶ Your family might hear you are Christ's follower before you planned to tell them, but God is in control of the situation and it will work for good.

Conclusion

Obeying today's teaching: What difference will this lesson make in your life?

- **Read together the practical task.** What will you share about Jesus?

Pray together: Ask learners to share in pairs about who knows about their faith, and then pray for wisdom for each other and strength to be good witnesses, especially in their families.

Appendix 2

A Lesson from "Life of Christ-1"

(Middle Level TEE Course)

This lesson is from Book 1 of the middle-level Life of Christ TEE series from Study by Extension for All Nations, or SEAN.[1] The series is based on Matthew's gospel and is also described as a Compendium of Pastoral Theology. Life of Christ has been used to equip many thousands around the world for practical pastoral leadership. Book 1 gives an introduction to the gospel and covers the infancy narratives; lesson 6A from unit 6 of Book 1 introduces three basic techniques of Bible study – observing, explaining and applying.[2] Unit 6 comprises lessons 6A, 6B, and 6C, and the whole unit may be found on the Increase website at https://www.increaseassociation.org/resources/LOC1-Unit6.

1. Pronounced say-an, an indicator of SEAN's origins in Spanish-speaking South America.
2. Reproduced here by permission of SEAN International. https://www. seaninternational.org.

Excerpt from Student Workbook

UNIT 6

Lesson 6A: The Three Basic Techniques of Bible Study (1)
Lesson 6B: The Three Basic Techniques of Bible Study (2)
Lesson 6C: The Announcements of the King's Birth (Matthew 1:18–25)

Goals for Unit 6

On completing this unit you should be able to achieve the following goals:

1. Name three basic techniques of Bible study in the order in which they should be used.
2. Take part in a group discussion on what the Scriptures teach us about the use of these techniques in Bible study.
3. From a list of given points drawn from a Bible passage, name the technique used in each case.
4. Explain simply to an inquirer how the Bible teaches that Jesus Christ is the only one in all the universe who can bridge the gap between God and humans.

Lesson 6A The Three Techniques of Bible Study (1)

In Lessons 6A and 6B we are going to learn how to use some of the basic methods of Bible study. This is SEAN's logo:

As you can see, the verse which SEAN has adopted as its vision is 2 Timothy 2:2.

"And the things that you have heard me say in the presence of many witnesses entrust to reliable men who will be qualified to teach others."

1. By now you should have a really good grasp of the overall pattern of Matthew's gospel. It is time, therefore, to take a closer look at some of the stories that he tells us about the Lord Jesus. This is important because God speaks to us through his Word, the Bible; he also has given us a helper who guides and counsels us in our understanding of what he is saying.

Read John 14:26.

Who has God given to help us? ______________________________

Let's pause to ask God to give us the help of his Holy Spirit in our study today.

2. The Holy Spirit helps us in each of the three basic techniques of Bible study. These are

1. The technique of **observing**: to spot the **main points in the Bible passage** that we are studying.
2. The technique of **explaining**: to **make plain the meaning**, especially of the difficult points.
3. The technique of **applying**: to find ways in which we can **put the teaching into practice** in our lives.

Which of these three basic techniques of Bible study is used in order to
a) make clear the meaning of the passage? ____________________
b) spot the main points in the passage? ____________________
c) put the main points into practice? ____________________

3. Let's take the story of how Jesus called the twelve apostles, in Matthew 10:1–4, as an example.
To which of the Five Steps in the life of Christ does this event belong? The chapter should tell you. ____________________

4. Now let's see how easy it is to make mistakes if we don't use these three techniques properly.

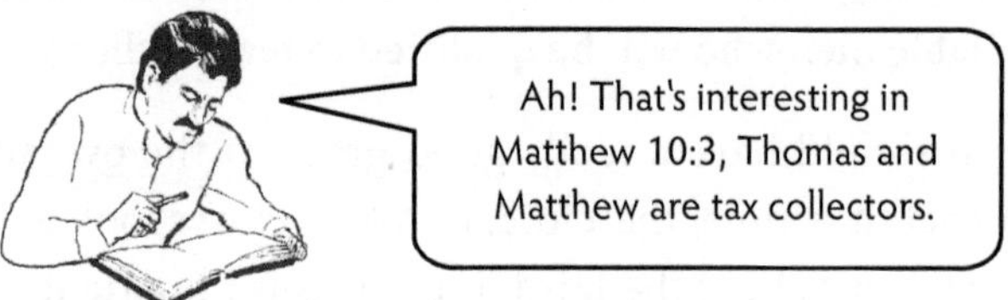

Do you see the mistake the student is making?

a) If we look carefully at what the passage says we can see that although Thomas and Matthew are mentioned together, only Matthew is the ____________________.
b) Clearly this student has made the mistake by not using well the technique of ________________.

5. Now look at this second mistake:

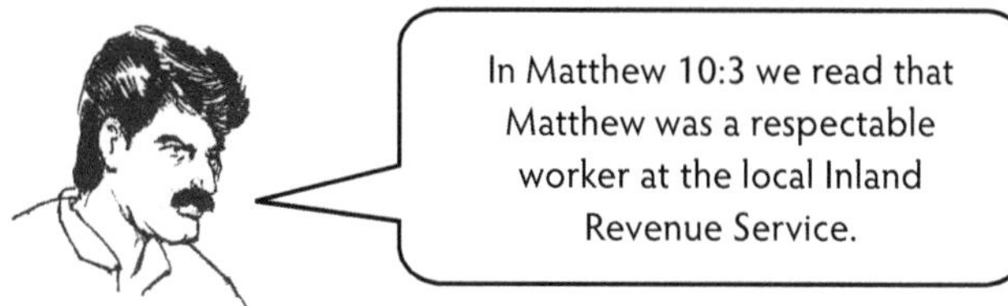

What is the mistake? Well, obviously the student was thinking of the kind of tax official who sometimes helps us fill out our income tax forms properly. He hasn't made clear that Matthew was collecting taxes for a foreign power and was therefore hated by his fellow Jews.

He has, therefore, not properly used the technique of_______________________.

6. Now look at this third mistake:

a) Is this student putting into practice in his own life what he had learned that morning from the example of Jesus in his Bible reading?_______

b) Which of the techniques is he not using properly? _______________

c) Why? Because the passage shows us that

- ☐ a. we ought not to let those who have sinned badly take part in church decisions, even though they are now repentant and believing Christians.
- ☐ b. we ought to accept such people as Jesus accepted Matthew.
- ☐ c. we only ought to let people with a clean past take part in church affairs.

7. These three examples give us some idea of the mistakes we can make if we don't use the three basic techniques of Bible study properly. Fill in the following spaces:

a) When I read the Bible I ought to pay careful attention to everything the passage says:
Technique of ______________________________

b) I need to make plain the proper meaning, especially of any difficult parts:
Technique of ______________________________

c) Finally, I must put what I read into practice in my daily life:
Technique of ______________________________

8. Now let's go back a little in the story of Matthew to the time when he began to follow Jesus. This will give us good practice in the three techniques of study. Read carefully Matthew 9:9–13.

In which step in the life of Christ did this event take place? ______________

9. a) Which of the following points are to be found in this passage?

- ☐ a. Jesus saw a man named Matthew sitting at the tax collector's booth.
- ☐ b. Four men fishing.
- ☐ c. Jesus called Peter, Andrew, James and John.
- ☐ d. Jesus invited Matthew to follow him.
- ☐ e. Matthew refused to follow Jesus.
- ☐ f. In Matthew's house, many tax collectors and "sinners" sat down with them at the table.
- ☐ g. The Pharisees asked why Jesus ate with such people.
- ☐ h. Jesus admits his mistake in eating with sinners.
- ☐ i. Jesus tried to hide the fact that he was eating with sinners.
- ☐ j. Jesus said, "*It is not the healthy who need a doctor, but the sick.*"
- ☐ k. Jesus said, "*I have not come to call the righteous, but sinners.*"

b) Which technique were you using here?

____

c) What are two of the most important points that you observed in Matthew 9:9–13?

Please use only your Bible; don't look back in your Workbook.

1) ______

2) ______

10. Let's continue studying this event.

a) What nationality was Matthew? ______

b) For which nation did he collect taxes? ______

c) From whom did he collect taxes? ______

d) In most countries today, officials who work in the Inland Revenue Service are not considered to be social outcasts! Why then did the Pharisees class them as such and show such disapproval of them?

______

______

______

e) Why do you think that Matthew invited tax collectors and sinners to his house to eat with Jesus?

☐ a. Because he still wanted to join in with their sinful ways.

☐ b. Because he wanted to introduce them to his new-found friend and master.

☐ c. Because he hoped they would persuade Jesus to join the ranks of the money-making tax collectors.

11. a) What were you doing in 6A.10 above?

☐ a. Observing what the passage said.

☐ b. Explaining some of the points that weren't quite clear by using things you had learned earlier in this course.

☐ c. Putting it into practice in your own life.

b) What technique were you using here? ______

12. In Matthew 9:11 there is a name that might not be clear to some people. They were members of a Jewish religious party who criticised Jesus. What were they called? ______

✏ **Note**: We will be finding out more about this religious party when we get to Book 2.

13. What are two of the points in this story which are hard to understand and which should be explained? (Try to answer, without looking above.)

____

____

14. Finally, what lessons can we learn from this story that we can put into practice in our own lives today?

- ☐ a. The value of inviting non-Christians to our homes with the aim of introducing them to the Lord Jesus.
- ☐ b. We can recognise Christ's tremendous love for us in spite of all our sin and trust in his ability to heal us.
- ☐ c. The importance of never having contact with non-Christians.
- ☐ d. Not to spend so much of our time with believers that we never make contact with those who don't know Christ yet.
- ☐ e. The necessity of putting Christ first in our lives before efforts to be a success in our business.
- ☐ f. The necessity of giving first place in our lives to earning money for ourselves.

15. a) Are the points you marked in 6A.14 above merely explaining things that aren't clear in the passage, or are they things that we should put into practice in our own lives today?

____

b) To which of the three techniques do they belong? ________________

16. What do you think is one of the most important lessons of this story that you can apply to your own life today?

____

____

(Compare your answer against 6A.14)

17. We should use all three techniques in every Bible study but always in their correct order.

- You cannot **explain** a point until you have first **observed** it accurately.
- You cannot **apply** a point properly until you have first **explained** it, or it could lead you into serious error.

In which order, then, must you use the three Bible study techniques?
1. Technique of ______________________
2. Technique of ______________________
3. Technique of ______________________

18. You need to be absolutely clear in your own mind about the difference between these three basic techniques of Bible study.

Which technique is used for
a) making the meaning clear? ______________
b) spotting the principal points in the passage? ______________
c) putting it into practice? ______________

19. Read Frame 6A.2 carefully again, thinking especially about what the words in bold print mean. Now what follows is a real test of your understanding of these three techniques. Keep clearly in your mind the differences between each technique as you tick the following points after reading Matthew 9:9–13. If you are not sure, check with the Answers after each point.

Write "O" for Observing; write "E" for Explaining and write "A" for Applying.

a) ______ Jesus saw Matthew, sitting at the tax collector's booth.
b) ______ Matthew was a Jew.
c) ______ He collected taxes from his own people, for the Roman conquerors.
d) ______ Jesus invited Matthew to follow him.
e) ______ I must put Christ first in my life, before all efforts to be a success in my job, just as Matthew did.
f) ______ Many tax collectors and "sinners" sat down with them at the table in his house.
g) ______ Matthew invited tax collectors and "sinners" because he wanted to introduce them to Jesus.
h) ______ We should not be afraid to invite non-Christians to our house to introduce them to Jesus, just as Matthew did.
i) ______ The Pharisees questioned the fact that Jesus ate with tax collectors and sinners.
j) ______ The Pharisees were members of a Jewish religious party.

k) ______ The Pharisees classed the tax collectors as sinners and showed their disapproval of Jesus eating with them because the tax collectors were really traitors to their country.

l) ______ Jesus said: "*It is not the healthy who need a doctor but the sick.*"

m) ______ Jesus said: "*I have not come to call the righteous, but sinners.*"

n) ______ We can rejoice because of Christ's tremendous love for us, in spite of all our sin and rebellion, and trust him to help and heal our weaknesses.

20. Now do Test 6A.

If you are taking a break between the parts of each lesson (which is always a good thing to do), remember to look back at the goals of the whole unit when starting each new part, to help you to pick up where you are in the whole study.

Answers to Lesson 6A

1. The Holy Spirit
2. a) Explaining b) Observing
   c) Applying
3. Year of Popularity
4. a) tax collector b) observing
5. explaining
6. a) No
   b) Applying c) b.
7. a) observing b) explaining
   c) applying
8. Year of Popularity
9. a) a. d. f. g. j. k.
   b) Observing
   c) Make sure that your 2 points are in Matthew 9:9–13
10. a) Jewish b) Roman
    c) The Jews
    d) Because they were traitors who took taxes from their own people to give to the foreigners and to line their own pockets with extra wealth
    e) b.
11. a) b.
    b) Explaining
12. Pharisees
13. • Matthew was a Jew
    • He collected taxes for the Romans
    • He was hated by other Jews, etc.
14. a. b. d. e.
15. a) Things for our own lives
    b) Applying
16. Feedback in 6A.14
17. 1. observing
    2. explaining
    3. applying
18. a) Explaining b) Observing
    c) Applying
19. a) O – The passage says this
    b) E – We are explaining something that the passage does not tell us
    c) E – Again we are explaining; the passage doesn't tell us this
    d) O – The passage tells us this. We are not yet applying it to our lives today
    e) A – Now applying it to our own lives. What we should do today
    f) O – The passage tells us this.
    g) E – The passage does not tell us why Matthew invited them
    h) A i) O j) E k) E
    l) O m) O n) A

TEST 6A

1. What are the three basic Bible study techniques? Write them in the order in which they should be used.

   1. ____________ 2. ____________ 3. ____________

2. Answer the following questions using your Bible but not your study unit.
   a) Who did Jesus see sitting at the tax collector's booth? ____________
   b) What did Jesus invite this tax collector to do? ____________
   c) What did the tax collector do? ____________
   d) Who sat down at table with Jesus and his disciples in the house?
   ____________ and ____________
   e) Who criticised Jesus for eating with these people? ____________
   f) According to Jesus, who needs a doctor? ____________
   g) According to Jesus, who did he come to call? ____________
   h) Who do not need a doctor? ____________
   i) Who did he not come to call? ____________
   j) In answering these questions, which of the three techniques of Bible study have you been using? ____________

3. a) To which of the five steps in the life of Christ does this event in Matthew 9:9–13 belong? ____________
   b) Why was Matthew's job so despised by the Jews?
   ____
   c) Why did Matthew invite some of his old tax collector friends to a meal in his house? ____________
   d) In answering these questions, which of the three basic techniques of Bible study have you been using? ____________

4. a) What lesson have you learned from this story that you could put into practice in your own life today? ____________
   b) In answering this question which basic technique of Bible study have you been using? ____________

Excerpt from Group Leader's Guide

GROUP MEETING 6

Lesson 6A: The Three Basic Techniques of Bible Study (1)
Lesson 6B: The Three Basic Techniques of Bible Study (2)
Lesson 6C: The Announcements of the King's Birth (Matthew 1:18–25)

Leader's preparation BEFORE Group Meeting 6

☐ 1. Prayer.

☐ 2. Read the Goals for Unit 6 in the Workbook.

☐ 3. Do Lessons 6A, 6B and 6C in your Workbook.

☐ 4. Work through the Guide to Unit 6 starting below and then return here to tick the box.

☐ 5. **Important:** Now do the Special Leader's Study for Unit 6 on pages 74 to 78. When you have finished, return here to tick the box.

☐ 6. **Optional:** Additional reading for group leader on Jesus, the unique and only Saviour:

John 3:16, 6:68, 8:24, 14:6; Acts 4:12; 1 Corinthians 2:2, 3:11.

☐ 7. Check your materials for the group meeting against the list on page 8. You will also need a Bible dictionary, a Bible commentary or an English dictionary (see goal C.3c of this Group Meeting).

Leader's Guide DURING Group Meeting 6

A. Opening: Review and Explanation (approx. 20 minutes)

1. Perhaps you could focus your time of prayer on the importance of the Word of God. Ask the Lord to help each one to be a faithful student of the Word.

2. **Any questions**

3. **Check the Exercises**

   Be sure that everyone has underlined, in green, the words: *"through the Holy Spirit"* in Matthew 1:18 and *"from the Holy Spirit"* in Matthew 1:20.

4. **Correct the Tests**

Test 6A

1. 1. Observing
   2. Explaining
   3. Applying
2. a) Matthew
   b) Follow him
   c) He obeyed and followed
   d) Tax collectors and "sinners"
   e) The Pharisees
   f) Those who are sick
   g) Sinners
   h) The healthy
   i) the righteous
   j) observing
3. a) The Year of Popularity
   b) Because he (a Jew) collected taxes from his fellow countrymen on behalf of the Romans (foreigners)
   c) To meet Jesus
   d) Explaining
4. a) One of the following: Frame 6A.14 a. b. d. or e.
   b) Applying

Test 6B

1. a) Is it right to pay taxes to Caesar or not?
   b) To trap him
   c) A coin or a Denarius
   d) Caesar's
   e) Give to Caesar what is Caesar's, and to God what is God's
   f) They were amazed
   g) Observing
2. a) The Pharisees tried to stir up strife between Jesus and his disciples, but Jesus used wisdom so that none were offended (or any of the points in 6B.12 to 14)
   b) Explaining
3. a) To be a peacemaker, like Jesus
   b) Applying

Test 6C

1. Two
2. Mary/ Luke
   Joseph/ Matthew
3. Nazareth
4. Angel Gabriel
5. At least 3 months
6. a) relative
   b) Elizabeth
   c) John the Baptist
   d) Judea (Judah)
7. a) father
   b) Mary / Holy Spirit
   c) God / Holy Spirit
8. a) Two
   b) Human / divine
9. one
10. He is the only one who has two natures, human and divine, and therefore can bridge the gap of sin between God and humanity
11. God with us

5. **Fill in the Register**

B. Discussion and Application (approx. 1 hour)

GOAL A: Bible Study

That all should be able to give a Bible example of what it means to use the technique of applying in a Bible study.

1. Ask the group: "What are the four techniques of Bible Study we have considered thus far?" *[Observing/explaining/applying/comparing.]*

2. Get the group to find John 14:23–24 and ask someone to read it in the New International Version of the Bible.
   - ☐ a) Ask the group: "To which technique do you think the words *'he will obey my teaching'* especially refer?" *[Applying.]*
   - ☐ b) Ask the group: "What blessing will we receive if we apply his word to our lives, according to these verses?" *[The abiding presence of the Lord.]*

3. Get the group to find James 1:22–26 and ask someone to read it.
   - ☐ a) Ask the group, "What does James mean by the words *'perfect law that gives freedom'* "? *[The good news of Jesus Christ.]*

- ☐ b) Ask the group: "To which of the three basic techniques of Bible Study does this passage refer?" *[Applying.]*
- ☐ c) Ask the group: "What can we learn from this illustration about how we can use the Bible as a mirror in the technique of applying?" *[Just as a mirror reveals dirt and untidiness, the Word of God can show us what is wrong in our lives and then help us make it right.]*

GOAL B: Bible Study

That all should be able to say exactly what we have to do when we use each of the three basic techniques of Bible study.

1. Now ask the group: "What do you actually have to do when you are using the technique of observing?" *[Spot the main points in the passage.]*
2. Ask: "What do you actually have to do when you are using the technique of explaining?" *[Clarify and expound on the meaning of any difficult or obscure points in the passage.]*
3. Ask: "What do you actually have to do when you are using the technique of applying?"
   [Put the lesson into practice in your own daily life.]

✎ **Note:** This objective is the foundation for all that is to come. Therefore make sure that everyone really grasps the difference between each of these three basic techniques before going on to Goal C.

GOAL C: Bible Study

That all will take part in preparing a Bible study on Matthew 8:5–13, and will apply its teaching to their own lives.

1. Ask the group to open their Bibles to Matthew 8:5–13 and ask one person to read this passage aloud, saying that this will deepen still further our knowledge of the Roman Empire in the time of Jesus.

2. **Technique of Observing**

- ☐ a) Say: "First we will practise the technique of observing by looking at the passage and stating some of the main points found in these verses. For example, in verse 5 there are two important points: The first is – Jesus entered Capernaum. What is the second?" *[Jesus met a centurion who came to him.]*
- ☐ b) Now complete the study by finding the rest of the main points in this passage, one by one.

  [The third main point is the centurion saying to Jesus, "Lord, my servant lies at home paralysed . . ." in verse 6. The fourth main point is Jesus offering to go to the centurion's house to heal his servant.]

- ☐ c) Continue listing the main points until you have reached the end of this passage in verse 13.
- ☐ d) When the students have finished, ask: "What technique did we just use to study Matthew 8:5–13?" *[Observing.]*

3. **Technique of Explaining**

- ☐ a) Say: "Now we will practise the technique of explaining. First, just name all the points that you think need explaining in this passage."

  [Capernaum (v. 5), centurion (v. 5), Israel (v. 10), Abraham, Isaac and Jacob (v. 11), Many from the east and the west (v. 11), The subjects of the kingdom (v. 12).]

- ☐ b) Ask someone to describe Capernaum. *[This should include a simple description of this lakeside town and its importance as a centre of Jesus's Galilean ministry during the Year of Popularity.]*
- ☐ c) Say: "One of the best places to find explanations of difficult or obscure points is in a Bible dictionary, Bible commentary, or even an English dictionary." Show the class how to use these.
- ☐ d) Have someone look up the word "centurion" in the dictionary and explain the definition to the rest of the group. *[A Roman captain over a 100 soldiers; "cent" is from the Roman word for 100, as in century: 100 years.]*

☐ e) Tell the group that they can follow the same procedure with the other difficult points they have identified. However, to save time, give them the following simple explanations before going on to the technique of applying.

Israel (v. 10)	–	Refers to the Jewish nation, which is named after one of their ancestors of this name
Abraham, Isaac, Jacob (v. 11)	–	Three ancestors of the Jews (Jacob was another name for Israel)
Many from the east and the west (v. 11)	–	Non-Jews who believed
The subjects of the kingdom (v. 12)	–	The unbelieving Jews

4. **Technique of Applying**

Say: "Now let's practise the technique of applying. What lessons can we learn from the example of the centurion which we should put into practice in our daily lives?"

Note: If the group has difficulty answering this, prompt them without actually telling them the answers. Some examples are given below. The group may have others. Only tell them the answer if they are unable to respond at all.

[a) Concern for the sick, especially those who are in our employment (v. 6).

b) Wisdom to come to Jesus in times of need (v. 5).

c) Simplicity and sincerity in prayer – the centurion just laid his need before the Lord without dictating the way to solve it (v. 6).

d) Humility – the centurion said, "I do not deserve . . ." (v. 8).

e) Clarity of thought – the centurion used a military illustration, which everyone could understand, as an example of the authority and power of God (vv. 8–9).

f) Greater faith – the centurion believed that Jesus could heal, even at a distance (vv. 8 and 10).

g) To expect the Lord to answer our prayers, as did the centurion (v. 13).

h) Look with joy to our promised reward. See what the Lord promised the centurion, i.e. to sit down with the father of the faithful, Abraham (v. 11; compare Galatians 3:7–9).]

5. Now invite the group to have a short time of prayer based on the lessons learned in this passage, before going on to the next Goal.

GOAL D: Bible Study

That all will take part in preparing a Bible study on Matthew 1:18–25 and will apply its teaching to their own lives.

1. **Technique of Observing**

Say: "Now let's practise the technique of observing."

☐ a) Ask everybody to turn to Matthew 1:18–25.

☐ b) Get the group to spot the principal points in the passage.

2. **Technique of Explaining**

Say: "Now let's use the technique of explaining:

☐ a) What was Joseph going to do, that proves that he was not Jesus's father? *[He was going to break off his engagement with Mary because he thought that she had been unfaithful to him by going with some other man. He would never have taken this attitude if he had been the father himself.]*

☐ b) What change do we see in Joseph that shows that afterwards he was completely convinced that Mary had not been unfaithful, and that no other man was the father of Jesus? *[He completely changed his attitude and took Mary as his wife, instead of breaking off their engagement as he had intended.]*

☐ c) What phrases in this passage show us that the real Father of Jesus was God?"

[The child's birth was through the Holy Spirit, in vv. 18 and 20. The child will be called Immanuel – God with us, in v. 23. A virgin will become pregnant, in v. 23.]

3. **Technique of Applying**
   Say: "Now let's use the technique of applying."
   Ask: "What benefits should these wonderful truths about Jesus bring to our Christian faith?"

   [A deeper sense of security regarding our own salvation because it doesn't depend on us but totally on the unique Son of God. A clearer understanding of Christ as Saviour which we can share with others, etc.]

GOAL E: Practical Activity 1.
The students should be able to give a knowledgeable answer to an interested person who finds it difficult to understand or believe that Jesus is the only one who can save us.

Practical Activity

1. Have someone read 1 Timothy 2:5–6 aloud.
   According to this verse, who is the only one who can bring God and humanity together? *[Jesus Christ.]*

2. Say to the group: "By answering the series of questions I am going to ask, you will learn how to answer someone who wants to know what the Bible teaches about Jesus Christ as the only mediator between God and humanity."

3. **Question 1**
   Which of the following suggestions would be the best way to begin to answer someone who is asking about the mediator between God and humanity?

a) "I am surprised that you are ignorant of such a basic fact of the Christian faith."
b) "I think the answer to your question might possibly be . . ."
c) "May I show you what the Bible very clearly teaches about this matter?" *[Discuss why (c) is right.]*

☐ **Question 2**

Say: "Perhaps the next thing to do would be to read aloud what the Bible says in 1 Timothy 2:5 and explain what a mediator is."

Have the group turn to Frame 6C.50 in their Workbooks and ask: "What good illustration of what a mediator is can be found in Frame 6C.50." *[A bridge.]*

☐ **Question 3**

Ask the group: "What examples of those who are not adequate mediators between God and humanity can you find in Frame 6C.51?" *[God the Father; the Holy Spirit; the virgin Mary; the Angel Gabriel; the minister or pastor of your church.]*

☐ **Question 4**

"According to the illustrations in Frame 6C.51, what do Drawings A, B, and D have in common, which indicate that they are all inadequate to serve as mediators between God and humanity?"

[None of the bridges in these drawings reaches both banks. That is, none of the people represented by these three illustrations have both a divine and a human nature.]

☐ **Question 5**

Ask: "Which drawing in Frame 6C.51 illustrates the only one in all the universe who can bridge the gap between God and humanity? Who does this drawing represent?" *[Drawing C; Jesus Christ.]*

☐ **Question 6**

Ask: "Can one of you briefly tell the story recorded in Matthew 1:18–25 to answer someone who asks you how Jesus Christ can bridge the gap between God and humanity?"

[Tell the story of the virgin birth. Explain how Jesus' birth is unique (born of a virgin by the Holy Spirit) and means that he alone is both perfect God and perfect man.]

4. Now say to the group:
   "I am going to pretend to be the person who is asking you to explain Jesus as the only mediator. I want ________________ (name one of the more confident members of the group) to reply, using the story in Matthew 1:18–25 and the illustration of the bridges in Frame 6C.51 to explain simply the meaning of 1 Timothy 2:5 (keeping in mind the questions I just asked you about this)."
   Now, playing the role of a person who wants an explanation, say: "I believe that Jesus is just one among many great leaders, such as Confucius or Gandhi. Why do Christians claim that he is unique?"
   [Refer to the answers given to Questions 1 to 6 you just asked the group.]

5. As always, allow the other members to respond by asking if anyone else has anything to add or correct in what has just been said.

GOAL F: Practical Activity 2.

The students will be able to list ways in which they can apply this biblical teaching on the uniqueness of Christ to their life and ministry.

1. Ask: "Which of the following would be ways in which you could apply this Bible teaching on the unique person of Jesus Christ?
   a) To explain simply to others (especially to those who don't know) how wonderful Jesus Christ is.
   b) To adopt a reserved attitude about the unique birth of Christ because you feel that such personal and intimate matters should not be discussed in public.
   c) To explain to a friend who thinks Christ is no more than a great man like Gandhi or Confucius, how the Bible teaches us that Christ is unique.
   d) To consider it a subject unfit for educated people and disproved by modern science.
   e) To meditate about it in your own devotional time in order to increase your confidence in boldly approaching God through this unique Saviour.

f) To help someone who has been deceived by a false sect which denies the divinity of Jesus Christ, by showing them what the Bible teaches about this truth.

g) To share what we have learned with other Christians who lack confidence in drawing near to God through prayer."

[a. c. e. f. g.]

2. As a group, pray that the Lord will open up opportunities for you to share this truth about the unique personality of Christ.

C. Closing and Assignments (approx. 10 minutes)

1. **Ministry Assignment**

☐ a) Say: "The fact that Jesus is the only mediator between God and humanity is the cornerstone of our faith. The more we ponder the biblical evidence, the stronger our faith will become. So do just that throughout the coming week, until its full significance overwhelms your heart and mind."

☐ b) Say: "It is surprising that so few Christians really understand why Jesus is the unique (only) mediator between God and sinful humanity. Still fewer can explain this in a clear and simple way to others. Pray that the Lord will lead you to someone who wants to understand, and seek to bring them to a deep and personal faith in Christ with the teaching of this lesson. In this way you, too, can be among those who make disciples of all nations (Matt 28:19). Each of us should do the work of an evangelist" (2 Tim 4:5).

2. **Home Study Assignment**

☐ a) Tell the group to complete Lessons 7A, 7B and 7C for the next group meeting, with their tests. Have someone read out the goals for Unit 7 in the Workbook.

☐ b) Say: "Unit 7 is perhaps the most important and central unit of the whole course because it deals with the doctrine of the person of Christ and what the Bible teaches about how he is perfect man and perfect God."

SPECIAL LEADER'S STUDY
(Associated with Unit 6)

The ability to ask good questions is an essential skill for leading a group discussion. Some leaders find this easier than others, but this special study should help you to improve your performance considerably.
In it you will see that your understanding of the three basic techniques of observing, explaining and applying, will not only help you in your devotional Bible study, but also in formulating matching questions of observing, explaining and applying. So let's practise this skill now.

Note: Cover the feedback with a piece of paper while you write your own answer on a separate piece of paper. Then check against the feedback.

1. In the first place, why do you think it is so important to be able to ask good questions in a group discussion?
[Because good questions stimulate the group to think, respond and discuss, and not just to listen.]

2. Now here is a teaser! Think carefully before answering. Which do you think would be the more difficult;
a) writing good questions?
b) answering good questions?
[It is usually more difficult to write a series of good questions. Although a good question makes us think, it is usually quite easy to answer – that is what makes it a good question. Formulating good questions is quite an art and requires much skill and practice to get it right.]
So let's get down to practising this important skill.

Questions of Observing

3. Each of the three basic techniques of Bible study has its own kind of question. The easiest kind of question to answer is one of observing.

Why do you think this is so?
[Because the answer is right there in the Bible passage for us to see.]

4. **Definition**
   Questions of observing are those that ask for one of the main points found in the actual Bible passage being studied.
   Exercise:
   Read the questions in Test 6A.2 in the Student Workbook. These are questions of observing. What do they all have in common?
   [The answers to them are all found directly in the Bible passage you studied on Matthew's call.]

5. Now turn to Matthew 8:5–13. Read the passage, then write a few questions of observing based on the main points in this passage.
   Note: Avoid writing questions which only require the answer "yes" or "no." A good question should draw out a fuller answer than that (e.g. questions that begin with "Why," "What," "Who," "How," "When," and "Where." Most questions that begin with "Did" or "Was" usually only require "Yes" or "No" answers.
   [Examples:
   - *What town did Jesus enter?*
   - *Who came to Jesus as he was entering this town?*
   - *What did this person ask Jesus to do?*
   - *What was Jesus' reply to this request?*
   - *Why didn't the centurion want Jesus to go to his house to heal the servant?*
   - *When was the servant healed? Etc., etc.]*

Questions of Explaining

6. **Definition**
   A question of explaining is one which leads us to clarify some obscure or difficult point in the Bible passage.
   Exercise:
   Read several of the questions of explaining asked in Frame 6A.10 in your Student Workbook.
   These questions correspond to Matthew 9:9–13.

a) The answers to these questions were not given directly in the Bible passage. They required the student to base the answer on previous knowledge gained while studying this course.
b) Remember, in questions of explaining, the primary purpose is to clarify the obscure or difficult points in a Bible passage.
[Did you complete the above exercise? (There is no feedback).]

7. Now return to the story of the Roman centurion in Matthew 8:5–13 and write a few questions of explaining on some of the difficult or obscure points mentioned in the passage.
[Examples:
- *What is a centurion?*
- *What is Jesus referring to when he speaks of Israel, in v.10?*
- *Who are Abraham, Isaac and Jacob?*
- *To whom is Jesus referring when he says, "many will come from the east and the west", in v. 11?*
- *Where was Capernaum located? Etc., etc.]*

Questions of Applying

8. **Definition**
A question of applying is one which asks how the teaching of the Bible passage can be put into practice in our own lives.
Exercise:
One example of a question of applying is found in Frame 6A.14. in your Workbook. Here it is:
What lessons can we learn from this story that we can put into practice in our own lives today?
Another example of a question of applying is found in Frame 6B.15.
[Did you complete the above exercise? (There is no feedback.)]

9. Again turn to Matthew 8:5–13 and write 3 or 4 questions of applying for this passage, based on the example of the centurion.
[Examples:
a) Notice the concern of the centurion for his servant in v. 6. How can we show our concern for those who are sick? What can we do to help them?

b) *In v. 8, notice how this important official, a centurion, considered himself unworthy for Jesus to come to his home. How can we demonstrate a similar attitude towards Jesus in our own lives?*
c) *The centurion recognised the authority of Jesus, in vv. 8 and 9. How can we acknowledge the authority of Jesus in our own lives? Etc., etc.]*

10. If you were leading a Bible study, which kind of question (observing, explaining, or applying) would you direct to:
    a) the more timid members of the group? *[Observing]*
    b) the slightly more confident members? *[Explaining]*
    c) the more advanced members? *[Applying]*

11. a) How could you improve the group discussion by putting a particular kind of question to a particular type of person?
    [By putting the simpler questions (e.g. of observing) to the more timid members, you help to build up their confidence.
    By putting the more difficult questions to the more advanced and confident students you stimulate them to think more deeply about the matter.]
    b) As your group grows in experience and becomes better acquainted with each other, which kind of questions would you want to ask more frequently? *[Explaining, and especially applying.]*

12. The plan for you as Group Leader of this course is to give you very full information, and then gradually to wean you from this as you learn to stand on your own feet. So although this Training Guide has a complete series of questions all laid out for you to use, this will be less so in the Leader's Guides for Book 2 and onward. This is why we are giving you this training in creating your own questions now.

    However, even at this stage there will always be times when you will need to supplement the set questions in this Guide with further questions of your own – for example, when a discussion drags.

    So spend a short time thinking of ways in which you can use what you have just learned to improve your skill in asking extra questions at the right time. Also use the set questions as models that you can copy in creating your own questions.

Appendix 3

A Lesson from "The Art of Teaching"

(Higher Level TEE Course)

This lesson is from the higher-level TEE course, The Art of Teaching. This course was written by Perry Shaw for inclusion in the curriculum offered by the Program for Theological Education by Extension, the PTEE, which serves Arabic-speaking Christians and church leaders. Week 5 gives a framework for effective lesson planning, "Hook," "Book," "Look," and "Took," and Week 5 Day 1 deals with the "Hook."[1] The whole of the personal study for Week 5, that is Days 1, 2, 3 and 4 may be found on the Increase website at https://www.increaseassociation.org/resources/Art-Week5. In this TEE lesson, expected responses are printed underneath the questions, and students are asked to cover these up, only revealing them after writing their own responses.

Excerpt from Student Book

The Art of Teaching Week 5 Day 1
Lesson Planning 1: Hook

OBJECTIVES:

At the end of this lesson you will be able to:

- briefly define what is involved in each of the four phases of effective lessons,

1. Reproduced here by permission of the author and the Program for Theological Education by Extension, ptee.org.

- state why "psychological ordering" is a particularly powerful approach to effective lesson preparation and presentation,
- briefly explain why the hook is a crucial element in effective lesson planning,
- give the three essential qualities of a good hook,
- give three pitfalls to avoid and four principles to apply in the formulation of effective lesson openings.

1. Throughout this course we have returned continually to the Educational Cycle as the essential framework for effective teaching ministry. By way of review, complete the diagram:
(See Week 1 Day 3 frame 3)

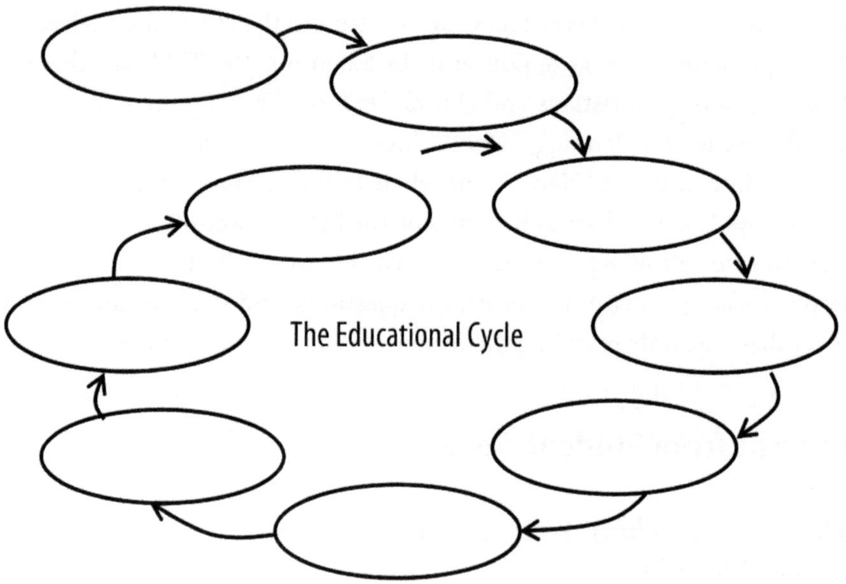

2. We began the course by coming to an understanding of the general goal of Christian teaching ministry, which is ______________________________
____
____

(to develop mature Christians in mature churches. See Week 1 Day 1 frame 10.)

3. An understanding of current needs emerged from an examination of _____

____

____

(the most significant developmental characteristics in the cognitive, social, emotional, and faith dimensions for each phase across the life-span. See Week 3.)

4. Last week you were required to develop a needs-based curriculum. Beginning with significant developmental characteristics, a specific and learner-centred current goal was developed. This goal became the foundation for the meaningful formulation of a program. What are the two main strengths of needs-based curricula?

(a) ____

____

(b) ____

____

(At the immediate level, learners will be enthused about a program if it meets a need that they recognise; at a deeper level, guiding believers to Christian maturity involves a step by step pilgrimage, learning to relate the Christian faith to each new developmental need. See Week 4 Day 1 frame 5.)

5. Over the next three weeks we will move to the nitty-gritty of lesson planning, first examining the basics of teaching Bible lessons, then the principles of developing effective topical lessons. Intertwined with these studies will be lessons designed to enhance your creativity in teaching methodology. The basic framework we will be using in lesson planning is the "psychological ordering" of "Hook, Book, Look, Took," suggested by Lawrence Richards in his now classic book *Creative Bible Teaching* (Chicago: Moody, 1970). Richards suggests that teaching effective lessons involves a continuous, systematic, but exciting process that embraces four phases. In brief these four phases can be summarized as follows:

- The ***hook*** segment helps students focus on the lesson topic in some interesting and pertinent manner. There are three basic qualities of a good hook: (a) it gets attention; (b) it gives the students a reason to attend to the whole lesson by setting a goal the students themselves want to reach; (c) it leads naturally into the Bible study. When a hook is developed with these three basic characteristics, then you have a good start on a creative class.

- In the ***book*** section the main subject is investigated and explained. Many methods could be used, but the purpose remains constant: a deepening understanding of the passage.
- Next, application of the subject is broadly explored in the ***look*** segment. The teacher guides the class to deeper insight into the relationship of the truth to life. The look segment addresses the question, "In general terms what are the implications of the text for today?"
- Finally, the lesson theme is privately addressed in the ***took***. The Scriptures are largely worthless without active response. While response may take place in class, even better is when the took can move out of the classroom into everyday life. Too often we leave church full of good intentions. We'll be more loving, more dedicated. But because the resolution is vague, because we haven't gone beyond the generalization to plan *how* we'll change, no change takes place. The creative teacher does not simply present a creative lesson, but also leads the students to plan ways in which they will put the lesson into practice.

In your own words, briefly define what is involved in each of the four phases of effective lessons:

(a) Hook: ____

____

(b) Book: ____

____

(c) Look: ____

____

(d) Took: ____

____

(a: The hook segment helps students focus on the lesson topic in some interesting and pertinent manner. b: In the book section the main subject is investigated and explained. c: The look segment addresses the question, "In general terms what are the implications of the text for today?" d: In the took phase the teacher leads the students to plan ways in which they will put the lesson into practice. Or similar responses.)

6. One of the great strengths of Richards' framework is that it recognizes the imperative of connecting the Bible with the world of our learners, and the reality that our learners' primary concern is the present and the future – the past only having relevance when it speaks to the present and gives tools for the future. This connectedness can be represented diagrammatically as follows:

Movement of a Lesson		
God's Word	Our World	
Past	Present	Future
	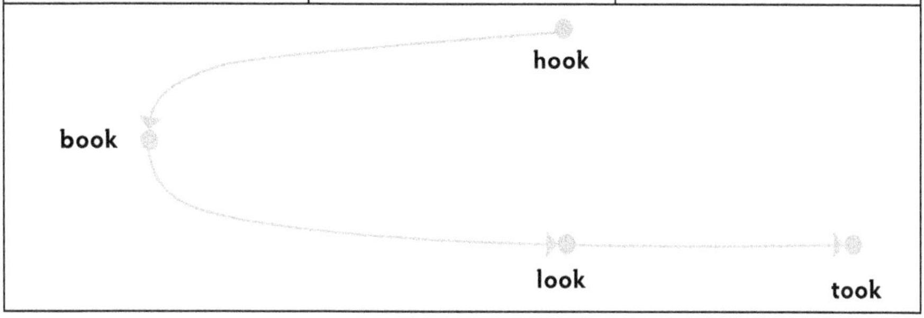 hook	
book		
	look	took

Why is Richards' "psychological ordering" a particularly powerful approach to effective lesson preparation and presentation? ______________________

____

____

(It recognizes the imperative of connecting the Bible with the world of our learners, and the reality that our learners' primary concern is with the present and the future.)

7. The "Hook, Book, Look, Took" approach takes seriously the need to connect the Bible with the world of our learners – issues of cognitive and behavioural learning. But it equally takes seriously the internal motivations of our students

to learn – an issue of affective learning. Although they rarely articulate their feelings, students come to class with three foundational questions:

(1) Why should I bother to pay attention to this lesson?

(2) Why should I continue to pay attention to this lesson?

(3) What relevance does this lesson have when I leave here?

How does Richards' psychological ordering address:

(a) Question (1)? ____

____

(b) Question (2)? ____

____

(c) Question (3)? ____

____

(a: The hook segment seeks to draw the student into the lesson in some interesting and pertinent way. b: Creative methodology used in the book and look segments helps to keep the student engaged in the lesson. c: The look and took phases seek to connect the Bible to today's world and give specific and tangible ways that the Biblical message works out in practice.)

8. One of the great tragedies of far too much Christian educational ministry is the teacher-orientation of the lessons: the teacher does virtually all the thinking, most of the talking, and is often the only member of the class who learns much from the lesson. Such teacher-centeredness emerges from attitudes such as the following: "If I as a teacher have spent many hours studying and preparing, I clearly know more than my students and they have much to benefit from my wisdom and knowledge." The unfortunate reality is that very few people actually learn much this way. The more passive the learning, the less content is learned, and the probability of applying the lesson in a meaningful way is next to nil. Our goal as Christian educators is not simply the transmission of information, but facilitating Christian maturation among those we are teaching. Consequently, a fundamental perspectival change needs to occur: lessons need to become learner-centred and learning-focused.

How would you respond to the following teacher comments:

(a) "I have done a theological degree, and the congregation need to be deepened theologically. The most systematic way to present theology is in organized lectures, so I am planning to do a lecture series on the Doctrine of God." ____

____

____

(b) "My primary job as pastor is to teach the Bible to the congregation. So I have a program of systematic Bible studies for which I spend hours in preparation. I prefer to lecture as I know my people don't have the time to study or prepare. I must admit, however, that I get tired of their superficial and often absurd questions. I wonder whether they even bother to listen." ____

____

____

(c) "My class of 10–12 year olds is excellent. I'm very strict with them, and they know that even the slightest misdemeanour will be severely punished. They always listen very carefully to my lesson – although I wish they would ask more questions." ____

____

____

(Your responses. In each case the most important question I would ask is, "What are your students actually learning?" This is an issue of both quantity and quality. If our students are passive, then it is improbable that much quantity is being received. If our focus is on transmission of information, then it is improbable that our people will be learning much about what it means to be mature Christians in mature churches. Unfortunately, the results of such approaches are seen everywhere: too much ignorance, or even where there is knowledge of content, too little application of that content in meaningful ways.)

9. As you sat down to begin working on today's lesson, how did you feel? Mark where you would have placed yourself on each of the following parameters.

Tense	←——→	**Relaxed**
Tired	←——→	**Awake**
Distracted	←——→	**Alert**
Sad	←——→	**Happy**
Anxious	←——→	**Calm**
Bored	←——→	**Excited**

(Your responses)

10. Your feelings as you approached the study of this lesson will have had a huge bearing on your readiness to learn the material I am presenting. Why is this so? ____

____

____

____

(Our feelings affect our learning – the affective domain impacts the cognitive domain. Or similar responses. Compare with Week 3 Days 1–2 frame 5.)

11. As a committed teacher, you enter the class prepared and enthusiastic. You've been gripped by the truth you want to teach. You've seen it work in your life. When you come to class, you're excited about the lesson. But your students aren't. They haven't had your experiences, and they aren't thinking about your lesson. They have their own interests and concerns. Some are happy, some are sad. Some have grave anxieties that are preoccupying their minds – the sickness of a loved one, an argument at work, financial problems. Many have come more to meet with friends than to listen to what you have spent hours preparing. In reality very few students ever arrive at class fully prepared to learn. Their minds are dominated by the affective domain – feelings and attitudes that generally are not well-focused on learning. You have to make them want to leave their thoughts and share yours. And so the hook. Fishermen use it to get the fish out of the lake into the boat. You use it to bring your students into the Word of life. The hook seeks to address the feelings and attitudes of our learners and turn their attention from that which is preoccupying their minds to a new phase of potential growth through the lesson at hand.

(a) Upon which of the learning domains you studied in Week 2 does the hook focus? Explain. ____________________

____

____

(b) Why is the hook a crucial element in effective lesson planning? ________

____

____

____

(Your answers. I would respond as follows. a: The hook focuses on the affective domain. The main purpose of the hook is to motivate students to turn from their own affective concerns – the feelings and attitudes with which they come to the class – and pay attention to the lesson. b: The hook is crucial because most of our learners do not enter the class ready to learn; their emotions and attitudes are elsewhere. The hook seeks to engage distracted learners into the lesson.)

12. The first quality of a good hook is that it gets attention. And the best way to get attention is to involve your learners physically or verbally. The moment a learner is doing something which you asked him to do, he is hooked in the class. The moment a learner has expressed her opinion in response to a controversial question or issue, she is hooked into the class. Involvement is the key to getting attention.

Consider each of the following openings to classes. Give each a grade out of 10, from 0 being deadly and uninspiring to 10 being an excellent way to gain the attention of the class:

	grade
• "Well, I think we should get started now. I'd like to begin by reading to you Philippians 2:1–11."	
• "I think everyone is here now. Let's call the roll before we get into the lesson."	

• The teacher writes on the board: "The Sermon on the Mount: Unreachable Ideal or Reachable Instructions for Christian Living." The class is divided in two and the teacher conducts a debate on the topic written on the board.	
• The teacher opens the class by reading a short extract from the week's newspaper which talks about the rising divorce rates in the Middle East, and then asks the students to say how they feel in response.	
• The teacher opens by reading a case study, and the class is divided into groups of 3–4 to discuss the case study.	

What factors made you favour certain openings over others? ______________

____

____

____

(Your responses. Discuss in class. I would favour the third and fifth openings are favourable in that the learners are more intensely involved from the beginning. The fourth has the strength of relating to the affective domain, but many learners would remain passive. The first and second are deadly openings all too often used in our classes.)

13. Getting attention isn't the only task of a good hook. The second quality of a good hook is that it sets a goal – it gives the learners an answer to the foundational question, "Why should I listen to this?" From the students' perspective this is a fair question: "If I am to pay attention, then this lesson needs to be about something important to me. Why should I pay attention to an irrelevant recounting of dusty data?" When your students have no reason to pay attention – that is, no reason that is important to them – then you'll find it hard to hold them. But if you set a goal *they* want to reach, then they will come with you. Consider again the class openings given in frame 12. Which of these five openings presents a goal – a reason – to engage in the lesson? Why? ____

____

____

____

____

(Your response. My observation is that the first and second openings provide no reason whatsoever for the students to pay attention. The third and fourth may only be of interest to learners for whom the respective issues of the Sermon on the Mount or divorce are already an issue. The fifth has the greatest potential: a well-written case study will draw the learners to identify with the story and give a very immediate answer to the question, "Why should I listen to this?")

14. A good hook should gain attention. It should also set a goal, giving the learners an answer to the question, "Why should I listen to this?" But if this is all the hook accomplished, it would be little more than entertainment. A good hook should also lead naturally into the Bible study. Consider again the five class openings given in frame 12. Which of these would easily and naturally lead into the Bible study? How and why?

____

____

____

____

____

(Your responses. My observations are as follows. The fact that it leads naturally into the Bible study is perhaps the only redeeming feature of the first opening. The second opening is again useless. The third opening clearly leads into the Bible study. The fourth and fifth may or may not, depending on the nature of the article and case study.)

15. David Edwards ("Designing Biblical Instruction," in *The Christian Educator's Handbook on Teaching*, eds. Gangel and Hendricks, 55–56) comments that "a group's readiness to learn is frequently determined within the first few minutes of a class session. During that time a "psychological set" is established that often persists through the entire period. Happily, that set may be positive as well as negative. Some common pitfalls you do well to avoid include:

- Consuming too much time with "administrivia" [administrative trivia] (taking roll, making announcements)
- Offering "dead time" with no expected activity (gathering materials, waiting for others to arrive)

- Stifling interest with a unoriginal or overused introduction ("Please open your Bibles to . . .")

Look for techniques that offer currency (a recent news article), reality (case studies, interesting physical objects linked to the lesson), drama (role play, audio tape), or vividness (pictures, slides) as a stimulus for attention. Some of these methods will be discussed later in this course.

Briefly state in your own words why great attention needs to be given to the first few minutes of a lesson – to the hook of the lesson. ________________

____

____

____

(Because the group's readiness to learn largely emerges out of the psychological mood established during the first few minutes of a lesson.)

16. By way of review, briefly define what is involved in each of the four phases of effective lessons:

(a) Hook: ____

____

(b) Book: ____

____

(c) Look: ____

____

(d) Took: ____

____

(See frame 5.)

17. Why is the "psychological ordering" of Hook, Book, Look, Took a particularly powerful approach to effective lesson preparation and presentation? ______

____

____

(See frame 6.)

18. Upon which of the learning domains does the hook focus? And why is the hook a crucial element in effective lesson planning? ____________________

____

____

____

____

(See frame 11.)

19. What are the three essential qualities of a good hook?

(a) ____

(b) ____

(c) ____

(It gets attention; it sets a goal; it leads naturally into the Bible study. See frames 12–14.)

20. Name three common pitfalls which should be avoided when opening your lesson:

(a) ____

(b) ____

(c) ____

(Administrivia, dead time, unoriginal or overused introduction. See frame 15.)

21. What four principles enhance lesson openings:

(a) ____

(b) ____

(c) ____

(d) ____

(Currency, reality, drama, vividness. See frame 15.)

Excerpt from Group Leader's Guide

The Art of Teaching – Week 5

Quiz: (10 Marks)

- The "psychological ordering" of Hook, Book, Look, Took is a particularly powerful approach to effective lesson preparation and presentation in that it recognizes the imperative of connecting the Bible with ____________ ________________________ of our learners? (2 marks) [the present and future world. See Day 1 frame 6.]
- Why is the hook a crucial element in effective lesson planning? (2 marks) [The hook is crucial because most of our learners do not enter the class ready to learn; their emotions and attitudes are elsewhere. The hook seeks to engage distracted learners into the lesson. Or similar response. See Day 1 frame 11.]
- Give the five key characteristics of a good main point (3 marks). [It is: the main point of the passage; short and easily remembered; stated in the form of a declarative sentence; positive in tone; focused on one idea. One half mark for each correct characteristic; an extra half mark if all 5 characteristics are given. See Day 2 frame 10.]
- What are the five characteristics of effective applications? (3 marks) [Specific, measurable, attainable, relevant, tangible. One half mark for each correct characteristic; an extra half mark if all 5 characteristics are given. See Day 4 frame 7.]

To the Tutor:

How well have ***you*** engaged the students in this PTEE class. Can you think of an effective way that you could "hook" your students into this lesson?

Class Discussion:

1. Begin the class by asking the students to respond to the affective taxonomy in Day 1 frame 9. Discuss the impact the students' moods as they entered the

class might have on their readiness to learn. Compare with the responses they gave to Day 1 frame 10.

2. Do students recognize that there is a problem with the traditional approach to Bible instruction in the churches? Spend some time discussing the teacher comments in Day 1 frame 8. What has been the students' own experience of sitting and listening to lectures? How often have they found their minds wandering in a Bible class because the teacher has not adequately engaged them? What about the ways in which they themselves teach? Do they seek to engage their students? What approaches have they found particularly effective?

3. What grades did students give the class openings shown in Day 1 frame 12? Ask students to explain why they gave these grades. How often have the students observed poor openings to classes? Can they give examples of particularly exciting class openings they have seen or given?

4. Ask students for their suggested main points (Day 2 frame 11). In each case have the other students evaluate the suggested main points in light of the five characteristics of a good main point.

5. The look phase is the key to successful Bible lessons. Consequently, you would do well to devote significant time to discussing this phase. Consider the following:

- How did the students see each of the four learning dimensions playing a role in the look phase? (Day 2 frame 3) Were they able to give suggestions beyond those given in the text?
- Spend some time discussing the lesson described in Day 2 frames 5–11.
  - Were the students satisfied with the chosen topic? (frame 5) Were they able to suggest alternate topics and/or passages? What reasons did they give for their choice? (frame 5)
  - Did the students have concerns with the youth leader's interpretation? (frame 6) What changes would your students like to make to the interpretative piece?
  - Did the students like the main point? Were they able to see its qualities? (frame 7) What suggestions did they give for an alternate main point?

- What cognitive, affective, and behavioural questions did the students suggest for this lesson (frames 10 and 11)? The design of divergent cognitive questions was discussed in depth in Week 2 Day 2 frames 12–16. You may like to review this material with your students. Note the description of affective and behavioural questions given at the beginning of frame 11. Your students' affective questions should clearly address feelings, attitudes, and motivations. Their behavioural questions should facilitate the connection between the Scriptures and daily life.

6. Few teachers are skilled at leading their students to specific and tangible responses to the message of the Scripture.

- Ensure that your students understand the problems associated with popular but vague applications, like those given in Day 4 frame 5 (a), (b), and (c). These sound good and spiritual, but they are too vague and general to lead to meaningful change.
- You may like to ask your students how many people they know in their churches that have listened to literally hundreds of sermons, but evidenced very little change in their lives. Then ask, "Why?"
- It would be valuable to spend time discussing the story given in Day 4 frame 8. Have your students ever asked their classes whether they have applied the message? Do they think it is a good idea? Why or why not?
- Why is it important for the teacher to experience the message personally before delivering it to his or her students? Ask your class to describe situations in which their teachers have spoken from their own experiences (Day 4 frame 12). In what ways (if any) did the teacher's experiences add power to the lesson?
- Devote significant time to the main points and practical applications suggested by your students (Day 4 frames 14–15).
  - Carefully evaluate the main points according to the principles given in Day 2 frame 10: the main point of the passage; short and easily remembered; stated in the form of a declarative sentence; positive in tone; focused on one idea.

- Carefully evaluate the applications, encouraging the students to work towards SMART (specific, measurable, attainable, relevant, tangible) applications.
- Ask the students what difficulties they experienced formulating main points and practical applications?
- Have students commit themselves to at least one action from the six practical applications they have suggested in frames 14 and 15 (see Day 1 frame 17).

What is the Increase Association?

Increase is an association of church-based training organizations rooted in and around Asia, most of whom use TEE. Increase is governed by an Asian committee and has a small serving base in Malaysia. It is an associate member of the Asia Theological Association and of the International Council for Evangelical Theological Education. It is a member of the World Evangelical Alliance's Global Theology Department.

Increase's vision is to see churches equipping all Christ's followers in their contexts, so that many millions are discipled and empowered for mission, ministry, and leadership.

Increase's purpose is to connect and strengthen church-based training movements across Asia and beyond. Together they:

- build a network of good relationships
- encourage collaborative projects and partnerships
- initiate and catalyze innovative approaches
- identify and share fruitful practice
- provide support, resources, advice, and training
- make a global contribution to theological education and adult learning
- connect with other church-based training associations and accrediting associations
- communicate widely the news and stories from Increase members.

Increase's work is carried out mostly by its members on a voluntary basis. For instance the Increase Equippers are experienced practitioners willing to pass on that experience through training workshops and in-person and virtual consultancy. Task groups focus on particular areas of innovation. The Intercessors Team support the work in prayer and Increase Trust UK in finance.
Increase's values guide its work:

- Sharing – through relationships and networking
- Inclusive – of all people, cultures and denominations
- Servant-hearted – in leadership and with each other
- Learning and changing – together and from each other
- Relevant – to local cultures and contexts
- Biblical – in how we work and act

Read more in http://www.increaseassociation.org.

ICETE International Council for Evangelical Theological Education

strengthening evangelical theological education through international cooperation

ICETE is a global community, sponsored by nine regional networks of theological schools, to enable international interaction and collaboration among all those engaged in strengthening and developing evangelical theological education and Christian leadership development worldwide.

The purpose of ICETE is:

1. To promote the enhancement of evangelical theological education worldwide.
2. To serve as a forum for interaction, partnership and collaboration among those involved in evangelical theological education and leadership development, for mutual assistance, stimulation and enrichment.
3. To provide networking and support services for regional associations of evangelical theological schools worldwide.
4. To facilitate among these bodies the advancement of their services to evangelical theological education within their regions.

Sponsoring associations include:

Africa: Association for Christian Theological Education in Africa (ACTEA)

Asia: Asia Theological Association (ATA)

Caribbean: Caribbean Evangelical Theological Association (CETA)

Europe: European Evangelical Accrediting Association (EEAA)

Euro-Asia: Euro-Asian Accrediting Association (E-AAA)

Latin America: Association for Evangelical Theological Education in Latin America (AETAL)

Middle East and North Africa: Middle East Association for Theological Education (MEATE)

North America: Association for Biblical Higher Education (ABHE)

South Pacific: South Pacific Association of Evangelical Colleges (SPAEC)

www.icete-edu.org

Langham Literature and its imprints are a ministry of Langham Partnership.

Langham Partnership is a global fellowship working in pursuit of the vision God entrusted to its founder John Stott –

to facilitate the growth of the church in maturity and Christ-likeness through raising the standards of biblical preaching and teaching.

Our vision is to see churches in the Majority World equipped for mission and growing to maturity in Christ through the ministry of pastors and leaders who believe, teach and live by the word of God.

Our mission is to strengthen the ministry of the word of God through:

- nurturing national movements for biblical preaching
- fostering the creation and distribution of evangelical literature
- enhancing evangelical theological education

especially in countries where churches are under-resourced.

Our ministry

Langham Preaching partners with national leaders to nurture indigenous biblical preaching movements for pastors and lay preachers all around the world. With the support of a team of trainers from many countries, a multi-level programme of seminars provides practical training, and is followed by a programme for training local facilitators. Local preachers' groups and national and regional networks ensure continuity and ongoing development, seeking to build vigorous movements committed to Bible exposition.

Langham Literature provides Majority World preachers, scholars and seminary libraries with evangelical books and electronic resources through publishing and distribution, grants and discounts. The programme also fosters the creation of indigenous evangelical books in many languages, through writer's grants, strengthening local evangelical publishing houses, and investment in major regional literature projects, such as one volume Bible commentaries like *The Africa Bible Commentary* and *The South Asia Bible Commentary*.

Langham Scholars provides financial support for evangelical doctoral students from the Majority World so that, when they return home, they may train pastors and other Christian leaders with sound, biblical and theological teaching. This programme equips those who equip others. Langham Scholars also works in partnership with Majority World seminaries in strengthening evangelical theological education. A growing number of Langham Scholars study in high quality doctoral programmes in the Majority World itself. As well as teaching the next generation of pastors, graduated Langham Scholars exercise significant influence through their writing and leadership.

To learn more about Langham Partnership and the work we do visit **langham.org**

Lightning Source UK Ltd.
Milton Keynes UK
UKHW022010161021
392327UK00002B/3